This Is PR

From the Wadsworth Series in Mass Communication and Journalism

General Mass Communication

Anokwa/Lin/Salwen, *International Communication: Issues and Controversies*

Biagi, *Media/Impact: An Introduction to Mass Media*, Eighth Edition

Bucy, *Living in the Information Age: A New Media Reader*, Second Edition

Day, *Ethics in Media Communications: Cases and Controversies*, Fifth Edition

Dennis/Merrill, *Media Debates: Great Issues for the Digital Age*, Fourth Edition

Fellow, *American Media History*

Hilmes, *Connections: A Broadcast History Reader*

Hilmes, *Only Connect: A Cultural History of Broadcasting in the United States*, Second Edition

Jamieson/Campbell, *The Interplay of Influence: News, Advertising, Politics, and the Mass Media*, Sixth Edition

Kamalipour, *Global Communication*, Second Edition

Lester, *Visual Communication: Images with Messages*, Fourth Edition

Overbeck, *Major Principles of Media Law*, 2007 Edition

Straubhaar/LaRose, *Media Now: Understanding Media, Culture, and Technology*, Fifth Edition

Zelezny, *Communications Law: Liberties, Restraints, and the Modern Media*, Fifth Edition

Zelezny, *Cases in Communications Law*, Fifth Edition

Journalism

Bowles/Borden, *Creative Editing*, Fourth Edition

Craig, *Online Journalism*

Hilliard, *Writing for Television, Radio, and New Media*, Eighth Edition

Kessler/McDonald, *When Words Collide: A Media Writer's Guide to Grammar and Style*, Sixth Edition

Poulter/Tidwell, *News Scene 2.0: Interactive Writing Exercises*

Rich, *Writing and Reporting News: A Coaching Method*, Fifth Edition

Rich, *Writing and Reporting News: A Coaching Method, Student Exercise Workbook*, Fifth Edition

Stephens, *Broadcast News*, Fourth Edition

Wilber/Miller, *Modern Media Writing*

Photojournalism and Photography

Parrish, *Photojournalism: An Introduction*

Public Relations and Advertising

Diggs-Brown, *The PR Styleguide: Formats for Public Relations Practice*, Second Edition

Hendrix/Hayes, *Public Relations Cases*, Seventh Edition

Jewler/Drewniany, *Creative Strategy in Advertising*, Eighth Edition

Newsom/Haynes, *Public Relations Writing: Form and Style*, Eighth Edition

Newsom/Turk/Kruckeberg, *This Is PR: The Realities of Public Relations*, Tenth Edition

Research and Theory

Baran/Davis, *Mass Communication Theory: Foundations, Ferment, and Future*, Fourth Edition

Littlejohn, *Theories of Human Communication*, Seventh Edition

Rubin/Rubin/Piele, *Communication Research: Strategies and Sources*, Sixth Edition

Scheufele/Babbie, *The Basics of Media Research*

Sparks, *Media Effects Research: A Basic Overview*, Second Edition

Wimmer/Dominick, *Mass Media Research: An Introduction*, Eighth Edition

This Is PR

THE REALITIES OF PUBLIC RELATIONS

Tenth Edition

Doug Newsom
Texas Christian University

Judy VanSlyke Turk
Virginia Commonwealth University

Dean Kruckeberg
University of North Carolina at Charlotte

WADSWORTH
CENGAGE Learning™

Australia • Brazil • Japan • Korea • Mexico • Singapore • Spain • United Kingdom • United States

This Is PR: The Realities of Public Relations, Tenth Edition
Newsom Turk Kruckeberg

Publisher: Michael Rosenberg

Associate Development Editor: Megan Garvey

Assistant Editor: Jillian D'Urso

Editorial Assistant: Erin Pass

Associate Media Editor: Jessica Badiner

Marketing Manager: Erin Mitchell

Marketing Communications Manager: Christine Dobberpuhl

Marketing Coordinator: Darlene Macanan

Content Project Manager: Lindsay Bethoney

Art Director: Linda Helcher

Print Buyer: Susan Carroll

Text Permissions Editor: Mardell Glinski Schultz

Production Service: Pre-PressPMG

Cover Designer: Grannan Graphic Design, Ltd

For product information and technology assistance, contact us at
Cengage Learning Academic Resource Center, 1-800-423-0563

For permission to use material from this text or product, submit all requests online at **www.cengage.com/permissions**. Further permissions questions can be e-mailed to **permissionrequest@cengage.com**.

Library of Congress Control Number: 2009920493

Student Edition:

ISBN-13: 978-0495-56882-7

ISBN-10: 0-495-56882-1

Wadsworth Cengage Learning
20 Channel Center Street
Boston, MA 02210
USA

Cengage Learning products are represented in Canada by Nelson Education, Ltd.

For your course and learning solutions, visit **academic.cengage.com**.

Purchase any of our products at your local college store or at our preferred online store **www.ichapters.com**.

Printed in Canada
1 2 3 4 5 6 7 13 12 11 10 09

To our students from whose questions, their observations and insights we continue to learn and to our colleagues, academics and practitioners, who explore with their research and share with their publications and conversations.

Doug Newsom, professor of journalism at Texas Christian University, is the senior coauthor of *This Is PR and Public Relations Writing*. She also is the co-author of three other books and the author of two others. She is former member of the Commission on Public Relations Education, is a former chair of PRSA's College of Fellows and is a past chair of the Accrediting Committee for the Accrediting Council on Education for Journalism and Mass Communications. She has been president of the Association for Education in Journalism and Mass Communication, Southwest Education Council for Journalism and Mass Communication, Texas Public Relations Association and both the Dallas and Fort Worth chapters of PRSA. Dr. Newsom has been national faculty advisor to PRSSA. She has been head of the PR Division of AEJMC and served as chair of its former PR division heads. Awards include the Institute for Public Relations' Pathfinder, PRSA Outstanding Educator, Public Relations Foundation of Texas's Educator of the Year Award, Texas Public Relations Association's Golden Spur and Association for Women in Communications Headliner. She has served Fulbrights in India and Singapore, given workshops in South Africa, Hungary, Bulgaria, Poland and Vanuatu and taught in Latvia and England. She has been chair of the Fulbright discipline committee, served 18 years on a gas research institute's advisory council and was one of the first women elected to the board of a publicly held company, where she served 24 years until reaching mandatory retirement age.

Judy VanSlyke Turk, professor of public relations and director of the School of Mass Communications at Virginia Commonwealth University, was founding dean of the College of Communication and Media Sciences at Zayed University in the United Arab Emirates. Prior to that she was dean of the College of Journalism and Mass Communications at the University of South Carolina and was director of the journalism and mass communication program at Kent State University. Dr. VanSlyke Turk is 2008–2009 president of the Association of Schools of Journalism and Mass Communication and is a past president of the Association for Education in Journalism and Mass Communication. She has represented both organizations on the Accrediting Council on Education in Journalism and Mass Communications. Dr. VanSlyke Turk is a member of the Commission on Public Relations Education and has been chair or co-chair of the Educational Affairs Committee of the Public Relations Society of America since 2007. She is a past chair of PRSA's College of Fellows and a PRSA outstanding Educator. She and coauthor Dr. Doug Newsom jointly won the Pathfinder Award from the Institute for Public Relations. She is associate editor of journalism studies and co-editor of a collection of international public relations case studies now in its third edition. She has consulted and lectured on public relations and journalism/mass communication in Eastern Europe, Russia and the Newly Independent States, the Baltics, the Middle East, Asia and Latin America.

Dean Kruckeberg is a professor in the Department of Communication Studies at the University of Northern Carolina at Charlotte and is director of that university's Center for Global Public Relations. He became co-author of *This Is PR* in its sixth edition and is co-author with Dr. Kenneth Starck of *Public Relations and Community: A Reconstructed Theory*. Dr. Kruckeberg is a member of PRSA's College of Fellows, is a past member of PRSA's national board and has been National Faculty Advisor of the Public Relations Student Society of America. He is the educator co-chair of the Commission on Public Relations Education, which recommends national guidelines for PR education. He is a former chair of the PR Divisions of the International Communication Association, the National Communication Association and the Association for Education in Journalism and Mass Communication as well as of PRSA's Educators Academy. He is a charter member of the Institute for Public Relations' Commission on Global Public Relations Research and is a former co-chair of PRSA's Educational Affairs Committee. Honors include PRSA's National Outstanding Educator Award, the Institute for Public Relations' Pathfinder Award, the Jackson Jackson & Wagner Behavioral Science Prize, the Iowa Regents Faculty Excellence Award, the Wartburg College Alumni Citation and NCA's first PRIDE award in the book category for his book with Dr. Starck. Dr. Kruckeberg has taught at the United Arab Emirates University and helped develop its PR curriculum. He also has taught in Latvia, Bulgaria, Sweden, Russia, Buryatia (Eastern Siberia) and Ukraine. He is author and co-author of numerous book chapters and journal articles that deal with global public relations and international PR ethics. He is a U.S. council representative to the board of the International Public Relations Association.

Brief Contents

Detailed Contents

The tenth edition is a milestone for this text that began in 1976 as a 318-page hardback in an unconventional shape. Credit for the birth of this book, and its continuity for many years, belongs to its first Wadsworth editor, Rebecca Hayden. Editors, publishers, and the industry have changed through the years but our main goals remain the same edition after edition. Our aim with each revision is to give you not just information about changes in public relations, but their impact on the field.

A major communication shift has occurred with technology, so much so that empowered publics have upturned research techniques and entangled tactics in a wired world. Along with constantly adapting to new technologies and the new methods of communication they facilitate, the he challenge today is talking about public relations in the global context in which it functions. Public discourse is global, and it is ongoing. Social media, universal in scope, are a significant part of both information and entertainment. Public relations practitioners as participants may be speaking for an international organization or a nation or giving counsel to those who do.

That strategic counsel has to come from practitioners who know global publics, including those often under-represented or unheard and respect the global truths embraced by all members of this global society.

We would like to thank the team at Cengage Learning that helped us develop and produce the new edition: associate development editor Megan Garvey, content project manager Lindsay Bethoney, publisher Michael Rosenberg, and assistant editor Jillian D'Urso. We'd also like to thank Sarah Wales-McGrath, copyeditor, Shannon Rhodes, proofreader, and Brenda and Kurt Grannan, cover design.

We greatly appreciated the suggestions from the following reviewers as we worked on the book:

Michele Bresso, *Bakersfield College*

Christopher Caldiero, *Fairleigh Dickinson University*

Lora DeFore, *Mississippi State University*

G. Faulconer, *Oklahoma City Community College*

John Fisher, *Northwest Missouri State University*

Margaret Fitch-Hauser, *Auburn University*

Teresa Holder, *Peace College*

Daniel Jorgensen, *Augsburg College*

Anne Lane, *Queensland University of Technology*

Debra Mayrhofer, *Edith Cowan University*

Melissa Motschall, *Eastern Michigan University*

Kathy Patterson, *St. Lawrence College*

Robert Taylor, *California University of Pennsylvania*

Katharina Wolf, *Curtin University of Technology*

CHAPTER 1

PR Roles and Specialties

"*All public relations should exist to preserve a consistent reputation and build relationships.*"

—Robert I. Wakefield[1]

- To understand the role and responsibilities of public relations—in public and private companies, nonprofit organizations, agencies and firms.
- To recognize the difference between strategic planning and execution that relies only on tactics and techniques.
- To appreciate the value of public relations in solving problems and making policy.
- To understand why individual as well as institutional credibility is critical to public relations practice.

When the PR practitioner arrived at her hotel in Lima, Peru, she plugged in her laptop only to find that her email box was flooded again. One email's attachment was a case study due at a journal, on which finishing touches had been added by a colleague and coauthor in Frankfurt, Germany.

She had less than a day now, considering time differences, to complete her editing and send the article electronically to her editor in London. Other messages involved meetings in Caracas, Venezuela, voice and text relays from the home office about other worldwide clients and a personal note.

She had experienced some difficulty using her mobile phone and its BlackBerry software to access her calendar, even though it was supposed to have global roaming capabilities. The hotel's business center made it possible for her to fax information to a coworker at home in Belgium, where a crisis was brewing for one of their clients. She gave the coworker her hotel room phone number and her appointment schedule so that they could talk strategy.

Prioritizing everything she had to do was her first and most important task. That's always the major decision every public relations practitioner must make. There is literally something to do every minute—no down time and very little personal space.

Diversity of tasks and high pressure are part of the public relations environment. Furthermore, for individuals who are comfortable only in one culture, a career in public relations is less and less a realistic option—if, indeed, it ever was. And, although some people like to do only one thing at a time, that never has been an option in public relations. It is even less so now that businesses are reducing staffs and having much of their work, including public relations functions, performed outside.

As the preceding scenario illustrates, technology has changed the way we communicate. Business cards carry phone and fax numbers and email addresses, as well as physical location addresses. The practice of public relations has emerged as a global phenomenon.

Some consistency of the practice, despite differences in the social, economic and political climates in various parts of the world, can be traced to the growing body of knowledge about and the general acceptance of what public relations is. The creator of public relations' international code of ethics, Lucien Matrat, offers these thoughts:

> *Public relations, in the sense that we use the term, forms part of the strategy of management. Its function is twofold: to respond to the expectations of those whose behaviour, judgments and opinions can influence the operation and development of an enterprise, and in turn to motivate them. . . .*
>
> *Establishing public relations policies means, first and foremost, harmonizing the interests of an enterprise with the interests of those on whom its growth depends.*
>
> *The next step is putting these policies into practice.*

This means developing a communications policy that can establish and maintain a relationship of mutual confidence with a firm's multiple publics.[2] ■

What Is Public Relations?

The **public relations (PR)** practitioner serves as an intermediary between the organization that he or she represents and all of that organization's publics.

Consequently, the PR practitioner has responsibilities both to the institution and to its various publics. He or she distributes information that enables the institution's publics to understand its policies.

Public relations involves research into all stakeholders: receiving information from them, advising

management of their attitudes and responses, helping to set policies that demonstrate responsible attention to them and constantly evaluating the effectiveness of all PR programs. This inclusive role embraces all activities connected with ascertaining and influencing the opinions of a group of people. But that is just the communications aspect. As a management function, *public relations involves responsibility and responsiveness in policy and information to the best interests of the organization and its publics.*

The First World Assembly of Public Relations Associations, held in Mexico City in August 1978, defined the practice of public relations as "the art and social science of analyzing trends, predicting their consequences, counseling organizational leaders, and implementing planned programs of action which will serve both the organization and the public interest."

The Public Relations Society of America (PRSA) defines public relations as a management function that involves counseling at the highest level and being involved in strategic planning for the organization. (The full statement, along with the organization's Code of Ethics 2000, appears in PRSA's *Blue Book*, part of the *One Source Directory*, discontinued in printed form in 2006.)

Yet another definition of public relations as "reputation management" has gained currency. The British Institute of Public Relations (IPR) offers this:

> *Public relations is about reputation—the result of what you do, what you say and what others say about you. Public Relations Practice is the discipline which looks after reputation with the aim of earning understanding and support, and influencing opinion and behaviour.*[3]

As a practical matter, good public relations involves confronting a problem openly and honestly and then solving it. In the long run, the best PR is evidence of an active social conscience.

Organizational Role and Function: 10 Basic Principles

As the definitions suggest, the result of public relations efforts must be the real behavior of the organization and perceptions of that behavior by its publics. Therefore, among the various titles now being used for the role of the public relations function are

Theory and Research Perspective

In attempting to agree on what public relations is, many researchers have wrestled with a definition that seems suitable and internationally acceptable. When some in the UK began to call public relations "reputation management," that caught on in the USA. The U.S. notion of "branding" that came from integrated marketing communications likewise caught on in Europe. In working on the European body of knowledge, researchers struggled for a paradigm that would cover private relationships, not just those in the public sphere, and broader social issues that public relations should address. This is not new to the social responsibility concept of public relations: being responsible first to a broader public welfare and then to the organization it represents.

Although that is understood, European researchers urge a reflective approach that looks at society's changing standards and values and then adjusts the organization's standards accordingly.

In terms of how public relations practitioners themselves define the discipline globally, a cultural-legal-economic model emerges that involves education, government, business and cultural norms including values—religion-based or not.

Read "On the Definition of Public Relations: A European View," by Dejan Verčič, Betteke van Ruler, Gerhard Butschi and Bertil Flodin in *Public Relations Review,* 27 (2002), pp. 373–87. Look at the Practice Matrix for the Cultural-Economic Model of International Public Relations Practice (Table 10-1) in Patricia A. Curtin and T. Kenn Gaither's *International Public Relations* (2007) and *Bridging Gaps in Global Communication* (2007) by Doug Newsom.

communications management (or sometimes strategic communications management), reputation management and relationship management. In delineating these, Fraser Likely, of the Canadian Public Relations Society, Inc., says all are managerial roles.[4]

We can describe the function and role of public relations practice by stating 10 basic principles:

1. Public relations deals with reality, not false fronts. Conscientiously planned programs that put the public interest in the forefront are the basis of sound public relations policy. (*Translation:* PR deals with facts, not fiction.)

2. Public relations is a service-oriented occupation in which public interest, not personal reward, should be the primary consideration. (PR is a public, not personal, service.)

3. Because the public relations practitioner must go to the public to seek support for programs and policies, public interest is the central criterion by which he or she should select these programs and policies. (PR practitioners must have the guts to say "no" to a client or to refuse a deceptive program.)

4. Because the public relations practitioner reaches many publics through mass media, which are the public channels of communication, the integrity of these channels must be preserved. (PR practitioners should never lie to the news media, either outright or by implication.)

5. Because PR practitioners are in the middle between an organization and its publics, they must be effective communicators—conveying information back and forth until understanding and ideally consensus are reached. (The PR practitioner probably was the original ombudsman or ombudswoman.)

6. To expedite two-way communication and to be responsible communicators, public relations practitioners must use scientific public opinion research extensively. (PR cannot afford to be a guessing game.)

7. To understand what their publics are saying and to reach them effectively, public relations practitioners must employ the social sciences—psychology, sociology, social psychology—and the literature of public opinion, communication, and semantics. (Intuition is not enough.)

8. Because a lot of people do PR research, the PR person must adapt the work of other, related disciplines, including learning theory and other psychology theories, sociology, political science, economics and history. (The PR field requires multidisciplinary applications.)

9. Public relations practitioners are obligated to explain problems to the public before these problems become crises. (PR practitioners should alert and advise, so people won't be taken by surprise.)

10. A public relations practitioner should be measured by only one standard: ethical performance.

PR and Related Activities

Public relations involves many activities. People's participation in the activities of public relations and their subsequent assertion that, therefore, they are "in public relations" often cause confusion in others' understanding of what public relations is. The activities of PR practice include press agentry, promotion, publicity, public affairs, research (primary and secondary), graphics, advertising, marketing, integrated marketing communications and merchandising support.

- *Press agentry* involves planning activities or staging events—sometimes just stunts—that will attract attention to a person, institution, idea or product.
- *Promotion* goes beyond press agentry into opinion making. Promotion tries to garner support and endorsement for a person, product, institution or idea.
- *Publicity* is placing information into a news medium. Publicity is not always good news. A PR writer may be crafting a response to an unpleasant situation. Publicists are primarily writers, one of the technical support teams for public relations. Publicists working for government are often called information officers.
- *Public affairs*, when the term is used by *government*, means the same thing as public relations with external publics. However, in companies or nonprofit organizations, it usually means the person responsible for that organization's relationship with all branches of government. Most of the activity is with the legislative and regulatory branches.
- *Research* is the foundation of all good public relations strategy. Much research involves publics and public opinion, although other research may involve the marketplace and the social, economic and legal climate in which a public relations activity is centered. Most research is digital, and includes monitoring as well as designing and implementing electronic inquiries, both quantitative and qualitative.
- *Graphics* are important because all public relations readers and viewers are "volunteers" who will reject any presentation that is visually unappealing and not "user-friendly."
- *Advertising* is usually commercial time or space bought in specific media to control the time, place and message. However, when nonprofits use advertising, the time or space may be donated by a medium, but what is lost is control over use and timing.
- *Marketing* is directed toward consumers of a service or product. In 2004, the American Marketing Association (AMA) defined marketing as "an organizational function and a set of processes for creating, communicating and delivering value to customers and for managing customer relationships in ways that benefit the organization and its stakeholders."[5] The AMA includes in that definition activities (ideas and services) of nonprofit organizations, as well as those sold for profit.
- *Integrated marketing communications (IMC)* began developing in the 1990s and emerged from what had been called Marketing/PR. Then IMC began to focus on branding to give instant recognition for a product or company. IMC talked about "relationship building," which sounded a lot like what PR was doing. Although some PR people accepted the development as IMC, other PR people agreed only that organizations should unify all communications to "speak with one voice"; what they called IC or integrated communication. As a result, IC and IMC terms began showing up in name changes for firms and in curriculum changes in some colleges and universities.[6]
- *Merchandising* is concerned with presentation. Its focus is the packaging for a product, idea or perhaps even a political candidate.[7] Technology has changed merchandising in the diversity of delivery: **compact disc (CD)** or **fax**, in addition to audiocassette or print, plus the direct response of online purchasing and cable-television shopping channels. Merchandising experts are strong in the application of graphics, color, tactile responses and emotional reactions to physical imagery. All of these are important elements in the "toolbox" of solutions to reaching publics. But public relations is something greater than just this collection of activities.

Changes in the environment for public relations can shift the emphasis from one activity to another over time. Recently, advances in technology—such as significant differences in the way the news media operate—have driven many of these shifts. Another result of these advances has been increased globalization, affecting both internal and external communication and significantly altering the way crises are handled. All crises now get global attention, which creates considerable urgency for appropriate organizational responses that are destined to be weighed in the world court of public opinion.

The Job of the PR Practitioner

Although the basic duties of a public relations practitioner have not changed much over the past several decades, the demands on the practitioner and the way the practitioner carries out his or her duties have changed and will continue to change. There is more call for depth and diversity in knowledge for this field now that it is functioning at a global level. There is more accountability for public relations actions and greater damage if risk management and crisis communication are mishandled. There's less tolerance for "hype." Practitioners need more command of a greater array of communication technologies, and **media relations** now demands greater sensitivity to multiculturalism.

But some things have not changed. Former PRSA president Frank Wylie, now a Santa Cruz, California, consultant, notes that "every beginner is a 'go-fer,' and it's important that you not only go for something, but that you bring back something usable."[8] The retrieval emphasis implies reportorial skills, including knowledge of research techniques.

Other skills Wylie stresses include thinking (first and foremost), writing of all types, speaking, being persuasive, understanding and appreciating media, knowing graphics and photography, respecting deadlines and developing an ability to deal with and solve multiple PR problems at one time.[9]

Three Basic Roles

The way a PR person applies his or her special skills depends on the role he or she plays in an organization. The three main roles are those of *staff member*, an *agency employee* and an *independent PR practitioner*, who might from time to time function as a *PR counselor*. We will consider each of these roles separately.

Staff Members Staff public relations practitioners are employees of commercial or nonprofit organizations or of divisions of government such as local, state and federal agencies. They perform highly specialized tasks in their organizations, but they get a paycheck just as other employees do, and they share the same corporate or institutional identity. Specific needs of the organization usually determine a staff member's job description.

Staff positions with small organizations often include responsibility for external relations. In the case of a small nonprofit organization, the PR person typically works either with volunteers who provide professional expertise of various kinds or with outside suppliers whose services may be bought on a limited basis or donated.

Staff positions with larger organizations can involve responsibility for all other communications functions that report to public relations, and in some instances for human resources (personnel) as well. Large organizations are likely to buy services such as research, audiovisuals (everything from employee training videos to video news releases and commercials) and perhaps even the annual report from outside suppliers. Outsourcing of special public relations services is increasing as companies cut back on their total number of in-house employees.

Commercial and Nonprofit Organizations Public relations people in institutions—whether commercial or nonprofit—may have skilled jobs in a PR department, may be middle managers of specialized PR activity, such as community relations or employee relations, or may function as general professional staff. Increased use of computer technology is likely to decrease the number of practitioners working at the lower-level jobs and increase the number working at the middle and senior managerial levels; the rather small number of positions at the most senior level of policy making is unlikely to be affected.[10]

Government Job descriptions for PR positions in government vary dramatically. Some people who are called "public information officers" are really publicists, whereas others with precisely the same title may have all the responsibilities of a corporate vice president for PR.

Firm/Agency Employees Each agency or firm has its own internal structure, but generally the president or CEO of the firm shares in handling accounts, as do the salespeople, who may also be account executives. A firm may employ a bookkeeper, a secretary, a publicity writer, an advertising or graphics specialist, an artist and a Web expert. In some instances, the writer may prepare both publicity and advertising copy, and the artist may be responsible for illustrations and layout. The Web expert suggests software to buy, handles technical problems, and may be the Web monitor too.

Large firms have copy editors, media specialists, Web site designers, several artists and a production facility. Most firms, even the largest ones, arrange contracts with printers, typesetters and photographers.

PR in Practice

Although the U.S. government is the world's largest employer of public relations practitioners, the government uses the term *public affairs*, not *public relations*. The reason for that is an October 22, 1913, act of Congress that is often interpreted as precluding governmental use of public relations talent. The last paragraph of the Interstate Commerce Commission statute reads: "Appropriated funds may not be used to pay a publicity expert unless specifically appropriated for that purpose." Because this was an amendment to a bill introduced by Representative Frederick H. Gillett, it is often called the Gillett Amendment in PR literature.

The intent was to be sure publicity was not used to propagandize U.S. citizens. PR people have tried a number of times to repeal this amendment, but not recently. The term *public affairs* is widely used in government to mean public relations, and in commercial and nonprofit organizations, it is part of the title for the person working on the organization's relationships with government at all levels, not just federal.

Digital publishing makes the jobs of writers and artists more efficient and easier to coordinate. Computer software programs that include type and graphics make almost instantaneous page makeup possible in-house. These systems usually make the writer the production person as well, because the writer actually develops the final format of publication, often including generic artwork available digitally. However, an artist usually provides original designs and artwork.

Independent Practitioners/Counselors The *independent* public relations practitioner is usually hired to accomplish a specific task—one that is ordinarily (but not always) predetermined. Payment may take the form of a flat fee, a fee plus expenses or a base fee plus hourly charges and expenses. The less experienced the independent practitioner is, the more often he or she will have to work for a flat fee.

Although some experienced independents prefer to bill for actual costs, they price a job based on the hours required to complete it multiplied by an hourly rate. They then increase these costs by a certain percentage to cover overhead and profit. Independent public relations practitioners sometimes function as PR counselors. Indeed, some independent practitioners work almost exclusively as counselors.

A PR counselor is called in at an advisory level and works for a consultant's fee, which he or she sets, with hours and expenses added. The counselor studies and researches a situation, interviews the people involved, outlines recommendations and makes a formal presentation of these. The program is then implemented by other PR workers at the organization or at an agency. (See Chapter 9 for details of billings.) Counselors may work independently, or

they may be associated with a firm as senior members. Some independent PR practitioners do various PR jobs, but most are strictly counselors.

Some counselors are sensitive about their roles because people tend to view them as behind-the-scenes influence peddlers. Another misconception is that counselors are simply unemployed would-be senior staffers. Public confusion is understandable, however, because counselors are *advisers* who possess special areas of expertise, most of it gained in agency or corporate work. Their value resides in their experience, in the people they know and are able to call upon and in their skill as researchers, analyzers, communicators and persuaders.

Some counselors develop reputations for helping institutions prepare for and handle crisis communication. Others are known for their ability to help institutions establish and maintain good government relations (at all levels, but primarily at the federal level). Still others are called on for their ability to help with internal problems, typically ones involving employee relations. Counselors, as senior practitioners, often develop staffs that include younger people who have particular strengths or specializations.

Specific Areas of PR Specialization

The breadth of PR services gives individuals a variety of career choices. Many practitioners are experienced in more than one area.

Nonprofit Organizations Nonprofit organizations offer a practitioner several advantages and opportunities, although the compensation is often less than in other areas. The structure of these organizations (small production staff answerable to a volunteer board of directors) means that the nonprofit PR person generally has a great deal of freedom in designing a program. An attractive program that does not require a large bankroll probably will be accepted.

This kind of PR work usually entails a considerable amount of promotional activity and sometimes also **fundraising** and seeking grants from foundations.

A particular plus, however, is the reception given to publicity materials by news media representatives, who are more likely to use information from nonprofit institutions than from for-profit organizations as long as the preparation is professional. Even nonprofit advertising gets a break, with special rates (sometimes called "church rates"). The only drawback other than a smaller budget is frequent dependence on volunteer support in many areas. Responsibility for training volunteers usually falls on the PR people, and they must recognize that volunteers' interest in and enthusiasm for the organization can be stimulated and sustained only by a viable program.

Outside the USA, nonprofit organizations may be called nongovernmental organizations (**NGOs**), although the World Bank notes that "there has been a deliberate shift away in the last few years from use of the term *NGO*, which refers more narrowly to professional, intermediary and non-profit organizations which advocate and/or provide services in the areas of economic and social development, human rights, welfare and emergency relief," and now "uses the term *civil society organizations* or *CSOs* to refer to the wide array of *non-governmental and not-for-profit* organizations which have a presence in public life, expressing the interests and values of their members or others, based on ethical, cultural, scientific, religious or philanthropic considerations."[11] Nevertheless, the term *NGO* in more casual usage still is applied to any nonprofit organization that is independent of government. These are typically value-based organizations that depend, at least in part, on charitable donations and voluntary service. Organizations that get some government funding are called near-state, nongovernmental organizations (known as **GONGOs**). Nonprofits all over the world include museums, hospitals, social service and health care groups, professional associations of all kinds, as well as activists groups, often known as private voluntary organizations or **PVOs**, such as Greenpeace and Oxfam.

Educational Institutions Educational institutions are usually nonprofit organizations as well, but they may be either public or private. The private institutions generally conform to the nonprofit organizational pattern. Although they have significant dealings with government, their work is quite unlike that of public institutions, which, being a part of government, are more open to the scrutiny of taxpayers and the whims of politicians. The type of PR practiced in state educational institutions is often suited to a person who enjoys dealing with the government.

PR people in all educational institutions are likely to be involved in development, which includes fundraising. The functions of PR and of development are separate, but the two groups must work closely together. In fact, the two functions are often lumped together under the umbrella term *institutional advancement* (a term used by CASE, the Council for the Advancement and Support of Education).

The title "vice president for development" or "director of university relations" is commonly assigned to the individual who supervises both the PR and the fundraising functions. Sports information may be included under public relations or kept separate from it in an athletic department; in the latter case, the person responsible for it reports to the athletic director who in turn reports to the president. However, this arrangement can cause problems because university sports can be involved in controversies that affect university relations.

Fundraising or Donor Relations Although many public relations people will tell you that they "don't do fundraising"—just as many others say that they "don't do advertising"—those who do it well are in great demand.

Fundraising is sometimes called donor relations. First and foremost, the fundraiser must identify sources of potential support through research. Then he or she must inform those sources of the value of the organization so that they will consider making a gift to it. In the case of individual donors, this usually means cultivating a relationship between that person and the organization over a period of time. If the source is a foundation, the informational task means writing a grant proposal that explains the value of the organization seeking the funds and identifies it closely with the mission of the foundation.

The third aspect of donor relations—the actual solicitation—takes many forms. It may involve an elaborate presentation book prepared just for that individual, or it may employ a videotape or DVD that can be used repeatedly in combination with personally directed appeals. It generally involves a series of letters requesting funds, and in broader appeals it may include **brochures** and telephone solicitations. Face-to-face meetings also are used for the personal appeal, and these can be one-on-one or one to a group of potential donors. In the case of large gifts, a strong tie is usually built between the institution (some element or some person in it) and the donor.

The next step is to provide some appropriate recognition for the donor that reflects the size of the gift and the nature of the appeal. (Nothing is more upsetting to a donor than getting an expensive "reward," because this signals that a good portion of the money raised is being spent on thank-yous instead of on the primary mission of the organization.)

Finally, the donor's relationship to the organization must be sustained in a way that is mutually satisfying. The fundraiser wants the donor to give again, especially if the organization has annual fundraising events (as public television stations do, for example). Even if the gift was substantial and there is no reason to expect another, the fundraiser still wants the donor to have an ongoing relationship with the organization and to feel good about having given. Donors often attract other donors, but only when they feel good about their experience.

Research: Trend Analysis, Issues Management and Public Opinion Evaluation

Some PR practitioners specialize in research that focuses on capturing information to help organizations plan better by anticipating currents of change. Some engage in analyzing trends to enable their organization to detect, adapt to and even take advantage of emerging changes. Issues management is centrally concerned with watching the horizons for change through many types of research. By determining in advance what developments are likely to become important to one or more of its publics, an organization can plan to meet the challenge, rather than be taken by surprise. Much of the research underlying trend analysis and issue anticipation consists of monitoring public opinion and evaluating the consequences of attitude changes to the organization and its publics.

Detection of emerging issues and surveillance of social and economic trends continue to be important PR functions. These skills cast PR people in the role of social scientist. Information and intelligent analysis of issues and trends can help restore public confidence. The challenge facing PR practitioners is to provide leadership in developing creative, pragmatic communication programs that provide their publics with complete, candid, factual and understandable information. Furthermore, PR workers must pioneer new skills to use in maintaining good relations with their publics.

International PR for Organizations and Firms

The globalization of news media, global economic dependence among countries and the emergence of multinational companies have helped expand this area of public relations. *International PR* is not limited to businesses, however, because many nonprofit organizations and associations are international in scope. PR firms often have offices abroad to represent both domestic and foreign clients. Corporate PR people abroad function just as their counterparts do at home, working with community leaders, government officials and media. They provide a crucial link between the branch organization and the home office.

International PR requires extra sensitivity to **public opinion** because practitioners deal with people whose languages, experiences and worldviews differ from their own. Areas of special concern are language (and knowledge of its nuances); customs affecting attitudes toward media, products/services and symbols that stem from customs; and laws. The last area is particularly significant, because incompatibilities between one country's laws and another's may make harmonious relationships difficult.

Financial PR or Investor Relations

This area includes such activities as preparing material for securities analysts to study, developing an **annual report** that is acceptable to auditors and intelligible to stockholders and knowing when and to whom to issue a **news release** that could affect corporate stock values. What this means in the USA is complying with the regulations for corporate disclosure of the Securities and Exchange Commission. Filing of the appropriate forms is usually a function for the chief financial officer (**CFO**) and the in-house attorney, but writing the accompanying news release and distributing it is the role of investor relations (IR). IR is a rather hazardous occupation because a wrong move can have such grave repercussions. In turn, it is exciting, remunerative and challenging.

Industry

Public relations for industry also requires a good feel for political PR–public affairs because so much of industry is regulated by government. A person working for a company that handles government contracts must develop a high tolerance for bureaucratic delay. One PR staffer for a defense contractor has said that the average time required to get an "original" release—one with all new material—cleared

Global Perspective

Wire services carrying public relations news releases and announcements are not new. The service dates to 1954, but what is new is the cultural and international expansion of the service.

Business Wire works with the Hispanic PR Wire and Black PR Wire to offer more culturally comprehensive services.

Internationally it has gained AFX News, a worldwide financial news service, through an agreement with The Press Association. The Press Association connection thus expands Business Wire outreach in the UK and Ireland.

for dissemination to the news media is 23 days. Because much of the emphasis in **industry relations** is on internal PR, and in particular on labor relations, a strong background in the social sciences and business helps.

Despite the trend toward deregulation in the utilities industry, PR practitioners still must work with both the government and consumers. They must also know financial PR and investor relations, because most utilities are publicly held. Finally, industry's PR practitioners may be involved in product promotion, which requires an understanding and appreciation of marketing and advertising activities.

General Business or Retail PR This area is somewhat broader than the term *retail* implies. It involves working with government regulatory bodies, employees, the community, competitors and, generally, the full complement of publics both inside and outside the company. Consumers represent an increasingly significant external public because they talk to politicians and can arouse public opinion against a business. Product promotion—of a service or of goods—is another common aspect of general business. For that reason, the business setting is a likely place to find the *marketing/public relations* or IMC title.

Government The four areas in this category all have the same focus, but their internal workings vary.

Federal, State or Local Government Employment
Although the federal government is prohibited from labeling PR activities as such, it (like state and local governments) uses PR talent under a variety of titles: public information officer, public affairs officer or departmental assistant or aide.

Nongovernmental Organizations' Government Relations The term *public affairs* is also used by institutions to designate the working area of staff members who deal with governments. Most institutions, whether commercial or nonprofit, have specialists who handle their relations with relevant departments of government on federal, state and local levels. In this context public affairs work consists of dealing with problems that come under the jurisdiction of elected or appointed public officials.

Political Public Relations Political PR involves working with candidates for office—and often continuing to work with them after their election—to handle problems, strategies and activities such as speech writing or publicity. Many PR practitioners will not support a cause or person they cannot conscientiously endorse. Others see PR advice as being like legal counsel and offer their services to anyone who is willing to pay for them.

For government, public affairs and politics, a strong background in government and history is useful. Political PR, like other areas of public relations, can be high-pressure, especially since the 1967 **Freedom of Information Act** has made government secrets more generally discoverable. In addition, restrictions on campaign financing mean that PR people must be even more judicious in collecting, reporting and spending money. State and federal laws must be obeyed to the letter.

Lobbying Many lobbyists are not public relations specialists at all (many are former government officials). But many public relations practitioners get involved in lobbying activities through their jobs with corporations or utilities. Some PR practitioners become professional lobbyists, at which point they generally represent a particular industry (such as oil and gas) or special interest (such as senior citizens or health care organizations). Lobbyists work closely with the staffs of federal and/or state representatives and senators, who depend on them to explain the intricacies and implications of proposed legislation. Lobbyists draw on information furnished by their

PR in Practice

Historical observations are always an opportunity to get media attention. Coca-Cola was invented in 1886 in Atlanta by a former Confederate army officer, John Pemberton, who was also a pharmacist. His bookkeeper, Frank Robinson, named the beverage, actually concocted in a bathtub, and created the script that is the drink's logo today.

When the 100th anniversary of Coca-Cola's arrival in Texas came about on June 10, 2002, news sections of papers covered the event. The company issued commemorative bottles, and a historical marker was placed on the site where the first bottling plant in Texas opened on Elm Street in Dallas. The bottling plant site, in what is now an entertainment center called Deep Ellum, had only three employees and a one-horse wagon but managed to sell 37 cases its first day of operation. Competing Dr Pepper, a native beverage from Waco, Texas, had a head start of 17 years on Coca-Cola.

Promotional events such as these anniversary observances are standard promotional public relations, and are usually part of an integrated campaign. The emphasis is on branding, although almost everyone in the world recognizes Coke. Still, Coke remains in a tight battle, not with its earlier competitor Dr Pepper, but with Pepsi-Cola. Interestingly, two days after this celebration of Coke, there was a wire service picture of the Afghanistan delegates to the grand council to form a new government and there, on the floor between the chairs of two delegates, was an easily identifiable bottle of Coke.

sponsors to try to persuade lawmakers to adopt a particular point of view.

Health Care Health maintenance organizations (HMOs), hospitals, other health care agencies (such as nursing home corporations), pharmaceutical companies, medical clinics, health-science centers and nonprofit health agencies (for example, those combating heart disease, cancer and birth defects) all employ public relations personnel. The demand in this field is for PR practitioners who either know or have the educational background to learn about medical science to translate that information accurately for the organization's publics. A heavy marketing component also exists in this area, which means that the PR person needs to have good advertising and public relations skills.

Sports Before sports became big business, the term *public relations* was sometimes used to describe a job that actually combined press agentry and publicity.

Today, however, business enterprises in professional sports are of such size and scope that the PR title is legitimate. Professional teams have intricate relations with investors, their own players, competing teams and players, stadium owners, transportation and housing facilities (at home and on the road), community supporters, media (with regard both to publicity and to contractual obligations, as in live

coverage) and other important publics. Most professional sports organizations employ full-time staff PR people, and they contract for special PR activities as well. Sports are also increasingly important to colleges and universities. Sports information officers in these institutions handle relations with media and fans.

Leisure Time The leisure-time market includes all recreation-related industries. It covers real estate promotion for resort locations; public park development; resorts and hotels; travel agencies; airlines and other mass transportation systems; sports, hobbies and crafts; and some educational, entertainment and cultural activities. The focus of PR activity in this market is promotion, and the only real hazard is the somewhat erratic international economy. Creative and inventive public relations generalists can function here quite comfortably.

Career, Job (Field) or Profession?

Some commentators argue that the very fact that anyone would question whether PR is a profession proves that public relations is *not* a profession. Another clue is the lack of practitioners' commitment to continuing education.

One criterion of a profession is that its practitioners have command over a *body of knowledge*.

PR in Practice

Some people resist considering lobbying a part of public relations, but it is. Sometimes it is difficult to decide what is lobbying and what is just public affairs practice. Public affairs is a public relations function that involves working with legislative and regulatory parts of government or working for government in conducting campaigns. When a public affairs person is working outside of government, that person is employed either for a company or nonprofit or for a firm that represents an organization as a client.

A good example of a public affairs campaign is the work that was done to get legislation that would permit airline pilots to carry guns in the cockpit, a post-9/11 issue. The PR firm that represents the Allied Pilots Association, Shirley and Banister Public Affairs, launched a campaign that involved talking to people in government who favored the idea to get them to introduce the legislation, a lobbying function. This is usually the way such campaigns begin, and the practice of pairing public affairs and lobbying is increasing. The reason is to find in government "ball carriers" who can move the idea forward, and then give them information that will support the proposed legislation. The idea has to be advanced to the public, too, through traditional and nontraditional media. Because the news media cover government, it is easier to get one of the supporters to lead off with the idea and get it covered by television and print news media.

The work only starts there. The staffs of government legislators and affected government regulatory groups have to be educated too. The public affairs people work with the actual contact persons, lobbyists, to be sure the knowledge is there to support the idea and to counter arguments. In working for their clients, public affairs firms write op-ed pieces for newspapers, and these often stimulate letters to the editor, so the idea gets into public discourse.

Often, media outside of Washington, D.C., have to be approached with a local angle to get coverage; sometimes the legislator's home state is an opening, or the community where the client is based.

Efforts such as this involve research, especially polling. Such campaigns involve lining up specialists to add credibility to arguments. They may involve advertising. All messages from whatever source must support the goal. This is strategic public relations at the most fundamental level, and the measurable outcome is getting policy adopted and implemented.

Although the PRSA has developed a body of knowledge, it is for the USA only and has been criticized by the International Public Relations Association for its parochialism. The Institute for Public Relations' Commission on International Public Relations is attempting to catalog and codify public relations literature globally. An additional criterion is general acceptance of a *standard educational curriculum.* Although this exists to some degree in the USA, what is being taught in the USA is not necessarily what is being taught elsewhere, where the availability of specialized education in public relations is growing at an explosive pace.

Another criterion is *control over entry and exit* to the field, and public relations, at least in the USA, lacks any such control. One aspect of that control consists of requiring continuing education of all practitioners to maintain standards of practice by ensuring that practitioners learn new developments and update skills. That is not a requirement for practicing public relations. In fact, there are no educational requirements that would preclude anyone from saying he or she is a public relations practitioner.

The Function of Public Relations in Business and Society

Traditionally, three functions have been ascribed to public relations. According to one point of view, public relations serves *to control publics,* by directing what people think or do to satisfy the needs or desires of an institution. According to a second point of view, PR's function is *to respond to publics*—reacting to developments, problems or the initiatives of others.

According to a third point of view, the function of public relations is *to achieve mutually beneficial relationships among all the publics that an institution has*, by fostering harmonious interchanges among an institution's various publics (including such groups as employees, consumers, suppliers and producers).[12]

Stephen A. Greyser, a Harvard University business professor and consumer researcher, calls this third view of the function of PR, in which the consumer is seen as a partner of business, the *transactional model*. Greyser has developed two other models: the *manipulative model*, which looks upon the consumer as victim; and the *service model*, which sees the consumer as king. According to Greyser, the consumer still sees some distance between the current marketplace and the ideal service model.[13]

The three traditional views of PR are each discernible in the history of public relations (see Chapter 2). Greyser's manipulative model describes public relations during the era of communicating and initiating. His service model describes practices that predominated during the era of reacting and responding. His transactional model describes public relations during the era of planning and presenting.

The current era of professionalism has seen practitioners beginning to control PR's development, use and practice. This concept of the uniqueness of public relations is well expressed in the following words of the late Philip Lesly:

> *Public relations people have the role of being always in the middle—pivoted between their clients/employers and their publics. . . . This role "in the middle" does not apply to any other group that deals with the climate of attitudes. Experts in other fields—journalists, sociologists, psychologists, politicians, etc.—are oriented in the direction of their specialties.*[14]

James E. Grunig, who edited *Excellence in Public Relations and Communication Management*, has defined public relations as "the management of communication between an organization and its publics."[15]

Another way of talking about the different approaches to PR is from the standpoint of practitioner self-description. PR educator Lalit Acharya suggests that environment might explain the self-perception of a practitioner.[16] Self-described roles, largely the conceptual work of Glen M. Broom and George D. Smith,[17] include *expert prescriber*, an authoritarian and prescriptive model; *communication technician*, a supportive, skills-oriented model; *communication facilitator*, a liaison model; *problem-solving process facilitator*, a confrontational model; and *acceptant legitimizer*, a yes-person model. Acharya examined these descriptions in terms of "perceived environmental uncertainty" for the practitioner and concluded that a public relations practitioner (as an individual) may play a number of these roles, depending on the environment in which he or she functions in any given case.

Actually these self-described roles may be telescoped into only two: manager (who supervises technical staff and participates in planning and policy making as counsel to management) and technician (who performs the skills jobs that PR demands). A test of this conceptual research that involved mailing surveys to 136 PR practitioners in Washington state suggests that this is the case.[18] If the roles really are more diverse, as the earlier descriptive work suggests, the particular roles chosen may depend on the degree of encouragement or discouragement for individual initiative present in the public relations practitioner's own environment.

Acharya's work describes practitioner behavior primarily in terms of the external environment of public opinion, but internal environments (such as open or closed communication systems) also can affect practitioner behavior. In fact, some research indicates that PR practitioners who work in participative environments (where employees make job-related suggestions and generally take a more active role in determining their work environment) see themselves as less constrained than those who work in authoritarian environments (where employee input is strongly discouraged).[19] It may be that the self-described "technician" doesn't have the option of being a manager because of authoritarian top management and a closed communication environment. Michael Ryan, who has investigated participative versus authoritative environments, observes:

> *Practitioners who work in authoritative environments might attempt to change those environments by educating management about the advantages— indeed, the necessity—of involving public relations persons in decision-making at the highest levels and of removing constraints on their freedom to act professionally.*[20]

Although Ryan recognizes that the task of transforming an organization from authoritative to participative might not be included in a PR person's job description, he notes that accomplishing such a change might be among the most significant contributions a practitioner could make. In any case, Ryan suggests that "public relations persons would do well to seek out participative environments and to avoid authoritative environments."[21]

Although most public relations practitioners accept the *idea* of there being distinct technician and manager roles due to the variety of activities that public relations incorporates, in reality public relations practitioners juggle the two roles most of the time. The delineation might best be used to describe which role occupies *most* of the practitioner's time.

Typologies Aside

These typologies are very useful; however, they often do not grasp the full range of factors affecting public relations practice. It makes a great deal of difference, for example, who is actually doing the PR. In many cases, public relations functions have been delegated to people from other fields: lawyers without any background in public relations or even communications, former media personnel who have been on the receiving end of public relations material but have no theoretical background, management-trained executives whose business school education did not include any courses in public relations or marketing experts who have no knowledge of the overall communications components. If management doesn't know what the public relations function should be—and many do not—the function becomes what the person doing the job knows how to do best. In other words, the *corporate communications environment*, the *education of the individuals* doing the job, the *type of organization* and the *culture* in which they function all significantly affect what actually happens under the name of public relations.

Internationally, much of what is called public relations really isn't. Often it is publicity, promotion or press agentry—all technical activities often included in public relations efforts. In many nations, you'll find something called "developmental public relations," and this is usually government-generated information or campaigns designed to get citizen compliance with or without prior consultation about the goals or objectives. A common tool found in the USA as well as abroad is what James E. Grunig has called "asymmetrical public relations practice," which means that feedback is used only to find out the best ways to persuade people and get compliance. Business

firms in highly competitive markets use this. Internationally, companies using this may even change products to meet consumer tastes and desires.

Grunig holds up a two-way symmetric model as the ideal because it involves negotiation with an organization's various publics to arrive at some mutually acceptable and beneficial policies and ways of doing business. The problem with the ideal is that negotiations depend too on a balance of power that is not present with some publics, such as employees. This is particularly true outside the USA.

Countries attempting to use the two-way symmetric model for best practices often find culture gets in the way of equalizing relationships. The two-way concept involves developing mutual understandings so that even when a public may not agree with management, at least there is an understanding of why management is saying or doing what it is. This can occur only if the public affected appreciates management's position, and if the culture is not too hierarchical to permit such practice.

The Value of Public Relations

The lack of consistency in PR practice is due to its rapid growth and its need to develop within the cultural, religious, socioeconomic and political context in which it is being practiced. The reason for its growth globally, though, is because it does have value to governments, commercial entities and nonprofit organizations.

- Public relations can represent the needs, interests and desires of the organization's various publics to management and then back from management to them, explaining management's perspectives. It opens a dialogue between an organization and the publics it affects.

    The dialogue can encourage mutual adjustments between an organization and the society it serves.

- Public relations focuses on society in the broadest sense and should work in the greater interest of society, rather than the narrow interests of the organizations it serves.

- In working toward the best interest of society, public relations has the opportunity to improve cooperation of an organization with its publics and perhaps avoid any arbitrary or coercive action on the part of government.

- PR provides useful information to people about various aspects of their lives.

Ethical Perspective

U.S. ethics are anything but universal, so it is easy to run into trouble practicing public relations abroad where ethical standards and practices are different. The opening of China to international public relations firms, U.S. professors teaching public relations in Chinese universities and increased flow of public relations material into China due to improvement in trade relations have exposed Western PR practitioners to something called **guanxi.**

Like many words from other languages, this word has no English equivalent, although *networking* is frequently used. It isn't networking as the term is used in the USA. It isn't even social networking, as most Westerners would understand it. Nor is it just a special interpersonal connection as the USA would equate with being "well connected" or having "strong connections" within an organization. Chinese who attempt to explain it to Westerners say it means a personal relationship with someone in power who can not only pave the way for what a PR person (or any other) wants to happen but who can actually get it accomplished by that person's power, status and access. There is reciprocity involved. But this is different from a Western understanding of "doing a favor" and "expect a favor," often expressed by "Okay, you owe me one" when someone accomplishes something for another. It's also more than *pulling strings*, a term used to mean that you got something to happen because of a person in power, but that is close. Although reciprocity is usually expected in any of these Western contexts, in guanxi, it means the return has to be greater than the deed.

Guanxi is common not just in China, but in many places where Chinese are a majority or a significant financial component of the population. The practice comes from Confucian principles, so it is culture-bound. Chinese are likely to believe their Confucian values are superior to Western values. In turn, many Westerners exposed to guanxi often worry about what seems to them to be ethical issues, because this is not what they would consider to be a "straightforward" transaction. To them, it appears almost like unethical influence peddling.

- Although PR people cannot be a conscience to an organization whose leadership has none, their role is to raise issues and concerns and remind management of ethical responsibilities.
- PR helps management formulate, advocate and teach objectives that are more sound.
- The principles of public relations reflect the basic cooperative natures of people, and thus PR people earn their reputation as problem solvers.
- Being socially responsible means upholding these obligations.

PR as Counsel for Social Responsibility

Management must be responsible and responsive to its publics; otherwise, it will have to combat a hostile environment. Unfortunately, the pattern of action has often been just the opposite, according to social scientist Hazel Henderson, who identified the following "normal" pattern of business response to social issues: (1) Ignore the problem. (2) If publicity calls widespread attention to the problem, admit its existence but present business as a victim of circumstances it cannot alter. (3) When the public takes the problem to lawmakers, lobby, testify in legislative hearings and advertise to get opinion leaders to believe that the proposed solutions constitute government interference in the private economy. (4) After new regulations are final, announce that business can live with the new law.[22]

Not only does such behavior justify public pressure for government intervention as the only way to achieve needed changes—just what business does not want—but it also undermines a company's credibility. First, the behavior is reactive, as the late William A. Durbin, former chairman of Hill & Knowlton, pointed out. Second, it is defensive, suggesting that there is a fundamental conflict between public welfare and industry. Third, the posture business takes in explaining how it is a victim of circumstances evidences a preference for quantification (as in talking about "nonproductive dollars") when the public is focused on something qualitative like "clean air." Fourth, the pattern of response concentrates on the means and ignores the end—an end that business might actually support, like clean air.[23]

All large institutions, not only businesses, are challenged these days: governments, schools and colleges, professional sports, churches, health care groups, fundraising groups and even the news media. With the prevalence of such crises in public confidence, the role of the PR practitioner becomes critical.

Probably the biggest obstacles to "ideal" public relations, as media scholars David Clark and William Blankenburg observe, are economics and human nature:

The plain fact is that managers are hired to make money for owners, and that a conscience can cost money. In the long run, it is money well spent, but many stockholders and managers fix their vision on the short run. Then, too, an abrupt change in corporate policy amounts to a public confession of past misbehavior—or so it seems to many executives. The natural temptation is to play up the good, and to let it go at that.[24]

As a result, in the 1970s a whole "new math" entered the corporate structure. Executives committed to being responsive and responsible attempted to explain social costs to chief financial officers, securities analysts and stockholders. *The Wall Street Journal* called it "the Arithmetic of Quality":

The social critics of business are making headway.

Increasingly, corporations are being held to account not just for their profitability but also for what they do about an endless agenda of social problems. For business executives, it's a whole new ball game. Now they're struggling to come up with a new way to keep score.[25]

With downsizing and restructuring that began in the 1980s and has continued into the twenty-first century, the job became increasingly more difficult.

Many examples of the problems of accountability can be found. How can a profit-and-loss statement be made to reveal on the credit ledger the good a company does when its personnel advise minority businesspeople struggling to succeed in a ghetto? How can the installation of pollution control devices at a factory be calculated as a positive accomplishment, rather than as a drag on productivity? How can the expense of hiring school dropouts and putting them

through company-financed training programs be manifested as a credit rather than as a debit? Conversely, how can the "bad" a company does (by polluting, using discriminatory hiring practices and the like) be measured and reflected as a negative factor in the company's performance?

Despite these problems, **social responsibility** is widely recognized today as an essential part of doing business in the USA. A good indication of how seriously major companies now regard "social accounting" is the big jump onto the "green" bandwagon that occurred in the early 1990s. According to *The Wall Street Journal*, many companies have appointed environmental policy officers.[26] But some of these companies were merely being duplicitous—promoting some environmental efforts while continuing to pollute in another area.[27] Perhaps the reason for this is that some who espoused the environmental cause and wanted to devote more than "window dressing" to it found that the social accounting was quite costly, because it entailed top-to-bottom organizational reform. Still, a company does better to anticipate environmental accountability than to ignore it and eventually face a fine from the Environmental Protection Agency (EPA), as Disney Industries did in 1990. The pressure comes from consumers.

Companies that claim to be doing good for society but aren't, and the public relations people who are their spokespersons, were soundly condemned in a 1997 book by John Stauber and Sheldon Rampton called *Toxic Sludge Is Good for You: Lies, Damn Lies and the Public Relations Industry*. Many practitioners were outraged at being included in what the book called "today's multibillion-dollar propaganda-for-hire industry." Nevertheless, the massive cover-ups by the tobacco industry revealed that same year should stand as a warning that deceit and misrepresentation have sometimes occurred on a massive scale in business and that PR people have been a part of it.

All of this criticism has meant that public relations has had to expand its role as (1) *a problem finder and problem solver or preventer* and (2) *an interpreter—a communication link*. Let's consider these two requirements individually.

PR as Problem Finder, Solver and Preventer PR people have to be problem finders and solvers and, preferably, problem preventers. Such work involves identifying issues and understanding what images are projected and how these are interpreted by global publics.

PR in Practice

The financial scandals of 2002 involving WorldCom, Enron and Arthur Andersen turned a bright light on two corporate board committees, the audit committee and the nominating and corporate governance committee, found in all publicly held companies.

Both are supposed to be composed largely of outside independent directors. The Securities and Exchange Commission began to focus on corporate governance because that is where outside directors should stop any management behavior that is contrary to good corporate citizenship.

The result of that focus is that many public relations firms began offering their services to publicly held companies to help examine the public relations implications—loss of confidence and credibility—that have come as a result of conflict of interest with supposedly outside directors, questionable accounting procedures and excessive executive pay packages, the oversight of another directors' committee—executive compensation.

The heavy focus on corporate governance as the place where major questions need to be asked of management has given PR firms, especially those with a strong public affairs department, a new business opportunity.

Now, in this twenty-first century, words from as long ago as 1965 by the late PR practitioner Philip Lesly remain valid. Lesly outlined the six major problems he saw for business in the second half of the twentieth century.[28] These most "intangible, immeasurable, and unpredictable of all elements affecting business problems," Lesly noted (that may also apply to large nonprofit institutions) were:

1. The main problem in production is no longer how to increase the efficiency of factories and plants, but how to deal with the attitudes of people whose jobs will be changed or eliminated by the introduction of more efficient methods.

2. The principal problem of growth through innovation is not how to organize and administer development programs, but how to deal with the reactions to the product of intended customers and dealers.

3. The personnel problem is not how to project a firm's staff needs and standards, but how to persuade the best people to work for the company—and then to stay and do their best work.

4. The financing problem is not how to plan for the company's funding, but how to deal with the attitudes of investors.

5. The problem in advertising is not how to analyze in minute detail the media, timing and costs, but how to reach the minds and hearts of the audience.

6. The problem of business acceptance is no longer how to demonstrate that an institution is operating in the public interest, but how to get people to understand that its array of activities works better when it has a minimum of restraints.

Each problem Lesly isolated suggests a need for awareness of and sensitivity to what is going on in the minds of publics that now are global. No longer primarily a communicator, today's PR practitioner tries to prevent crises and, once they occur, tries to keep them from getting out of hand. The measure of performance is not only how effectively the client's message gets across but also whether a flare-up that might injure a client's business can be avoided. Often these flare-ups are electronic, instant and global. One major obligation is to help clients conduct their businesses in a way that responds to the new demands made by concerned scientists, environmentalists, consumerists, minority leaders, employees and underprivileged segments of the community.

The most valuable type of public relations activity involves anticipating problems, planning to prevent problems or at least trying to solve them while they are still small.

PR as Interpreter and Communication Link Perhaps, as suggested by Daniel H. Gray, a management consultant noted for his work on the social role of business, social accounting doesn't exist.[29] Indeed, the system needed may well be more concerned with communication than with accounting.

Communication audits—internal, external or both—have become common for institutions trying to track problem areas. Philip Lesly observed that institutions must function in a human climate, and thoughtful managers recognize that they don't have the expertise to deal with this element unaided. As human patterns become more complicated, they demand greater expertise and experience. Consequently, Lesly said, "Communications sense and skills, which have been vital and have always been scarce, are becoming more vital and scarcer still."[30]

This is where the PR practitioner comes in, of course. He or she must act as an interpreter or communication link between an organization and its publics. Lesly added,

Public relations is a bridge to change. It is a means to adjust to new attitudes that have been caused by change. It is a means of stimulating attitudes in order to create change. It helps an organization see the whole of our society together, rather than from one intensified viewpoint. It provides judgment, creativity and skills in accommodating groups to each other, based on wide and diverse experience.[31]

In 1972, David Finn, cofounder of the PR firm of Ruder & Finn, wrote:

Twenty years ago public relations had its eye on the social sciences, with the full expectation that new discoveries would soon be made which would elevate the art of mass communications into a responsible profession. Ten years ago some of us thought computer technology was going to do the trick and the phrase "opinion management" emerged as a possible successor to the long-abandoned "engineering of consent." As things turned out, it is not the technique of public relations which has changed so much as the subject matter with which we are concerned.[32]

Emphasizing PR's role as a communication link, Finn focused on four developments that he held to be true of the job: (1) resolving conflicts may require modifying many opinions, including those held by the public relations consultant and the client; (2) patterns of communication in the future may revolve increasingly around smaller groups;

(3) the random benefits of public relations activities not directly tied to corporate interests will increase; (4) new methods of research now being developed will be especially relevant to situations where opinions change rapidly.[33]

His words were prophetic of the instant global communication system in which PR practitioners now work.

Public relations, one writer notes, does not "create the corporate image or reputation"; rather, "it interprets and advocates the policies, statements, and activities which qualify the corporation for its reputation."[34] In other words, PR cannot fabricate a corporate image; it must start with reality and seek to match the image to the truth. Many people wrongly assume that public relations is preoccupied with image-making in the sense of creating a false front or cover-up. Unfortunately, this misperception of public relations is reinforced by periodic reports of just such behavior on the part of individuals identified as public relations specialists. For example, the term *spin doctor*, which suggests media manipulation through "doctored" (that is, deceptive) accounts or interpretations of events, was introduced in the late 1980s and gained currency in the 1990s.[35] In fact, a *New York Times* story about a media relations course being taught in business schools was headlined "Media Manipulation 101."[36]

At least most media relations instructors are teaching better answers than the following response received by a reporter investigating the troubled Los Angeles-based Security Pacific Bank: "[A] bank spokeswoman says that regulators aren't at the bank; she added that if they were, she wouldn't be permitted to say so."[37]

Discussion Questions

1. Why is public relations a management function? What makes it strategic?

2. What tactics, techniques and roles are suggested by PR's various specialties?

3. What field of public relations interests you most? Why?

Points to Remember

- The practice of PR is now global, but some basic principles apply to it regardless of the culture and the geopolitical area where it is practiced.

Calvin and Hobbes   by Bill Watterson

Although humorous, the cartoon makes the point that many people think of PR as **spin**. Public relations professional Thomas J. Madden called his 1997 book *Spin Man*, and Larry Tye named his 1998 biography of Edward L. Bernays *The Father of Spin*. In today's world of pervasive media, spinning is likely to bring counter information and undesired publicity. CALVIN AND HOBBES © 1990 Watterson. Dist. By UNIVERSAL PRESS SYNDICATE. Reprinted with permission. All rights reserved.

- Because a PR person has only credibility to offer, he or she is only as good as his or her deserved reputation. The organization's credibility is always at stake, too, hence the term *reputation management*.

- PR involves responsibility and responsiveness in policy and information to the best interests of the organization and its publics.

- Demonstrating an active social conscience is the best PR.

- Whatever the title for the public relations function—communications, reputation management or relationship management—it is a *strategic* management function.

- Public relations activities may include press agentry, promotion, publicity, public affairs, research, graphics, advertising, marketing and merchandising support.

- The public relations function has an impact on the organization's policy.

- Use of the term *public relations* for activities such as publicity or other tactics is confusing and misrepresents the function.

- One exception is the term *public affairs* as used by government, which usually does represent the function of public relations.

- PR practitioner roles include being a staff member in a variety of institutional settings, being an agency or firm employee or being an independent PR practitioner.

- Public relations lacks the three major ingredients that qualify a field of activity as a profession: body of knowledge, standard educational curriculum and control over entry and exit.

- Specific areas of PR specialization include nonprofit organizations, educational institutions, fundraising or donor relations, research, international, investor relations, industry, general business, government, health care, sports and leisure time.

- The three traditional interpretations of the function of public relations—controlling publics, responding to publics and achieving mutually beneficial relationships among all publics—correspond to the manipulative, service and transactional models of PR.

- Various typologies attempt to describe what public relations people do. However, who is doing the job, in what kind of communications environment, in what type of organization and in what culture all determine what is being done in the name of public relations.

- PR offers at least eight measurable values to society and the institutions it serves, most of them centering on PR's role in working out institutional and social relationships.

- Social responsibility, once ignored by most institutions, now is viewed as being an essential "cost" of doing business.

- PR people have to be interpreters, functioning as a communication link between an institution and all of its publics.
- Many people wrongly assume that public relations means image-making in the sense of creating a false front, cover-up or "spinning" facts.

Go to the Web site for this book at **www.cengage.com/masscomm/newsom/thisispr10e** to find more Web links on this subject.

Related Web Sites to Review

Professional associations:

Public Relations Society of America
   http://www.prsa.org

International Public Relations Association
   http://www.ipra.org

International Association of Business Communicators
   http://www.iabc.com

National Investor Relations Institute
   http://www.niri.org

Sources for information about PR:

Institute for Public Relations
   http://www.instituteforpr.com

PR Newswire http://www.prnewswire.com

PR Museum http://www.prmuseum.com

About Public Relations
   http://advertising.about.com/od/publicrelationsresources/

Reprinted with permission of King Features Syndicate.

CHAPTER 2

PR's Origins and Evolution

"It's now a very good day to get out anything we want to bury."

—Jo Moore[1], former Labour Party media adviser to Britain's transport secretary, in an email to colleagues an hour after the first hijacked airplane crashed into the World Trade Center in New York Sept. 11, 2001.

OBJECTIVES

- To appreciate that public relations in some form has been a part of societies throughout the history of humankind.
- To recognize how public relations practice has influenced how society has evolved throughout history.
- To understand the critical importance of public relations in a free and democratic society.
- To develop a sensitivity about why public relations evolved, not just in business, but also in government and in a wide range of nongovernmental organizations.
- To create a heightened awareness of how public relations has matured as a professional occupation.

New names for public relations abound, such as integrated communication. Old ones have become more prominent, such as corporate communication.

Arguments exist that not all public relations tasks provide the practitioner with an appropriate claim to the umbrella title of "public relations." Public relations, by that view, should be reserved only for management jobs that involve strategic planning.

Given that the occupation continues to have difficulty defining itself, it should be no surprise that authorities disagree about where and when public relations started and how it got its name. Some historians credit Thomas Jefferson in 1807 with first combining the words *public* and *relations* into *public relations*. Others say that the term was coined by lawyer Dorman Eaton in an address to the Yale graduating class of 1882.[2] Regardless, *public relations* was not used in its modern sense until 1897, when it appeared in the Association of American Railroads' *Yearbook of Railway Literature*.[3] The real success of the term can be credited to Edward L. Bernays, whom Irwin Ross calls "the first and doubtless the leading ideologue of public relations."[4]

Bernays was the first to call himself a "public relations counsel," which he did in 1921. Two years later, he wrote the first book on the subject, *Crystallizing Public Opinion*,[5] and taught the first college course on PR at New York University. Thus it was around the turn of the twentieth century that

PR came into being as a term, as an occupation and as an academic discipline.

Like his uncle Sigmund Freud, Bernays devoted his career to the study of the human mind. His specialty was mass psychology—how the opinions of large numbers of people can be influenced effectively and honorably. When he arrived on the scene, public opinion was considered the province of philosophy. Sociology was in its infancy, and Walter Lippmann had just begun to define what Bernays called "the American tribal consciousness." Bernays' approach to psychology is exemplified in the advice he gave the Procter & Gamble Company when it came to him with a problem: a boycott of its products by black people. Bernays advised Procter & Gamble to eliminate its racist advertising campaign, to hire blacks in white-collar jobs and to invite black people to open-house gatherings at the plant.

The Bernays style was often subtle. For example, he helped the Beech-Nut Packing Company sell bacon not by promoting bacon itself, but by promoting what all America could respond to—a nutritious breakfast. In 1918, Bernays even changed the course of history by convincing Tomas Masaryk, the founder of Czechoslovakia, to delay announcement of that country's independence by a day in order to get better press coverage.

Bernays, who died in 1995 at the age of 103, adamantly believed that public relations is more than mere press agentry. He was not, however, above staging events. In 1924, he helped President Coolidge counteract his aloof image by staging a White House breakfast, to which Al Jolson and several other movie stars were invited. In 1929, he publicized the fiftieth anniversary of the electric light bulb by having Thomas Edison reenact its discovery in the presence of President Hoover.

On the other hand, Bernays turned down an appeal through an intermediary to provide PR assistance to Adolf Hitler in 1933, just before Hitler came to power. A correspondent for the Hearst newspapers told Bernays, however, that—during an interview with Joseph Goebbels, Hitler's minister of propaganda, some years later—he saw Bernays' 1923 book, *Crystallizing Public Opinion*, on the Nazi's desk.[6] ■

Seeking the PR "Source Spring"

For all his influence on the field of public relations, Bernays is not its "founder." In fact, some authorities say Bernays learned public relations while serving on George Creel's Committee on Public Information, which was dedicated to gaining popular support for the U.S. war effort during World War I.

Public relations probably has no single founder, but many public relations practitioners in the USA see Ivy Lee as the first practitioner of a modern-style public relations practice. Most of Lee's early efforts were strictly publicity, but later he and others working in this early era were called for some "media relations" assistance when a crisis occurred. More strategic planning and counsel developed in the Bernays' era.

Without a doubt, public relations developed faster in the USA than in other countries.[7] Historian Alan R. Raucher attributes this to the nation's social, political, cultural and economic climate, as well as to the power of its media to render all large public institutions vulnerable to public opinion.[8] Public relations practice also has become an important service globally, as other nations have adopted or adapted U.S. practices and have developed their own versions of the practices.

Public relations as a concept has no central, identifying founder, national origin or founding date because it focuses on efforts to influence—not only opinions but behavior. This very element has created the greatest criticism of public relations. Historians who view public relations as a significant positive influence regard it as a broker for public support of ideas, institutions and people. Others, however, contend that this role entails the sacrifice of individual freedom, which is usurped by majority decision, that is, "the tyranny of the majority." Of course, the same trade-off is central to the nature of democracy itself; but this does not dispose of the problem that public relations and attempts to influence public opinion can be misused (see Chapter 5).

PR Functions Throughout History

Because the effort to *persuade* underlies all public relations activity, we can say that the general endeavor of public relations is as old as civilization itself. For society to exist, people must achieve some minimum level of agreement, and this agreement is usually reached through interpersonal and group communication. But reaching agreement often requires more than the simple act of sharing information; it demands a strong element of persuasion on the part of all parties involved in the decision-making process. Today persuasion is still the driving force of public relations, and many of the tactics that modern PR people use to persuade have been used by those having power and those seeking power and influence in society for thousands of years.

Monuments and other art forms of the ancient world reflect early efforts at persuasion. Pyramids, statues, temples, tombs, paintings and early forms of writing announce the divinity of rulers, whose power derived from the religious convictions of the public. Ancient art and literature also celebrated the heroic deeds of leaders and rulers, who were considered gods or godlike. Speeches by the powerful or powerseeking used what could be called institutionalized rhetoric (artificial or inflated language) as a principal device for persuasion.

Looking at some of the early techniques and tools used in persuasion can help put today's PR activities in perspective. Certainly such an overview will reveal that, in the process of its development, PR has amalgamated various persuasive techniques that have proved their utility and effectiveness through the centuries.

As Theodore Lustig, a retired professor and former Sun Chemical Corporation communications manager, points out:

> *The ancients had to make do with what they had. Two media, sculpture and coins, were particularly effective, and their use for political ends was refined between the fourth century B.C. and the establishment of the Byzantine Empire in the sixth century A.D., the beginning of the Dark Ages.[9]*

Lustig cites as an example Philip II of Macedonia. By 338 B.C., Philip had subjugated all the city-states of the Hellenic peninsula under his dominion.

Gold and ivory statues of Philip adorned temples along with those of the gods. Philip was thus a good role model for his son, Alexander the Great. In the 13 years of Alexander's reign and conquests (336–323 B.C.), he managed to erect idealized images of himself across Africa, Asia Minor and India. According to Lustig, these image-making lessons were not lost on the first Roman emperor, Augustus.

All Roman emperors, from Augustus on, made use of the ultimate promotion campaign: They proclaimed themselves gods and required the people to worship them.[10] Augustus also had Virgil's *Aeneid* published for propaganda purposes. This epic poem glorified the origin of the Roman people and, by implication, the house of Caesar.

PR Uses and Strategies Throughout History

Throughout history, PR has been used to promote wars, to lobby for political causes, to support political parties, to promote religion, to sell products, to raise money and to publicize events and people. Indeed, most of the uses modern society has found for public relations are not new, and modern PR practitioners have learned a lot by studying the strategies employed by earlier experts.

In 1095 Pope Urban II promoted war against the Muslim caliphate to the east. He sent word through his information network—cardinals, archbishops, bishops and parish priests—that to fight in this holy war was to serve God and to earn forgiveness of sins.

Global Perspective

PR's Early Best Sellers

St. Paul wrote his *Epistles* to encourage membership growth and to boost the morale of the early Christian churches, which were spread about the Roman Empire. His PR campaign was a great success, and his slogans and words of encouragement are still quoted.

The Islamic prophet Mohammed would seclude himself briefly during certain periods of social conflict or crisis and emerge with *suras* (verses) attributed to divine authorship that offered arguments pointing toward a particular resolution of the controversy at hand. These and various more meditative suras became the text of the collection known as the *Koran*.

Dante Alighieri wrote his *Divine Comedy* in Italian rather than in Latin to reach a wider local audience. In the book, Dante, a political activist, eloquently put forth his moral, political and intellectual views.

William Shakespeare's historical plays contained poetry and ideas for the intellectuals and jokes and violence for the rest of the audience. But they also appealed to those in power by glorifying and reinterpreting the War of the Roses to justify the Tudor regime.

John Milton spent much of his career writing pamphlets for the Puritans. He also wrote for the Cromwell government. His greatest work, *Paradise Lost*, is a beautiful and influential statement of Puritan religious views.

PR in Practice

To truly understand public relations practice, it is necessary to view the practice from a global perspective. Many Americans think that public relations evolved in the USA, and it is true that the USA has contributed greatly to public relations theory and practice. However, other countries and regions also have had a long tradition of public relations practice, although sometimes in different forms or with different tactics. Van Ruler and Verčič report that European public relations has existed for more than a century, with the Krupp Company establishing a press relations department in 1870; the beginning of the practice in England was in the 1920s, and the first departments appeared in The Netherlands at the beginning of the twentieth century. The Dutch have the oldest public relations professional association in the world, established in 1946.1 Some Arab-Muslim public relations scholars argue that Mohammed was the first public relations practitioner in their culture, although in the Arab world, public relations and advertising reportedly date back to the 1930s.2 Hung says that public relations in China started thousands of years ago.3 Anantachart says that, in Thailand, the evolution of public relations began in 1283, when the King developed the first Thai alphabet and governed in a style in which public relations techniques were used.4 He established a two-way communication system with his people by setting up a big bell in front of his palace. Citizens could ring the bell, and the king would judge, help or otherwise solve people's problems. Some of the tactics and techniques from around the world and throughout time might seem strange to today's practitioners, but in many ways the goals and objectives of public relations have remained much the same.

Sources: [1]Betteke van Ruler and Dejan Verčič, *The Bled Manifesto* (Ljubljana, Slovenia: Pristop Communications, 2002).

[2]Badran A. Badran, Judy VanSlyke Turk and Timothy N. Walters, "Transformations: Public Relations and the United Arab Emirates Come of Age," in *The Global Public Relations Handbook: Theory, Research and Practice*, ed. Krishnamerthy Sriramesh and Dejan Verčič(Mahway, NJ: Lawrence Erlbaum Associates, Inc., 2003).

[3]Chun-ju Flora Hung, "Public Relations in China." Paper presented at the pre-conference workshop of the conference of the International Communication Association, Seoul, Korea, July 2002.

[4]Saravudh Anantachart, "Understanding Public Relations in Thailand: Its Development and Current Status." Paper presented at the pre-conference workshop of the conference of the International Communication Association, Seoul, Korea, July 2002.

It also gave Christians a once-in-a-lifetime chance to visit the holy shrines. The response was overwhelming, even though the Crusades were not an unqualified success.

In 1215 Stephen Langton, Archbishop of Canterbury, used promotion tactics to lobby for a political cause. He mobilized an influential group of barons to stand up for their rights against King John, and these men ultimately forced the king to agree to the terms of the Magna Carta—a document that has been used as a political banner ever since by people combating political oppression and control. In the fifteenth century Niccolo Machiavelli, an Italian statesman and political philosopher, used his talents as a publicist to support a political party in power. His *The Prince* and *Discourses* are essentially treatises on how to govern people firmly and effectively. Machiavelli's political psychology seems quite modern. His work for Cesare Borgia relied heavily on propaganda and

attempts to influence public opinion—techniques that can be associated today with "issues management."

PR-related activities have been used to promote religion throughout the ages. In 1622 Pope Gregory XV established the *Congregatio de propaganda fide*, the Congregation for Propagating the Faith, to handle missionary activity. From that institution we have retained the word ***propaganda***. In 1351 John Wycliffe called for reform of the Catholic Church and, in particular, for an English translation of the Bible to give the word of God more directly to more people. Wycliffe took his campaign to the people themselves, addressing them on the streets and in public places. Although it was forbidden, he and his followers also distributed books, tracts and broadsides.

Public relations scholars are aware, however, that a "battle/kings" approach to the history of famous people and remarkable events cannot totally explain the evolution of public relations; insights into societal developments are required for such understanding.

PR Tactics Throughout History

Various functions and uses of public relations have certainly existed throughout civilized history. The same cannot be said, however, for many of the *tactics* of twentieth-century PR, because these often depend on relatively recent inventions. For example, much of modern PR relies on electronic communication—telephone, fax, even satellites—and on electronic mass media—movies, radio and television. PR also has been radically affected by the rise of the computer, especially with the advent of the **Internet** and its new social media as well as internal **intranets**.

Of course, not all tactics of modern PR are of recent origin. PR still uses *rhetoric*, which is as old as human speech; *symbols*, which have been around as long as the human imagination; and *slogans*, which date back to people's first consciousness of themselves as groups.

Before the Industrial Revolution the most significant period in the development of PR tactics was a 100-year period starting about 1450. During that time the Renaissance reached its height, the Reformation began and the European rediscovery of the New World occurred. These events gave people a new view of themselves, of one another and of their environment.

The period also marked the beginning of the age of mass media. Around 1450 Johann Gutenberg invented printing from movable type, and the press was born. Few other inventions have had so profound an effect on human culture, at least until the birth of primitive forms of electronic communication at the end of the nineteenth century and the birth of the Internet and the World Wide Web in the late twentieth century. Spinoffs of this innovation in printing have been used by PR practitioners ever since in books, advertising posters, handbills, publicity releases, party publications, newspapers and so on. Of course, these media existed before Gutenberg and his press, but never before could they be produced so efficiently to reach and persuade so many people at once.

The Beginnings of PR in the USA, 1600–1799

As Figure 2.1 indicates, the USA has witnessed five periods or stages in the development of public relations.

During the early colonization of America, PR was used to sell real estate. The Virginia Company in 1620 issued a broadside in England offering 50 acres of free land to anyone who brought a new settler to America before 1625. In 1643 PR was used in the colonies to raise money. Harvard College solicited funds by issuing a public relations brochure titled "New England's First Fruits."[11] Another college was the first to use a

---

Figure 2.1   **Capsule History of PR in the United States**

In the USA the development of PR has gone through five distinct stages:

1. **Preliminary period**—an era of development of the channels of communication and exercise of PR tactics (publicity, promotion and press agentry)
2. **Communicating/initiating**—a time primarily of publicists, press agents, promoters and propagandists
3. **Reacting/responding**—a period of writers hired to be spokespeople for special interests
4. **Planning/preventing**—a maturing of PR as it began to be incorporated into the management function
5. **Professionalism**—an effort by PR practitioners to control PR's development, use and practice on an international level

These stages of evolution are marked by particular periods in U.S. history, which fall into the following divisions:

1600–1799
Initial Colonization, American Revolution

1800–1899
Civil War, Western Expansion, Industrial Revolution

1900–1939
Progressive Era/Muckrakers, World War I, Roaring Twenties, Depression

1940–1979
World War II, Cold War of the 1950s, Consumer Movement

1980–Present
Global Communication

publicity release in the New World to publicize an event. King's College (now Columbia University) sent an announcement of its 1758 commencement to various newspapers, where the item was printed as news.[12] Even sports sponsorship is not new. The first recorded intercollegiate competition was an 1852 rowing match between Harvard and Yale, sponsored by the Boston, Concord and Montreal Railroads.

By the time of the American Revolution, substantial advances had been made in public relations uses and tactics. Although public relations as such did not exist in 1776, many of PR's functions, uses and tactics were already well developed by that time. The patriots who promoted the American Revolution overlooked no opportunity to use PR in their efforts to persuade— that is, to boost the war effort and to rally support for their new political plans. To this end they employed a wide variety of PR tools—**newsletters**, newspapers, heroes, slogans, symbols, rhetoric, organizations, press agentry and publicity—as well as rallies, parades, exhibitions, celebrations, poetry, songs, cartoons, fireworks, effigies and even crude lantern slides.

American patriots made the most of heroes (George Washington, Ethan Allen), legends (Yankee Doodle, the Spirit of '76), slogans ("Give me liberty or give me death!"), symbols (the Liberty Tree) and rhetoric (the speeches of John Adams and the writings of Thomas Jefferson, including the Declaration of Independence). They founded public-spirited organizations (the Sons of Liberty, the Committees of Correspondence). They grabbed every opportunity to interpret events in a light most favorable to their cause: A brawl on March 5, 1770, in which five unruly Bostonians were shot, was billed by the revolutionary press as the "Boston Massacre" and denounced as an atrocity to inflame passions against the British.

When there was no event to exploit, the patriots didn't hesitate to create one. On December 16, 1773, a group of them put on war paint and feathers, boarded a British ship and tossed its cargo of tea leaves overboard. The Boston Tea Party, the main function of which was to attract attention, has been called an early example of American press agentry. Historian Richard Bissell states, "Of all the crazy hooligan stunts pulled off by the colonies against England, the Boston Tea Party was the wildest."[13]

Following independence, another massive effort at persuasion was necessary to push for reform of the short-lived Articles of Confederation. The men who drafted the Constitution conducted an intense PR campaign to sell the document to their colleagues and to the American people. Their propaganda took the form of 85 letters written to newspapers. These letters, by Alexander Hamilton, James Madison and John Jay, became known as the Federalist Papers, and they did much to shape the political opinions of citizens of the young nation. The Bill of Rights, a propaganda piece supported by that spectacular campaigner Patrick Henry, guaranteed citizens numerous rights against the federal government, including freedom of the press. The resulting climate of free interchange encouraged the evolution of public relations into a full-fledged practice. If the Bill of Rights, especially with the provisions of the First Amendment, had not been adopted, public relations would never have become what it is today.

Communicating/Initiating: The Era of Press Agentry and Publicity, 1800–1899

Although PR tactics were initially used in the USA for political purposes, as the nation developed and the nineteenth century progressed, all aspects of life fell under the influence of two PR tools: press agentry and publicity.

Government and Activists

In the 1830s, political sophistication got a boost from the PR innovations of Amos Kendall, the first person to function (although without the title) as a presidential press secretary—to Andrew Jackson. Kendall, an ex–newspaper reporter, held the official position of fourth auditor of the treasury,[14] but in fact he wrote speeches and **pamphlets**, prepared strategy, conducted **polls**, counseled the president on his public image, coordinated the efforts of the executive branch with other branches of government and with the public and constantly publicized Jackson in a favorable light.

PR techniques were also important in the heyday of the political machine. By the late 1850s the Tammany Hall organization of New York was using interviews to gather information about the public mood. This marked the beginning of polling by special interest groups for strategic planning and publicity.[15]

Although public relations had always been employed in political campaigns in an effort to persuade, the 1888 Harrison–Cleveland presidential race showed a growing sophistication in its use. First, far greater use was made of the press—newspapers, pamphlets, fliers and the first official campaign press bureau—during that election year. The political campaign grew even more sophisticated during the 1896 race between Bryan and McKinley.[16] Both parties established campaign headquarters and flooded the nation with propaganda. Campaign trains and public opinion polls were also used extensively.[17]

Politicians were not the only ones to sell their ideas through PR. Agitators of many persuasions discovered that publicity could help change the nation's thinking. By relying mainly on appeals to public sentiment, groups such as the antivivisectionists, the American Peace Party and the Women's Christian Temperance Union met with varying degrees of success. Leaders of the women's suffrage movement publicized their cause at the 1876 centennial celebration in Philadelphia; on July 4, Elizabeth Cady Stanton, Susan B. Anthony and Matilda Joslyn Gage staged a demonstration to dramatize that their rights as citizens had not yet been won.[18]

The most compelling protest movement of the nineteenth century was the abolitionist or antislavery movement, which consisted of many allied organizations. These organizations found that their cause was helped not only by news releases and press agentry stunts but also by getting public figures and newspaper editors to endorse their efforts and ideas. Forming an editorial alliance with a mass medium extended the reach of their message and gave it prestige and credibility.

Harriet Beecher Stowe used the partisan press to publicize the antislavery cause. Her best known work, *Uncle Tom's Cabin, or Life Among the Lowly*, was first published in serial form in an abolitionist journal. When the novel appeared as a book in 1852, some 300,000 copies were sold above the Mason–Dixon line, the cultural boundary between the northern and southern states.

The fund drive, a very successful PR practice first used to raise money for military purposes, came into existence during the Civil War. During that war, the Treasury Department put Jay Cooke, a banker, in charge of selling war bonds to the public. Not only did the bonds finance the army, but the mass sales effort also roused public opinion in support of the Union cause.[19] Similar fundraising programs were later used to finance war efforts during World Wars I and II.

National Development

PR also was an important factor in the westward development of the USA. The Western frontier was sold like real estate by the forerunners of modern PR practitioners, who made the most of legends and heroes. As early as 1784, for example, John Filson promoted land deals by making a legendary figure out of Daniel Boone, an unschooled, wandering hunter and trapper.[20] Almost a century later, George Armstrong Custer was likewise made into a hero—partly to justify U.S. policy toward the Native Americans, partly to promote the settling of the West and partly to sell newspapers and dime novels.

In the 1840s various publicists actively encouraged interest in the West. Perhaps the most effective publicist of Westward expansion was *New York Tribune* publisher Horace Greeley, whose editorial "Go West, Young Man, and Grow Up with the Country" changed the lives of many people and the demographics of the entire nation.

But if the West was sold by PR techniques, it also was exploited by some of those same techniques. Press agent Matthew St. Clair Clarke brought Davy Crockett, the frontier hero, to the public's attention in the 1830s and used Crockett's glory to win political support away from Andrew Jackson. Two generations later, the adventures of Western personalities such as Buffalo Bill, Wyatt Earp, Calamity Jane and Wild Bill Hickock were blown out of all proportion (to the benefit of their promoters in the Eastern press) to give people a glamorous picture of the American frontier. Even outlaws like Jesse James became adept at using the press for glory—and to mislead the authorities.

Entertainment and Culture

The role of PR in the growth of America's entertainment industry was substantial. In fact, the PR tactic of press agentry grew up with the entertainment business in the nineteenth century, a flamboyant era of road shows and circuses. P. T. Barnum was one of many circus show people who employed press agentry.

Publicity stunts were even used occasionally to attract attention to books and their authors. For example, in 1809 the *New York Evening Post* ran a story about the mysterious disappearance of one Diedrich Knickerbocker from his residence in the Columbian Hotel. In follow-up stories, readers learned that Knickerbocker had left a manuscript, which the hotel's owner offered to sell to cover the cost of the unpaid bill. Later, the publishing house of Inskeep & Bradford announced in the same newspaper that they were publishing the manuscript, titled *Knickerbocker's History of New York*. The whole story was a hoax, a publicity campaign conducted by the book's real author, Washington Irving.[21]

In the field of education, the value of PR was recognized even before the Revolution. In the nineteenth century, the trend continued. In 1899 Yale University established a PR and alumni office, showing that even the most established institutions were ready to enlist the budding profession to help them create favorable public opinion.[22] In 1900 Harvard University hired the Publicity Bureau—the nation's first PR firm, formed in Boston in 1900—but refused to pay the bureau's fees after about 1902. Nevertheless, the bureau continued to service the client for the resulting prestige.

Business and Industry

The development of industry during the 1800s brought about the most significant changes in the history of PR. The technological advances of the Industrial Revolution changed and modernized the tactics and techniques of PR. Steam power and inventions such as the Linotype, a "hot metal" type line-casting machine, made newspapers a truly democratic, nationwide mass medium.

Although the early industrialists used advertising to sell their wares and services to a growing market, they were not very interested in other functions of public relations. The prevailing attitude of the "robber barons" of the latter half of the nineteenth century was summed up by William Henry Vanderbilt, head of the New York Central Railroad: "The public be damned."[23] J. P. Morgan, another railroad tycoon, echoed this sentiment when he said, "I don't owe the public anything." During the years between the Civil War and the turn of the century, industrial profit and power controlled and reshaped American life. Industrial magnates were answerable to no one and were immune to pressure from government, labor or public opinion.

An example of the corporate attitude at that time was the behavior of steel tycoon Andrew Carnegie during the Homestead Strike of 1892. When labor problems in his steel plant erupted into violence, Carnegie retired to his lodge in Scotland, 35 miles from the nearest railroad or telegraph. Carnegie wanted to be known as a cultured philanthropist,

---

PR in Practice

Phineas Taylor Barnum (1810–1891)

The most famous and successful of nineteenth-century press agents was P. T. Barnum, who created, promoted and exploited the careers of many celebrities, including the midget General Tom Thumb, singer Jenny Lind and Chang and Eng, the original Siamese twins. Early in his career, in 1835, Barnum exhibited a black slave named Joice Heth, claiming that she had nursed George Washington 100 years before. Newspapers fell for the story, intrigued by its historical angle. Then, when public interest in Joice Heth began to die down, Barnum kept the story alive by writing letters to the editor under assumed names, debating her authenticity. Barnum didn't care what the papers said, as long as he got space. When Heth died, an autopsy revealed her age to be about 80. With the fraud exposed, Barnum claimed that he also had been duped.[1] Was this true? Why not? After all, "There's a sucker born every minute."

The great circus showman was himself often the center of public attention, for which he credited his own press agent, Richard F. "Tody" Hamilton.[2] However, the term *press agent* was first formally used by another circus. In 1868 the roster of John Robinson's Circus carried the name W. W. Duran with the title "press agent."[3]

Barnum's circus museum in Bridgeport, Connecticut, celebrated its centennial in 1993.[4]

Sources: [1]Edward L. Bernays, *Public Relations* (Norman: University of Oklahoma Press, 1952), pp. 38–9.

[2]Dexter W. Fellows and Andrew A. Freeman, *This Way to the Big Show* (New York: Viking Press, 1936), p. 193.

[3]Will Irwin, "The Press Agent: His Rise and Decline," *Colliers,* 48 (Dec. 2, 1911), pp. 24–5.

[4]Craig Wilson, "These Days Life Is but a Scheme," *USA Today* (August 31, 1993).

and he let the London press know that he remained aloof from the labor struggle only to protect his company from his own generosity. But professionally, he had not amassed a fortune of $400 million by worrying about the working or living conditions of his poorly paid employees, and he was content to have his right-hand man, Henry Clay Frick, crush their strike and their union with the help of the state militia.[24]

Nonetheless, even in the 1800s, a few large corporations recognized that in the long run they would have to woo the public's favor. In 1858 the Borden Company, a producer of dairy products, set a PR precedent by issuing a financial report to its stockholders.[25] In 1883 an even more important precedent was set by Theodore N. Vail, general manager of the American Bell Telephone Company. Vail wrote to the managers of local exchanges, urging them to reexamine the services they were offering and the prices they were charging.[26] His letter is significant because it shows concern for the consumer and an interest in improving relations between the telephone company and the public.

In 1877 Jay Gould opened a "literary bureau" for the Union Pacific Railroad, for the purpose of attracting immigrants to the West.[27] In about 1888 the Mutual Life Insurance Company hired an outside consultant, Charles J. Smith, to write press releases and articles to boost the company's image.[28] In 1889 the Westinghouse Corporation established, under the directorship of ex–newspaperman E. H. Heinrichs, what was essentially the first in-house publicity department in the USA.[29]

This was also the period when department stores first appeared in the USA. The originator of the concept, John Wanamaker, was also the best in the business at public relations. When his Philadelphia store opened in 1876, Wanamaker used publicity to generate interest in the new idea of a store that covered a full 2 acres. He gave visitors copies of a self-printed 16-page "souvenir booklet" that explained the store's departments, hiring policies and dedication to customer service. Salespeople were instructed in how to capture quotes from visitors that could later be incorporated into news releases.[30] Wanamaker also founded the *Farm Journal*, which he published for years, and he began publishing the *Ladies Home Journal* to sell ladies' fashions.[31] Macy's, Bloomingdale's, Lord & Taylor and Marshall Field's quickly caught on and began publishing their own magazines and souvenir books.[32]

Press Agents and Publicists

It has often been said that twentieth-century public relations primarily grew out of nineteenth-century press agentry. In some ways this is true. Certainly, many early PR practitioners got their start as press agents. Although few of these PR pioneers were as flamboyant as the great showman P. T. Barnum, many were publicity writers whose main target had always been the press. The greatest of the publicity consultants was Ivy Ledbetter Lee.

Press Agentry Press agentry really began in about 1830, with the birth of the penny press. When newspaper prices dropped to a penny each, circulation and readership boomed, but so did the price of newspaper advertising. To reach the huge new audience without paying for the opportunity, promoters and publicity people developed a talent for "making news." The object was simply to break into print, often at the expense of truth or dignity. Press agents exploited "freaks" to publicize circuses, invented legends to promote politicians, told outrageous lies to gain attention and generally provided plenty of popular entertainment if not much real news.

The cardinal virtue of press agentry was its promptness. Indeed, it was often so prompt that its practitioners spent practically no time verifying the accuracy or news value of its content. But ultimately the effectiveness of a press release depended on its creator's imagination, and imagination remains a necessary talent for effective PR today.

Publicity Many early publicists were no more careful with the facts than their press agent contemporaries; neither were many journalists of that day. Most publicists continually tried to "plant" stories in newspapers, hiding their sources. In that respect, Ivy Lee represented a new kind of publicist. Perhaps the essential difference can be found in Lee's "Declaration of Principles" (1906), in which he defined the important ideals of public relations, his new profession: "Our plan is, frankly and openly . . . to supply the press and public of the United States prompt and accurate information concerning subjects which it is of value and interest to the public to know about."[33]

Lee's career spans the earlier era of communicating/initiating and the subsequent era of reacting/responding (1900–1939). At the dawn of the twentieth century, PR's incubation period had drawn to a close.

America was now a powerful, industrialized nation with sophisticated mass media and a well-informed public. The time was right for a model of practice that would synthesize and coordinate the various talents—publicity, promotion, propaganda and press agentry—that had developed in tandem with the nation's growth.

Reacting/Responding: The Time of Reporters-in-Residence, 1900–1939

Public relations developed significantly in the first four decades of the twentieth century, as publicists became spokespersons for organizations. As the

Ethical Perspective

Ivy Ledbetter Lee (1877–1934): "The Father of Public Relations"

After graduating from Princeton, Ivy Lee became a reporter in New York City but soon gave that up to become a political publicist. Then in 1904 he and George F. Parker formed the nation's third publicity bureau. By 1906 he was the most inspiring success in the young field of PR and found himself representing George F. Baer and his associates (who were allied with the J. P. Morgan financial empire) in a public controversy over an anthracite coal strike. Lee tried a radical approach: Frankly announcing himself as a publicity consultant, he invited the press to ask questions, handed out news releases and presented his client as cooperative and communicative.[1]

Lee's "Declaration of Principles," issued in 1906 to city editors all over the country, won respect for public relations (and didn't hurt the Baer bunch either). That same year, Lee represented the Pennsylvania Railroad when an accident occurred on the main line. Instead of hushing up the incident, Lee invited the press to come, at company expense, to the scene of the accident, where he made every effort to supply reporters with facts and to help photographers. As a result, the Pennsylvania Railroad and the railroad industry got their first favorable press coverage in years.[2]

Lee's remarkable, straightforward style came from his frank admiration of industry and capitalism, and he made it his goal to get big business to communicate its story to the public. By the time he was 30, Lee had sired a profession, chiefly by introducing and promoting its first code of ethics.

Lee's career continued to be successful, if not so influenced by high ideals. He began working for the Rockefeller family in 1913, when he presented the "facts" about a coal strike in Colorado that resulted in an incident known as the Ludlow Massacre. Lee later admitted that the "facts" he handed out about the bloody affair were the facts as management saw them, and that he had not checked them for accuracy.[3]

Lee's many later clients included the American Russian Chamber of Commerce and the German Dye Trust, from whom he earned $25,000 a year and a sticky PR problem of his own—how to defend his work for a Nazi organization. He was also heavily criticized for his support of Stalin-era Soviet Russia and his encouragement of U.S.–Soviet ties.

Lee once wrote, "The relationship of a company to the people . . . involves far more than *saying*—it involves *doing*."[4] Nevertheless, it is perhaps an example of Ivy Lee's public relations talent that he is now remembered not so much for what he *did* at the height of his career as for what he *said* when he was still in his twenties.[5]

Sources: [1]Frank Luther Mott, *American Journalism* (New York: Macmillan, 1950), pp. 179–80.

[2]Irwin Ross, *The Image Merchants* (Garden City, N.Y: Doubleday, 1959), p. 31.

[3]Ibid.

[4]Ibid., p. 32.

[5]For a defense of Lee's often-criticized international activities, see the letter to the editor of *PR Review*, 13(3) (Fall 1987), pp. 12–13, by James W. Lee, his son.

age of unchecked industrial growth ended, industry faced new challenges to its established way of doing business. The new century began with a cry of protest from the "muckrakers"—investigative journalists who exposed scandals associated with power capitalism and government corruption. The term *muckraker* is a metaphor taken from John Bunyan's *Pilgrim's Progress*. It was first used in its modern sense by Theodore Roosevelt, who applied it pejoratively to journalists who attacked the New York Police Department in 1897, while he was commissioner. Later as president, with a consumer protection platform and a trust-busting program, Roosevelt came to appreciate the muckrakers.[34]

The Turn of the Century

Perhaps the first of the muckrakers was Joseph Pulitzer, whose editorials supported labor in the Homestead strike of 1892. "The public be informed," his slogan for an earlier campaign in support of labor, parodied the contemptuous attitude of William H. Vanderbilt.[35] But the great age of muckraking journalism began in the twentieth century.[36]

Lincoln Steffens, staff writer for *McClure's* magazine, wrote articles and books exposing corruption in municipal politics. Frank Norris, who covered the Spanish–American War for *McClure's*, took on the railroads and the wheat traders in his novels *The Octopus* (1901) and *The Pit* (1903). Ida Tarbell's *History of the Standard Oil Company* (1904), which began as a series for *McClure's* in 1902 and consisted mainly of interviews with former Rockefeller employees, exposed the company's corruption and its unfair competition with smaller companies. In 1906 Upton Sinclair described the unsavory conditions that existed in the meat-packing industry in his novel *The Jungle*. These articles and books resulted in social legislation that remains the law of the land today.

Big business also was under fire from the government. President Theodore Roosevelt considered it the federal government's job to uphold the public interest in the battles that flared among management, labor and consumers. Using the Sherman Antitrust Act of 1890, he challenged big business—including U.S. Steel, Standard Oil and the Pennsylvania Railroad—to respond to popular displeasure.

An era of social consciousness was dawning. Proof that the former "public be damned" attitude was giving way came in 1899 with the founding of the first national consumer group, the National Consumers

League (NCL), which was formed from state consumer leagues by Florence Kelley and Dr. John Graham Brooks.[37] The fledgling NCL supported the work of Harvey W. Wiley, a Department of Agriculture chemist who for more than 20 years gathered information to prove the need for a federal food and drug law. The first Pure Food and Drug Act was passed in 1906.

Industry *had* to respond. It could no longer afford simply to ignore the public and the press. Threatening to withhold advertising from uncomplimentary media did not have the desired effect. No longer could the railroads placate the press by giving free passes to reporters. No longer would the public buy statements like that of coal industrialist George F. Baer, who in 1902 told labor to put its trust in "the Christian men whom God in His infinite wisdom has given control of the property interests of the country."[38] When the coal industry came under fire again in 1906, the coal owners had learned their lesson. Instead of relying on puffery and rhetoric, they enlisted the talents of the young ex–newspaper reporter, Ivy Lee.

It is no coincidence that most of the first generation of public relations specialists came from newspapers. Newspaper advertising had long been the only way that many companies communicated with their markets. Newspapers also were the medium in which many companies were being attacked. And newspaper coverage had been the main goal of nineteenth-century press agents, whose legacy inspired the first publicity agencies of the twentieth century.

The first publicity firm, the Publicity Bureau, was formed in Boston in 1900.[39] The idea of publicity caught on quickly, and soon several such firms—composed largely of ex–newspaper people—had appeared, including the firm of William Wolf Smith in Washington, D.C., which specialized in publicity aimed at influencing legislators.[40] From a historical standpoint, however, the most important publicity bureau during this period was the one operated by George F. Parker and Ivy Lee. Although that company lasted only four years, it launched the career of Ivy Lee.

Before long, publicity became a standard and necessary tool for many businesses, individuals and organizations. Big businesses especially, such as communication companies, railroads and the automobile industry, found that publicity agencies and in-house publicity bureaus improved their relations with both the public and the government. In 1904 two major universities—the University of Pennsylvania and the University of Wisconsin—set up publicity bureaus.[41]

Publicity also proved valuable for public service organizations. The Young Men's Christian Association (YMCA) employed a full-time publicist to call attention to its fund drive in 1905.[42] The National Tuberculosis Association started a publicity program in 1908, and the American Red Cross followed suit the same year.[43] The U.S. Marine Corps established a publicity bureau in 1907 in Chicago.[44] In 1909 the Trinity Episcopal Church in New York City hired Pendleton Dudley as a public relations counsel to help combat criticism of its ownership of slum tenements.[45] Three years later the Seventh-Day Adventist Church established a formal publicity bureau to answer complaints about its opposition to Sunday closing laws.[46]

Publicity in support of a product was used by National Cash Register founders John and Frank Patterson, who employed newsletters, brochures and flyers in the world's first direct-mail campaign.

Many useful tactics and techniques were developed during this early period. One PR pioneer who contributed a number of new ideas was Samuel Insull, publicity expert for the Chicago Edison Company.[47] Insull had a demonstration electric cottage constructed in 1902 to show how convenient the new technology was. In 1903 he communicated with the company's customers via bill stuffers and a house publication that was distributed to the community. In 1909 Insull became the first person to make PR-related movies.[48] (This was appropriate, because Thomas Edison himself was one of the first movie tycoons.)

Larger organizations, such as the Ford Motor Company, helped broaden business' interest in the public relations function. In 1908 Ford established a house publication, *Ford Times*.[49] In 1912 the company began using public opinion surveys for market research.[50] And in 1914 Ford established the first corporate film department.[51]

The first formally designated press bureau in the federal government was founded in 1905 by the U.S. Forest Service.[52] The aggressiveness of its promotions is said to have been one of the elements leading to the 1913 federal ban on hiring public relations people.[53] However, Walter Lippmann's concern over the infiltration of German propaganda into American newspapers in the years immediately preceding World War I was another contributing factor, as was the growing resentment by newspaper reporters and editors of publicists.[54]

Making the World Safe for Democracy

By the time the USA entered World War I in 1917, the war had been going on for several years (since 1914), and PR had proven itself an effective weapon of persuasion for Europeans. The British, in particular, directed a "hands across the sea" propaganda campaign at the U.S. government and people, urging them to join the fight. They publicized the Allies' view of the *Lusitania* incident, for example, characterizing the Germans (whose submarine had sunk the ocean liner) as vicious "Huns." When President Wilson finally gave up his policy of peacemaking and neutrality, the USA entered the war with money, military might and a massive public relations effort. This PR effort was seen as essential to gain popular support in a country with many German immigrants and first generation German-Americans.

In selling the war as one destined "to make the world safe for democracy," the U.S. government solicited cooperation from many sources. The government convinced AT&T that the government needed control of the phone company for the war effort.[55] The press was persuaded to exercise self-censorship and to contribute free advertising space for the war effort.[56] Academics served too. College professors acted as a force of Four-Minute Men, meaning that they were prepared to speak for that length of time on propaganda topics relating to the war. The world, not just the classroom, was their forum.

The government also solicited cooperation directly from the public: Herbert Hoover's Food Administration persuaded American citizens to conserve food during this time of emergency. The greatest example of the government's salesmanship, however, was the Liberty Loan Drive, which financed the war.

The genius behind America's wartime public relations effort was George Creel, a former newspaper reporter whom President Wilson appointed as chairman of the newly formed Committee on Public Information. The success of the Liberty Loan Drive and the effectiveness of U.S. wartime propaganda at home and abroad were both attributable to the Creel Committee.

The committee also created a legacy for the PR profession. Many members of the committee who learned their craft in wartime went on to practice it in peacetime. Included among these were Edward L. Bernays[57] and Carl Byoir.[58] As assistant chairman of the Creel Committee, Byoir publicized the draft and was in charge of distributing the *Red White and Blue Textbooks*, which described the goals of the war. He went on to become one of America's most successful public relations practitioners.

The Roaring Twenties

Public relations as well as advertising grew in scope and in stature during the 1920s. Books and courses were offered on the subject, and social scientists began to take notice. Among them was Walter Lippmann, a former adviser to President Wilson, who expressed concern over the implications of public opinion molding. In *Public Opinion* (1922), he wrote that the public no longer formed its own opinions, particularly about government policy; instead, people's opinions, like their knowledge, were fed to them by the media in the form of slogans and stereotypes.[59] He pointed out, however, that opinion molding is a two-way street. Society contains "innumerable large and small corporations and institutions, voluntary and semi-voluntary associations, national, provincial, urban and neighborhood groupings, which often as not make the decisions that the political body registers."[60]

Social scientists' interest in public opinion was shared by industry. Many companies, including AT&T, had learned from their experiences in World War I that social responsibility was good for public relations and hence good for business.[61] Thus the field of opinion research grew as companies developed tactics for finding out what their stockholders, their markets and the general community wanted. AT&T's cooperation with the government during the war had earned it the confidence of the government and of the pro-war public. When Arthur W. Page joined the company in 1927 as vice president and in-house public relations expert, he stressed several opinions that have affected modern PR ever since: that business begins with the public's permission and survives because of its approval; that businesses should have public relations departments with real influence in top management; and that companies should find out what the public wants and make public commitments that will work as "hostages to performance." Page insisted that PR is built by performance, not by publicity.[62]

The New Deal

The mood of the 1930s differed drastically from that of the 1920s. Following the stock market crash of 1929, the U.S. economy plunged into a depression from which it did not fully recover for 10 years. Public relations during this time faced many challenges, as industry was forced to defend itself against public distrust, a discontented labor force and strict regulation by the Roosevelt administration. The greatest challenge to PR, however, was the job of selling good cheer to a confused and frightened populace. The challenge was felt by government, and successive presidents responded by trying to convince the country that a return to prosperity was just around the corner and that the only thing to fear was fear itself. The challenge was also felt by industry, and in 1938 the National Association of Manufacturers and the U.S. Chamber of Commerce conducted a comprehensive campaign based on the slogan "What helps business helps you."[63]

PR continued to develop as a field of practice during the 1930s. The National Association of Accredited Publicity Directors was founded in 1936. The American Association of Industrial Editors, founded two years later, was an indirect descendant of earlier groups, including the Association of House Organ Editors, which had been formed in 1915. The American Council on Public Relations (ACPR) was founded in 1939 by Rex Harlow,[64] but it had no chapters. The National Association of Accredited Publicity Directors, which changed its name in 1944 to the National Association of Public Relations Counsel, had chapters and requirements for professional experience. This group merged with Harlow's ACPR in 1948 to form the Public Relations Society of America.

Another significant development during the 1930s was the institution of the Gallup Poll, which gave a boost to the sophistication and credibility of opinion research.[65]

The Increasing Influence of U.S. Presidents as Opinion Makers

The management of news by U.S. presidents goes back to George Washington, who leaked his Farewell Address to a favored publisher who he knew would give it a good display. When Thomas Jefferson was in Washington's cabinet, he put a newspaper reporter on the federal payroll to establish a party newspaper that would represent Jefferson's point of view; later, when he became president, he relied heavily on his "party press" and limited other newspapers' access to him.

Abraham Lincoln sought out newspaper editors who he believed might convey his ideas sympathetically to the people and thus help win their support for his policies. The significance he placed on public opinion is apparent in his famous statement, "Public sentiment is everything. With public sentiment, nothing can fail; without it, nothing can succeed. Consequently, he who molds public sentiment goes deeper than he who enacts statutes or pronounces decisions."

Theodore Roosevelt developed the "trial balloon" device, calling favorite reporters to the White House to get their reaction to his ideas before trying them out on the public. He was sensitive to media coverage and once waited to sign a Thanksgiving Proclamation until the Associated Press photographer arrived.[66]

However, Calvin Coolidge is credited with having arranged the first pure photo opportunity, some 20 years later, on the occasion of his fifty-fifth birthday. The taciturn president liked photo sessions because he didn't have to talk during them.[67]

Woodrow Wilson developed the first regular formal press conferences, although he later regretted

the idea, for he was a reserved man and never won popularity with the press. He also complained that the press was interested in the personal and the trivial rather than in principles and policies—to which the press responded that presidents just want journalists to print what they tell them, not what the public wants to know.

Franklin Roosevelt's candor and geniality delighted reporters, but even he sometimes regretted holding press conferences; once, in a pique, he said that he would like to award a Nazi Iron Cross to a news reporter whose stories he felt had earned it. Roosevelt staged a great many photo sessions so that photographers wouldn't take candid pictures that called attention to his paralysis.[68]

Roosevelt, more than any of his predecessors, used public relations tactics to sway public opinion, and the development of mass media technology during the 1930s enhanced his efforts. In the decades following his death, he drew increased retrospective criticism for "managing news," as have more recent presidents and their spokespeople. There may be some justification for this criticism, because the executive branch can end most independent reportorial investigations into its affairs by claiming "executive privilege." No one expects to find out too much from the judiciary branch,

PR in Practice

PR at AT&T—A Long History

In 1938 Arthur Wilson Page, first vice president for public relations of the American Telephone and Telegraphy Company (AT&T), told an international management congress that "the task which business has, and which it has always had, is of fitting itself to the patterns of public desires." A familiar saying of the PR pioneer was that in a democratic society no business could exist without public permission nor long succeed without public approval. Page also helped to popularize opinion survey techniques. In doing so Page was following through on the philosophy of a predecessor who was very conscious of public opinion: Theodore Vail, AT&T president in the early 1900s, had sent a series of questions about service to Bell telephone exchange managers to inquire about how well Bell was serving its customers. He understood the power of public opinion, noting that it was based on information and belief. When public opinion was wrong, it was because of wrong information, and Vail said it was "not only the right, but the obligation of all individuals . . . who come before the public, to see the public have full and correct information." The long history of PR at AT&T makes even more amazing the public support of the 1982 consent decree that separated individual Bell companies from each other and from AT&T. Page's philosophy and views of public relations are kept alive today by members of the Arthur Page Society, a professional membership organization founded by Bell public relations practitioners.

Sources: E. M. Block, "Arthur Page and the Uses of Knowledge," Inaugural Lecture, Arthur Page Lecture and Awards Program, College of Communication, University of Texas at Austin, April 22, 1982. Reprinted with permission of E. M. Block.

because of restrictions on what can be discussed, in keeping with the American Bar Association's code of judicial conduct; but, in the legislative branch, what one party won't tell, the other will.

Planning/Preventing: The Growth of PR as a Management Function, 1940–1979

With the advent of the 1940s, the nation's mood changed again. The country was soon at war, and, as in World War I, the most conspicuous public relations efforts either served the war effort directly or were obvious byproducts of a wartime economy.

World War II

When the USA entered World War II, PR firms quickly seized the opportunity to enlist in the cause. Hill & Knowlton, for example, firmly established itself by representing war industry groups such as the Aviation Corporation of America, the American Shipbuilding Council and the Aeronautical Chamber of Commerce.[69] Overall, the PR effort during World War II was much more sophisticated, coordinated and integrated than the one during World War I.

Communications scholar Charles Steinberg believes that World War II caused public relations to develop into a "full-fledged profession."[70] In 1947 Boston University established the first full school of public relations,[71] now part of the College of Communication. By 1949 more than 100 colleges and universities across the nation were offering courses in PR.

Two significant events in government affected the future of public relations. One was the appointment of former newscaster Elmer Davis as director of the Office of War Information (OWI)—the forerunner of the agency that would become the U.S. Information Agency that was disbanded in October 1999. Davis' program was even larger than George Creel's had been, but it was focused exclusively on the task of disseminating information worldwide. Unlike Creel, Davis was not an advisor to the president. At OWI evidence of government-planted disinformation began to appear.

The second event to affect PR practice was the creation of a War Advertising Council, which handled war-related public service announcements and created slogans like "Loose lips sink ships." The two organizations were tremendously successful in winning support for the USA at home and abroad, in helping to sell war bonds and in winning cooperation from the public, from industry and from labor.

Ethical Perspective

PR Stands for President Roosevelt

Franklin Delano Roosevelt used every possible public relations device to sell the radical reforms of his New Deal to the American people. Advised by PR expert Louis McHenry Howe, FDR projected an image of self-confidence and happiness—just what the American public wanted to believe in. He talked to them on the radio. He smiled for the cameras. He was mentioned in popular songs. He even allowed himself to be one of the main characters in a Rodgers and Hart musical comedy (played by George M. Cohan, America's favorite Yankee Doodle Dandy). Of course, FDR's public image didn't succeed with everybody. But in general, the American people liked FDR, and they showed it by putting him in the White House four times.

   Louis McHenry Howe also encouraged First Lady Eleanor Roosevelt to expand her public activities. She had joined the National Consumers League as an 18-year-old volunteer and was very interested in public issues. With Howe's help, she developed news conferences for women reporters only—"news hens," they came to be called. Nevertheless, they got exclusives from Eleanor, despite being excluded from most other news meetings because of their gender.

Source: L. L. L. Golden, *Only by Public Consent.* Copyright © 1968 by L. L. L. Golden. Used by permission of Dutton, a division of Penguin Group (USA) Inc.

The use of films for PR purposes expanded greatly during this period. In 1943, for example, Frank Capra made a documentary film for the U.S. Signal Corps to inspire patriotism and build morale.[72] The government was not alone in using film for PR, however; Hollywood also made countless movies glorifying American fighting forces. The persuasive power of film was not lost on industry officials. In 1948 filmmaker Robert Flaherty made the documentary *Louisiana Story*[73] for Standard Oil.

Individual companies adapted to the war in different ways, often with the help of PR. Because of wartime ink shortages, the American Tobacco Company had to change the color of the Lucky Strike package from green to white. Thanks to PR, the change caused the company only a moment's regret. It launched a new campaign promoting a new slogan: "Lucky Strike Green Has Gone to War." Lucky Strike smokers everywhere were proud of their new white package because it signified that their brand was doing its part for America.

For Standard Oil of New Jersey, the war created a public relations crisis. At hearings of Senator Harry Truman's Committee on National Defense, Assistant Attorney General Thurman Arnold charged Standard Oil with "acting against American intent."[74] The charge involved a deal that Standard Oil had made with a German company many years earlier. In response, the oil company's marketing director, Robert T. Haslan, mounted a public opinion campaign, sending letters to customers and stockholders and hiring Earl Newsom as outside PR counsel. Eventually, Standard Oil beat the charges and came out of it with public support.[75]

In 1945 the same public relations fervor that helped sell the war effort contributed to the postwar industrial recovery. In that year, Henry Ford II, the new president of Ford Motor Company, hired Earl Newsom as a PR consultant. Newsom helped Ford compose a letter to the United Automotive Workers (UAW) during a strike at General Motors, urging the union to be reasonable and fair. He also helped Ford with his speech to the Society of Automotive Engineers in January 1946 and with an important antilabor address to the Commonwealth Club in San Francisco the following month. With Newsom's help, young Ford became a public figure—a respected and publicized spokesperson for responsible business management.[76]

The Fabulous Fifties and the Military-Industrial Complex

During the 1950s America again experienced a booming economy, this time based largely on rising production of consumer goods. The population was growing faster than ever, and more and more people were getting good educations and entering the white-collar workforce. Technology progressed on all fronts: television, satellites, atomic energy and the mainframe computer. Industry, despite "labor pains," continued to grow at home and abroad. Yet the mood of the nation reflected fear—of Communists, Russians, the atomic bomb, McCarthyism, technology, juvenile delinquency and mass conformity, to name a few. In 1955 Sloan Wilson examined society and described the American white-collar worker in his best-selling novel, *The Man in the Gray Flannel Suit.* The hero, Tom Rath, was an in-house PR person for a large broadcasting corporation.

Public relations grew with the economy. That Wilson's typical businessperson was a PR practitioner shows how well established public relations had become. In 1953 the International Chamber of Commerce set up a commission on public relations, and in 1954 the Public Relations Society of America (PRSA) developed its first code of ethics.[77] A year later the International Public Relations Association was founded. Its individual members currently represent more than 96 countries. Many public relations organizations in other countries also trace their founding to the period from 1955 to 1960.

By the end of the 1950s, a number of women had entered the field, including several who ranked among the nation's top PR people: Doris E. Fleischman Bernays, early PR pioneer; Denny Griswold, former editor and publisher of *Public Relations News*; Jane Stewart, then president of Group Attitudes Corporation; and Leone Baxter, former president of Whitaker and Baxter International in San Francisco.[78] In 1957 President Eisenhower appointed Anne Williams Wheaton his associate press secretary, drawing nationwide attention to PR as a potential career for women.[79]

The affluence of the 1950s encouraged businesses to find new uses for their money, and one job of public relations was to help them reinvest it in society—not only in tax-sheltering foundations, but also in health and community interest campaigns, public service drives and educational seminars. By encouraging corporate investment in society,

PR gained greater respect and increased its own influence within corporations.

Television, which conquered America in the 1950s, had an enormous effect on the growth of public relations. This powerful medium's capacity for persuasion was evident from the start. Social scientists criticized television's pervasive control over public opinion, but it soon became clear that TV could create harmful as well as helpful PR. For example, Joseph McCarthy's credibility was weakened when his hectoring manner and his beard's five o'clock shadow were exposed to the scrutiny of viewers across the nation. The Revlon Company first enjoyed glorious PR from its sponsorship of the nation's most popular TV program, but when the "$64,000 Question" was exposed as a fraud, Revlon suffered acute embarrassment and a wave of public criticism for its failure to meet its social responsibility.

Honesty in public relations became a serious issue during the 1950s and led to PRSA's first code of ethics, a very brief statement in 1954. In 1959 PRSA adopted a Declaration of Principles and a more developed code of ethical behavior.[80] To avoid being accused of creating a paper tiger, PRSA established a grievance board in 1962 to conduct hearings whenever a PRSA member suspected another member of violating the code.[81] Two years later PRSA approved a voluntary accreditation program open to all members of the society. This was simultaneously the first step in recognizing a level of professional accomplishment in public relations and the first step toward establishing and policing standards of behavior among practitioners.

Transition in the Turbulent Sixties and Seventies

The 1960s and early 1970s were years of great crisis and change in the USA. Public relations talent was called on to cope with the drama and the trauma. Modern PR practitioners needed a broad knowledge of the social sciences, as well as communication and management skills. In addition, nonmarketing problems received new emphasis, more attention was given to the worldwide consumer movement, corporate–government relationships were scrutinized, PR people gained increasing responsibility within the corporate structure, a more demanding role emerged for PR in multinational companies and cries for help came from all sectors in dealing with dissident youth and minorities. Communication

satellites, the awesome power of nuclear weaponry and the emergence of electronic information storage for data processing had made the globe smaller but had not diminished its problems.

One fundamental change in the USA actually began in the 1950s, signaled by the U.S. Supreme Court's landmark school desegregation decision of 1954, *Brown v. Board of Education of Topeka*, and involved a reassessment and legal reform of black and white race relations. During the 1950s in Montgomery, Alabama, Martin Luther King, Jr. began expressing his vision of what U.S. society could achieve if racism were ended. He used many public relations techniques to gain support for his cause, and he was skillful in working with the news media. His "I Have a Dream" speech and other eloquent sermons and addresses, as well as his adoption of nonviolent protest patterned on the approach developed by Mahatma Ghandi, helped launch a civil rights movement that produced many social changes, especially in the 1960s. King's assassination in April 1968 shocked the nation and made his name a rallying cry for supporters of the continuing movement to achieve racial equality in the USA.

The nation seemed to divide on one point after another: civil rights, disarmament, the space program, the Vietnam War and the peace movement, conservation, farm labor, women's liberation, nuclear energy, the Watergate affair and on and on. In the debate over each of these issues, public relations was important to both sides. For example, PR professionals conducted seminars to train people within the power structure in how to respond directly to activists and how to answer them indirectly through news media and other public channels of communication. But the activists used PR just as effectively, capturing public attention with demonstrations, organizations and powerful rhetoric. Conservatives charged that the Chicago riots of 1968 smacked of press agentry. Radicals retorted that the same could be said of the Gulf of Tonkin incident, in which the North Vietnamese ostensibly attacked an American ship.

The Rise of Consumerism

In the USA, the consumer movement produced much criticism of institutions. Because of its increased visibility, many people assumed that the movement was new. It wasn't. The first national consumer group, the National Consumers League, had been founded from 90 state affiliates in 1899. Early issues it supported were minimum wage laws, improved working hours, occupational safety, abolition of sweatshops and child labor and improved working conditions for migrant farm workers. In supporting the 1906 Pure Food and Drug Act, the league formed food committees that set standards for food manufacture, inspected food manufacturing establishments and certified their safe working conditions by affixing a White Label, a logo similar to today's union label, to products.

Another organization that has been a longtime consumer advocate is the Consumers Union of the United States. It began as part of Consumers' Research, Inc., the first product-testing organization supported by consumers, and was established as a separate entity in 1936. Consumers Union is an independent, nonprofit organization that tests and evaluates such products as appliances, automobiles and packaged food. Since its founding, it has published the results of its tests in a monthly magazine, *Consumer Reports*, along with articles designed to help consumers spend their money more wisely and to make them aware of current consumer problems. The organization has always pressed for increased consumer protection by calling attention to what it believes are unsafe products. It has also concerned itself with weaknesses in consumer legislation and with the reluctance or failure of government regulatory agencies to act on behalf of consumers.

Sarah Newman, executive director of the National Consumers League from 1962 to 1975, pointed out the major tactical differences between consumer-oriented organizations of earlier periods and those of the 1970s. For one thing, consumer advocates in the 1970s were more program-oriented. Consumer advocates during earlier periods did not resort to militancy. They also had to do much of the watchdog work themselves, because no regulatory agency was responsible for ensuring the safety of most consumer products. By the late 1970s Newman's own group was involved in supporting such reforms as equal credit, no-fault insurance and uniform beef grading. The NCL also pushed for creation of an agency for consumer advocacy.

Consumerism has been called "buyer's rights,"[82] "a cause or movement that advances the rights and interests of the consumer"[83] or a movement "seeking to increase the rights and powers of buyers in relation to sellers."[84] Whatever its title and definition, the essence of consumerism was clearly expressed by the late Margot Sherman, a former senior vice

president of McCann Erickson (a New York agency), who had been in charge of setting up the agency's division of consumerism:

On this business of consumerism, I suppose as a concept it was probably born in March 1962, when President Kennedy declared, "Every consumer has four basic rights—the right to be informed, the right to safety, the right to choose, and the right to be heard!"

Helping to craft those four rights was consumer advocate Helen Nelson, who produced a video documentary in 1995 chronicling the history of the movement, *Change Makers: The Struggle for Consumer Rights*. Accompanying the video, which took her 3 years to write, was a teacher's guide of edited conversations with 35 consumer leaders interviewed for the video.[85] President Kennedy had identified consumers as the only important group in contemporary society that was not effectively organized. He then appointed 10 private citizens to serve on a Consumer Advisory Council, including Nelson. Also he placed a consumer adviser, Esther Peterson, on his staff. Every U.S. president since Kennedy has followed his lead in having a staff consumer advisor.[86] Nelson advised two presidents and Congress on consumer matters and was California's first governor-appointed consumer advocate, from 1959 to 1966.[87]

The Sentiment Behind Consumerism The sentiment behind the consumer movement was best defined by Ralph Nader:

Indeed the quality of life is deteriorating in so many ways that the traditional measurements of the "standard of living" according to personal income, housing, ownership of cars and appliances, etc., have come to sound increasingly phony.[88]

The sentiment was in fact a reaction to a "hostile environment." And the movement's character at any particular point in time, according to Edgar Chasteen, depended on the behavior of the "enemy," as defined by the movement.[89]

The enemy was business. In bewilderment, business looked on as a generation of consumers whose basic needs had been satisfied reacted adversely to old methods of persuasion. Evidently, the techniques that sold products also created expectations that could not be satisfied. A gap materialized between reality and the anticipation of rewards. In addition, consumer dissatisfaction was both the cause and the effect of another wave of investigative (or muckraking) journalism.[90]

To measure the intensity of consumer satisfaction/ dissatisfaction, business used five common techniques: (1) statistics such as sales, profits and market share; (2) behavioral measures such as repeat purchases, acceptance of other products in the same line and favorable word-of-mouth publicity; (3) direct observation; (4) dissatisfaction indices such as recorded complaint data; and (5) surveys and interviews to unearth reticent respondents. The hazards of using these techniques and the difficulties involved in measuring consumer satisfaction and dissatisfaction are legion.[91]

A thorough look at the activist requires a look at the adversary as well. Ralph Nader has said that the principal concern of the consumer movement has always been the "involuntary subeconomy"— unwritten price-fixing for goods and services and inflationary agreements with labor and suppliers. These factors force up the costs of consumer goods and services, and the higher costs must be accepted because no other sources of the goods or services exist. Because there are no controls and no choices, the system is "involuntary"; because it underlies the economic structure, it constitutes a "subeconomy." Writing in 1973, Nader noted that the consumer movement had had limited success in improving regulatory action and encouraging private litigation. Its main achievement had been to create an awareness among consumers that they were being cheated and endangered. Nader conceded that the consumer movement had yet to devise an economic and policy-making framework to counterbalance or deplete the power of corporations to impose involuntary expenditures:[92]

To some extent, consumerism as we know it was born of public frustration during a period of social turmoil, which saw unrest over civil rights issues and a divisive war in Southeast Asia. We entered a strobe-light existence, and with every blink of the flashing light, society had changed a little more before our very eyes! In short, the storm of the 1960s blew away many of the road signs that had helped us find our way comfortably along in the more predictable decades that came before.[93]

The Impact of Consumerism Most consumer activists of the 1960s and 1970s were members of what has been called the "silent generation." This generation was proportionally small because its members were Depression or post-Depression babies.[94] For it, quality of life was understood in terms of a standard of living.[95, 96] But not until confronted with the hostile accusations of the "antimaterialistic" younger generation of the 1960s did the silent generation recognize two salient questions: (1) At whose expense does a better living come? and (2) What is the real value of all this? Robert Glessing has perceptively commented that "the unpreparedness of the silent generation was at least part of the cause of the student protest movements."[97]

But after taking a careful and critical look at its own lot, the silent generation began borrowing tactics from the youth revolt. Suddenly meat boycotts were being staged by matrons who were definitely over 40.[98] Although Rachel Carson's *Silent Spring* was published in 1962 and Ralph Nader's consumer statistics tips to Congress began appearing in 1960 (even before his 1965 publication *Unsafe at Any Speed*), the consumer movement did not become formidable until the early 1970s.[99] In 1972 and 1973, however, the Public Relations Society of America appointed a task force to examine the impact of consumerism on business.[100] By this time, class action suits were being filed, pressure was being brought to bear on regulatory agencies to enact stricter criteria and to enforce them, stockholders' meetings were losing their predictability because minor shareholders were appearing and demanding social accountability and employees were more likely to become litigants than loyalists.[101]

By 1967 President Lyndon Johnson had decided that consumer complaints were so politically significant that he appointed Betty Furness as his consumer advisory counsel.[102] By 1971 there were four national consumer organizations: the Consumer Federation of America, the Nader Organization and the two older associations, the National Consumers League and the Consumers Union.[103]

Communication Problems and Public Opinion The consumer movement clearly demonstrated some lack of communication between business and consumers, a deficiency that the following statement makes clear:

The consumerism movement not only mirrors the inability of the business sector to discern what factors of inherent consumer motivations promulgate (dis)satisfaction, but also reflects a growing concern for the "quality of life," which seems to be a popular cause, as well as a goal to collectively attain.[104]

In commenting on a 1977 Louis Harris survey, financial columnist Sylvia Porter asked how closely the views of senior business managers, consumer activists and government regulators matched the views of the general public. The answer was "not closely," with senior management "less in touch with public opinion than are any of the other groups." As Porter said:

> Consumer activists would prefer to concentrate on electric utilities, the advertising industry, nuclear power plants and banks.
>   Business executives want reforms in hospitals, the medical profession, garages, home building and the legal profession.
>   Only one common perception is shared by every group surveyed: mistrust of the honesty and accuracy of advertising.[105]

The Harris survey had found that more than one third of all adults were bothered by poor quality or dangerous products that failed to live up to advertising claims. They were distressed at the failure of companies to show legitimate concern for the consumer. They were bothered by poor after-sales service and repairs and by misleading packaging or labeling. More than half of the respondents thought they were receiving a worse bargain in the marketplace than they had been getting ten years earlier. Moreover, consumers expected things to get worse in three areas: product durability, product repair and the reliability of manufacturers' claims for products. Although the public expressed a desire for more information about subjects relevant to consumers, the poll found little public confidence in the accuracy and reliability of media news.

The Scope of the Problem   The word *corporate*, as used in the consumer movement, should be interpreted in its broadest sense. Under fire, in addition to businesses, were all large institutions—hospitals, fund-raising public health associations, major-league sports teams, public and private educational institutions at all levels and religious groups. The biggest guns of all were leveled at government administrators. The news media suffered from adverse public opinion, too, as did newsmakers themselves, due to lawsuits, public attacks and threats of government intervention.

The harsh realities are clearly set forth by mass media scholars David Clark and William Blankenburg:

> *The sturdiest obstacles to "ideal" public relations are economics and human nature. The plain fact is that managers are hired to make money for owners, and that a conscience can cost money. In the long run, it is money well spent, but many stockholders and managers fix their vision on the short run. Then, too, an abrupt change in corporate policy amounts to a public confession of past misbehavior—or so it seems to many executives. The natural temptation is to play up the good, and to let it go at that.*[106]

The Impact of the Sixties and Seventies on Public Relations

The urgency of the problems that PR practitioners handled during the crises of the 1960s and 1970s and the expectations of those hiring PR talent gave the role new dimensions. But the new demands also created a crisis of confidence inside and outside public relations. In 1968 the Public Relations Student Society of America was formed,[107] and, as public relations continued to gain status as an academic discipline, the field for the first time became dominated by people specially trained for the job.

In 1973 the U.S. Supreme Court handed down a decision that fundamentally changed the role of the PR practitioner. In the *Texas Gulf Sulphur* case, the Supreme Court upheld a 1968 decision of the U.S. Circuit Court of Appeals in New York requiring immediate disclosure of any information that may affect the market value of stock in publicly held corporations.[108] This ruling meant that PR had to concentrate more on dealing with public information and less on selecting what information to make public. The Supreme Court also ruled that PR practitioners involved in such cases were "insiders" and therefore were subject to the same trading restrictions as other members of the corporation whose knowledge of special circumstances prohibited them from buying or selling stock.[109] The insider trading scandals of the 1980s severely tested the Securities and Exchange Commission's (SEC's) ability to enforce insider trading rules.

The Growth of Public Skepticism   Between 1966 and 1977, public confidence in corporate leadership dropped by 31 percentage points. While many executives besieged by negative public opinion bunkered down or toyed with the idea of resigning, one public relations officer decided to take the offensive. Mobil Oil's Herb Schmertz, a lawyer, began running Mobil's issue advertising in 1970. Following the oil shortages of the 1970s and the price acceleration they caused, Schmertz expanded Mobil's aggressive ad program and sought favorable opinion by convincing the corporation to sponsor public television's *Masterpiece Theatre*.

Pulling together as many communication devices as possible to influence public opinion was a response to deepening public disaffection and distrust, including the beginnings of widespread genuine mistrust of government. This development was not without foundation. Throughout the 1960s and 1970s valid grounds for public skepticism existed. Although the term *disinformation* didn't gain currency until the 1980s, the U.S. government was giving its citizens a good bit of it all along.

The Seventies in Summary The Middle East garnered a great deal of attention in the USA in the 1970s. The effects of the oil shortage created by policies of the coalition of oil-producing nations (OPEC—the Organization of Petroleum Exporting Countries) began to be felt as world demand for oil outstripped the supply from non-OPEC sources. In Iran the Ayatollah Khomeini and his fundamentalist Islamic followers overthrew the U.S.-backed shah. Soon thereafter, on November 4, 1979, the American Embassy in Tehran was seized and its staff held hostage by "revolutionary guards" whose exact relationship to the new Iranian government was never satisfactorily clarified. Some former hostages said in the summer of 2005 that they recognized Iran's new president-elect as one of their captors, a claim that was denied. Other acts of terrorism in the region suggested that the U.S. government was unable to defend its interests in that part of the world.

Problems in the Middle East added to a loss of confidence in the U.S. government at home. Another contributing factor was double-digit inflation, which eroded the economy and caused a serious decline in the standard of living. The nation's first military defeat, in Vietnam, drained people's feelings of nationalism, although the 1976 bicentennial helped revive these to some extent.

During the 1970s the cultural monopoly of the traditional American family disappeared. More couples lived together outside marriage, and some were of the same sex. Married couples divorced at high rates, and after the 1950s "baby boom," fewer children were born each year, especially to white couples.[110] The ethnic mix in America changed as the black and Hispanic populations, respectively, grew at twice and six times the rate of the white population.

The Hispanic community was enlarged by numerous political and economic refugees from Latin America. Southeast Asian refugees, fleeing their homelands in the wake of communist victories there, added another ethnic piece to the American mosaic.

Although consumerism and environmentalism both made great strides during the decade, the main social movement of the 1970s was the women's movement. Opponents succeeded in blocking modification of the Equal Rights Amendment to the Constitution, but the movement helped bring about some fundamental changes in society. Women began to view themselves as complete equals to men and demanded equal treatment in the workplace. Of the 3 million new people in the workforce, 2 million were women; almost half of all married women were employed, one fourth of them with children younger than the age of 6. Women's wages, though, were only 60 percent of men's. Women in legal careers doubled. Women getting medical degrees accounted for 22 percent of all those who sought such degrees in traditional medicine and 23 percent in veterinary medicine. The percentage of financial officers who were women rose from 18 percent to 30 percent in the decade, and women economists increased from 11 percent to 23 percent. Women in operations system research and analysis more than doubled, and women entered the public relations field in unprecedented numbers. Betsy Plank became the first woman president of the Public Relations Society of America in 1973, and she was the first person to receive PRSA's two top professional honors: the Gold Anvil as the nation's outstanding professional in 1977 and the Lund Award for exemplary civic and community service in 1989. At Ameritech (formerly Illinois Bell), she became the first female to head a company department, external affairs, directing a staff of 102.

Professionalism: PR in the Era of Global Communication, 1980–Present

The 1960s was a time of tremendous social and economic upheaval. The 1970s was a decade of uncertainty. Most Americans worried about economic problems and shortages of natural resources, especially energy. Many people also lacked confidence in American institutions. These concerns continued into the 1980s, giving impetus to planning based on predictions of internal company development and external social, political and economic conditions.

The confrontations, challenges and turbulence of the 1960s and 1970s led to polarization in the 1980s. This polarization crossed every imaginable social and political boundary. The resulting struggles increased global as well as national tensions between fundamentalists and secularists. At the same time, the centrist position narrowed dramatically.

The Reagan Eighties

President Ronald Reagan's deputy press secretary, Pete Roussel, said he faithfully adhered to what he called the "Press Secretary's Prayer": "Oh, Lord, let me utter words sweet and gentle, for tomorrow, I may have to eat them."[111] Roussel was one of several public-opinion–sensitive specialists on Reagan's staff. Reagan came to be called "the Great Communicator." Recognizing that some people who didn't like what Reagan said nonetheless continued to like him, Colorado Congresswoman Pat Schroeder nicknamed him the "Teflon" president: Nothing unpopular that his administration did seemed to stick to him personally. Reagan's administration also employed pollster Richard Beal, whose job was to look at public views on questions likely to arise as issues in the future.

In doing this, Reagan was following a trend that started with John F. Kennedy's use of polling, according to Sidney Blumenthal, author of *The Permanent Campaign*.[112] Blumenthal called Reagan "Communicator in Chief" and made this observation:

> *Reagan is governing America by a new doctrine—the permanent campaign. He is applying in the White House the most sophisticated team of pollsters, media masters and tacticians ever to work there. They have helped him to transcend entrenched institutions like the Congress and the Washington press corps to appeal directly to the people.*[113]

In addition to filling the administration's major public relations posts with experienced professionals, Reagan appointed PR pros to many positions not traditionally considered public relations jobs. Of the three top advisers to the president, two were lawyers and one, Michael Deaver, was a public relations professional. Deaver was indicted for influence peddling after he left the White House, and Bernard Kalb of the State Department left in protest when the government got involved in a disinformation campaign.

After press secretary Jim Brady was severely injured in the assassination attempt on Reagan March 30, 1981, Larry Speakes became acting press secretary. Speakes sometimes felt that he wasn't sufficiently informed by other administration officials, and some news people agreed. However, Speakes said, not knowing is the lesser of the two sins of a press secretary; lying was a "cardinal sin" and unforgivable. Then, after he left the administration—first to work for a large public relations firm, and then to direct public relations for a major brokerage firm—Speakes acknowledged he had "made up" quotes he attributed to President Reagan!

The Reagan presidency was one of the most controlled in the history of the office. One indication of this was the number of orchestrated photo opportunities.[114] In addition, during the Reagan administration, the U.S. Information Agency (USIA) and its companion U.S. Information Service (USIS) in other countries grew in power and influence.

But USIA was disbanded in October 1999, with many of its functions being absorbed by the U.S. Department of State. Since 1994 the International Broadcasting Bureau (IBB) has provided administrative and engineering support for U.S. government–funded nonmilitary international broadcast services, including Worldnet Television and Film Service. Originally part of USIA, the IBB was formed by the 1994 International Broadcasting Act, and the IBB was established as an independent federal government entity.

> *Concern about Worldnet was expressed in 1987 by Florida Congressman Dan Mica, who observed that it had an "untapped and unlimited potential." The Congressman was concerned "that a particular administration could use Worldnet as its private propaganda vehicle."*[115]

Integrated Communication Trend Begins

Beginning in the late 1970s and early 1980s, several large public relations firms were acquired by advertising agencies. In one transaction, J. Walter Thompson acquired Hill & Knowlton for $28 million. In another important merger, Dudley-Anderson-Yutzy, a PR firm, became a part of Ogilvy & Mather, an advertising firm, which was renamed the Ogilvy Group. Then, in 1989, the Ogilvy Group and J. Walter Thompson merged, through a hostile takeover, into the British-owned WPP Group. WPP grew even faster than its chief competitor at the time (also

British), Saatchi & Saatchi PLC. In addition to owning what was then the world's largest PR firm, Hill & Knowlton, WPP got the largest custom market research company, Research International, and the largest direct marketing company, Ogilvy & Mather Direct.[116]

Mergers also created giant communications operations with advertising and public relations capabilities. For instance, Young and Rubicam bought Burson-Marsteller and Marsteller, Inc., for about $20 million, and Benton and Bowles acquired Manning, Selvage and Lee for $2 million. The first big merger (1978) was of Carl Byoir & Associates (one of the oldest PR firms) with Foote, Cone & Belding.

Many advertising agencies moved into related fields: public relations, specialized advertising to and for select groups (doctors, for example), merchandising (including package design), direct marketing and/or sales promotion. Some agencies bought successful companies to put under a corporate umbrella. Others created their own divisions. Some integrated the various units into a super team. Others operated the units separately and independently but found an advantage in presenting themselves as a "full-service" agency. The late PR counselor Philip Lesly expressed a fear that the trend could limit PR to a narrow communications role, subservient to marketing and stripped of its counseling role. Although some agencies used PR mostly for product/service support, others allowed PR free rein to pursue its full range of functions.

The intertwining function that these mergers produced was recognized by some colleges and universities, which combined the academic programs of advertising and PR, sometimes calling them integrated communication or integrated marketing communications.

Global Impact on Public Relations Practice and Education in the 1980s and 1990s

The growth and evolution of public relations practice and of education for public relations internationally continued at an even faster pace during the 1980s and 1990s. Technology connected the world as never before, and this emphasized the need for and use of communication. Cultural awareness became increasingly important—not only in international communication, but also within nations—as political and economic disruptions the world over created a tide of refugees. Natural disasters added to the displacement of people from their homelands.

The formal integration of advertising and public relations tactics that began in the 1970s increased. The results were greater emphasis on "strategic planning" to coordinate the integrated communication elements and greater awareness of the need to integrate an organization's different "voices" to ensure consistency of message statements and to enhance credibility.[117] To put this phenomenal global growth of public relations into perspective, we must look at the social and political environment in which it occurred.

Historical Developments in the 1980s and 1990s

The interconnectedness and shared experience of our global society were demonstrated in international reactions to everything from natural events such as the return of Halley's comet (1985–1986) to calamities like the Chernobyl nuclear power plant accident in the Ukraine (April 25, 1986) to the world stock market disaster of Black Monday (October 19, 1987), which was precipitated by a drop of 508 points in the Dow Jones industrial average. Individual investors fled the marketplace and complained bitterly about the havoc wreaked by the speculators. In 1989 the "Big Board" in the USA initiated a major public information campaign aimed at the 47 million Americans who owned stocks or shares in mutual funds. By 1991 there was some evidence that individual investors had returned to the stock market.

Discoveries of a supernova and of a superconducting substance, as well as breakthroughs in genetic coding research, revitalized American confidence in its ability to understand and shape the world. But the proliferation of the deadly virally induced condition AIDS (acquired immunodeficiency syndrome) was humbling and defied explanation and control. Both in the USA and abroad, advertising and public relations programs were undertaken to educate the public about AIDS and to impede its progress into a pandemic.

Faith in U.S. institutions was severely shaken in 1986 by a series of events. The first of these was the January 28 explosion of the *Challenger* space shuttle, which temporarily ended human space explorations by the USA. NASA's return in 1989 was with the launches of the *Magellan* and *Galileo* space probes and with the brilliant success of *Voyager 2*'s flyby of Neptune at the conclusion of its 12-year journey. Then there followed the first-ever pictures of the surface of Venus. Despite these successes, however, NASA was forced by the national budget crunch to economize, sometimes to the detriment of its projects. Nothing typifies the agency's mixture of triumph and fallibility better than the launch of the Hubble telescope in 1990. A simple mathematical error produced a flawed lens shape, which for a time prevented the remarkable telescope from transmitting the exquisite views of the heavens it had been expected to provide. Subsequent delicate (and expensive) maneuvers in space brought the telescope to its full operational capacity.

Falling oil prices in 1986 caused such economic chaos in the Sunbelt states that more banks failed that year than ever before in the nation's history. The drop in oil prices hurt not only the banks themselves and U.S. oil-producing states, but also Latin American countries that had used their petroleum assets as collateral for loans from U.S. banks that they suddenly had no means of repaying.

Worldwide television audiences witnessed the exposure of an unelected sub-government in the USA during the Iran–Contra hearings, which investigated unauthorized sales of overpriced arms to Iran, supposedly in exchange for American hostages held in Lebanon, with some of the profits from the sales going to the Nicaraguan Contras. President Ronald Reagan claimed to have been unaware of these activities, and Marine Lieutenant Colonel Oliver North of the National Security Council enjoyed a brief career as a national hero before being indicted and sentenced in 1989. (His convictions were overturned later when an appeals court decided that the evidence proving his guilt had not been sufficiently insulated from testimony North gave to Congress under a grant of immunity from prosecution. North pronounced himself "totally exonerated" by this ruling and ran [unsuccessfully] for the Senate in 1994.) Before the dust from the Iran–Contra debacle had settled, a new (but lesser) scandal involving Pentagon defense contracts further eroded public confidence in government.

Television audiences also watched the downfall of TV evangelists Jim and Tammy Bakker and Jimmy Swaggart and the collapse of the Bakkers' organization, an event that indirectly led to Jerry Falwell's resignation as head of Moral Majority, the leading fundamentalist organization in the USA.

In the face of falling U.S. prestige, Soviet Prime Minister Mikhail Gorbachev introduced a new climate of *glasnost* (openness) in the USSR. He sent young, effective communicators to represent his nation in preliminary peace talks and agreed to many U.S. positioning statements, much to the dismay of U.S. diplomats. In 1987, he came to the USA and showed that he, too, knew how to handle a media event. But by 1991 Gorbachev was in serious trouble at home, trying to keep the USSR glued together as one state after another voted for independence. By year's end the Soviet Union was defunct, and Gorbachev was head of a Russian "think tank."

The USA hosted another important world leader in 1987, Pope John Paul II, who found his followers in a restive mood as he refused to modify his conservative views on the issues of marriage for priests and nuns, abortion, birth control and homosexuality. The world of public relations got directly involved in that issue because the United States Catholic Conference (USCC) asked Hill & Knowlton to represent it in a public antiabortion campaign. Robert L. Dilenschneider, then president and CEO of Hill & Knowlton, agreed to take the account, but he didn't anticipate that USCC would announce that fact before he had a chance to tell employees about it. Many of his staffers were quite upset, and some even quit. Dilenschneider later conceded that the internal handling of the affair was not ideal, but he defended his decision to accept the account as a first amendment issue—a rather problematic line of argument because it implies that, much like lawyers, PR practitioners have a societal duty to provide their services to anyone who wants (and can pay for) professional help in framing and disseminating ideas, regardless of how repugnant those ideas may be. Taken to an extreme, this reasoning would find an obligation to provide PR services to hate groups, on the theory that the First Amendment guarantees them not merely the right to free speech, but the right to effective speech. In the fall of 1991, Dilenschneider resigned, citing loss of control to the parent company, WPP Group PLC.

Hill & Knowlton also had the account of the Citizens for a Free Kuwait, which it obtained shortly after U.S. troops started their campaign to recapture that country on January 16, 1991. The Desert Storm war, perhaps because of its brevity, success and multinational force, restored a strong feeling of patriotism to citizens of the USA. However, the war's aftermath, especially the Kurdish refugee situation, reminded the international community of the lingering horrors of war. The war also left a substantial number of Kuwaiti oil fields on fire (the last of these fires was put out some six months later) and an oil-drenched, ecologically damaged Persian Gulf. Cynicism replaced patriotism in some quarters after the war, as people became more aware that the "reality" of the coverage they had been exposed to more nearly resembled managed news. The backlash among media personnel against PR control of war information was strong.

The stock market collapse of Black Monday in 1987 represented a frightening but graphic example of imagery and public opinion. The lingering weakness of the market was attributable in part to global discomfort at the U.S. debt, which had reached trillions of dollars, and at the deadlock between the Reagan administration and Congress over how to deal with it. The friction in philosophies between the executive and legislative branches was apparent in the Iran–Contra hearings, the budget negotiations and most dramatically in the Senate's refusal to confirm strict constructionist Robert Bork to the Supreme Court. Opposition to his nomination revived the activism of civil rights and feminist constituencies. Four years later the nomination of Clarence Thomas to replace Thurgood Marshall on the Supreme Court opened a rift within the black community when law professor Anita Hill's allegations of sexual harassment by Thomas created a national furor over the nature and prevalence of this previously ignored type of crime. Although many people found Hill's testimony at the resulting hearing both plausible and compelling, the U.S. Senate's 98 men and 2 women narrowly voted to confirm Thomas' appointment to the court.

The most dramatic historical development of the late 1980s was the downfall of Communist regimes in Eastern Europe. In the spring of 1989, with neighboring borders relaxed, East Germans began leaving the state in droves. Then in November the East German government resigned en masse, and on November 10 the Berlin wall began to come down. Pieces of the wall sold as souvenirs in U.S. department stores at

Theory and Research Perspective

Research by Katerina Tsetsura, a public relations scholar who is an assistant professor at the Gaylord College of Journalism & Mass Communication at the University of Oklahoma, has demonstrated that American public relations theory has greatly influenced Russian theory. In the past, authors of Russian textbooks were either not familiar with, or chose to ignore, some major theoretical concepts of contemporary American public relations theory. Up to this day, Russian textbooks have tended to analyze public relations practice more so than theory and many times have substituted theoretical explanations with practical suggestions, tactical elements and "how-to" tips. In general, European- and U.S.-published textbooks are more theoretically oriented than are the textbooks published in Eastern Europe. Because the Russian texts are the first original Russian textbooks in public relations, they have a tendency to concentrate their efforts on explanations of the origins of public relations, general functions and placement of the field among other fields rather than on an expansion of the study of public relations as a separate professional area of communication. This tendency was also present in the early U.S. textbooks and sometimes can still be found in textbooks that are published in Eastern Europe.

Another trend in Russian textbooks is their in-depth description of the importance of government and government relations, or GR, in public relations practice. Previously, Russian textbooks extensively covered election campaign strategies, but recently they have switched from political public relations to government relations, reacting to changes in the Russian political environment. Recently, attention also has been given to corporate social responsibility, reputation management and issues and crisis management, among other areas. Yet today, for many Russian practitioners and scholars, public relations is associated with integrated marketing communication. Such a point of view can potentially ruin the modern idea of public relations as a study of effective communication management between organizations and publics, Tsetsura argued.

Russian texts also provide more practical applications and general explanations of possible fields with which public relations can be associated. Tsetsura says it is extremely important for Russians and other Eastern European practitioners and scholars to develop, study and apply new theoretical concepts to public relations practice. And this shared meaning of the significance of public relations theory should be recognized by scholars of the twenty-first century all over the world, she concluded.

Source: Katerina Y. Tsetsura, "Conceptual Frameworks in the Field of Public Relations: A Comparative Study of Russian and United States Perspectives." (Master's Thesis, Fort Hays State University, 2000). Reprinted with permission from Katerina Y. Tsetsura.

prices from $15 to $25. By 1990 the USIA had opened the first "American University Bookstore" in East Berlin. The two Germanies were united in October 1990. Another notable development in November 1989 was Hungary's withdrawal from the Warsaw Pact; and later in the same month, Hungarians voted in their first free election in 42 years. In Czechoslovakia voters elected prominent dissident playwright Vaclav Havel president in 1989. But within 4 years, the national government gave in, reluctantly but peacefully, to the secession of Slovakia from the union with the subsequently renamed Czech Republic in 1993. The Solidarity trade-union leader Lech Walesa was chosen premier of Poland in August 1989. By 1990 the Voice of America had opened its first Polish office, in Warsaw. Meanwhile, in Bulgaria, seeing the tide of change in 1989, Communist party leader Todor Zhivkov resigned.

The most dramatic climax may have been in Romania. In December 1989, after his Communist government had collapsed, Nicolae Ceausescu was captured, tried in secret and, along with his wife, executed by a firing squad on Christmas Day. Mass graves of suspected government opponents were exhumed, and U.S. families began to adopt orphaned and abandoned Romanian children. This turned out to be a problem by 1991 when it became clear that many private adoption homes in Romania were placing children who had been relinquished (either abandoned or sold) by poor families. The U.S. State Department responded by refusing for a time to grant adopting parents visas for the children.

In the Western hemisphere, Fidel Castro began issuing visas that permitted some people to leave Cuba legally for the first time under Castro's regime.

With restraints loosening in much of the Communist world, the Western world was shocked to watch on television as Chinese students participating in a pro-democracy movement were attacked by armed troops and tanks near Beijing's Tiananmen Square. Especially apprehensive were the Chinese citizens of Hong Kong, because that island city would revert to China in 1997. Many of the students who weren't captured in the subsequent crackdown escaped with the help of an underground movement operating out of Hong Kong.

Two unique elements in the tragic event point out the globalization of today's world. First, the students in revolt were receiving fax messages from Chinese students and sympathizers abroad; second, the authorities later used television footage to identify the students and track them down. Some received lengthy prison sentences. This led some U.S. citizens to push for revoking China's "most favored nation" trading status, but President George H. W. Bush opposed this measure and committed the administration to a policy of keeping the market open. The subsequent Democratic administration of Bill Clinton did not reverse the Bush policy on China.

The mostly nonviolent revolutions of Eastern Europe were followed in 1991 by the disintegration of the Soviet Union into its constituent republics (loosely allied as the Confederation of Independent States). A destructive secessionist movement occurred in Yugoslavia, where 45 years of cooperative existence between neighboring states gave way to older enmities and bitter warfare. In 1990 the former Yugoslavia had begun to disintegrate when two Yugoslavian republics, Slovenia and Croatia, decided to secede from the federation, resulting in warfare with Serbia and Montenegro for 5 years until 1995.

The world's turbulence and turmoil opened markets and new opportunities for public relations practitioners who could cope with the demands of global communications. The new Russian commonwealth presented a particularly challenging opportunity. In response to the new European Union market formed by the Maastricht Treaty, the USA, on President George H. W. Bush's initiative, opened expanded trade with Canada and Mexico, as a part of a "united continent" concept. The North American Free Trade Agreement (NAFTA) was ratified in 1994. A year later, the U.S. Congress approved a General Agreement on Tariffs and Trade (GATT), which further opened up international trade and had significant domestic economic consequences as well. The GATT agreement vote in the U.S. Congress came after voter anger in the 1994 elections had ousted many politicians and put both houses of Congress into Republican hands for the first time in 40 years. The level of public hostility and distrust toward government (including President Clinton) was at a 1960s level. However, the GATT agreement, like some other legislation of the period, showed some new political alignments being forged in an effort to find out what citizens wanted. In Latin America, the new Southern Cone Common Market (Mercosur) began to attract other nations.

Advances in technology dominated the early 1990s, especially with regard to computers. Even hotels and airplanes had to accommodate computer users. The key phrase *information superhighway* created all sorts of opportunities and problems. Facsimile messages went all over the world and became almost as commonplace as telephones in some countries. Voicemail message systems meant 24-hour answering, even at home. Telephones went on board airplanes for in-air use, and countries without reliable permanent phone systems found handheld mobile phones in great demand. Many addresses on business cards and letterheads included both phone and fax numbers and, in addition to a physical location, an email address and a professional or personal home page URL, that is, its address on the information superhighway. International travelers used money cards in electronic machines for access to their accounts and moved money across national boundaries with ease.

Friendships also moved across national boundaries as people began communicating across borders and continents via email. As computer network "correspondents" plugged in internationally, whole new publics and media, in a public relations sense, developed. Teenagers could communicate with people their age all over the world, and the elderly found a whole new group of friends worldwide at the touch of their keyboards. In addition to these new publics, new media developed. Some "publications" became available only electronically, and traditional "library" information became available in CD-ROM format as well as in electronic databases, with some libraries becoming virtually "electronic libraries." "Desktop publishing" meant not only publishing at home by an individual who wanted to create a newsletter, but also having the capacity to send that information electronically around the world.

The problems technology brought involved, among other things, disputes over copyrights, something ignored by certain countries, and laws involving pornography, libel and slander. Computer networks had developed some protocols or procedures to which users generally adhered. These protocols worked fairly well when there were few users, but they fell into an abyss when many users came online.

PR Developments in the 1980s and 1990s

During the 1980s, PR newswire services responded to the new technology by using satellite transmissions. "Clipping" services functioned electronically too. In addition to the greater dispersion and collection of information, computer technology brought the microcomputer to the public relations office and, with it, an array of microcomputer techniques. Desktop publishing improved the look of in-house publications and made possible sophisticated graphics for reports, speeches and ads.

The World Wide Web has created a whole new medium for public relations, presenting new opportunities and problems. From home pages and chat rooms to email and listservs, all sorts of institutions and individuals have a presence on the Web. Within organizations, the email intranet systems have also deeply affected employee relations, because these internal email networks have become a powerful means of internal communication.

The Web has significantly changed media relations as well. A good Web page gives basic information about the organization and access to additional information and includes text, pictures and graphics, as well as video. News releases are often posted on organizations' Web pages, and media can seek sources from a number of different sites.

The media's use of their own Web pages to release stories that may be speculative has created new difficulties for public relations people. Individuals can also use the Web to circulate rumors that often have serious consequences. With their lack of editors, chat rooms and independent Web pages, as well as Web logs (blogs) and the new social media, can pose problems even more troublesome than stories released by major media organizations. Anyone and everyone can easily and inexpensively have his or her own Web log, or blog, to express any opinion about any subject. And, while the Web has become a preferred fact-finding tool because of its easy access, misinformation is rampant on the Internet and the verifiability of Web information remains a problem.

Improvements in computers also added to the explosion of the PR research industry. Its dependence is such that a major concern of the 1990s was to bring computers into compliance with Year 2000 (Y2K) standards. Most of the older programs could not cope with any date after 1999. Changes in the economy throughout the world created a situation in which many companies began to cut their numbers of employees and to depend on suppliers for services previously provided within the institution, often on other continents. This outsourcing also affected public relations. Many public relations practitioners began to work for themselves because they were let go by organizations that had employed them; as independent contractors, they established their own clientele, servicing many customers, often including their previous employers. The electronic technology that had allowed their employers to reduce the number of in-house employees also made it possible for public relations practitioners to work from their homes and service clients all over the world.

PR in Practice

For many Americans, the twenty-first century began on 9/11/01. Terrorist attacks in the USA required expert public relations practice as the U.S. government attempted to reassure Americans; to explain its position on increased security while addressing concerns about the potential erosion of civil liberties; and as airlines and tourist destination sites attempted to reassure Americans that they could travel safely due to increased security. Victoria Clarke became one of the most recognized public relations practitioners when she was U.S. assistant secretary of defense for public affairs—that is, as public relations practitioner for the Department of Defense.

But many other events during the years surrounding the new millennium have required professional public relations practice, for example, the demise of the dot.coms; the Bridgestone/Firestone tire recall and the allegations that this tire company and Ford Motor Company knew about the defects in advance; financial irregularities and the demise of large corporations, with a devastating impact on stockholders, other companies and the nation; the disappearance of pensions for employees of large companies; a 6-year-old boy, Elian Gonzalez, who became a symbol of the hostilities between the USA and Cuba; the death of 118 Russian submariners on the *Kursk*; the shooting rampage in Columbine High School; and the AIDS pandemic in Africa. More recently have been the shootings at Virginia Tech and at Northern Illinois University; massive floods, cyclones, tornadoes and other weather-related devastation throughout the world; global concerns about the economy, rising food and fuel prices and a host of other events and issues that have required the use of public relations knowledge and skills.

Worldwide, new democracies have continued to emerge and develop, often resulting in much confusion and social and economic upheaval, and other countries have become far more oppressive toward their citizens; diversity problems have increased as different ethnic groups have either attempted or resisted living together; and high-profile lawsuits have illustrated public health issues ranging from smoking to obesity.

In this global environment, companies have increased their global marketing and branding efforts, requiring public relations support. Public relations strategies and tactics have also been used in nation-building and in promoting the goals of nongovernmental organizations (NGOs), also known as Civil Society Organizations (CSOs). The continuing and increasing sophistication of public relations practice is occurring in regions and countries of the world including Russia, the Republic of Buryatia (Siberia), the People's Republic of China, Hong Kong, the Republic of Korea, Malaysia, Singapore, Brazil, Ukraine, India, Israel and the United Arab Emirates.

Starck and Kruckeberg have pointed to three phenomena that have continuing effects on humankind and that have tremendous implications for professional public relations practice: (1) communication/transportation technology, (2) multiculturalism and (3) globalism. They point to the immense societal changes that have occurred during recent years as a result of the escalating development of these linked variables. They note that teachers, governments and parents have difficulty knowing what knowledge and skills students will need to live in a future world that in many ways is impossible to predict and thus difficult to prepare for.

The need for professional public relations practice throughout the world is increasingly obvious, and those who are now studying public relations in colleges and universities (and who are reading this textbook, that has also been translated into Russian, Chinese and Romanian) will practice public relations at a time in history when public relations will be needed throughout the world as never before and hopefully will be appreciated and recognized for its importance as never before.

The global aspect of public relations was underscored by the demand throughout the world for public relations expertise both in the practice and in the classroom, with much of that demand coming from transnational corporations that operate truly without borders, obtaining their raw resources from throughout the world, their labor from throughout the world and their markets likewise throughout a borderless world. Developing nations with a growing middle class began to expand public relations activities, and newly democratized nations found a need to talk to citizens who had new liberty to make political and economic decisions. As a result, the International Public Relations Association began to develop a global body of knowledge designed to be more comprehensive than the PRSA body of knowledge, and there is much sharing of knowledge among public relations scholars/educators and practitioners worldwide who realize that they have much to learn from one another. Textbooks such as this one are translated into multiple languages. This textbook, either in its international English edition or in foreign languages, is used in countries ranging from South Africa to Buryatia, Siberia, and is found on practitioners' desks ranging from Moscow to China.

With the globalization of public relations, educational standards for public relations and the body of knowledge on which these would be based are more diverse than ever before. The code of ethics is a bit of a problem, too; although the IPRA code has broad international acceptance, it lacks the specificity of the PRSA code. A code that was developed by the International Association of Business Communicators (IABC) has attempted to deal with contemporary international issues; PRSA is working with other communication-related organizations to create a universal PR code of ethics, and the Global Alliance for Public Relations and Communication Management ethics project team in 2002 developed a Global Protocol on Public Relations Protocol for its member associations worldwide.

Public relations practitioners in the USA now compete with practitioners throughout the world and will continue to do so. Lack of international experience is a problem for some public relations practitioners who might never have imagined they would need it. More and more companies and nonprofit organizations are involved in international activities.

Another trend in public relations was the continued stream of women into the field, as documented and examined in *The Velvet Ghetto*.[118] Although male PR practitioners moved into CEO slots, women did not. Most women in public relations held lower-status positions and earned considerably less than men in similar positions. Most women at the top reached it by heading their own agencies, although there were exceptions such as Betsy Plank, executive vice president and treasurer of Edelman Public Relations and department head of Ameritech, and Jean Way Schoonover, former vice chair of Ogilvy Public Relations Group. Alma Triner was vice president of corporate communication for Arthur D. Little, Inc., until she and several others went into business handling the promotion of entrepreneurial ventures.

Internationally, the female spokesperson who gained the highest visibility in the early 1990s was the articulate Hanan Ashrawi. As spokeswoman for the Palestinian delegation to the U.S.-initiated Middle East peace talks from the time they began in early 1991, she commanded world attention and praise for her ability to present the Palestinian case effectively in the court of public opinion.

Another highly visible international appointment occurred in the USA. In 1989 the Episcopal Church (Anglican Communion) elected as its first woman bishop a former public relations practitioner, Barbara Harris. The African-American activist broke a 2,000-year-long barrier for women in Anglican communion.

Another trend of the 1990s was the growth of ethnic public relations organizations. The consolidation of people of like backgrounds in these organizations almost certainly highlights the failure of inclusiveness and diversity in the longer-established public relations organizations. However, it may help ethnic practitioners to eventually get a better foothold in other firms, because they will be more identifiable to those companies and institutions that want to diversify and are looking for talent.

It is difficult to study the careers of women and minorities in the field because public relations careers are not high profile. The role of the public relations practitioner in fact often requires avoiding the spotlight. The result is that public relations history has produced only a few identifiable personalities, even though the histories of all institutions, profit and nonprofit, have embedded in them the influence and work of men and women from a variety of ethnic backgrounds and nationalities.

Media coverage of public relations in the 1980s and 1990s was extensive and often hostile—usually because of the perceived manipulation of public attitudes by sophisticated PR campaigns. An unpublished PRSA survey showed that most CEOs evaluate the quality of their public relations as being only fair. The principal weaknesses they cite are their internal and external public relations advisers' inability to grasp

Global Perspective

Public relations scholars Marina Vujnovic, Anup Kumar and Dean Kruckeberg argue that to better understand the exertion of power in a social system, public relations practitioners must consider three dominant social actors—corporations, governments and NGOs—that engage in a communication exchange through the mass media, which serve as a limited public sphere. This does not imply that numerous other publics do not exist; however, the three major actors often marginalize such publics' position. Media serve as a "turf" for debate, rather than as social actors in their own right, although they can have a powerful role in privileging dominant voices and marginalizing lesser voices. While media have an active role in the construction of the social reality of the debate, they rarely engage in the debate as the actors themselves.

In July 2006 a nongovernmental organization (NGO) in India, the Centre for Science and Environment (CSE), released the results of its analysis of harmful chemicals in Coca-Cola and Pepsi-Cola products in the Indian market. CSE claimed that its tests showed that Pepsi-Cola and Coca-Cola products had high levels of pesticides, to an extent beyond that permitted by law. The allegation that was made by CSE, which was extensively covered by the news media, resulted in outrage among people, and civil society exerted pressure on the government to ban these products. Some local governments even went ahead and did so! Pepsi-Cola and Coca-Cola responded to the allegations with their own public relations campaigns in the press and eventually succeeded in blocking the efforts to ban their products.

The three constituents in the interaction had different goals. CSE was trying to protect the public interest by cautioning against the violation of safety standards by cola companies. The cola companies, Coca-Cola and Pepsi-Cola, were trying to counter the claims that were being made by CSE and to get the message out that their products adhered to safety standards. And the government was trying to get the message out that it was upholding the law of the land and was also protecting the public interest. The mass media functioned as a neutral turf on which the three constituents to the crisis staked out their claims and engaged in the public debate to come out favorably in the eyes of the public.

Just as in the case of any other civil society organization, CSE was given deference by the news media, and the news media by and large did not question the CSE findings. And the news media reported the CSE rebuttals to the criticism that came from the government and corporations. CSE countered the criticism that questioned the reliability and validity of its study on scientific grounds. To the criticism that had been made by the scientists flown in by Coca-Cola from CSL of London, CSE was reported in the press to have said that that cola companies were making a counter claim by using tests done by a foreign laboratory, which was "patronizing and bordering on racism."

The consequences of the case were:

1. Coke and Pepsi avoided immediate damage and were able to override the crisis within a matter of four weeks.

2. The government instituted a committee to set standards for soft drinks separately from drinking water.

3. The state governments that had banned the products withdrew the ban for the time being.

4. CSE was able to raise an important issue to the level of public discourse and affect public policy.

5. CSE learned a lesson about rules and procedures for carrying out a scientific study.

The authors argue that in the mediated public space where these power interactions were played out, all constituents tried to use the crisis situation to protect their images; yet, at the same time, they used the crisis for promotional, that is, consumer, purposes. The government, by arguing for the benefit of citizens, tried to strengthen its power position; both corporations tried to protect their investment in the production industry; and CSE, although ostensibly more interested in the benefit of

Global Perspective (continued)

society, tried to maintain its image of an organization whose main interest is the public interest. The authors suggest that when the media allow public debate among governments, NGOs and corporations, none of the three constituents exclusively or independently will be able to exert sufficient power to override the public interest. The authors recommend that public relations practitioners think more about the active, live societal interactions among powerful societal players to determine what really defines socially responsible behavior, with less emphasis on static corporate, governmental and non-governmental definitions of socially responsible behavior.

Source: "An 'Organic Theory' as a Social Theory of Public Relations: A Case Study from India" by Marina Vujnovic, Anup Kumar and Dean Kruckeberg. Used by permission of the authors.

management's needs fully, to understand the institution's goals and to chart a way to meet these goals.

In 1998 the Association of Public Relations Firms, which has its own code of ethics, was established with Jack D. Bergen as its first president. Longtime public relations practitioner Kathy Cripps was appointed president in 2002. Now renamed the Council of Public Relations Firms, this is the first trade association to represent the professional, ethical and financial interests of the U.S. PR industry.

Although the term *public relations* is widely used now, it is often misapplied and misused. Public recognition of the term without full knowledge of what it means in its accepted professional sense allows many people on the fringes of or outside the field to inappropriately call themselves public relations practitioners.

A close examination of how media use the term *public relations* nevertheless shows that, overall, positive references outweigh negative; most of the focus is on agencies, publicity and support to marketing. Probably because of that, the most attention to public relations by news media occurs in New York, Los Angeles and Washington, D.C. The government's use of public relations is not always seen positively—as, for example, in the negative reactions to the government's handling of information about the present war in Iraq and the Katrina hurricane that devastated New Orleans and other U.S. cities on the Gulf of Mexico. Writers for the mass media still refer to "putting public relations spins" on news and using "PR **gimmicks**."

Nevertheless, the use of public relations talent worldwide is increasing daily, and education for public relations continues to grow steadily in the USA and elsewhere. More universities throughout the world have begun adding public relations courses to their programs, and professional public relations organizations are providing continuing education for public relations. Much global attention has been paid to *The Professional Bond: Public Relations Education for the 21ˢᵗ Century*, the November 2006 Report of the Commission on Public Relations Education, which has a dedicated Web site (www.commpred.org) that has been accessed from throughout the world.

The outlook appears good for students who are preparing for careers in public relations. The *Occupational Outlook Handbook* of the U.S. Department of Labor's Bureau of Labor Statistics states that employment of public relations specialists is expected to increase by 18 percent from 2006 to 2016, which is faster than the average for all occupations, although entry-level positions will nevertheless be competitive because the number of applicants is expected to exceed available career opportunities. The *Handbook* notes that an increasingly competitive business environment should spur demand for public relations specialists in organizations of all types and sizes and that employment in public relations firms should grow as firms retain agencies rather than support full-time staff.[119]

PR Developments in the Twenty-first Century

Without question, at no time have public relations practice and the values that it brings to society been more important than in the twenty-first century. A highly festive, but relatively uneventful, global welcoming of the year 2000 was soon superseded by the dramatic calamity of 9/11, which in many ways defined the USA's new challenges in balancing openness and positive relationships with domestic concerns

Ethical Perspective

When former White House Press Secretary Scott McClellan released his book, *What Happened: Inside the Bush White House and Washington's Culture of Deception*, in May 2008, many people used his allegations to criticize the practice of public relations. CBS legal analyst Andrew Cohen in a television broadcast noted on June 1, 2008:

> . . . *in every tragic drama comes a moment of comedic Zen. And in L'Affair McClellan, that has come from the public relations community, where some now wonder whether the former flack violated the "ethics" of his craft.*
>
> *Apparently, an industry the very essence of which is to try to convince people that a turkey is really an eagle has a rule that condemns lying.*
>
> *The Public Relations Society of America states: "We adhere to the highest standards of accuracy and truth in advancing the interests of those we represent. . ." This clause strikes me as if the Burglars Association of America had as its creed "Thou Shalt Not Steal."*
>
> *Show me a PR person who is "accurate" and "truthful," and I'll show you a PR person who is unemployed.*
>
> *The reason companies or governments hire oodles of PR people is because PR people are trained to be slickly untruthful or half-truthful. Misinformation and disinformation are the coin of the realm, and it has nothing to do with being a Democrat or a Republican.*
>
> *So McClellan is a liar. Big deal. Thomas Jefferson was a liar, and so was Franklin Roosevelt. John Kennedy lied and so did Richard Nixon.*
>
> *During the time it took me to write this essay I'll bet dozens of PR people blatantly lied to their audiences, despite the presence of proclamations declaring that they should not.*
>
> *You can't try to convince someone that a milk cow is really a racehorse without lying. You can't build a profession based a deceit and spin, then create "ethics" rules that call for honesty, and then criticize McClellan. . . .*

On June 2 the Public Relations Society of America reacted to both the book and to Cohen's assessment of the overall integrity of public relations practitioners, calling for government reform and challenging the 2008 presidential candidates to adopt a communications policy engaging principles such as those in the PRSA Code of Ethics. The following day, and specifically in response to Cohen's characterization of public relations, PRSA chair and CEO Jeffrey Julin issued a video response to the CBS legal analyst's commentary. Julin refuted Cohen's broad-stroked condemnation of the practice of public relations and reinforced the role of the PRSA Code of Ethics as a guide for public relations practitioners. The vast majority of public relations professionals do not deal with misinformation and disinformation, Julin said. Rather, practitioners inform, educate and serve the best interests of the public. Julin argued that true professionals embrace strong ethics in how they think, what they say and how they advise their organizations' management. Honest, respectful and transparent communication and trustworthy behavior and relationship-building are what public relations practice is about, Julin said.

McClellan is not a member of PRSA, and some could argue that his position as White House Press Secretary was more a political role than a public relations role. Nevertheless, the actions of prominent communicators such as McClellan reflect on public relations, and all practitioners suffer when wrongdoing in the public relations role and function occurs.

Sources: The Flak Over Flacks. http://www.cbsnews.com/stories/2008/06/01/sunday/main4142947.shtml, retrieved June 18, 2008. McClellan Book Prompts National Public Relations Organization to Call for Government Reform and Candidate Code of Ethics http://media.prsa.org/article_display.cfm?article_id=1177, retrieved June 18, 2008. PRSA CEO & Chair Jeffrey Julin Issues Video Response to CBS Legal Analyst Andrew Cohen http://media.prsa.org/article_display.cfm?article_id=1179, retrieved June 18, 2008.

Multiple sources cited on manuscript page 2-90 (new to this edition) about safety and security, as well as increased suspicions about people different from Americans. An increasingly diverse nation in which at least four states, Hawaii, New Mexico, California and Texas, as well as the District of Columbia, do not have a white majority; the aging and beginning retirement of post–World War II baby boomers; a global environment that includes war in Iraq as well as political tensions elsewhere throughout the world; the threat of continuing terrorism; evidence of U.S. troops' torture of war prisoners in Guantanamo Bay, Cuba, and the Abu Ghraib prison in Iraq; the loss of life and other devastation caused by tropical cyclone Nargis in Myanmar (Burma) in May 2008; and the winter storm and earthquake that caused the worst flooding in 50 years in the People's Republic of China in 2008; drastically rising prices of food and oil worldwide; concerns about global warming; and many other global happenings have created a twenty-first century that is filled with high anxiety and much uncertainty among the world's population. Public relations practitioners in the twenty-first century are being asked to deal with relationship problems of immense magnitude that such world and national events are presenting.

Public relations practitioners have been both facilitated and challenged in their responsibilities by today's communication technology and people's creative use of this technology. MP3 players, iPods, mobile phones (called "cell phones" in the USA, a contraction of "cellular phones"); virtually everyone's reliance on the Internet in their day-to-day activities; and pervasive marketing of and quick acceptance of a host of rapidly evolving communication technologies that most people wouldn't have dreamed of even a few years previously have drastically changed both how people communicate and how they live.

Edelman Public Relations' 2008 Trust Survey observed that trust in business is higher than in government in 14 of 18 countries, with the USA experiencing the widest divide between business and government in the survey's 9-year history. Trust in media as an institution is at a high point in the survey's history. However, trust in media is rising because the definition of media has broadened to encompass social media, which is more highly used and trusted by 25- to 34-year-old opinion elites. Wikipedia ranks as the number 2 source of credible information among these young elites.[120] Mid-career public relations practitioners have long ceased to rely on traditional means of monitoring their organizations' publics and no longer rely on traditional mass media relations in communicating with these publics.

Entry-level public relations practitioners and today's students who are studying public relations must continually keep up with not only global events and trends that affect all of society, but also communication technology that directly influences the relationships of people, organizations and governments in an increasingly complex and challenging world.

Discussion Questions

1. What factors have influenced how public relations has been practiced at different times throughout the history of humankind? In what ways have they affected how public relations is defined and what strategies and tactics have been used?

2. What changes do you predict in public relations practice in the near future of your country? Of the world?

3. How can students prepare for public relations practice in the future when the future is difficult to predict?

Points to Remember

- Although public relations practice as we identify it today has existed only since the beginning of the twentieth century, it has grown from ancient practices.

- The particular political, economic and social climate in the USA allowed public relations to establish itself here first, so the practice is now firmly identified with the USA.

- Historians who view the practice of public relations positively see it as a broker for public support of ideas, institutions and people, but critics say this is done at the expense of individual autonomy.

- In the USA, the development of public relations has gone through five distinct stages, each related to the type of public relations predominantly practiced during that period.

- The U.S. government's effort to get support for World War I through the Creel Committee resulted in on-the-job training of many of the founders of the first public relations firms.

- The economic crash of the 1930s stirred industry's concern for social responsibility as a way to regain public esteem and confidence.

- The PR effort during World War II was much better focused than that during World War I, but it also injected an element of disinformation; unlike Creel, Davis was not a presidential adviser.

■ The post World War II period saw PR counseling come into prominence and begin to develop toward professional status.

■ The fractionalization of the nation in the 1960s and 1970s underscored the need for public relations people who were good social scientists and good social counselors.

■ The consumer movement was the origin of current environmentalism, which has general public support, although hype by institutions has created some skepticism about its positive value to the public.

■ Business lost consumer loyalty during the post World War II period, and employee loyalty became almost nonexistent.

■ The stage of the 1980s and 1990s saw technology transform the world into a global neighborhood; this stage created an international demand for public relations talent, especially in developing and newly democratized nations.

■ This need for public relations practitioners is being met by continuing education for practitioners by professional associations and by public relations courses added to university curricula.

■ The high visibility of public relations, due to its stature and the increasing pervasiveness of news media, has resulted in increasing criticism.

■ Many users of public relations talent don't think PR people understand their organization's real needs and goals and how to help meet these.

■ Cutbacks in employees, partly as a result of technology, have resulted in the out-sourcing of many services, including public relations.

■ Many public relations practitioners who have left institutions have gone into business for themselves, keeping their former employers as clients and adding clients throughout the world, which they can service easily through technology.

■ The continuing and increasing sophistication of public relations practice is occurring in regions of the world.

■ Three phenomena have continuing effects on humankind and tremendous implications for professional public relations practice: (1) communication/transportation technology, (2) multiculturalism and (3) globalism.

Go to the Web site for this book at **www.cengage.com/masscomm/newsom/thisispr10e** to find more Web links on this subject.

Other Related Web Sites to Review

Association for Education in Journalism and Mass Communication (AEJMC)
http://www.aejmc.org

Council of Public Relations Firms
http://www.prfirms.org

Global Alliance for Public Relations and Communication Management
http://www.globalpr.org/

International Communication Association (ICA)
http://www.icahdq.org

Public Relations Student Society of America (PRSSA)
http://www.prssa.org/about/history.asp

CHAPTER 3

Trends in PR

- To appreciate the need for cultural literacy.
- To recognize the implications of technological transparency.
- To understand the realities of integrated communication.
- To develop sensitivity to the potential for global impact in seemingly local actions/events.
- To create a heightened awareness of the tie between credibility and reputation.

. . . (T)echnology will continue to transform the rituals of everyday life—sometimes in startling ways.

—Introduction to "Thinking About Tomorrow," in the *Wall Street Journal's* special section on how technology will change the world in the next ten years, Monday, January 28, 2008.[1]

How we learn to live in a world where technology every day is erasing more and more walls— making it so much easier to communicate, trade, and integrate, but also so much easier for small groups to reach around the world and wreak great havoc thousands of miles away—is the great challenge of the new century.

—Thomas L. Friedman, *Longitudes and Attitudes: The World in the Age of Terrorism*[2]

The twenty-first century corporation will be predicated on constant change and not stability. The corporation will be organized around networks and not rigid hierarchies, built on shifting partnerships and alliances, not self-sufficiency. . . . In this much looser business environment, control gives way to persuasion and reputations will be paramount. We, as PR people, will be in strong demand.

—Gavin Anderson, Chairman, Gavin Anderson & Company, USA, October 23, 2000[3]

Today's technology suggests a future when fewer and smaller devices make almost all information available, including some that is "private," and individual experiences of the moment are captured and sent immediately anywhere. The problem for public relations is identifying and organizing what is needed, creating and formatting information for all publics and building relationships electronically as well as personally. For the organization, it means being transparent in its operations so that all it says and does increases its credibility at all levels and improves its reputation with all publics. Sound impossible? Not really, because technology offers opportunities for those who anticipate potential obstacles.

Being citizens in a global world is reinventing public relations in practice and in name. Electronics has shrink-wrapped the world. Public relations practitioners are planning and coordinating strategies and tactics with partners around the world, so getting and sending information is constant and can be stressful with increased demand and smaller staffs. The move of public relations toward more strategic planning and meeting demands of the clients and employers to detail return-on-investment (ROI) has gone into overdrive with constant changes in the political and economic climates at home and abroad.

Because Web sites are available internationally, content must be updated at least daily, hourly in some cases, and carefully vetted to avoid conflicts with the laws, cultures or customs of recipients around the world. Issues anticipation is even more demanding with increased sensitivity to events that signal potential crises. The instant availability of information has heightened the need for cultural awareness in media relations.

Maintaining and improving reputations, for both nonprofit as well as profit-making organizations, is a challenge at home and abroad because "truth" has different meanings in different value systems—a difficulty that impacts being socially responsible. The different truths we must learn to live with and respect are being assisted by worldwide associations of public relations practitioners and educators that set some standards for global practice, and by the partnering of practitioners around the world to localize public relations campaigns while maintaining their global focus.

Associations are also assisting educational institutions in the continuing education of practitioners and are exposing interns and graduate students to the application of theories and research. Today's practitioners must understand business, politics and other cultures to contend with the complexities of a global society.

An increased awareness of the need for public relations has contributed to its reinvention and also has given its practitioners some new titles. "Corporate communications" is often the title used in business, but in some nonprofits the title is likely to be "marketing communications" because of a greater emphasis on messaging than planning. In all cases, integration of all messages means command of more skills and understanding the consequences of both citizen journalism and the convergence of traditional media.

The push for more diversity in public relations practice continues, but that doesn't mean just gender, race and ethnicity. Most important is diversity in perspective and points of view. ■

Cultural Influences on PR

The world is connected by interlocking economic structures, political treaties, transnational companies and nonprofit groups of all types, from the Red Cross to Greenpeace. Therefore, public relations functions in a global environment. The culture of one country or region inevitably influences how PR is practiced

somewhere else. What is local can become international instantly with the Internet, satellite television and the 24-hour global news delivery of satellite television and wire services. As public relations in strategic management increases and the numbers of women in public relations likewise increase, a gender gap remains in positions, status and pay—even though most students studying public relations in U.S. colleges and universities are now women. Minorities also find their practice isolated as a specialty and rightfully resent people's assumption that they only practice in and are primarily interested in practice for minority clients or publics.

Restructuring PR Roles

The role of the public relations professional as counsel to management has increased. Monitoring issues and anticipating what problems to avoid have taken precedence over problem solving. Although problem solving certainly still is in demand, it now is seen as solving problems with various individuals or publics to avoid conflict or a crisis. (See Chapters 4 and 5.)

With so much emphasis on economics, investor relations in publicly held companies has grown beyond what the name implies. Investor relations practitioners are expected to maintain a steady flow of information on the state of the organization to regulators, banks, securities analysts and the financial as well as the trade press. They are counted on to work with internal and external auditors and the board's audit committee to protect the economic reputation of the company. Because reputation and risk are closely connected, they also must work with corporate risk managers. Furthermore, because employees are also investors, investor relations practitioners are expected to alert this internal public first to any economic issues that might have an impact on the company. Of course, they are legally bound to alert the entire investment community, which really means everybody, if there is something **material** that affects stock values.

Given the importance of any profit or nonprofit organization's reputation, increasingly public relations practitioners are being required to either earn law degrees or to learn enough about the law to recognize a potential problem. Also, with many cases being tried now in the court of public opinion before going to court, public relations practitioners are the ones who must work with lawyers to present the organization's position to its publics.

These practitioners often carry the title "vice president of corporate communication." Restructuring also has occurred in the areas of tactics and techniques. A promotion, a news release or an ad can cause serious damage if practitioners are not culturally literate and sensitive. Practitioners have to know how messages, art, music and other symbols are likely to affect not only intended publics, but also unintended recipients such as people in other countries.

Another problem can occur if all messages from the organization are not consonant. The result of these concerns has been further integration of organizations' communications. Internationally, integration is more likely because public relations and advertising have been used by the public sector, that is, by government, for decades. One of the most significant areas of public relations growth abroad has been public affairs. This is largely in the context of communication by a government, but increasingly reference to the role of public relations in public diplomacy has emerged because communication originated by public relations contributes to public discourse. Reputation management has also become both a focus and a specialization of public relations, with an emerging literature, and with some corporations even establishing a position of "chief reputation officer."

Changes in PR Practices

Most practitioners are working across time zones and borders daily. Much of their work is through electronic communication, especially **email**. The difficulty is that email messages often are sent without the care that goes into crafting a printed message.

Spelling, grammar and punctuation sometimes get less attention than they should. Slang that may not be understood correctly gets incorporated. Perhaps more important, the tone of the communication is not always considered. In the rush to communicate, anticipation of the recipient's reaction may be overlooked. Public relations practitioners always have been spokespeople for their organizations, but now what they say and how they say it goes around the globe in real time. What people see and hear in their own contexts, not necessarily that of the organization, is critical to their assessment of the organization.

Public relations people are now developing specialties much more than in the past because of the increasing complexity of many fields. Health care is one; science is another. Companies look for public relations people who have a background sufficient to understand what that company does well enough to interpret and explain it clearly to anyone at any time. When a crisis occurs or an issue arises, there's no time to learn the background needed to put a response into context.

Social responsibility and ethics are inextricably tied to an organization's reputation. Credibility is critical. Increasingly, publics want to hear an explanation from the top. So public relations practitioners who have been involved in giving media training to management now find it imperative to be sure the "boss" is good under fire in both words and gestures that will be seen around the world.

If you see a need for PR practitioners to be flexible in meeting these demands, you have gotten the message. Some people are just not emotionally suited for the field. Although flexibility always has been an issue, the global workplace has made it imperative.

PR in Practice

The Commission on Public Relations Education that included representatives from all of the major U.S. communication associations issued "Public Relations Education for the 21st Century, The Professional Bond: Education—Public Relations—Practice" in November 2006. Although the report was developed primarily for the USA, it is being used as a model for other countries and is available from the Public Relations Society of America in other languages. The executive summary was released in Arabic, Portuguese, Spanish and Russian, and the full report in Chinese.

The purpose of this report is to offer guidelines for developing some educational standards for public relations practice to move the field forward toward professional status.

Commission co-chairs for the report were John L Paluszek and Dean Kruckeberg, and the editor was Judy VanSlyke Turk. The report is available online at http://www.commpred.org.

Theory and Research Perspective

Muhammad I. Ayish, dean of the College of Communication at the University of Sharjah, United Arab Emirates, notes that communication study has been dominated by Western-oriented perspectives that arose in the context of media perceptions in Western Europe and North America, and that Western communication theories have been promoted around the world as possessing a strong element of universalism. He notes:

> For decades, Arabism and Islam have been enigmatic to the Western mind. Century-old Western images of Arabians as barbaric, fanatic, lusty, and ruthless people have spawned contemporary stereotypes of Arabs as terrorists, fundamentalists, or as greedy and uncivilized. At no time have these perceptions been more well-entrenched than in the post-9/11 era, when mutual mistrust seems to have degenerated into a clash of civilization game, in which universal values and norms shared by both sides of the divide have been prime casualties. Religious fanaticism and neo-colonial war mongerism have combined to preclude voices of reason and arguments for balance emanating from global, intellectual debates on human coexistence in the context of cultural diversity. As the world seems headed for more ideologically motivated, head-on collisions between civilizations, the role of culture in international relations seems to be taking a hard beating, while the intellectual community is marginalised in the ongoing confrontation. When hard-core ideologues on both sides are perceived as heroes, chances for harmony and coexistence seem slimmer than ever before.

He concludes:

> In this critical time of Western–Arab Islamic disharmony, the elaboration of normative culture-based perspectives on how people on both sides of this divide manage their communication acts and rituals should serve to narrow gaps of misunderstanding and misperception.[4]

Professor Ayish's emphasis about the importance of realizing cultural differences in "worldview" is an important one to learn for public relations students in the USA, whose cultural perspective may be considerably different from those of others throughout the world. To be successful public relations practitioners in a twenty-first-century global society, students must learn to understand and appreciate different perspectives, that is, "worldviews," to search for universal values and norms and to provide voices of reason as well as arguments for balance to ensure human coexistence in the context of cultural diversity.

Gender and Minority Issues

Although the number of women practicing public relations has increased dramatically since the 1980s, women all over the globe still do not receive the same salaries as men with the same educational background and experience. Why is this important to public relations? Women represent a different perspective, a fact for which there's considerable evidence. In most scientific polling in the USA, women, regardless of generation, reflect different values than men.

That is an important component of decision making within any organization.

More women in the USA are appearing as spokespeople for organizations, yet still they are not equal to the number of men. Furthermore, they are not represented proportionally in the total number of public relations practitioners. Some of this is attributable to the increased demand on CEOs to speak for their organizations. Most of them, still, are men. Although women comprise the majority in the world in terms of numbers, they are not all that visible in the public sphere. Female public relations practitioners in some countries have even more serious problems than they do in the USA.

Minorities of both genders are likely to find themselves practicing public relations in a ghetto, that is, they are hired by companies to work with other members of their ethnic group, or they work for organizations that are considered experts in communicating with Hispanics, African-Americans or Asians. The separation is obvious in organizations for public relations practitioners that are exclusive to their ethnicity. Compensation, too, is often discriminatory. A change may come now that public relations practitioners are using technology in which the gender or ethnicity of the communicator is not identifiable.

Technology's Impact on Strategy and Tactics

Constant changes in technology such as new equipment and software upgrades mean that practitioners are always on a learning curve, having to constantly master just enough technology to accomplish their tasks. Expectations must be met, such as deadlines, wherever they are and regardless of what might be going on. The need to be fast and accurate is imperative.

Electronic Communication

Walk along the beach at a vacation resort, and you will see guests holding their sunscreen in one hand and a BlackBerry in the other so that executives can stay in touch with their offices via wireless email, telephone, Web sites and SMS (short message service). Indeed, *BlackBerrying* has become a verb, just as *Googling* has.

Such electronic forms of communication continue to evolve and have become a part of everyone's life. Indeed, do you know anyone without a mobile phone? Versatility in cell/mobile phones gives users many communication options, including BlackBerry functions. What about a computer? Many have more than one, a laptop and a desktop. A fax at work is usual, and at home too for some, although facsimile transmission has been replaced by computer-based electronic transmissions. These all are basic forms of electronic communication that many regard as essential. These examples tap only the *surface* of what is available and what will evolve. Satellite transmissions and teleconferences are an everyday occurrence, and video conferencing is common too.

What organization doesn't have a Web site? Many individuals have Web sites as well. So how has all this interconnectedness affected strategies and tactics?

Organizations are warned by some public relations practitioners not to "go digital" unless the effort can be supported. What that means is that corporations must be prepared to frequently update their **Web sites** and have personnel respond to email messages promptly, cogently and accurately. It also means using infographics to communicate clearly and to convey complex information at a glance with tables, charts, graphics and interactive manipulative devices. For example, now you can look at clothes in an online catalog, electronically "try them on" and buy them. You can go through houses or business buildings that real estate agents have for sale without leaving your computer. You also can tour galleries and "visit" university campuses.

The caution is: These applications must work all the time and work well. Easy-to-follow instructions have to be available. If people are conveying private information, such as health or financial information, sites have to offer encryption for security.

Investor relations people offer online interviews with CEOs and CFOs for analysts who want to ask questions and for all investors to just listen in. Having conference calls that attract investors to listen in on the Web cuts down on costs to the organization and makes the information available to more people.

Corporate PR people have to be sure information is on the **intranet** so that employees won't find out anything about their company from the mass media before they've been told. For employees not connected to a computer, one way or another, there should always be a blast phone message that will reach them on their cell phones. Web sites are especially useful in a crisis because information on the sites gives people needing information immediate access. Email access from the site must work easily.

Databases also make research and connecting to resources easier. The problem is pulling meaning out of these, most of which contain mostly numerical data. Fortunately text analytic software can find needed material such as concepts, trends and problems and provide it in a useful format. Access to electronic information is so much easier now that many facilities have "live" spots, which provide access without plugs for computers.

Computers do pose some impediments to communication. Attachments often can't be opened by the receiver unless the receiver has the right software. Some pages look different if accessed by different browsers. Many problems still occur across **Macintosh operating systems** and **Windows**. A PR person has to be sure multiple opportunities exist, or publics trying to reach them will be as frustrated with the computerized system as they are with some phone messaging systems.

Although telephonic communications can make it easier to keep from missing messages, this method can make getting information nearly impossible. You have probably had the experience of getting phone menus with submenus and then sub-submenus. The risk in setting up technological communications is that you can get one without the other: You can get the technology but fail to communicate.

(Go to http://www.clickz.com/stats/ to get the latest statistics on the number of Internet users by nation, gender, age and so on.)

Integrated Communication

Advertising and publicity/press agentry/promotion grew up together and then grew apart, as you read in Chapter 2. Public relations then developed apart from advertising until the late 1970s, when the two began coming back together, thanks in large part to technology and all that it has made possible. Not everyone was thrilled about this, least of all some public relations practitioners. However, in practice, both public relations and advertising always have been used to solve problems. A good illustration is the growth of Burson-Marsteller (public relations) and Marsteller, Inc. (advertising). Harold Burson and Bill Marsteller recognized the usefulness of both PR and advertising as strategies and as tools.

Something called *"integrated marketing communications"* came out of the effort of advertising agencies to incorporate public relations tools. In the 1970s and 1980s, advertising agencies began buying public relations firms. Sometimes the purpose was to integrate tools to help clients. Some motives were economic. Ad agencies saw PR as impervious to economic downturns. Certainly that seemed to be the case when high-tech businesses took off in the 1990s. Part of these businesses' big push, especially for **IPOs** (initial public offerings), come from public relations. However, when the recession began with the failure of many **dot.coms**, the public relations businesses that had helped fuel the whole industry began to fade as well. Ad agencies with public relations/public affairs components realized anywhere from 5 to 25 percent downturns in profits in 2002.

Another side of this economic aspect has been the consolidation by clients of their ad/PR dollars. Companies with a number of different products used different agencies and PR firms. When money got tight, clients concentrated their money in one place. Actually, this is what many public relations people would endorse because they see the biggest benefit of integration is giving an organization one voice for credibility.

The concept is that the organization's advertising, promotions, media relations, employee communications, investor communications and Internet presence will all be coordinated and pulled from the mission statements and positioning statements to give consonance to all the organization says and does. Thus, public relations people prefer the term *integrated communication* because not all that the organization does is marketing. Integrated communication is so prevalent now that it is unlikely the concept will be discontinued in the near future.

Convergence of another kind has occurred in the news media. A journalist covering a story will develop the story with words, sound and pictures and then transmit that instantly and electronically for all media. Furthermore, citizen journalists contribute to the news product from mobile phones. Individuals may send material instantly from a site to the medium that makes it available, or the person may put his or her coverage, sound and pictures in a personal electronic space, such as a blog or social media location (for example, YouTube), where it is available to all.

Whereas public relations practitioners have tried to identify which media different publics receive and find credible, the job now is to get the publics' attention electronically because people are their own editors and publishers, finding information they want and increasingly accessing it on handheld devices.[5]

Future Focus and Problems

Major issues such as identifying and connecting with publics offer an array of technological choices. There's no single solution in sight, although one might emerge. Globalization is another issue that can both create and confound relationships. Although some people react with the observation that globalization is a fact, not an issue, it is a fact with consequences, some of them unintended. Another major issue is what some call transparency and others identify as ethical behavior based on acts being fully disclosed. Also a concern is professionalism of public relations practice on a global level.

Globalization

Globalization does not have a positive meaning for large numbers of the world's population. Instead of suggesting synergy, as it does in many developed nations, the word instead implies for many a loss of culture, language and arts due to homogenization.

Some smaller nations refer to it as a second colonization.

Others, individuals as well as groups (for example, women), worry about the marketing emphasis of the global economy. Some women in emerging democracies say their lives were better under communism because they were treated equally. A market economy, they say, is paternalistic and places less value on women's work, which also gives them less opportunity.

Some international organizations see a free-market economy as stimulating and condoning unethical behavior, and they condemn what they see as an international division of haves and have-nots. The latter complaint is also voiced by some workers in countries formerly under communism. Workers, who could always count on sufficient incomes, now are poor. The privatization that has come with a global marketplace is also criticized by workers. Workers in some countries such as Bulgaria and Romania have physically attacked their new owners and have tried to destroy remodeled factories. Capitalism is seen by these workers as just another form of totalitarianism, like fascism and communism.[6]

For some, this may seem puzzling—especially those in the USA who are accustomed to free

Ethical Perspective

Each year Edelman Public Relations issues a "trust barometer." Research for the ninth (2008) was conducted with 30 minute telephone interviews during October and November 2007 by StrategyOne.

For the first time, opinions of 25–34 year olds in 12 countries were solicited concurrently with those of 35–60 year olds. The younger respondents included 100 in the USA; 75 in China; and 50 each in the United Kingdom, Germany, France, Russia, Mexico, Brazil, Japan, South Korea, Canada and India. In the older generations, respondents from 18 countries included 400 in the USA; 300 in China; and 150 each in the United Kingdom, Germany, France, Italy, Spain, the Netherlands, Sweden, Poland, Russia, Ireland, Mexico, Brazil, Canada and Japan. The report says, "Respondents were college educated, had a household income in the top quartile of their country, and reported a significant interest in and engagement with the media, business news, and policy affairs."

These are some of the results from the 20-page 2008 study:

- In both groups, there was more trust in business than in government.
- Actions speak louder than words in terms of company reputations.
- Youth were more willing to hear different points of view through a number of different channels. Their most trusted sources are analysts, academics and "a person like me."
- In 17 of the 18 countries, technology was the most trusted sector.
- Traditional media, rather than corporate, are the most widely used source of information about companies, and access came from CNN, BBC and Google.
- Younger respondents were more likely to demand immediacy and transparency, share their opinions online and spread the word when they had a bad experience.
- Some identified as TrustHolders™ act or influence others too, said the president of StrategyOne, Laurence Evans. These are a special public that needs to be carefully identified, considered—especially on issues—and engaged through media sources they rely on. "Through focused research, a company can identify a unique mix of TrustHolders for any market or situation and create a communication strategy that will engage them."

For rankings of trust in different countries shown in bar charts and other details, go to http://www .edelman.com.[7]

markets, the freedom to execute commercial transactions individually or collectively and the free flow of information. But U.S. activists also have been complaining about the environment, work being taken to places where labor costs are lowest (and stay low) and international labor standards (child labor laws among them). These complaints have found an international billboard: the Internet. Companies are attacked daily, sometimes directly by opposition Web sites with confusing titles. Often people are sent to these opposing sites rather than to the official site of the company the other sites are attacking.

Some protests are demonstrations that get global coverage through news media sites on the Internet and satellite television. Although it is always comforting to listen to words of support and praise, it is a hazard to ignore words of criticism.

In response to this criticism, organizations become more aware of issues and the risks these pose and consequently will invest more in research. Monitoring and evaluating are essential to avoid crises, to address issues of increasing regulation at both national and global levels as well as to mitigate damage to corporate reputations. The credibility of all institutions rests on public perceptions of their accountability and social responsibility. Corporate governance has become a global issue, not one restricted to only a single nation. Nations, too, are viewed in terms of their social responsibility to the planet and other governments, so public affairs practitioners are going to be busy around the clock.[8]

Global Perspective

Information is distributed globally in real time. Most public facilities and educational institutions have "live" or wireless reception areas. Personal channels of communication make it easy to keep with friends, family and businesses 24/7. Mass communication channels are on the same schedule. You can go into hotel rooms all over the world and get CNN on television.

Organizations, profit and nonprofit, keep up with employees anywhere in the world by intranet and with their business contacts—buyers, suppliers, distributors and investors—by Internet. The communication tools are there, but what makes a difference in the transfer of understanding are the sources and systems, their concepts, economics and politics.

Concepts are important because there are two levels of decision making in any culture: individual and personal. A culture may determine, though, which dominates. The government system's structure provides an infrastructure for communication and provides for or restrains individual freedom to communicate. The economic aspect is another consideration. Information may be commercially based, that is, messages usually are competitive. Or information may be government-based and supportive of government systems.

What is communicated is intended for both individual and communal decision making. Some societies are more dependent on one than the other, but in either case, making some meaning of messages has to be done by individuals. The context for their attention to and use of information depends on their cultural, social, political and economic circumstances.

Cultures convey values that influence how people react to and act on information. Exposure to information often is dependent on government structures and their stability. Structures and stability vary and, within them, individual freedoms and responsibilities. Economies are either commercially based and competitive, or government-based and supportive. An individual evaluating the significance of a message with economic consequences ranks it according to personal experiences with an economic structure or structures. In a competitive marketplace information about the economy is more likely to get attention than in a government-based system where the individual may be somewhat protected from economic turbulence unless the political system becomes unstable.[9]

Exerpted from *Bridging Gaps in Global Communication*, by Doug Newsom. Used with permission.

Defining Ethical Behavior

The emphasis on ethical behavior comes with built-in problems because ethics is rooted firmly in values that are strongly affected by family, faith and culture. Some accepted patterns for global behavior will be forged in this hot environment. The outcome will be some accepted relationships for companies and their investors, for managers and their employees, for governments and their citizens—especially relationships built on humanitarian treatment of immigrants and refugees from natural disasters and political chaos. Other norms will be established for diversity of lifestyles, with more emphasis on individual choice.

A serious consideration now and increasingly true for the future will be work and its relationship to the health of workers, respect for their family obligations and protection of their economic well-being. Laws will become more global, perhaps with more international courts. Even without legal systems at the global level, more agreements may be forged on laws such as copyright, which the Internet has challenged. Privacy protection is another issue created by the digital age. None of these issues will be settled easily. Conflicts have to be negotiated and resolved for the global community that we are, for better or worse.

Some progress has been made, in part through the Global Alliance for Public Relations and Communication Management, an organization of public relations associations worldwide (see its Web site, http://www.globalpr.org/). Its international ethics committee considers important issues surrounding ethical practice in public relations and communication management and provides advice about ethical questions. Also, the Global Alliance has been exploring the feasibility of global curriculum standards for public relations education.

Professionalism

In terms of the professionalization of public relations practice, as yet public relations does not meet the necessary criteria to be considered a profession. There is progress, though. An agreed-upon body of knowledge is evidenced today, not only by the ever-growing body of literature of public relations worldwide, which is being catalogued globally by such groups as the Institute for Public Relations' Commission on Global Public Relations Research. The USA and the UK have developed bodies of knowledge—separately, but at least these are available. When a global body of knowledge for public relations is complete, we'll have something to draw from in teaching and in PR practice. Education for public relations in universities is growing dramatically all around the world, but on-the-job training remains the norm in some countries. Until there is some standardization of education for the field, public relations will remain outside the qualifications for a profession. But, again, there is progress. Standardization of curricula exists in the USA, through the Accrediting Council on Education in Journalism and Mass Communications, the Certified in Education for Public Relations program of the Public Relations Society of America and criteria that must be satisfied to establish chapters of the Public Relations Student Society of America and student chapters of the International Association of Business Communicators. Considerable consistency can be found in the selection and adoption of textbooks by U.S. public relations educators. The Report of the Commission on Public Relations Education (in November 2006 and its predecessor in October 1999) has added much standardization to public relations professional education in U.S. colleges and universities.

Accountability is another issue. The degree to which PR practitioners in different locales are held accountable varies widely. Standards for ethical practice have been set up in public relations foundations, institutes and associations around the world. This helps. Also, many associations endorse other associations' codes for behavior, such as those by **PRSA** and **IPRA**, and in addition they craft their own. Furthermore, many associations of public relations professionals have or are developing accreditation processes so that public relations professionals will be tested for their expertise.[10]

PRSA's accreditation program originated in 1964, but in 1998 the Universal Accreditation Program was formed to administer the program's examination. UAP includes associations of specialized as well as geographical practice such as the Agricultural Relations Council, public relations associations in Florida and Puerto Rico. Writing about the future is like looking through a crystal ball, darkly, because the global environment changes, and with it the practice of public relations. No one knows for sure when or how much change will occur. However, it is important to remember that, as is the case with the traditionally recognized professions (for example, medicine, law and the clergy), society is the primary stakeholder of public relations practice and its education because a complex modern global society needs professional public relations practitioners. The second most important stakeholder is the professional community, which has a watchdog role for society in ensuring that aspirants admitted into its community are worthy of professional membership.

Discussion Questions

1. What makes a public relations person culturally literate, and what are some ways a PR practitioner can gain cultural literacy?

2. What do you think is the solution to discriminatory practices toward women and minorities? How is the solution different when we look at only one country as opposed to looking across cultures and at countries with different practices?

3. What effect do you think technology, not just the Internet, will have on public relations practice in the future?

Points to Remember

- Culture crowding and technological transparency affect U.S. public relations work.

- Technology makes it possible to have a virtual office.

- Web sites make organizations accessible globally 24 hours a day, and email messaging eliminates the need to fit contacts into global time zones.

- Public relations is and always has been a 7-day-a-week, 24-hour-a-day function.

- The world is connected by interlocking economic structures, political treaties, transnational companies and nonprofit groups of all sorts, from the Red Cross to Greenpeace.

- Social responsibility and ethics are inextricably tied to an organization's reputation. Credibility is critical.

- As public relations in strategic management increases and the numbers of women in public relations likewise increase, a gender gap remains in titles, status and pay.

- Minorities find their practice isolated as a specialty.

- Organizations should not "go digital" unless the effort can be supported. Web sites that don't work and emails that go unanswered only create problems.

- Public relations practitioners always have been spokespeople for their organizations, but now what they say and how they say it can go around the globe in real time.

- What people see and hear in their own context, not necessarily that of the organization, is critical to their assessment of the organization.

- Public relations people are developing specialties much more than in the past because of the increasing complexity of many fields.

- Integrated marketing communications came out of the effort of advertising agencies to incorporate public relations tools, for client opportunities and economic reasons.

- Public relations people support all communication elements of an organization "speaking with one voice" but prefer the term *integrated communication* because not all organizational goals are market-driven.

- *Globalization* does not have a positive meaning for large numbers of the world's population. To some, instead of suggesting synergy, the word implies a loss of culture, language and arts due to homogenization.

- In response to criticism, organizations will become more aware of globalization issues and the risks these pose and will invest more in research.

- An emphasis on ethical behavior comes with built-in problems because ethics is rooted firmly in values that are strongly affected by family, faith and culture.

- In terms of the professionalization of public relations practice, PR is still a long way from meeting the requirements to be called a real profession: global body of knowledge, standardized preparation for the field (education and continuing education) and standards for practice (accreditation or licensing).

Go to the Web site for this book **www. cengage.com/masscomm/newsom/ thisispr10e**

Other Related Web Sites to Review

Global Alliance for Public Relations and Communication Management
http://www.globalpr.org/

For Internet users by country, try
http://ww.internetworldstats.com/top20htm
and http://www.clickz.com/stats/web.worldwide

CHAPTER 4

Research

Planning, Processes and Techniques

Public relations practitioners need to understand the research process—not that they will conduct research daily (some will), but they will have to make important and informed decisions about hiring research firms, evaluating their proposals and end products, as well as helping to determine how that research benefits the "bottom line."

—Don W. Stacks, *author and professor, University of Miami, Coral Gables*[1]

OBJECTIVES

- To understand the role of research in public relations practice.
- To appreciate the need for ongoing research and the cyclical pattern of PR research.
- To realize when it is best to go outside to an individual or firm for research needs.
- To evaluate secondary research and determine its use in a PR situation.
- To know how to do primary research for PR fact finding.

Public relations research is fundamental to every PR operation. Every public relations activity—strategic or tactical—begins with some preliminary facts, gathered through research. Initial research is generally secondary—making use of facts already compiled. Primary research involves gathering new information.

The basic fact finding begins with an organization's own records, which have to be kept meticulously, accurately and promptly. Keeping is one thing; retrieving is something else. Records must be kept in a format in which they are quickly retrievable, electronically sorted and combined to get organizational patterns. Records also must have some protections for the privacy of individuals' information and restrictions on corporate confidentiality. Records have to be backed up at least every 24 hours and transferred electronically to another location for safety. Buildings can burn. Hackers can intrude and change information. Print or electronic files can be lost, illegally removed or destroyed.

Another part of the fundamental research process is knowing how to locate needed information from other sources. The **World Wide Web (WWW)** is within easy access, even if you don't know what you are looking for. Web addresses change, not as often as email addresses, but they do change. However, that's what **search engines** are for: to find for you what you need. Fortunately, they are easy to use if you put in simple, basic information. You may have to refine some searches to get on the right path, but that doesn't take too long either. Also, you'll find that some materials from academic and professional publications as well as materials from the mass media are online.

The key to research is knowing precisely what you want to find out and how you plan to use the information you get. Most public relations research is done to find out about issues, publics, media contents and media audiences and to evaluate public relations results. When the economy is tight, internal resources are not going to be allocated until the budget request is accompanied by some evidence of value for dollars spent.

Two types of research are employed: informal and formal. Just because something is informal doesn't mean it lacks structure. Informal processes do have research designs and protocols. Formal research designs and protocols are more rigorous and are subjected to **testing**. Two types of formal research exist: qualitative and quantitative. Both have advantages and disadvantages. In an overall public relations research effort, the best type of research is a mix of qualitative and quantitative (statistical) research. In research, *quantitative* is the *what* and *qualitative* is the *why*. You need both. You'll be using research for problem identification and analysis and for program development, implementation and assessment. ■

The Basics: Record Keeping and Retrieving

Getting started with a new public relations job or a new client means doing a lot of preliminary research and setting up a system for accumulating and accessing information. Some large organizations have information systems officers and librarians. Information systems officers manage the current flow of information generated by the organization. Librarians maintain past records and archives such as files and documents. You will find that both are invaluable as you gather the information you need.

Keeping Records

The kinds of records you will need to accumulate fall into several categories: information about the organization itself (when it was begun, its mission statement, what it makes or does, its history), information about personnel (biographies of current and past

leaders) and information about ongoing organizational activities. You will need file copies of all of the organization's formal communication—magazines, newsletters, annual reports, all publicity including serially numbered news releases, advertising, films and videotapes. These may be on file in the organization's library, but you will also need to have all the current information readily accessible in your office.

Retrieving Information

Systematic record keeping—fact collecting—can be an interesting and fun part of your job, because you are being paid to learn. It also can supply critically needed information (such as a record telling you what you did last year when the same problem cropped up), help you plan (by telling you what you need to put on your calendar) and help you flesh out stories or identify a news peg. Maintaining a file on all major activities, as well as a general how-to file, facilitates planning and reduces strain on the nerves—provided that you can find what you filed.

Recorded information must be kept in a logical, well-organized and easily retrievable form. It is not valuable unless you can quickly find it. For example, suppose that you have been touting the high nutritional value of your company's canned peaches, and a competitor releases a "market study" showing that its frozen peaches have more nutritional value because much nutrition in yours is destroyed in canning. A newspaper food editor calls you for a comment. If it takes you too long to find the nutritional information you need, the competition may win the headlines that day, and you may have to settle for a less prominent display of your "second-day" story.

Finding and Using Research Resources

There are two broad categories of research sources: scholarly and commercial. Academic institutions and faculty do scholarly research, sometimes with funding from the government, from foundations or from professional associations. Government research in the USA and in many other nations is free and available in print or off the World Wide Web. A problem with electronic data from the U.S. government, and probably that from the governments in other countries too, is that information in the public databases is not updated regularly. You need to crosscheck electronic information found in government sources with other data on the topic, both electronic and print. Commercial research is done by research firms, advertising and public relations firms/agencies and other public relations/marketing–related companies. Much of it is also available in publications such as annual reports and on Web sites.

Research results that are funded by academic institutions or by professional associations or societies are usually published in scholarly or professional journals and made public. The Institute for Public Relations has a *Bibliography of Public Relations Measurement* available free from its Web site, http://www.instituteforpr.com. This bibliography, developed by Tina Carroll and Dr. Don Stacks, includes research topics, measurement scales and scaling techniques, reliability tests, cases and research reports, peer-reviewed journals and other published sources on public relations measurement. The results of much commercial research are proprietary and generally are not made available to others. Scholars, however, may be given limited access to the results. Normally, research findings are withheld unless the commercial organization sees some benefit in releasing them.

Web Sources

Carefully used, the World Wide Web is an excellent research tool. There's reliable information on most established sites, but personal Web sites, **listservs** and newsgroups often have less valid information. Organizational sites are more dependable. You'll need to watch sites that depend on survey research, including election surveys and the census. These two frequently used sources have problems that are fairly typical for all survey research. Issues arise from how the question was worded, when it was asked, of whom, how representative the responses are and so on. The Web is full of information, not all from survey research.

Finding information on the Web is sometimes a challenge. You'll find all sorts of professional guides for research from newsletters and organizations.[2] You are familiar with the search engines that pop up on your screen when you initiate a search: Yahoo, AskJeeves, LookSmart, Lycos, AltaVista, Google. In addition, there are **meta search engines**. The difference is that meta search engines, instead of maintaining their own database, search other sites, many simultaneously. They sort out the information, delete what's redundant and organize a response. One such site is Zuula.com, which compiles and organizes results on a specified topic from blog search engines such as Bloglines or Technorati.

If you are comfortable with Web searches, try the All-in-One Search Page (see the list at the end of this chapter), which is updated about every 48 hours and compiles information from the World Wide Web, general Internet, desk references, other publications/literature and other interesting searches/services. Each entry gives you a brief description and search strategy.[3] Google, the search engine that began as a Stanford University research project, has an agreement with Oxford University and major U.S. libraries to convert their holdings to digital files that are freely searchable on the Web. Librarians estimate the project may take a decade, at least.[4] An unofficial manual of strategies for using Google's capacities more efficiently by Sarah Milstein and Rael Dornfest, *The Missing Manual*, was published in 2004 by O'Reilly Media in the UK.[5]

Search engines will get you to Web sites; you will find a few of them listed in each chapter's Web site section for convenience. The problem with the search databases, though, is that they are sometimes organized by people who collect and categorize information on a volunteer basis (http://www.dmoz.org). That's why it's difficult sometimes to find what you are looking for. This is also a problem for your company. Some Web editors include their own opinions and associate your Web site with "opposing" sites that are critical of your company. Companies register their sites with database editors and generally add the word *official* to their title so that activist sites with a similar name are not considered a corporate source. Monitoring how search engines find your organization's information is essential. Usually the editors will accept a correction if your organization is miscategorized.[6]

Your organization is likely to be one that is searched for information, just as you, as a researcher, may go to the U.S. Department of State for travel warnings about certain parts of the world or to the Securities and Exchange Commission for access to corporate filings online. *Forbes* magazine offers daily updates of the Dow Jones and other stock market indices, as well as copies of its current and past publications. Maybe you want to check to see if an issue you've been following is making the news, so you'll go to CNN online. Emerging trends may come from places like the United Nations.

Formal research organizations such as Opinion Research Corporation, founded in 1938, offer comprehensive reports compiled from various surveys—its own, Roper's and others. It is a subscription publication. Other research groups are member-based, as is the Newspaper Advertising Bureau. Publications of the U.S. Government Printing Office cover a multitude of issues and topics and are available on the Internet and in university libraries that are government document repositories. Much of the printed reference material you might need is available on **CD-ROM**.

Academic Journals, Professional Publications, Mass Media

Academic journals contain a wealth of research useful to public relations. Most of it is theory-based, and that type of research is in short supply in the working world. One difficulty with academic research is that because funds are limited and research is expensive, university professors often use an available subject pool: students. Not only do students vary, significantly, from university to university, but also, they are educationally elite. When comparative studies are made, these students differ significantly even from the same age group of nonstudents. There's some excellent applied research done by companies for clients, but it is proprietary. Some scholarly publications are free, and those that require subscriptions can be accessed in most university libraries and some public ones. Many are available online, and abstracts of scholarly research are generally online and free. Likewise, professional publications attempt to offer continuing education of sorts. Some, such as *PR Tactics* from PRSA and *FrontLine 21* from IPRA, are membership-based. Others, such as *PR Quarterly* or *PRWeek*, go to subscribers.

More than news is available through the mass media. Both print and broadcast media conduct surveys that are useful. Permission is required, of course, to use the results.[7]

Using Research for Planning and Monitoring

Understanding how to use existing research is essential. U.S. Census data are a lodestone of information about who lives where and with whom, gender, educational level, ethnicity and race, as well as their money and mobility. Some national surveys can be adapted for your organization. Often you can get permission to use the same questionnaire and methodology to compare your **publics** with the nation at large. Before you decide to use a survey, though, you need to ask two questions. First, is it valid? That is, does it measure what you want to measure? Second, what do the survey's findings mean to your organization or to your client? If some but not all of the survey is applicable, you may want to use only the relevant portion.

If you are considering using the results of a survey, you need to know who sponsored the survey; how the survey subjects were chosen; the dates of inquiry; how the survey data was gathered—online or by phone (landline only or mobile and landline), by post or in person; who did the interviewing if in person; the wording of the questions; the population surveyed; the size of the sample; the size of the subsample if only a part was used; and how many of those who were asked actually responded.

Telephone interviews using landline systems give inadequate results. With laws restricting unsolicited calls, telephone identification systems and voicemail, this is becoming a less reliable way to gather information. The question of using landline phones only is being raised because people with landlines often don't answer their phones, but just use an answering device and determine whether to respond. When auto-dial programs are used, there is a good chance that respondents will be elusive. Younger members of the population may be using only mobile phones, and the reason these are not considered very often for phone surveys is cost—double or triple a landline. The calls have to be made individually, rather than using an auto-dial system, and the respondents have to be compensated for the minute charges if not on an unlimited calling plan. Furthermore, mobile users may be in an inconvenient place or distracted when responding, and thus may be reluctant to be connected very long.

Electronic surveys are much easier to manage now that software is available to manage them. You still have to choose the publics, of course, and plan the questions, but often tools such as SurveyMonkey can help you explore opinions from special audiences.

In looking at research data or planning for studies, you need to think about the group in which you are interested. Consider the population in terms of its **demographics**—hard, factual data such as age, gender, educational level; the **psychographics**—a likeness in audiences that is unrelated to demographics, such as lifestyle, music preferences, hobbies; and **geodemographics**—where people live, such as zip code areas.

Finding Out About Trends and Issues

For both planning and monitoring, you need to know what people are thinking about and doing relative to your organization or your client's business. In planning, you need to know where you are initially, a benchmark, before you implement a new strategy; otherwise you have no way of evaluating progress toward goals. Furthermore, you need to know the environment in which your strategy will be implemented. (See Chapter 9 on management.) Research for benchmarking the current status and research for initial **scanning** of the environment helps in developing a strategy and planning message statements.

Once you have implemented a public relations program or campaign, you need to watch the environment to see if anything undergoes a change that calls for a different approach. In 2005 a new nutritional pyramid from the U.S. government caused many organizations such as food and fitness commercial firms as well as nonprofit health groups such as the American Heart Association to adjust their strategies. Scanning also helps to identify underserved markets. The British Broadcasting Corporation (BBC) began its American BBC service when it found a market niche that it filled by modifying its presentation but maintaining its worldwide reputation for reliable reporting.

What You Want to Know About Publics

The backbone of successful public relations efforts is understanding an organization's publics. The difficulty that organizations have in dealing with publics is the fact that these publics have conflicting interests. In a university setting, for example, the students and the regents or trustees may not react the same way to a situation or an issue (such as tuition increases).

That means that although an organization typically has its publics prioritized, in different situations and with different issues, priorities usually change. To effectively set priorities, you must know what these publics know and what they think they know about the issue or situation at hand and the organization as a whole. You need to understand the dynamics of the organization, too, which can also change in any given situation or with any issue. Organizations that have more open communications systems with their publics generally get fewer surprises than those who have relatively closed communications systems. Surveys to examine **attitudes** and **beliefs** often surprise closed-systems managers because they've isolated

themselves from their publics. Increasingly, an organization's long-term relationships with its various publics are seen as being responsible for its image, its reputation. (See Chapter 9.) In giving names to publics, such as students or employees, it is easy to forget that publics are not homogeneous. In trying to get out the vote in the 2008 election, three publics seen as critical by both parties were voters of color, women and youth (18–24 years old). The unpredictability of voters' choices soon became apparent. Researchers were using demographics to attempt to predict an outcome. People vote for people they think will take actions on issues the way they would, that is, the way their values lie. Psychographics are critical because no nominative public has homogeneity.

No public is static either. That's why publics must be monitored in an ongoing way. Messages have to be designed for them and tested with them, and media must be chosen to convey those messages.

Social Media and Traditional Media

The shift in the power balance between organizations and their publics has also changed PR practioners' choice for sources of information. The annual survey Media, Myths and Realities by Ketchum (http://www.ketchum.com) with the USC Annenberg Strategic Public Relations Center explores the use of traditional and social media in the USA, Brazil, Russia, India and China. Results show a shift in media choice, not only to digital media but within digital media for information from social media and interpersonal contacts to word of mouth. Corporate Web sites are far down the list of information sources, and in the USA, consumers are skeptical of most media. Publics are personalizing their media choices and engaging in conversations, not behaving simply as recipients of messages. That means examining carefully which media are chosen and with what results.

What Media Analysis Can Tell You

National and international research firms can do sophisticated analyses for an organization, and it's worth it unless your concern is very limited. Organizations may just need to know where their publics get their information. A church deciding to put much of its information on its Web site has to find out first who wouldn't get the information if it only appeared electronically.

For global projects, or even more regionally limited ones, commercial research firms such as Cision provide media analyses and distribution systems such as Medialink Worldwide that help you place data and check its use. Content analysis of media is useful in determining which audiences might be reached through which media, what the best message would be for the public reached by each medium and the tone of that message. Once material is in the media, the results are evaluated for potential image, given the size and placement of the material and the audience at that particular place, day, time and so on. It's not just general mass media that can be analyzed, but also trade press and professional publications.

In this respect, media analysis examines all levels: input into the messages; actual output, meaning what was used, where and how many people were exposed; and the possible outcome. This, though, is only exposure. Other survey research is needed to find out the *So what?* You need to know how many people heard the message, found it credible, acted on it and changed as a result.

Media Audience Information

News media have to do research for their own marketing and content planning. What is available to media clients is advertising research. Newspapers and magazines are selling subscriber information and circulation figures. The latter are verifiable through the Audit Bureau of Circulations **(ABC)**. These publication profiles are available from salespeople wanting to sign a contract for advertising. While most of the information in the profiles is strictly demographic and geodemographic, some newspapers do readership surveys that are made available. Such surveys tell you who reads what part of the publication and how often, and thus somewhat indicate psychographics. Online publications count on "hits," or how often people visit a site and are thus exposed to information and advertising content. You may have seen, when you entered a site, that you were the 1,578th visitor that day or something like that. Of course this is an automatic tabulation and not entirely accurate. If you visit Amazon.com four times in one day, each time you are a "new" visitor for the day.

Broadcast media use **rating services** to gather information about who is viewing what and when. To be effective and useful, ratings must be comparable from market to market. This requires that the ratings be tallied by national rating services. Ratings are available from a number of such services, the most familiar being **Nielsen**, which measures Internet as well as television use. Nielsen Online research looks at online video use, now a standard source for both news and entertainment from network and user-generated sites that post clips. For television Nielsen DigitalPlus in 2008 added a new feature to its set-top boxes that determines who is watching as well as what is being watched second by second. It may be possible later to tie second-by-second information to other data bases for more specific user information. Other services use set-top boxes too and some set boxes also may use program analyzers so that selected participants can record their specific reactions to different parts of programs.

Broadcasters still use two older systems: diaries and phones. A diary requires one person in a selected household to keep a written log of radio and television use. It doesn't cover when the set is playing to an empty room, though, so it generally shows higher use than a technical device like the mechanical recorder.

Nielson is trying to replace all of its diaries with people meters, small boxes on the TV that record what channels are being watched at any given time. The device is supposed to be more accurate, but it depends on the viewers responding with a remote control to a red flashing light to check in and then to check out. The change is costly to Nielson and the stations; furthermore, the meters have resulted in an undercounting of minorities in the sample because some don't want to use the meters or perhaps due to language problems use them incorrectly.

Nielsen now has some serious competitors. For example, TNS Media Research uses set-top boxes from Direct-TV households that capture second-by-second information for programs and commercials, as opposed to Nielsen's measure by minutes. Also TNS is using 100,000 households to Nielsen's 14,000 audience panel. With the 2009 change to digital from analog television distribution, households without new digital TV sets will have a top box anyway. Yet another competitor for audience information is TiVo. Nielsen's agreement with Comcast allows it to measure video-on-demand use, so the measurement of TV audiences continues to change. In 2008 Nielson bought IAG Research, Inc., a private company that uses an online panel to find out how well commercials are received and how much the products being advertised in them are remembered.

Radio measurement ratings are changing too as Arbitron moves from paper diaries to Portable People Meter, an electronic mechanism about the size of a pocket pager. One advantage is that Abritron can use a larger sample and captures real listening, including station changes. Results often surprise even radio stations that do their own monitoring.

Using Research to Plan and to Evaluate Outcomes

Anytime you consider a public relations plan, you should closely examine everything that can go wrong. Looking at these possibilities early on might prevent some missteps in the planning process. You also need to examine the possibility that some unexplored areas or opportunities exist. Then you have to make a decision about cost and time to determine how critical the missing information is.

Preliminary research helps with planning but doesn't mean you can neglect pretesting. Pretesting messages and illustrations, especially among diverse publics, can prevent some unwanted attention.

You've probably been part of a pretest at some time. If you got a sample size of a new product in the mail and you were then queried about your opinion, you were in a **test group**. Or you might have gotten some coupons in your newspaper that not everyone got. Marketers use **split runs** of publications to test. You might even have been interviewed at the mall, where you were asked to look at something or read something and react to it. The compensation for a person's time in this situation is generally a coupon for a refreshment in the food court.

Final evaluations must be comprehensive to be useful. The interpretation is just as important because the research may have some indicators for redirecting the organization. (See Figure 4.1.) Research is critical to internal evaluations as well, especially in employee development. (See Chapter 9.)

As you can see, the public relations planning process begins with research. Research is used for monitoring a PR effort's progress and for fine-tuning.

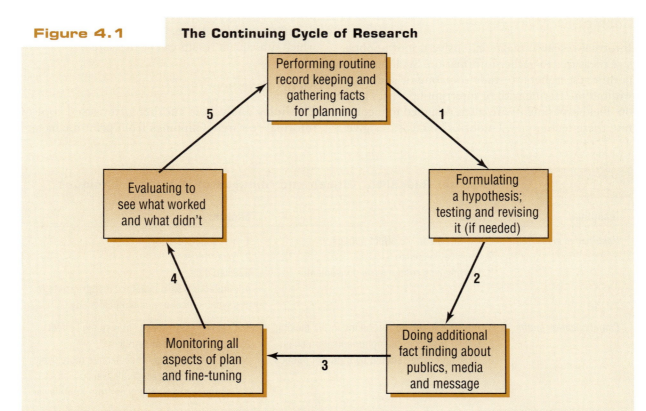

Figure 4.1   **The Continuing Cycle of Research**

Research begins as routine study to assist in public relations planning, moves on to testing and revising hypotheses, necessitates further fact finding and methodology assessment, shifts to monitoring the ongoing program and concludes with a final evaluation of the public relations plan, which provides information to help in planning for the future, thereby completing (and restarting) the cycle.

At the end of a project or campaign, research is used for a final evaluation. The evaluation shows the current status of the product, service or relationship. That information is a major factor for future planning. Thus, PR research is cyclical. (See Figure 4.1)

Informal Research

Informal research generally is conducted without agreed-upon rules and procedures that would enable someone else to replicate the study. The results of such research can be used only for description, not for prediction. (See Table 4.1.) Among the categories of techniques frequently used in informal research are unobtrusive measures, communication audits and media research. There are risks and responsibilities involved. Experience and intuition play a role, and ethical considerations must be given full weight in all research endeavors.

Unobtrusive Measures

Informal research makes extensive use of unobtrusive measures to gather information. Such measures permit researchers to study someone or something without interfering with or interrupting what's going on. Field experiments are often designed to incorporate these techniques. Unobtrusive measures give a researcher a general notion of what has occurred, but no real proof. If, for example, you use several different sources to issue color-coded tickets to an event, you can count how many people used each color of ticket, but you cannot tell from where they got them.

Communication Audits

Informal research also makes wide use of **opinion** audits and communication audits. The typical procedure for either type of **audit** is identical (see Figure 4.2). Opinion audits may be social, economic or political. Some opinion audits use survey research, but many concentrate on observational data such as economic indicators, trends that note what is happening but do not explain why and experiential reporting (people recounting individual experiences).

Communication audits attempt to evaluate various publics' responses to an organization's communication efforts (see Figure 4.3). Opinion audits and communication audits can both be done with publics inside or outside an organization. Moreover, either can be used prior to a change (such as at the beginning of a campaign) to establish a benchmark or baseline against which subsequent results can be measured.

Media Research

Publicity analysis is another often-used tool of informal research. Clippings from print media and

Table 4.1	Informal Research: Pluses and Minuses of Various Techniques	
Technique	**Pluses**	**Minuses**
Unobtrusive measures	1. No "intrusion" to affect publics 2. Physical evidence 3. Usually less costly, more convenient	1. Investigative error 2. Recorder error 3. Fixed data 4. Limited physical evidence inappropriate to psychological or sociological study
Communication audits	1. Possible to locate "problems in the making" 2. Detect breaks in the communication chain 3. Develop images shared by different publics	1. Special sensitivity to "guinea pig" effect 2. Sensitivity to confidentiality 3. Those who are less educated are more likely to give "socially acceptable" responses 4. Responses to visible cues from interviewer
Media research	1. Evidence of efforts (outputs) 2. Suggests other opportunities	1. Same as for unobtrusive measures 2. Often incomplete documentation 3. Difficult to put in context 4. Not a measure of audience impact

Figure 4.2 **Communication Audit**

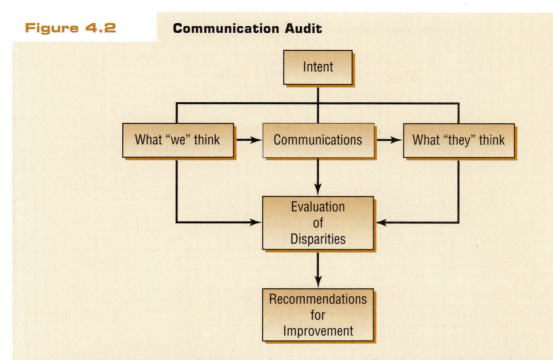

A communication audit for an organization involves searching for differences in opinion about the organization among various publics to improve the "fit" so that publics develop the same ideas about what the organization is, does and should be.

Source: Reprinted with permission of Jim Haynes.

transcripts from broadcast publicity can be analyzed to determine the quantity and quality of coverage. Analysis is usually broken down by audience, medium, message and frequency. The prestige of the publication or broadcast source is often taken into consideration as well, to weigh the value of the publicity to intended audiences.

Risks and Responsibilities

The validity of sources used in informal research is always a serious issue. For example, in looking at audiences that media claim to reach, figures should always be suspect. When using secondary information, always cross-check information with at least three sources before accepting its validity. Your responsibility in using and disseminating information from informal research is especially critical because other researchers are less likely to check the results. There's not the process of replication that formal research offers.

Final Evaluation Procedures

1. Check the effects of the PR activity on each public, or at least the priority publics if not all.

2. Evaluate what goals were met and how these affect the organization's future plans. A shift in emphasis could occur.

3. Determine any possible effect on the organization's directions or its mission.

4. Measure the impact in three areas: (1) *financial responsibility*—going beyond market share to the various publics' perceptions of how an organization gets and spends its money; (2) *ethics*—the perception by publics of an organization's standards of behavior, a moral judgment of the consequences of what it says and does; and (3) *social responsibility*—publics' perceptions of whether an organization is a good citizen, that is, a contributor to social, economic and environmental health.

Figure 4.3   **Typical Audit Procedure**

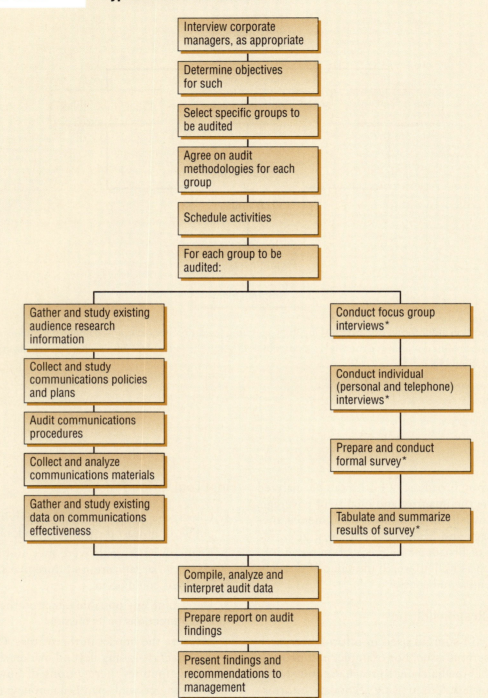

This audit procedure applies to either opinion audits or communication audits. It uses both formal and informal research techniques.

*As appropriate for the methodology selected

Source: Reprinted with permission of Jim Haynes.

Theory and Research Perspective

A college professor told a class that publicity benefited from third-party credibility. The seeming logic to that concept is that publicity is "vetted" by journalists before it is published. It undergoes the editing process and is checked for verification. Beyond that, it is material submitted that doesn't have to be published at all. It appears only because editors have decided that not only is it accurate, but also that it has news value.

The professor told the class that advertising was seen as a message with a vested self interest of the organization. Because the time or space is paid for, the organization may say whatever it wishes, within legal limits. There are penalties for outright false advertising, but none for exaggeration. It is true that advertising serves an organization's vested self interest. It is not true that publicity benefits from third-party credibility. The professor told the class that publicity had more credibility than advertising by a factor of seven, that is, it is seven times more credible. Wrong.

Research has indicated that the credibility of publicity or advertising depends on a number of factors, but whether it is editorial matter or advertising content is not a factor.

See Kirk Hallahan, "No, Virginia, It's Not True What They Say About Publicity's Third-Party Endorsement Effect!" *Public Relations Review,* 25(4) (Fall 1999), pp. 331–50.

In doing your own research, you must pretest even exploratory experiments. You will be dealing with respondents' interpretations of your questions, so you need to discover any misconceptions that might skew results or cause discomfort or distress. Most institutions doing research have review boards to vet all research using human subjects to stay inside the legal boundaries of using human subjects. Be sure your experiments are reviewed before you launch them.

Upholding ethical standards in gathering information is important too. You must be sure respondents understand how the study is being conducted, what the purpose is and how the results will be used. You should protect respondents by guaranteeing them anonymity.

Anonymity is especially critical in the audit process, which is usually done with employees. It's important, too, in processes that use employee suggestions, either put in boxes or sent by email. Another process for gathering ideas to identify problems or to solve them is the Crawford Slip-Writing Method (CSM). The CSM asks participants (customers, employees, volunteers or any other public) to write a response to a focused question in 5 to 10 minutes. The process can use as many as three questions, resulting in a 30-minute session. The involvement of the public in the process gives management special insights and creates public participation, but it also raises expectations. Beyond that, sorting the slips is a concentrated, analytical and evaluative process that can

be time-consuming. However, research shows that 4–6 percent of the ideas generated are immediately usable. The important thing in this process lies in keeping confidences. More ideas are generated when anonymity is promised. Therefore, confidences must be kept.

The Role of Intuition and Experience

Much informal research is conducted to confirm or deny the validity of concepts that are ultimately based on intuition or experience: Someone simply feels that something is true or that something is happening. Research typically cannot *prove* that the intuition or experience is valid or invalid, but often it can *indicate* that it is. Intuition and experience are very important because they may lead to a larger and more formal study that does yield scientific evidence.

While some people assert that formal research proves only what everyone already knows, the results of formal studies sometimes reveal that "common knowledge" is in error—indeed, that it is little more than shared myth.

Formal Research

The two types of formal research—qualitative and quantitative—can be conducted either in the laboratory or in the field (see Table 4.2). Qualitative research

Table 4.2	Formal Research: Pluses and Minuses of Various Techniques

QUALITATIVE

Technique	Pluses	Minuses
Historiography, case studies, diaries	1. Give insight into situations 2. Suggest further research to examine the "whys" that the research indicates 3. Provide detail that can put other research into perspective	1. Difficult to generalize from 2. Often lack rigor of scientific method 3. Time-consuming and require boiling down a lot of data that are sometimes selectively presented
In-depth interviews	1. Allow interviewers to follow up on new lines of questioning 2. Permit respondent to describe in detail so that more information is available 3. Permit questions to be broader, more comprehensive	1. Difficult to transcribe and code for content analysis 2. Interviewer sometimes leads the witness or otherwise influences responses 3. Responses often include basically meaningless information
Focus groups	1. Some are quick and less expensive than other research methods 2. Flexible in design and format 3. Elicit more in-depth information and often point out "whys" of behavior, as well as showing the intensity of attitudes held	1. Often used as conclusive evidence when they are merely tools to be used with other research 2. Sometimes not handled well by moderator, so not all participants express opinions 3. Sometimes not representative of the population
Panels	1. Same as for focus groups 2. May be chosen to represent a population	1. Same as for focus groups 2. Same people used over time "learn" some of the reasons for difficulties and cease to be representative

QUANTITATIVE

Technique	Pluses	Minuses
Content analysis	1. Shows what appeared, how often, where and in what context 2. Allows comparison with other data, especially about publics 3. Useful in tracking trends and in monitoring change	1. Expensive and time-consuming 2. Provides no information about the impact of messages and audiences 3. Some information may not be in the media
Survey research	1. Flexible 2. Varied—administered by mail, telephone, computer, personal or group interview 3. Capitalizes on enjoyment of expressing opinion	1. Respondents may not tell the truth, because they don't remember accurately or because they want to appear different from how they really act 2. Inflexibility of instrument doesn't allow for in-depth expression and intensity of true feelings 3. Wrong questions may be asked of wrong people

describes, while quantitative research measures (by counting). However, it is now possible to code qualitative research for computer analysis, so much data previously dependent on individual interpretation and analysis now is open to more scientific replication. Both types of research follow the same general steps, and in both the researcher is responsible for representing the study honestly, maintaining confidentiality and interpreting data objectively. The responsibility is great because many people are suspicious of research.

Steps in Formal Research

The formal research process usually consists of the following steps:

1. State the problem.
2. Select a manageable (and measurable) portion of the problem.
3. Establish definitions to be used in the measurement.
4. Conduct a search in published literature for studies similar in subject or research approach.
5. Develop a hypothesis.
6. Design experiments.[7] This step includes defining the universe or population you want to study and then choosing a sampling method and a sample.
7. Obtain the data.
8. Analyze the data.
9. Interpret the data to make inferences and generalizations.
10. Communicate the results.

Stating the problem with precision certainly aids in the second step. Deciding which part of the problem most requires study or which part lends itself to testing that may cast light into other dark corners. Because they ignore this step, many inexperienced practitioners design unwieldy research projects that attempt to examine too much at once.

A realistic researcher usually designs simple projects that keep the significance of the research in proper perspective. This involves, in each case, isolating a testable portion of the problem and knowing specifically what information is needed. You must take care to spell out what you want to know. Don't set a goal such as "Find out how to establish effective communications with employees" when you really want to know whether they would like to have an employee publication. If the latter is the question,

find out what kind of publication they want, how often it should be published and what subjects it should cover.

By establishing definitions, you also set parameters for your research. If you want to find out what people think about the Center for Battered Women, first decide what you mean by "people"—Social workers? Battered women? Everyone in the city or county? Residents of the neighborhood in which it is located? The purpose of your study is the determining factor in establishing these definitions.

Conducting a literature search simply means seeing if someone has already done some work for you. Has someone conducted research that you can apply or use as a model? To answer this question, you must consult relevant research journals in the social sciences, communication and business. Buried deep in one or more of these may be precisely the information you need to obtain a unique insight into your research project.

Qualitative Research

Many people are more comfortable with qualitative research than with quantitative, because they are suspicious of statistics and feel that numbers neglect the human side of the story. Undeniably, statistics can be used to obscure, distort or exaggerate. Consider, for example, the debates about how many homeless people there are in the USA and how many people may go hungry here (not necessarily the same people). The percentages might be comparatively small, but whatever they are, the human suffering involved is indeed intolerable.

Although much formal research could be classified as qualitative, three distinct techniques are generally employed in qualitative work: historiography (including case studies and diaries), in-depth interviews and focus groups.

Historiography, Case Studies, Diaries People who write biographies or historical narratives about actual happenings must first collect facts from informed sources—both secondary sources (books, articles, journals and so on) and primary sources (people who were involved in some way). The researchers then organize these facts to provide the necessary background for understanding the problem or issue they are examining. When PR people produce background papers or position papers, they rely on this methodology and reporting technique—called *historiography*—which reconstructs the past in a systematic and orderly manner. It involves recording, analyzing, coordinating and explaining past events.

Case studies use all available factual data to examine issues, events and organizations systematically. Diaries are used in field studies and consist of detailed reports of personal experiences and actions.

All of these approaches are so much easier now that there are search engines to help. You can search a topic anywhere and everywhere on the Web with Google Alerts (http://www.google.com/alerts). Other search approaches are identified at http://www.googleguide.com/advanced.operators.reference.html. The Internet also helps in locating sources for additional information, such as that gathered by interviewing.

In-Depth Interviews As is the case with informal audits, most in-depth interviews are conducted with a specifically chosen audience. But in these formal interviews, the questions are pretested and are usually asked of all respondents. The questions are designed to produce open-ended responses that the researcher must interpret. The respondents selected are encouraged to talk freely and fully. This technique is used extensively in motivational research—the study of the emotional or subconscious reasons that lie behind decision making. However, motivational research requires highly trained interviewers and skilled analysis.

Open-ended questions are often used with in-depth interviewing because they give the **interviewer** an opportunity to follow up equivocal answers with more probing questions. For example, while trying to ferret out employer bias toward hiring members of minority groups, some in-depth interviewers asked general questions at first and then zoomed in with questions such as this: "If you had two applicants absolutely equal in terms of educational background and experience, and one was a woman or a member of a minority race, or both, which would you hire?" The employer's answer could then be interpreted directly, based on a particular response.

Some researchers also feel that open-ended questions reduce error in reply, because the **interviewee** can respond in his or her own words rather than having to fit his or her answer into a category set up by the researcher. Errors are often made in evaluating such questions, however, because interviewers may interpret responses in light of their own opinions.

Consequently, most researchers prefer that the answers be coded in the office rather than in the field by the interviewer. This reduces the impact of **interviewer bias**.

Problems with field/onsite interviews have been reduced over time. Interview questions are created for electronic response and sent to interviewees who were contacted earlier by email and agreed to respond. Sometimes the questions are simply included in an email message, especially if they are brief, but occasionally an electronic instrument is used for the questions, though in an essay, not survey, format.

Focus Groups In the focus group technique, the interviewees chosen generally represent one specific public, because homogeneous groups usually converse more freely. Alternatively, however, focus groups may include representatives from each of a number of different publics. In a university setting, such publics might include faculty, staff, administrators, students, alumni and perhaps parents, regents or trustees. Generally, a focus group consists of 12–15 interviewees.

The key to the session's success is the moderator, who must be a skillful interviewer, adept at keeping the conversation moving and tactful when acting as referee or devil's advocate. Research groups often videotape these sessions, too, and they often use a live monitor so that viewers—the researchers or the client—can slip notes to the moderator during breaks in the session and get additional questions on the agenda. Focus groups can be used to pretest and posttest message statements before and after communication campaigns. The focus interview is often used as a prelude to developing a questionnaire.

Misuse of this technique appears when reported results are the basis of judgments made without benefit of more specific research. Focus groups should be used only as a *preliminary* or *guidance* technique. Prior to technology making social networks so available, the problem of getting respondents to complete questionnaires pressed researchers to go with focus group data only. Now acting on focus group information alone is not necessary.

Focus groups are not the same as panels, although the two research techniques share some advantages and disadvantages. Panels (groups of people queried on several occasions) are sometimes used for discussions in issue development, but they generally are not considered appropriate for formal research. Focus groups are.

Five steps are followed in focus group research, some of which are identical to the steps involved in overall research methodology[8]:

1. Define the problem to be examined.
2. Choose the part of the problem to be looked at by the participants.
3. Decide how many focus groups are needed and choose the participants. (Because group selection methods are likely to create nonrepresentative groups, more than one group is necessary in almost every situation.)
4. Work out all the details of the session, including notification of the participants, selection of the moderator, physical arrangement of the interview area and compensation of the participants.
5. Prepare all materials that the group will need, including a list of basic questions to serve as a guide for the moderator.

Recruiting focus groups is increasingly difficult because people have so little extra time and because the compensation is usually product gifts, not money. Personal contacts work best, or drawing from a company's clients. The corporate Web site can be used to offer visitors a chance to participate. Email is another way. It is difficult to get people to participate unless you schedule a convenient time. Always there are "no shows," so consider that when choosing participants.

Measuring Qualitative Research

Although **textual analysis** has been used to measure qualitative research, many researchers are uncomfortable with analysis of interviews, open-ended responses to questionnaires, results of panel discussions or transcribed focus groups discussion. The more formal process involves transcribing data, determining what it is to be measured against some theoretical background and detailing what is being examined such as themes running through the qualitative materials or concepts the information seems to present or represent.

Then the coding of the information begins. Not counting, but coding. Coding means creating units of data that capture the specifics as well as the complexities that qualitative material yields and that are significant to interpreting what is said. Coding involves keeping in mind what computer program to use. The complexity of coding has turned many qualitative researchers to what is called the grounded theory model, which involves coding every portion systematically. This model is generally used in developing or enriching, rather than testing, a theory. Using open coding, as some do, often doesn't capture consistency. A number of computer programs exist to help with this endeavor, and it is best to find one that will produce the type of analysis you need.

Quantitative Research

The difference between qualitative research (which is based primarily on description) and quantitative research (which is based primarily on measurement) is that quantitative research offers a higher degree of predictability. It is easier to generalize from results of this research to make predictions about the larger population from which the participants were drawn. Quantitative measures include content analysis and survey research based on descriptive and inferential statistics. (Descriptive statistics describe data by intelligible category; inferential statistics help the user draw conclusions, often about a population, from the sample studied.)

Content Analysis Transcripts of panel discussions or interactions, in-depth interviews and focus group interviews are often subjected to **content analysis**, as are broadcast media transcripts and newspaper and magazine clippings. Content analysis allows for the systematic coding and classification of written material that relates to the public relations practitioner's organization or client. Content analysis tells what has been published or broadcast and the context in which it was presented. This provides helpful clues to the kinds of information various publics are being exposed to (although not necessarily what they consume and believe).

As a data-gathering technique, content analysis can also be used to assess what is being said about the goals set by the organization and about its specialized areas of interest, such as proposed legislation. The main difficulty with the technique consists in setting up a model that will give an unbiased analysis.

The classic definition of content analysis was provided by Bernard Berelson, who called it a research technique for the "objective, systematic, and quantitative description of the manifest content of communication."[10] The content analysis research procedure developed by H. D. Lasswell is one of the earliest quantitative measures of communication and follows Berelson's definition. It is *objective* because categories used in the analysis are both precise and normative, with no evaluative terms (good–bad) used. It is *systematic* because selection proceeds by a formal, unbiased system that does not permit subjective collection of data. It is *quantitative* because the results are usually expressed in some numerical way—in percentages, ratios, frequency distributions, correlation coefficients or the like. It is *manifest* because it is a direct measure. No effort is made to figure out the intent of the person using the words; only the fact that the words were used is registered. Some content analysis research designs are more complicated, because they apply symbol or phrase coding to allow for mention of the "context" of the words used.

Content analysis uses variables related to the medium: typography, makeup and layout for print; and camera angles, editing, shot selection, pace and scene locations for broadcast. PR content analysis usually is concerned with the time or space given to an organization and its spokespersons. In broadcasting, the concern is with whether the spokesperson does the talking, the announcer describes the situation or the two work in combination.

Hypotheses can be tested with content analysis, and comparisons can be made with normal or real situations by designing a representation of the "normal" or "real" world. Sometimes the comparison shows how a group is represented, in contrast to their real role in society. An example might start with a television drama that depicts a family with two working parents and two children. This might then be compared to the current reality, which is often a family headed by a single parent who works.

Some research steps in content analysis are different from those in the basic research process. Once you format the research questions, construct a hypothesis, identify the population and select a sample, you must go on to define a unit of analysis, construct the categories to be analyzed and write descriptions of the categories. After you establish a way to uniformly choose material for the various categories, you must train coders and make sure they categorize the items the same way. You can test that ability by applying a coder reliability formula that measures whether the definitions are consistently applied. After the collected data are categorized, you analyze them, draw conclusions and then try to develop some statements indicating a situation or circumstance that supports your hypothesis.

Survey Research Survey research attempts to measure the practices and preferences of a specified public by tabulating responses to a standardized series of questions. Such research has become an essential basis for assessing a public's actions and opinions. Two types of statistics are used in survey research: descriptive and inferential. With descriptive statistics, data is discussed in manageable ways. Inferential statistics lets you use what you found in the sample to draw conclusions about a population.

Basics of Quantitative Research

A PR practitioner must master at least the basics of quantitative research. These basics include a practical understanding of sampling, probability and how to pose research questions.

Sampling Because a public normally contains a large number of people, it's usually possible to question only a representative sample of this population to determine what the public as a whole thinks. The **sample** need not be large. Large samples cost too much, and they do not improve the investigation's accuracy much, once a certain sample size is reached. At very small sample sizes, predictability increases rather dramatically with each additional member of the sample; however, once the sample reaches a certain size, error becomes a factor. (**Sample error** is the degree of discrepancy between the representativeness of the sample and the larger population.) Thus, a sample of 1,000 is not likely to be much better than a sample of 500, although a sample of 100 is considerably more reliable than one of 50. Researchers do this work within a margin of allowable error. The size of the sample depends on how much error can be tolerated in the results—that is, how close a call you need to make.

Sampling is more than a matter of convenience. A universe is everyone you would want to be included in a study, and you're not likely to reach everyone unless that universe is small.

Probability Sampling is based on **probability**. The researcher is gambling on how probable it is that a sample accurately represents a population. But the gamble is not wild. The people selected for a sample can be chosen *randomly*, and a **random sample** is usually free of bias or substantial error with regard to such things as the income of those chosen. The use of a mechanical method for random selection eliminates any bias that the researcher might have or any peculiar homogeneity that might exist within a group or segment of a group selected for study. (*Bias* is the tendency of an estimate to deviate from the true value.) In a random sample, each member of a population has an equal chance of being selected. For example, students in a mass communication class were used as subjects for a survey on media use. To select a random sample from the class, the researcher gave every *other* student seated in the classroom a survey to complete. Because seating was a matter of the students' choice, and not simply assigned, every student had an equal chance of being selected for the sample. This is random selection.

But although this group of students constitutes a random sample of the population of students in the room, it does not constitute a sample of people living in that area or of students attending that college or even of students taking classes in mass communication at that college. The population from which the sample was drawn was one particular classroom of students, and that remains the population to which information discovered in the sample survey can legitimately be extrapolated.

In dealing with any large number of events that occur by chance, we can make predictions (or at least educated guesses) based on the relative frequency of occurrence of certain events among all events that are observed. This involves applying rules of probability. To return to the example of the student survey, because every other student in the classroom was chosen, half of the students (one out of every two) completed the questionnaire. Thus, each student had a 1:2 (or .5) chance of being selected, and this is the probability that any given student would be chosen.

Two types of errors can occur in research that uses probability sampling: sampling errors and nonsampling errors. Sampling errors are the chance difference between an unrepresentative sample and the larger population from which it was drawn. They can occur if a sample is too small for the audience or population being sampled or if the selection is not random enough. *Nonsampling errors* are simply mistakes made by the research team in gathering, recording or calculating data. Nonsampling errors are reduced when fewer data have to be recorded and calculated—another argument for using a small sample size.

Not all samples are chosen randomly. In fact, three major types of **nonprobability** or **nonrandom sampling** exist: accidental, purposive and quota. A reporter who stands outside the campus cafeteria and asks people leaving what they think of the food is getting an **accidental sample**; it is accidental because those who come out at that time may not be representative of everyone who eats there. (Suppose you catch all the members of the football team, and they all liked the ground round?) A *purposive* sample, for example, could be conducted by a reporter who interviews teachers and students in the food and nutrition department about the quality of food in the college cafeteria. (They have been chosen because of their particular expertise or background, and they can be expected to have different ideas about food from their counterparts in, say, engineering.) A *quota* sample is used, for example, by a reporter who tries to match the school's population in miniature, that is, the proper proportion of freshmen, transfer students, sophomores, juniors, seniors, staff and faculty. The sample in this case would be improved if the reporter already knew what percentage of these different groups ate regularly in the cafeteria. Each group could then be represented in the sample in the same proportion as its presence in the entire population of students who ate in the cafeteria.

Stratified sampling is similar to quota sampling in that both recreate the population in microcosm and both have population representation. However, the selection process is different. In **stratified sample measurement**, selection is random but the overall population has been divided into categories or strata. Selection is, therefore, a matter of probability. In quota sampling, the interviewer selects participants nonrandomly.

Posing Research Questions Most quantitative research attempts to answer "What if…" or "I wonder if…" questions or speculations. Research questions are often asked about matters that haven't been looked into often or in depth. Such *exploratory* research looks for indications, not causes. It attempts to get preliminary data so that research questions can be refined for future study and so that hypotheses can be proposed. You might wonder, for example, what conditions (if any) could change the results of your exploratory research, or how other elements of the research questions are related. In doing this, you are attempting to make a prediction (hypothesis) that states your assumption of what is or could be. The reverse of that assumption—what is not or could not be—is called a *null hypothesis*. It expresses the assumption that there is no relationship.

Prediction comes after preliminary or exploratory research and before hypothesis testing. At the exploratory stage, you are saying, "I wonder…" At the prediction stage, you are saying, "I think…" When you start to test an idea or a hypothesis in quantitative research, your particular research project will dictate whether you should use parametric or nonparametric statistics. You will use **parametric** statistics for interval and ratio data—data about populations, means and variances. You will use **nonparametric** statistics for nominal and ordinal data. The numbers contained in **interval** data reflect the existence of meaningful, consistent-sized increments between numerical values of each variable. **Ratio** data are similar to interval data but in addition possess a true zero reference point. **Nominal** data are organized into exhaustive and mutually exclusive categories for each variable. **Ordinal** data are arranged by rank order of the underlying measurements.

Hypothesis testing is always done within some theoretical framework. Most public relations people use communication or persuasion theories. There are five commonly accepted bases for communication theories and two general bases for persuasion theories. (See Chapter 6.)

The five-step procedure for testing a hypothesis is quite simple:

1. State your hypothesis—what you think is true of the population or universe (generally a PR public) in general. Make sure that the variable you want to measure in your population can be quantified or counted.

2. State the opposite of your hypothesis—the null hypothesis. This is simply a statement of what would be the case if your hypothesis were not true.

3. Determine the probability that you would see the same differences in the population or universe that you see in your sample, if the opposite of what you believe turned out to be true. This is the null hypothesis's probability of being true, based on your sample's results.

4. If that probability is slight—less than .05, say—then you can reject the null hypothesis, with (in this case) at least 95 percent confidence that what you thought was true is true.

5. If the sample probability that the null hypothesis is true is significantly larger—even though it is much less than .5 (that is, 50/50)—you should not reject the null hypothesis, because you can't be sufficiently confident that your original hypothesis is true.

Hypothesis testing uses descriptive and inferential statistics.

Audience Information

Most sampling relies on a small subgroup of the audience that the researcher uses to represent the larger group. The subgroup is chosen with the characteristics of the larger **audience** in mind. The most familiar processes for data gathering by samples are cross-section surveys and survey panels. The most frequently used instrument is the questionnaire, which has many formats.

Cross-Section Surveys Three types of samples are widely used in cross-section surveys: probability samples, quota samples and area samples.

In a *probability sample*, people are chosen at random—ordinarily by using a random number table or a mechanical formula such as every *n*th name on a list together with a random start, a method called "systematic sampling" or "interval sampling."

In a *quota sample*, a population is analyzed by its known characteristics, such as age, sex, residence, occupation and income level. A sample selection is made by choosing a quota of people with desired characteristics in the same proportion as these characteristics exist in the whole population.

In an *area sample*, geographical areas, such as cities or units of cities, are used. An area sample can be designed by using city directories as sources for housing units. Using a *cluster plan* in an area sample may reduce the time and money spent on travel, although it also reduces the randomness somewhat. (In a cluster plan, areas are selected and small sample block clusters from each area are drawn. A random sample may then be drawn from each cluster.)

Survey Panels

Businesses and institutions often use survey panels, such as consumer panels, in their research. One unusual consumer panel employed by a toy company consists of panelists five years old and younger. Once a panel is selected, the members are interviewed several times over the duration of the panel. The toy manufacturers get around verbal communication problems by watching their consumer panel. Some research firms videotape panel sessions so that the client can see the results without inhibiting the panelists by being there. (Using one-way glass in the viewing area doesn't fool many panelists.) Videotaping aids in analyzing the sessions, too, because it permits body language as well as words to be evaluated.

Survey panelists are usually selected on a cross-sectional basis and generally by quota, which is effective for controlled experiments. Seldom, if ever, are panelists chosen randomly. One disadvantage of panels is that, over time, they tend to become less representative. For example, newspaper editors have found that citizens chosen for small panels of readers from the community tend to become less critical as they learn more about the problems of getting out a daily paper.

Not all survey panels physically meet. Some may participate through teleconferencing. Some may respond only to mailed inquiries of various types, including diaries and questionnaires. Sometimes a panel represents people with vested interests, presumably participating with the inducements of improved goods or services. But members of some panels are rewarded with gifts.

Questionnaires

The most familiar survey data-gathering device is the **questionnaire**. A questionnaire is often administered in face-to-face personal interviews,

with the interviewer asking the questions and noting the interviewee's responses on a form.

One important benefit of face-to-face contact is the ability to better understand the questions. Research has shown that even listeners whose hearing is not impaired understand better if they have visual cues. Telephone surveys have declined in usefulness, even in polling, because more households use mobile phones exclusively and their owners worry about using up minutes with unsolicited and unwanted calls. Some people don't even have landline phones. The computer is a good way to administer a questionnaire because results are so much easier to tabulate. But one difficulty is getting the correct email addresses for the sample. Another problem is with nonrespondents who may delete the request. If you do have addresses, though, you may use a Web-based survey company to handle the whole survey for a fee. Some companies help with the design and others may let you piggyback some questions on some of their larger survey instruments.

If you are doing the survey yourself, using information from social or professional network sites allows you to pose questions directed to identifiable interests and use electronic survey instruments such as survey.monkey that make possible quick responses with easy to tally results.

Questionnaires sent by direct mail can increase the proportion of responses by enclosing a self-addressed, postage-paid envelope. Such questionnaires can be longer than those used in telephone or personal interviews, but a long, formidable-looking questionnaire will draw few responses. The problem is that the questionnaire itself may be discarded with other unsolicited, unwanted mail.

One important factor in the rate of return for any survey is the respondent's interest in the subject. When people don't have a vested interest, offering them money to cooperate is the best way to elicit a response. For years, researchers have provided monetary incentives to encourage people to respond to questionnaires. For affluent respondents, a gift in their name to a charity may work.

Increases in postage rates have forced researchers to examine content and systems very carefully to stay within budgets. Some research agencies use listserves or other electronic mail systems for both speed and cost. However, there is always the "delete" choice of the respondent to consider.

How to Prepare a Questionnaire The best way to encourage a good level of response to a survey is to

Ethical Perspective

A university class was working on a project for an outside "client" that was underwriting the research costs. The students chose the sampling method, wrote the questions, pretested them, drafted the survey, had it approved by the client and then got copies of the survey printed. Some students bought clipboards and went to malls to "trap" passersby. Others went to the airport to survey people waiting for their friends and relatives outside the security area. Fine. That was appropriate for the methodology chosen.

There was one problem, though. Some grade consideration was given for the student who brought back the largest number of completed, usable surveys. One student who intended to get the best grade "hired" a few friends to help him complete a large number of surveys. He escaped detection and got the highest grade. It was only when the surveys were given to the client as part of the whole package with the report and recommendations that one member of the client's research team looked carefully at the returned surveys. One of the "hired" respondents had marked multiple surveys with a dark blue, nearly navy-colored pencil. The surveys were the kind you often get in the mail where it doesn't matter whether you use an *x* or a check mark in the box. It wasn't like the scanner sheets you use for tests or to vote.

The instructor had accepted the survey sheets but didn't look carefully at them before putting them with all of the others to be tabulated, so the professor didn't notice that many surveys were obviously marked with the same instrument, the dark blue pencil. Several students were working on the tabulations, so none of them caught the problem. What a problem it was! The client was dismayed at such unethical behavior on the part of university students.

The professor was embarrassed. The student was disciplined.

This was a blatantly unethical act. Professionals may be less obvious but just as unethical when they skew results to please a client or don't respect and protect the confidentiality of respondents. Often they don't get caught. Let this serve as a warning to watch all research done for you, whether it is done in-house or comes from an outside contractor.

PR in Practice

Because public relations is problem prevention and problem solving, a lot of the research is exploration to find out if there are problems and what these might be. Researchers know that how the question is asked is important.

In counseling a friend who had done some research in a church congregation and found only negative comments about a new minister at the end of the minister's first year, James E. Lukaszewski gave her some good advice. Lukaszewski told her to go back to the same people and, instead of asking for "constructive criticism," as she had the first time, ask the church members to give a single positive suggestion to achieve the church's goals. He warned her that 20 people's responses might yield only one usable suggestion. She was successful in her second effort. She got positive suggestions, and the minister implemented the suggestions and kept his job.

Lukaszewski's advice addressed a broader topic than research. Positive approaches yield positive responses; negative approaches yield negative responses.

Source: For more of what Lukaszewski said, see "Public Relations Is a Transformational Force: It's Up to You," *Vital Speeches*, LXV (20) (August 1, 1999), pp. 623–25.

write a good questionnaire (which is usually called the "instrument" by social scientists). The questionnaire should be clear, simple and interesting. You must decide whether the questions should require specific answers or be open-ended to elicit free response. (The latter type is much more difficult to tabulate and usually demands time-consuming content analysis to codify responses.)

Some formats dictate the type of questions. In all cases, though, you must try to elicit all pertinent information easily, quickly and in analyzable form. It takes skill to break a general question down into its logical parts. Questions should be definite and separate, not overlapping, and they should invite answers. Be especially careful of your phrasing because personal queries often meet with some resentment.

It is important to group questions in a logical sequence so that the arrangement encourages response and doesn't condition it. As an example, a class was working on a mental health awareness campaign for the campus and was using as a baseline and for a final measure a national mental health organization's survey because it had been vetted by mental health professionals, which reduced the clearance time for use in classrooms at the university. However, in evaluating the results from the baseline survey responses, a problem of question ordering appeared. Opinions about the causes for clinical mental illness, not behavioral problems, were solicited by a series of agree/disagree responses, one of which was: "Mental illness is caused by improper parenting/not enough attention as a child." Many agreed either strongly or somewhat with this postulate. The following question was: "Mental illness is caused by chemical imbalances in the brain." This is the statement that is actually true, and it received mostly strongly agree or somewhat agree responses. You can't agree with both statements. Although the original questionnaire was used again as a baseline measure, the class tested three classes not involved in the original baseline survey and found that reordering the questions to put the chemical imbalance first changed responses to the parenting question and to other related questions about mental illness being a lack of self-control or character flaws. Although this was a different population, it wasn't demographically different. Nevertheless, after responding to the question about chemical imbalance being a cause, the other causes received only scatterings of affirmative responses. It's difficult to make assumptions, but this suggests that, if the true statement is first, the other responses are more representative, because the students had

a limited time to respond to the survey instrument and didn't go back and change answers as they might have done if given an academic objective test where one question following others suggested changes in previous responses.

If a respondent is to fill out a questionnaire unaided, the instructions must clearly specify whether responses are to be checked, underlined or crossed out. Many survey results have been skewed because respondents put x's by choices they thought they were deleting. Every question must be accounted for, but there should also be an allowance for "Other," "Do not know," "Do not wish to answer" or "Omitted."

Another source of skewed results is artificial polarization of opinion in which response options are framed as narrowly and starkly as possible. Otherwise, the interviewees tend to adopt a noncommittal position, not because that reflected their true views but because they thought that by giving such an answer they could evade the responsibility of defending their real opinions.

Some questionnaires that require a specific response provide no gauge for measuring the *intensity* of the response. However, researchers can use semantic differential scales or summated ratings to get at intensity.

Always pretest questionnaires. Words change meaning in different contexts, for one thing. For example, the word *family* has many meanings. A biological family means parents and their children, but the term *family* by itself can include formally adopted children. Other references to the family unit are *nuclear family*, *natural family*, *immediate family*, *primary family* and *restricted family*.

Choosing the term that conveys the right meaning is problematic even when the language, such as English, is the same. Translations create even more hazards. However, even if all of that is done carefully, respondents still may be puzzled by the wording of the question. Surveys using clarifying phrases have proved more reliable. Sometimes the choice of one word over another makes a difference in the response. The Roper Center publishes compilations of different surveys on the same issue and compares the different phrasing of questions and the different responses these elicit.

These problems are compounded when researchers are gathering information in other countries. Survey research may need to be handled differently for both cultural reasons and because of differences in infrastructure. There are also many governments that do not permit collection of opinion data of any kind.

The most sensitive, of course, is political polling. Even some governments that permit opinion polls on social, economic and political issues restrict or limit their publication. If an election is in the near future, many governments, including Western democracies, put restrictions on the publication of opinion data.

Questionnaire Formats The way respondents are asked to answer survey questions also affects the type of answers. Some questionnaires mix different types of formats for responses. Evaluative formats you might consider are semantic differential, summated ratings, scale analysis and respondent-generated questionnaires.

Semantic Differential Scales A semantic differential questionnaire accounts for intensity by measuring variations in the connotative meanings of objects and words. Some researchers disagree, saying semantic differential scales measure degree of *response*, but not *intensity*. But others argue that degree itself reflects intensity.

In this procedure, the respondent rates the object (person or concept) being judged within a framework of two adjectival opposites with seven steps between them. In rating a person, for instance, adjectival opposites might be active–passive or strong–weak. A political pollster may use a semantic differential scale in asking respondents to select qualities, positive or negative, they attribute to persons or issues.

Complex questionnaires and tests have been designed, using the semantic differential technique, to measure changes in attitudes, personality, knowledge and behavior against a background of such variables as education, income, religion, social status, gender, occupation and race. One writer has listed the following measurement dimensions and examples of semantic differential adjectives for each:

- *General evaluative dimension:* pleasant–unpleasant, valuable–worthless, important–unimportant, interesting–boring
- *Ethical dimension:* fair–unfair, truthful–untruthful, accurate–inaccurate, biased–unbiased, responsible–irresponsible
- *Stylistic dimension:* exciting–dull, fresh–stale, easy–difficult, neat–messy, colorful–colorless
- *Potency dimension:* bold–timid, powerful–weak, loud–soft
- *Evaluative dimension:* accurate–inaccurate, good–bad, responsible–irresponsible, wise–foolish, acceptable–unacceptable

- *Excitement dimension:* colorful–colorless, interesting–uninteresting, exciting–unexciting, hot–cold
- *Activity dimension:* active–passive, agitated–calm, bold–timid

Summated Ratings Summated ratings are similar to semantic differential scales. Here, however, the responses to a series of statements are selected from among the options strongly approve, approve, undecided, disapprove or strongly disapprove. A weight from 1 to 5 is assigned to each option so that the high score consistently represents one of the two extremes—for example, 5 for strongly approve and 1 for strongly disapprove. After testing, the weights are totaled and each individual is given a single numerical score. Those who score high and those who score low are selected for further study. Then each question on the questionnaire is evaluated by determining whether the high scorers responded to the particular item with a higher score than did those who are low scorers. Internal consistency in the questions ensures that no correlation of answers appears between these extreme groups. If correlation is found on some questions, these are deleted from the scoring so that only the items reflecting consistent divergence of opinion are used as a scale.

Scale Analysis In its simplest form, scale analysis involves dichotomous questions—such questions as "Is your grade point average 4.0 (yes or no)?" and "Is it 3.5 (yes or no)?" Questions of this type often appear on questionnaires about salary and position in relation to years of experience in professional fields. Other questions may be posed along lines of increasing or decreasing agreement or disagreement. These may be presented in a multiple-choice format.

Respondent-Generated Questionnaire: The DELPHI Process Developed by a Rand Corporation research group, the **DELPHI** process is a method of polling an audience to reach a consensus. An organization's management might use this method to improve relations with employees. The process involves six steps. First, a questionnaire is designed to allow open-ended responses. Second, the sample is chosen on the basis of cost and acceptable level of sampling error. Third, the questionnaire is sent to respondents in the sample as individuals—not handed out by a supervisor or given to the respondents in a general assembly. Fourth, the responses received are organized into a single composite list. Corrections in spelling and grammar are made as a common

Global Perspective

The USA is an open society, and that is not common to all nations or cultures. If you are doing research in other countries, you need to know the culture thoroughly. One problem to consider is the fact that in many countries there are no street addresses. Forget about looking at residence codes to figure out sampling. Another issue is literacy. Even if you get something translated into one of the government-recognized languages, it does not mean that everyone can read it. There are often countless dialects; some speakers may not be literate in any of the government languages, and perhaps not even in their own.

Culture is really a serious issue. Many nations, especially Asian nations, protect their women and children. If you are going to interview a child, you'll have to go through a system such as a school where the teacher administers the survey. If you are trying to interview a woman who is not in a work-place, you are likely to get answers from a male member of the household answering for her—that is, if you are allowed into the house at all.

There is yet another difficulty in less open societies. People are often afraid to give their opinions. They often don't trust promises of confidentiality, usually from experience, and they may fear retribution for honest answers that don't fit the government line. Also, some countries have sedition laws. Any criticism of something for which the government is responsible is a serious act.

Research, by its nature, is invasive. You must know what is permissible and what to expect. Language barriers are the least of your problems, although "translations" that are only literal translations and not genuine interpretations can get you some strange answers.

courtesy, but no value judgments are made, such as discarding an idea because it is too costly or has been tried before. Fifth, each respondent is given a copy of the composite list of responses, together with a rating scale, such as high to low from 5 to 1, and asked to order the responses. Tabulations of this second series of responses—that is, a ranking of items on the list—can be made on a computer. When a number of issues from the list are rated in the highest category, they are grouped according to some relationship of ideas. Once categories of ideas have been developed, the items can be rank-ordered within the categories, according to what the responses were. Sixth, a copy of the ordered list is sent back to each respondent along with his or her individual responses. Of course, this cannot be done if the responses are anonymous; however, if the respondents' anonymity is important, you can provide an automatic copy that they tear off and keep to compare with the overall results.

One result of the DELPHI process is that employees can see if their opinions are shared by the majority of their peers. If the results of the polling are to be reported to management for some action, those in the minority may want to present a minority report also. This opportunity to participate in issue description and prioritization has given employees a greater sense of contributing to the organization's overall planning, and it certainly aids in communication.

Some Basics in Quantitative and Qualitative Research and the Mix

Research conducted within an organization is often done informally. When formal, it usually mixes qualitative and quantitative techniques: conferences with employees involved in a particular problem, studies of the organization's records, reviews of employee suggestions and surveys of employee opinions. Some internal research also may take into account external opinion: ideas of opinion leaders that affect the organization's management; incoming mail; reports from field agents or sales personnel; press clippings and monitoring reports on electronic media; opinion polls, elections and legislative voting patterns or similar reflections of public opinion that may be shared by internal audiences; and the work of advisory committees or panels of people experienced in a particular field. The trouble with internal research is that it is seldom representative and almost always lacks objectivity.

External research is almost always formal. It may involve public opinion—that is, the opinions of large groups of the public (such as a nation), which are usually described demographically—and it always involves monitoring specific target audiences outside the organization that are of particular significance to it. Both qualitative and quantitative methods are used.

Research and Problem Solving

Three types of people don't want to hear about an institution's problems: the ones responsible for them, because the problems make them look bad; the ones whose egos are involved, because the problems are a threat to their expertise; and the helpless, who are usually employees or suppliers, because they can't do anything about the problems and are likely to become victims of any institutional shakeup. When people don't want to hear about a problem, they may either ignore the information that points to it or deny that the information is accurate.

In either case, the messenger who draws attention to the problem—for example, a public relations practitioner armed with information obtained through research—is always at considerable risk. People who feel threatened are likely to lash out at the most convenient and visible target. To avoid getting involved in battles that can't be won, you must be a diligent fact-finder and an expert communicator. You also must be sensitive to the natural resistance to certain messages that exists within each public, and you must compensate for the resistance. Finally, you must anticipate that some resistance will be put up in response to any action that you or your organization takes to solve problems.

An organization's reaction to its problems is determined in part by its structure and its corporate culture, which also influence how it communicates about its problems. Organizations maintain either closed or open systems of communication.

Research for Problem Identification

A good way to begin identifying problems is to ask an organization's insiders about them. Employees know an institution better than anyone else. They may know only parts of it expertly, but they also interact with people in other sections of the organization, and they talk among themselves. Listening to the voices of dissent within an institution often provides good information. Unfortunately, this is a little-used technique, perhaps because it strikes management as being subversive. Public relations practitioners, of course, recognize that employees are the front line for public relations because they *are* the institutional image. They have a strong sense of what an institution really is, what its problems consist of and what its customers think about it. They also represent the institution to its publics. In their neighborhoods and among their friends, they are the authority on the institution. Finding out what employees know or think they know about an institution is a critical monitoring operation.

Employees respond to an external environment, as the public relations practitioner well knows. Anticipating reactions of various publics under certain circumstances is part of the job of the PR person as a social scientist within management. Unfortunately, this role often calls for the PR person to become a devil's advocate, posing hard questions about proposed actions. Anticipating problems and dealing with them while they are small are two major public relations contributions to management. Policy changes (indeed, changes in general) usually mean problems. The role of the public relations practitioner is to help smooth the way for changes by eliminating surprises and building interest and anticipation. The PR person also may have to assume the role of negotiator to help effect a change.

Research for Problem Analysis

Dissecting a problem sounds simple when you work step-by-step through the procedures. Yet what is initially identified as the problem rarely turns out to be the problem. It's usually an effect or result of the underlying problem. The only way to get to the root of the situation is to describe in clear declarative sentences what has happened or is happening. Then you have to do some research—formal or informal (and probably both)—to see if you can get at the true cause or causes.

Once you have identified the problem, you should be able to express it in one simple sentence. The next step is to state what you want the outcome to be, again in one simple sentence. Even if the situation is as complex as an attempted takeover, you should express the desired outcome in a simple statement.

If the desired outcome cannot be stated, you should set down some possible outcomes as goals, together with the consequences, positive and negative, of each. This step involves selecting strategies and the tactics to implement them, as well as research techniques for measuring progress toward your goals. The research can be unobtrusive (such as monitoring phone calls or mail) or formal (such as a survey). Once your action strategies are set, you must identify the publics and the appeals likely to affect them. Finally, you must choose the media most likely to reach those publics.

Now the easy part begins. You have to orchestrate the organization's efforts so that it carries out the strategies and tactics needed to meet the goals, on a timetable and within a reasonable budget.

Constraints on time or resources may force you to modify your goals, but creative thinking usually will enable you to overcome these constraints. On the other hand, even when resources are unlimited, you have to set some priorities. This entails deciding what you need to achieve first for a strategy to work.

Once you have decided that, you can begin work on a more mechanical timetable that tells you what has to happen first. If not done properly, the whole deal could be torpedoed. Once you have made this determination, the mechanics become clear. Meeting with various publics helps to set messages before they appear in any medium.

In problem situations, your concern is to influence public opinion in a positive way. Case histories show that successful plans to influence opinion share five problem-solving steps: assessment of the needs, goals and capabilities of target publics; systematic campaign planning and production; continuous evaluation; complementary roles of mass media and interpersonal communication; and selection of appropriate media for target audiences. The success or failure of all of these steps depend on sound research.

Research for Program Development and Implementation

When you develop a program to address a problem, you focus on three major components: the publics involved, prioritized and described in terms of demographics and psychographics; the message statements to each of these publics, slanted for special appeal to each public—but essentially the same, so that the institution speaks with one corporate voice—and phrased as simple statements; and the media to reach each public, primary and secondary, evaluated for their usefulness in delivering the message in an appropriate, economical and timely manner. You should plan the program in parts and set achievement goals for each part. Research techniques are built in, so you can measure how well the plan is working. Any plan has to be flexible enough to allow for changes as you work through it. The purpose of measuring (monitoring) your achievement as you

PR in Practice

Most professional competitions in public relations require that those who submit projects for judging state measurable goals and then show how those goals were met with some serious evaluations. Judges reviewing those documents submitted by firms and agencies as well as nonprofit organizations and corporations look at the goals first, skip the main content for the time being and go to the conclusions to check the validity of the measurements. Many projects get rejected at this first check because they have not used valid research measurements to show results.

One of the most common reasons a contestant is rejected is because he or she equates publicity space with ad space. What occurs is that the contestant counts the number of column inches of publicity and the number of minutes of television time and multiplies these by the medium's ad rate. This is invalid on the face. All print media rates vary for size, placement and contract specifications—discounts come with the number of inches purchased in a contract. Broadcast rates change with the time and frequency as well as a contract for total amount of commercial time. If the organization is a nonprofit, then the public service announcements (PSAs) were donated time/space or perhaps sponsored by a company. The whole concept is a farce.

In any case, this type of measurement is not a real measurement of anything except *exposure.* Just because something appeared in a news medium doesn't mean anyone saw it, paid any attention to it, came to any judgments or took any action as a result.

For more on this topic, see Julia Hood, "Measuring Up," in *PR Week* (April 1, 2002), and "How PR Can Document Its Overall Value to the Organization by Measuring Outcomes, Not Outputs," *pr reporter,* 45(17) (April 29, 2002), pp. 1–2.

go along is to fine-tune the plan by eliminating what is not working. This kind of midcourse correction research may also reveal at some point that you must go in an entirely different direction. If this happens, you must be prepared to make the necessary changes in course.

The danger in measuring results as you go along, however, is that you might draw erroneous conclusions, especially regarding cause and effect. For instance, you might conclude that because customers said in a survey that they liked your product, they can be expected to buy it. In the social sciences, you deal with people who respond differently under different circumstances. As a result, cause and effect are difficult to determine without extensive replication. In this kind of research, you also run the risk of throwing out information that seems irrelevant but may later turn out to be meaningful. On the other hand, you can become confused and led astray by information that you think is useful but is fundamentally unrelated to the problem.

Deciding which research data are relevant and which are irrelevant is critical to objective thinking. Ego involvement always presents a major problem in any effort to think objectively. The problem is lessened if plans are made by a group rather than by an individual. Information about progress can then be shared with all members of the group. At some point, however, someone has to make critical decisions. It may be the public relations person, or it may be someone else in the management group, acting after receiving an appropriate recommendation from the public relations person.

In any case, the best way to proceed is to make your recommendation as objectively as possible, based on your research findings, anticipating as you do so the positive and negative effects it may have on various publics. These potential effects should not be guessed at. They should be anticipated based on past responses in similar situations and on what research has shown is likely to happen.

Discussion Questions

1. What sort of day-to-day fact finding and retaining needs to go on in a PR job?
2. What are some good sources for secondary research?
3. How would you construct a PR audit?
4. What are the advantages of combining qualitative and quantitative research?

Points to Remember

- The two basic categories of research methods are secondary and primary.
- Secondary research involves gathering already available information, such as from books, articles and journals. Primary research is gathering original information, usually from people who are involved in some way with what is being studied.
- The two fundamental types of formal research are qualitative and quantitative.
- One practical difference between qualitative research (based primarily on description) and quantitative research (based primarily on measurement) is that quantitative research offers higher predictability.
- Records the public relations practitioner must accumulate include information about the organization, its personnel and its ongoing activities.
- Information systems officers manage the current flow of information generated by an organization; organizations' librarians maintain past records and archives such as files and documents.
- The ability to retrieve information in a timely way is essential, and having critical information stored in multiple locations is necessary in case of disaster.
- Two broad categories of research sources are scholarly and commercial.
- Much research is available in electronic data banks, and some is accessible to users of personal computers through CD-ROM and through the Internet.
- The key to successful interpretation of surveys and polls is a realistic and objective viewpoint.
- *Demographics* provide "hard" factual data about a population: its gender, level of education, occupation and so on.
- *Psychographics* reveal the personality traits of a public.
- *Geodemographics* identify geographic areas that are populated by consumers who share demographic and psychographic characteristics.
- Using research for planning and monitoring means looking for trends and issues that are likely to affect your organization.
- You need to know about your publics—what they know and think they know and how they relate to the organization.

- Content analysis of a medium can tell you the educational level, the interests and the economic and social background of the audience.

- Media collect information about their audiences that is useful to PR practitioners.

- Evaluation of results from public relations activities helps in the analysis of what worked well and what didn't, and what that signifies for the future.

- Because informal research doesn't follow established rules and procedures, rely on it for description, not prediction.

- With informal research, you need to cross-check secondary sources to verify the validity of information.

- Informal research may use unobtrusive measures for some sense of a situation.

- Communication audits may use both formal and informal research methods with both internal and external publics.

- Media research can offer some insight into where publics get information.

- Informal research can confirm or deny intuition and experience.

- Of the two fundamental types of formal research, quantitative and qualitative, only quantitative is truly measurable.

- Survey research attempts to measure the practices and preferences of a specified public by tabulating responses to a standardized series of questions.

- Sampling is based on probability. A random sample is relatively free of bias or substantial error. Bias is the tendency of an estimate to deviate from the true value.

- Three major types of nonprobability or nonrandom sampling are accidental, purposive and quota.

- Pretesting a questionnaire helps to avoid ambiguous questions and questions that may generate resentment. Pretest by asking some people to complete the questionnaire before distribution. The more diverse the pretesters are in terms of culture and ethnicity, the better.

- Pretest questionnaires that have been translated to another language to be sure the intended meaning is conveyed by the word choice.

- The six-step DELPHI process is a method of polling an audience to reach a consensus. It begins with a questionnaire designed to allow open-ended responses.

- Research done internally is often done informally, whereas external research is usually formal but undertaken with a mix of qualitative and quantitative techniques.

- Defining a problem means being able to express it in one simple declarative sentence. From that point, the desirable outcome(s) can be stated, goals developed and a timetable established for achieving them. Recognition of constraints in meeting goals is an important factor in achieving success. Be realistic.

Go to the Web site for this book at **www.cengage.com/masscomm/newsom/thisispr10e** to find more Web links on this subject.

Other Related Web Sites to Review

Institute for Public Relations: How to Set Objectives
http://www.instituteforpr.org

KDPaine & Partners offers updates on measurement at its Web site,
http://www.themeasurementstandard.com

UK-based Chartered Institute of Public Relations online guide for information, research, case studies, tools and models for measuring public relations effectiveness on the CIPR Web site. *Subscription newsletter about interactive PR from Ragan Communications*
http://www.ragan.com

Information Sources:

CIA World Factbook
http://www.odci.gov/cia/publications/factbook/index.html

CNN News
http://www.cnn.com

Dow Jones
http://www.factiva.com

Forbes
http://www.forbes.com

General Social Survey
http://www.norc.org/GSS+website

LexisNexis
http://www.lexisnexis.com (also http://www.nexis.com, http://www.lexis.com or http://www.lexis-nexis.com/universe)

U.S. Census Bureau
    http://www.census.gov

United States Government Printing Office
    http://www.gpo.gov

U.S. Securities and Exchange Commission
    http://www.sec.gov/ (the Securities and
    Exchange Commission site will get you
    other government sites)

References:

Leadership Directories
    http://www.leadershipdirectories.com
    (14 address books for governments,
    corporations, nonprofits, professionals)

Search help:

All-in-One Search Page
    http://www.searchmonger.com

Reprinted with permission of Universal Press Syndicate.

CHAPTER 5

Publics and Public Opinion

OBJECTIVES

- To appreciate the similarities and distinctions among the public relations terms *stakeholder, public* and *audience*.
- To recognize and be able to identify priority or "target" publics for an organization.
- To understand how priority publics can be described nominatively, demographically and psychographically.
- To develop sensitivity toward minority publics such as women and those of different ethnic and religious backgrounds.
- To be able to identify potential issues that may create problems for an organization.
- To understand the complexity of opinion formation and the fragility of public opinion.

[P]ublic opinion no longer refers to opinions being expressed in public and then recorded in the press. Public opinion is formed by the press and modeled by the public opinion industry and the apparatus of polling. Today, to get ahead of the story, polling (the word, interestingly enough, from the old synonym for voting) is an attempt to simulate public opinion in order to prevent an authentic public opinion from forming.

—James Carey, *"The Press, Public Opinion, and Public Discourse," in James Carey: A Critical Reader*[1]

Public relations or communications? Just as what to call the person handling a public relations job is undergoing some changes, so too is the subject of that public relations activity. You'll find many references to **stakeholders**, rather than *publics*. The idea comes from the term *stockholders*, who have bought into a publicly held company and thus have a vested interest. However, there are many others with vested interests in an organization, such as employees who may or may not actually own stock. Thus the term *stakeholders* has evolved to capture that broader concept.

Stakeholders can be employees, suppliers, customers, government, investors, a local community or even many local communities where an organization operates, special interest groups affected by the organization and others interested in the organization and its activities including activist groups, local and global, with some perceived adversarial relationship. The concept is a good one because stakeholders have expectations of an organization and the organization owes them some level of accountability. Stakeholders have more than the peripheral exposure to an organization that some publics might. Stakeholders may have a financial investment, but their investment could be intangible: time, energy, loyalty, self-identification, dependency. Thus, public opinion is the collective opinion of various publics. ∎

Identifying and Describing Publics

In any public relations situation, whether it is at the public relations management or public relations technician level, you can't even start without first identifying your publics.

Every discipline seems to develop its own terminology; sometimes, the same term is used in different ways by people in different disciplines and professions. In this book, one exceedingly important term is *public*, which has a very specific meaning in public relations. It is essential that a practitioner grasp the distinction between a "public" and an "audience."

The term *public* has traditionally meant any group (or possibly individual) that has some involvement with an organization. Publics thus include the organization's neighbors, customers, employees, competitors and government regulators. Publics and organizations have consequences for each other. What a public does has some impact on the organization, and vice versa. You might imagine that "public" and "audience" are synonymous. But in important ways they are not.

From a public relations perspective, the term *audience* suggests a group of people who are recipients of something—a message or a performance. An audience is thus inherently passive. But this conflicts with the goal of most public relations programs, which is to stimulate strong audience participation. To help resolve the semantic conflict, the term *public* evolved to distinguish between passive audiences and active ones.

In public relations, the term *public* ("active audience") encompasses *any group of people who are tied together, however loosely, by some common bond of interest or concern and who have consequences for an organization.* The best way to understand this concept is to think of various publics that you, as an individual, might be part of.

First, you belong to a group of consumers that, no doubt, has been well-defined by marketing people. You may, for instance, be in the 18- to 24-year-old "college" market. This market receives a great deal of attention because—although you may not believe it—it is responsible for a vast outlay of cash. Second, you may have an organizational identity. For instance, if you belong to a preprofessional, social or civic organization—the Public Relations Student Society of America, a sorority or fraternity, a service club, a political action group or an athletic team—you are a member of a public. You also belong to

other publics because of your race, religion, ethnic group or national origin. You probably would not want to be thought of as a member of "the general public," and you're not. No one is. *No such public exists.* Instead, you are a member of many definable, describable publics. It is the job of public relations practitioners to identify these publics as they relate to the practitioners' organizations.

Publics are often identified nominatively, but while we can name them, it's important to remember that any public has no homogeneity. All members of that public are not alike. Making that assumption can create problems. Perhaps it helps to remember that another way to look at publics is by their demographics and psychographics. Psychographic ties among people create a sense of shared identity. Although that's usually positive, or at least benign, such as scuba divers or football fans, it can be negative, as we know from teenage gangs.

In traditional public relations literature, publics are divided into two categories: external and internal. **External publics** exist outside an institution. They are not directly or officially a part of the organization, but they do have a relationship with it. Certain external publics, such as government regulatory agencies, have a substantial impact on the organization.

Internal publics share the institutional identity. They include management, employees and many types of supporters (investors, for example). Occasionally, the term *internal publics* is used in public relations practice to refer exclusively to employees—that is, workers. This usage is unfortunate, however, because it results in employees being considered as unrelated to management instead of as part of the same team. Such thinking has a marginalizing effect that creates serious communication problems. In a strong union situation, the separation is real and a team concept is not as likely. Still, the adversarial relationship can be healthy as long as communication between the two groups is maintained.

Realistically, the categories *internal* and *external* are too broad to be very useful in identifying publics. More definitive typologies are needed for planning purposes. Jerry A. Hendrix identifies major publics as media, employees, members, community, government, investor, international, special and integrated marketing. However, even a term such as *media* has become more complex with mass media convergence, community journalism concepts and the participation of "citizen journalists" in the news process. Many specialized media exist only electronically, so that category is broader than ever. Each organization needs to thoughtfully compile a comprehensive list of its publics.

Any particular public, regardless of its broad category, may become the focal point for a public relations effort. When that occurs, the public singled out for attention is called a **target public** or a **priority public**.

Not everyone approves of the connotations of the term *target* in the context of an important public. The "dean" of communication researchers, Wilbur Schramm, was one authority who early on disparaged it.

> *For nearly thirty years after World War I, the favorite concept of the mass media audience was what advertisers and propagandists often chose to call the "target audience." . . . A propagandist could shoot the magic bullet of communication into a viewer or a listener, who would stand still and wait to be hit! . . .*
>
> *By the late 1950s the bullet theory was, so to speak, shot full of holes. Mass communication was not like a shooting gallery. There was nothing necessarily irresistible about mass communication or mass propaganda. Many influences entered into the effect of the mass media. The audience was not a passive target; rather, it was extraordinarily active.*[2]

Certainly most PR practitioners would agree that a *target public* tends not to be passive and may exhibit unpredictable behavior. Still, the idea behind the term is valid—as a silhouette or a statistical profile, and not as a life-size, full-color portrait. Although *priority public* might be more accurate, the term *target public* continues to be used today to signify some definable audience for whom advertising and information are specifically prepared. The "mass audience" is indeed a myth, and using the scattershot approach to reach target publics is both foolish and uneconomical.

Identifying Priority Publics

As a public relations practitioner, you must carefully study your comprehensive list of publics and identify each priority public that is especially pertinent to your particular project. You must also designate publics not on your initial list that might be affected in the future. One way to isolate these peripheral publics (which are not normally a part of your contact list) is to determine how you would get names, addresses and phone numbers if you needed to contact *each* member of that public directly.

The PVI (public vulnerability importance) index has been developed to help organizations identify target or priority publics. The potential *P* of a public plus the vulnerability *V* of the organization to action from that public equals the importance *I* of that public to the organization and to its public relations program (see Figure 5.1).

The key to identifying and rank-ordering (that is, prioritizing) target publics accurately is *research*—finding out who these publics really are and what they actually think. The danger of not doing research and only *assuming* what a priority public thinks or knows is quite serious. Alert public relations practitioners consider not only the collective or majority opinion of each public, but also the opinions of dissenters.

To develop sensitivity to the attitudes of various priority publics, a PR person must develop empathy for each one, much as an actor studies a role and then becomes the character. The PR person must ask, "If I were this public, with this background, these situations, this set of concepts, how would I react to the

---

Figure 5.1 Prioritizing Publics

Prioritizing publics may be done in several ways. One informal method is called the PVI index: *P*, the organization's potential to influence a public, plus *V*, the organization's vulnerability to that public (which may change over time and in different situations), equals *I*, the impact of that public on the organization. The higher the *I* value, the greater the impact. Here is a tabular form for "computing" a PVI index.

	P	+	V	=	I
Audience or Public	Potential for Organization to Influence (Scale 1–10)		Vulnerability of Organization to Being Affected (Scale 1–10)		Importance of Audience to Organization

Source: Reprinted with permission of Jim Haynes.

set of circumstances being introduced by the institution I represent?" Developing such empathy for a public—trying to imagine how that public will react—not only helps in planning for a specific situation, but also helps in media selection.

Each institution has its own particular **primary publics**, all or many of whom are *priority* publics—although the terms are not necessarily synonymous. A business, for example, has internal primary publics (stockholders, employees, dealers and sales representatives) and external primary publics (customers, government regulatory agencies, suppliers, competitors, the financial community—security analysts and investors in addition to their own stockholders—and the local community). At any time, depending on the issue or situation, one or more of these primary publics can become a target (that is, a priority) public.

Describing Priority Publics

Priority publics can be described in any of three ways: nominatively, demographically or psychographically. The nominative form of description consists merely of giving the public a name, such as "stockholders." The demographic approach involves looking at the public's statistical characteristics such as age, gender, income, education and so on. The psychographic method examines the public's defining emotional and behavioral characteristics. These psychographics often show how one primary public resembles another in interests, attitudes, beliefs or behavior.

Such descriptions are becoming more and more important as the diversity of publics increases. Telling evidence of that appeared in *The Wall Street Journal* in a story about jury selection.[3] In the USA one is supposed to be judged by "peers," which has meant that lawyers selecting a jury have used demographics. However, some lawyers realize that demographic profiles corresponding to those of their clients may not yield as favorable an opinion as expected, despite the attitudes attributed to certain groups. One assumption, for example, has been that women are less likely to vote for a death sentence than men. This cannot be relied upon. According to research by the American Bar Association, demographics account for no more than 15 percent of the variation in jury verdict preferences. Then why are demographics so commonly used? Because they're easy. Marketers frequently make the same mistake. Assumptions about demographics are risky. Religious preference, or the lack thereof, often is assumed from demographic

data to be an indicator. Perhaps religion does suggest a value system and maybe some lifestyles, such as food choices or attire, but not always. Religion can't be discounted, but yet another demographic might need to be considered at the same time, such as age. Generations approach religion differently, and not just in the USA.

Sophisticated approaches to publics examine core personality traits such as values and look at attitudes as well as lifestyles. An example is the psychographic casting done by SRI International, which uses a system called VALS™.[4] Adults responding to the SRI questionnaire are placed in one of eight types: Innovators, Thinkers, Achievers, Experiencers, Believers, Strivers, Makers, Survivors. The VALS™ framework has two dimensions: primary motivation and resources. SRI says the following of these two:

Primary Motivation: Consumers buy products and services and seek experiences that fulfill their characteristic preferences and give shape, substance and satisfaction to their lives. An individual's primary motivation determines what in particular about the self or the world is the meaningful core that governs his or her activities. Consumers are inspired by one of three primary motivations: ideals, achievement and self-expression. Consumers who are primarily motivated by ideals are guided by knowledge and principles. Consumers who are primarily motivated by achievement look for products and services that demonstrate success to their peers. Consumers who are primarily motivated by self-expression desire social or physical activity, variety and risk.

Resources: A person's tendency to consume goods and services extends beyond age, income and education. Energy, self-confidence, intellectualism, novelty seeking, innovativeness, impulsiveness, leadership and vanity play a critical role. These personality traits in conjunction with key demographics determine an individual's resources. Different levels or resources enhance or constrain a person's expression of his or her primary motivation.

Another psychographic approach was the media cross-referencing used in a Roper Starch Worldwide global study that surveyed the views of 1.5 billion people. Roper interviewed 35,000 people ages 13 to 65 in 35 nations on all continents using 1-hour, 1,000-answer questions in face-to-face interviews. The questions were based on what Roper called 58 "guiding principles" for their lives. From these 58, the top 10 global values were: (1) protecting family,

(2) honesty, (3) respecting ancestors, (4) authenticity, (5) self-esteem, (6) friendships, (7) freedom, (8) health and fitness, (9) stable personal relationships, and (10) material security. These values are used to describe six psychographic categories, including important variations in patterns of media use.[5] The way these patterns are interpreted by public relations practitioners may be dramatically affected by the increased use of the newest medium, the Internet.

Psychographic researchers realize the difficulty of predicting behaviors from attitudes, but attitudes remain easier to measure than behavior (without invading privacy). To improve educated guessing before a final decision is made, demographic and psychographic information should be cross-referenced with other statistics. Numerous firms correlate such data with the outreach potential of various forms of the media. The study by Roper Starch Worldwide described previously, for example, was one that effectively used media cross-referencing.

Media Research, Media Use

Audience research is used by media to help sell advertising time and space and by media buyers to determine how to maximize their budgets to most effectively reach their publics. Some media specialty firms offer combined databases that they sell to media buyers. Research information firms often supply these data at a lower cost than subscribing to all of these databases, some of which might be used only occasionally; certainly this is easier than trying to maintain a usable library of information in-house. Media relations people also use media specialty firms, some of which also offer placement of both advertising and publicity. An important service that specialty firms can provide is interpretation of information from the databases. A serious consideration for both placement of advertising and publicity is the falling interest in news from traditional media. Newspapers have fewer readers and television news programs per se have only somewhat larger audiences than newspapers. Radio news gets the smallest audience. With traditional broadcast media, the falling statistics are related to news of international, national, state and local events, not entertainment news or entertainment programs that include issues. These have higher ratings, as do talk shows and commentaries. Magazines and books are being read, but not those about public affairs. Although the number of people exposed to news from traditional media sources continues to decline, people do get news—from the Internet.

A confounding problem for media use researchers is how to interpret "audiences" on the Internet. Although Web pages abound on the World Wide Web and "hits" can be counted, it can be difficult to determine who is doing the hitting. Web pages are set up by organizations to put out information, publicity and advertising, and to engage publics, especially priority publics, in responding. Exactly who is accessing Web page information and responding is becoming increasingly significant to know in a global society composed of fragmented publics.

One aspect of this fragmentation is the growing number of people, especially in the USA, who feel inundated with information from all kinds of media. Specialized media invade their privacy with phone calls and unsolicited, unwelcomed mail—postal and electronic. Of course, part of this comes from the ability to electronically track all kinds of personal information about people from just their daily living: credit card use, telephone calls, plane and hotel reservations, banking services and the like. The result of all of these data is the growth of services that sell information about individuals, some of which is sold on the Web. Buyers of this personal data can be anyone, but usually it is someone trying to sell something. The effect on marketing and market research has been great enough that the Direct Marketing Association now requires its members to publicly disclose how they gather and use data.[6]

Many people have responded by effectively "tuning out" all of these media, mass and specialized. Additionally, as noted in the research chapter, mobile phones have replaced landline phones, and the numbers are not as easily available and are more likely to change. Some of these changes are simply the result of technology, others are backlash against intrusions into privacy. Whatever the reason, organizations trying to reach publics with messages have resorted to new methods, especially more personal and more participatory approaches. Also increasing is the use of intranets within organizations and listservs on the Internet to reach special publics. Participation is the key that media users hope will facilitate messages getting through.[7]

That sort of participation on the Internet, though, serves to underscore the fragmentation of publics, inasmuch as it works through the building of definable constituencies. For example, one of the appeals of the Internet to teenagers is its anonymity, a quality which is also appealing to fringe groups afraid to speak openly on controversial issues. For the elderly, who were written off early as not likely users of the Internet, it has become a way to socialize and keep up with family, and to focus on issues that concern them, such as Medicare and Medicaid.[8]

Social Security is another item for concern but the audience for that information, of interest to the government, politicians, insurance companies and the entire medical community, requires a careful definition of what kinds of information go to which groups and who constitutes those groups. Not carefully defining publics has led to incorrect assumptions. For example, the group called the Baby Boomers—those born from 1946 to 1964—is not at all a cohesive group owing to dramatically different economic, political and social climates in those years. Also, the assumption that people already drawing Social Security are bystanders in the issue is also wrong. These individuals worry about diminished resources for their children and grandchildren. Contributing to the public discourse on this topic is the declining middle class in the USA, many of whom are college graduates with considerable Internet savvy. The Internet savvy of teenagers, on the other hand, is overrated. They may play video games, but when it comes to getting information on the Internet, they want simple, not flashy, sites that are easy to use and that provide helpful information and services.

The benefit of having these groups on the Web has been significant for public relations people who can use Web sites and chat rooms as part of their issues identification and monitoring procedures. The downside of the Internet for public relations people is that constituencies can attack the organization directly by setting up rogue Web sites, for example, which mimic the real site but which contain negative information.[9] In other cases, the constituencies coalesce in much the same ways that any fragmented, disenchanted public does. They are outside the bounds of traditional institutional spheres of influence and can affect an organization's operations and well being.[10] Included in these constituencies are some important conventional publics, such as employees or customers of a particular ethnic group or women who have had some relationship with the organization, as well as those who may become concerned about an issue and use the Internet as a platform to attract others to their concerns.

Important Publics: Employees, Women and Minorities

Employees are always an important public because they are any organization's public relations "front line." Employees are seen as knowledgeable about the organization with the special insight of an insider's experience and information, so they are credible to other publics. In addition, employees often have direct contact with other publics, such as customers or suppliers. Women and minorities may be a part of an employee public, but additionally, from a broader perspective, they constitute significant publics who can damage an institution's reputation. Insensitivity to women and minorities in all types of relationships has cost profit and nonprofit groups both money and status.

Employees Employees have incredible job pressures. A headline in *The Wall Street Journal* in 2001 asked, "Can Workplace Stress Get *Worse*?" The answer seems to be "yes," according to a number of studies examining the cost of stress to national economies. Contributing to this stress in most Western nations is financial uncertainty because of the economy, mergers and downsizings, and the ability of managers to monitor individuals' job performance. Information overload comes from technology that makes employees reachable anytime and increases demand for instant responses.[11] Long hours and cramped quarters are other factors contributing to "desk rage," which can range from lost tempers such as yelling and verbal abuse to physical violence. Overwork is blamed, as is crowding. Employees are packed tighter than in the past, often in cubicles like those in the Dilbert cartoons. High housing costs mean that some people must commute long distances from affordable homes.[12]

However, most employees will respond with loyalty to their employers when they are made to feel valued.[13] The key to feeling valued for most employees is not salary and benefits as much as it is the quality of their work life—space and improved communication from management, which helps build stronger relationships. PR people can make important contributions in this area.

Women Women in the workplace are more likely to feel stressed than men, and although some women say it is the combination of family and job pressures, for many it is a problem of lack of power. Although women are a majority of the world's population, many, if not most, are in economic, social and political environments in which they are a minority in terms of power. Because most women are working in male-dominated environments in which they have little authority, many experience sexual harassment. Only a fraction of those complain about it, but in the USA some of those cases have resulted in class action lawsuits with high-profile trials. The damage is not just monetary. A company that gets a reputation for abusing women as employees or customers may fail to get both. This is an issue that needs to be addressed in any organization before it creates a problem. The same is true for treatment of minorities.

Minorities Minorities can be ethnic or religious groups, and they can be physically present in a nation or represented by a constituency abroad—one now connected to its counterparts any place in the world by the Internet. This is an important consideration in issues identification and monitoring. Although an issue can cause diverse groups of any religion or ethnicity to coalesce, it's important to remember that these groups often have no real homogeneity.

Hispanics, for example, now constitute the largest minority in the USA. The greatest number is of Mexican origin, but there are large groups from other places, such as Cuba and Puerto Rico. These groups should not be casually lumped together—not by politicians, advertisers or public relations people. Spanish is common, but not at all uniformly spoken.

The problem is finding the right Spanish for each Hispanic audience, but there also needs to be some confidence that the translated message fits the culture. The California Milk Processors Board, for example, discovered that their "Got milk?" campaign couldn't be literally translated because the result meant something like "Are you lactating?" Worse than that, the notion of running out of milk in the household was not funny because it implied that the provider had failed to meet family responsibilities. A California-based Hispanic ad agency was hired to develop a campaign just for that state. Rather than focusing on deprivation, the campaign by Anita Santiago Advertising, Los Angeles, instead showed milk as an important ingredient in recipes handed down from grandmother to mother to daughter in traditional Mexican families.[14] The research showed that simply translating the original campaign not only would have been confusing, but also could have been very embarrassing.

Hispanic cultures and histories are very different. Moreover, the gulf between recent immigrants and those whose families have been in the USA for many generations often can be even more significant than differences of national origin. The need to be sensitive to the differences created by the diversity of cultures exposed to messages is part of what makes the role of issues identification and monitoring so important.

Issues: Identification, Monitoring, Evaluation and Management

Identifying issues that are likely to create problems for a company or nonprofit organization is the first step in the process of monitoring not only the issue but also the socioeconomic and political climate for any event or development that could have an impact on any of the organization's publics. Not everything that appears on the PR radar can be dealt with, but each must be evaluated for its potential to create some serious problem or to offer an opportunity. Monitoring helps management foresee when opinion is likely to build around incidents or trends.

Anticipating problems makes it easier to deal with them before a major difficulty arises and a crisis ensues. Not all problems result in crises. Some issues can be managed, at least from the perspective of the organization's response. In many cases, the emergence of an issue creates an opportunity, and even a crisis may in the long run be turned into a beneficial experience. Increasingly, issues are arising from global situations. Typically these have come from nongovernmental organizations (NGOs), some of which may be lobbying groups. Many, though, are private voluntary organizations (PVOs) that have a narrower focus, that of social goals. These include some well-known names such as Oxfam, Greenpeace and Amnesty International.[15]

Handling issues demands an integrated approach to communication. The issue, the public and the situation in which an issue develops all require that an evaluation consider strategies that use any communication tools available. This is where the artificial barriers in an organization, especially among its communication units, can be extraordinarily detrimental. The organization needs to speak with one voice, and that voice must be clear and unambiguous.

PR in Practice

A worldwide focus on terrorism caused social psychologists to look at suicide bombers beyond what was known about their demographics and at their admiration of martyrdom. What they found was that group dynamics are the determining factor. Terrorist groups create a pseudo family for their recruits, says Todd Stewart, retired USA Air Force general who directs the Program for International and Homeland Security at The Ohio State University. It is for this family that the bombers are willing to sacrifice their lives.

The concept that identification with a group, more than individual personality, often determines behavior that exists without peer pressure. Robert Cialdini gives the example of a woman visitor to the petrified forest in Arizona who picked up a piece of forest there, despite admonitions to the contrary posted everywhere by foresters. As someone who wouldn't have taken even a paper clip from her office, she told her astonished boyfriend that taking a piece of the forest was normal behavior for visitors and she was just doing what everyone else did—conforming to the group norm.

The lesson for public relations practitioners is to look beyond however publics are classified and examine group norms and how closely individuals accept and identify with those norms.

Source: Sharon Bagley, "Alternative Peer Groups May Offer Way to Deter Some Suicide Bombers," in *Science Journal*, *The Wall Street Journal*, October 8, 2004, B1. Reprinted with permission.

Issues

The handling of issues once they have been identified is not a linear action that concludes when a favorable solution is achieved. Instead, it is a cyclical process with five steps: (1) sensing the problem (research), (2) defining the problem (through judgment and priority setting), (3) deriving solutions (through policy and strategy selection), (4) implementing them, and (5) evaluating outcomes (see Figure 5.2). The process can recur as each portion of a solution is worked through. The feedback causes adjustments in the plans, which in turn cause the next step of the solution to return to step one each time.[16]

Issues Evaluation and Management

In many instances, the appropriate strategy to use depends on the life-cycle stage of the issue, according to John F. Mahon of the Boston University School of Management.[17] He suggests three strategies: (1) containment, for an emerging issue; (2) shaping, for an issue that has media attention and therefore is on the public agenda; (3) coping, for issues that face legislative, regulatory or interest-group action. When an issue is emerging, Mahon recommends dealing directly with it, or with those who are promoting it, to defuse the situation.

The most aggressive stance an organization can take is to shape or define the issue in its own terms. Shaping strategies include total resistance, bargaining, capitulation, termination and cessation of activity. If the issue has reached the coping stage, Mahon says, the organization has no choice but to change its behavior substantially.

Accepting the cyclical nature of issues, many theorists argue for the revised catalytic model (see the theory for this in Chapter 6). In this model, the issue is guided through its life cycle toward a resolution that is in the organization's favor. This takes into consideration an intense examination of the publics involved in the issue and their potential receptiveness to information about the issue, how that message can be presented, and how the organization can frame the issue and set the agenda for public discussion to gain a favorable resolution.

One of the hardest parts of handling issues is convincing management that an issue needs to be addressed. The late Richard Long suggested a four-step process: (1) state the issue or problem in the most specific terms possible and describe the various effects it can have on the organization, (2) identify adversaries and friends, (3) develop a strategy that includes deciding whether to take the initiative, and (4) determine whether to involve coalitions.[18]

Figure 5.2

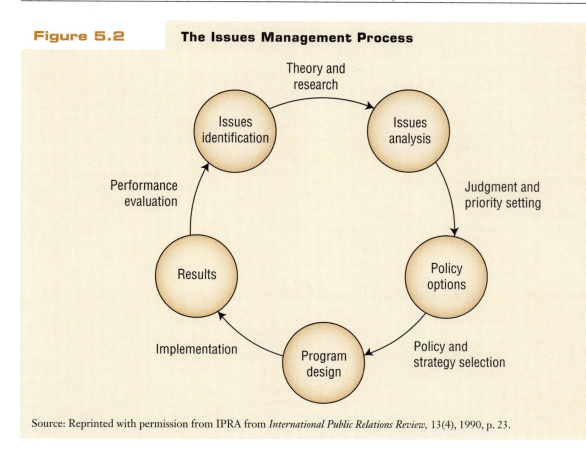

The Issues Management Process

Source: Reprinted with permission from IPRA from *International Public Relations Review*, 13(4), 1990, p. 23.

Issues and the Role of the PR Practitioner

More than any other executive (except the chief executive), the PR practitioner must know what is going on inside and outside the organization and how the organization's activities and functions interrelate and relate to those of others. He or she also is expected to bring awareness and objectivity to the job and to inject unvarnished, usable facts into the decision-making process.

The PR person learns about what is happening outside the organization by being exposed to pressures generated by various groups seeking support. The role of the practitioner here is sensitive and complex. Sometimes the PR practitioner must play devil's advocate, raising all salient arguments against a proposed course of action and explaining which decisions will adversely affect certain groups. Sometimes actions must be taken that will offend a major public, and management should be warned in advance and offered some way of successfully explaining to the public why the action is necessary.

Years ago, no one foresaw the role public relations now plays in relation to current issues and social crises. No longer primarily a communicator, the PR practitioner must act as an intervener and relationship-builder who tries to prevent a potential problem from getting out of hand. Indeed, the most valuable public relations activity consists of formulating plans and convincing management to take steps designed to prevent problems or at least to solve them while they are small.

Some of the tools the PR practitioner uses remain the same, such as personal contact and mass media. The proper measure of performance is not how effectively the client's message gets across, however, but whether a flare-up that can stop a client's business can be avoided. The public relations practitioner has an obligation to help employers or clients conduct their business in a way that responds to the new demands made by concerned scientists, environmentalists, consumerists, minority leaders, underprivileged segments of the community and employees.

Internal and External Publics

Management's perception of priority publics—both internal and external—is not always accurate. Knowing who your target publics are implies knowing what to say to them and how to say it (see Figure 5.3). You need to know how your messages are likely to affect the various publics you depend on for goodwill.

Awareness of publics and their responses requires heightened sensitivity, constant alertness and a lot of guessing, unless you have and regularly update a statistical profile of these publics. There has been a trend in public relations away from the artistic to the scientific. More and more clients ask practitioners to back up their advice with scientific evidence. As Wayne Danielson summarizes:

> The point is simply this: Interest in science and in asking the scientific question is part of the spirit of our times. Professional communicators cannot avoid these questions. They encounter them all the time. They frequently ask them themselves. And they cannot indefinitely avoid giving a scientific as opposed to an artistic answer.
>
> This is basically what communication research is all about. It is an attempt to give scientific answers to scientific questions about communication.[19]

Figure 5.3   **Internal and External Publics and Media**

	Internal	**External**	
Publics	Management (top and middle) Staff and employees (union and employee organizations—nonunion) Stockholders Directors	Direct (marketing communications) Customers Sales representatives Traders and distributors Suppliers Competitors	Indirect (institutional communications) Potential customers Potential investors (stockholders) Financial community Special community of institution Government (local, state, federal) Community (environmental)
Media	Personal (person to person/person to group) Audiovisual (specialized media: films, slides, videotape, closed-circuit TV, computer networks—that is, on intranet) Publications (specialized media: books, magazines, newspapers, newsletters) Direct mail Exhibits (including posters and bulletin board materials internally displayed as well as personalized items such as pins and awards) CD-ROMs Email Fax (or facsimile) CD-ROMs Web pages	Personal (person to person/person to group) Audiovisual (Web pages with art and sound, films, slides, videotape, mass media, specialized media available to external audiences such as externally distributed CD-ROMs, videos, etc.) Publications (mass and specialized, including controlled and uncontrolled publicity as well as institutional and commercial advertising) Direct Mail (personalized, institutional and sales promotion) Exhibits (mass and specialized externally displayed and product packaging, graphics, including point-of-sale promotions) CD-ROMs Broadcast fax ListServe (email) Internet site (on World Wide Web)	

Source: Reprinted from Doug Newsom and Jim Haynes, *Public Relations Writing, Form and Style*, 8th ed. (Belmont, CA: Wadsworth, 2008), p. 8, an adaptation of a model used in *pr reporter*, 33(30), July 30, 1990. *Public Relations Writing* Copyright © 2008. Reprinted with permission of Wadsworth, a division of Cengage.

Being aware of publics and their opinions depends on having ready access to information that helps give an accurate picture of where they stand on issues facing an organization. Institutions accumulate a wealth of information in their daily operations. Unless some thought is given to how that information might be used, it is useless.

Research for sound public relations planning can be built into a record-keeping system, provided that retrieval is also carefully considered. Information about PR audiences is critical. (See Chapter 4 on research.)

Internal Publics and Perceptions of the Organization

One important aspect of an organization's internal publics is their perception of the organization: its image in their eyes. The collective perceptions of *all* publics for an organization—based on what it says and does—constitute its image. A word needs to be said about "image" in connection with public relations. Most PR practitioners would gladly ban use of the word *image* because it's so often misused and misunderstood and because they don't like being depicted as "image makers." Nonetheless, *image* does describe the perception of an organization or individual, and this perception is based largely on what the organization or individual does and says. Of course, the organization seldom is perceived in exactly the same way by all of its publics at any given time, but we will return to this aspect of the subject a bit later.

A major contributor to virtually every public's perception of an organization is the organization's employees. To complicate matters, employees are themselves an organizational public that has its own perceptions of the organization. The role of employees is a significant concern in most PR efforts.

The lack of homogeneity in any public poses problems for the public relations practitioner trying to evaluate it. This is especially true of employees, because they exist on many different levels: salespeople, clerks and receptionists, technicians, professionals, administrators. Moreover, within each group, some people see themselves as embarked on a career while others see their work only as a job. Beyond that, subgroups exist in all of the main categories; professionals, for instance, may include engineers, researchers and lawyers.

The way these people work together and the way the administration works with them create a corporate or organizational culture, which strongly affects how employees behave in relationships with each other and with outsiders. This in turn affects how the organization is perceived. Furthermore, with increased diversity in the workforce and with increasing international ownership and operational linkages, such differences among employees can be profound.

Although the best way to find out what various publics think is by conducting scientific research, you can also ask a few questions: (1) If the institution has an image, does it live up to it? Or does it say one thing and do another? (2) If the organization has a favorable image, can employees live up to it? Or do conflicting demands, low pay or other factors render this impossible? (3) When an image change is necessary, have the employees been helped to make the change through participative management? (4) If the company has no recognizable image, does this result in confusion, limited identification and disparate values?

Internal publics are likely to be particularly sensitive to how an institution is presented to an external public because, as a part of that institution, their ego is involved. All sorts of communication from the organization to other publics must reflect most employees' experiences as closely as possible, especially the institutional presentations such as Web pages and advertising. Furthermore, all internal publics are seen as authorities on the organization, which is the reason they need to have access to as much information as possible.

Realizing that each member of an internal public is a potentially significant public relations asset could make most public relations directors' jobs easier. The best way to promote the use of internal publics as PR's front line is to make employees feel involved. PR researcher James E. Grunig says that a person involved in a situation seeks information, and that a person motivated to communicate about a situation is also motivated to develop a solution for it.

Internal surveys to find out what employees think of their organizations are now as common as external ones. Evidence suggests that labor strife can be reduced by *regular* employee attitude surveys. Such surveys often influence organizational decisions on personnel policies, work practices, communication, productivity, compensation, organizational structure and physical plant improvements.

The organizational behavior of employees, who produce the corporate or organizational culture, contributes significantly to the organization's image.

"Is there any way you PR people can improve our image without our being able to tell you anything about ourselves?"

Source: Reprinted with permission of Punch Ltd.

Joseph F. Coates has described the concept of corporate culture as recognizing that every stable human organization has consistent patterns of behavior reflecting implicit and explicit beliefs and values. Coates says that the cultural characteristics of an organization are usually expressed in positive terms by employees, who often fail to see how outsiders may perceive the same company behavior or policy in negative terms—for example, as "paternalistic," "moralistic" or "intrusive into personal matters," rather than as "offering counseling" or "genuinely concerned."

Coates identifies two widely held beliefs regarding the corporate culture. One is that the culture comes from the top down. The other is that it determines or strongly influences a corporation's willingness to embrace change, promote innovation, tolerate dissent, encourage criticism, experiment and allow for other qualities that characterize a competitive firm. Organizations with especially strong corporate cultures *may* enjoy a more cohesive image, but they tend to be less flexible and don't adapt well to change. Furthermore, the influence of the corporate culture is also shaped by its environment (location), its business (for example, TV or manufacturing) and the primary societal culture of its employees (for example, American or Japanese).

Typically, PR practitioners are not asked to persuade employees that they should accept the corporate culture. People usually try to work in a place where they are comfortable. The more common problem public relations must deal with is *changing* a corporate culture when new leadership arrives.

Coates recommends that employees be "brought along" with a change in corporate culture through discussions and requests for their input, although he concedes that the job is not easy. Philip Lesly expressed more pessimism. He said it is akin to "turning over an elephant with a shoe horn."[20] People are more likely to change their jobs than to change their values.

External Publics and Perceptions of the Organization

External publics are not the exclusive property of any institution. Any external public may become a target for public relations activities. Prospective candidates, for example, might be students in community colleges and working people who might want to return to school or enroll for the first time.

Looking at the different subsets of people who constitute an organization's external publics helps PR practitioners avoid the fallacy of considering external publics as a "mass public." There is no such thing as a mass audience or public. External publics

Theory and Research Perspective

Persuasion is a major component of public relations efforts, and information is the tool. Although most practitioners will agree that it's not as easy as it sounds, what might cause further dismay is that people will believe whatever they want to, even if it's clearly false and they know that it is.

We believe what we want to believe, and a 2005 international study reinforces the fact that we also choose to remember what fits our beliefs. People build mental models, says Stephan Lewandowsky, psychology professor at the University of Western Australia, by way of explanation.

The study took five "events" from the invasion of Iraq—three had occurred and two hadn't, but they had been reported as fact and then later corrected. Even people who recalled the retractions or corrections still contended that the events did happen as initially reported because that belief fit their mental model.

PR practitioners, especially those attempting to respond to false accusations or trying to correct rumor, might look at who among their publics is likely to believe them.

Source: Sharon Bagley, "People Believe a 'Fact' That Fits Their Views Even If It's Clearly False," in *Science Journal*, *The Wall Street Journal*, February 4, 2005, B1. Reprinted with permission.

---

usually consist of larger segments of people than do internal publics, but never should external publics be thought of as an undifferentiated "mass."[21]

External publics may be a supportive constituency—like the residents of cities that have a professional sports team—or they may be adversarial—as antinuclear advocates are to electric utilities that use nuclear energy. Both types must be considered in public relations planning and communication strategies. External publics also have a great deal to do with an institution's image. When external publics and internal publics share similar perceptions of what the institution is and what it should be, the institution's image is likely to be sound because it is consistent.

The perception of an organization's image may vary from public to public, and it may change over time, owing to significant economic, technological and demographic changes in the business environment. Organizations should always monitor perceptions of their identity, but they must reexamine their identity under the following circumstances:

- When public perceptions of a company do not reflect reality. Vestiges of past management mistakes, poor earnings, environmental problems and the like may still be having a negative impact.

- When external forces such as a new competitor, a breakthrough product, deregulation or an existing competitor's new identity require identification countermeasures.

- When competitors are slow to form clearly defined and effectively projected corporate and/or product presentation. In this sense, identity is opportunistic and can become a competitive advantage in itself.[22]

In looking at relationships with external audiences, keep in mind the differences between attitudes, opinions and beliefs. Although some people use the terms *attitudes*, *opinions* and *beliefs* interchangeably, social scientists generally define each of them differently. *Attitudes* are tendencies or orientations toward something or someone—a state of mind, a manner, a disposition, a position. *Opinions* are expressions of estimates or judgments—generally something not as strongly held as a conviction, but articulating a sentiment or point of view. *Beliefs* are convictions firmly fixed in the bedrock of one's value system, embodying one's sense of truth.

Priority Publics and Planning

Tailoring public relations programs to fit various priority publics requires careful and specific identification of the publics and their characteristics (through both formal and informal research methods), translation of this information into a sensitive understanding of each public's needs and knowledge of how to communicate with each. To develop a program that is both real and realistic—not merely a facade of imagery that produces disillusionment and alienation when its insincerity is detected—you must have respect for and empathy with the target publics.

A public is a priority, not only when it is centrally affected by a PR recommendation, but also when it is the group most influential in determining whether an idea, policy, event, decision or product recommendation will be accepted. Once identified as a priority public, the group must be studied for its other relationships. Insensitivity to the composition of publics, their interrelationships, their relationships with members of other publics (as well as to your organization), their ideals and their attitudes may lead an organization to waste much time, effort and money on public relations programs that bore or offend the intended recipients or have a negative effect on unintended recipients.

The news media are often overlooked as a target public by PR practitioners in their planning. Those who regard the press as "the enemy" generally find this attitude reflected in news coverage of their organization. In contrast, consider a corporation that had always cooperated with the news media and that continued to do so when its plant was wracked by explosions. The explosions received front-page coverage, but only for one day—and the coverage was generally sympathetic to the business. Media reports described what the company was doing to help the victims and how it was attempting to discover the cause of the explosions. Clearly, PR practitioners can benefit from keeping in close contact with both mass and specialized media such as trade, industry and association publications.

An important but seldom mentioned public is the competition. The competition is an important public to know, communicate and work with. Institutions that maintain fair and honest dealings with their competitors usually establish this relationship through trade or association organizations. It is harder to insult someone you know personally. In addition, mutual respect within an industry or profession helps prevent open hostilities that could damage everyone.

Perceptions and Public Opinion

An American Airlines pilot training manual contained copy that proved embarrassing when it was made public in 1997 during a pretrial hearing in a lawsuit over the crash of one of the airline's planes in Cali, Columbia, in 1995. The manual said that Latin

American passengers are frequently unruly and intoxicated. Some Latin American passengers, it said, may even call in a false bomb threat to delay a plane if they are running late. On the other hand, it also claimed that Latin Americans generally don't expect to depart on time. To make matters worse, the *Latin America Pilot Reference Guide* contained instructions for flying into Latin American airports that fell below U.S. safety standards.

For an airline that is the leading carrier in the Latin American market, this was an unfortunate disclosure. The airline's senior vice president for Latin America and the Caribbean, Peter Dolara, himself a Latino, said he was offended by the manual, which he noted got its bad information from Eastern Airlines when American acquired Eastern's Latin American routes in 1989! A spokesperson for the airline expressed regret over the generalizations and promised that they would rewrite the guidebook to delete any inaccuracies and misrepresentations.

That was seen as superficial action by some members of the offended communities who flew on the airline to Latin America and the Caribbean. "When we caught them, they supposedly apologized. How many other stereotypical beliefs do they have in place that haven't been revealed?" asked Rosa Martha Zarate, co-manager of Quetzal Travel in San Bernardino, California.[23]

Public relations can help develop the proper management philosophy by listening and responding effectively. When listening and responding effectively go together, the conscience of management takes on a new perspective. In an institution whose policies are inconsistent and whose management lacks integrity, no public relations effort can be effective.

American Airlines' problem with its pilot training manual came to light in a pretrial hearing for a lawsuit brought against it. Often before and during a trial, the case is taken by the lawyers to the court of public opinion. This has been called, variously, *litigation journalism* (because the media are used) or *litigation public relations* (because the lawyers are acting as spokespersons for their clients and talking to news media in a media relations role).

What this means for those involved in the conflict is a battle for the minds and hearts—because the appeals are often emotional—of a variety of publics. (For more on litigation journalism/public relations, see Chapter 8.) All media are used in these battles, and the Internet is becoming increasingly important. Attempts to influence public opinion are made in formal settings such as news release postings on

Global Perspective

Transnational corporations long ago learned that their actions in one part of the world can easily and quickly create negative public opinion elsewhere, and this is particularly true in this age of instantaneous global communication. Whole nations are not exempt either. Global communication that compresses time and space helps create empathy among people around the world. Actions in distant corners of the world only a few decades ago might have gone by-and-large unnoticed elsewhere. Today those same actions can quickly become part of the news agenda worldwide as well as subjects of public discussion that helps create or change public opinion that, in turn, can affect goodwill toward the company as well as sales of its products and services.

After recalls of pet food, human food and toys that had been made in China for export, that country has a job of untangling internal problems that created the situations as well as external difficulties as they work to reassure importers of its products that safety issues have been addressed. The nation faced a problem of changing an image created by this series of problems, all in 2007, that the Made in China label is not a cautionary warning not to buy or use.

Difficulties such as the recalls of Chinese-made products can occur to a country, an industry or an organization—profit or nonprofit. Each situation offers learning examples that can be part of policy and procedure changes.

In 2001 students on U.S. college campuses were organizing "teach-ins" to protest drug companies' pricing and patent practices; states were threatening price-control legislation; longtime business allies were organizing campaigns to seek reduced drug prices; and federal prosecutors were investigating an alleged industry-wide scheme to defraud the federal government health care plans Medicare and Medicaid. Further, the Federal Trade Commission was probing whether the industry had engaged in anticompetitive practices by blocking access to generic drugs, and some members of Congress were discussing whether new Medicare benefits should contain price restrictions. These public relations problems, many believed, were to a great extent because of the African AIDS crisis two continents away.

In the previous two years, the pharmaceutical industry had responded to international calls for lower AIDS drug prices in poor nations with several actions that had created negative public opinion, damaging drug companies' reputations in the USA and elsewhere. The pharmaceutical industry's actions also dramatized the companies' profit margins when drug manufacturers lowered prices to the point where they claimed there was "no profit"—revealing that some medicines were priced 8 to 10 times what they cost to manufacture and distribute. Also, activists were drawing attention to the South African lawsuit in which 39 drug makers were trying to block a law that would facilitate the purchase of patented drugs from generic makers. In what was called one of the industry's "more visible public-relations stumbles," the lawsuit named as a defendant Nelson Mandela, the antiapartheid hero who was president of the country when the law was passed. These actions in one part of the world created negative public opinion elsewhere throughout the world, a lesson that no public relations practitioner should forget.

Source: Gardiner Harris, "AIDS Gaffes in Africa Come Back to Haunt Drug Industry at Home," *The Wall Street Journal*, April 23, 2001, pp. A1 and A6. Reprinted with permission.

established Web sites, on special Web sites often with links to media Web sites, and informally in chat rooms. A guide for evaluating the impact of Internet news outlets and Web sites on perception of an organization is available from the Institute for Public Relations on its Web site (http://www.instituteforpr.com). *A Primer in Internet Audience Measurement* was written by Bruce Jeffries-Fox, whose firm conducts media studies and a range of public relations research.

Keeping information available and monitoring the media are essential in these cases that are tried in the court of public opinion. This is true not only for particular cases; issues can be tried in the court of public opinion too. As noted in *pr reporter*, "When unfair, greedy or antisocial actions or policies become sufficiently widespread to cause outrage, the public turns its wrath onto *institutions*. This contrasts with attacks on specific organizations, which is perpetual and more immediate."[24]

Getting a Handle on Public Opinion

Public relations practitioners function in a climate of public opinion that often conditions their own perceptions and responses. Climates of public opinion can be as broad as that of the international community with regard to a nation's presumed leadership in an arms race or as narrow as that of securities analysts when a company's bonds are re-rated downward.

Public opinion is what most people in a particular public think; in other words, it is a collective opinion of, for instance, what voters or teenagers or senior citizens or politicians think about a specific issue. Bernard Hennessy said, "Public opinion is the complex of preferences expressed by a significant number of persons on an issue of general importance."[25] Hennessy, who does not distinguish between opinion and attitude, says that public opinion has five basic elements. First, public opinion must be focused on an issue, which Hennessy defines as "a contemporary situation with a likelihood of disagreement." Second, the public must consist of "a recognizable group of persons concerned with the issue." A third element in the definition, the phrase *complex of preferences*, Hennessy says, "means more than mere direction and intensity; it means all the imagined or measured individual opinions held by the relevant public on all the proposals about the issue over which that public has come into existence." The fourth factor, the expression of opinion, may involve any form of

expression—printed or spoken words, symbols (such as a clenched fist or stiff arm salute) or even the gasp of a crowd. The fifth factor is the number of persons involved. The number of people in a public can be large or small, as long as the impact of their opinion has a measurable effect. The effect may be as much determined by the intensity of opinion and the organization of effort as by the size of the public. Hennessy's definition of public opinion does not deal with what could be called "*latent public opinion.*" He reserves that term for "describing a situation in which a considerable number of individuals hold attitudes or general predispositions that may eventually crystallize into opinions around a given issue." In any case, public opinion has to be expressed to be measured.[26]

Public opinion expresses beliefs based not necessarily on facts but on perceptions or evaluations of events, persons, institutions or products. In the USA, many people assume that "public opinion is always right." Perhaps this view should be expected in a democracy, in which elected officials must be concerned with public opinion. Long before the pollsters were on the scene, nineteenth-century essayist Charles Dudley Warner said, "Public opinion is stronger than the legislature, and nearly as strong as the Ten Commandments."

Obviously, public opinion can be misused or manipulated—as Adolf Hitler's master propagandist, Joseph Goebbels, demonstrated. And it can be based on a lack of accurate information—as in the period before World War II when many Americans applauded Mussolini's efforts at "straightening out the Italians" (tourist translation: getting the trains to run on time), while many Italians were beginning to live in fear of the black-shirted fascist militia.

Public opinion also is notably unstable. That is why the "bottom line" for political strategists is election day itself, when the actual votes are tallied, not public opinion poll results from earlier in the campaign. Public opinion's reliability as a measurement resembles that of body temperature. For accuracy, doctors say, "The patient's temperature was 101 degrees at 7 a.m.," not "the patient's temperature is 101 degrees" (unless the thermometer has just been read). PR people would be a lot safer in their judgments if they would take the same precautions. Exposure to new information or events can quickly change public opinion, rendering recent polling research obsolete.

To keep pace with constantly changing public opinion, you must accept a few basic precepts.

Not everyone is going to be on your side at any one time. The best you can hope for is a majority consensus. To achieve this, you need to retain the partisans you have, win at least provisional support from the undecided or uncommitted bloc and neutralize or win over the opposition.

Winning over the opposition is the most difficult part. Most of us read and listen for reinforcement of our own ideas. We do not like to hear ideas that conflict with our own, and we make every effort to reject them. For example, we may simply tune out and fail to hear or remember what we have been exposed to. We may discredit the source, without objectively determining the legitimacy of its evidence or argument. We may reduce the conflicting argument to a crude caricature whose fallacious elements we have no difficulty pointing out. We may distort meanings so that what we hear or read conforms to what we believe. No doubt you have seen letters to the editor of a magazine from two different people, each complimenting the publication for an editorial they interpreted in opposite ways; the readers simply read into the editorial what they wanted the publication to say.

Public Opinion as a Moving Target

The importance of the private, individual "opinion" (attitudes and beliefs) that underlies public opinion was described as follows by Daniel Katz:

> *The study of opinion formation and attitude change is basic to an understanding of the public opinion process even though it should not be equated with this process. The public opinion process is one phase of the influencing of collective decisions, and its investigation involves knowledge of channels of communication, of the power structures of a society, of the character of mass media, of the relation between elites, factions, and masses, of the role of formal and informal leaders, of the institutionalized access to officials. But the raw material out of which public opinion develops is to be found in the attitudes of individuals, whether they be followers or leaders and whether these attitudes be at the general level of tendencies to conform to legitimate authority or majority opinion or at the specific level of favoring or opposing the particular aspects of the issue under consideration. The nature of the organization of attitudes within the personality and the processes which account for attitude change are thus critical areas for the understanding of the collective product known as public opinion.*[27]

The capriciousness of public opinion is due to its fragile base in perceptions. Celebrities know (or soon learn) how fickle public opinion is. Influencing it requires constant effort directed toward viable—that is, credible and supportable—positioning of the organization (or person) vis-à-vis the competition. Positioning can sell a product, as Bernays proved when a promotional campaign he developed made smoking in public socially acceptable for young women—a feat he later felt less proud of. Positioning can also sell a person, as many elected officials can testify.

Ideas can be sold, too. During World War II, a massive PR effort by government and industry convinced the American public that the international situation made it appropriate for large numbers of single and married women to enter the paid labor force.[28] That effort put women in jobs never before imagined as "women's work," but it also returned them to hearth and home when those jobs were needed by returning veterans. In moving from one major model of American womanhood to another—each based on American myth—the tide of public opinion was manipulated each time to suit the government's perceived needs.

Measuring Public Opinion

Because public opinion changes so often and can be influenced so easily, measuring it is big business. Most public relations people make use of published public opinion surveys, and many buy public opinion research. Published surveys, for instance, are available by subscription from both Gallup and Roper. For Gallup, go to The Gallup Organization's Web site, which charges now but soon may be offering its services free. For Roper, go to the Roper Center for Public Opinion Research. Issues of its *The Public Perspective* are also available online in Nexis (file PUBPER). It often includes polls, such as those taken by Louis Harris, George Gallup or news organizations, which sample the nation's moods and pass on the information through public outlets. Other public opinion research is offered by a variety of groups for a fee. Some studies—many done by academics or research institutions—are available without charge, or at minimal cost.

Public relations practitioners often perform similar research themselves, although this is usually proprietary—owned by the organization paying for it, and unavailable to other firms or clients. Even when no original research is done, however, familiarity with research methodology is essential to be able to successfully apply the many published surveys to a particular company, market or client.

Walter K. Lindenmann, a prominent researcher, observed that the most sophisticated public relations practitioners measure outcomes—that is, changes in opinion, attitude and behavior. Practitioners rely on such techniques as before-and-after polls; experimental research designs; observation, participation and role-playing; perceptual mapping; psychographic analysis; factor and cluster analysis; and multifaceted communication audits.[29]

Although attitude research must be used promptly because opinion is so unstable, old data should not be discarded. Information from old polls can be used later in developing simulated tests that will yield some probable responses. For instance, when John F. Kennedy was running for president in 1960, his campaign strategists used cards from the Roper Public Opinion Research Center in Williamstown, Massachusetts (depository for the old cards of the Gallup and Roper polls) to design a program simulating how people around the USA would react to various critical questions and issues, based on how they had reacted in the past. In fact, the simulation came closer to predicting the November election outcome than did the public opinion polls taken in August. The reason, Philip Meyer explains, is that the simulation, designed by Ithiel de Sola Pool,

was acting out how the voters would react to a [campaign] strategy that had not been fully implemented. After it was implemented and the voters began to react, the polls began to reflect the results and came into closer correlation with both the simulation and the final outcome.[30]

The reliability of polls has from time to time been questioned. Nevertheless, both the Gallup and Harris organizations claim that polls are generally accurate. The Gallup organization claims that, since 1948, it has, on average, been off the actual balloting in important elections by a little less than one percentage point.

The problem with public understanding of any poll, but particularly political polls, was stated succinctly by authors and researchers Charles Roll and Albert Cantril:

There is nothing immutable about the results of a poll. The way polls are treated by the press and politicians, one might be led to think otherwise. However, what

a poll provides is a picture of the public's view at only one point in time and on only the questions that were asked. Yet, inferences of sweeping proportion are frequently drawn from a poll, leading to fundamental misunderstandings of what the state of public opinion really is.[31]

Something else may be going on as well. The very act of communicating an opinion has consequences on public opinion. For example, a male candidate for governor in one U.S. state appeared to be leading until the final hours of the election, but his opponent, a woman, won without a runoff. What was going on with the pre-election polling? Two factors may have come into play. First, early polls had asked how the respondent was going to vote and what he or she thought others would do. While many women said they intended to vote for the woman candidate, they doubted that other women would. Misperception of others' opinions is a common phenomenon. People often see themselves as holding opinions that are different than those of their friends and neighbors.[32]

The second element that skewed the early projections involved social relationships theory.[33] Not only were women talking with other women about the election, but they were getting more ideas from these discussions than from the mass media. People often won't talk about how they feel or are going to vote if they think their friends, family, neighbors and others close to them will disagree. Many women were not saying openly (in mixed company) that they intended to vote for the woman candidate because they didn't want to argue with male family members, office colleagues or bosses.

Some might say that another contributing factor is embodied in the Noelle-Neumann "spiral of silence" theory.[34] This theory, which assumes a "powerful effects model" for media, states that media can suppress public expression of opinions opposed to those presented in the media, creating a "spiral of silence" that grows until the media's picture of reality becomes reality itself.

Public Opinion Research and Public Relations

The difference between public opinion researchers and PR people was stated many years ago by Fred Palmer, a partner in the PR firm of Earl Newsom and Company: "The public opinion researchers' function is to know, measure, analyze, and weigh public opinion. The practitioners' function is to help people deal constructively with the force of public opinion."[35]

Research on Public Opinion

The study of public opinion ties public relations research to both behavioral psychology and economics. Opinion research reflects seasonal and other types of trends in attitudes that raise questions about behavior patterns, and these in turn often require researchers to look at the economic picture to determine whether the roots of the problem might be there. Anyone who questions this sort of correlation might find some adequate, if unscientific, support in simple observation. Read the front-page headlines of the newspaper, and check the Dow Jones averages. Any securities analyst or stockbroker will tell you that a correlation exists between news on the AP wires and subsequent information on the Dow Jones ticker.

The study of public opinion is particularly important to public relations people for another reason. Information and opinion are fundamentally different. Appreciating that difference means recognizing how understanding and knowledge differ, Hadley Cantril, public opinion authority and pollster, observed that public understanding is "knowledge that

Theory and Research Perspective

A broad collection of theories support the idea of changing opinions to change behavior, but how to do that in a global society is a complex undertaking. Culture bequeaths a collection of assumptions about reality from a person or groups of people that are passed along from generation to generation, even though environments and situations may change.

What this means in terms of public opinion is that understanding reactions to events, products or policies has to be anticipated by using empathy to imagine someone experiencing them through a different "lens," or mind-set. In counseling corporations on preparing for a crisis when management seems reluctant to consider it, one question usually gets management's attention: "If you wanted to wreck this company, what would you do?"

That is the kind of training the U.S. military in Afghanistan is now receiving in counterinsurgency classes. In the fall of 2007, groups of 60 military personnel at a time began attending intensive 5-day sessions training them to "think like the Taliban." In April 2007, the U.S. Army gave the teaching job to a 26-year-old Rhodes Scholar, Capt. Dan Helmer. Capt. Helmer tells his students of all ranks, enlisted and officer, that the important battles are 80 percent political and just 20 percent military.

The Wall Street Journal reporter Michael M. Phillips summed up the job in the following manner. The academy's principal message: The war that began to oust a regime has evolved into a popularity contest where insurgents and counterinsurgents vie for public support and the right to rule. The implicit critique: "Many U.S. and allied soldiers still arrive in the country (Afghanistan) well trained to kill, but not to persuade."

Writer Claire Villareal, a student of Asia and particularly Buddhism, has noted that it is important to use a "culture map" to understand people "living in their unique cultural space." While Villareal is writing to improve understanding and empathy, and to encourage respect for other traditions, she reinforces the concept of the necessity of looking at the world and what is going on in it through the lens of others.

You can't persuade people you don't understand. Persuasion always has been the instrument of public diplomacy.

Sources: Claire Villareal, "Cultural Relativity: My World, Your World, Our World," *Journal of General Semantics*, July 2007, pp. 230–234; Michael M. Phillips, "Course Correction: In Counterinsurgency Class, Soldiers Think Like Taliban," *The Wall Street Journal,* November 30, 2007, pp. 1, A13.

is functional, that has been built up from experience, that has been tested by action."[36] Public knowledge, on the other hand, is more in the nature of intellectual data that do not play a role in concrete perception. Cantril suggested that public opinion surveys should watch for occasions when "knowledge" is used for "understanding" and should inquire into the reasons for its being linked to purpose and brought to bear on decision making.

The first three of Cantril's "laws" deal with the impact of events on public opinion and provide guidance not only for researchers who need to know that an "event" is going to condition responses, but also to spokespeople responding to issues and crises. Their responses also are "events" that can sway the opinions of publics, especially those stakeholders most involved and impacted. That is reinforced by Cantril's fourth and sixth laws about the potential for what they say to have greater force while public opinion is yet unstructured and that self-interest is a major component in responses of publics. But the eighth law about when self-interest is involved opinion is less likely to change suggests that the response of a spokesperson is likely to "set" opinion on an issue for those publics. The fourteenth opinion fits somewhat with self-interest because it says that when opinion is based mostly on desire, it tends to move sharply with events. The seventh law, which says only self-interest or continuing events are likely to sustain public opinion, can be good news except that self-interest groups may sustain an issue by continuing events, especially if they want change. However, the ninth law about public opinion usually being ahead of official policy offers an opportunity to have a greater impact by changing policy in response to the situation, and if it is government policy that needs changing, having some influence on that change. The tenth law suggests that an organization needs to move quickly when an issue arises or a crisis occurs because when an opinion held by a slight majority is unstructured, an accomplished fact moves opinion toward acceptance.

The idea presented in Cantril's fifth law that people react to emergencies, rather than anticipate them, has a connection to the eleventh law that at critical times people are more sensitive to the adequacy of their leadership at these times. The twelfth law that people are more inclined to go along with policy changes if they have a role in decision-making also is a factor here as well as in times when there's not a crisis.

Finally, the thirteenth law states that people have an easier time forming opinions that relate to goals than to the means to reach them. And the fifteenth law points out that the important psychological dimensions of opinion are direction, intensity, breadth and depth—an important point to remember in considering polls and other opinion measurements.

There is still no continuing system of measurement for the "climate of public opinion." Specific tests measure public opinion on a particular issue at a given time, but no continuing study of a public's state of mind exists to reveal, for example, how much they are willing to sacrifice in craftsmanship in return for less expensive, mass-produced products. Who knows what the real religious temper of the nation is, what spiritual values are held and by whom and why and when these values change? Such attitudes can have political consequences, as the Italians demonstrated in 1974, when they finally voted to provide a legal process for divorce in that Roman Catholic country.

How much freedom are people in the USA willing to relinquish in return for security? This question has become even more critical since the terrorist attacks on September 11, 2001, as Americans have had to consider how to balance homeland security with the personal freedoms and security they previously enjoyed throughout their history. This question also was raised repeatedly in 1994 political campaigns throughout the USA, in discussions on topics ranging from gun ownership to teenage curfews. It is a question politicians and businesspeople alike would benefit from knowing the answer to.

In recent years, the advertising industry has shown an awakened responsiveness to public opinion. The ad agencies have been forced to meet the mood of consumerism, which demands that ads tell what a public wants to know about a producer or service, rather than what the company wants to tell.

Dealing with Public Opinion

Many publics share knowledge or work together on various issues. Hence, organizations sometimes find, to their dismay, coalitions of unlikely political partners involved in a boycott or other hostile action against them. Computerized information banks, electronic mail (email), facsimile (fax), video teleconferencing and special interest organizations create loosely affiliated publics with strong emotional ties to particular issues. Because of crossover of communication among these loosely connected publics, it pays to make sure that a message designed to respond

Ethical Perspective

If you live and attend college in the USA, what is your university's ranking by such publications as *U.S. News & World Report*, one of the most respected news publications?

It seems that some universities are "cooking the books," so to speak, in counting their alumni donor contributions, one of the major ranking indicators. The alumni-giving rate is being inflated faster than grades, according to a 2007 *The Wall Street Journal* report that offered such manipulations as extending a donor on the list beyond an original gift by spreading the one-time gift over several years to keep the donor on the list. Another guise is including graduating senior gifts with those of actual alumni donors. Yet another device is to simply not count alumni with whom the university has lost contact. While that is generally seen as reasonable and approved by rankers, what is not is to deliberately ignore locating alumni whom it is assumed would not give.

Nonprofit institutions, like universities, have a greater risk than commercial for-profit institutions in losing favorable opinion over questionable ethical behavior because money given to them is given in trust. A number of nonprofit institutions—such as the American Red Cross, which was criticized for its 9/11 blood donation decisions—can testify to the problems of restoring trust and credibility.

Source: Daniel Golden, "Math Lessons: To Boost Donor Numbers, Colleges Adopt New Tricks," *The Wall Street Journal*, March 2, 2007, pp. 1 and A9.

---

to one public doesn't offend another.[37] Many subsets of very tightly woven communities are tied together by common experiences (for example, children of alcoholics, or CoAs) or situations (for example, disabilities or illnesses) or interests (for example, animal rights). These webs of relationships are interlocking even for a single individual.

Even though different publics often share some common interests and values, it is increasingly dangerous to assume that people share common sets of values. Thus, an organization trying to determine a socially responsible course of action must simultaneously try to respond to special interest groups interested in changing broader public opinion. An example is a revision of a high-school history textbook that discusses Abigail Adams's role in the American Revolution at greater length than that of her husband. The book's author, Henry F. Groff, says the changes resulted from his having raised two daughters and from scholarship that has illuminated the historical role of women (women's studies and the women's movement).[38]

The PR manager often feels caught in a force field of special interest groups. But allegiance to a mission statement can keep PR efforts from being scattershot and can work, instead, to strengthen the organization's image and the public's perception of its organizational values.

In dealing with public opinion, the organization counts on maintaining credibility, accomplished through trust. People trust people, not organizations, according to advice on trust from *PR Week*. That trust comes from experience—direct contact from an organization not when using its products or services, but with its employees. Trusted employees are those who feel that they can speak with authority for a company and do so knowledgeably and confidently. Publics are also very forgiving when an organization has a crisis, as long as it acts honestly and communicates often. And they are more likely to trust information from news, rather than ads, especially when the same news content comes from multiple sources.[39]

Discussion Questions

1. What do you think of when you hear the word *public*? How do you define public opinion? Can you think of ways your opinion as part of some public has been formed around certain issues? What about the opinions of your friends? How many publics do you belong to?

2. Think of three or four publics at your school. What are the best ways to communicate with these publics, that is, what media is best? What else influences these publics' opinion?

3. How do you think culture could affect an opinion of a public? Gender? Race and ethnicity? Religion?

4. How much influence do you think public relations practitioners have on public opinion? Defend your answer with examples.

Points to Remember

- The term *public* ("active audience") encompasses any group of people tied together, however loosely, by some common bond of interest or concern and who have consequences on an organization. No "general public" exists. *External publics* exist outside an institution; *internal publics* share the institutional identity. An *audience* is a group of people who are recipients of something—a message or a performance.

- A "mass audience" is a myth, and the scattershot approach is both foolish and uneconomical.

- *Publics* can be described in three ways: nominatively, demographically and psychographically.

- Priority publics are those most important to an organization in terms of their potential impact on the organization.

- Certain priority publics are stable, such as employees (who are always important), but others may change as issues or situations develop.

- Psychographics are increasingly important for describing diverse publics. One system for analysis of U.S. consumers is VALS™ (values, attitudes and lifestyles), which puts consumers into eight categories. An international study by Roper Starch Worldwide uses six psychographic categories and identifies a list of "top ten global values."

- Increasingly people are not using traditional media, which furthers the fragmentation of publics.

- The "tuning out" of traditional media, mass and specialized, is partly the result of saturation, including messages that people perceive as violations of their privacy.

- Organizations are trying to reach some fragmented communities by using intranets and listservs to benefit from interactive participation.

- The newest medium, the Internet, is drawing more use because it is participatory, offers anonymity and affords the development of "communities."

- Many of the communities develop into constituencies that can be online critics of organizations, even to the extent of setting up rogue Web sites and otherwise using the Web to legitimize their criticism.

- Employees are always an important public because they often have direct contact with a number of other publics. With their insiders' experience and information, they are perceived as knowledgeable and credible. Keeping employees informed and loyal is crucial for maintaining this PR "front line."

- Women in the workplace and women customers can create serious problems with an institution's reputation if they are victims of harassment or discrimination and make that case publicly.

- Minorities can be ethnic or religious, and it should not be assumed that they represent any sort of homogeneous public. Failure to recognize that they can be in the nation or represented by a constituency abroad is also a serious mistake.

- Sensitivity to a minority culture is as important as being aware of and using the language of that minority effectively.

- Identifying issues that are likely to create problems for a company or nonprofit organization is the first step in the process of monitoring not only issues but also the socioeconomic and political climate for events and developments that could affect any of the organization's publics.

- Handling issues demands an integrated approach to communication. The issue, the public and the situation in which an issue develops all require that an evaluation consider strategies that use any and all available communication tools.

- Issues are cyclical in nature. Understanding that cycle helps to determine at what stage it is important to act.

- The catalytic model aims to seize the opportunity to frame the issue and to guide it through its life cycle toward resolution in the organization's favor.

- One of the most difficult parts of handling issues is convincing management to address an issue in a timely way.

- More than any other executive, other than the president or chief executive officer (CEO), the staff public relations practitioner needs to know what is going on both inside and outside the organization and how the organization's actions and plans will relate to its publics.

- The job of the PR person is to bring awareness and objectivity to the job and to inject unvarnished, usable facts into the decision-making process. This is not always a popular position, but it is essential for the PR person's role in strategic planning.

- The type of information known about internal and external publics and the media used to reach them must be as verifiable as possible, which means using research that employs a mix of scientific measurements.

- *Image* describes the collective perceptions of an organization or individual by all of its publics, based on what it says and does, which constitute its image.

- The way employees and management work together creates a corporate or institutional culture that strongly affects how employees behave in relationships to each other and to outsiders. This, in turn, affects how the organization is perceived.

- The corporate culture has an impact on the image that external publics have of an organization. Mergers and acquisitions can, consequently, create some confusion about the new entity.

- An external public may be a supportive or adversarial constituency. The perception of the organization varies from public to public and may change over time due to significant changes in relationships or in the environment.

- *Attitudes* are tendencies or orientations toward something or someone—a state of mind, a manner, a disposition or a position. *Opinions* are expressions of estimates or judgments—generally something not as strongly held as a conviction but articulating a sentiment or point of view. *Beliefs* are convictions firmly fixed in the bedrock of one's value system, embodying one's sense of truth.

- *Public opinion* is a collective opinion—that is, what most people in a particular public think.

- Public opinion expresses beliefs based not necessarily on facts but on perceptions or evaluations of events, persons, institutions or products.

- Tailoring public relations programs to fit various priority publics requires careful and specific identification of the publics, an understanding of their needs and knowledge of how best to communicate with them.

- A public is a priority not just because the organization says so, but because the public is influential in the success or failure of an idea, policy, event, decision or product.

- Attempting to influence publics means being sensitive about their reaction to imagery, going to them instead of expecting them to come to you, not assuming attitude change is necessary for behavior change, using moral arguments only as adjuncts and not as main points, embracing the attitudinal public mainstream and not offending the people you want to change.

- Insensitivity or unawareness of the interconnectedness of publics is a formula for failure.

- Knowledge is power. That is why fact finding is so important, and why understanding how organizations and institutions work is critical.

- Often overlooked in research about publics are the news media and competitors, two publics that have the potential to do the most harm.

- Not everyone is going to be on your side at any one time. The best you can hope for is a majority consensus.

- There is still no continuing system of measurement for the "climate of public opinion." Specific tests measure public opinion on a particular issue at a given time, but no continuing study of a public's state of mind exists.

- Internal communications can become public communications, so these should always be prepared with a consideration for the sensitivities of all publics, not just those for whom they are written.

- Perception is the reality for publics, so when image and experience conflict, opinion of the institution takes a nosedive.

- Public relations people who think they can be only image-makers or spokespersons for whatever management wants to say are borrowing trouble and abdicating their role as institutional strategists.

- Public opinion is what most people in a particular public think—a collective opinion. Groups of those publics can be seen as having an opinion about an organization or institution. In order to be measured, however, public opinion has to be expressed.

- Public opinion is unstable and is only as good as the information involved in its formation.

- Pollster Hadley Cantril developed some concepts about public opinion that have stood the tests of time and theoretical assessment.

- Public relations practitioners measure outcomes, changes in opinion, attitudes and behaviors to determine the effectiveness of persuasive efforts.

of the ways to measure opinion is by using polls. But to interpret results correctly, public relations people must understand the mechanics of polling as well as communication theories that affect gathering information.

- Some information about public opinion is available in public sources, and other information can be bought; but research done by firms for clients or done by companies for their own use is proprietary and is generally not available.

- Public opinion researchers know, measure, analyze and weigh public opinion; but the PR practitioners' job is to help their organizations and clients deal with the *impact* of public opinion.

- Information and opinion are different. Appreciating that difference means recognizing how understanding and knowledge differ, and being careful about which are used in decision-making.

- Different publics may share some common interests and values, but it can't be assumed that there is enough homogeneity in a public to make assumptions about how fully values are shared.

- Organizations depend on the opinions of their publics, so they need to be sure that these publics get accurate information and can communicate with the organization, especially about decisions that may have an impact on them.

Go to the Web site for this book at **www.cengage.com/masscomm/newsom/thisispr10e** to find more Web links on this subject.

Other Related Web Sites to Review

EUROPA Public Opinion Analysis
http://europa.eu.int/comm/public_opinion/

The Gallup Organization
http://www.gallup.com/

International Journal of Public Opinion Research
ijpor.oxfordjournals.org/

PollingReport.com
http://www.pollingreport.com/

Public Agenda Online
http://www.publicagenda.org

Public Opinion Strategies (POS)
http://www.pos.org/

The Roper Center for Public Opinion
http://www.ropercenter.uconn.edu/

Reprinted with permission of King Features Syndicate.

CHAPTER 6

Theoretical Underpinnings for PR

Thank God, communication isn't a disease, because we know so little about it.

—Bill Marsteller, *Former Chairman and Chief Executive Officer, Marsteller, Inc.*

OBJECTIVES

- To understand that theories are just that, and not principles.
- To learn what theories might apply to particular PR situations.
- To test theories in PR practice to refine theoretical models.
- To realize that PR functions in organizational structures and particular communication environments, and depends on volunteer readers, viewers and participants.

Public relations theory borrows from a number of disciplines. Because PR is a management function and works in an organizational environment, it draws on organizational theory and management theory. Because public affairs is also a major element of public relations practice, it also uses political theory.

Because much of public relations is also one-on-one as well as within groups, interpersonal communication is an important source for PR application of theory.

Communication theory certainly is as relevant as theory about persuasion.

You'll find, though, that all of these theories are fairly "young" as theories go. Their roots are primarily in sociology and psychology, although math, biology and physics have contributed too. But, you'll be looking at them here in another context. We'll focus in this chapter on two basic underlying disciplines—sociology and psychology, plus some communication models and persuasion theories. Then, we'll examine the communication process from sources of information, to messages, to what a combination of sources and messages creates, to media used and finally to message receivers with their reactions and feedback. In reading this chapter, remember these are theories, most tested and revised and rethought. You can do that too as you read and think about this chapter.

ou learned in Chapter 5, public opinion is the collective opinion of groups of people. You can count on two things about public opinion: first, it will change; second, those who hold an opinion were somehow persuaded to think as they do. Although people do sometimes respond collectively, as when they applaud or join in a boycott of a product or store, they always initiate their responses individually. These individual responses indicate attitudes that reflect feelings or convictions. Each person decides individually to clap or not to clap, to buy or not to buy and to patronize or not to patronize. Consequently, we must look at individual reactions first. Then we try to figure out how these reactions of individuals affect the reactions of other individuals to produce a collective response. It is important to keep in mind that responses are always individual before they are collective. Many faulty mass communication theories have been based on the mistaken idea that there is only a mass response. Looking at publics collectively can create a number of difficulties for public relations practitioners, as can looking at what publics say without explaining what they *do*. ■

Origins in Sociology and Psychology

Four general theories drawn from sociology help us understand how people respond to communication from mass and specialized communication. Two others come from psychology.

1. *Structural functionalism* (Plato's *Republic*, Durkheim, Merton, Parsons): This theory holds that the organization or structure of society provides its stability. As a result, the forms of media and mass communication depend on their society and contribute to social equilibrium.

2. *Evolutionary perspective* (Darwin, Spencer): This theory holds that social change follows a set of natural laws and that mass communication systems have grown and developed with technology and with decision makers' needs for communication.

3. *Social conflict* (Hegel, Marx, Engels): This theory holds that social struggles occur between groups with competing needs and goals. The mass media are competitive and active in a number of areas of conflict, such as being a watchdog over government.

4. *Symbolic interactionism* (Charles Horton Cooley [environment over genes] and George Herbert Mead [language symbols in collective and individual life]): This theory holds that the media present constructs of reality that offer information from limited sources, resulting in individual and collective creations of reality.

These general theories are social paradigms (sets of assumptions or systems of beliefs).

Some competing psychological theories are usually discussed as a single framework, chiefly because in the study of mass communication the first four theories provide a good launching pad for discussions of collective action or effects. Nevertheless, we have to turn to a psychological paradigm for the effect of communication on the individual. Several approaches can be isolated within the psychological framework. One is the neurobiological approach, which concerns itself with the effects of communication on the nerves and the brain. Another is the comparative approach, which focuses on the effect of communication on humans versus its effect on other living creatures. A third focus is the behavioral approach, which derives from stimulus–response psychology and is closely related to the neurobiological and the comparative. A fourth is the psychoanalytic approach, which studies unconscious reactions. A related fifth orientation is the cognitive approach, which examines what people do to and with sensory input. This is the most commonly used approach in studies of the effects of mass communication.

The two general persuasion models are as follows:

1. *Sociocultural paradigm:* This model attempts to account for sociocultural variables that enable a particular individual to interpret or present reality as in the mass media.

2. *Psychodynamic model:* This model, based on the cognitive paradigm, studies how an effective message makes a person do something (deliver an overt response) that the communicator desired as an effect. One of the most valuable theories drawn from this model is Ball-Rokeach's Theory of Value Change. People who are given a value test and who are then compared with others like them or whom they want to be like will change specific values to accommodate the others' values.[1]

Organizational Theory

The basis for organizational theory lies in general systems theory. The theoretical concept can be found in works by Georg Hegel. His idea of a power struggle provided by tensions of opposing ideas was picked up by Karl Marx who applied it to labor versus capitalism. To some extent Darwin's work on evolution was not exactly a survival of the fittest, a sort of power struggle, but he saw species adapting to pressures from their environment. Biologist Ludwig von Bertalanffy used systems theory for his expansion and adaptation of the idea to general systems theory. His belief that all life forms, social as well as biological, are organized for dynamic interaction to sustain life was picked up by therapists who used the life systems theory in their interactional theory of communication. Max Weber's work looked at how organizing occurred, and Rensis Likert's theory indicated the importance of communication. In mass communication, information theory draws from systems theory in that it considers the interfacing of corresponding systems. Wilbur Schramm noted that the mathematical model from Claude Shannon was structural, whereas human communication systems are functional. Communication researchers apply systems theory in a broad context.[2]

Systems theory embraces an organization and all of its publics. The idea is that all parts of a system are interrelated and function as an organized whole that is greater than the sum of its parts. These systems are open to change from the outside environment, but the amount of change is relative to the degree of openness of the system. You'll hear organizations referred to as having open or closed communication systems, for example. All systems try for but never gain real equilibrium, or stability.

Many theories have evolved from this basic concept, including open systems theory,[3] but one that is of particular interest to us is cybernetic systems theory developed by Norbert Wiener in 1948 for physical systems but later found applicable to organizational systems. This is one of the sources for the idea of goal setting within an organization and the notion of using feedback to adjust actions directed toward achieving that goal. Here's the way it works. A system's control center directs behavior toward a goal and system mechanisms are used to change system behavior when feedback suggests that the goal is not being met.[4]

Systems approaches are not the only ones used and not the only sources for communication theory. Two others are especially important: cultural and critical/postmodern.

PR literature often refers to the impact on PR practice of organizational culture. The primary basis for the organizational culture is its values. That's why you read so much about good public relations practice being aligned with an organization's mission statement—its

reason for being—and its values either stated or implied by the practices and behaviors of its employees. Organizational cultures change because they depend on the interaction of participants in them, but the most direct influence is the organizational leadership. Sometimes a change of leadership changes the culture.

All members of the organization may not share the organizational culture, or at least not to the same degree. All organizations have subcultures that exist within the broader culture, and some may be connected to the particular skills or knowledge of a subgroup. In a university setting, for example, even though there is an overall mission statement, colleges and departments also have mission statements, and often the "culture" of one department is totally different from that of another.

The study of cultures usually involves qualitative research that you'll remember being discussed in Chapter 4. One such measure not mentioned in the research chapter that deals with social science research is ethnography. Ethnography treats the study of culture as a text to be read and draws observations from direct involvement in the organization to gain personal experience. The theory about the organization then is "grounded" in direct experience.[5]

Critical and postmodern approaches also have had an effect on theory in the field. For example, systems theory attempts an objective approach to understanding organizational dynamics, whereas cultural theory tries to experience an organization as an insider so as to interpret it to outsiders. Critical theory, with its origins in Karl Marx, looks at organizations as power structures of dominance.

Critical theory examines sources of power in an organization and questions control of organizational discourse such as whose view of reality is it? Also, where is the control in gender issues? The philosopher–sociologist Jurgen Habermas examines the interplay of work, interaction and power. Habermas often is cited in discussions of ethics because power can distort communication, but marginalized groups can empower themselves by understanding the dominant ideologies. Habermas has said, "Reality is constituted in a framework that is the form of life of communicating in groups and is organized through ordinary language. What is real is that which can be experienced according to the interpretations of a prevailing symbolic system."[6]

Postmodernists believe that an historical break occurred sometime in the mid-1960s to move us into a postmodern world. Postmodern characteristics include a global economy, the dominance of popular culture and the power and control of organizations

...ple. Postmodern theorists see scientific ...ods and rational critical inquiry as inadequate for examining today's society.[7]

Another critical theorist whose name you will encounter in public relations literature is Michael Foucault.[8] Foucault talks about discursive structures that are embedded in our identity, the way we think about things and the way our society works. He sees Western societies as concerned about independence and individualism, whereas other societies such as Hispanics, Asians, Africans and African Americans are collective societies that frame their members' identity and relationships. You'll also see Foucault's name in women's studies because he sees discourse as ruled by power structures that say who can talk and who can't. Women who feel silenced in their culture, including Western ones, tend to agree.

The major criticism of postmodern theory is that it is nihilistic, rejecting all moral principles—with no basis for social orders, values, or moral conduct. As theories are viewed, though, postmodernism is considered "new," and a theoretical frontier.

Communication Theories, Three Models

The attitudes and opinions of publics greatly interest the PR practitioner, but even more important is what these publics are doing. This point is reflected in the replacement of the communication model by the behavioral model as the theoretical underpinning of public relations (see Figure 6.1).[9]

Figure 6.1   **Two Theoretical Models Underpinning Public Relations Practice**

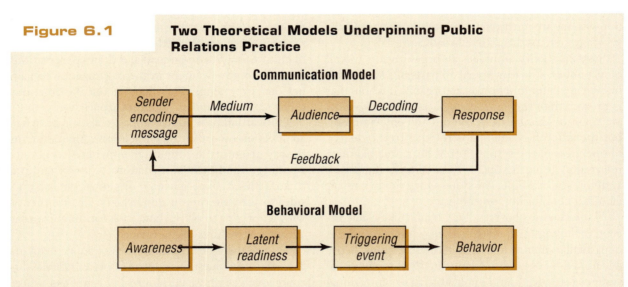

According to *pr reporter*, the behavioral model "basically shifts the objective, and with it the focus of thinking, strategizing and planning, away from the traditional model's emphasis on creating or retaining awareness."[1] Step 1, **awareness**, may involve creating awareness, changing levels of awareness or maintaining awareness, but in every case relevance to the individual is the key to getting attention. In this step, the diffusion process of communication—the two-step flow—contributes either positively or negatively to the next step. In other words, information goes *from* mass media *to* opinion leaders and is then passed along to individuals who have some contact with the opinion leader. Step 2, **latent readiness**, precedes action and involves referencing existing experiences, information, attitudes, values and beliefs and every other resource. The mental computer of each member of the target public is checking and matching, confirming or rejecting. In Step 3, the **triggering event**, some circumstance arises, accidentally or intentionally, that causes action. Step 4, **behavior**, is that action. The initial action may only be preliminary to the final action—the ultimate, desired behavior. This is a modification of the six-step persuasion model (see Example 7.2, where the behavioral response to each phase of the symmetrical process model of persuasion is represented as a boxed event).

[1]"Behavioral Model Replacing Communications Model as Basic Theoretical Underpinning of PR Practice," *pr reporter*, 33(30) (July 30, 1990), pp. 2–3.

Source: Reprinted with permission of *pr reporter*, Exeter, N.H., 33(30), July 30, 1990, p. 1.

Edward L. Bernays held this view all along, which is why he insisted that public relations must be viewed as a social science. To be useful and appropriate for public relations practitioners, a communication model must encompass publicity, publications, advertising and special events that attract attention. All of these practices serve either to create or to maintain levels of awareness, and all emphasize messages designed to affect attitudes and opinions; but as pr reporter notes, "Every dieter facing the dessert tray understands the difference between attitude and behavior."[10] The behavioral model also suggests that communication in public relations should focus less on "mass" appeal and more on direct, personal impact on members of a defined public. Still, the behavioral model suggested here does not allow for the type of reciprocal action envisioned in the symmetrical model for public relations. The behavioral model is clearly asymmetrical, although it could be modified to accommodate symmetrical behavior (see Figure 6.2).

Best practices in public relations suggest that a symmetrical system for communication is desirable in an organization. The two-way symmetrical model allows for more input from publics that can provide innovative solutions and corrective discourse, both essential for sound strategic PR management.

Prior to the Internet's becoming the principal communication medium, an impediment to the symmetrical model was an imbalance in power among the publics and in their relationship to management. An adjustment to the balance of power has occurred, significantly changing all types of relationships.

Although the three traditional models are presented herein, you should realize that most theories provide some sort of schematics that "model" the theory to show you how it works.[11] When a researcher tests a new application for a theory, the older model is used to show suggested modifications. New media are forging the development and testing of new communication models.

Persuasion and Change

When someone holds a strong opposing opinion, you are probably wasting your time trying to win that person over to your view. Usually, all you can hope to do is to limit whatever effects the person may have on others who are undecided or uncommitted. In particular, you should not waste time on recent converts to the opposition, because new converts to anything react with more emotion than

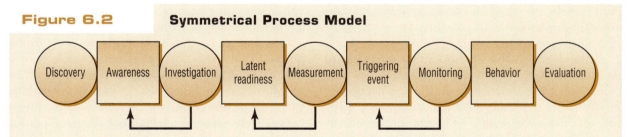

Figure 6.2 **Symmetrical Process Model**

Discovery — Awareness — Investigation — Latent readiness — Measurement — Triggering event — Monitoring — Behavior — Evaluation

The symmetrical behavioral model involves five steps (represented as circles in the preceding schematic diagram): first, **gauging** existing levels of awareness and discovering conditions under which publics are likely to respond positively to an effort to create, enhance or increase awareness of some desired behavioral goal; second, **investigating** responses to attempt to create, raise or sustain awareness, to determine any problems with the desired behavior goal that may already be apparent and should cause goal modification (or even abandonment) with respect to one or more publics; third, **measuring** latent readiness to act, so that the action's direction can be anticipated, depending on certain conditions; fourth, **monitoring** responses to the triggering event, to anticipate the level of resulting behavior, and interceding with action or communication or both if the behavior seems likely to be undesirable; fifth, **evaluating** behavior to determine why that particular action was taken, whether it is likely to be sustained and (if it is desired) what is needed to sustain it. Each of these five stages builds in the opportunity for publics to communicate their desires, needs and concerns so that goals can be adjusted or at least a mutual understanding can be negotiated.

Source: Reprinted with permission of *pr reporter, Exeter, N.H.*, 33(30), July 30, 1990.

...d are almost impossible to reach with fac-
...aterials, much less with a persuasive argument.
You should concentrate your efforts, then, on preserving what favorable opinion exists and on winning
over undecided individuals to your point of view.

There are three basic ways to get people to do what
you want: power, patronage and persuasion. Power
involves the use of authority and the implied or overt
threat of compulsion. One obvious source of power is
the legal system, which has laws that demand compliance. Other sources of power may be more subtle, but
they are equally binding. For example, employees may
not be legally bound to follow a supervisor's suggestions, but if they don't they may soon be looking for
other jobs. Because groups can exert substantial pressure internally, peer groups are also a strong source of
power. (If you don't believe that, consider how often
you hear, "But I must have one. Everyone else has it.")
Public relations practitioners use power, for example,
in helping promote blood donation drives, where they
rely on the tactic of asking employers to get commitments from their employees. The request is for a
good purpose—an honest cause, certainly—but it still
involves the use of power.

Forms of patronage used as a means of changing people's behavior may be as crude as bribery, or
they may be quite delicate, particularly if a favorable
opinion is sought or if there is an implied threat of
denial. Patronage may involve paying a celebrity
money to make advertising endorsements or public
appearances on behalf of a campaign, or it may involve making a substantial contribution to a civic improvement project in a key neighborhood or area.[12]

Persuasion involves using communication to
win people over. Whatever the goal of the persuasion, there are essentially six steps in the persuasion
process—not that each act of persuasion necessarily
follows these sequentially.[13] The first step is *presenting*. A person must be in a position to receive a persuasive message—that is, both physically accessible
and mentally receptive. You can present something
and have the presentation ignored, however, so the
second step in the persuasion process is *attending*,
which means that the receiver must pay attention
to the persuasive message. Beyond attending to the
message, the receiver has to understand it. Therefore,
the third step is *comprehending*. To satisfy this step, the
message must be presented in symbols the receiver
can understand. The fourth step is *yielding*, in which
the receiver accepts the message and agrees with the
point of view it expresses. The next (fifth) step is *retaining* the transmitted information, which explains

why repetition is so fundamental to the persuasion
process. People have to be reminded of the message,
even after they have accepted it. The sixth and final
step is *acting*. The persuader must be able to observe
the results of persuasion in the receiver's behavior.

Some strategies that will get receivers to one
point in the process will not carry them all the way
through to the final step.[14] So persuasion strategy has
to be planned and monitored to ascertain whether it
is having the desired effect at each stage, and if it is
not, why not. Parallels between the persuasion model
and the behavior model are easy to see. The behavior
model's awareness stage incorporates the persuasion
model's presenting and attending. The latent awareness stage corresponds to comprehending, yielding
and retaining. The triggering event essentially offers
a demonstration of the receiver's retention, resulting
in some sort of behavior. If this behavior matches the
desired action, the persuasion process has succeeded.

Despite the protestations of some practitioners
to the contrary, public relations frequently employs
the techniques of persuasion to articulate a point of
view that differs from that of members of a public.
Examples include public relations or advertising
campaigns, which are generally highly visible because of the attendant publicity. In persuasion, the
critical factor in opinion change usually is information or the lack thereof and how this information is
presented or withheld. Information is power, as the
late social scientist Herbert I. Schiller pointed out,
and information resides in controllable sources—
among the upper echelons of government, business
and education. It tends to be made available to the
public, Schiller says, through public relations people
who have the power to control its flow. Their access
to information and their selective use of it combine
the tools of power and persuasion. Schiller railed
persuasively against such "mind managers," but his
arguments failed to take into account the social responsibility exercised by these institutions or their
representatives, plus the social responsibility assumed
by news and advertising personnel in the media.[15]

Persuaders and Their Appeals

We have all practiced persuading others to do our
bidding since we discovered as babies that crying
brought us a bottle. As adults, we persuade people to
come with us to see a film they don't want to see, or
to take us to pick up our car at the shop or to come
for us when the car breaks down. Although these
may be considered deeds of friendship, they actually

are negotiations. We used something in the bargaining process, stated or unstated. If you doubt that, think of the times you have heard, "I'd have to call in some chits (favors granted and not yet returned) to get that done," or "I don't have any leverage with her. You're in a better position to ask." You might even say in response, "I'll ask. She owes me one."

Personal Persuaders Organizations and authorities, family members and what sociologists call "significant others"—people you care about—exercise leverage over you. Organizations that you belong to ask for money regularly, and you usually give. They ask you to obey certain codes of conduct and to be present for certain events, and you comply. As a member, you probably get most of your messages in a List-Serve, and/or directly from the organization's Web site. You may belong to the organization for social, religious or political reasons or for economic reasons (as with the organization that employs you). At your job, most communications come to you in your email or from the organization's intranet. In the workplace, certain people are in positions of authority—those who have special responsibilities. When you work for someone or when you are a conscientious member of an organization, you generally comply with the requests of those in authority. You also generally do what close friends and members of your family ask you to do. Recognition of authority in families is long-lived when it grows into respect or when someone has the leverage of purchase (that is, inheritance). Often personal persuaders can get you to do things contrary to your own desires, best interests or values. Their persuasive control is potent.

Impersonal Persuaders Less potent and influential are the impersonal persuaders. These are found through the Internet in blogs or Web sites, usually information on destinations you bookmark for frequent reference. In traditional print mass media, persuasive messages usually appear in the form of editorials, columns and advertisements. However, news stories can also "frame" the information so that it takes an advocacy position. Although this also can occur in broadcast news, in broadcasting these "framed" messages generally are on talk shows, in commentaries and in commercial content—paid programming, public service announcements and commercials. They also are found in the content of various types of entertainment and among persons who perform. They are found as well in educational and governmental institutions and in the commercial institutions that

we depend on for goods and services. In some countries, all of these may be operated or controlled by government. These impersonal institutions may persuade you through your fear of the punishments that they have available for noncompliance or because of the personal persuasiveness of their representatives. An individual teacher in a school or an individual sales clerk in a favorite store moves the relationship beyond the impersonal and into the personal.

Some of these impersonal persuaders qualify as opinion-makers because they influence significant numbers of people. Some are opinion-makers because of their public status (as in the case of celebrities and other newsmakers), and others because they manage the news. Some of the most visible opinion-makers are both public figures and news managers.

Opinion-Makers and News Managers A news manager may be someone who creates an event that becomes news when it is made to happen, usually on a carefully detailed and prearranged schedule. The event may be the public appearance of an organizational mascot or other human representation of a cartoon character. The event could also be less benign, such as the terrorist attacks on a major city, building or system somewhere. The event may be one that continues over an extended period of time, as did the 1979–1981 hostage crisis at the American Embassy in Tehran, Iran; the O.J. Simpson trial involving his wife's death; the impeachment hearings of former presidents Richard Nixon and Bill Clinton; the weapons of mass destruction (WMD) debate related to the Iraq invasion—all still "recalled" occasionally in current news stories. A news manager may also be someone who focuses media attention on an event that might otherwise be overlooked. In addition, a news manager may attempt to control information, as former U.S. Attorney General Alberto Gonzales did in Congressional hearings about the treatment of accused terrorists being held by the USA. This is not new, however. As media critic William L. Rivers noted, "Nothing is quite so absurd as thinking of news control by government as a modern phenomenon. . . . Information policy has been at the very center of governing the United States from the beginning."[16]

Public Relations and Opinion-Making

What is true of news management by government is true of any group in business, science, education or elsewhere that possesses specialized information: Those in command of information

PR in Practice

If you want people to find your Web site when they don't know your name or that you provide a product or service they want, you might want to hire a linguistics professional—make that a linguistic professor, because most linguists are professors. E-businesses are using linguists to build databases of words that will help them respond to requests for information or help. Linguists are building the database lexicon that can sort out a searcher's intent by relating words by concept, distinguishing between multiple meanings of words, or even asking questions of the searcher.

Technology has made communication faster, but not always easier. Searches can be exasperating and sometimes fruitless. PR practitioners work with Web designers to be sure the content is there and accessible, but you want to be sure your Web site can be found, too. The lexicographers, knowledge engineers and vocabulary-resource managers don't come cheap. Experienced ones are commanding $100,000 in their first high-tech jobs.

The alternative is to learn linguistics theory, which is not a bad idea. Linguistic concepts can help any wordsmith.

See Daniel Golden, "No Longer Just Eggheads, Linguists Leap to the Net," *The Wall Street Journal*, May 30, 2000, pp. B1, 20.

---

control its dissemination. The public's only defense lies in being aware that someone is always trying to influence its opinion. A sophisticated person will ask, "What am I being asked to think? What am I being asked to do? By whom? Why?"

In a democracy, these questions often are raised by members of some opposition, resulting in a struggle for favorable public opinion. That struggle confounds some other nations whose form of government makes it possible to ignore public opinion. But the freedom to compete for public opinion is inherent in our concept of democracy. PR practitioners become involved in such struggles because each side in a controversy employs them as professional advisers or spokespersons. Practitioners usually represent the side corresponding to their own beliefs, although some ethical practitioners will, like lawyers, serve any client with loyalty whether or not they personally subscribe to the client's position. What differentiates the professional practitioner from the unprofessional news manager—who unfortunately is often mistaken for the PR person—is strict adherence to a code of ethics that upholds a strong sense of overall social responsibility. Professional public relations practitioners never lie to the news media, although in the interests of a client they may sometimes have to say to the press, "I know, but I cannot tell you." The success of those who control certain areas of information in affecting public opinion is only as strong as their credibility. Credibility is thus among the most important assets a public relations practitioner possesses.

Propaganda and Persuasion Appeals

People who want to sway opinions use a variety of persuasion appeals—not all of them honest. The following list identifies some propaganda devices commonly used to mislead publics:

1. *Name calling:* The characterization can be positive or negative. Someone can be called "wise and conscientious" or "a liar and a cheat" (or the matter can even be left open to interpretation, as with "He's a character!").

2. *Glittering generalities:* Many nebulous words can be used here—for example, "enthusiastic crowds" or "throngs of greeters."

3. *Transfer:* This occurs when a movie star or other celebrity campaigns for a politician or product with the result that some of the famous person's aura is transferred to the less well-known person or product.

4. *Testimonial:* This is an actual endorsement, as opposed to a transfer device. A common advertising technique, it involves having professional athletes and other celebrities encourage consumers to buy a product by saying that they use it.

5. *Plain folks:* A favorite of politicians, this device involves using homey language or appeals to

PR in Practice

Although Edward L. Bernays deplored use of the word *image*, it remains linked with PR practice, and has even garnered some attention by researchers. Now the U.S. government has made it official with the establishment of an Office of Global Communications, which charged with coordinating the administration's foreign policy message and supervising the USA's *image* abroad.

Although the first designated official public relations counselor to a U.S. president, Karen Hughes, left her office to return to Texas, her influence continued in the George W. Bush presidency and she was named to the State Department in 2005 as an under secretary of public diplomacy and public affairs. The Office of Global Communications was her idea. The administration says the office has the primary responsibility of telling America's story abroad. The office is designed to add thematic and strategic value, along with presidential clout, to the efforts of other government agencies. The agency expands the White House Coalition Information Center, established after the U.S. military campaign began in Afghanistan in the fall of 2001. As Hughes left office in December 2007, she had put in place new exchange programs and "rapid response" teams to comment on breaking news, and she established media hubs in London, Brussels and Dubai.

Critics have commented that it was too little too late and that lack of changes in U.S. foreign policy tested the credibility of the messages. Others said that her efforts couldn't compensate for Clinton administration decisions to incorporate the U.S. Information Agency (USIA) into the State Department and the loss of the independence of Voice of America and the U.S. government–backed Persian-language Radio Farda. Hughes, in 2008, joined Burson-Marsteller as a vice-chairman.

(See stories on her departure from the State Department in print news media from December 2007 as well as stories in public relations publications of the same period, including coverage of her participation in the PRSA 2007 convention.)

down-to-earth concerns to convince a public that, despite their high office or aspirations thereto, the politicians are still "one of us."

6. *Bandwagon:* This compelling device is used to sway undecided people to go with the majority, however, slight the majority might be. The bandwagon device is considered so powerful that networks avoid telecasting projected results of election returns in the East until polls close in the West. Some research evidence indicates, however, that such coverage has no impact on people who have not yet voted.

7. *Card stacking:* Telling "one side of the story" involves selecting facts that represent one point of view, while obscuring other facts. The result is distortion and misrepresentation.

8. *Emotional stereotypes:* These evoke all kinds of images, and are so designed: "good American," "housewife," "foreigner" and so on.

9. *Illicit silence:* This device is a subtle form of propaganda, like innuendo, suggestion and insinuation. It involves withholding information that would correct a false impression.

10. *Subversive rhetoric:* An offshoot of card stacking is the device of discrediting a person's motivation in order to discredit the idea, which may be good and useful. For example, someone may discredit the mayor's plan to build a bridge on grounds that the mayor owns property on the other side of the river. In the meantime, viewed objectively, the bridge-building plan may still be a good one for opening up commerce, traffic or tourism.

Obvious forms of these propaganda devices are easily recognizable, but history offers numerous examples of skillful users wielding them with great subtlety and effectiveness. Anyone who communicates may employ propaganda devices—spoken, written, pictorial or whatever. Such devices also may take the form of synthetic events. Demonstrations are all propaganda devices.

Although it encompasses some techniques that are used to mislead, the word *propaganda* should not be thought of as totally negative. Indeed, when one of the authors was working professionally for a large organization, a European colleague always introduced him as a member of the organization's

of propaganda, meaning no insult. Cer-
~~~~, there is nothing inherent in the nature of
propaganda that prevents it from being used to
change attitudes and behavior in a constructive
way. Propagandists differ from educators in that
educators try to teach people how to think, but
propagandists try to teach people what to think.[17]
Propaganda also has been used to appeal to basic
human emotions in order to effect opinion changes
in the public interest.

Emotions and Persuasion Social legislation, income tax,
Medicare, civil rights laws and other public policy initiatives all reflect changes in public opinion that were
sensed and acted upon by politicians. Generally, such
public opinion is an emotional response to information
or events. Social psychologist Hadley Cantril developed some "laws" purportedly governing this emotional response. Although critics say that no law can
account for something with as many variables as public
opinion, Cantril's laws do suggest five basic ideas that
seem common to all studies of opinion expression:
(1) events are most likely to affect opinion; (2) demands
for action are a usual response; (3) self-interest must
figure heavily if people are to become involved;
(4) leadership is sought, and not always objectively and
critically; and (5) reliability is difficult to assess.

Another five elements have been isolated by
psychology professor Robert Cialdini, who identifies these as being elements of self-persuasion, the
strongest and most effective type of persuasion. All
are tied to the social persuasion strategy discussed
earlier. Cialdini explains the elements as follows[18]:

1. *Consistency:* After committing themselves to a
   position, even in some trivial way, people are
   more likely to perform behaviors consistent with
   that position. When people decide to comply
   with a request, they check to see if they have already done something that is consistent with the
   request. For example, in one American Cancer
   Society charity drive it was found that homeowners who had previously gone on record as
   supporting the Cancer Society (by accepting and
   wearing a small lapel pin for a day) were nearly
   twice as likely as others to give a monetary donation a week later when the charity drive began.
   However, not all small, initial commitments are
   equally good at producing consistent future behavior. They are most effective in this regard
   when the commitments are active, public and
   not coerced.

Consistency draws from two basic theories:
the theory of cognitive dissonance developed by
Leon Festinger[19] and the theory of beliefs, attitudes and values from Milton Rokeach.[20]

Festinger's cognitive dissonance theory says
that information is judged in one of three ways:
irrelevant, consistent or inconsistent, which he
calls dissonant. Whatever information or persuasive effort proves dissonant to someone, the result is a pressure to change, which causes stress.
Someone telling you to clean off your desk so
that the office looks orderly produces stress. You
know where things are and your order is someone else's chaos. Dissonance causes avoidance
behavior. You shut your office door so that no
one can see your organized chaos. If the edict to
clean up your desk is repeated, perhaps with a
formal note from a supervisor, you try to reduce
the stress. Most additional theory and research
in this area focuses on such forced compliance,
initiation of an effort, social support for change
and an effort to make the change.

Festinger thought of at least five ways you
might choose to reduce the stress. One, you
change your behavior or your attitude. You decide that a clean desk probably is a good idea.
You put a lot of effort into it. That makes you
rationalize the value of having done it. Two, you
get more information that adds to the tension
one way or the other. For instance, you read that
a clean desk reflects an orderly mind or perhaps
you lose some important papers. Three, with the
loss of the papers and time finding them, you
decide that a clean desk is for people who don't
have much to do. Four, you might seek some
benefits. Perhaps someone helps you reorganize
your office and you actually find it easier to locate things than you imagined. The social support increases your acceptance. Fifth, you distort
the information to suit yourself. Your reorgani-
zation involves stacking material and putting a
label on the top of each pile.

A couple of variables matter in this theory.
The first is how important the decision is. If
you are going to get fired if you don't clean up
your desk, that's a pretty strong persuader. Another is the attractiveness of an alternative, such
as getting an award or bonus for keeping a clean
desk. Third, the more you like the unchosen alternative, the greater dissonance you'll have: if
you really don't want to clean up your desk but
do it anyway, you'll suffer dissonance. If you had

to do it, it's worse. Dissonance is really strong if you are forced to violate your value system, unlikely in the clean desk illustration, but possible if you were told to fire someone on the telephone when you think a personal interview and discussion would be kinder.

Values are central to Rokeach's Beliefs, Attitudes and Values theory, a concept you find in the exploration of publics with the VALS™ approach: values, attitudes and lifestyles. Rokeach said people have some beliefs that are central to the core of their being, and some that are peripheral. Core beliefs are resistant to change. Attitudes are beliefs with a focus, he says. The focus might be toward an object or a situation. Your behavior is a combination of these two. You might not like modern art, but you go to an exhibit with a friend and pretend to enjoy it because you don't want to offend your friend and host.

Values come from those core beliefs, and the most important have to do with your self-concept. Rokeach thinks the only real behavior change occurs with inconsistencies in self-concept that cause such self-dissatisfaction that self-regard is achieved through change. Dieters who retain their weight loss often cite self-regard as the primary ingredient for the change in their eating and exercise habits. Self-regard is often cited over health.

2. *Reciprocity:* One question people ask themselves before agreeing to another's request is, "Do I owe this person something?" If the answer is "yes," they are more apt to comply, often when they would otherwise have declined and even when what they agree to do is more significant than what they received earlier. For this reason, charities mail unsolicited token gifts.[21]

3. *Social validation:* People are more influenced to perform an action or hold a belief when they see that others are doing so. An important piece of evidence people inspect in deciding what is appropriate conduct for themselves in a situation is how others are acting. For this reason, advertisers love to include the words "fastest growing" or "largest selling" in their product descriptions. They don't have to say directly that the product is good; they only need to say that others think so, which seems to be proof enough.[22]

4. *Authority:* People are more willing to follow the suggestions of someone they consider a legitimate authority in terms of knowledge and trustworthiness. Demonstrating knowledge can usually be accomplished by showing evidence of superior experience, training, skill or information. Establishing trustworthiness is trickier. One device, in pitching a story to an editor, is to back off from this week's story but promise real newsworthiness with the following week's item—for example, "I know this item isn't exactly what you want, but wait until you see what we have for you next week!"[23]

5. *Scarcity:* People try to seize items and opportunities that are scarce or dwindling in availability. This accounts for the success of the "deadline," "limited number" and "can't-come-back-later" sales tactics. Research indicates that people want a scarce item more than ever when they are in competition with others for it, or when they believe they have an exclusive.[24]

Personal Identification, Involvement, Credibility and Trust Earl Newsom's four principles of persuasion build on the concept of personal identification with an idea or problem, and suggest actions that people will take in response to a personal appeal:

1. *Identification:* People will relate to an idea, opinion or point of view only if they can see it as having some direct effect on their own hopes, fears, desires or aspirations.

2. *Suggestion of action:* People will endorse ideas only if the ideas are accompanied by a proposed action from the sponsor of the idea or if the recipients themselves propose it—especially a *convenient* action.

3. *Familiarity and trust:* People are unwilling to accept ideas from sources they don't trust, whether the sources are people or institutions. Thus a goal of PR is to ensure that an institution deserves and obtains such confidence, that it increases the trust of many people and that it keeps the trust of those it counts as friends.

4. *Clarity:* The meaning of an idea in an event, situation or message has to be clear in order to be persuasive.[25]

Successful advertising copywriters certainly know the importance of the last two principles—namely, that the people doing the buying have to trust those doing the selling, and that those doing the selling must communicate clearly to have any effect at all.

The element of trust needs to be emphasized in any study of opinion change. All of us are more likely to assume attitudes and accept ideas uncritically from persons we love and trust. Observers predicted all kinds of voting patterns for 18-year-olds in the USA before they were given the right to vote. What actually happened? Most youths voted like their parents—probably because they loved and trusted them. However, even if they did not love and trust their parents, they did receive information from them over a long period of time. One communication theory—called the "sleeper effect"—suggests that the source of a persuasive message, even if it is a distrusted source, is apt to be forgotten after a long period of time, leaving a residue of information accepted as fact.

Identification and suggestion of action are also important. As for identification, most of us feel an association with others—by education, religion, occupation, social or economic status or other category. What our identification groups say and do suggest courses of action for us. These associations have potential power because, when events so demand, opinion can be mobilized along lines of self-interest.

Leadership for Opinion Change
According to Philip Lesly, such mobilization can be activated by highly visible leaders.

Lesly said that at least three separate groups are discernible in the "leader" category:

1. *Vocal activists* who devote themselves to high profile advocacy of cause.
2. *Opinion leaders*, both mass-media and individual thought leaders throughout society.
3. *Power leaders*—legislators, government officials, judges and regulators who have the power to take actions that affect organizations and society.

Increasingly, the focal group in persuasion is the power leaders. They have the ability to make things happen. Vocal activists, influential individuals and groups, the media and the general public provide input to the power leaders, but they have little power themselves. The input that reaches the power leaders is much greater from vocal activists and from opinion leaders than from the public and from most private organizations.[26]

Opinion mobilization by a leader creates a pressure group. Even if we are not directly involved in a particular controversy, we are still likely, because of our personal loyalties, to side with the pressure group that claims to represent us. For example, during the 1970s strife in Northern Ireland, international problems resulted when Americans of Irish descent became involved in gunrunning.

Persuasion Strategies
Persuaders use one or more of five specific strategies to enlist compliance: stimulus–response, cognitive, motivational, social appeal and personality appeal.

The stimulus–response (S-R) strategy, borrowed from behavioral research, presupposes that audiences can be conditioned to respond automatically to certain stimuli, such as answering the phone when it rings. But sometimes S-R doesn't work as planned. For example, capricious association may occur, in which the stimulus elicits a different response from the one desired because the mind makes a different (and unexpected) connection. Another problem arises from the need for repetition before learning can occur. If not enough repetition takes place, the response can differ markedly from the one anticipated. A third problem is that the exposure necessary for repetition is usually expensive and is not always cost-effective, because the association may be forgotten. Nonetheless, long-term payoffs from embedded recall do result when S-R works.

Anticipating an S-R response of some kind can affect the type of message sent, according to Glimpse, a now discontinued newsletter of the International Society for General Semantics. The newsletter noted that this anticipation can lead to another propaganda technique:

> *Once told that an event or action signals a particular response, we may assume uncritically that earlier learning has established such a connection, as the word signal suggests. Unaware how we do so, we may come to believe that a particular event or action serves as a signal because someone labels it a "signal."*
>
> *Thus our reasoning and conclusions may be shaped by this propaganda ploy.*[27]

The *cognitive* strategy reasons that learning factual information in the context of a message can persuade if the information is retained. However, this strategy works only with individuals who have no stake in the outcome or who have no negative preconceptions about what they are being persuaded to do. Additionally, because it is cognitive, suitable alternatives have to be proposed, and the persuasion has to be presented in a context, as part of a bigger picture. For example, the purpose of exercise is not just to lose weight; it may also make you feel and think better.

The *motivational* strategy involves creating a need or stimulating a desire or want. It relies on a learned behavior, and not everyone that you want to reach can be motivated. To succeed, this strategy must offer a real or at least a perceived reward.

The *social appeal* strategy concentrates on calling attention to social conditions. Many appeals to alleviate conditions for the poor and needy use this strategy, as do appeals designed to correct behavior (such as those sponsored by Mothers Against Drunk Driving). Often the appeals are tied to job-related norms.

The *personality appeal* strategy is designed for people who are outer-directed rather than inner-directed. It is based on tolerance (as opposed to intolerance) levels. Some nonsmoking and smoking appeals are personality-based, as is the appeal that promotes self-employment: "Own your own business; be your own boss."

Effectiveness of Persuasion In making persuasive appeals to various human motives, you must consider two possibilities: that cognitive dissonance could occur, and that truth may be personal.

According to Stanford University psychology professor Philip Zimbardo, subtlety is sometimes the best persuader. He believes that more attitude change can sometimes be produced by *less* social persuasion. If people think themselves free to make decisions that run counter to their values, they sometimes need only a gentle push to take the plunge. Some smokers, for example, abandon their habit when subtly persuaded that smoking impairs the health of others, such as expectant mothers and small children. No one had to pressure them to abandon the habit; they simply became aware of the health hazard through media reports. They view themselves as having made a free choice and remain unaware that they were coaxed into changing by gentle social persuasion.[28]

To see that truth is personal and value-oriented, we need only look at the religions of the world. All disciples claim that their religion represents *the truth*, yet there are obviously many conflicts in doctrine among different sects and denominations. Certain objective truths are generally accepted—for example, football is a contact sport—but many less definitive "personal truths" exist as well, and these are often circumstantial, such as the different definitions of "sex" that arose in the Clinton-Lewinsky scandal.

Is manipulation of public opinion only a matter of communication skills and knowledge? Not always. PR practitioner Earl Newsom pointed out an example of a major failure in a 6-month "skilled persuasion" effort in an Ohio city. The campaign distributed 59,000 pieces of literature aimed at getting people to view the United Nations in positive terms. But it failed miserably because, during the campaign, the United Nations itself was particularly ineffective. It is not true, Newsom said, "That if you have enough money to pay for printing, advertising, and 'propaganda,' you can change people's minds."[29] It is also possible to overcampaign, arousing suspicion and backlash when people notice that a lot of money is being spent on the media.

Overcampaigning probably also occurred in the effort to control smoking. Smokers clearly understood that their addiction caused cancer, but after a certain point the campaign against smoking began to falter. Then coalitions of antismokers began to obtain results that the original campaign could not produce. These groups brought about restrictions on smoking in public places by pressuring airline management, government officials and private business owners. Today, it is difficult to find an indoor public place where people are permitted to smoke.

The perceptual aspect of communication is the way an individual responds to an event or the communication of or about an event and that is dependent on assumptions, point of view, background and such. In the world of instant global transmission of information, cultural factors based on education and experience are major factors in responses to such events as 9/11, the treatment of prisoners at Guantanamo Bay, Cuba, and what may or may not have happened to copies of the Qu'ran there. This transactional way of looking at perception is much more common in mass communication research today than it was in the 1950s when George Gerbner developed his communication model that included both personal and mediated communication.

Critical Thinking and Responsibility Recipients of information have obligations and responsibilities, not only to themselves but also to others. All persuasion efforts should be subjected to critical thinking: Is that true? Where's the evidence? Does this fit with my experience? How might I assimilate this into my life? What are the consequences of doing what I've been asked to do?

The idea of evaluating information in a variety of ways was introduced by social psychologists Richard

Petty and John Cacioppo who called it the elaboration likelihood theory. This theory about persuasion that says you may apply critical thinking to a proposition or argument or you may not based on your motivation to examine something carefully and your ability to do so, or perhaps through your casual, or peripheral, processing where you make a judgment based on cues, usually whether or not you agree with the message.

A need for precision in framing messages is one of the reasons public relations practitioners use the term *publics*, rather than the term *audiences* often used by media. PR practitioners assume that people *choose* to expose themselves to all kinds of information, persuasive appeals included. A PR practitioner accused of being a "manipulator" by a verbal antagonist calmly replied, "I wish." The PR person elaborated by saying public relations and advertising persuasive efforts don't always cause results; if so, all of those in the business would not only be rich, they'd be running the world.

Another view comes from what Charles Larson calls an assumption by many that all public communication is untrustworthy.[30] It isn't, but the truthfulness or the ethics of the communication are often in the mind of the beholder. What responsible public relations people count on is the kind of feedback that you see in the symmetrical model.

A Way to Look at Media: Source, Message, Source+Message, Media, Receivers

Persuasion occurs face to face and through mass media. But while interpersonal persuasion can result in cognitive changes, mass media tend to focus their efforts on channeling attitudes and existing behavior changes in a particular direction.[31]

Mass and specialized media provide a constant flow of information, but how much of it gets to the intended publics and with what effect still makes useful the classic question posed by political scientist Harold D. Lasswell:

> *Who*
> *Says What*
> *In Which Channel*
> *To Whom*
> *With What Effect?*[32]

The Lasswell formula, one of the earlier communication models, ignores feedback, but understandably, because communication research was in its infancy at that time. In addition, feedback was not considered in the model developed by mathematician Claude Shannon and modified with co-worker Warren Weaver. The Shannon-Weaver model that appears in many books today was developed in 1949, a year after Lasswell's. DeFleur added feedback to the Shannon-Weaver model, but you seldom see his more complex, but also more viable, model developed in 1966.[33]

What we know today is that research is needed at every level, and that every level is affected by feedback.

Source

What research tells us about the source for communication is important to public relations because we get to choose the source for messages. Is it better to have the CEO announce a new product or the research and development director or the engineering team or, well, you get the idea.

Research gives us some insight into the two areas in which we are most interested: credibility and effect. Credibility is important and we want something to happen because in public relations we are involved in purposeful communication. We know that attractive sources are more effective than unattractive ones, but source credibility has more impact. The CEO may be better looking, but the product developer knows the product. That helps with our choice.

Experts tend to be believed. Expertise adds more to persuasive impact than trustworthiness, and we are more likely to be influenced by experts than our peers. Obviously biased sources, though, are less likely to be believed even if they are experts. But powerful, attractive, biased sources can be more effective than unbiased sources in reinforcing opinions. Remember that when activists challenge your organization.

Credibility of a source does not affect message recall, and information from low-credibility sources does not increase over time. Unattractive sources are more effective when they advocate unexpected positions, such as when someone who might be presumed to be negative about something advocates it, and we also know that retention of a message is higher if it comes from an unexpected source. High-credibility sources, when recalled as the source, produce more opinion change.

Change is an effect, and sometimes to be sure of an effect, a threat is considered. Health communicators must always consider the merits of a threat. Sources that offer more rewards than threats are more effective, but a source that threatens one of several punishments for noncompliance may be as persuasive as one that promises rewards. Mild threats may be internalized and may lead to compliance, whereas strong threats stimulate defiance. Something else is at work here too. Internalization—self-persuasion—seems to be the most permanent source of persuasion, followed by identification and compliance.

Finally, source credibility may not matter if the messages themselves present reasonable arguments.[34] That means we have to consider the message carefully, which we will after we look at some theories that relate to the source.

Source Orientation

People tend to believe sources that are like them, like they want to be or like they perceive themselves to be. People also seek authority in sources, most of the time. But they can be emotionally swayed into accepting someone else's advice. For example, the U.S. Surgeon General's initial appeal to people in the 1980s to use condoms to avoid possible contagion from the AIDS virus had only a marginal effect. Planned Parenthood could have told him that the appeal would have little impact. Planned Parenthood has been trying for years to prevent unwanted pregnancies, but it often has to compete with someone emotionally close to the decision-maker and with the decision-maker's own emotions. Part of the acceptance of authority is credibility, much of which is based on trust. People almost always trust someone close to them more than they do any authority figure. Some analysts contend that the influence of traditional authority is generally in decline—both because of cultural changes among baby boomers and "Generation X," and because electronic communication and globalization have tended to erode institutional hierarchies.[35]

Some research has suggested that source credentials may not matter as much as a message's plausibility and message quality, at least when the reader is not highly involved in the topic. In this view, questions of source expertise and bias tend to have less influence on people's beliefs than the quality of the message itself.[36]

Messages

Anyone who clicked New Document in a word processing program, then spent some time looking at a blank screen can testify that finding the best beginning to a message is a test of creativity, imagination *and* patience. Knowing the medium is essential, of course. Media have particular formats that all PR practitioners have to know, from billboards and business letters to zealous sales proposals, for your own PR firm or a client's business. You start with the format for the medium, and that gives you structure, but not content. It's the content that has consequences.

The way the information is presented has an impact on the effect. When good news is presented first, it increases the acceptance of the message, which may also include bad news. Telling both sides of a message (telling the other side and refuting it) is advisable if the recipient is educated, is likely to hear the other side anyway, is familiar with the issue or is opposed to the side being advocated.

In persuasive messages such as a blog, a broadcast commentary, a piece for the OpEd page or commercial content copy such as a public service announcement or an ad/commercial itself, repetition is a consideration. With the increasing convergence of all mass media content, the repetition of messages is increasingly likely. That suggests some rethinking of all media effects theories—whether mass media effects on audiences are "weak" or "strong."

Learning does increase with message repetition. A risk is that counterargumentation may increase and favorable thoughts decrease. Also, repeated exposure to a message, while it may increase agreement, can be so excessive that it leads to boredom and reduce agreement. A period of nonexposure can overcome effects of overexposure, and that's why in planning a campaign, you may want to decrease appeals periodically.

As always, the effects are the whole point of the communication. Increased comprehension of a message increases agreement, so you want to be sure your messages are clear and easy to understand. Remember that exposure is voluntary. No one is going to work too hard to find out what it is you want them to know.

In comparative materials—your client's product or services or your own company's versus another's—it won't matter whether you take that approach or a noncomparative one unless the material is going to be on television. Showing differences is especially effective in making the argument on television.

Comparative approaches are better, too, if the service or product is new, the market share small and the public you are appealing to has no preferences.

Generally there's no difference in the persuasive impact of emotional versus rational appeals, but that may depend both on the medium and the content of the message. The threats mentioned earlier regarding the source are important in both message structure and effect. High-fear appeals can be more effective than low-fear ones if receivers are not very anxious or don't see themselves as vulnerable, and when recommendations are specific, clear and easy to follow.

The increased appearance of information on the Internet, with its pervasiveness in all communication, indicates that reinforcement of fear messages may originate with and receive emphasis from message recipients who respond and participate in the public dialogue.

In creating warning messages, always tell people what you want them to think or do. Messages with explicit conclusions are more effective than messages that allow the recipient to draw his or her own conclusions.

In your writing style, always keep in mind the person whom you want to receive the message. Individuals are complex. William McGuire says people approach material with their heads (cognitive) and their hearts (affective). Their response is related to their need for the information or to some provocation for seeking it, and the response may be active or reactive.[37]

Message Orientation To be persuasive, a message has to present something of value to the target public. It must also be compatible with that public's motives. If your public has to make some adjustments to accept a new or different idea, you must provide a clear statement of that adjustment and the rationale for making it. In a free society where communication is open, the person being persuaded chooses which messages to attend to. If your message challenges your public's sense of security or self-image, you must provide an ego defense; otherwise, members of the public will repel the argument, instinctively defending their egos. If you are suggesting acceptance of something that has been rejected before as socially taboo, you must offer a value that can be adopted to replace it or rationalize it. For instance, although it may be difficult to get white Americans to adopt American-born children of other races, they may adopt *foreign* children of other races because of an emotional appeal to guilt or conscience. Some of this can be explained by the theory of *cognitive dissonance*.

News media often are credited with the ability to bring about change in a free society. Agenda-setting theory studies say media give importance or significance to a message or to an issue by giving it news coverage.[38]

Research suggests that media coverage can be crucial throughout the life of an issue, although perhaps less so when publics are split on their support. Thus, public agenda-setters might want to keep up bursts of coverage to maintain the popularity of a position on an issue. Also, agenda-setters can influence issue priorities by increasing media coverage of those issues that are international or otherwise unobtrusive, that is, those issues that people cannot experience directly.[39] Agenda-setting research indicates that not only do news media give significance to the message, but also suggest to people what to think about the message.

Another media theory is tied especially to television. Cultivation theory, developed by George Gerbner, suggests that television offers people a shared world vision and thus is more of a cultural than media effects theory. The homogenizing abilities of television seem to be diminished with the fragmentation of media, except for global news coverage. The exposure certainly is there, but the "shared" vision often is not because global audiences are watching through the prism of their values, based on their education, and their experience.

The Purpose of a Message The purpose of a message depends on the objective of the communication. What do you wish to accomplish? The goal should be something measurable, such as increasing the enrollment of a university, and not something nebulous, such as improving the image of the institution. PR pioneer Edward L. Bernays was adamant about refusing to use the word *image* in a public relations context. Bernays said the word suggests that PR deals with shadows and illusions when in reality it deals with changing attitudes and actions to meet social objectives.[40]

Some problems of institutional credibility cited by the late PR practitioner Philip Lesly can be attributed directly to peddling images instead of dealing with realities.[41] Some data indicate that deceptive persuaders are more likely to use rationale or explanation than are truthful persuaders, who tend to employ positive and negative attributes of a situation.

Once the purpose of the message has been clearly defined, the motivation and inspiration decisions are easier. Psychologist Abraham H. Maslow devised a hierarchy of human motives that, although no longer held as reliable as it once was, suggests ways for a message to appeal to the appropriate needs at each level within this hierarchy:

- *Physical needs*—for food, drink, sex, rest and such—are the most fundamental motivations.

- *Safety* is the need for protection against violence, economic hazards and unpredictable reality.

- *Love* is more than a need for affection. It encompasses the need to belong to a group and the longing for a friendly social environment. The strength of this motivational need pulls young people, particularly teenagers, together into a seemingly impenetrable peer group.

- *Self-esteem* includes the needs for achievement and for recognition of that achievement by others. It also involves the face-saving compromises we often engage in to rescue our self-regard, such as settling for a fancier title instead of a salary increase.[42]

- *Self-actualization* is the need to develop individuality and to make constructive use of one's abilities. This extends to creativity and aesthetic appreciation. One subtle aspect of this motive is the need to know and to understand.

Some principles go along with these needs. One is *homeostasis*. People constantly make an effort to maintain their own status quo. Another is the principle of *deprivation*. Related to physiological needs, it never wanes in intensity. If people are deprived of a physiological goal (for instance, food), they will continue to seek it. (One compulsive chocolate eater explained that a childhood allergy had deprived her of the pleasure of eating chocolates when very young!) When deprivation involves social goals, however, it often retains its effectiveness as a motivation only up to a point.

Beyond that point, it loses intensity and people may abandon a goal; for instance, they may resign themselves to a certain social class or status. The principle of *satiation* weakens physiological drives and can weaken social motives, but it seems to have no effect on emotions—good news for lovers, perhaps. The principle of *goal evaluation* is based on tension, as in straining to achieve something—to earn a Karate black belt, to be a master at bridge. Goals that are not socially acceptable, however, either must be abandoned or must find support from another principle. This occurs also when certain goals prove impossible to achieve. For example, if you can't be an "A" student, perhaps you can be a "solid B" student. One other principle works in these basic motives: the *barrier* principle. A barrier placed between people and the fulfillment of their goals will enhance the appeal of the goal unless the barrier proves too great, in which case they will probably change their goals.

Our goals are tied closely to what we want to be. An advertising creative director, for example, may steadfastly maintain that everyone is a snob of one kind or another—for example, if well-educated, probably an intellectual snob. The promoter of a national magazine keyed to intellectuals (*Harper's*) adopted that very thesis in a mailing piece sent in a "plain brown envelope" that carried this question in the lower left corner: "Should you be punished for being born with a high IQ?" The envelope probably was opened by most recipients. What we value is often a key to our personality.

The Texture of a Message Once you know which needs and values you want to appeal to, you understand the purpose of your message and which persuasive appeal is likely to work; then you can choose the texture of the message for its persuasive effect. The medium dictates to some extent the range of textures. Television has a wide range—color, design, movement and sound. A computer has all of these, plus interactive control. But pictures and sound on computers are still not as good as TV. In print, the size, shape and feel of an object—as people trained in graphics know—may determine whether a brochure is picked up (much less read), whether a package is taken off a supermarket shelf and whether an ad catches people's attention.

Motivational studies involving texture need to be interpreted by public relations practitioners as well as by marketing people in approaching particular problems. Regarding color, for instance, most businesspeople will not respond to a questionnaire printed on hot pink, will make little response to one on blue, but will give many answers to a questionnaire printed on green, beige or white.

Most of us psychologically favor certain colors. This is likely to manifest itself in our choice of colors for clothes, cars and furniture. The public relations person needs to know which colors will appeal to a particular audience and how well those colors reproduce in the medium chosen for communicating with

Ethical Perspective

Doublespeak is so common to our public discourse that "gobbledygook" is often mistaken for meaning. As the primary commentator on doublespeak, William Lutz has said, "Doublespeak is incongruity, the incongruity between what is said or left unsaid and what really is." Gobbledygook is using many words instead of the few that would suffice or just using a long word instead of a shorter one. According to semanticist Stuart Chase, *gobbledygook* was created in 1944 by Maury Maverick, a Texas congressman who compared Washington bureaucrats' language to the meaningless gobbling of turkeys.

"Corporate speak" is what doublespeak sometimes is called, although, as Maverick suggested, the government may have the most skilled practitioners. In public relations or public affairs, there is considerable environmental pressure to use the "acceptable" language. It's another form of "correct" speech. The problem is that people are often misled, if they understand anything at all, and that is unethical.

"Microsoft Trial Prompts an Outbreak of Doublespeak," reads a front page headline in *The Wall Street Journal*'s Marketplace section (April 15, 2002), pp. B1, 3. A subhead on the story by Rebecca Buckman and Nicholas Kulish reads, "Company and Competitors Say One Thing in the Courtroom, Sing Different Tune in the Marketplace."

The examples appear in a box called, "Spin Cycles." What is usually referred to as "spin"? Public relations. The comment in the box is "Microsoft and its rivals tailor their messages one way in court and another way for investors and consumers." Of course. Public relations teaches practitioners to adjust the message for the audience, but the messages, though different, must be consonant for credibility. This story is about what happens when they aren't.

The implication is that Palm, the rival, is talking from both sides of its corporate mouth. The two quotes the reporters used are as follows. "We believe that the handheld opportunity remains wide open. Unlike the PC industry, there is no monopoly of silicon, there is no monopoly of software," Palm CEO Eric Benhamou on an analyst conference call. Compare that with the following from Palm executive Michael Mace at the Microsoft trial: "We believe there is a very substantial risk that Microsoft could manipulate its products and its standards in order to exclude Palm from the marketplace in the future." Can't have it both ways, Palm.

Translation from doublespeak:

CEO—The future is bright, invest.
Exec—We're going to lose our shirts. Stop Microsoft.

It's not just a matter of speaking clearly, it is a matter of telling the truth, whatever the venue.

Doublespeak also made *The Wall Street Journal's* front page of the Marketplace section March 27, 2006 in Carol Hymowitz's column, "In the Lead," under the headline: "Mind Your Language: To Do Business Today, Consider Delayering."

The "layering" she illustrated is among business buzzwords that mislead. One example is "delayering," which although suggesting a cake, she says is nothing sweet because it means firing employees. Another example is a business's saying it has "a limited downsize," which really means things can't get much worse.

Doublespeak counts on receivers' lack of critical thinking. Understanding persuasion theory, even if you never use it, helps hone critical thinking skills.

See William Lutz, *The New Doublespeak: Why No One Knows What Anyone's Saying Anymore*, New York: HarperCollins Publishers, 1996. The quote is from page 4.

For more on gobbledygook, see *The Revenge of Anguished English* by Richard Lederer, 2005, St. Martin's Press.

that audience. One despairing art director, after having to change colors for a campaign owing to problems in reproducing them in different media, said with some resignation, "I'm ready to go back to the basics: red, white and blue," a safe choice after 9/11.

Nonverbal symbols are also part of a message's texture. Be particularly careful to avoid those that suggest bias, such as a woman standing beside a man seated at a desk or an ethnic or racial minority in a subservient posture in relation to a majority figure. Nonverbal cues say things that words do not, and today's diverse and culturally sensitive audiences will be quick to notice them. Be sure that the symbolism your message projects matches your intentions. Well-chosen nonverbal cues can greatly enhance the message communicated by the accompanying words. Carelessly chosen cues can completely destroy an intended message and alienate an audience.

The Language of a Message Problems in communication are often caused by semantics. The words you use must mean the same thing to the receiver that they do to you. It doesn't matter whether the words you use to say something are the ones that *you* think sound the best or most authoritative; rather, you must focus on what words have the most forceful and desirable impact on the viewer or listener. Only people can bestow meanings on words, says communications specialist Don Fabun, adding, "When we act as if we believed that a word symbol is the event that was originally experienced, we ignore all the steps that have made it something else."[43]

Jargon and obfuscation abound in government, education and elsewhere, as the Lutz Doublespeak example illustrates. Important factors in language choice include clarity, emotional impact and context. A message's consistency with other messages from the same source and its level of repetition are also significant.

Clarity has almost been lost. Obscurity in language has reached ridiculous proportions in American usage, as today's technical society embraces an entire vocabulary of words that would not have been understood even a decade ago. And because PR practitioners are not around to explain what their messages mean, the language they use had better be self-explanatory. You must choose your words with a feeling for the associations that the receivers will make, based on their individual frames of reference; the images the words will conjure up for them, based usually on stereotypes they hold; and the simple fitness of the word itself. As an instance of clarity,

John F. Kennedy's inaugural address ("Ask not what your country can do for you . . .") was written almost entirely in single-syllable words and was comprehensible, as well as elegant and eloquent, to almost all who heard it. Readability can be tested. Computer software can be used to check the clarity and reading level of your writing.[44]

The emotional impact of language has nothing to do with clarity; it depends on emotional association. Emotional impact is, of course, a significant weapon in all propaganda battles. In World War II, Axis Sally and Tokyo Rose, two sultry radio personalities and propagandists, tried to entice American defections; however, two incomparable commanders of the English language, Winston Churchill and Franklin D. Roosevelt, urged their countrymen on with eloquent propaganda, raising the morale and resolve of those on the front lines as well as those at home.

The emotional impact of icons—emotionally arousing images, events or verbal metaphors—is an important mechanism for affecting public opinion. Although this is not a revelation, as anyone who has seen Leni Riefenstahl's film for Hitler, *Triumph of the Will*, can attest, there are some new studies of emotional campaigning. Robert Blood, strategic communications analyst in the United Kingdom, says "Icons infect people's beliefs and they replicate by communication—they are the viruses of persuasion." His studies indicate that three factors influence the rate at which an icon spreads through the public consciousness: emotiveness, resonance and benignity. Emotiveness is the icon's measure of emotional arousal; resonance, its degree of agreement with existing beliefs and anxieties; benignity, its lack of a direct effect on the individual exposed to it. The actual cost of a new environmental policy, for example, may be quite benign for an individual, because often the government and/or businesses are most directly affected. This factor can be separated from whether the policy has any emotive or resonant qualities. Blood's analysis helps explain how public opinion is affected by pressure groups and the news media.[45]

The context of messages—their verbal settings—is also important. As one writer advises:

There is no easy way of choosing words. They must not be so general in meaning as to include thoughts not intended, nor so narrow as to eliminate thoughts that are intended. Let the meaning select the word.

A word is ambiguous when the reader is unable to choose decisively between alternative meanings, either of which would seem to fit the context.

Reprinted with permission of Copley News Service and Mike Thompson.

A great deal of unclear writing results from the use of too many broad, general words, those having so many possible meanings that the precise thought is not clear. The more general the words are, the fainter is the picture; the more special they are, the brighter.[46]

Because people both seek and avoid messages, it is important to consider the significance of *repetition* and *consistency* in public relations messages. Repetition increases the opportunity for exposure. Consistency helps increase credibility. Communication scholars who have conducted experiments on cognitive discrepancies and communication call the act of seeking "information search" and the act of avoiding a message "information preference."

Making sure that a message gets through to an intended receiver is the first goal, and repetition increases your chances of accomplishing this. Making sure that the message is believed is the next goal, and consistency helps here. But both of these techniques are based on a time element, and communications scholars have made some disquieting discoveries in this area. First, they found that, when pressed for time, people often make decisions based on less information than they would normally require (an especially significant fact in political PR). Second,

writers must decide whether their target public needs information piece by piece (which is all right if members of the public already have made their decisions) or whether they need an evaluative structure or frame of reference to permit making comparisons between alternatives.[47]

Other Considerations in Message Strategy With the diversity of our society in the USA plus the fact that most messages are globally accessible, culture is an important consideration. Messages don't always travel well across cultures, not to mention national borders. One of the first casualties is humor. Humor separates those who "get it" from those who don't, and can offend different cultures and social groups.[48] Another difficulty occurs with values, discussed previously, that divide as well as connect. Freedom of expression is not a universal value, for example.[49]

In personality promotions, creating personal identity is a sensitive task. For instance, the personal identification campaigns for women politicians was given structure using Foucault's theories of self.[50]

Two theories regarding messages for organizations that include a model of positive deviancy and reflective practice have useful application. The positive deviancy model singles out organizations that

Theory and Research Perspective

The idea of "authentic" communication is a concept that what one is reading or hearing is indeed true, genuine. Certainly PR messages that win that sort of acceptance have a good chance of being believed.

PR practitioner, now professor, Bojinka Bishop decided to test attributes of "authentic communication" that she called the "ten essential elements." A national survey of 960 large water utilities in the USA asked how successful the respondents considered their communication programs to be and correlated that information with their ranking on a four-point scale of the ten attributes: (1) truthful, (2) fundamental, (3) comprehensive, (4) consistent with other words and action, (5) made relevant, (6) clear, (7) timely, (8) accessible, (9) allows for feedback and discussion, and (10) shows care.

Nine of the ten showed "extremely" high correlations with success and "being consistent" ranked high, but not as high as the other nine. This would suggest checking your communications for these ten attributes.

Bojinka Bishop is Sloan Professor of Public Relations, E. W. Scripps School of Journalism, Ohio University. A summary of her research appeared in tips & tactics supplement to *pr reporter*, 38(15), November 13, 2000, p. 1.

---

are doing extraordinarily well and flourishing with the same resources that others in the same environment have but are less resourceful in using. The positive model can help others see where they are failing without that criticism having to come from outside where it might be rejected.[51] Another internal organizational effort is suggested by reflective PR practice, where assumptions are challenged as well as the values on which these are based, with the idea of improving the organization.[52]

Source+Message

The mix of source and message is key to acceptance and credibility. Communicators are evaluated more favorably to the extent that their messages have the following qualities: listenability or readability, human interest, vocabulary diversity and realism. If you have a message for which there is little supporting evidence, source credibility is more important.[53] Often the organization provides that credibility.

When organizations are under flux as they are in the high tech environment, it's important to remember that publics are subjected to the same sorts of disorder. A new symmetrical and ethical approach to increase credibility, crafted from postmodern and complexity theory as well as chaos theory, offers a communication structure that gives publics as stakeholders more input. Chaos theory, borrowed from physics, suggests that organizational boundaries are constantly changing such that they become blurred

and that external factors, including stakeholders and perhaps especially government, define the parameters. Such change gives flexibility to an organization to change with its environment and thus survive.[54]

An organization's credibility is also at risk in multinational organizations maintaining offices all over the world. One chemical company's public affairs officer, when asked whether a corporate policy widely stated in the USA was accepted abroad, said quite candidly, "We have different message statements on that depending on the country." Not a good idea, because all is available on the Internet. A research paper exploring the integration of parent companies and their subsidiaries or sister companies showed they can achieve a balance between integration and localization of communication strategies, certainly a help for maintaining credibility.[55]

Media

Media, especially traditional mass media, have been studied for decades, and the Internet now is under academic scrutiny. The ubiquity of the Internet with its mix of words, pictures and sound offers many research opportunities, especially because many of the pictures are electronically engineered. This mix of messages is occurring in the traditional news media as well and will increasingly be a source of consideration with the convergence of mass media content—where a single message (report) is adapted for print, broadcast and other electronic presentations through the Internet.

At this point, without some verification of "new" media observations that suggest new theories, here is what we do know from past research. First is that if you have a complex message, you're better off with print media. But when the message is simple, video presentations are much more effective. Video or live presentations are most effective if attitudes on an issue are changing. Next in order of effectiveness are audio messages. Least effective in that environment is print. Television, Marshall McLuhan's "cool medium," involves its audiences more than radio and far more than print. Because computers are interactive, probably they will rank higher than TV as the quality of computer presentation of video continues to improve.

The media orientation of publics is critical information, because media deliver the messages. Public relations involves deciding what to tell, whom to tell it to, how to tell it and through what media to communicate. The choice of medium is critical. It must be believable, able to reach the priority public and technologically capable of carrying the message. Television, for example, has high credibility and mass penetration. Safety officials who want to alert residents about an impending hurricane invariably take to the airwaves. But something complicated like a change in Social Security benefits cannot be communicated as well through this medium. All television can do is alert people to the change and tell them where to find the information: a print medium is better at explaining details.

People also turn to different media for different types of gratification and rewards. Many different measures have been used in examining *media use* and *gratification* motives, but three seem especially well-suited: environmental surveillance, environmental diversion and environmental interaction.[56] According to these measures, people use media to see what's going on that might interest them or for sheer entertainment or to prepare for anticipated conversations or interactions with others.

How people use media for gratification may change as they change, as their circumstances change and as their relationships with others change. A young woman normally not concerned with athletics might become an avid searcher of sports information while she is in a relationship with a sports enthusiast. A young man might begin to subscribe to computer magazines if he becomes interested in a young woman who is a computer scientist. In either case, the individual's interest in the specialized medium may not outlast his or her enthusiasm for the human relationship being pursued at the moment.

Reception Test for Media   Although media research departments can show tables of statistics that theoretically profile their audiences, you should still ask some probing questions. For example, are the selected "receivers" chosen from a physical or from an intellectual base? A university (for instance) may define all those to whom it mails its alumni magazine as "readers," yet a substantial number are probably "nonreceivers" (they throw the publication away without ever lifting the cover) and another segment may be "lookers" (they thumb through the magazine but never read anything except photo captions). The real readers are those who read at least one article per publication in the time period sampled. The same applies to news releases. To quote former Ohio State University PR professor Walter Siefert:

> *"Dissemination [of news releases] does not equal Publication, and Publication does not equal Absorption and Action! Which means, in simpler words: All who receive it won't publish it, and all who read or hear it won't understand or act on it."[57]*

Credibility Test for Media   Another relevant question concerns a medium's credibility. How much do surveys couched in terms of numbers reached tell you about reception? If you send a news release to the media, not all media will use it, and many people who ultimately are exposed to the information will not pay any real attention to it. For instance, a presentation designed by the Magazine Publishers Association to show the impact of magazine advertising claimed that certain ads reached women in the 25- to 35-year-old bracket who, it was asserted, do most of the buying. The presentation offered supporting data to show such women's response to and recall of specific advertising messages, but it did not state the proportion of readers recalling these messages. And just as some people read editorial content and ignore advertising, others do just the opposite.

Ethnic and religious media tend have a higher credibility with their audiences than other media do with theirs. Industry, trade, association and professional print media also rank high with their selected audiences. Suburban and small-town weekly publications (generally newspapers) rate next highest in credibility. Specialized magazines also rate high—again, perhaps, because their readers have a concentrated interest in the subject matter. Recent studies tested readers' *affinity* for a publication—an emotional reaction, rather than an intellectual one.

Global Perspective

Antiglobalism activists are diversified. They appear to confront the WTO (World Trade Organization) and the WHO (World Health Organization), for example, and organize protests at McDonald's operations (animal cruelty, mad cow disease) or ExxonMobil (global warming) or any number of other commercial establishments.

Who are "they"? Many different organizations, mostly nongovernmental organizations (NGOs), are involved. Often they work separately but sometimes form coalitions, some formal alliances. This is not new. It was apparent in the 1960s in the USA with the heightened visibility of the consumer movement. Results are often damaging boycotts and humiliating publicity. Of course the question always to be asked: How much of their accusations have a basis in fact that can be addressed and corrected? The other question: Is the difference in political perspective so great that the problem is not likely to be resolved? The situation is different for the two different groups.

The important aspect for public relations practitioners is to understand the activists' strategy. Activists can be individuals or organizations. It was an individual, Saul Alinsky, who codified the rules for activists in his 1969 *Reveille for Radicals* and his 1971 *Rules for Radicals*. If the objective is really to engage the organization to change policies, the activists are open to negotiation but expect real change as a result. That activism uses new and traditional media systems, a combination of mass and interpersonal communication to achieve its objective. The objective, on the other hand, may be simply to damage the company, maybe enough to put it out of business. What the organization intends is to capture media attention, counting on its thirst for conflict, especially in highly competitive markets.

Propaganda is a strong tool for activists, especially the card stacking and glittering generalities techniques. The testimonial is used too, generally that of a former employee or a victim of corporate abuse. Data is distorted and facts replaced by exaggeration and emotionalism. Symbolism is important, so you see unnerving posters like the cow's head with the changed logo "Murder King" for Burger King and the words: "Have it your way. How much cruelty can you stomach?" Cognitive dissonance is used too. The idea is to create enough tension or pressure for change. This is what make boycotts work. Someone who likes animals and supports animal rights may justify eating hamburgers because the animals were raised for that. However, they expect humane treatment. If they think the treatment is not humane, either in the raising or in the slaughter, they can be encouraged to join a boycott.

Grassroots organizing is another strong point of activism, one that plays on social validation. Getting a strong spokesperson also provides followers with identification. The call to action also is always clear, much clearer, usually, than corporate responses.

To deal with activists, companies first have to separate the groups based on their seriousness about negotiating for change. With serious groups, identify a leader. Be prompt in responding through that leader(s), listening carefully and supplying substantive, provable data. When change is possible, it should be discussed. When it can't be implemented, or there will be a considerable delay, some understanding or agreement needs to be arrived at and announced by both in a joint news release. The risk is to ignore the serious and perhaps clear up a problem that can only get worse and be the source of continuing problems.

Now, the enemies. There are those who really don't want change. They want the company out of business, never mind the employees it will put on the streets, the taxes that won't be there to support the community, etc. There is no logic here. You can't fight fire with fire, so to speak, because aggression looks like the powerful attacking the powerless. Crisis specialist James E. Lukaszewski encourages companies to "Wage peace relentlessly."

The Internet has offered a powerful organizing tool for global activism. Their targets can't afford to dismiss them, but must think of strategies of their own to use in the battle for customers and credibility.

For more see Douglas Quenqua, "When Activists Attack," *PR Week*, June 11, 2001, and James Lukaszewski, "Activism: Preparing Counteractive Strategies," in "strategy," supplement to *pr reporter*, November 12, December 18, 2000, pp. 1–4.

The strength of that affinity is a measure of how high the credibility of the publication is with its reader.[58]

Among mass (as opposed to specialized) media, television dominates. Possible reasons for this are the widespread belief that "seeing is believing" and TV's capacity to disengage the critical senses. Daily newspapers have more credibility than their critics often are willing to concede and a higher persuasive impact than their publishers and editors may be willing to admit. Some of that impact is indirect because opinion leaders exposed to the information transmit it to others, usually in a different format and without attribution. Radio stations, owing to their specialized appeal and the emotional impact of the medium, significantly affect their own loyal audiences, but these are comparatively small. At the bottom of the credibility ratings come company publications and Web sites, which get mixed reviews for credibility, perhaps because they are so diverse in quality. In an era when everything else about the government seems suspect, government publications consistently get rather high credibility ratings—particularly those that include unbiased consumer-oriented studies.

An understanding of the agenda-setting role of mass media is also valuable to the public relations practitioner. The term *agenda setting* refers to the variable degrees of attention the mass media give to certain ideas, issues or themes, lending them more or less significance. A symbiotic relationship (mutually beneficial coexistence) seems to exist between message source and medium, in that mass media may pick up ideas that seem likely to represent broad appeals and then popularize them. The media agenda may also suggest to leaders some exploitable public concerns, although some evidence suggests that the power of agenda setting is diminished when the issue is abstract (federal budget deficit) rather than concrete (drug abuse).[59] There is increasing evidence that agenda setting goes beyond telling us what to think about and tells us also what to think.[60]

Receivers

A public relations mantra is that perception is reality. Research offers a more conditional statement: Perception is often subjective. Even when information is not adequate, receivers tend to use what is there or what they perceive is there to serve an immediate need or purpose. Even a message that contradicts an existing opinion won't be rejected out of hand if it seems to reward the receiver in some way. However, there is no solid evidence of selective retention of information based on the receiver's attitudes and behaviors. Publics tend to disregard supportive messages that are easy to refute and nonsupportive messages that are difficult to refute.

Adjusting messages to minimize differences between the source and extreme receivers facilitates greater acceptance. Most mental and personality traits of receivers have diametrically opposed effects on message reception and yielding. Intelligence, for instance, facilitates reception but inhibits yielding. Accurate and favorable perceptions of a message can be facilitated by establishing early bonding with the intended public. Familiar symbols, objects, categories and message cues that are easy to recognize help message receivers.

Receiving and Accepting Messages   Evidence suggests that people who have grown up with lots of television (which means most readers of this book) learn to tune out messages they do not wish to receive. Everyone does this to some degree—otherwise we would all be drowning in noise. But the high degree of unconscious selectivity exercised by members of the electronic generation poses particular challenges to the PR person trying to reach them.

Great stock was once put in the two-step flow theory, which holds that ideas flow from opinion-makers down to the public at large.[61] The theory suggests that opinion leaders attending to mass or specialized media are early adopters of new ideas. Their adoption influences others, starting with people who are like themselves—those in the same occupations or social/economic class. In the past several decades, however, politicians have successfully conducted public opinion studies to see what people are interested in and concerned with and then have enunciated those feelings as ideas or policies. Presidential programs reflecting this upward flow are John F. Kennedy's War on Poverty, Lyndon B. Johnson's Great Society, and Jimmy Carter's New Foundations, as well as Bill Clinton's tax revision efforts. Currently health care initiatives, both physical and mental, are under scrutiny.

How publics perceive the source of a message is a significant factor in whether they accept the message. Perception can be looked at two different ways. One focus is on attending to the environment. Another focus is on interpretation—stressing language and mental activity. The human transaction model includes an attended-to present, a remembered past and an anticipated future. Each—present, past and future—has four aspects: physical, extending potential, cognitive and affective. Most people are able to separate past and future, but nevertheless bring them to bear on their present. Our perception processes affect what we discover, give name to, classify mentally, attach significance to and communicate.[62] Our perception affects how we react to an important source for messages: people.

We are in almost constant conversation with people, and the information we get this way has a higher credibility than any other—depending on the attitude we hold toward the speaker. Is it someone we like? Respect? Consider smart? Is it someone who resembles us or who accepts and likes us? Credibility ratings of people by their occupations is common, and nationally this changes with events. Rankings of trust for occupations usually rate teachers high, small-business owners next, then police officers. Journalists and CEOs of large corporations share the lower ranks with car dealers and now government officials.

We tend to seek out as sources, not only people but media, that reflect our opinions and attitudes. For this reason, many PR veterans recommend not trying to persuade vehement opponents to change their minds, but instead trying to neutralize them so that they will do minimal harm.

Everyone seems to recognize that a sender must encode messages—that is, translate information into something personally meaningful to an intended receiver. However, we tend to forget the static and interference created by competing messages, credibility disturbances and the interference of selectivity on the part of the receiver. If the receiver does accept the message, it must be decoded, after which a response to the message may be encoded.

Considering the environment of distortion that exists in our family, social, educational, religious and ethnic life, it is a wonder that any communication gets through to us at all. And of course, many messages do not get through. In other instances, our intended messages are contraindicated by our body language or other symbols.[63]

Nonverbal communication expresses our subconscious, and thus gives off cues when we are not telling the truth, which means loss of credibility. Clues come from eyes, head, voice and hands, so recipients can tell when a source is not being truthful and thus credibility is lost.[64]

Indeed, symbols are important—whether in advertising or in art, or whether as trademarks or as company logos—in conveying the meaning we intend. In utilizing symbols, we often resort to stereotyping, a mental shorthand that can be useful in processing information. The word *chair* makes you think of a certain type of chair because you have *all* chairs filed under that mental image. Often this is adequate for communication and for understanding a situation. However, the context may make you seek a particular symbol. Thus your mental image may go from your basic chair to a desk chair in a classroom setting.

But stereotypes—the pictures in our heads— are personal and may misrepresent reality. As a result, communication, imprecise at best, takes on an even greater risk when using stereotypes.[65] If you were dealing with a clearly defined target public and you had a well-grounded knowledge of which stereotypes you could use effectively and appropriately with this audience, you might proceed with some confidence. But there are some monumental examples of the hazards of stereotyping.

For example, look at various situations where ways of representing women resulted in boycotts, demonstrations and even loss of elections. The stereotyping of females in advertising, television programming and news columns and by public speakers (especially politicians) has lessened in the face of activity by women's groups, but it is still evident. The main criticism of using stereotypes to represent roles people perform or to view groups of people is that, for many, the image becomes the reality. During the civil rights movement in the USA, for example, objections by blacks to racial stereotyping were based on concerns that people who had limited contact with blacks accepted the representation as the reality. In the ongoing international religious tensions with the Muslim faith, adherents are making the same argument.

Responses to a Message Responses to the presentation of a message vary too. Different message stimuli are used to increase involvement. That's the reason pop-ups appear on your computer screen when you are doing a search or looking at an especially active Web site. Images move to get your attention. Sound is another stimulus on Web sites, and especially with electronic greetings. Print greeting cards sometimes have "voice" too—words or music. And, occasionally scent is added. Advertisers use scent as well. Catalogs, even bills, may arrive with a fragrance. McCormick Foods for years has scented its annual report.

Anticipation, expectations and assumptions all are ingredients of how we respond to messages. For many years both advertisers and publicists thought that recipients of messages in the mass media gave higher credibility to publicity than advertising. The idea that some sort of third party endorsement accrued to publicity because it had been accepted by editors gave rise to estimates of increases in impact by a factor of three or seven or any number. Recent research indicates that implied third-party endorsement doesn't occur. PR scholar Glen Cameron's research indicated that there is some effect in delayed memory of a message but not enough to be significant. Scholar Kirk Hallahan's research found that people knew the ads were trying to sell them something but they preferred to get product information from ads, and were not sure how much to trust information in the news media without question, especially when the product or issue was important to them.[66]

What about the impact of news media at all? Increasing criticism of news media as doing more entertaining than informing has many asking how important the mass media are to recipients. The argument is not new. You'll find it in effects theories of mass communication. Some argue that mass media have very strong effects on recipients and others say the effects are not so strong. Researchers have examined this for decades, from the magic bullet concept that a message sent through a medium hit its target to later worries over whether it hit at all and with what impact.[67] Neither end of the spectrum seems to have an edge at this point in terms of research evidence.

Information processing is critical in evaluating the impact (or potential impact) of communication. Carl Hovland established the idea of changing attitudes in order to change opinions, and this became known as the Yale approach to persuasion. He pointed out that effective communication involved attention, comprehension, acceptance and retention. Using Lasswell's model of who said what to whom with what effect, Hovland identified source, message, audience and audience reaction as the elements of the processing cycle. The source had to evidence power, competence, trustworthiness, goodwill, idealism, similarity (to audience) and dynamism. The credibility (trust, goodwill, idealism, similarity) and authority (power, competence, dynamism) of the source are the major conceptual factors in the Yale model.

William McGuire saw a flaw in the Yale information-processing theories. Hovland and his associates, McGuire felt, had ignored the relationship between comprehension and acceptance. Instead of emphasizing the *source*, McGuire focused on the *receiver*. His modifications clarified the relationship between comprehension and acceptance, indicating their separate effects on a persuasive message's impact. Personality traits of message recipients, he said, affected comprehension, acceptance of messages and persuasion in general. McGuire reduced the steps of the Yale model to two—receiving message content and yielding to what is comprehended—arguing that, to make a change of attitude or opinion possible, a person has to receive a message effectively and then yield to its point.

McGuire, like Hovland and associates, assumed that new cognitive information was learned from the content of the messages. That supposition was challenged by Anthony Greenwald, who said that people did not learn message content, but rather created their own covert messages idiosyncratically in response to the original message. However, Greenwald's cognitive response approach tells more about "the *covariation* between self-generated messages and their effects than it does about *why* covert conditions generate cognitive realignments and behavior changes."[68]

Other theories of social and cognitive behavior also help explain message effects. We know that messages are incorporated into an individual's agenda if they help that person meet a particular goal. Planning theory is considered when public relations practitioners analyze audiences to find the information seekers. Planning theory, developed by Charles Berger, was designed to explain how individuals plan their communication not only just seeking information but also in communicating. For example, students often arrange a meeting with their instructors not to get information but to express their concern about their performance and convey their goal to be successful in the class. Asking how to accomplish that is a communication behavior designed to convince the instructor of their efforts more than to gain cues for improving their performance. Planning is used to accomplish all sorts of goals, social as well as personal. Think of how often you have said that if plan A doesn't work, you'll go to plan B.

Social psychologist Kurt Lewin observed that people process information and "compute" attitudes to make logical combinations.[69] *Group dynamics* are important in this process because individuals try to adjust their opinions and perceptions in response to group norms and pressures toward uniformity. Motivation, said Lewin, is socially based, which means that the group has the power to reward for compliance or to punish for deviation. Leon Festinger's *theory of cognitive dissonance*, discussed previously, states that people strive to reduce discrepancies that exist within their own cognitive system.

Explaining people's efforts to make sense of others' behavior is called *attribution theory*. According to Fritz Heider, two types of causes are used to explain behavior: situational (external) causes and dispositional (internal) causes. The type we choose depends on some suppositions. If people often do unusual things in different situations for reasons we can't discern, we may attribute their behavior to an internal or dispositional cause. The problem with such assumptions is that analysts tend to oversimplify and overestimate people's consistency in behavior and tend to see an internal reason when the external situation might have had more bearing. Clearly people do take behavior cues from their environment, and they also have some reason to explain their behavior. The question is which comes first: the reason or the behavior?

Social learning theory holds that continuous reciprocal interaction and continuous feedback occur between a person's internal cognition and the situation. What we learn through experience, observation, listening or reading and establishing symbolic relationships teaches us to expect different consequences in different situations for the same behavior. In addition, according to the theory, reinforcements are different for various people, depending on such factors as value systems. Another element of social learning theory states that, in order for learning to occur, a person must remember and expect something to occur again. Extinction is one way to change behavior. Extinction may occur when the anticipated result of an action is withheld (for example, when a parent does not respond with attention to a child's tantrum as the child expects). Rules, instructions or communications can also be used to change behaviors.

The public relations practitioner thus has a choice of several theories to apply in planning message strategy to reach a goal. The option selected may be to encourage people to belong (Lewin). It may be to avoid a message that conflicts with values or—if people are already in a state of cognitive dissonance—to help them reconcile the value conflict through rationalization (Festinger). Self-persuasion, remember, is the most successful form of persuasion. The strategy might also be to provide environmental cues (Heider) that are likely to appeal to a target group (such as using an impressive setting—for example, a black-tie event—to mark the opening of a new building). Or it may be an ongoing

educational program to develop expectations (as in the case of antismoking campaigns that aim at making smokers feel uncomfortable whenever they light up in a public place).

Some researchers feel that a model devised by Martin Fishbein is useful in predicting group attitudes. The Fishbein model can be used to identify and categorize consumers according to criteria that are significant to the consumers themselves, and for this reason it may have practical implications for marketing specialists in particular.[70]

Fishbein himself has contended that his model can measure both a person's emotional evaluation of a concept or object and his or her beliefs about that object. He has asserted further than it can be used to demonstrate that a person's belief may change independently of attitude, with the result that two people may differ in belief but have similar attitudes.[71]

Some researchers say that opinions and facts both represent answers to questions, making it impossible to draw a sharp line between them. A fuzzy line may separate opinions and attitudes as well, although opinions can be verbalized, whereas attitudes often cannot (they may be subconscious).

The opinions, attitudes and actions of people are all affected by family, friends, informal work groups and formal groups such as clubs and organizations. Group influence and pressure become particularly apparent during controversy, according to research evidence. When issues are clear, group pressure influences at most only one third of the people, with two thirds standing firm. If even a small countervailing voice comes in, the third shrinks away. Only when ambiguity and confusion reign can you count on a bandwagon effect, which means that factors other than the propaganda device itself determine media effectiveness.[72]

Getting people to believe something is easier than preventing them from accepting something you don't want them to believe. One popular idea is that early exposure to some opposing arguments will inoculate hearers against future belief in the opponents. Other evidence suggests, though, that any preliminary message may weaken the impact of a persuasive opposing attack that might follow. Some evidence also suggests that trying to elicit a critical viewpoint in a public can either inhibit or enhance the effect of a message that is to come. If you try to turn people against a message or against the messenger, your efforts could have the opposite effect of inoculating them against further negative criticisms. The effect could be to make them more vulnerable to future persuasive appeals by opponents. But reception and acceptance of a later persuasive appeal are determined by both the target of criticism and the nature of the critical act. Therefore, the situation could be manipulated to have some bearing on the outcome.

The purpose of a persuasive communication is often concealed, becoming apparent only after careful examination. Comparing the obvious content with its intent may be done in examining such organized propaganda campaigns as those launched internally by a government or directed by one government against another, as in psychological warfare. Psychological warfare is as old as war itself. Although it has become more sophisticated, its goals remain basically the same: first, to convert subjects from one allegiance to another; second, to divide the opposition into defeatable groups; third, to consolidate existing support; and fourth, to counteract or refute another propaganda theme.[73]

Certain kinds of persuasive language can diminish people's critical thinking skills, although such language doesn't completely eliminate the ability to think critically. Rather, persuasive language triggers mental processes that are related to memories, imagery and emotion more so than to analytical thought.

Regarding retention of information, researcher Carl Hovland finds that, during an initial period, people forget verbal material rapidly; this forgetfulness gradually decreases until little further loss is noticeable. (Sometimes, in fact, the amount remembered over a period of time actually increases.) He also has found that people retain meaningful material better than obscure material, but that overusing even good material in order to emphasize it can have a boomerang effect. Moreover, the more completely people learn material initially, the longer they will remember it. Hovland also found that repeating a message up to three or four times usually increases the degree of people's attention, but that too frequent repetition without reward is likely to lead to inattention, boredom and disregard of the communication.[74]

Communications researcher Steuart Henderson Britt developed a whole set of learning principles that apply to consumer behavior:

1. Unpleasant appeals can be learned as readily as pleasant ones.
2. Appeals made over a period of time are more effective.
3. Unique messages are better remembered.
4. It is easier to recognize an appeal than to recall it.

5. Knowledge of results increases learning of a message.
6. Repetition is more effective when related to belongingness and satisfaction.
7. Messages are easier to learn when they do not interfere with earlier habits.
8. Learning a new pattern of behavior can interfere with remembering something else.[75]

One thing is certain about communication: You can never tell whether you have achieved understanding of your message unless you provide the recipient with a way to respond. Measuring understanding—rather than just message reception—was the task undertaken by two researchers, M. Beth Heffner and Kenneth Jackson.[76] They used pictures and verbal descriptions of the pictures to see whether the verbal descriptions resulted in the same mental impressions on readers as the pictures. Results showed that understanding seems to occur independently of the messages received verbally (which can occur without their being understood). Conversely, understanding can occur when messages are altered. The researchers also found that having a cognitive frame of reference helped students determine meaning. If students had the same basis for organizing information, it increased their comprehension of the messages' meaning. Some verbal descriptions were more reliable than the picture themselves. Another thing noticed was that symbols can be misunderstood. This has happened occasionally when American advertising has been "exported" without due research into the culture or mores of another country.

The complexities of operations in an international community are heightened by the sophisticated technology of instantaneous satellite communications and the Internet. Although the satellite picture or email message might be technically clear, the message can be easily misunderstood. This increases the communicators' responsibility to ensure the fidelity of message reception through conscientious research, attention to research findings and cultural sensitivity.

Because information processing is such a critical factor in communication, models that predict behavior successfully are important in planning a communication campaign. James E. Grunig has considered publics along a spectrum from active to inactive and characterized their behavior toward information in each category to predict what type of person would be seeking information or just processing it.

The significance of this to public relations people is that some publics are just not going to respond to information. Those that need to get information are latent publics—groups that share a common concern or interest, but are not aware that others do because they are not likely to seek the information but will be responsive to it. It's a useful model.

Research supports two aspects of Grunig's model. The research shows that individuals are more likely to seek and process information if they anticipate that it will help them solve a problem and if they are personally involved in trying to solve the problem. The research also supports the prediction that people who are constrained (and therefore would not be free to implement a solution if they had one) are less likely to seek or process information, although this relationship was largely explained by other independent variables. Another factor, beyond the individual's inclination, is the organization. An integrated model of the two concepts can be instructive in employee communications.[77,78] Because most companies now have an intranet for their employee communication, there have been attempts to make that intranet part of corporate strategic communication, but so far only in high-tech companies.[79]

Much of a public's response to persuasive information in a situation that requires a behavioral change has to do with where it lies in the diffusion process. The diffusion process has six phases:

Phase I: Awareness (also called *presenting*, as in presenting information)—The public learns about an idea or practice but lacks detail.

Phase II: Information (also called *attending*, as in getting someone's attention)—The public gets facts, develops interest, sees possibilities.

Phase III: Evaluation (also called *comprehending*, an understanding of the appeal)—The public tries it mentally, weighs alternatives.

Phase IV: Trial (also called *yielding*)—The information achieves social acceptability, experimentation.

Phase V: Adoption (also treated as one aspect of *retaining*)—The public adopts the information for full-scale use.

Phase VI: Reinforcement (also treated as the other aspect of *retaining*)—The public displays continued, unswerving commitment.[80]

Other studies show that when there's a conceptual match between attitudes and behavior, there is a stronger relationship between the two.[81]

Discussions about how people's behavior can be affected through persuasion make many of us uncomfortable, even though most of us have been doing it all our lives. You learned as an infant what kind of behavior gained attention. As you got older, you learned the right words and the best timing to use in asking for money from a parent.

Behavioral psychologist B. F. Skinner made the following observation about the positive aspects of affecting what people do:

I am concerned with the possible relevance of a behavioral analysis to the problems of the world today. We are threatened by the unrestrained growth of the population, the exhaustion of resources, the pollution of the environment, and the specter of a nuclear holocaust. We have the physical and biological technology needed to solve most of those problems, but we do not seem to be able to put it to use. That is a problem in human behavior, and it is one to which an experimental analysis may offer a solution. Structuralism in the behavioral sciences has always been weak on the side of motivation. It does not explain why knowledge is acquired or put to use; hence, it has little to tell us about the conditions under which the human species will make the changes needed for its survival. If there is a solution to that problem, I believe that it will be found in the kind of understanding to which an experimental analysis of human behavior points.[82]

Not only did Skinner point to a critical flaw in the effort to use today's theoretical knowledge to predict what people will actually do, he also alluded to another difficulty. Today's problems are global, but today's theories are culture-bound. Most research has been done in Western societies; and even within them, little attention has been paid to nonwhite minorities—who, of course, are the majority in much of the world. One way to compensate for this gap is to read refereed scholarly journals on a regular basis. Many articles offer updates and new insights into the application of theories through testing them, and increasingly scholarship from other countries that tests application of theory in another culture is adding significantly to the potential to use theory as it should be, the underpinnings of practice.

Discussion Questions

1. What questions does organizational theory suggest you need to ask about an organization's communications climate before you go to work there, or work with the organization as a client?

2. Who is the best person to talk you into doing something you'd really rather not do? What theories suggest why that person is likely to be successful?

3. What media are your major sources for news? Why? What theory or theories explain this best?

4. Do communication theory models created and tested in the USA apply in other cultures?

5. If you are doing some research to find out what people think and you suspect you are not getting what they really think, what theories might explain this?

6. Have you observed or experienced something that you think might provide a new theory? What do you think is going on, that is, what is your hypothesis? Why do you think so? Are there some theories you've read about here that might apply? What are they and how are they applicable?

Points to Remember

- Current theories about media are undergoing reconsideration as a result of "new" media and convergence within traditional media.

- When someone holds a strong opposing opinion, you are probably wasting your time trying to win that person over to your view. Usually, all you can hope to do is to limit whatever effects the person may have on persons who are undecided or uncommitted.

- There are three basic ways to get people to do what you want: power, patronage and persuasion.

- Public relations involves persuasion as well as accommodation. At the least, public relations involves articulating a point of view that may differ from that of members of a public.

- To be persuasive, a message has to present something of value to the target public.

- Theories applied to public relations practice come from a number of different disciplines and have been adapted for PR. Of six most-used theories, four come from sociology and two from psychology.

- From general systems theory, cybernetic systems theory is often applied to PR.

- Two other especially important theories are: cultural and critical/postmodern. Because most theories take some time to be applied, tested and modified, their origins are "old," and in fact, postmodern theory, although dating from the mid-1960s, is considered too "new" to have many tested applications.

- Three communication models are used most frequently to explain what happens in PR practice: a standard communication model (media-related), a behavior model (persuasion-related) and a symmetrical model (strategic management–related).

- What we know today is that research is needed at every level, and that every level is affected by feedback.

- What research tells us about the source for communication is important to public relations because we get to choose the source for messages.

- Message content has consequences, and the way the information is presented has an impact on the effect.

- The media orientation of publics is critical information because media deliver the messages.

- The PR practitioner's view of the recipient is often what advertisers have used: reach, recall and reaction.

Go to the Web site for this book at **www.cengage.com/masscomm/newsom/thisispr10e** to find more Web links on this subject.

Other Related Web Sites to Review

International Communication Association
   http://icahdq.org

Institute for Public Relations, USA
   http://www.instituteforpr.com

Institute of Public Relations, UK
   http://www.ipr.org.uk

CHAPTER 7

PR Ethics and Responsibilities

OBJECTIVES

- To appreciate the complexity of public relations ethical decision making in a twenty-first-century global, multicultural and technological society.

- To recognize the wide range of stakeholders to whom public relations practitioners and their organizations have ethical responsibilities.

- To understand that public relations practitioners have personal, as well as professional, responsibilities in ethical decision making.

- To develop a sensitivity about how unethical conduct can create public relations crises.

- To create a heightened awareness of potential ethical problems that can occur within an organization.

[T]he crisis in communication facing the United States and, to varying degrees, the entire world, is one aspect of the broader crisis emanating from the tension of combining a highly concentrated corporate-driven economy that generates significant social inequality and insecurity with an ostensibly free and democratic society.

—Robert W. McChesney, *Rich Media, Poor Democracy: Communication Politics in Dubious Times*[1]

Two Wolves (Unknown Author)
One evening an old Cherokee told his grandson about a battle that goes on inside people. He said, "My son, the battle is between two 'wolves' inside us all.
"The one wolf's name is Evil. It is anger, envy, jealousy, sorrow, regret, greed, arrogance, self-pity, guilt, resentment, inferiority, lies, false pride, superiority and ego.
"The other wolf's name is Good. It is joy, peace, love, hope, serenity, humility, kindness, benevolence, empathy, generosity, truth, compassion and faith."
The grandson thought about it for a minute and then asked his grandfather:
"Which wolf wins?"
The old Cherokee simply replied, "The one you feed."[2]

A public relations professor approached a colleague in philosophy to ask about offering a communications ethics course that would be cross-listed with philosophy, offering the philosophy professor some codes of ethics from journalism as well as from public relations. The philosophy professor shook his head incredulously, saying, "I didn't know you folks had any ethics."

Outside the university, others question the attempt to teach ethics in college courses in general. One argument is that it's too late by the time people reach college age. Another is that ethical behavior is culture-bound. Certainly culture is a factor in what is considered ethical behavior.

Ethics are founded on moral principles that are themselves grounded in effects. This holds true whether you subscribe to the idea that a moral judgment must fulfill only *formal* conditions that are universal and prescriptive or whether you think it must also meet a *material* condition for the welfare of society as a whole. In either case, "ethical behavior recognizes and rests within a shared interest," according to Ivan Hill, writing for the Ethics Resource Center.[3]

Judgments about an organization's standing are made in three areas: ethics, social responsibility and financial responsibility. An organization's sense of commitment toward its publics (which often have conflicting interests among one another) has to be articulated and demonstrated.

When Arthur W. Page was hired by AT&T in 1927 as the first corporate vice-president of public relations ever in the USA, he advocated this philosophy: "Be sure our deeds match our words"—and vice versa.[4]

Ethics and responsibilities are public relations concerns on two levels. We have to consider the behavior of the individual practitioner and that of the institution she or he represents. Public relations has been called the "conscience" of management, which underscores PR's role in reminding an organization of its social responsibility to all of its publics.

Actually, most research supports the idea that top management sets the ethical tone for an organization. Management, after all, chooses both inside public relations staff and the outside firm or agency that may be employed to complement or supply public relations work. If those public relations people see themselves as simply functionary "order takers" for management,

and that management is unethical, then there's little hope for financial and social responsibility. Highly visible ethical lapses by organizations with PR staff or contracted firms have received a great deal of public attention in books, magazine articles and television shows. Such attention has not done much to improve the reputation of public relations people who are supposed to be advising management of ways to gain and maintain their own good reputations.

The challenge for internal and external public relations people is to guide those who hire them to responsible actions that are founded on integrity. To maintain standards of practice for public relations that don't allow representation of unethical behavior means having the courage to stand up for ethical codes as well as having a strong set of personal values. It also means having the courage of one's convictions and refusing to do what is unethical.

Theory and Research Perspective

Ethics at theoretical and strategic levels can be exceedingly complex; intuitive "do the right thing" answers may not always be the correct ones. One fundamental question is whether corporations can be held ethically responsible for their actions in the way that individual people are held accountable. Some people argue yes, because corporations can control their actions and make rational decisions from a range of options that are available to them. However, being moral is more complex for an organization than for an individual—partly because corporations have a tremendous effect upon society. Amitai Etzioni, for example, says that corporations in the USA cannot impose conditions of employment that are unconstitutional. However, can corporations ban individuals' conduct outside the workplace, as well as any other private behavior that may affect the health care costs that these corporations must pay?[1] What about values? Paul Kennedy maintains that dominant corporate value systems must adhere to Western rationalism, scientific inquiry, legal theory and capitalism. Thus, he questions whether those companies sharing cultures of some developing societies can compete in the global economic arena.[2] However, it would be dangerously naïve to assume that the corporate model based on Western culture will always prevail globally or that such a perspective is necessarily the most moral. *The Economist* observes that companies are now paying elaborate attention to corporate social responsibility, appointing corporate social responsibility (CSR) officers, consultants, departments and initiatives. However, it argues that there is much to be said for leaving social and economic policy to governments, which are accountable to voters. The British news magazine argues that, if companies want to make the world a better place, they should concentrate on discharging their obligations to shareholders, the people who are paying their wages.[3]

---

[1]Amitai Etzioni, *The Spirit of Community: The Reinvention of American Society* (New York: Touchstone, 1994).

[2]Paul Kennedy, *Preparing for the Twenty-First Century* (New York: Vintage Books, 1993).

[3]"The Good Company," *The Economist*, 374(8410) (January 22, 2005), pp. 3–4.

Source: Dean Kruckeberg, "The Public Relations Practitioner's Role in Practicing Strategic Ethics," *Public Relations Quarterly*, 45, Fall 2000, pp. 35–9.

It is not difficult to find examples in news from throughout the world of organizations' and individuals' ethical abuses or perceptions of abuses and wrongdoing. New York Governor Eliot Spitzer resigned amidst allegations that he had sex with expensive prostitutes.[5] National Football League Commissioner Roger Goodell penalized the New England Patriots and the team's head coach after an assistant was caught videotaping New York Jets defensive signals from the sidelines, a violation of league rules.[6] Syndicated journalist Armstrong Williams was found to have accepted cash payments for covering and promoting the government program No Child Left Behind. The payments were funneled through a large respected public relations agency.[7] Congress and at least two states investigated questionable relationships between colleges and student loan lenders, including arrangements in which lenders routed a percentage of student-loan revenue back to the schools that recommended them as preferred lenders together with allegations that a lender had given stock grants or paid consulting fees to financial aid officers at schools that recommended the lender to their students.[8] Two medical journals suggested that Merck & Co. violated scientific-publishing ethics by ghostwriting academic articles and minimized patient deaths in its analyses of some human trials of a drug later linked to cardiac problems.[9]

Although extremely complex, the study of ethics falls into two broad categories: **comparative ethics**, which is the purview of social scientists; and **normative ethics**, generally the domain of philosophers and theologians. Comparative ethics, sometimes called *descriptive ethics*, is a study of how different cultures observe ethical standards. Both diversity and similarity are of interest to social scientists. However, the social

PR in Practice

The late professor Rich Long, who taught at Brigham Young University, noted recent examples of how to ruin a corporate reputation: break the law, lie to the news media and to others, ignore warnings, don't consider the opinions of critics and sacrifice employees and retirees for the benefit of bonuses and stock benefits to top management.[1] Professor Long pointed to Enron, a once $100 billion (*Fortune* 10) company whose stock plummeted from $83.00 to $0.25 per share. In addition to the harm done to Enron and its stakeholders through its corporate misbehavior, there also has been a tremendous "spinoff" effect on other corporations, including Arthur Andersen, Enron's former accounting firm. That highly respected firm was accused of shredding evidence related to Enron. Although the firm fired its auditor in charge of Enron's business, the discharged employee claimed he was only following orders.[2] One member of Arthur Andersen's outside public relations team reported he had been so busy because of the Enron crisis that he hadn't been home in 18 days, leaving his apartment with a two-day supply of clean clothes, but having to make trips to Florida and Washington. A reporter for *The Wall Street Journal* called all the work that was created "the Enron effect." Workplaces throughout the country have extra income from Enron's misfortune. Fallout from the demise of this huge company has lasted for years, of course.[3] The late public relations educator Bill Adams, a longtime senior corporate practitioner, said most senior-level public relations practitioners are ethical. However, when in a company having an arrogant, closed culture, there are only two things a practitioner can do: (1) try to help change the culture, pointing out the benefits of doing so, both internally and externally, or (2) quit. But he added rhetorically, "Can you do the job of a professional public relations person within an organization that disdains two-way communication and mutual understanding?"[4]

[1]Rich Long, "Countering Corporate Arrogance," *Public Relations Strategist,* 8 (Spring 2002), pp. 6, 7, 9 and 10.

[2]Rich Long, "New Challenges Arising From Enron," *Public Relations Strategist,* 8 (Spring 2002), p. 8.

[3]"Enron: Crisis—and Opportunity," *The Wall Street Journal*, January 23, 2002, p. B1.

[4]Long, "Countering Corporate Arrogance."

scientist looks for evidence that can be verified, and in a study of ethics such questions as whether ethical behaviors are a part of human nature spill over into other areas, such as theology and philosophy.

PR educator Hugh Culbertson observes that the philosopher and author Sissela Bok takes a near absolute position that decisions are either morally right or wrong.[10] But there is another basis for decision making—what is referred to as **situational ethics**, which sees ethical standards not as constant but as varying or flexible in application to specific occasions or situations. Culbertson's observations of students suggest that they lean more toward situational ethics. Bok, too, recognizes that lies can sometimes serve a good purpose, says Culbertson. (One example is protecting Jewish houseguests from discovery by Nazi soldiers by lying about their presence. A more common and less dramatic example might be telling a friend who asks your opinion that you think her new and expensive outfit is becoming when you think it isn't.) But, Bok asserts, in choosing between lying and truth telling, the presumption is always against lying, for the following reasons:

1. Dishonesty leads to lack of trust and cynicism—such as when a reporter later discovers that a PR person has told half-truths, resulting in an inaccurate story.

2. Lying is an exercise in coercion, forcing someone to act differently from the way he or she would have behaved if given the truth.

3. Lying is resented by those deceived, even if the deceived are liars themselves.

4. Dishonesty is likely to be discovered, and no climate for credibility can be reestablished.

5. Decisions about when to lie are often made without calculating either alternatives or consequences.

6. A lie often demands another lie to cover it up, and then others to maintain the prevarications.[11] Dishonesty is seldom ambiguous, but some public relations actions are. ■

Complexities in Ethical Decision Making

Part of the problem for public relations people trying to behave in an ethical way is that they are hired to be advocates, whether they are employees of an organization or employees of a firm hired to represent an organization. Public relations people have a role to play as educators or informers, telling what an organization is and does, but also as persuaders, convincing publics to support that organization, which, of course, must deserve this support.

One reason the two-way symmetrical model for public relations, discussed in Chapter 1, is seen as desirable is that it allows for input from all affected publics and for negotiations about policy decisions. The reality, however, is that negotiation with all of an organization's publics is simply not practical. Nothing would get done! In practice an organization should try to act in such a way that even when its actions negatively affect one or more of its publics (such as through the closing of an unprofitable facility), those who are affected will understand and accept the decision, even if they don't like it. Furthermore, publics can change the organization as much as the organization's public relations efforts can change the beliefs, attitudes, opinions and even behaviors of publics.

Ethics and Values

Certainly someone who is ethical would tell the truth, right? One problem is inherent in the use of the word *truth* to mean factually accurate, in which case one can be factually accurate and still deceive. The other problem is that for something to be a fact, it has to be something about which most people agree. There still is a Flat Earth Society (http://www.theflatearthsociety.org), even after photos from space testify to the earth's roundness. Most people accept the photos and other evidence that the earth is a sphere. This is a verifiable truth. Some "truths" are actually people's perceptions of events, **data** and pictures. Our own bias or view of the world affects how we see things and react to information. Then, too, our beliefs and personal values influence how we define "truth." (If you don't want to accept that, just think for a moment about why we have so many different religions in the world. Which one has the monopoly on the "truth"?)

Many individuals and organizations have strong positions on such issues as drinking and abortion, for example. Sometimes, organizations compromise, however. After admitting defeat in convincing students that drinking can be dangerous, many higher education institutions are emphasizing moderation over abstinence, and alcoholic beverage manufacturers are pleased to help spread this message, investing money and other resources into these programs.

"Social-norms marketing," oftentimes referred to as "social marketing," involves placing advertisements in campus newspapers and displaying messages on posters, T-shirts, coffee mugs and screen savers to stress that students should drink sensibly, that is, not more than four or five drinks a week. Colleges and universities thereby must decide whether their partners in these campaigns against alcohol abuse should be the very companies that make and market the beer and liquor that young people drink. Drinking on campus, of course, has frequently been linked to fatalities, rapes, drunk driving incidents and vandalism.[12] Sometimes opposing groups do not compromise. When the early abortion pill known as RU-486 became available in the USA, after years of controversy, proponents of abortion rights were funding projects to boost access to the drug regimen, whereas opponents were barraging doctors with mail noting potential hazards.[13]

As a practical matter, Arthur W. Page offered six management principles that lead to ethical behavior:

1. Tell the truth. Let the public know what's happening and provide an accurate picture of the company's character, ideals and practices.

2. Prove it with action. Public perception of an organization is determined 90 percent by doing and 10 percent by talking.

3. Listen to the customer. To serve the public well, you need to understand what it needs and wants. Keep top decision-makers and other employees informed of public reaction to company products, policies and practices.

4. Manage for tomorrow. Anticipate public reaction and eliminate practices that create difficulties. Create goodwill.

5. Conduct public relations as if the whole company depends on it. It does. Corporate relations is a management function. No corporate strategy should be implemented without considering its external and internal public relations impact. The PR practitioner is a policy-maker, not just a publicist.

6. Remain calm, patient and good-humored. Lay the groundwork for public relations miracles with consistent, calm and reasoned attention to information and contacts. When a crisis comes, you will be prepared and know exactly what to do to defuse it.

These principles underscored the Page philosophy: "Real success, both for big business and the public, lies in large enterprise conducting itself in the public interest and in such a way that the public will give it sufficient freedom to serve effectively."[14]

An organization's standing depends on its actions, and an organization's *good* standing depends on its acting in an ethical manner. An organization also is judged on how ethical its publics *perceive* it to be. For example, if your organization's board of directors adopts an antitakeover device—a poison pill—and your news release says that the pill is not to prevent takeovers, whom are you kidding? If your organization is a bank that is reported to be failing, and you deny that you are looking for help to avoid failing, how do you think you look to the people who are considering helping you? Depositors fearful of losing their money will withdraw funds immediately because you obviously can't be trusted.

Once again, beliefs are important to the public perception of an organization. When you measure a public's view of your ethics, you are asking if it thinks you deserve to exist. Don't be surprised if your organization is seen as undeserving.

Ethics are often defined as just "doing what's right." But, in different cultures, "right" may be "wrong." The fact that ethics are culture-bound creates some difficulties for global public relations practice. The view of an organization's ethics is likely to be based not so much on a definition of morality as on an understanding of the consequences of what the organization says and does, which are seen as either moral or immoral by its publics. Beliefs about social responsibility strongly influence whether and to what extent publics see the organization as being a good citizen, either locally or globally.

Public Consent

PR pioneers Arthur W. Page and Edward Bernays both emphasized that organizations in democratic societies exist with the consent of their publics. In that light, it is appropriate to look at the issue of responsibility in detail.

Social responsibility, another term for good citizenship, means producing sound products or reliable services that don't threaten the environment, and contributing positively to the social, political and economic health of society. It also means compensating employees fairly and treating them justly, regardless of the cultural environment in which you operate. It means protecting the pension plans of employees as much as possible. Clearly translated, this means no poorly paid "slave" labor and no discriminatory or "sweatshop" practices in an organization's home country or elsewhere around the world. It means never offering overpriced or potentially dangerous junk in the guise of a high-quality product. It means refusing to misuse this small planet and its creatures, both human and nonhuman. It means restoring and protecting the earth and its natural resources as well as anything else your organization might damage or threaten during its business operations.

Financial responsibility generally refers to an organization's fiscal soundness, as indicated by such measures as market or audience share; but it also includes how the organization interacts with investors and investment advisers. Public relations has its own financial responsibility: to measure and evaluate its own contribution to the bottom line (an organization's profit margin).

These traditional measures of responsibility are important, of course, but just as significant are the perceptions people have about how a for-profit or nonprofit organization gets and spends its money. These facets of financial responsibility are too often overlooked in attempts to measure public images. Yet beliefs about an organization in these areas are strongly tied to confidence, trust and loyalty. For example, should we try to measure loyalty? If our organization becomes embroiled in a takeover fight, investors' loyalty may be absolutely critical. How many of our large individual stockholders will retain their holdings in the face of escalating offers?

As public relations people, we hope that our organization's image will influence our stockholders to retain their confidence in the organization's leadership. And the same goes for "stakeholders." Suppose that you represent a nonprofit organization—a museum, say—and you are trying to recruit volunteers to serve in it at a time when it is receiving heavy public criticism. You must rely on the long-standing goodwill of the public toward the museum and on the ability of current volunteers to reinforce this in the community. The goodwill must be a strong resource, however, because you'll need it to bolster current volunteers' morale. The key point here is that traditional measures of financial responsibility most often are *not* adequate.

In all three areas—ethics, social responsibility and financial responsibility—publics are likely to believe that public relations people are trying to influence them. The fact that PR does work to change people's views causes the individual practitioner's ethics to be closely entwined with the

organization's social responsibility. The frequent tension inherent in the role is clearly articulated by journalism professor Marvin Olasky. He says that free-market competition forced PR practitioners (as voices for corporate America) to seek government regulation as a means of eliminating competition while they spoke publicly of supporting free enterprise. But the very pursuit of "social responsibility," Olasky says, has fostered the popular notion that there are no "private" areas of business—that is, no areas that are off limits to public scrutiny. In attempting to say *something* while at the same time protecting an organization's business, the PR person often deceives, according to Olasky. Olasky also asserts that, the closer business moves toward government, the more likely it is to try to affect the political process.[15]

Corporate philanthropy will not necessarily guarantee goodwill; and not all efforts to be socially responsible are necessarily perceived in a favorable light. On June 11, 2008, Wal-Mart announced a $500,000 commitment to help with relief efforts in the wake of flash floods in the Midwestern USA. The retailer's commitment, a combination of both cash and merchandise donations, helped flood victims throughout Illinois, Indiana, Iowa, Nebraska and Wisconsin. The American Red Cross and The Salvation Army each received a portion of the funds, and Wal-Mart worked with both organizations to provide food, water and other life-sustaining products to those who had been affected by the floods.[16] Despite a history of generous support for many worthy causes, Wal-Mart is frequently criticized for its effect on local economies and is accused of providing low-paying jobs with poor benefits and of undercutting prices by importing merchandise from foreign countries. *The Wall Street Journal* in May 2008 reported the results of experiments indicating that consumers would pay a slight premium for ethically made goods, but they would buy unethically made products only at a steep discount. The researchers concluded that companies should segment their market and make a particular effort to reach out to buyers with high ethical standards, because those are the customers who could deliver the biggest potential profits on ethically produced goods.[17]

Responsibility to Whom?

There will always be some people in the business world who are convinced that all they need is a lawyer

Global Perspective

Media bribery is a global phenomenon that directly affects public relations practice, the integrity of the news media and the citizens of countries where it occurs. And it occurs throughout the world. Toni Muzi Falconi, a senior counsel at an Italian management consultancy, reports the following information in his blog about paying bribes to place news releases in the media, which is sometimes called black PR.

An April 2007 study of the business community in Lithuania about the role of black PR revealed that:

■ Thirty-five percent believe that all public relations agencies indulge in those practices and 50 percent say that those practices are mostly used to gain direct advantages for their clients. Forty-percent say that they are used to smear their clients' competitors.

■ Thirty-three percent of the sample say that they themselves have been victims of black PR and the same number believe that in Lithuania the practice is more widespread than elsewhere.

■ There is some optimism in the 32 percent who say the phenomena is decreasing while 28 percent insist that it is instead increasing.

■ Finally 47 percent believe black PR is not a crime, 40 percent indicate that it is less serious than bribing a public official while 10 percent say it is the same.

Inga Latkovska, from Latvia, was quoted as saying that in her country it was easy to bribe the media, and Yaryna Klyuchkovska, from Ukraine, estimated that "some 50 percent of the PR spent goes in those practices, without even considering political PR where it certainly was much higher." Thorsten Lutzler of the DPRG, the German public relations association, said that 54 percent of the German public believes that PR is propaganda. Thorsten described recent cases of black PR in his country, including the millionaire lobbyist who was found having the same bank account as the defense minister, media coverage for money, television soap opera producers paid by companies to plug their products and paid blogging practices. He questioned whether certain related marketing tactics were not also to be considered as black PR. Thorsten said that the DPRG had a new policy to go out in public and denounce every bad practice. In 2006 there were 28 DPRG council decisions, 24 of which ended with public reprehensions. This is more than all the previous 20 years of the association's history.

Yaryna Klyuchkovska, former chair of the board of the Ukrainian Association of Public Relations (UAPR), which is a professional association of young reformist-minded professionals, reports in the collaborative blog *PR Conversations* that "The Ugly Side of Eastern European PR. I Wish It Were a Joke":

"Here is an ad that a Ukrainian firm mails to prospective clients. It's self-explanatory, really. 'SmartManager company offers:

1. Placing PR-materials in the elite pool of publications that usually decline to publish paid-for materials without marking them as advertising.

2. Placing stories in Ukrainian media (television, Internet, press, radio) on the most attractive terms.

3. Producing high quality PR texts effectively forming the public opinion without being identified as paid-for. We write with a deep knowledge of the specifics of the Ukrainian market and the local mentality.

4. Securing comments from Ukraine's leading economists and political experts in the format required by the client.

5. Possibility of purchasing comments from leading Ukrainian politicians.

6. Mitigating the effect of negative PR stories. Intercepting negative stories.

7. Monitoring the effectiveness of the impact the paid-for stories have on the position of the media.

N.B. We can publish a paid-for story without marking it as advertising in every single media outlet registered in Ukraine at very attractive prices.

(continued)

Global Perspective (continued)

Our partners include:

State government bodies

International organizations

Political parties of Ukraine'

"No, I really must say that this generated a genuine outrage among Ukrainian PR practitioners. A lively discussion ensued in blogs and forums. I sincerely hope this is some sort of a hoax devised to disclose the unethical practices. Otherwise, I don't really understand what is happening to the world if in 2007 people openly advertise these "services" and call them "public relations.""

Sources: Toni Muzi Falconi, "Blogging from Vilnius on Black PR. A Really Freezing Shower for All of Us!," PR Conversations, April 19, 2007, accessed June 20, 2008, from http://www.prconversations.com/?p=210#more-210 and Yaryna Klyuchkovska, "The Ugly Side of Eastern European PR. I Wish It Were a Joke," *PR Conversations*, June 27, 2007, accessed June 20, 2008, from http://www.prconversations.com/?p=265.

to keep them out of jail and a PR practitioner to keep bad news out of the paper.

Actually, public relations must create constant awareness by management of the institution's responsibility to all its publics. Most professional PR practitioners recognize that they and their organizations have ethical responsibilities to at least 10 different publics:

1. *Clients:* Being responsible to a client means not only being judicious with his or her money, but also (sometimes) saying no, because the customer is *not* always right. When a client is wrong, it is important to say so—to tell truths substantiated by facts discovered through honest research.

2. *News media:* These deserve honest and valid use of their channels; that is, you should not involve them in compromising situations, such as by lying or feeding them misleading or incomplete information. PR practitioners are accused by news media more often for sins of omission than of commission. A responsible PR person may not be expected to call news media attention to bad news but should be expected, when asked, to respond with a straightforward and complete presentation of the facts when the news media are pursuing an unfavorable story. Exceptions might occur in legal cases where specific or complete disclosure is required by law (for example, Securities and Exchange Commission [SEC] regulations) or is prudent (where events are matters of public record or otherwise legally accessible).

3. *Government agencies:* The PR person should be a source and resource for authoritative and accurate information that is needed and required by the government.

4. *Educational institutions:* There should be a good two-way system for sharing research, ideas and resources and for offering learning opportunities for students. Both sides can enhance their riches through close, professional cooperation.

5. *Consumers of your client's products and services:* An increasingly skeptical and demanding customer public can be exasperating, especially to those watching the profit-and-loss sheet, but sincerity and quality go a long way here. Consumers have a right to expect goodwill and integrity in products and services.

6. *Stockholders and analysts:* Many PR practitioners owe their jobs to investors in their business and to those who counsel such investments, because such investors provide the economic framework and the overall climate of confidence in an organization. Both investors and investment counselors need adequate information to make good decisions, and this calls for lucid interpretations of financial status, reliable annual reports and full explanations of company developments.

7. *Community:* Because the local community often provides critical elements such as utilities, tax breaks, cooperative zoning plans and chamber of commerce promotion, a community has a right to expect environmental protection, a fair tax return, employment of local people and corporate

contributions of funds and executive time to community projects.

8. *Competitors:* Other businesses have a right to expect from PR-advised firms a fair competitive environment that stays within the limits of the law and does not violate individual rights or privacy.

    The obligations of PR practitioners are set forth in the codes of ethics or standards for behavior promulgated by various professional PR organizations. (The Public Relations Society of America's Member Code of Ethics, with Interpretations, the International Association of Business Communicators [IABC] code and the IPRA code are included in the *Instructor's Manual* for this text.)

9. *Critics:* Public relations practice is likely to generate criticism from all of the preceding publics, but its very existence as an organizational role and function is criticized from at least two philosophical points of view. One set of critics complains that public relations practitioners impede rather than facilitate corporate social responsibility by rationalizing corporate actions and manipulating public opinion. For these reasons, they add, corporations do not bear the full measure of hostility they deserve from their various publics for ignoring quality-of-life factors that economic indicators may not reflect. These critics may not be fundamentally opposed to the capitalistic system, only to what they consider to be its abuses. They think the institutions of our society should voluntarily provide improvements in quality of life as well as economic well-being. They see public relations people as a cushion between management and the public's demand for social responsibility.

    Another philosophical set of critics might be categorized as human rights defenders, who are oftentimes members of nongovernmental organizations (NGOs), more recently called civil society organizations (CSOs). This group tends to speak out against public relations practitioners who represent unpopular clients—for example, leaders of countries that are reputed to be repressive.

10. *Public relations practitioners:* Other practitioners in the field itself expect practitioners to uphold standards of behavior that will win respect for the practice of public relations. This impulse provides the basis of the PRSA, IPRA and IABC codes and lies at the root of the discussions of licensing.

Public relations codes of ethical behavior or standards of practice have been called self-serving, but they do provide guidelines and, in some cases, an argument against pressures in the workplace.

Hadley Cantril succinctly identified the basis for appraising ethical public relations conduct:

> The "morality" or "ethical" nature—the correctness or rightness—of any action . . . is to be judged in terms of the degree to which it includes and integrates the purposes, and provides for the potential development of those purposes for all other people concerned in the action or possibly affected by it.[18]

Responsibility in Practice

Some areas of public relations practice considered legitimate by most practitioners nonetheless cause public concern and arouse criticism. Among the most obvious of these are how to conduct research (and how to use the resulting information), how to handle internal battles you lose with management and what to do about international activities when these involve working with foreign governments and corporations that operate according to codes of ethics that might conflict with your own.

Research and Persuasion Research is critical in all areas of public relations. (Chapter 4 of this book is devoted to the subject.) Finding out all that you can about the demographics and psychographics of your publics enables you to reach and communicate with them effectively. However, the uses of PR research and the purposes of persuasion must be examined by the practitioner to minimize opportunities for abuse.

The first ethical problem to resolve is how to collect the data. Whether you do the research yourself—in-house—or buy research services, you have to maintain certain standards toward the subjects used in the research. Earl Babbie, a highly respected social science researcher, identifies the following practices that must be safeguarded in a research study: (1) ensuring the voluntary participation of all subjects, including employees when the research is of internal publics; (2) preventing harm to the subjects, either psychologically (through participation itself or as a result of facing issues they would prefer to avoid) or through analysis and reporting (when self-identification could cause damage to self-image); (3) protecting participants through anonymity and/or confidentiality, the latter occurring when

Ethical Perspective

High fuel prices and record profits are a public relations disaster for the world's oil companies. They have responded with a series of public relations advertisements to counteract negative public opinion. In the following release, National Public Radio (NPR) examines the strategy used in this public relations campaign. Is the argument the oil companies are making valid? Do you think the advertisements are effective? Why or why not?

Slick Oil Ads Aim to Bolster Industry's Image By Yuki Noguchi

As oil companies rake in record profits, their public relations problems seem to grow deeper.

During a hearing last month, Senator Dianne Feinstein (D-CA) told oil executives they lacked an "ethical compass" for racking up huge profits while consumers pay more for their gasoline. Gas prices above $4 a gallon have inspired various energy bills in Congress, some of which propose a windfall-profits tax on the oil industry.

In the face of its political unpopularity, and in an effort to address its poor consumer image, the oil industry has been increasing its advertising spending. During the first quarter of this year, the industry spent $53 million in radio, television and print ads—a boost of more than 17 percent from the comparable period a year ago, according to TNS Media Intelligence, a firm that tracks ad spending.

The American Petroleum Institute launched a series of ads in April called "Do You Own an Oil Company?" which cites a commissioned study showing that 41 percent of oil company stocks are held by investors in mutual funds, pensions or "other investments." The API spent $3.8 million during the first quarter of this year on advertising, according to TNS.

The ad about owning oil companies is particularly powerful because it suggests the average American investor is a partner in the oil company's business, said Robert Thompson, director of the Center for the Study of Popular Television at Syracuse University. In selling this message, the industry is trying to slow the growing chorus of complaints against it, in part by linking its business success with the good of the American economy.

According to Morningstar, an investment research firm, 75 percent—or 3,126 of the 4,164 mutual funds it follows—are invested in some form of oil or gas stocks.

API President Red Cavaney says the industry isn't trying to come out smelling like roses. But it wants to educate the public about its point of view, he says. Cavaney also cited a Gallup Poll from last month showing that 20 percent of Americans blame oil companies for the high gas prices—that's down from 34 percent last year.

Source: Yuki Noguchi, "Slick Oil Ads Aim to Bolster Industry's Image," National Public Radio, June 20, 2008, accessed June 20, 2008, from http://www.npr.org/templates/story/story.php?storyId=91700175.

the researcher identifies the participant but does not reveal the information; (4) avoiding deceiving participants, something not always possible but highly desirable; and (5) reporting and analyzing results fairly and accurately so that others are not misled by the findings. Incidentally, when you buy research, you should know that members of the American Association for Public Opinion Research are pledged to uphold a code of professional ethics and practices.[19]

The second ethical problem in research involves the actual accumulation and storage of information.

Probably no PR practitioner can match any level of government in its accumulation of data on an individual. Most people are in at least 10 to 30 local and state databases as individuals. In addition, the U.S. government classifies individual citizens according to more than 8,000 separate record systems. Many government records are supposed to be off-limits to commercial researchers, although there have been cases where confidentiality has been breached. Also, Internet activity increasingly can be monitored, for example, CenturyTel Inc., a Monroe, Louisiana, phone company, uses technology that could change the way the $16.9 billion Internet ad market works, bringing new concerns about consumer privacy. Its system observes and analyzes the online activities of its Internet customers, keeping tabs on every Web site they visit. The equipment is installed into the phone company's network, and the system's manufacturer takes the information it collects and offers advertisers the chance to place online ads targeted to individual consumers. The manufacturer and CenturyTel get paid whenever a consumer clicks on an advertisement. This form of behavioral targeting can track all sites a consumer visits and can deliver far more detailed information to potential advertisers.[20]

Of course, people voluntarily give up their privacy in the new social media, such as Facebook.com and MySpace.com. Such accumulated data offer an opportunity for compilations that can profile individuals and families.

Concern over possible misuse of this kind of data was partly why legislators passed the Freedom of Information Act (FOIA) in 1966 and the U.S. Credit Bill of Rights that allows people to see just what information government and business have compiled on them. Nevertheless, both public and private institutions continue to gather substantial data, owing to the many different types of public registration (auto and boat licenses, building permits and so on) and mailing lists that are maintained.

A third problem has to do with how research information is used. Harrah's, a Las Vegas-based company in the gaming industry, has conducted thousands of clinical-style trials to determine what gets people to gamble more. Based on its findings, Harrah's has developed marketing strategies that are tailored individually to "low-rollers" who make up its bread-and-butter business. A mathematical model tells Harrah's marketers how to appeal to gamblers based on collected data that track customers' previous behavior in casinos. The data are gathered from electronic frequent-gambler cards that customers present before they play; the mathematical model calculates their "predicted lifetime value" to Harrah's.[21]

Internal Battles and Defeat Public relations people generally try to persuade management to act in socially responsible ways toward all publics. Occasionally, though, the interests of two or more publics conflict, or the profit interests of the company conflict with the interests of one or more of its publics. Management decisions are not always in line with

what the PR person recommends. What happens then? The PR person can first try to reach a compromise (if one is possible). If that doesn't work, he or she must review the situation to decide just how serious the conflict is.

Public relations practitioners are constrained in their efforts to influence management by at least four factors: (1) lack of access to management; (2) restraints on information collection; (3) roadblocks to dissemination of timely, accurate information; and (4) a narrow definition of the role of public relations. Of these factors, the first two pose the most serious problems. Researcher Michael Ryan concludes that practitioners need to find environments suitable to them. The most innovative practitioners should seek the most constraint-free environment; those who prefer routine tasks may be able to function well in an environment where management imposes considerable constraints on employees' behavior.[22]

The September 2007 Walker Information *Loyalty Report Executive Summary* noted that 63 percent of employees agree their company is highly ethical and 57 percent believe their senior leaders are ethical; the study also showed a clear link between employees' perceptions of company ethics and employee loyalty.[23] David C. Korten, a critic of corporations, argues, "There are plenty of socially conscious managers. The problem is a predator system that makes it difficult for them to survive."[24] An April 12, 2005, story in *The Wall Street Journal* reported that schools offering master of business administration (MBA) degrees were still struggling with how to teach ethics more effectively. A professor at Columbia University said, "What we want to give students are strategies for protecting their integrity in the workplace. We aren't trying to teach them right from wrong."[25]

Employees must assume responsibility too. Some practitioners label themselves "team players" and carry out each management's decision as though it were their own. Others may carry out decisions imposed from above, but not as effectively as they would have worked on their own—a subtle form of sabotage that raises an ethical question in itself. The alternative is to move on to another place where the ethical climate is more compatible.

One practitioner asserts that leaving is difficult to do. "Your ethics may be as good as your credit rating. No one with a big mortgage and lots of bills takes too many risks for a 'cause.'" But this is not always a valid rule. Doing something you feel is wrong is often worse for you personally and professionally than having to go job hunting. Moreover, if the action taken violates the PRSA or IABC code, you have to leave. If you don't, you risk being reported for the code violation by another practitioner. Fortunately, crises of confidence rarely occur because most people gravitate toward managements with ethical standards compatible with their own.[26]

Foreign Governments and Locations Working within, with or for foreign governments poses some complex ethical questions because of different cultural patterns. That doesn't mean that other countries are less ethical than the USA. For example, in January 2008 Norway's Government Pension Fund, which is one of the world's biggest sovereign-wealth funds, was considering broadening its ethical-investment program after having already divested holdings in arms-makers, mining companies and U.S. retailer Wal-Mart. The Norwegian central bank that oversees the $369 billion Norwegian Government Pension Fund began a year-long review of ethical guidelines, and investments in tobacco companies, pornographers and the gambling industry were likely to be considered for exclusion, as well as corporations from countries with human rights abuses.[27]

In response to the surfacing of "questionable payments" by corporations doing business abroad, legislation was passed in the USA making bribery illegal. But where do you draw the line between bribes or kickbacks and such traditionally acceptable practices as tips, gratuities and gifts? When do these become conditions for doing business? Even in foreign countries where bribes and kickbacks are illegal, such practices may exist in custom, which is difficult to work around. At the European Public Relations Congress in Kiev in October 2007, Pravda Award recipients were first "washed" by people in surgical garb to indicate that the public relations practitioners there did not use bribery to have their news releases published, and a journalist was given an award for being honest and not taking bribery, evidence that many public relations practitioners worldwide do not want to participate in bribery or other unethical professional practice.

However, the same month, *Corporate Watch* noted that Chevron's public relations campaign—titled "The Power of Human Energy" to position itself as a leader in environmental and social responsibility—suffered a setback when the company was forced to pay $30 million to settle federal charges that it had made illegal kickback payments to prewar Iraq in connection with crude oil purchases under the United Nations' Oil-for-Food program. Siemens

earlier had to pay a fine of about $300 million in a global bribery investigation by a German court.[28] Following the documentation of 100 cases between April 1994 and May 1995 in which U.S. firms lost contracts valued at $45 billion to foreign companies that pay bribery, an editorial in *The Wall Street Journal* commented that it doubted that a global antibribery law was workable. Corruption, it noted, is just "the usual slime found on the still waters of any system."[29]

Some companies, such as multinational Ingersoll-Rand, have tried to protect themselves by establishing a committee of outside directors charged with investigating all business practices. From an outside director's point of view, the role of adviser is probably preferable to that of police inspector. However, all companies—multinationals, in particular—are trying codes of conduct, outside directors and anything else they can think of to undergird corporate morality. Multinationals have a social responsibility to all of their publics, not just to the nation in which they were originally chartered.

Furthermore, public relations firms in the USA are being purchased or merged with agencies based in other countries, which creates the potential for differing cultural beliefs.[30] Ethical conflicts in these areas can arise over the status of women and children, hiring practices (especially where sex, class or caste are factors), job descriptions (especially ones that might violate some religious observances), conditions for promotion, the treatment of animals and contracts or agreements with suppliers or the government, just to name a few.

Working directly for foreign governments poses even more ethical questions. Some questions have been raised about U.S. political strategists, pollsters and political PR campaign managers who handle candidates in other countries—even when the elections are free and open. Although attorneys represent clients with public and professional impunity (in fact, their services are supposed to be available to all), public relations firms share the image of their clients. Not only the firm, but also the individual handling the PR account, may find it difficult to defend working for a country that has a reputation for being repressive.

Many countries with records of human rights violations have turned to U.S. public relations firms for help. And the desire to look good in world public opinion is not the only reason for doing so. Aid payments from the USA are bigger to nations with better reputations in this area. Tourism may increase as well. Some companies accept only foreign clients with reputations as responsible world citizens; but as one executive said in discussing the Iranian takeover of 1979, such a judgment gets more and more difficult to make.

Foreign governments rely increasingly on U.S. (and British) public relations firms for both government contracts and media relations. Some media people say that the PR firms aren't effective and that the embassies of the countries could do the same job. Others consider the embassies less skilled at media relations. Apparently the only effective PR people are those whom media people accept as credible sources. When their own media contacts haven't worked, foreign countries have often turned to advocacy advertising.

The ethical practices of the world's media are yet another issue because they factor in the media relations aspect of public relations and have an impact on opinions. From data collected in fall 2007, public relations scholar Katerina Tsetsura found that a large majority of journalists and public relations practitioners throughout the world said it was not professional for media to accept payments from news sources in return for coverage. Nevertheless, more than one in three public relations practitioners and one in five journalists said it was generally considered okay in their countries for national media to accept such payments. Only 60 percent said that paid-for material was always or often identified as advertising in national daily newspapers.[31] The role of media ethics is significant, not only because of editorial content, but also because of the advertising.

Responsibility in Advertising and Sponsorships

The People's Republic of China made every effort to ensure that coordinated groups of spectators would not wear uniforms or branded clothing during the Olympic Games in August 2008, ensuring "clean," that is, noncommercialized, sports stadiums. Authorities also controlled billboards in prominent locations to give priority to official sponsors, and athletes and coaches were not allowed to lend their images to marketing without prior approval from Olympics officials.[32] In a far less restrictive environment, a Carl's Jr. and Hardee's television commercial presented in the style of an MTV performance in 2005 featured celebrity actress Paris Hilton in a revealing swimsuit washing a Bentley luxury automobile. The commercial, which aired during the television program *American Idol* and at other prime times, stood out among the 3,000 commercials being broadcast nationally at the time. But it also raised an uproar among citizens groups that questioned its appropriateness for general television audiences. The commercial was pulled from the West Coast, where Carl's Jr. stores operate, in mid-June, but later that month began airing in the Midwest and Southeast to promote Hardee's restaurants' Spicy BBQ Burger.[33]

Such advertisements may at least be direct, but what about subliminal advertising? Subliminal advertising comes up for discussion from time to time, often in a classroom setting. Books have been written on the subject. However, most social scientists discount the effectiveness of such advertising, and mass media gatekeepers (advertising directors in particular) deny that such ads, if submitted, would be published. Nevertheless, subliminal suggestion is possible. You can buy tapes that supposedly help you learn while you sleep, relax or are otherwise occupied. The eye can physically detect and relay to the subconscious symbols (words and art) that the conscious mind doesn't react to at the time. But it is unlikely that subliminal advertising is created on any significant scale, much less that it abounds.

Responsibility in advertising also extends to the agencies involved in developing the campaigns and in buying time and space.

The harshest critics of advertising say stimulating people to buy what they do not need or to buy something instead of spending or saving prudently is also unethical. These kinds of choices, though, seem to be a permanent feature of the free marketplace.

Protecting the Client

Just as a client's name should be respected, so should its rights to a trademark, logo and trade name. Protecting these forms of property can be difficult. For one thing, only the name of the specific design may be protected; there is no law against stealing general ideas. This may explain the similarities often found in symbols, names and even in advertising ideas.

The only recompense for a copied idea is the realization that imitation is the sincerest form of flattery. If your trademark or logo is copied, you may be able to sue for damages, but only if the *precise* design is used. In general, it does not make any difference legally that the public might fail to distinguish between your design and the thinly disguised copied one.

For instance, the symbol of the famous Texas Boys Choir, a silhouetted choirboy in bowtie holding an open music book, was appropriated by a civic girls' chorus. In the altered design, the choirboy's ears were covered with shoulder-length hair and the pants legs were filled in to resemble a skirt. A copyright authority stated that the changes were sufficient to prevent a suit. The alternative was simply for the Boys Choir to stop using the symbol it had created, which it did for several years until the other group's use of it declined.

If you are watchful, you can find numerous examples of close copies, especially with logos or creative advertising concepts and designs. Packaging similarities are found in crayons (green and yellow box with old-fashioned lettering), in bleaches (white plastic container with predominately blue label) and corn chips (red and yellow packaging)—all prompted by imitation of very successful brand-name products.

Trade names are also legally entitled to protection, but this often becomes virtually impossible to enforce when they fall into generic use, such as Kleenex, Band-Aid and Xerox.

Protecting the Consumer

Efforts to protect the consumer cover a wide range of areas, but we will focus on three: products, politics and promotions.

Products A PR person should warn a client when his or her product is being erroneously confused with another (thus violating consumer confidence) or when the product itself is creating a consumer problem.

Criticized for using the cartoon character Joe Camel to sell cigarettes, RJR Nabisco launched an educational campaign advising children not to try the product until they were old enough to make a "mature" decision about smoking. The company refused to stop using its popular character (which has high recognition and appeal among youngsters) in advertisements until legally compelled to do so.

Constrained at home, U.S. tobacco companies are moving abroad to increase sales where restrictions are considerably fewer. The question this effort raises is how responsible is this? In addition to the health risks, other countries complain about the well-financed campaigns that compete with their own national products and actually are more pervasive in their exposure than their companies can afford to be.

The impact of media content, editorial and advertising, cannot be underestimated. For example, corporate advertising when a company is in litigation can cause legal problems, as discussed in Chapter 8 under litigation journalism, but it also can raise ethical issues. For example, when Dow Chemical was going on trial in New Orleans over silicon breast implants, Dow began running ads on TV and radio playing up its corporate citizenship. One spot was placed by a nonprofit organization. A little girl was shown with a life-saving silicone shunt in her brain, and her mother says, "Silicone is not the problem. The personal-injury lawyers and their greed is the problem." A New Orleans attorney for the breast implant plaintiffs accused Dow of trying to influence the jury, but the state judge refused to take any action against the company.[34] Product placement is all around us, for example, the clearly identifiable automobiles in the movies *Iron Man* and *Sex and the City*. However, such product placement can be inappropriate in some circumstances, for example, food makers are facing growing criticism over their role in childhood obesity and are exploring voluntary restrictions to reduce product placement in television shows that target children, the use of licensed characters in advertising and packaging and "advergaming," the practice of promoting candy, soft drinks and cereals on online games.[35]

Mars stopped airing its controversial 2007 Super Bowl ad after complaints by the Gay and Lesbian Alliance Against Defamation condemned it as anti-gay. Produced by Omnicom Group Inc.'s TBWA/Chiat//Day, the ad showed two mechanics eating from opposite ends of a Snickers candy bar until their lips touched. They then ripped out their chest hair to "do something manly." Mars canceled an elaborate follow-up for the spot. A General Motors Super Bowl ad showing a robot envisioning leaping from a bridge was also harshly criticized for its trite depiction of suicide.[36] "Guerrilla marketing" suffered a setback at about the same time when a stunt caused a bomb scare in Boston, where subway, river and highway traffic was halted and thousands of people were frightened by 40 blinking boxes promoting the "Aqua Teen Hunger Force" television show. These boxes had been placed near bridges, depots and other locations.[37]

Most publications adhere to standards of ethical behavior, and these standards may also cover their ability to reject advertising that they see as offensive or objectionable. Standards of ethical behavior in advertising are set forth in the advertising profession's own code and in an elaborate two-tiered mechanism to deal with truth and accuracy in national advertising—although, of course, there is nothing to prevent those who do not subscribe to it from plying their trade. But even if advertisers ignore their own code, the media may provide the restraint—at least in matters of taste.

Politics Although the Internet has yet to yield to any meaningful or far-reaching legal restraints, legal and ethical issues can be controlled on intranets, those internal computer systems within organizations.

The California Supreme Court was asked in 2002 to hear the case concerning Intel Corporation and Ken Hamidi, who was fired in 1995. The issue was whether Hamidi was trespassing electronically or simply using his right of free speech. In addition to dressing like a cowboy and going on horseback to distribute printed versions of his messages to employees entering the company's Folsom, California, facility, he also spent two years criticizing the company in emails that he sent to thousands of his former co-workers.[38]

What are the ethical issues here? What about harassment, hate speech and such? The Internet culture is fiercely protective of freedom of expression, but intranets are another issue.

The digital age has created another monster of sorts in new televised political ads as well as political content in the new social media, the latter by bloggers and other content providers exploiting the by-and-large unregulated Internet. Some standard techniques accepted in commercial ads such as speeded up or slowed down motion or sound can be devastating in political advertising, of course, But particularly damaging can be the misuse of the new social media. Presidential candidate Barack Obama used a dedicated Web site, *Fightthesmears.com*, not only to disprove rumors, but to actually track down those spreading them.[39]

Broadcast stations historically had less flexibility in rejecting political advertising because of the **equal-time provision**. This provision appeared in the 1934 Broadcast Act through the incorporation of language from the 1927 Radio Act stating that if a licensee permits any person who is a legally qualified candidate for any public office to use a broadcasting station, the licensee has to give equal opportunity to all other such candidates. Furthermore, the licensee (broadcast station) has no power of censorship over the material broadcast. This stipulation was regarded somewhat ruefully by Atlanta, Georgia, broadcast-

ers, who in 1974 had taken the advertising of one political candidate and then, under FCC regulations, had to accept the spots of his opponent, Democratic candidate J. B. Stoner. Stoner's taped messages said: "I am the only candidate for the U.S. Senate for white people. The main reason why niggers want integration is that niggers want our white women. I am for law and order. You can't have law and order and niggers." The messages, broadcast over radio station WPLO and WSB-TV, evoked a deluge of protesting phone calls, but the spots ran for a week anyway.

The equal-time provision was amended in 1959 by the *fairness doctrine*, which stated that legally qualified candidates can appear on bona fide newscasts, news interviews, news documentaries or on-the-spot coverage of news events without the licensee having to provide equal time to opposing candidates. But another clause proved more difficult to interpret: Because stations are supposed to operate in the public interest, they must afford reasonable opportunity for the discussion of conflicting views on issues of public importance. The fairness doctrine had been interpreted to include advertising as well as program content and was the basis on which two networks, ABC and CBS, refused Mobil's explanatory advertising on the 1970s energy crisis.

The FCC discontinued the fairness doctrine in 1987. Print media supported the broadcasters in their effort to get rid of the requirement. Congress then tried to enact the fairness doctrine as law, but the bill was vetoed by President Reagan.

The problem for public relations people involved in politics is that people tend to see all campaigns as "public relations" efforts, regardless of who actually runs them. The campaign for a risky candidate usually involves strict control of exposure, limited access to media and voters, no discussion of issues or philosophy of governance and as much television commercial time as available money allows. The unfortunate consequence of the last feature is that only candidates who have money or the ability to raise it can even compete. This narrows the field.

During an election campaign period—which now lasts at least a year, and sometimes extends to 18 months or longer—the "public relations" tactics employed by various candidates arouse a great deal of resentment toward public relations practice in general. In fact, however, many political election campaigns are not handled by mainstream PR practitioners, who adhere to the highest standards of professional practice. There may be several reasons for this.

First, if the PR practitioner is a member of PRSA, he or she should comply with specific standards governing the practice of public relations. Unfortunately, everything that goes on in a political race is called "public relations." Public relations counselors now find themselves wondering how to deal with the problem of negative campaigning itself, the popular perception that public relations people are responsible for it and the notion that these are "legitimate" public relations practices. Another worthwhile item to put on the agenda might be an effort to make individuals who hold the nation's top public relations jobs (such as press secretaries) accountable to a code of professional practice, a need evidenced by the issues raised by former White House Press Secretary Scott McClellan in his 2008 book, *What Happened: Inside the Bush White House and Washington's Culture of Deception.*

Promotions Most promotions are part of a larger campaign, and in some cases are highly creative and engaging. In late 2007 CBS Corp. promoted a real-life version of the puzzle "Chain Factor," which had been featured during an episode of the television show *Num3rs*, in which participants spent hours on the Web and on the streets searching for clues that would help them solve a complex puzzle. Working collaboratively, players shared clues on an online forum. The goal with such scavenger-hunt games is to build buzz among an audience. Other games have been affiliated with ABC's *Lost* and CBS's *Jericho*.[40] Are any misuses of such promotions possible or likely, for example, such as the panic that Boston experienced in the guerrilla marketing example cited earlier in this chapter? Drug makers' "direct-to-consumer" advertising remains both popular and controversial. Evidence suggests such advertising of prescription drugs increases sales and helps to avert underuse of medicines but leads to potential overuse. The Food and Drug Administration (FDA) has been criticized for weak enforcement of laws regulating this advertising. Spending on direct-to-consumer advertising has continued to increase in recent years despite such criticisms.[41] "Direct-to-consumer ads often portray drugs through rose-colored glasses by including more information about a drug's benefits than risks," said American Medical Association (AMA) President-Elect Dr. Nancy Nielsen.[42]

Some promotions are deceptive because they are personalized. An advertising tearsheet arrives with what appears to be a handwritten sticky note attached that says something like the one that came to one of the authors of this textbook: "Douglas, Try this it works! Y" The signature could have been a "T." In any case, it was attached to an ad about making speeches. As it turns out, the "signature" must have been a "J" because James Durham, who was director of business development for the law firm Mintz, Levin, Cohn, Ferris & Glovsky, sent his second email in two years to members of the firm explaining that he is not the "J" on the sticky note that had people calling him from all over the country, asking him if they really should buy the book that was being recommended on the sticky note. Presumably it was a book about law or some legal issue. In any case, the Better Business Bureau of Washington, D.C., has issued a cease and desist order to the Georgetown Publishing House responsible for this promotion.[43]

Another deceptive promotion practice is to blur advertising and editorial photographic formats, something increasingly common in magazines, where product advertising seems to enjoy making a mystery of what is being offered for sale. These single documentary-like photos or photo essays in some cases simply show the photos and the advertiser's logo, often in a very subtle presentation. Preliminary research shows these to be more memorable, a key factor in advertising. But is this ethical?[44]

The challenge for public relations practitioners involved in promotions is to test their own value systems for what they are advocating. A critical issue lies beyond that: Is it responsible?

Responsibility in Publicity

The ethical question of when and how to acknowledge the PR source of news is extremely important. In 2007 one Russian newspaper published an article claiming that beer-drinking was good for consumers, news that probably was met with joy by many readers. However, a tiny icon at the end of the story referred to a legend several pages later that indicated the story was placed by a beer-brewers' association, an effort in transparency that nevertheless was greater than perhaps many editorial placements in media throughout the world. Critics question the ethics of having news appear in the mass media precisely in the form submitted by a PR person. They feel that PR-originated news should carry some identifying label to alert the reader or viewer. Many PR and media people regard this as impractical and (for different reasons) undesirable. They argue that it is the job of newspeople to know the source of the information they use and to employ discrimination and good editorial judgment about what to disseminate and whether to include attribution.

PR as a Source

The relationship between PR people and newspeople is rarely the kind of contest in which the PR practitioner plots to sneak misleading or nonnewsworthy material into print, and the reporter tries to "get" the PR practitioner's client. Publicity is supposed to *facilitate* the news-gathering process. PR people expect newspeople to regard news releases critically and to use or not use the news releases at their own discretion. The release can be rewritten, incorporated with other materials, or not used at the time and used at a later date, sometimes in an unflattering way that is not so helpful. That is part of the risk in being a source.

The same is true of **video news releases**, although some people have accused public relations people of deceiving the public. Video news releases go to news directors who can decide, the same as any other newsperson, what, if any, should be used. The television station can, and often does, identify the footage they use as supplied by a company or organization. But the practice is seen as deceptive because many people may not realize that public relations people are the source for some of the information.[45] In summer 2005, PRSA responded to the FCC's call for a review of existing rules and regulations regarding prepackaged news materials involving financial or promotional considerations for broadcasters who aired them and those involving "controversial" or "political" subjects. The FCC inquiry was in response to instances in 2004 in which some broadcasters aired government-sponsored VNRs on controversial presidential initiatives without identifying the source of the materials. Then-PRSA president Judith Phair argued that most VNRs and other prepackaged materials were, in fact, being clearly labeled when they were delivered to broadcast organizations and that the FCC inquiry as well as legislative initiatives in Congress were in response to a "procedural breakdown" in which identifying labeling had been removed when materials were distributed by a network to local affiliates.[46]

Complaints sometimes are legitimate. For example, a content analysis of tobacco industry information in two children's publications, *Weekly Reader* and *Scholastic News*, showed that the industry's viewpoint predominated in *Weekly Reader*, as did coverage about the issue whether smokers' rights and that the new tax and smoking laws were unfair.[47] It is reasonable to question why the industry tried to place stories in either children's publication. And what was the responsibility of the editors in presenting what some parents said was unbalanced coverage of news that involves a product that is a health risk for children?

One deceptive publicity practice that has invaded the magazine field (coming perhaps from small newspapers) involves specialized magazines and is relatively transparent. A company that buys an elaborate ad—always four-color, usually **doubletruck** (two pages side by side), and sometimes with a foldout—is almost always featured in an article with several pictures in the same issue. Sometimes the article carries no byline. When it does, the professional identity of the writers is seldom disclosed. In all likelihood, the writers are publicists for the advertisers. In one case, an aviation magazine that carried a prominent four-color advertisement for an airplane manufacturer's new model also published an illustrated four-page article on the plane and gave it the cover.

Some magazines that compete with commercial publications for readership and advertising are actually public relations tools themselves. Among these are American Express's publications *Travel and Leisure* and *Departures*. *Ford Times* was published from 1908 until January 1993.

Although professional communicators express concern over the lack of a clear division between news and advertising copy, the public seldom seems to give it a thought. Study after study has indicated attention to *content*, with little understanding of the difference between commercial content and editorial content. Or perhaps this just shows an advanced level of calloused disbelief.

World Wide Web pages further blur the lines between advertising and publicity. Many organizations use their Web page to post news releases, illustrate information with graphics such as financial charts, show pictures, engage Web surfers with games, offer opportunities for questions to be asked and give information about new products, services or promotions. Of course, there's no deception in that, because anyone logging on to the organization's page will know the source of the information. Problems begin when others use the information there too, such as newspeople. Whether or not they credit the source is their responsibility.

A phenomenon to which public relations practitioners must pay increasing attention, to the point where it has become a major resource for monitoring issues that cannot be ignored by practitioners, is that of Web logs, known as blogs. Easy for anyone to originate, develop and maintain, blogs are used not only by traditional mass media, such as newspapers whose reporters engage in dialogue with readers, but also by private individuals who record their thoughts and seek feedback about any interest or obsession. Many thousands of these blogs already exist, and new ones are being introduced on the World Wide Web each day. Although some blogs might go virtually unread, many have developed large readership and participation. Incorrect information and unfavorable opinions toward public relations practitioners' organizations, together with search engines that are greatly improved in identifying these blogs, mean that practitioners must realize that blogs can be far more influential than just one person's unread opinion.

Art/Photos

The digital world offers opportunities in terms of photos and art, but these opportunities can pose ethical issues. It's not that pictures haven't been manipulated before. Certainly they have, but now it's easier to do and more difficult to detect. Some organizations have published standards for altering imagery, but others will do anything that's effective. People in fashion may improve a model's physical characteristics; political ads have used morphing (showing a candidate turn into someone else); and news media have altered images to emphasize a point or get a laugh.[48]

News organizations have different standards, just like other organizations, for what they will and won't change, and if *National Geographic* will move the pyramids closer together for a good cover, then what can you expect? Photo fiction is likely to continue, and that expectation has led the photography profession to suggest some way to keep its credibility by telling people when an image has been manipulated.[49] The trouble is, not everyone will. The amount of photo manipulation that had been connected to the O. J. Simpson 1995 trial for the murder of Nicole Brown Simpson and Ronald Goldman is a good indication that it won't—everything from the bruises on Nicole Brown Simpson's face to the unflattering *Time* magazine cover of O. J. Simpson. Using photo illustrations or digitally enhanced images of any kind calls for the viewer to interpret the symbolic intent instead of accepting it as reality.[50]

That may not always occur. When it doesn't, the viewer is deceived.

Money Matters

What happens when you, as a publicity writer, have a story accepted by a publication? Are you entitled to compensation for the story or pictures? No! Publicity is free; magazine editors know it and won't offer payment. Many will give you a byline, and some will identify you as a guest writer in that issue. But make sure your identification as the writer indicates your relationship to the organization or other client about which you are writing.

The PRSA Member Code of Ethics 2000 guidelines say a member shall "preserve the integrity of the process of communication" and "preserve the free flow of unprejudiced information when giving or receiving gifts by ensuring that gifts are nominal, legal, and infrequent."[51]

What if a magazine staff writer writes a story suggested by a PR firm and allows her or his expenses to be paid by the firm? What if the writer accepts a fee as well as expenses from the firm? The ethical problem here is not only that the magazine staffer is "on the take," but also that the PR people are inducing the misconduct. It is permissible for a public relations practitioner to suggest a story to a publication, and if the idea is accepted and a writer assigned, the practitioner may make arrangements for accommodations and may see that all expenses involved in getting information for the story are covered. Almost all publications permit such arrangements on expenses, but many want to pay for transportation and accommodations themselves. Some are flexible about the accommodations.

Criticism remains about junkets—all-expenses-paid excursions for movie reviewers to the location of a filming, for travel editors to the opening of a new resort hotel or amusement park, for fashion editors to the site where a new line (cosmetics, shoes, sportswear, anything) is being introduced or for real estate editors to the opening of a new luxury development in a remote area. Critics charge that such junkets amount to the purchasing of editorial talent. Many PR practitioners see nothing wrong with them, however, particularly because there is no control over what the wined-and-dined reporters write. And most practitioners use a careful screening process to separate the professionals from the freeloaders. Sometimes a strict publication will allow its reporter to go but will insist on paying for the transportation and accommodations. Others permit these items to be paid for if the reporter acknowledges the fact in his or her copy. Still others permit reporters to accept trip packages because they believe the gratuities will not affect how the reporters handle the story. Increasingly, bloggers are being invited on these junkets.

Many newspapers don't accept stories from subsidized trips. A lot of newspapers have a don't ask-don't tell policy about subsidies. Magazines may be less stringent in their policies, although *Conde Nast Traveler* and *Travel & Leisure* are among those with strict no-subsidies policies. They pay for their reporters' travel.[52]

Broadcasters appear to have more flexibility, especially in situations where it's clear to the viewer that the resort area featured in the travelogue obviously cooperated in the production. Features of this type are usually broadcast on special channels or in quasi-commercial programming. But how do these TV magazine format features differ from newspaper travel sections?

The Society of Business Writers was the first to respond to this problem. It adopted a code of ethics that specifically outlaws junkets and "freebies." A member may not accept any special treatment or any gift of more than token value; all out-of-town travel must be paid for by the writer's employer. Other professional journalism organizations followed suit, as did individual newspaper corporations. Most publications had already prohibited outright gifts to their editorial staff members, either directly or through people in their own advertising departments. Some specialized publications, though, such as *Car and Driver*, ended staff freebies only in 1991.

There is another side to this, though. Public officials are also on PR gift lists. Many companies have certain public officials they want remembered and tell their PR person to "buy something." Many city, county and state governments have strict regulations about what public officials may accept, but just as many don't. Common prudence suggests that all gifts should be "token" rather than substantial. One executive who shops the catalogs every year for gifts to suggest to his clients offers this rule of thumb: "When I choose something, I always think, how would I feel if I suddenly saw this on the 6 p.m. news? That curbs my buying sprees considerably."

Another kind of remuneration—one that inflates the ego as well as the pocketbook—is the awarding of prizes, and this affects both press and public officials. Does a reporter embark on a series about arthritis to

enlighten the newspaper's readers or to increase the writer's chances for tangible recognition from the Arthritis Foundation? Does a local television station do a documentary on possible fire hazards during the summer to warn its viewers or to receive recognition from the Firefighters Association? Does a network choose its documentary for overriding public interest or a chance to win an Emmy or Peabody? Does an ambitious lawyer offer to head the local symphony drive for the arts out of love of music or because her eye is on a civic club's annual outstanding citizen award? Commercial as well as nonprofit institutions engage in these incentive programs, but these seem to meet with greater editorial acceptance than junkets, even though many awards are cash prizes.

A more blatant type of remuneration is the moonlighting that some reporters and photographers do at part-time publicity jobs. Although most media executives do not condone the practice, few actively try to stop it. As one newspaper's photo chief said, "Are you kidding? All my good people would quit. They can't live on what this paper pays them." Nevertheless, there are all sorts of ethical ramifications. For instance, does a feature photo taken by a photographer working part-time for a public relations department get published in the community newspaper because of her favored status as a full-time news photographer for that publication?

Favor can also be shown by PR people in the gifts their organizations make to nonprofits. Public relations people often control more than their own departmental budgets. Generally the corporation's investments in the community—gifts to civic, social, even national organizations—are within the control of the PR department. This is especially true of national organizations to whom the company gives its support. These relationships are scrutinized by special-interest groups that monitor such gifts to ensure that minorities and other disadvantaged groups are not excluded. Their reviews can also put an institution in a bad position if its funds go to groups that do exclude minorities, that practice discrimination or that have labor policies that could be criticized as unfair.

Public relations practitioners are accustomed to providing for the media, but usually on a temporary basis. The situation is different for public affairs officers in government. In 1978, attention became focused on the facilities provided for news media in public places (government centers), such as courthouses and state capitols. In many of these places free parking spaces, a paging system and a complete writing facility with desks, typewriters, telephones and even attendants were provided. The taxpayer was picking up the tab, of course. Much of the furor over such perquisites ("perks") originated in the Washington, D.C., news media's criticism and exposure of congressional perks. Suddenly government perks for reporters came under scrutiny everywhere, much to the consternation of some government people hired to handle the news media. When the reporters moved out, the working relationships of these staffs with the news media became a lot more complicated. However, news agencies could preserve their integrity by paying rent for the facilities and furnishings.

Some state governments, whose constitutions required them to provide the media with free space and prevented reimbursement, found themselves in a bind. However, few people working in the public relations role for government saw the facilities issue as a threat to the free press system, and several pointed to an observation made by some newspeople themselves—that lack of facilities really inhibited news coverage. The bigger organizations could afford to foot the bill, but some of the smaller media, whose reporters tend to look carefully at what their constituents' representatives are doing, were forced to abandon coverage and use the more general wire-service copy.

PACs: Political Action Committees

Political Action Committees (PACs) PACs are clearly identifiable legal organizations registered and incorporated in states to raise money for politicians whom they favor. The corporate political war chests they command are sizable but are regulated at both the state and federal levels. PACs are also developed by unions and by activist groups ranging from antiabortionists to homosexuals. Most states require that PACs maintain public records of their names, affiliations and assets and the names of those who make donations to them above a given amount. However, in some cases the information is not easy to get. Public relations ethical questions arise over how the money is raised (through pressure put on employees, for example), how the money is spent (on political candidates who may not behave in the best interests of society), how much information is made public about the institution's PAC and whom it supports. Although big business and big labor dominate PAC activity, many professional and trade associations are also involved. These institutions defend their right to bankroll the candidates they feel will support them

most staunchly when in office. Critics of PACs insist that they invite abuse of the electoral process.

News Media and Political PR

Politicians and the news media are natural adversaries. The cause for conflict, as journalism educator William Blankenburg identifies it, is that "undefinable thing called news that mixes two combustibles, timely disclosure and objective truth, one of which is chaotic and the other coercive."[53] Often the problem with unauthorized information is that its release would make certain individuals in positions of authority look bad. The PR person is always suspect and therefore occupies a high-tension spot. The tension is heightened by the way public officials use the news media and vice versa.

In international PR practice, media play by different rules. Demand for payment to disseminate news releases has been coined *zakazukha*, a Russian slang word that can be translated as "pay-for-publicity." However, Russian journalists and their newspapers who participate in this practice have many counterparts elsewhere throughout the world. Public relations practitioners and their clients do not wish to pay bribes that are solicited or demanded by news media to ensure the dissemination of news releases that public relations practitioners feel have value to the consumers of news media. Professional public relations practitioners believe that news releases placed in consumer news media should have "newsworthiness." In many countries throughout the world, no factors other than newsworthiness influence placement of public relations practitioner–generated news releases.

However, media extortion of public relations practitioners does occur regularly worldwide. Public relations practitioners must pay "bribes" if they want their news releases to be disseminated in many consumer news media, despite the obvious or apparent newsworthiness of these subsidies. Such solicitation oftentimes comes from journalists who are supposedly unbiased and neutral in their role as "gatekeepers"; that is, these journalists promote the illusion among consumers of the news they package that relative newsworthiness is the sole criterion for placement of editorial content into their consumer news media. (See *Global Perspective* in this chapter.)

The Public's Right to Know

The media's right to know is related to the public's right to information. The FOIA has given individuals access to certain types of information, and the media derive their right to that information from the public's right. The act, however, protects certain kinds of information from public exposure. Information that the government believes is important to national security remains confidential, as does information that pertains to ongoing criminal investigations. Of course, the act has nothing to do with financial and commercial information generated by private sources. Other state and local regulations, such as the open-meeting and public record laws, also protect certain kinds of information. Governmental bodies still have the right to discuss such things as collective bargaining and certain personnel matters in executive session.

Although some information remains hidden from the media, some critics believe that the media are now privy to too much information. Other critics maintain that the media do not treat privileged information with sufficient discretion or respect.

Many problems that the news media encounter are attributable to the fact that we as a public do not agree on what we want or need to know. We do not agree because our basis for deciding what we want to know is a value system; because we have different value systems, complete agreement appears to be impossible. Nevertheless, the law says we have a right to know everything that does not invade an individual's privacy—and the privacy of public figures in some instances—and that information should be available so long as if it does not violate laws such as libel, protected trade secrets, and so on.

The limits on these two crucial freedoms—to be informed and to be left alone—have been set, but they continue to evolve in court cases, because these rights come with obligations. The news media are not the only ones who fail to uphold their obligations to tell the public what they need to know in order to make rational decisions. In the past, the commercial sector has often withheld health and safety information from consumers and employees. Additional examples continue to come to light.

Promotions and Public Opinion

McDonald's suffered not only global embarrassment, but also litigation, because its U.S. French fries still contained flavoring from beef fat, a tremendous offense to some of McDonald's 43 million daily customers in the USA. A Seattle, Washington, Hindu brought a multimillion dollar legal action against the fast-food chain, accusing McDonald's of misleading

customers in the USA. He started eating the French fries only after McDonald's announced in 1990 that it had started cooking its fries in vegetable oil rather than beef fat. A co-plaintiff from Los Angeles said, "I have made a vow to God not to eat meat, fish or eggs." Even though beef fat is not used in India to make French fries, in Delhi, the McDonald's restaurants had windows smashed and statues of Ronald McDonald smeared with dung. Some politicians called for the company to be expelled from the country.[54]

In what is considered a classic public relations case study, the issue of whether and how infant formula should be made available to poor African mothers pitted the United Nations and its member agency United Nations Children's Fund (UNICEF), which is charged with protecting the interests of children, against the $3 billion infant formula industry. One major formula maker said it was ready to donate tons of free formula to HIV-infected women, who can give AIDS to their children through breast-feeding. Another large company said it also would donate. But UNICEF refused to approve the gifts because it didn't want to endorse an industry it had long accused of abusive practices in the developing world. Haunting the good intentions of the formula makers was the distrust that had developed between them and UNICEF since the 1970s when Nestlé and other formula makers routinely used advertising in developing countries that featured fat formula-fed babies and gave out free samples in maternity wards to attract new mothers to the product. By the time the free formula was consumed, women's own breast milk had usually dried up. Few could afford to purchase the formula, and those who could diluted it to make it last longer—sometimes starving their babies in the process. In protest, activists organized a worldwide boycott of Nestlé products, and UNICEF refused to accept cash donations from the big formula makers.[55]

Individual Responsibilities

Ethical performance amounts to doing what's right to preserve your integrity, in accordance with your value system. But values are culture-bound, which is why difficulties often arise across cultures. In the USA, honesty is valued, but it isn't rewarded very well. As any "whistleblower" can tell you, there's not much reward for ethical behavior. (*Whistleblowers* are individuals who call public attention to problems within their own industry, business or organization. As a result of their revelations, they often lose their jobs and have trouble finding other employment. Women and minorities who file antidiscrimination lawsuits often encounter the same difficulties, even when they "win.")

Individual Decisions

Two writers for the *Harvard Business Review*, seeking to test the hypothesis that "honesty pays," found the opposite to be true. Their study led them to conclude that "power can be an effective substitute for trust." According to these researchers, "Trustworthy behavior does provide protection against the loss of power and against invisible sniping. But these protections are intangible, and their dollars-and-cents value does not make a compelling case for trustworthiness." Then why be trustworthy? The authors say, "Only our individual wills, our determination to do what is right, whether or not it is profitable, save us from choosing between chaos and stagnation."[56]

There may be faint comfort in that. These writers' research suggests that conscientious public relations practitioners must attempt to function ethically and responsibly in settings where a different culture may support different values, in a larger society in the USA that lauds ethical behavior but seldom rewards it, and in situations where others are using entirely different standards reflecting divergent underlying values. In fact, the student views discussed earlier in this chapter may signal that values in American society are changing.

There may be a difference between ethical decisions and what Joseph L. Badaracco, Jr., calls a "defining moment." Ethical decisions, he says, are between right and wrong, while defining moments present choices between two ideals in which we deeply believe, and have no truly "correct" answer. However, the way these decisions are made over a period of time defines one's character. The question "Who am I?" can be a corporate one, "Who are we?" The answer is in the values of the organization, which is why most organizations faced with a difficult decision go to their mission statements for guidance.[57]

What many public relations professionals do is turn to their codes of ethics or standards of behavior. The problem with most of these is that they are seen as self-serving. The problem for public relations professionals is that they must uphold not only their own code, but the codes of news media. These codes are a form of self-policing, so they are not infallible.

But what efforts to be responsible in all relationships do is establish a level of trust.

Reciprocal Trust

An area of major importance in PR involves keeping confidences with the media and with other publics. For example, a reporter on the trail of a story deserves the exclusive he or she is ingenious enough to identify and develop. A PR practitioner should not pull the rug out by offering a general release before the reporter has had an opportunity to use the material. Also, a news medium has the right to expect a practitioner to be entirely aboveboard in offering information. Feature ideas, suggestions and pictures should be offered on an "exclusive use" basis. Certainly magazine editors expect stories and pictures submitted to be exclusives. A magazine editor who finds the same or a similar story in another magazine will never trust you again.

A story issued in printed form "for general release" notifies an editor that other news media have the story. However, a story marked, for example, "Special to the *Charlotte Observer*" should be just that. No other news medium in that circulation area should receive the story. (If you do send it to other newspapers, you should let the editor know.) The quickest way to destroy your welcome in the newsroom is to plant the same story all over the place. Even if the same story is given to the morning and evening editions of the same newspaper, you are in trouble. Each deserves different stories with different approaches. The best way to do this is to take separate stories to one person at each newspaper. Decide where each story would most appropriately appear or who on the paper would most likely be interested. If it is a column item and more than one newspaper is involved, you should determine which columnist would be most likely to use the piece and plant it there—only there.

News media should also be able to trust you to have cleared publicity pictures submitted to them by securing a release from those who posed. They should also be able to trust you to protect them from copyright complications and libel and lottery laws that can be violated in publicity copy.

When you supply news to the media, you are bound, ethically and morally, just as they are, by the codes to which their members subscribe. By the same token, the news media owe public relations practitioners a responsibility to honor agreed-upon release dates and times (so-called "embargoed" releases). Most do. If a story appears in the media earlier than was requested, try to discover why. Often it is an accident. However, if a publication frequently has "accidents," don't give future stories to that publication until there is no jeopardy to your client. Do this quietly, without any warning and certainly without threats. It won't take the publication long to figure out what is happening and why.

Crisis situations are the most trying for relationships because both sides are under pressure and both sides are generally frustrated. Journalists accuse PR people of misrepresentation and covering up information. PR people accuse reporters of bias and inaccuracies. Part of the problem resides in how the "truth" appears to each side. PR commentator and practitioner David Finn has observed:

> One of the most disturbing discoveries public relations people can make about themselves is that learning "the facts" doesn't always tell them what they should believe. As citizens and readers of newspapers and television viewers, they have opinions on as many things as anybody else.
>
> But sometimes their convictions run counter to positions held by a client. Then they study "the facts" and listen to what their client's experts have to say, and those passionate convictions become surprisingly less convincing. They see another point of view and find it more persuasive than they imagined.
>
> The first time this happens, public relations people don't mind admitting they might have been wrong. But when it happens again and again they begin to wonder whether any point of view can be supported by a given set of facts and a particular group of experts. And they fear that a lifetime of listening to all the experts who support their clients' positions weakens their capacity to make independent judgments.[58]

The question of corruption of judgment is a serious one for public relations people. Often the heart of a dispute is not over facts but over the interpretation of facts and over conflicting value systems. In these situations, the best guide for the PR person is to return to the formula for socially responsible public relations decision making. Who are the publics? What are the interests of each in the decision or situation? How will an institution's policy, position or action affect each of these publics? What social values are involved? What values are in conflict? What will the effects be? Can the effects be defended? The PR person who loses the public's perspective has foregone public responsibility and become the persuaded instead of the persuader.

Discussion Questions

1. From where do you think you have learned your personal values that will help you to practice ethical public relations? From where have you learned your preprofessional values?

2. Can ethics be taught? Can practitioners know ethical behavior, that is, what is right and wrong in professional practice, but yet not practice such behavior they know to be right? Explain your answer. Do you think practitioners become more ethical or less ethical or remain about the same in their ethics from the time they begin their careers to the time they are senior-level practitioners? Why?

3. How can students prepare for ethical public relations practice? What types of education (for example, coursework) would be helpful? What types of other resources would be valuable to help you learn what is ethical public relations practice?

4. Who is ultimately ethically accountable for the ethical behavior of a corporation—the organization or its individual employees? Provide reasons to explain why you answered the way you did.

Points to Remember

- Ethics are founded on moral principles that are themselves grounded in effects.

- Judgments about an organization's standing are made in three areas: ethics, social responsibility and financial responsibility.

- Ethics and responsibilities are public relations concerns on two levels. We have to consider the behavior of the individual practitioner and that of the institution she or he represents. Public relations is often called the "conscience" of management, but can't be if top management has none.

- Top management sets the ethical tone in an organization, and the challenge for internal and external PR people is to guide those who hire them to responsible actions that are founded in integrity.

- Although extremely complex, the study of ethics falls into two broad categories: comparative ethics (sometimes called descriptive ethics), the purview of social scientists, and normative ethics, generally the domain of philosophers and theologians.

- Some hold decisions about what is right or wrong to be absolute; others say the situation is a factor.

- Part of the complexity in ethical decision making for public relations practitioners is that they are hired to be advocates; they play a role as educators, but also as persuaders.

- Some truths are verifiable and commonly accepted, but others are actually perceptions. Furthermore, beliefs and personal values influence how "truth" is defined. Thus ethics are inseparable from values.

- Page's management principles stress conducting public relations as if the whole company depended on it. It might, because the belief that publics hold in organizations validates their organizations' existence.

- Responsibility has two facets: social and financial. People's perception of how well an organization is fulfilling these gives the organization legitimacy.

- Social responsibility means producing sound products or reliable services that don't threaten the environment, and it means contributing positively to the social, political and economic health of society. It also means compensating employees fairly and treating them justly.

- Financial responsibility includes how the organization interacts with investors and investment advisers.

- The fact that PR works to change people's views causes the individual practitioner's ethics to be closely intertwined with the organization's social responsibility.

- Political PR people often find themselves caught in the middle of conflicts resulting from use of news media by public officials and vice versa.

- Conflicts often arise over interpretation of social and financial responsibility in a global setting.

- Most professional PR practitioners recognize that they and their organizations have ethical responsibilities to at least 10 different publics: clients, news media, government agencies, educational institutions, consumers, stockholders and analysts, community, competitors, critics and other public relations practitioners.

- Ethical problems that must be resolved in public relations research include how to collect the data, how to accumulate and store information and how to use research.

- As a consenting agent of attitude change, you need to consider what you are trying to change, and you must ask whether the attitude change is one that will benefit the involved publics.

- Public relations practitioners are constrained in their efforts to influence management by at least four factors: (1) lack of access to management; (2) restraints on information collection; (3) roadblocks to dissemination of timely, accurate information; (4) a narrow definition of the role of public relations. Of these, the first two pose the most serious problems.

- Senior executives are sometimes accused of talking about ethics but failing to follow through. Practitioners who see themselves as "team players" may be swept up in a bad ethical environment and jeopardize their own credibility.

- To be a professional and maintain the standards embodied in a code of professional ethics often take courage, as well as a strong set of personal values.

- Ethical conflicts among multinational corporations include issues of the status of women and children, hiring practices, job descriptions, conditions for promotion, treatment of animals and contracts or agreements with suppliers or the government. Working directly for foreign governments poses even more ethical questions.

- Responsibility in advertising and sponsorships includes assuming personal responsibility in protecting the client and the customer regarding products and in political issues.

- The PRSA Member Code of Ethics 2000 focuses on conducting business in the public interest, dealing fairly with the public, adhering to standards of accuracy and truth and not knowingly disseminating false and misleading information or corrupting the integrity of the channels of communication.

- Responsibility in publicity means being honest and faithful as a source of information, as a supplier of illustrations and as the finder of information and space or other considerations.

- The problem for public relations people involved in politics is that people tend to see all campaigns as "public relations" efforts, regardless of who actually runs them.

- Increasing criticism has been voiced about junkets—all-expenses-paid excursions for movie reviewers, travel editors, fashion editors and real estate editors.

- Political Action Committees (PACs) are clearly identifiable, legal organizations registered and incorporated in states to raise money for politicians whom they favor.

- The media's right to know is related to the public's right to information. The Freedom of Information Act (FOIA) has given individuals access to certain types of information, and the media derive their right to that information from the public's right.

- Promotions can have a significant impact on public opinion about the organization. Be sure the impact is a positive one.

- Ultimately the ethical, responsible practice of public relations is a personal choice.

Go to the Web site for this book at **www.cengage.com/masscomm/newsom/thisispr10e** to find more Web links on this subject.

Other Related Web Sites to Review

Canadian Public Relations Society (CPRS)
http://www.cprs.ca/AboutCPRS/e_code.htm

Council of Public Relations Firms (CPRF)
http://www.prfirms.org/

index.cfm?fuseaction=Page.viewPage&pageId=532&parentID=472

Institute for Public Relations (IPR)
http://www.instituteforpr.org/essential_knowledge/detail/ethics_and_public_relations/

International Association of Business Communicators (IABC)
http://www.iabc.com/about/code.htm

International Public Relations Association (IPRA)
http://www.ipra.org/detail.asp?articleid=24

National School Public Relations Association (NSPRA)
http://www.nspra.org/

Public Relations Society of America (PRSA)
http://www.prsa.org/aboutUs/ethics/index.html

Radio-Television News Directors Association and Foundation (RTNDA) Code of Ethics and Professional Conduct
http://www.rtnda.org/pages/media_items/code-of-ethics-and-professional-conduct48.php

Society of Professional Journalists (SPJ)
http://www.spj.org/ethicscode.asp

CHAPTER 8

PR and the Law

The law is the last result of human wisdom acting upon human experience for the benefit of the public.

—Samuel Johnson, *Miscellanies*

OBJECTIVES

- To understand the legal environments of PR practice.
- To be familiar enough with the law to stay within safe boundaries.
- To develop an appreciation for working with legal counsel.
- To be sensitive to the impact of litigation on public opinion.

You are public relations director for a toy company that has its own line of electronic educational toys with a very distinctive character called "cyber cadet" used in the promotions. One of your staff members tells you that the local library in the city where your corporate headquarters is located is using the cyber cadet figure on its Web page. Is this illegal? Should you talk with the corporate attorney about filing a lawsuit?

As your PR firm's account executive for a pharmaceutical company client, you are working on a competitive strategy to respond to another company's new product. You learn that this product is expected to be approved soon by the U.S. Food and Drug Administration (FDA). When that occurs, it will seriously challenge your client company's product. Your boss tells you to run your strategy by the client's in-house attorney because that way it will be "privileged" information and thus not ever publicly disclosed. Is that the case?

You are the staff public relations person for a school district that has just bought a new fleet of buses and vans in which to transport students. The manufacturer sends you some information about the safety of the buses and the adaptability of the vans for use with handicapped students. Your employer encourages you to put this in the school district's newsletter. Is this a good idea? Would the school district be responsible if some safety problems later appeared? ■

You've been asked to write a publicity release that downplays your organization's financial crisis. Can you do that?

One of your clients spent a lot of money for a distinctive logo that you promoted with stories in the trade press describing its development. Now you find an advertisement in *The Wall Street Journal* for an organization with a logo very similar to that of your client's. What can you do?

You've been asked to write the script for an **infomercial** (a program-length commercial) that mimics a talk show program to the extent of simulating "commercial breaks." You don't know anything about the product or the doctor being "interviewed" on this infomercial—other than information you've been given by your boss. Can you write the script?

Your lawyer client calls to tell you that she's just completed a week of special seminars and received a certificate. She wants to know if she can add the certification to the letterhead of the stationery you helped design for her. What do you tell her?

You're trying to create a full-page ad for a special newspaper section that will call attention to the annual outdoor sports event you handle. Thus, you need a photo of people attending an event that has yet to occur. Last year's news coverage included a good picture of a couple inflating a raft. Can you use the picture?

Your organization's human resources person calls to ask if you have model releases for the pictures of employees used in the last magazine. One of those pictured doesn't work for your organization anymore. You don't have a release. Is this a problem?

As the public relations director for a publicly held children's book publisher, you oversee all of the promotional materials for the books as well as the corporate publicity, advertising and promotions. The company has an investor relations manager who handles all of the financial news and the annual report, although you have helped him with that. He is going on a cruise and tells you that the news release about the second quarter earnings needs to be written while he is gone. He says the chief financial officer (CFO) has agreed to go over the earnings report with you when it is ready and will clear the news release once you've written it and send it for you. You agree to do that; it sounds simple. A week later, the CFO brings you the report and reviews it with you. You then write the release, which he approves and sends. That evening you have dinner with your brother who is a financial analyst, and you tell him about your new experience. In doing so, you tell him that the earnings were down, but the company

had expected that because a new series of children's travel books that was expected to do well has not. This is simply innocent dinner conversation, right?

These are all legal questions that PR practitioners in the USA encounter. While the laws governing what is and is not legal in PR vary from country to country, all countries have laws with which PR practitioners need to be familiar. Furthermore, because so much of PR practice is global today, although this chapter deals with U.S. law, PR practitioners must know laws governing what they say and do in all countries in which they are working. Because legal questions sometimes catch you unaware, it's wise to have a close working relationship with your organization's attorney.

Indeed, most public relations practitioners in independent practice have their own attorneys. Of course, sometimes the legal difficulties PR people encounter are of their own making. In the mid-1980s, the president of PRSA was accused of insider trading, and for the first time in history, a PR firm was charged with the same offense. PR people are faced with countless temptations, and the practice of public relations is a legal minefield.

The Liabilities of Practicing PR

PR practitioners are more conscious than ever of their legal exposure. An Oklahoma City counselor says he now buys malpractice insurance, a business expense he never considered until the mid-1970s. The policy is his response to three areas of exposure identified by attorney Morton Simon: (1) normal legal exposure, like that encountered by any other person, encompassing civil and criminal matters, including conspiracy; (2) work-oriented legal exposure, such as that found in the course of normal PR or publicity activities; (3) extraneous legal exposure, including everything from testifying as an expert witness to getting sports event tickets for a client to lobbying without registering as a lobbyist or reporting income and expenses from such activities. This third category also includes allowing the corporation to use the public relations office as a conduit for illegal corporate political contributions and, in the international arena, allowing it to use the PR office as the locus for bribes or other illicit activities.[1]

Liabilities have increased as outsourcing has become more common. Organizations always have been responsible for anything done by their contract workers. The "work for hire" is considered the same as "in-house" work. If a photographer hired by the company failed to get permission to take someone's picture, that always became the company's responsibility once the photo was published. But now the photographer may be giving the picture to a PR boutique that is producing the brochure, magazine or newsletter for the company. The company is still responsible for the results, but monitoring the process is a lot more difficult.

PR consultant and educator Marian Huttenstine says public relations itself has its functional roots in commercial speech, advertising, traditional speech and the press, and, as a result, statutory and case law for public relations is constantly evolving in all of these areas.[2]

PR developed in the USA largely because of the country's specific social, economic and political climate, and the last of these depends heavily on constitutionally protected freedom of speech and of the press. Huttenstine notes that some of the laws governing public relations practice would not be in place if First Amendment guarantees had not been found to apply to commercial speech.[3]

Legal Problems: Civil and Criminal

Civil suits involving PR practitioners may occur in relation to communication activities—for example, copyright infringements—or physical activities, such as accidents during plant tours. In addition, the practitioner may incur statutory and administrative liability in connection with dealings with government administrative agencies (SEC, FTC, FDA, ICC and others). A publicity release, for example, may violate SEC regulations, cause the company's stock to be closed for trading and result in court action. A carelessly worded ad can result in fines and perhaps court action. The statutory responsibilities are substantial. Sometimes a civil case results from failure to do something required as a matter of compliance (such as obligatory disclosure of certain information), rather than from doing something wrong—failing to disclose information, for example. Or it might be an entirely internal matter, such as a letter to employees advocating management's position on a unionization effort. The National Labor Relations Board (NLRB) takes a dim view of persuasive communications that sound coercive.

More so than ordinary citizens, PR practitioners are also exposed to many opportunities for criminal actions such as bribery, price fixing, mail fraud, securities manipulation and even perjury. To yield to these opportunities, however, is to risk criminal charges,

particularly for conspiracy. It is imperative, therefore, to understand the PR person's legal standing as the agent of the client. As Morton Simon explains:

Whatever the PR practitioner does, he usually does by reason of his retainer by his client and in concert with the client. Joint or multiparty action is therefore almost indigenous to the PR function. This is the root of the conspiracy charge.[4]

Simon lists five situations in which a PR practitioner may be subjected to a conspiracy charge. These occur when the practitioner (1) participates in the illegal action; (2) counsels, guides and directs the policy behind it; (3) takes a large personal part in it; (4) sets up a propaganda agency to fight enemies of it; or (5) cooperates to further it.

A civil suit and a criminal prosecution can and often do grow out of the same legal situation. Protection from double jeopardy, being tried twice for essentially the same infraction, no longer covers defendants facing both civil and criminal action. In 1997, the Supreme Court ruled that defendants who contend that they have already been sufficiently punished by a civil suit now must offer very clear proof that their civil penalty is the equivalent of a criminal penalty (see *Hudson v. U.S.*). When a company is fined in civil court it isn't always likely that its executives will also face criminal action. However, parallel civil and criminal proceedings are becoming common because Congress has provided for a number of different types of civil penalties in cases involving securities regulations, banking, environmental codes, government fraud and drug laws. The government may prosecute and try to impose regulatory fines, order forfeiture of property or keep a company from doing business with certain entities.[5]

Legal Cases

Simon suggests that PR practitioners are usually involved in four specific kinds of cases: the big case, the human interest case, the routine case and testimony. The big case, as he describes it,

[M]ay be antitrust action directed at [a company's] entire marketing program, a labor relations hearing involving thousands of employees, suits involving product liability—especially those which deal with basic safety or acceptability of a product—minority stockholders' actions charging mismanagement or fraud, and other litigation basic to the continued success of the company.[6]

The human interest case may not involve much money, but by its nature it has a particular appeal to the news media. Simon lists the following examples:

[A] minor civil rights charge, a local zoning conflict, a right of privacy suit by a "glamour name," air or water pollution charges, suits against a company by a retired employee seeking a large pension, and myriad other kinds of litigation which may concern either an individual or some community interest.

The routine types of litigation are commonplace results of being in business. They include "actions for breach of contract, workmen's compensation claims, tax refund matters." Routine suits rarely involve such public relations activities as the preparation of documents, publicity releases or media conferences for executives. Therefore, most routine litigation is unlikely to need staff PR involvement or the PR firm's help (if the company is a client). Of course, the PR person who owns a firm or works as a consultant is subject as such to all the routine and normal potential litigation of being in business.

Cases calling for a PR person's testimony typically involve his or her participation in the company program at issue in the legal action or his or her status as an "expert" witness. These may vary from "cases growing out of preparation of the company president's statement before a congressional committee to a $200 supplier claim for tables and chairs used at a company picnic." Cases may also involve a high-profile client or a company executive accused of some illegal act.

The potential now for any case—not just the ones Simon calls "big" or "human interest" cases—to attract attention is greater due to litigation journalism. Carole Gorney, the public relations educator who defined the term in an article in the *New York Times* in 1992, says litigation journalism is the use and/or manipulation of the news and information media to advance the positions of plaintiffs in civil lawsuits and/or to promote the practices of trial lawyers by attracting new clients for class action litigation.[7] This promotion also has occurred in high-profile criminal cases.

Litigation Journalism/Public Relations

What Gorney identified as litigation journalism also has been called "litigation public relations" because the situation is one in which lawyers simultaneously act as both lawyer and publicist/spokesperson for their clients. Law firms have become mediawise in the last 10 years; some now have their own public

relations practitioners, and some have marketing staffs to promote the firm. Members of the law firm that engage in litigation PR often get very well known, but their law firms don't. Sometimes the law firm with a really unpleasant case doesn't want publicity and that creates problems for their PR people who have to deal with the media in any event, regardless of what the law firm wants.

Large corporations have their own lawyers, and sometimes their role in a litigation/PR case, often with activists, is difficult because to large numbers of the media public, a lawsuit means guilty, whatever the outcome (see Chapter 13). There are also constraints on what the corporate lawyer can do without getting into trouble with the judge.

Two high-profile events put litigation PR in the forefront. One was the George W. Bush versus Al Gore presidential battle that got very complex in Florida, where Bush's brother, Jeb, was governor. The nitty-gritty details of voting machines and state rules on voting had the public and the news media bogged down, as well as the campaign communication staffs who suddenly found themselves in another game—litigation PR.

An expert in the practice, and one of the best known for it, is Robert L. Shapiro, who represented O. J. Simpson in his murder case. "When we are retained for these high-profile cases, we are instantly thrust into the role of a public relations person," Shapiro wrote in a 1993 article, "Using the Media to Your Own Advantage." Although Shapiro does not recommend lying to the news media or making up facts, he does say that the calculated manipulation of the news media is essential for a defense attorney to counter what he (as a defense attorney) considers the natural advantage of the prosecutor.[8]

Prosecutors also have used litigation journalism. Thus, a case may be tried in the court of public opinion at the same time it is being tried in the courts. The consequence is a conflict between the First and Sixth Amendments, the latter of which protects a defendant's right to a fair trial. Using public relations practitioners for high-profile cases is not new. The joint practice by lawyers of public relations and law is.

With regard to civil suits, legal concerns have grown for PR practitioners in connection with what Marian Huttenstine calls the duty or legal obligation for clear and accurate communications, detrimental reliance (ill effects of depending upon someone to keep confidences), vicarious liability and respondeat superior (being responsible for the action of others) and fair use.[9]

Theory and Research Perspective

Disagreements between public relations practitioners and lawyers often are centered in what has been called the "legal turn of mind." What that means is a focus on winning.

PR people are trained to see the many facets of a situation and try to work out "win-win" arrangements, which means their perspective is accommodation and negotiation. Both are important in public relations because the publics of any organization seldom are in total agreement on policies or practices, so negotiation is needed. Success is when a public that really doesn't like something the organization is doing or planning to do accepts the situation and agrees not to fight it.

One semanticist, Paul Globus, says those with a legal turn of mind also tend to be "poor listeners, highly opinionated, righteous, arrogant, and harshly judgmental." His observation comes from their talk in terms of polar opposites, right or wrong, guilty or innocent. That's a small step, Globus says, from the "I-know-better-than-you-about-everything" syndrome. "Words, in fact, are symbolic utterances whose meanings reside in the minds of those making them. Meanings of words evolve over time," Globus says.

A legal climate fills public discourse with confrontational stances and verbal sparring that prevent listening calmly to the ideas and opinions of others without needing to refute them.

Source: Paul Globus, "The Legal Turn of Mind," *ETC, Journal of General Semantics*, Winter 2000–2001, pp. 451–454. Reprinted by permission.

Duty is the civil legal obligation to act in a way consistent with what might be expected of a "reasonable person," as assessed by a judge or jury. Problems in this area generally have had to do with risks and warnings or misleading communications. The determination hinges on the interpretation of whether the reader or listener acted on the message "reasonably." The consequences of reliance have to be something detrimental (and quantifiable in terms of money damages) for the case to be actionable.[10]

Detrimental reliance may occur when relied-upon information is faulty or when a promise is broken. One example consists of relying on information from others such as research and development people supplying product information for publicity and advertising that proves to be less than entirely accurate. Another involves using or distributing information from a supplier that later turns out to be flawed. Detrimental reliance also may occur if a PR person is a source for information to news media or others on the basis of a promise of confidentiality that later is broken and the results are damaging to the source.[11]

Being responsible for the acts of others under contract to your organization has always been a legal obligation. But now there is more of a responsibility on the part of the organization to be sure that those working for the organization either directly as employees or indirectly as contractors don't do anything illegal. Most communication today is electronic, and that means all material ever on a computer can be recovered, even if deleted. Organizations today have greater difficulty meeting this obligation because whole tasks are contracted out and because those under contract often subcontract for special services. An example would be a contractor engaged to do the weekly newsletter who then subcontracts for art or distribution. For anything the subcontractors do, the organization for which they are ultimately doing the job—not just its contractor—is responsible.[12] The fair use aspect of copyright law has become increasingly complicated because of the use of electronic transmissions.[13] We examine this question in some detail later in this chapter.

Working with Legal Counsel

Most large institutions, businesses and news media have legal counsel. If your client retains legal help, use it. The client's own counselor is as eager to stay out of trouble as you are. One word of caution, though. Some attorneys are not knowledgeable in communications law, and their instinct is to have a client or the organization say nothing. This is usually not the best public relations response. You need to know where to go for specialized legal counsel.

Many practitioners have also built up libraries of cases and regulations relating to both public relations and their clients. In addition, many PR firms have prepared manuals for their employees to alert them to legal trouble spots. Clients, too, may have manuals; the PR person should ask for them and examine them carefully for areas where misunderstandings might create problems.

The public relations person within a corporation needs to establish a liaison with the corporate attorney, advises Morton Simon. Simon suggests that some CEOs ask PR practitioners to do "Machiavellian" things because they don't understand what a PR person is supposed to do, because so many "loose" descriptions of the PR job are floating around and because PR activities are difficult to define.[14]

Another reason for establishing a liaison with the corporate attorney is that the top PR person holds a seat within inner management councils, helping to formulate policy that will affect the organization's various publics, with special concern for how that policy will be understood and accepted by those publics. Therefore, the corporate PR person is in a good position to assist corporate counsel in planning strategies and suggesting how the various publics are likely to receive legal actions.[15] The PR person also needs legal counsel's help, especially in reviewing financial materials, even if trained in investor relations and also in crises. Determining the appropriate action in a crisis is clearer if attorneys can talk about actions that can be taken and alternatives, perhaps citing similar cases and their conclusions, noting particular similarities and differences. Their experience with the courts also allows them to set some timetables and help develop the company's message.

Transparency is important because legal discovery procedures bring out all sorts of hidden information that will get introduced in the public forum of the courtroom.[16] Any of these documents may later be disclosed. Even documents prepared by in-house lawyers may not be secure if they contain advice to management that is strategic but is essentially non-legal in nature. The material must be primarily legal advice for it to deserve attorney/client privilege from disclosure.[17]

For these reasons, the relationship between the PR person and the company attorney needs to be complementary, not adversarial.

Ways to Stay Out of Trouble

Maintaining a good relationship with the organization's attorney is one of the best ways to stay out of trouble, but attorney Morton Simon identifies five others:

1. Recognize your individual responsibility for your actions—none of this "I only did what the boss said." The law won't look at it that way.

2. Know your business.

3. Ignore the vague lines between advertising and PR, because the law often does.

4. Decide how far you are willing to go to run a risk of jail, fine, a cease and desist order or a corrective order.

5. "Know your enemy," especially which government agency is likely to go after you. It helps to get on the agency's mailing list and read all speeches its administrators give. Often these provide the first hint of troubles for your company or industry.

Simon notes three general types of legal involvements. The first consists of meeting federal, state and local government agencies' regulations on everything from antitrust matters to building permits.

The second consists of government-related activities—activities that hinge on laws or regulations such as those governing libel and slander; right of privacy; contempt of court; ownership of ideas including copyright, trademarks and patents; publicity; political views, registering political activity as lobbying and representing foreign governments; contract disputes; stockholder actions; fair trade problems; use of photos of individuals and groups; preparation of publicity releases, advertising copy, games and giveaway promotions; and financial collections.

The third type consists of contracts with clients and suppliers of goods and services. These deal with such matters as who owns the music for a commercial jingle if the client moves his or her account from the agency that created the commercial and what recourse you have if the photographer you hired to make enlargements messes up the color negatives you provided.[18]

In any of these three types of cases, a PR person outside the situation is likely to be called by either side as an expert witness. When this occurs, you must devote considerable time to research—gathering facts in the case, not just relying on what you are told. (Most PR testimony consists of fact finding, in the discovery part of litigation.) Additionally, most PR people alert their own attorneys, who can advise them of any legal traps or personal jeopardy. Litigants generally pay fees for expert witnesses. However, excessive fees tend to invalidate the testimony. (The opposition generally tries to get the precise sum made public, usually as a part of the deposition.)

The legal zones of greatest danger to a PR person are business memos and letters, proxy fights, use of photos, product claims, accusations that might be ruled libel or slander, promotions involving games, publicity that might result in charges of misrepresentation, and political campaigns. You should keep handy a checklist of laws covering areas such as contracts, releases, statements of responsibility and rights of privacy.

Most important, don't guess. Get legal assistance. Talk with the organization's legal counsel. Work closely with media and organization attorneys. The New York Stock Exchange encourages calls and other inquiries. Query any government body involved, and get a statement of legal precedent or request an informal ruling.

Getting government advice and assistance won't work, though, with one of the biggest sources of difficulty for an organization—lawsuits initiated by an employee, a "whistleblower" who has called attention of authorities, usually government regulators, to some legal problem. Laws at the federal, state and local levels constrain communications in whistleblower cases, so normal strategies may not work. For example, federal laws place a 60-day secrecy on the existence of a whistleblower. In some cases, an organization can be under investigation for a year or more before the situation is made public, and then it is usually the government entity involved that makes the announcement. All PR communication, then, can be only reactive. The same is true if information about the case is "leaked." Leaks may originate outside the organization from someone knowledgeable about the situation, but there is always a court seal on such cases affecting both the organization and the whistleblower.

At the national level, whistleblowers get their power from the U.S. Federal False Claims Act that allows citizens to "blow the whistle" on an organization's misdeeds, to start sealed lawsuits on the government's behalf and to get 25 percent for themselves of what the government collects. At the state and local levels, the government's primary role is to protect the whistleblower from some kind of retaliation, usually getting fired. Whatever branch of government joins the whistleblower's suit, the organization is in a default position. The government has both authority and power behind it, and public opinion often supports the whistleblower who is seen as the responsible citizen calling attention to organizational wrongdoing.[19] (See Chapter 13 for more information on whistleblowers.)

Government Regulations

As a practitioner, you may find yourself working with any of hundreds of government agencies. Of this multitude, five are particularly important due to their influence on how PR is practiced: the U.S. Postal Service, the Securities and Exchange Commission (SEC), the Federal Trade Commission (FTC), the Food and Drug Administration (FDA) and the Federal Communications Commission (FCC).

Postal Service

Postal Service regulations prohibit dissemination by mail of obscene materials, information about a lottery (two important elements: consideration and chance) and material that would incite riot, murder, arson or assassination. A 1975 law exempts newspapers and broadcast stations from prosecution in publicizing state-operated lotteries. However, newspapers may not carry information on another state's lotteries in editions that are mailed.

Certain state laws prohibit the circulation of magazines carrying particular types of advertising, so space buyers have to beware. Furthermore, although substantial specifications exist for inserts in magazines mailed second-class, the total reference to the subject in the Postal Service Manual with respect to controlled circulation publications is one sentence: "Enclosures are not permitted."

All mailing pieces face multiple regulations regarding size, weight, thickness and where an address may appear. It is best to have the design of a piece checked by the post office, or to use standard shapes and weights already approved.

A sender's freedom to reach publics by direct mail has been limited by a 1970 decision in a U.S. District Court, which has been upheld by the U.S. Supreme Court.[20] Senders may be compelled to delete an address from their mailing list and may be prohibited by law from sending or having an agent send future mailings to an addressee at the addressee's request.

The case began when a mail-order business challenged a California regulation stating that the recipient has a right not to have to receive "a pandering advertisement which offers for sale matter which addressee in his sole discretion believes to be erotically arousing or sexually provocative." If a violation occurs, the addressee may report it and the Postmaster General will inform the sender, who then has an opportunity to respond. An administrative hearing is held to see whether a violation has occurred. The Postmaster General may request the U.S. Attorney General to enforce compliance through a court order.

Three points here are significant:

1. The law allows a person absolute discretion to decide whether he or she wishes to receive any further material from a particular sender. (The material need not be erotic.)

2. A vendor does not have a constitutional right to send unwanted material to someone's home. A mailer's right to communicate must stop before the mailbox of an unreceptive addressee.

3. The law satisfies the due process rights of the vendor who sends the material. It provides for an administrative hearing if the sender does violate the prohibitory order from the U.S. Postal Service, and a judicial hearing is held prior to issuance of any compliance order by a district court.

As a result, the Postal Service now provides two relevant forms. Form 2150 is directed to a particular sender and is usually requested when a person has received obscene or sex-related materials in the mail. Form 2201 is a request that a person's name be removed from all mailing lists. In an effort to counteract legislation that might be directed toward controlling unsolicited mail, the Direct Marketing Association has asked that all persons who wish to be removed from the lists of their members send their name and mailing address to the DMA (1120 Avenue of the Americas, New York, NY 10036–6700, or 1119 19th Street NW, Washington, DC 20036–3603; http://www.the-dma.org). The DMA then contacts individual mailers and asks that they delete the name. (The DMA in 1998 merged with Association of Interactive Media, a leading cyberspace trade group that is now operating as a subsidiary of DMA.)

Securities and Exchange Commission (SEC)

Public corporations (those whose stock is publicly traded and owned) have to be concerned with SEC regulations, and all corporations must be aware of and sensitive to personnel and financial information that might be released. The larger the company, the more likely it is to let something escape that should not have. This is particularly true when the corporation must coordinate its information dissemination with one of its clients (especially in the case of companies with government contracts) or when releases are prepared by an outside firm.

It is wise to have a procedure for clearing news releases so that no one is confused about what to do and (it is hoped) so that no one jumps the gun and releases a story before it has been cleared (see Figure 8.1). Some institutions release only the information required, but a case can be made for using releases as early warning signals (such as for possible bankruptcy filing) and as timely announcements of good news. Taking the offensive in takeover battles became a PR tactic. However, financial abuses have pushed the SEC to take a more active role in policing disclosures.

The SEC is concerned with:

- Initial public offerings (IPOs) when a company decides to become a publicly held company
- The information a publicly held company gives for investment evaluation, formerly given only to analysts now required to be publicly available
- Regular reporting of financial condition on a quarterly basis
- Special filings when material issues arise
- Annual report and 10K

Public relations practitioners are involved in all five of these, and if you are not handling investor relations, you may be working for a firm or agency that has a publicly held company as an account, or you may be the PR person in a company that has an investor relations practitioner with whom you need to have a solid working relationship, which means understanding his or her role and functions.

In an effort to clean up bad business practices and return public trust to publicly held companies, the government enacted in 2002 the Sarbanes-Oxley corporate reform law.[21] The law's aim was to bring transparency and responsibility to business practices. It has been costly to companies because it requires extensive examination of internal audit systems that began to have to be researched, documented and reported in 2004. The act also requires CEOs and CFOs to sign off, personally, on the validity of all financial reports. Corporate board committee charters and corporate codes of ethics must be posted for public access, and companies are required to have a direct whistleblower line to the board of directors. The law has affected all of the publicly held public relations and advertising conglomerates, of course.[22] Although intended for publicly held companies, SOX has also affected nonprofits because many of the larger ones, including schools such as Juilliard

Figure 8.1   **Procedures for Clearing News Releases**

Handling of Product News Releases

1. First draft of copy to primary sources for preliminary approval.
2. Draft of release to corporate secretary for approval.
3. Revised copy to legal department for approval.
4. Draft to division general manager for approval in certain instances. (Group public relations manager should make judgment in this instance.)
5. Copy of approved news release is then mailed to the company handling news releases, along with media selection sheets for distribution.
6. Media covered will depend on the nature of the product, its importance to the various markets and industries and the marketing philosophy behind the development. (Distribution should be as broad as possible without covering media that would obviously not be interested in the development.)
7. Internal distribution of the news release to be determined by the group public relations manager.

Approval Chain for Agency-Prepared Releases

1. Clear with primary source at division.
2. Send cleared draft to group public relations manager for corporate clearance.
3. Following approvals at corporate level, distribution may be made through agency channels.
4. Copies of completed release to all involved in clearances. (News releases that must be approved at the corporate level include features, case histories, new product releases and any other product-oriented information released to magazines or other news media.)

Handling of Personnel News Releases

1. First draft of copy to individual named in release to check accuracy of facts.
2. Draft of release to source requesting release.
3. Draft of release to division general manager or individual's immediate superior at corporate level.
4. Draft to corporate secretary and legal department for legal clearances.
5. Draft to group vice president in cases of key promotions at divisional level. In instances of key corporate promotions, the chairman, president, executive vice president, general counsel and appropriate group vice president must clear release.
6. Media coverage should include plant cities, corporate headquarter's city, the individual's home town, association publications and appropriate alumni publications, as well as trade magazines covering industries served by the division or group with which the individual is associated.
7. Internal distribution determined by group PR manager and, in cases of key corporate promotions, by public relations director.
8. Copies of news release should be sent to everyone included in the chain of approval.

Note: These procedures depend on the organizational structure and policy. Each organization will develop its own clearance procedures.

and institutions such as The International Swimming Hall of Fame, have adopted Sarbanes-Oxley practices to reassure donors and supporters and to enhance credibility.[23]

IPOs have been troublesome for the SEC because the initial offering of dot-com stocks, and continue to be so. Because companies are offering their shares for the first time, they have to disclose all of their business and prospects for this offering. PR practitioners were in demand when the dot-coms first began offering their shares because a business without bricks and mortar and a tangible product was expected to be a hard sell. The dot-coms sold well due in part to public fascination with the technology and in part to strong publicity. What happened, though, was information in the high-tech world got passed along informally in chat rooms and bulletin board postings. Most of that was uncontrolled, as is characteristic of the Internet. Enthusiasts were doing their own promoting and using poster names that didn't really identify them. It wasn't long before the realization came to some of them that what they posted could affect the shares of stock, any stock. Other unauthorized posters use news releases to engage in stock fraud. Why do you need to know this? Companies have to watch for fake, maybe even libelous, information that appears in chat rooms and on bulletin boards daily. Any of these can precipitate a crisis for the company.

Simultaneous disclosure (Regulation FD) is now the rule for all material information. Financial briefings used to be given periodically to financial analysts, especially those following the company closely.

The briefings were usually given by the CEO and CFO with the investor relations person sitting in. An August 10, 2000, ruling by the SEC requires that material information be disclosed publicly at the same time as it is given to large institutional investors and any securities professionals, analysts and money managers. The rule applies only to information given by senior executives, not other managers and supervisors in contact with suppliers and customers. All of these briefings are now followed by a news release.

To accommodate the rule's requirement for full and simultaneous disclosure, companies have broadened access to conference calls so that individual investors are given a call-in number that allows them to listen but, usually, not to ask questions as all of the securities community (large and small investors) is allowed to do. Access is also provided through the Internet with the time and date of the call posted on the company's Web site. There anyone can listen in and then send emails for explanations or additional information. The news release covering the hour or longer conference call follows as closely as possible and is also posted on the Web site as well as sent to the financial wires and general news wires.

Compliance has increased corporate use of Web sites. Investors may vote their proxies online, and get the annual report and 10K and any other filings by email or fax. Site visitors can sign up to receive all kinds of company announcements by email, if they wish, and the result of Regulation FD (for fair disclosure), has pushed investor relations into using technology more.[24] IRs turn to technology mainly because if material information is accidentally released, the company has only 24 hours to make it publicly available. The rule initially was not favorably received by the National Investor Relations Institute (NIRI) to which most IR practitioners belong. However, Reg FD has managed to save companies money and has made it easier for CEOs and CFOs to control the timing and positioning of information, a consequence probably not intended by the SEC. It has increased the responsibilities of the IR person.

Quarterly financial reports (10Q) are required by the SEC, although critics say this encourages companies to look short-term, rather than long-term, to keep stock prices going up rather than down. In the Enron and WorldCom debacles the need to keep the stock price climbing was a contributing factor, but that's no excuse for fraudulent behavior. In fact, that is exactly what quarterly reports are supposed to prevent. These earnings reports are prepared by the CFO and reviewed by corporate audit committees, the majority of which are supposed to be outside, independent directors knowledgeable about financial matters. Each quarterly report is accompanied by a news release interpreting the data, and usually written and released by the IR officer. As a result of the financial scandals of 2002, as mentioned earlier, CEOs have to sign the reports as testimony (an oath) to their having read and approved them with penalties for fraud (civil penalties or jail time) if the reports are later proven to be inaccurate or misleading.

Special Filings, such as an 8K, are to alert the SEC, investors and potential investors to any changes in the financial climate that are likely to affect earnings and/or the price of the stock. In other words, anything material. The company has 15 days from the event, such as an unfavorable court ruling in a lawsuit, sale or acquisition of significant assets to disclose. A delay may be requested if trade secrets or competitive data are at risk. However, most companies in light of RegFD release the material information as promptly as possible. What is important for PR people to remember is that the news releases accompanying these are considered by the SEC to be as important as the forms filed. A misstep, even unintentional, can cause serious consequences. (To his credit, David Duncan, Enron's chief auditor at Arthur Andersen, warned Enron against putting out a news release with "misleading" information in its third-quarter earnings report, but was ignored by Enron management.)

If a leak occurs or the event is likely to cause a flurry of activity for the stock, the exchange will stop trading, but only briefly. A judgment to withhold can't be made to defraud, and there must be no downplay in reporting good or bad news.

The other occasion for the exchanges to control trading is when large investors, usually major retirement or mutual funds, use computerized sells that automatically put shares on the market, usually in response to special events that push prices down. This policy was instituted after Black Monday in 1987 caused a precipitous drop in stock prices. Called **program trading**, the market curbs go on when the volume of trading causes a 180 point drop in the Dow Jones Industrial Average. Trading actually shuts down if a market declines by 950 points before 2 p.m. Eastern time.

Annual reports and 10Ks are the year's summary of the company's activities, the 10K being the required form that must be filed with the SEC. For annual report and 10K requirements, go the SEC's Web site. Also look for the Financial Accounting Standards Board **(FASB)** rules on accounting for postretirement benefits **(OPEB)** other than pensions. The present value of OPEB must be declared as a liability. Those provisions took effect in 1992. Because of the corporate failures of 2002, a few companies—Coca-Cola was the first—now are declaring as liabilities stock options that are available but not yet taken by management and/or directors.

The annual report and the 10K are usually prepared by IR officers, PR staffs or firms. Annual reports have become promotional tools used by investment brokers and the company itself in presenting the company to all members of the financial public, from banks to analysts. When annual reports are distributed, a news release summarizing the main points and announcing the report's publication is also sent out (see Figure 8.2). The annual report may include the 10K as the best way to integrate management messages with financial reports.

In annual reports and the news releases that accompany them, the SEC also allows speculative claims. These are called "forward-looking statements" and must be identified as such in the report and the release. In addition to the SEC, which

administers six major federal statutes in this area, other federal agencies important to financial institutions include the Federal Deposit Insurance Corporation (FDIC), which insures bank deposits, and the Federal Home Loan Bank Board (FHLBB), which is responsible for savings and loan associations.

Major court cases have shown that corporate officials and employees must understand the legal obligations of proper corporate disclosure.[25] This is particularly true of the corporation's relationship with financial analysts and the investment community. In the *Texas Gulf Sulphur* case,[26] a federal district court ruling that the U.S. Supreme Court let stand, an insider was defined as anyone who has access to information that, if disseminated, might influence the price of a stock. A PR person who writes a news release, then, could be considered an insider. A PR firm must therefore disclose in its news releases that it is acting on behalf of an issuer and is receiving consideration from the issuer for its service. Richard S. Seltzer, former SEC special counsel, writes:

The SEC apparently believes that fraudulent schemes initiated by corporate insiders may be facilitated by the action—or deliberate inaction—of outside professionals: the accountant who "stretches" generally accepted

Figure 8.2 SEC Requirements for Annual Reports and Interpretive News Releases

The SEC offers guidance for management's discussion of a publicly held company's financial condition and the results of its operations. The Sarbanes-Oxley Act increased internal diligence as support for such statements (MD&A, management's discussion and analysis of the 10K and 10Q filings). In the news release that accompanies these documents, the National Investor Relations Institute (NIRI) suggests that a summary of the MD&A and other critical information for investors be incorporated into that release. Information that investors need includes material changes to the financial statement and other required disclosures, resources and liquidity status (assets and debts), high-risk items and potential threats to the company's overall financial health. Included with this news release, as with all earnings data in news releases that accompany quarterly reports, should be the company's income statement, with some historical information for investors to make comparisons of profits and losses, and a balance sheet that shows assets and

liabilities. NIRI also argues for plain English to be used in news releases. That is an important recommendation because some SEC report language is somewhat arcane except to the most experienced investors.

Financial releases usually include a prospective or forward-looking discussion of operations and finances that includes market data and trends of the industry, corporate-specific demands and commitments as well as any other uncertainties that could have material effects on the financial condition and results of operations. Forward-looking statements fall under the SEC's "safe harbor" rule that protects companies from liability if such required statements are made on a "reasonable basis," in "good faith," and if underlying assumptions are disclosed. A news release that is judged to be false or misleading may be found to be fraudulent, in which case it falls under SEC action.

accounting principles; the lawyer who is willing to "overlook" material disclosures; and even the public relations practitioner who seeks to portray a convincing, but inaccurate, picture of corporate events.[27]

Another federal court decision has affected financial public relations significantly. Pig 'N' Whistle, a Chicago-based restaurant and motel chain, was headed by Paul Pickle, who had previously been sentenced to 3 years in prison for misapplication of federally insured funds. Pig 'N' Whistle was brought before the SEC in February and March of 1972 to answer charges of having distributed two untrue and misleading press releases concerning stock transactions and acquisition of property in 1969. The firm was also charged with illegal stock registration.[28] The two releases, one made on September 8 and the other on December 30, contained untrue or misleading statements about the purchases of the Mary Ann Baking Company and the Holiday Lodge near Lake Tahoe. Pig 'N' Whistle stock shot up to $18 per share after the two releases—which came from Financial Relations Board, Inc., a public relations company—were printed. Pig 'N' Whistle had been a client of Financial Relations for 8 weeks in 1969.[29] The statements released by Financial Relations were handled by only one member of the firm. The president of Financial Relations stated that Pig 'N' Whistle had not provided the firm with proper SEC registration papers for the stock. The PR firm was told by Pig 'N' Whistle lawyers that immediate disclosure of the purchase made by Pig 'N' Whistle was necessary to comply with SEC disclosure requirements.[30] Thus, the releases couldn't wait for registration papers to be filed.

The SEC investigated the actions of both Pig 'N' Whistle and Financial Relations and ruled that Financial Relations had not exercised due caution in establishing the truth about the information furnished by Pig 'N' Whistle. The SEC said that Financial Relations should have done independent research before allowing any release to leave its offices. As a result, Financial Relations established within 30 days new procedures for reviewing the credentials of any new clients and for verifying the facts given to it for publication. This verification of facts covers any information that might affect investment decisions by stock purchasers. The SEC also ordered Financial Relations to cease any contact with Pig 'N' Whistle.

In the 1970s, following the *Pig 'N' Whistle* case, the SEC began reviewing possible new disclosure regulations designed to protect the stock purchaser.

The most important outcome of this, from the point of view of public relations, was that the kind of information released has to be more detailed and exact. Statements must be registered and must include a budget and cash flow projection for the company.[31] It is an SEC violation to issue a false and/or misleading release, whether or not a profit is realized as a result.

Public relations practitioners have to provide more information and be more certain now than in the past that the information is true. Further, the people who do the research and write the releases now assume the same liabilities as does the company about which the releases are published. The information the public relations department or firm releases—the financial operations, history, future outlook, management and marketing structure of the company for which it is working—must therefore be carefully considered. The SEC has placed a heavy burden on public relations practitioners by holding them accountable. Financial releases must also be considered in the context of other public information put out about the company. This underscores the need to speak with one voice, to ensure that no information is misleading. Especially important is pro forma accounting in earnings reports. Earnings reports now must be explained in the news releases from publicly held companies. The investor relations officers are on the front line here.

More on Follow-Up and Executive Compensation Disclosures Follow-up or additional disclosure is necessary under four circumstances:

1. New information must be updated when new events make previous statements misleading.

2. Responses to outside reports must be made if these are misleading and come from people in a position to have had the information approved by the company, such as an underwriter, director or large shareholder.

3. Trading of shares held by executives and all insiders, including the company itself and company-managed pension plans, must be reported unless all material information about the stock's value already has been made available to the public. (The company is liable if it has given material nonpublic information to outsiders.)

4. Acquisition and merger information must be disclosed when negotiations reach agreement in principle.

The SEC in 1992 changed policies regarding disclosure of compensation for senior executive officers in proxy statements. This includes the CEO and the four most highly paid senior executive officers who earn more than $100,000 per year in salary and bonus and requires details of other kinds of compensation awards and payouts such as stock options. The SEC also requires disclosure in proxy statements of employment and severance agreements of payments exceeding $100,000 for senior executive officers. The statements must also identify standard compensation arrangements for directors and information on interlocking directorships. In the proxy report, the SEC requires inclusion of a chart showing the total return of stock to shareholders (stock price appreciation plus dividends) in comparison with the returns on a broad market index, such as the Standard and Poor's 500, as well as with a peer group index, depending on the company's line of business. Other changes in the proxy rules involved unbundling proxy proposals so votes can be taken on separate issues, reporting the number of yes and no votes and allowing dissident stockholders to nominate their own candidates. Complete voting results have to be printed in the annual report and the 10K. Regulations requiring more transparency were put in place by the Sarbanes-Oxley Act of 2002.

Rumors, Leaks and Insider Information with Disclosure

When you are faced with rumors or leaks, you have three options: you can admit and disclose, you can make no comment or deny or you can dodge and mislead. Courts have disagreed over where to draw the line clearly between exploratory preliminary talks and serious negotiations.[32] The former may be reported in a relatively leisurely manner, but the latter should be reported quickly because information about them almost always leaks. Two bills introduced into Congress in 1987 would have amended the SEC Act of 1934 on this point. One would have required a "yes" or "no" response in talks about a tender offer. The other would have made misleading statements illegal but would not have outlawed the "no comment" response, which could cause speculative buying.

It is just as important to understand the SEC's view of information to which there is "equal access." People who have knowledge that others do not have access to are called insiders. Thus, an insider, viewed broadly, is anyone who has information "everyone" else doesn't have (for example, information not generally available) that would give that person an advantage in buying or

selling a company's stock. The court's rather narrow definition in the *Texas Gulf Sulphur* case stipulated that an insider is an "officer, director or beneficial owner of 10 percent of any class of equity or security." This definition has never been accepted by PR people, who looked with horror at headlines such as "Press Release Goes to Court."

Insider trading means using inside information to buy or sell securities or to buy puts, calls or other options on securities. This is considered insider trading whether the action is taken in the name of the person initiating the transaction or in the name of someone else. The U.S. Supreme Court upheld lower-court insider trading convictions of former *The Wall Street Journal* reporter R. Foster Winans and two co-conspirators on November 16, 1987. The SEC viewed the ruling as an affirmation of its efforts to halt insider trading, efforts that had become very aggressive in the 1980s. The Court's opinion upheld the convictions of the former reporter for securities, mail and wire fraud. The Court refused to reject the misappropriation theory, which holds that information may be misused no matter how it is obtained. (In this case, the reporter had obtained it in the course of writing his "Heard on the Street" column.) The misappropriation theory strengthens the SEC's broad interpretation of insider trading.

The SEC's interpretation is expected to cover the gray areas of the insider trading law, including informed tips received directly or indirectly from or through associates, from raiders, from overheard conversation or from prepublication access to news stories.

Even before the ruling in the *Winans* case, however, the SEC had charged a PR firm with insider trading. That case involved Ronald Hengen of R. F. Hengen, Inc., a financial public relations firm hired by Puritan Fashions Corporation (which was later bought by C. K. Holdings, Inc.). Andrew Rosen, Puritan's president in 1983, had issued an earnings projection of $3.25 per share on annual sales of $300 million. The SEC said in its complaint that both Rosen and Puritan's chief financial officer knew that the projection would not be met and so did Hengen, who told a stockbroker, who told another stockbroker. The two brokers allegedly engaged in $2 million worth of trading in Puritan stock before the public announcement that the earnings and sales projections were incorrect.

In 1998, the SEC's rule on insider trading got some criticism from the courts. The Eleventh U.S.

Court of Appeals ruled that in insider trading cases, the SEC must show that a corporate insider "used" material, nonpublic information when trading. The SEC's stance is that "knowing possession" of such information is enough. Proof of use is more difficult, and the court recognized that in saying that the SEC could make "knowing possession" a rule, this would become a standard in judging such cases.[33]

As soon as a company becomes aware of any insider trading, the SEC and the exchange must be notified, and if the situation is somewhat vague, consultation is available. When a decision is made and a news release prepared, the SEC and the exchange must receive the information before it is made publicly available through any medium. Then the release must go to all of the news and business wires as any other disclosure would.

SEC rules on insider trading that were put in place in 2000 clarified the law and also gave better information to people who want to know when corporate directors, executives and other insiders are buying or selling their company's stock. The rules were part of Reg FB and are the first to deal specifically with insider trading. Rule 10b5-1 says that insiders only have to be "aware" of confidential material information, in contrast to some previous decisions in which insiders used the information to buy or sell stock. Knowing means not selling or buying until the information is publicly available. Rule 10b5-2 extends the rule to family members and any other individuals in nonbusiness relationships who got the confidential information and agreed not to disclose it. This helps honest corporate insiders. If they had a regular program for exercising stock options or buying shares, timed for tax advantages, for example, they can still use that plan, even though in the intervening time they have become aware of sensitive information. What the SEC will look for is irregular trading.[34]

If new stock is to be issued, there is a registration period during which two types of publicity are forbidden: any estimates (dollars or percentages), even in broad or general terms, of earnings or sales for the industry or any product lines, and any predictions of increases in sales or earnings from any source. In 2006 an effort began to have the SEC exert more control over disclosure by lawmakers and staff of their trades and explicitly prohibit them from using information for insider trading. Also, the proposed congressional legislation would have firms gathering information on legislation and its status to register with the House and Senate. Such a rule would affect any group engaged in lobbying and/or public affairs.

Accounting Reform Bill Congress passed a corporate reform bill July 26, 2002, largely in reaction to the Arthur Andersen/Enron situations. The bill's components set the following in place: Corporate fraud that involves altering or destroying documents is a federal crime punishable by a $5 million fine and up to 20 years in prison; a five-member nongovernment board with subpoena power has been created to oversee accounting companies; new rules have been imposed on financial analysts to prevent conflict of interest; an accounting firm's consulting services are restricted when the firm is the company's outside auditor; personal loans from companies to top officials or board members have been prohibited; the time for defrauded investors to sue the company has been extended and a federal account for defrauded investors, with the funds to come from payment of civil fines and company assets, has been created. This puts additional responsibility on the IR person to keep a watchful eye on corporate processes as well as actions.

Federal Trade Commission

Although the SEC looks out for the rights of investors, another equally alert agency, the Federal Trade Commission (FTC), looks out for the rights of both investors and consumers. On the investor side, it monitors compliance with antitrust legislation and has been very aggressive in monitoring proposed mergers that impinge on antitrust laws. On the consumer side, the FTC's scrupulous surveillance has resulted in charges of false claims relating to publicity releases as well as to advertising. As in advertising, both the client making the assertions and the PR department or firm disseminating them are legally liable. This can fall under the previously discussed area of duty and detrimental reliance. The only protection is to take prudent precautions.

Consequently, the publicist should seek some verification for product or service claims before publicizing them. One suspicious (or cautious) publicist insists on trying a product before he writes the release. "If it works, and works well, I write a better story. If it doesn't work, I don't write it!" This is fine if the thing to be publicized is tangible, but often it is not. Services must be carefully explored, too. Some professionals, such as lawyers, have been sued for deceptive ads. Since the writer is legally responsible, some PR writers, especially those in independent firms (as opposed to corporate staff), require notarized statements from research and development staff of product attributes.

The conscientious publicist is less concerned with the action of government agencies than with consumers' wrath or loss of confidence, but he or she should still be aware that fraud or misrepresentation, as it applies to advertising, is watched over by the FTC, the local Better Business Bureau and state and local law enforcement authorities. And the PR person should certainly be aware that payola and similar illegal promotional activities are grouped by the law in the category of "bribes."

Among the promotional activities monitored by the FTC are infomercials—program-length commercials that are scripted to simulate standard entertainment or educational features. The FTC now has guidelines for infomercials. Instead of attempting to prosecute the producers of the products (miraculous aging cures) or services (making $1 million in real estate), the FTC has decided to go after the producers of the infomercials. The FTC guidelines require that the infomercial producers have "reliable, scientific evidence" before making any claims for a product's efficacy or safety. The FTC also requires disclosures that the infomercial is a paid commercial if it runs longer than 15 minutes. These disclosures have to appear at the beginning and end of the program, as well as before any ordering information.[35]

The FTC has also made some infomercial production companies more cautious. TV Inc. of Largo, Florida, says that it will no longer create infomercials for anything that has to be ingested, whether foods or medicines.[36] Even if they were not cautious before, all of the recalls of China-produced toys, drugs and food for both pets and humans that occurred in 2007 should put everyone connected with promoting such products on the alert. Responsibility to consumers creates a broad brush approach.

An FTC policy holds celebrities accountable for the statements they make in advertising. The first example of that FTC policy was a 1978 case resulting in a consent agreement of May 11, 1980, with singer Pat Boone. Boone was a spokesperson for Acne Statin, a skin preparation manufactured by Karr Prevention Medical Products, Inc. The FTC accused Boone of making false claims that the product cured acne, that it was superior to competitive products and that some members of his family had used the product with good results. Boone agreed to contribute to any restitution the FTC might order, but he didn't deny or admit to the charges.[37] Under the Reagan administration, the FTC became less aggressive, and Boone was even quoted as saying he would go back on the air to support the product. But while Boone had personal knowledge of this particular product, many celebrities endorse products without knowing anything about them; their only contact might be in having the product shipped free to their home or office. Advertising drugs directly to consumers has created all manner of problems, and stirred ethical issues as well. After Merck got into legal problems with its Vioxx over the drug's connection with heart failure, Pfizer decided to limit its advertising of new drugs to consumers until the products have been on the market for six weeks. Also 23 of the drug companies agreed to an advertising code of conduct in August 2005.

Food and Drug Administration

Like the FTC, the U.S. Food and Drug Administration (FDA) is active in protecting consumers. For instance, the FDA developed guidelines for consumer advertising initiated by drug companies. The first prescription drug advertising in the fall of 1983 appeared on cable TV shows aimed at physicians, but there is no way to exclude the lay public from exposure to the same advertising.

In September 1987, Sandoz Pharmaceuticals placed 25 full-page ads in newspapers nationwide to call attention to its antiallergy medicine Tavist-1. *The Wall Street Journal* noted, "the Sandoz ads are the first to mention a prescription drug by name in general-interest publications."[38] The FDA reviewed the Sandoz ads and proclaimed them legal. The FDA requires that ads mentioning a drug by name be balanced and contain the sort of prescription information doctors get about side effects and possible problems.

Physicians have expressed some concern that ads such as this will show only the advantages of the product. Nevertheless, the marketing, promotion and advertising of prescription drugs already has the drug companies' PR people heavily involved.

In 1991, the FDA told doctors who serve as paid agents of the drug industry that they too would be targets of FDA surveillance. At the same time a warning went out to the pharmaceutical industry to stop touting (in promotional brochures and articles) FDA unapproved uses for products. Complicating the whole matter is evidence that some substances in the body, even at low levels, can cause brain disorders, even cancer, in some people, especially children. The FDA considers the images, and, in broadcasting, the audio, including the use of music.

The FDA is getting pressure from food and drug industries to loosen their restrictions in the name of corporate free speech, but there's opposition to that. Of special concern to consumer advocates and the health industries is the publicizing of "off label" or unapproved uses of products. Although the FDA approves products for specific uses, sometimes research indicates additional benefits for something that may or may not be directly related. The FDA has moved away from a previous stance of keeping sales representatives from even giving such research reports to physicians, but it still does not permit wide dissemination of such materials. A series of food and pharmaceutical crises in 2006 and 2007 regarding Chinese involvement in production of both food and drugs for U.S. markets has put consumer pressure on the FDA to get involved in more, rather than less, surveillance.

The lesson here is that promotions and news releases, as well as advertising, can get you in trouble with the FDA. For safety, the FDA needs to be in the preapproval loop so the company won't get into trouble for "misleading" the public.[39]

Federal Communications Commission (FCC)

In 1981, the Federal Communications Commission **(FCC)** deregulated broadcasting—an action that primarily affected its public affairs programming requirements and the fairness doctrine for television and radio. In 1987, the FCC did away with the fairness doctrine altogether, as discussed in Chapter 7.

The deregulation has made it more difficult to get public service time because broadcasters are not required by the FCC to broadcast public service announcements (PSAs). Also, the demise of the fairness doctrine has made broadcasters more hesitant to accept issue advertising in any form, whether purchased time or public service announcements, because avoidable controversies can hurt advertising revenues.

The fairness doctrine required a station to provide reply time to any person or group who thought the presentation of a controversial issue had either attacked them or not presented their point of view. In October of 2000, the FCC repealed the only "fairness" rules left—the personal attack and political editorial rules—because these were based on the long gone fairness doctrine.

Still in force is the equal time rule, section 315 of the Communications Act, which requires stations to give equal access to political candidates during elections. The FCC also requires stations to give political candidates the lowest rates, to charge the same rates to candidates for the same office and to offer them an equal amount of time. Political ads are not subject to censorship for any reasons. Stations are protected because they may not be sued for any libel or slander in the commercials.

Many people forget that the FCC also regulates telecommunications, including telephone and computer networks and satellite communications. This means that PR's electronic communications also fall under the scrutiny of this government agency. So far the FCC has not weighed in on Internet activities, but with fraud claims being leveled against some of the e-commerce, there is always that opportunity. In 2008 the FCC held an auction of airwaves with major purchasers being companies interested in building broadband wireless networks for hand-held communication devices of all kinds. A block of airwaves in the auction that were set aside for public-safety groups such as firefighter and police did not sell and will have to be re-auctioned.

Court Rulings and Legal Responsibilities

Many aspects of PR are affected by court rulings and a variety of civil and criminal laws. Here we will touch on those that seem particularly important. One aspect of almost all of the legal responsibilities resulting from these is the presence of truth as a required element. Johnson & Johnson's Tylenol was the subject of a civil suit settled in May 1987.[40] Actually, what was being contested was Johnson & Johnson's slogan for the product: "You can't buy a more potent pain reliever without a prescription." The slogan was not true, said Judge William C. Conner, and he accused Johnson & Johnson of false and misleading claims in its advertising for Tylenol that exaggerated its superiority over other pain relievers. The judge reviewed all of Tylenol's ads and said the case pointed out five good lessons for consumers and advertisers:

1. Don't be fooled by headlines and pictures.
2. Beware of every word, even the smallest ones.
3. Numbers don't mean much, even the big ones.
4. Know the ingredients behind the product.
5. Repeating a slogan doesn't make it true.

A 1990 case involved a special event. Volvo had spent 24 years building a favorable image of its cars as the safest and strongest on the road. The special event was a monster truck contest in San Antonio, Texas, one aspect of which involved driving the monster trucks over several cars, including a Volvo. The other cars caved in, but the Volvo stood tall, and was hardly affected. The reason, brought to light later, was that Volvo's advertising agency, WPP Group, had had steel reinforcing pillars placed inside the Volvo and had weakened the other cars' tops with cutting torches so they would collapse.

Footage of Volvo's "successful" performance was used in commercials. When the truth became known, however, WPP Group's actions for Volvo cost them the account, Volvo suffered a serious loss of credibility and other public relations problems resulted from this deceitful action.

Special events have also captured the attention of the Internal Revenue Service (IRS). A 1991 IRS ruling would tax, at the rate of 34 percent, donations that nonprofit organizations receive from corporate sponsors. Athletic events got the first warnings, but also liable are cultural events that enjoy corporate sponsorship. The ruling was directed at Mobil Oil Company for the Mobil Cotton Bowl and John Hancock Insurance for the John Hancock Bowl. The potential reach of the ruling rallied all nonprofit groups to seek exemptions. The repercussions of the IRS ruling are indeed broad, extending even to universities that name endowed chairs or buildings for donors.

Another area to watch is the increasing number of discrimination and bias suits being filed by both employees and customers. One of the highest-profile cases was the suit filed against Texaco after internal tape recordings of conversations that denigrated African-American employees were made public. To the company's credit, Texaco Chairman Peter Bijur publicly stated that this was unacceptable behavior, and an "equality and tolerance task force" was given "extraordinary powers" to change personnel policies and practices.[41] In addition to the issue of race, gender continues to be a problem with some women working in very uncomfortable environments where sexual harassment is accepted behavior. Mitsubishi Motors in 1998 agreed to pay $34 million to settle claims filed by female workers who claimed that they were insulted and groped on the job. High-profile cases in these areas not only cost firms financially, for fines and recompense, but also make it more difficult for them to attract qualified employees. Some actions may even inspire boycotts, which keep the issue alive in the court of public opinion.

Investor relations is another area of growing importance, especially in terms of public confidence in a company. For example, ValueJet was already suffering from a decline in public confidence after a May 11, 1996, crash in the Florida Everglades when it was hit with a shareholder lawsuit alleging that it deceived investors about its operations and maintenance.[42] In the case of *Fundamental Service Corp.*, the regulatory arm of the National Association of Securities Dealers leveled the highest fine ever for misleading mutual fund advertising. In addition to the fines, it suspended three executives held responsible for the ads which, according to NASD, "overstated the fund's stability and safety and understated its risks and potential volatility."[43]

Court decisions regarding the bankruptcies of WorldCom and Enron will continue, although most of the problems with these two companies were addressed immediately as reflected in the SEC discussion. Arthur Andersen's relationship with Enron is largely responsible for the Accounting Reform Act of 2002. For further discussion of these 2002 cases, see Chapter 13 on crises.

Free Speech and Organizational Voice

Whether or not you, as a PR practitioner, are involved in preparing your organization's advertising, you share responsibility for maintaining the organization's credibility. This is especially true in relation to handling the publicity resulting from any lawsuit, because it is bound to have some impact on both consumers and investors. Such situations are exactly what public relations practitioners have in mind when they argue for speaking with one organizational voice and coordinating all communication efforts.

The freedom of that organizational voice may be jeopardized by legal actions, primarily against some forms of marketing and advertising. And although all courts have long recognized that organizations, like individuals, have a "voice," some Supreme Court decisions have restricted commercial freedom of speech in ways that have threatened to muffle organizational or institutional voices.

In recent decades, court rulings on commercial speech have gone up and down; some have been favorable, some restrictive. On the favorable side, in 2001, the Supreme Court struck down a Massachusetts law that restricted tobacco advertising on the basis that the state failed to prove that its regulations were not more extensive than needed to prevent underage use of tobacco. Massachusetts prevented cigarette ads within 1,000 feet of schools and children's facilities.

Confusing the issue is a 2002 claim by Nike that commercial speech does not include news releases or letters to editors and others. Nike, in trying to recover from the accusation that it runs sweatshops in poor countries, contracted with APCO Worldwide for a social responsibility PR campaign.

That was before the California Supreme Court decided to allow a case against Nike to go forward. That decision, that PR has the same obligation to truth as advertising and is commercial speech, was upheld at the next level, so Nike decided to take the case to the U.S. Supreme Court. Nike had sent letters to editors and to universities saying that all of its employees in China, Indonesia and Vietnam were paid twice the minimum wage, had a healthful and safe work environment and got free food and medical care. The company also had issued news releases explaining the situation with their factories.

The case against Nike was brought by Mark Kasky, a San Francisco activist, who said that news release statements should be regarded the same as advertising. Kasky's claim was that Nike violated laws prohibiting false or misleading statements in commercial free speech. Integrated communication (or IMC) has always accepted the idea that news releases and advertising are both commercial free speech and has supported free speech for all corporate communications. After an appeal to the U.S. Supreme Court was denied, Nike settled the case with Kasky in 2003 by agreeing to pay $1.5 million during the next three years to the Fair Labor Association based in Washington, D.C. that includes consumer groups, human rights organizations, companies and universities. The funds were for worker education and training, to create a global reporting standard for factory conditions and to monitor factory processes.[44]

A 1977 case had distinguished between strictly commercial advertising and newsworthy advertising that served the public interest. That same year lawyers got the right to advertise, and in 1980 a New York regulation that prohibited an electric utility from advertising was struck down. Other decisions in the 1980s were not so positive. But in Puerto Rico in 1993, it was determined that magazines could be distributed from free-standing racks on public property. Also that year, broadcast lottery advertising was allowed in states that had lotteries, although it was still banned nationally and in nonlottery states. In 1995, the courts determined that brewers may not

be forbidden to publish alcohol content on labels.[45] (The result, though, had ethical implications, as consumers sought beverages for their "kick.")

Restrictions The first major restriction on institutional voices involved the banning of tobacco advertising on television. (There are efforts now to ban the advertising of all tobacco products in all media.) The free speech counterargument is that, as long as the product is legal, producers should be permitted to advertise it. (In fact, farmers are subsidized to grow tobacco. There seems to be some inconsistency in government policy, at least.)

In 1995 lawyers were restrained from "ambulance chasing" by mail for 30 days. In that ruling, standards from the 1980s *Central Hudson Gas & Electric Corp v. Public Service Commission* were applied. Basically, these are: the speech must be accurate and not misleading; the government must establish a substantial interest in regulating the speech; the regulation must advance the government's interest; and the regulation must be narrowly written so as not to trample unnecessarily on other rights.[46]

The early 1990s saw a flurry of legal action against artists and arts organizations—much of it centered on the National Endowment for the Arts (NEA), which had funded some exhibits and artists that provoked controversy over obscenity. The NEA was not the only focus for challenges to First Amendment rights. The rap group "2 Live Crew" was arrested while performing, and some record and tape store owners were arrested for selling the group's recordings, in both cases because the lyrics were alleged to be obscene. The eventual legal decisions in all of these most recent cases came out in favor of free speech, but the controversy is not over.

Observers see a threat to individual freedom in another case, involving a suit by the Attorney Registration and Disciplinary Commission of Illinois against a lawyer who listed his certification by a trial lawyers' group on his stationery. The American Advertising Federation filed a brief in court supporting the lawyer, saying that the certification mention doesn't constitute advertising, and even if it did, the restriction is far too broad. In any case, the Federation urged, restrictions can't validly be placed on speech unless the speech is misleading.[47]

One reason for what appears to be court vacillation on the issue of corporate speech doctrine may rest with the mixed will of the people in the country. Periodically polls indicate that there is some waning of public support for unlimited "free speech" by individuals or corporations. Public evidence of a desire for limits on corporate speech are such things as the federal no-call list, which is enforced by the FTC and the FCC. Although some organizations argue that this is an abridgement of corporate speech because political and nonprofit charities are exempt, as well as some businesses (credit issues), most people are relieved to have at least their landline phones and faxes quieter. On the judicial side, a problem may be in trying to decide what is in the best interest of the individual or the community. (See ethics on communitarian vs. utilitarian ethics.)

Contempt of Court Contempt may occur when you comment on a case that is pending before a court in such a way that it can be construed as an attempt to influence a jury or prospective jurors. When a case is in its pretrial stages, you should avoid putting your argument in advertising or publicity. A company with its case in court can't take it to the public by issuing releases or buying ads explaining its position. It can't send out a mailing if the judge has ordered that no public comment be made on the trial. If the news media's coverage of a trial erodes public confidence and hurts the company, it still can't respond. Failure to comply may result in a contempt citation. Even **issue advertisements** can cause problems. Aetna Insurance's ads about damage suits running up the cost of insurance created problems subsequently in choosing a jury that had not been "exposed."

The tobacco industry that is still involved in injury lawsuits due to appeals needs to tell investors what to expect, but can't because of gag orders placed by judges hearing many of its cases. Trial courts are restricted from blanket gag orders unless a fair trial might be compromised. However, the court is expected to decide whether new evidence can be admitted and to put a time limit on the restriction. So, the tension is between the company trying to fulfill disclosure rules on material information and gag orders in courts where it is trying cases. While this is a tobacco industry problem at the time of this writing, it could become a problem for any company that is involved in jury trials.

Just how much advertising can influence juries is the issue, and research findings are on the side of those who say it does. (Recall the Chapter 7 discussion of Dow's argument for First Amendment freedom in the silicone breast implant case.) But even if influence can be shown, does this necessarily impair the plaintiff's right to a fair and impartial hearing? Judges have not always agreed. In Maryland, a state

court sided with Keene Corp., which bought a full-page newspaper ad on the eve of a big asbestos trial criticizing the litigation as "lawyer-inspired." That judge said careful instructions to the jury would avoid any ill effect on the proceedings. A Los Angeles judge, on the other hand, ordered Northrop Corp. to stop running ads promoting its quality controls in making fighter jets the week before the company was to stand trial on criminal fraud charges that it falsified test data on jet parts.[48]

Many companies, nevertheless, see the need to launch defensive action in the face of the litigation journalism/public relations mounted by plaintiffs. In one case, Sony mounted a campaign to counter adverse publicity stemming from its sale of blank videocassettes, which consumers might use to create "pirated" versions of prerecorded tapes. However, this campaign didn't begin until the case was on appeal. A lobbying effort to change the copyright law was going on at the same time Sony was arguing that current law permitted its videotapes to be made, sold and used by the public. The Supreme Court upheld Sony's position. However, the fight to change the copyright law's treatment of videotapes continues.

Publicizing Political Views State laws cannot prevent firms from publicizing (or advertising) their position on political issues that materially affect their property, business or assets. In 1978 the Supreme Court found unconstitutional a Massachusetts state law that prohibited companies from making contributions to support a political viewpoint.[49] Thus, on referendum issues, corporations, like individuals, have the right to convey information of public interest, whether or not the issue directly affects the company.

The Supreme Court has not ruled on whether corporations can support candidates. However, because corporate campaign contributions are illegal in most states, corporations have developed political action committees (PACs), which can gather funds and do have some impact. Recently, controversy has arisen over the power of these groups, and future regulations may limit their current freedom through federal and state laws. PACs, although they report to the Federal Election Commission, are also required to advise the IRS of their purpose, and report annual contributions of $200 or more and expenditures of $500 or more. That decision came from a bill passed during the Clinton administration in an effort to reform political campaigns (http://www.fec.gov/pages/cflaw98.htm). Gifts by unions and corporations also were affected by H.R. 2356, passed in the Bush administration during 2002 in an effort to curtail "soft" money contributions. This bill calls for more, and more prompt, disclosure.

Contrary to popular belief, charities can lobby unless they are churches. For guidelines, a charity needs to go the IRS Web site or contact it, because that is the government unit that controls its tax-exempt status. Basically, the charity can't spend a "substantial" amount of its activities on lobbying, and the IRS has a sliding scale based on the charity's budget that determines what can be spent. Well-funded groups may spend up to $1 million on lobbying and up to $250,000 on grassroots lobbying.

For churches, the line between legal and illegal is a bit fuzzy, but the IRS handbook "Tax-Exempt Status for Your Organization" offers guidance affecting 501(c)(3) organizations. The handbook says churches can get involved in nonpartisan voter education activities or public forums. Religious institutions also can separately incorporate organizations, under 501(c)(4) rules. Such organizations have more freedom to engage in partisan activities.

In 1988, the Supreme Court ruled unconstitutional a District of Columbia code provision that had made it unlawful to display within 500 feet of any foreign embassy any sign that would bring a foreign government into "public odium or public disrepute." It also found unconstitutional a lower-court ruling that protesters could not congregate within 500 feet of a foreign embassy. The ruling came after the Soviet embassy had been picketed with signs saying "Release Sakharov" (the physicist and human rights activist), and after a group outside the Nicaraguan embassy had carried signs that said, "Stop the Killing."

In another case of free speech, *Hustler* [magazine] *v. Falwell*, the Supreme Court ruled that, as a public figure, Jerry Falwell could not recover damages from an ad that was an obvious parody. The court ruled that public figures are not entitled to recover even for emotional distress unless the publication contains a false statement of fact made with actual malice.

A 2006 Supreme Court case, *Garcetti v. Ceballos*, held that public employees lose their first amendment rights too if they make statements involving their official duties because in that case they are speaking as representatives of the public institution hiring them and not just themselves. The American Association of University Professors (AAUP) has asked a federal appeals court to clarify that the case does not apply to professors in public institutions for fear that it will restrain campus speech including discussions of policies or the hiring of faculty.

Individual Practitioners' Responsibilities

Public relations practitioners must register with the U.S. government when they represent a foreign government or act as a lobbyist, and they are personally legally liable for the accuracy of statements they write for advertising and publicity—regardless of who directed them to write the material. They are also responsible for material and information they provide as a news source. Additionally, they are personally and individually responsible to their employer, organization or client, and can go to federal prison for their misdeeds such as fraud.

Registering Political Activity Public relations practitioners representing foreign governments must be registered with the U.S. government as foreign agents. (When the Justice Department took the PR man for the French-made Concorde SST to court for failing to register, he responded by putting a "foreign agent" identification on his Christmas cards.[50]) Complexity created by globalization adds to this problem and contributes confusion to the ban on internal audiences receiving messages crafted for propagandizing international audiences. (See information about the Gillett Amendment in Chapter 1.) In what is being called "public diplomacy," many public relations practitioners are involved in creating messages as a part of relationships with other parts of the world that inevitably cross national boundaries because of the Internet. All sorts of issues arise, such as transparency and figuring out what communication activity falls under the need to register.

Lobbyists functioning at all levels of government usually have to be registered, although laws vary. For example, New York City requires registration of anyone who attempts to influence city legislation or is responsible for "articles or editorials designed or intended to influence directly or indirectly any municipal legislation."[51] On the federal level, lobbying activities consist of (1) payment to a legislative agent of $500 or more in a given calendar quarter to lobby; (2) making twelve or more oral lobbying communications per quarter through paid officers, directors or employees with senators or representatives from districts other than those in which the principal place of business is located; (3) reporting all lobbying expenditures, including loans, of $10 or more.

Product Liability and Publicity and Advertising Calling consumers' attention to a product that later harms them raises liability concerns among public relations writers and advertising copywriters who handle publicity. Many writers now ask for certification of product reliability before writing news releases and ad copy, as assurance that the product will perform as claimed and will not cause harm. Agency managers and in-house managers who were previously reluctant to ask for such protection for their ad and publicity copywriters might reconsider now that many media are doing so. Media have been characterized as "conduits" for harmful product or service information in judicial proceedings, and they don't like the idea of facing expensive lawsuits.[52]

Complying with Consumer Rights

People have sought legal means to obtain information that will help them make rational decisions about their lives.

Freedom of Information Act The FOIA brings much government-held information within the reach of the news media and the public in general, including reams of data provided by corporate executives to meet the regulatory requirements of various government agencies, commissions and bureaus. The public relations corporate staff officers should know what information is filed with these various government offices, to anticipate any that might cause problems if released under an FOIA request.[53]

Corporate lawyers will advise you about what confidential material is protected under the law, but generally the only types of information exempted from disclosure under the FOIA are trade secrets (narrowly defined) and confidential, commercial or financial data obtained from outside government. Competitive disadvantage is a legitimate argument for protecting confidentiality, but it must be proved; the mere possibility of harm to a competitive position is not adequate. Some portions of otherwise protected material still may have to be released if, after critical portions are eliminated, the basic confidentiality is protected. Another way to justify confidentiality is to show that release of the information will make it difficult for the government to get the same type of information in the future.

Right to Know Many states have enacted "right to know" laws patterned on the FOIA. These make information available to the public regarding the presence of hazardous substances in the environment or other social threats. Some of the information becoming available under such laws is being released as a result of court rulings in favor of company management against regulatory agencies such as the Occupational Safety and Health Administration (OSHA).

Open-Meeting Laws PR people need to be aware of which of their organization's meetings must be announced and open to the public. "Sunshine laws" require that almost all government meetings, except those dealing with personnel matters, be open. Very unfavorable publicity can result from violations.

In many states, it is impermissible to say only "personnel matters" or "closed" on the notice of a meeting. The matters to be discussed must be specifically listed on the agenda, even though that part of the meeting may be closed. Federal law requires that governmental bodies keep a tape recording of any executive session that is closed to the public. However, anyone who makes that tape recording or a portion of it public is subject to civil and criminal penalties. (Guides to different states' access laws are often published in *Quill*, the magazine of the Society of Professional Journalists.)

In their role as a news source, PR people often respond to calls from media representatives or initiate calls to share information that may or may not be about their client(s) or organization. If their statements are false or misleading, they may find themselves involved in litigation—even if confidentiality has been promised by the media.

Copyright Laws

Copyright laws protect a creative work, both in form and in style, from publication in any manner.[54] Before quoting from copyrighted works, you must ask for permission. There are some exceptions to this general rule, however.

If artistic efforts (writings, art, graphics, photos or other creative work) are done on company time by an employee using company resources, the material belongs to the organization (the person's salary constitutes his or her compensation). In some cases, an organization will make an arrangement for one-time use and permit the artist to earn extra money by subsequently selling the work elsewhere. However, the artist can only sell work done on company time when a prior agreement exists between employer and employee.

If the organization wants to use other work by the employee that is not a part of his or her regular duties or that doesn't qualify as "work made for hire," permission must be obtained. An example would be a piece of art produced by an employee privately and on his or her own time that is to be used on a company holiday greeting card.

When work is purchased from an outside person (as supplier), there can be confusion later unless an agreement is drawn up. Most PR people either buy file rights or one-time rights (which are nonexclusive). But even then you should make sure there is a written agreement when the work is ordered.

A Supreme Court decision issued in 1989 said that written agreements between a freelancer and the commissioner of the work are valid only if the work fits under one or more of nine definitions found in the law: work created within the scope of employment; collective work (ads); part of an audiovisual work; a translation; a supplementary work; a compilation; instructional text; a test or answers to a test; or an atlas.

The transfer of ownership of the copyright is defined as an assignment—a transfer of exclusive license to reproduce the work; to prepare a derivative from it; to distribute copies by sale, rent, lease, loan or transfer of ownership; and to perform or display the work in public. A written assignment has to be filed with the Library of Congress, just like copyrights the originator would file.

Publishers going online got a surprise in 1999 when the courts ruled that **freelancers'** work they had paid for nevertheless needed permissions. Publishers cannot put freelancers' work on CD-ROMs or into online materials without going back to them for permissions, which means the publishers have to pay them again. This includes all freelancers: writers, photographers, musicians and fine artists unless the freelancer specifically gave up that right in the contract. What companies have done is craft "all rights" contracts for print and electronic reproduction. Google had to backpedal on a promise to provide an electronic library and decided, in August of 2005, to delay scanning copyrighted materials into digital formats. Some libraries involved in the project had only provided works in the public domain.

Extent of Protection Copyrights cover written and recorded (audiovisual and photographic) work and are an intangible property right that begins when an original work is created. Copyright protects the specific expression of the idea. A person who wishes to copyright an original work must use the copyright symbol (©) on a substantial number of copies that are publicly distributed. In addition, two copies must be sent within 3 months of publication or recording to the Copyright Office of the Library of Congress,

with a request for an application for registration for copyright. Fees vary with the size of the work being copyrighted (http://www.copyright.gov/circs/circ04.html). The copyright owner has exclusive rights of reproduction, adaptation, distribution, performance and display. Copyrights that were secured prior to January 1, 1978, are protected for 28 years and may be renewed during the 28th year for an additional 47 years.[55] Public Law 105-298 increased protection by 20 more years, so now copyrights can extend for 95 years. Individual works not done "for hire" are automatically protected from the time of creation until 70 years after the author's death. Company publication copyrights are good for 75 years from the year of first publication or for 100 years from the year of a publication's creation if it is never published. When copyrights expire, the works they covered enter the "public domain" and become available to all for any of the previously restricted purposes.

In 1983 to 1984, news media contended that videotapes of news broadcasts constitute a copyright infringement. Some companies regularly supply clips of television exposure to clients, and other PR people capture their own. Implicated in the same issue was the legality of home videotaping with videocassette recorders (VCRs). The issue was resolved in 1984 when the Supreme Court ruled that Sony was not directly contributing to copyright infringement by making and selling VCRs, because VCRs have substantial noninfringement uses.[56]

The Copyright Office in 2000 approved protection of creative material on the Internet (companies have the right to limit access to their content when it is offered on the Internet) and made illegal hacking around those protective barriers. At issue still are situations on the Internet where one Web site traps another's site in its site, known as in-line linking. The argument is that the presentation is not what the author intended.

Another protection has been developed in the digital age. Thirty nations have signed a treaty that protects written works and are close to agreement on a second treaty that will protect artists and musicians.

In a digital age, though, copyright is subject to modification and interpretation. Part of this comes from international pressure to free up intellectual and creative property, a perspective that includes all protections such as copyright, trademark and patent laws. Google got involved in this dispute in 2006 over making available creative materials that can be downloaded without copyright permissions. Google is arguing fair use. But the U.S. government is looking at use without permission as piracy. Google says it can't police sites such as YouTube for permissions. Google's position is that of facilitator and says that individuals contributing the material hold a responsibility to get permission. Digital disputes seem destined for the courts.

Although the application of laws to the Internet is uncertain at best, copyright holders have been vigilant in surfing to discover infringements. The Internet poses a different kind of threat to copyright holders because it can disperse an endless number of free copies of all sorts of material from software to songs and everything in between. "To lose control over the material can be death," said Eileen Kent of Playboy Enterprises, which found students posting its photos on the Internet using their university accounts. Some companies like Sony Music Entertainment send notices to fans who use Sony images on their Web pages and give them licenses to use the images as long as they don't change the images in any way.[58]

To reduce confusion about copyright on the Internet, there has been a push for changes in copyright law that would define digital transmission as a form of publication and that would allow an electronic encoding of copyrighted material to alert copyright holders when it is being used. Another argument is that much of the material is being modified, and thus its use is not an infringement because it has been transformed.

Even arrangements where boundaries once seemed clear no longer are. For example, in 2007 the red cross symbol became a point of contention between the nonprofit Red Cross agency and the commercial company Johnson & Johnson. One has the rights to use the symbol for nonprofit and the other for commercial use, but the borderline got blurred in 2005 when the nonprofit began licensing its logo to commercial makers of safety products.

Copying or "copycatting" is a common problem in advertising; but because ideas cannot be copyrighted, there is seldom a legal case in this area. The form that ideas take, not the ideas themselves, is entitled to copyright. However, a 1989 Supreme Court decision enables advertisers to copyright individual ads separately from the copyright that covers the publication in which they appear. If an advertiser brings a previously composed ad to a newspaper for publication, the advertiser owns the copyright unless there is an explicit agreement to the contrary.

However, if the staff of the newspaper or magazine prepares the ad, the periodical owns the ad and can copyright it. Such an ad can't be published elsewhere without permission from (and compensation to) the publication that created it. Of course, for the copyright to be enforceable, the published ad must carry a copyright notice.

Fair Use Violation of any copyright is an infringement, but one defense against infringement is fair use.[57] This includes use of one or more parts of the work in criticism, comment, news reporting, teaching, scholarship or research. Many publishers filed suit against Kinko's Copies because of copyright violations in preparing "textbooks to order" for professors. Most Kinko's outlets are now extremely cautious about checking copyrights and asking professors to get permission, in writing, from the copyright holders before they will copy such materials.

Public relations people might be tempted to send published information to people they think need to see it as attached documents in email. This could be a violation. Texaco, for example, found itself in court because it had been copying articles from scientific and technical journals to use in the collection of research data. The legal case centered on one researcher who had made single photocopies of eight complete articles from a research journal in the Texaco library and put these copies in his personal files. Texaco had paid for three subscriptions to this journal at the institutional subscription rate. Texaco claimed this was fair use. The Court disagreed, ruling that the researcher made the copies for commercial reasons, to improve profitability, and cited the number of articles copied, each in its entirety. The Court also found that the plaintiff, the Copyright Clearance Center, had lost revenue under its photocopy licensing system, so it accepted the publishers' argument that they had suffered substantial harm.[59]

Abuse of copyright should not be confused with plagiarism. Plagiarism is the use and passing along as one's own original work someone else's created material, which may or may not be copyrighted. A student taking term papers off the Internet and submitting them as personally created work is plagiarizing, but may or may not be violating an established copyright. A nonprofit group trying to publish a cookbook of recipes from performers who had appeared at its theater found an abundance of situations of plagiarism, some of which were also copyright violations. The same discovery was made by writer Anne Fadiman, who noted that, "The more I've read about plagiarism, the more I've come to think that literature is one big recycling bin." Of course, the frequency of plagiarism, even in established literary works, does not make it legitimate.[60]

Since so much public relations work is farmed out to freelancers, public relations freelancers should realize that they don't own works they were paid to produce. This includes work produced by employees within the scope of employment and work commissioned for use as a part of a collective work, if the parties agree that it is work "for hire."[61]

Copyright infringement applies also to music, which explains why more and more songs for everything from sales meetings to commercials are being written "for hire." Unless music is in the public domain, it may not be used. Even if the music itself is not copyrighted, the words may be. With regard to music, copyright infringement means using music, words or both—or similar-sounding versions—without express permission. And although permission may have been given to use the composition and the words, an additional copyright may exist on the specific arrangement or version of the composition.

If you want to use a recording, you may have to pay for performance rights. You can't just choose music you like and use it. Furthermore, if you are determined to use a particular piece, be prepared for long negotiations for clearance and sometimes very costly permission fees, especially if you are going to broadcast it. The term broadcast has its own definition, which does not necessarily include using mass media. For example, sponsors of any form of public dancing in an entertainment establishment that uses records instead of live music have to pay the copyright holders a fee, and musicians who perform have to pay to use the compositions they perform in public or for recordings. Nonprofit organizations can usually obtain permission to use music in a public relations campaign either free of charge or by paying a small fee. However, they still have to get permission.[62]

Fair use means occasions when copyrighted material can be used without permission. The nature of the copyrighted work and the proportion of the work used always have been important; thus, quoting a single verse of a long poem or a few lines from a song constitutes acceptable fair use, but reproducing most of the poem or song does not. Use for nonprofit purposes generally has been permitted. However, the accessibility of copy machines and the ability to "publish" electronically by putting something (words or art) into electronic computer networks (usually through bulletin boards) have generated more restrictive interpretations. One major key in recent interpretations of the law is the effect of use of the copyrighted material on the market value of the original. Another is use for commercial purposes, now defined not just as making money but as profiting through "appropriating" someone else's creative effort.

In the fall of 1994, the federal government issued a draft report updating the law on intellectual property. Motion picture, software, songwriters' and publishing groups supported the draft, while electronic computer services such as CompuServe and other commercial online services opposed it because it holds them responsible for what some subscribers might put on line.[63] One proposal to counteract this would hold the electronic services accountable for a copyright violation on their system only after they have been notified of it.

Confusions: Patents and Trademarks Patents are often confused with copyrights. Patents are government grants that offer protection for inventions and novelties; trademarks are distinctive, recognizable symbols (word, design or a combination of the two) protected from infringement, previous claim or use without permission. In this sense, trademarks are like a company's brand name or identification (logo). To use a patent or trademark, you must check with the government registry and ask the owners for permission to use. The Patent Office of the U.S. Department of Commerce administers laws dealing with patents and trademarks.

Is a trademark infringement really an infringement if you can't see it? Maybe, if it's on the Web. Web managers have been implanting trademarks on their sites with invisible coding so that visitors to the site don't see the trademark, but it is identified by search engines that then guide the unknowing Web user to the site. The first court ruling on this issue occurred in 1997 when a San Francisco federal judge ordered invisible coding of *Playboy* magazine to be removed from two adult-oriented Web pages. The suit was filed by Playboy Enterprises when it was discovered that the two sites were located by search engines whenever they looked for "Playboy" or "Playmate." This may turn out to be more than trademark infringement. Other cases suggest it may involve unfair trade practices in that it is considered unfair to pass off someone else's business as your own.[64]

Defamation: Libel and Slander

There are two kinds of libel: civil and criminal. Libel (written or otherwise published defamation) was originally confined to statements made in the print media, but it now applies to statements made in the broadcast media as well. The courts have interpreted libel as a more serious offense than slander (spoken defamation).

Civil Libel Civil libel is defined as tortious (that is, noncriminal) defamation of character by malicious publication tending to tarnish the reputation of a living person so as to expose him or her to public hatred, contempt or ridicule. It also means injuring the person in his or her trade or profession. Use of "alleged" or other subtle qualifications offers no protection. Civil libel law encompasses all forms of defamatory communication about a person's character, including headlines, tag lines and all artwork (photographs, cartoons and caricatures). It also applies to errors that may result in libel, such as incorrect initials or the wrong name with the wrong photo. If the defamation occurs in an accurately quoted statement that contains a libelous statement, the person or medium publishing the statement may still be held responsible.

In libel cases involving public officials and public figures, "actual malice" must be proved. But don't count on plaintiffs' being held to that standard of proof. Definitions of all three designations—libel, malice and public figures—remain subject to individual interpretation in the courts.

Publication in libel suits is defined as dissemination of more than one copy. Consequently, office memos, letters, telegrams and broadcasting scripts are all subject to libel laws, just as newspapers, newsletters and brochures are. Anyone who takes part in the procurement, composition and publication of libelous material shares responsibility for the libel, although the original publisher is not responsible for subsequent publications by others. Even persons who bring the matter to the attention of anyone connected with possible publication are subject to being sued for libel (see Figure 8.3 for a guide to determining what is libel). Copying and distributing a libelous piece can result in additional action against the person or persons responsible in the organization.

Slander is spoken defamation. It does not always apply to broadcast defamations, however, because multiple copies of a script may have been produced; thus, even though the copy is eventually spoken, the offending scripts constitute publication and are therefore libelous, not slanderous.

Criminal Libel Criminal libel—breach of peace or treason—involves inciting to riot or some other form of violence against the government or publishing an obscenity or blasphemy. Charges of criminal libel are rarely pressed, and one writer suggests that such a prosecution might be unconstitutional.[65]

Defense Against Libel Charges There are three traditional defenses against charges of libel:

1. Truth: substantial proof that is admissible in court.
2. Privilege: a fair and true report of a public, official or judicial proceeding.
3. Fair comment: statements made in an honest (albeit erroneous) belief that they are true; also, statements with some element of exaggeration or irony in them that nonetheless do not overstep the bounds of reasonable civility; however, it is up to the jury to decide the issue of "fairness." Guidelines are (1) sufficient public interest in the subject addressed by the author; (2) intent to serve a just cause; (3) a reasonable and supportable conclusion drawn from the reported facts.

A constitutional protection, if not a defense, is provided by the Supreme Court's 1964 decision in *New York Times v. Sullivan*,[66] which involved publication by the *New York Times* of a political advertisement that made various (false) allegations about a sheriff. The newspaper evidently did not attempt to verify the substance of these allegations prior to publishing the ad. The Supreme Court's opinion in the case held that a public official must prove malice in a libel suit, rather than some form of negligence. The trial court decides the question of "malice," but basically it involves an intent to harm. The primary significance of the *New York Times v. Sullivan* case lies in its implication that the Supreme Court may look at libel judgments to make sure that constitutionally guaranteed freedoms have not been denied. In addition, because the defamatory statements in the case were contained in an advertisement, the court's decision signaled that the standard of proof it was imposing applied to commercial speech as well as to noncommercial speech. Finally, the Supreme Court said it was limiting the power of all states to award libel damages for statements about public officials. In the court's opinion, actual malice was defined as either knowledge that the libelous statement was false or a reckless disregard for whether it was true or false. Thus, what

Figure 8.3 **A Guide to Libel**

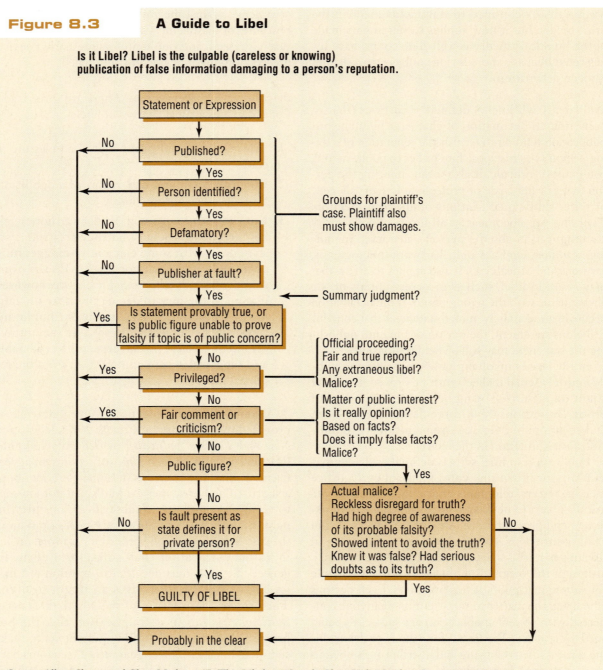

Is it Libel? Libel is the culpable (careless or knowing) publication of false information damaging to a person's reputation.

Source: Albert Skaggs and Cleve Mathews, "Is This Libelous? Simple Chart Helps Student Get Answer," *Journalism Educator*, Autumn 1982, pp. 16–18. Revised chart (1992) reprinted with permission of Cleve Mathews.

the writer thinks about the truth or falsity of the statement becomes a central question in assessing its actionability.

A subsequent case extended this requirement to "public figures" other than government officials—that is, to anyone who has put him- or herself in the public arena, such as a United Fund chairperson. However, in a 1974 decision,[67] the Supreme Court held that information conveyed by the press that falsely maligns a person—such as by leveling unprovable accusations—is still subject to a jury determination of negligence, regardless of the public figure's status or voluntary involvement. What this means to PR people is that careless overstatements in a news release can be costly.

A Duluth, Minnesota, state court ruling, if reinstated by the U.S. Supreme Court, could make it even more costly. The case involved a public figure about whom all the statements made in the *Duluth News-Tribune* were true, but the plaintiff claimed that he had been defamed by implication—that is, by a false impression. The Minnesota Supreme Court overturned the lower state court's ruling in May of 1990. In February 1991, the U.S. Supreme Court declined to hear the case.[68]

The U.S. Supreme Court has ruled that public figures must prove statements false, defamatory and published with knowledge that they were false or with reckless disregard for their truth or falseness. Private figures in most states must prove negligence to recover actual damages, and all plaintiffs, whether private or public figures, must prove reckless disregard for the truth or calculated falsehood to recover punitive damages. Because releases typically go into more than one state, you have to assume that a private plaintiff will only need to prove negligence to recover actual damages. However, the writer of the release might be in one of a few states that imposes a higher standard of proof.

The standard itself is interpreted differently in some states. Some use the "prudent person" standard, while others use the "prudent publisher" (which applies the standard of care set by the media).[69] One defense to an action filed by a private individual is that if the person has read and approved an article about himself or herself before its publication, he or she cannot later claim to have been libeled.

Another limit to libel charges is the statute of limitations, which provides that a person cannot be sued after a certain period of time has elapsed. (States have varying periods of from 1 to 5 years.) In the past, if the defamed person died, the suit would often be dropped, on the theory that the dead could not be harmed by false reports. But more courts are now accepting libel suits (and slander suits) on behalf of the dead, reasoning that their name or reputation could be defamed even if they themselves could not be materially injured.[70]

Fair comment has been interpreted in the past to apply to opinion pieces such as editorials, commentaries and reviews of all kinds. A 1990 Supreme Court decision rejected the idea of a distinction between fact and opinion, ruling that statements of opinion can be libelous if they contain false facts.

A 1994 case tested that ruling. The case involved a review of Dan E. Moldea's book about football called Interference. When it was panned by a reviewer at the *New York Times* who said that it involved "sloppy journalism" and contained "unfounded insinuations," Moldea demanded a correction or at least publication of a letter to the editor from him. When the newspaper refused, he sued. A federal district court judge in Washington, D.C., threw the case out; but a federal appellate court reinstated it, saying that criticism isn't protected from libel suits.

According to an article in *The Wall Street Journal* on the situation, people in the news media are unhappy at the prospect that a new area of libel litigation may open up, and book publishers are afraid that newspapers will simply get rid of book review sections.[71] Many public relations repercussions are involved, and these are not limited to book reviews—especially if all opinion pieces with factual errors are found to be actionable. Three rather spectacular cases in the 1990s put some different twists on suits against the media. In 1995, beleaguered by what appeared to the company to be war against the tobacco industry, Philip Morris sued ABC for its "Day One" television magazine story that claimed cigarettes were "spiked" with nicotine to make users addicts. The very aggressive response by Philip Morris resulted in an apology by ABC, because the process of taking out nicotine, combining it with alcohol, and then putting it back in for flavoring could not be accurately characterized as "spiking." Philip Morris ran full-page ads touting the apology in 700 publications.[72]

Another widely touted media apology followed an NBC "Dateline" story that showed footage of a General Motors pickup exploding in flames after a side-impact collision. Painstaking research on the part of GM proved the footage to have been rigged by attaching toy rockets to the fuel tank, creating an explosion that would not otherwise have occurred. GM won the libel lawsuit. NBC apologized, paid GM's legal bills and fired three "Dateline" producers.[73]

A third case might have been a libel case, but was not, and that's what makes it interesting. ABC's "20/20" news magazine had employed undercover investigative techniques to report improper handling of food by Food Lion. In response, Food Lion accused ABC not of libel but of civil fraud because the two field producers who went undercover as employees had lied on their job applications. Food Lion also accused the two of breach of duty and of loyalty that employees owe employers, and trespass for getting into the supermarket under false pretenses. Without a libel suit, Food Lion couldn't ask for compensation for damages to its reputation. Food Lion did win a $5.5 million jury award, but that was overturned by a federal district judge who ruled that the award was out of proportion to the actual harm done on the basis of the suit. To collect the larger damages to reputation, Food Lion would have had to sue for libel under the *Times v. Sullivan* rule and prove the story false. The grocer never tried to do that.[74]

Because of the freedom of the Internet, gossip columnist Matt Drudge had been getting by with much more than traditional media could hope to until he libeled Sidney and Jacqueline Jordan Blumenthal. The couple filed a $30 million defamation lawsuit when Drudge reported an untruth: that White House recruit Sidney Blumenthal had a spousal abuse past that had been covered up. The Blumenthals were public figures. Drudge made no pretense to check the truthfulness of his material, and he was a known detractor of President Bill Clinton. Within 24 hours, Drudge apologized and took the item off his Web site. But what about America Online (AOL), which carried the column on its service? Is AOL a common carrier like a phone company? If so, it has no responsibility. Is it a publisher? The Blumenthals think it is. It might even be argued that AOL is an employer, because it pays Drudge and promotes his site.[75] The new medium is causing new rules to be made.

The Internet is also enabling traditional media to evade some rules. Many news media are putting "hot" stories, for which all of the verification is not quite there, on their Web sites before using them on the air or printing them. Many media declare that they do this to "protect the free flow of information." They are afraid that by asking they risk a court injunction that would restrain them from using the information. Such was the case when the *Dallas Morning News* chose to publish the purported confession of Timothy McVeigh, later convicted in the Oklahoma City bombing. Other newspapers noted that this was an interesting use of the newspaper's Web site and that in the future, a U.S. medium might even bypass a judge's order by passing the story off to a foreign counterpart who could post the story on the Internet.[76] Many laws will change as a result of the Internet, including those governing privacy. A May 27, 2002, court decision making its way through the appeals process could make it possible for online publishers to be sued for defamation in any state or country. (See Global Perspective box in this chapter.)

Right of Privacy

The right of privacy applies only to people, not to organizations. Violations of the law take four forms: (1) intrusion into solitude; (2) portraying someone in a false light (making the person appear to be someone or something he or she isn't); (3) public disclosure of private information; and (4) appropriation (using a person's name or likeness for commercial purposes without the person's consent).[77] Unlike the other three, appropriation does not have to breach decency or cause mental anguish or ridicule. It is the privacy violation that causes most PR problems. Model and photo releases are usually obtained in order to avoid these problems.

A picture, letter or name of a living person cannot be used in advertising or publicity without his or her consent. For instance, a cereal company once used an artist's representation of a woman that showed her pregnant. Because the real woman was neither pregnant nor married, she sued.

Photos taken at an event for publicity purposes may later be used innocently or ignorantly in a brochure about the event. The photo might even be used in an ad, perhaps because it just happens to be available. Using such photos in an ad can lead to legal problems. Furthermore, even in a publicity situation, people may not be aware that their picture is being taken and for any number of reasons may not wish to have their photograph used.

Most attorneys for public relations people advise that releases should always be obtained. In most states, consent is the best defense; typically, newsworthiness is a more difficult rationale to defend. For example, employee pictures and names can be used internally; but if distribution is external, newsworthiness is lost as a legal defense. Even photos for internal use must be germane to the job—for example, giving information about promotions—or an employee who has not given consent may sue for invasion of privacy. Furthermore, use of an employee's name or image must end when the person leaves the organization's employment.

Employees must be treated both as employees and as private individuals who should not be forced to pose for annual report pictures if they don't want to. The company doesn't have the right to use their photos without permission. Furthermore, if they leave the organization and have not signed a permission

Global Perspective

A global automotive dot-com based in Irvine, California, sells cars through local dealers and offers financing and insurance. The vice president for international development, Joshua McCarter, said the company couldn't have opened its doors for 3 years if it had "complied with every possible law that could affect its operations in Europe."

What McCarter did do for Autobytel was research all of the laws and regulations affecting consumers, marketing, licensing, financing, insurance and local regulations wherever its Web operations might be subject to legal purview. In an effort to avoid legal problems, McCarter set up a separate Web page for each country, in the local language. Using the laws he found in his research as a guide, he made each country's page reflect local business practices.

Then, in making arrangements with local partners, the agreements specified responsibilities and liabilities. The length of the agreements surprised Autobytel's European partners, but McCarter is still not certain he's avoided all legal problems. The difficulty is that anywhere the Web site can be accessed, it is subject to local laws.

The uncertainty is created by a case in which France prosecuted the USA-based Web site Yahoo!, saying its suit was justified because Yahoo! was targeting France. The distinction is that passive sites not actually trying to do business and only presenting information don't have to comply with local laws. Sites inviting transactions do.

However, in Germany during the 1990s, CompuServe's subsidiary there was prosecuted for a bulletin board posting that violated the country's child pornography laws. The executive was tried and convicted, but on appeal the case was overturned due to a technicality.

For more on this, see Erika Morphy, "Ecom Risk, How Local Can You Go?," *Global Business*, March 2001, pp. 20–2, 24, 26, 28.

---

form for the use of their picture, using it anyway can create a serious legal problem.

In one privacy suit, a photo became part of the product. A photograph of a prominent Chicago-area nun, Sister Candida Lund, chancellor of Rosary College in River Forest, showed her in nun's attire and seated in a chair. The photograph appeared on a greeting card produced by California Dreamers, Inc., of Chicago. The words above the photo, which does not identify Lund, say, "It's all right if you kiss me." Inside the card are the words, "So long as you don't get in the habit." The Dominican nun does not know where the card company got the photo, which certainly was used without her permission. She charged that the card demeaned her morals, violated her exclusive property rights (by using the picture without permission) and embarrassed her and the college. Apparently Rosary College alumni had seen the card in gift shops from Alaska to Texas.[78]

The courts have upheld the use of celebrity look-alikes under the First Amendment privilege, as long as it is clear that the real celebrity is not involved.

A "false light" invasion of privacy suit in 1986 was ruled to state a claim similar to a suit for libel. The particular case (*Eastwood v. Cascade Broadcasting et al.* in the Washington State Supreme Court) was subject to the 2-year statute of limitations for filing on libel.

The availability of information online has created serious concerns about privacy. America Online permits users to have aliases when using their service, but when faced with a subpoena, the company will comply by supplying names and information about subscribers. Critics maintain that while a criminal subpoena leaves no recourse but to respond, civil subpoenas should be resisted. AOL says it notifies subscribers when court requests are pending so they may fight it if they wish. And while subscribers' names may not be protected, AOL says their email is.[79]

Another Internet privacy issue arose over a **database** of personal information operated by Lexis-Nexis called P-TRAK. The database is used by the legal community to find litigants, heirs and others involved in a case. Some have claimed that it gives more information than just name, address and phone number, that it also gives social security numbers. That was originally intended to be part of the service, but was disabled shortly after P-TRAK was put into place due to complaints. It is still possible, though, to dial in a social security number and see to whom it belongs. In response to criticism, Lexis-Nexis does permit people to have their names removed from the database.[80]

An issue that brought privacy to the forefront came with the public discovery of "cookies," tags deposited on the hard drive that identify visitors to Web sites and register what they "click on," so that pitches from the company can be personalized when you click back on and are recognized. This became disconcerting to some, although others liked it. You can get around this, and perhaps that is what is saving companies from being accused of privacy violations.

What is of increasing concern, though, are efforts by law enforcement to get records of what people read. This effort is not new, but before a law enforcement officer had to confront a librarian, almost always hostile to the idea, or a book dealer, usually not too agreeable either. Many states have laws that protect librarians, although not booksellers who can be subpoenaed.

Contracts and Consents

A PR practitioner need not get involved in a lot of permission forms and contracts, but he or she ought to know about at least five such forms: the **model release**, the employee contract, the photo agreement, the work for hire (usually writing) and the printing contract.

Major elements of a consent release are identified by Frank Walsh as written consent of all parties (employer, employee and parent of employee if a minor); consideration (something of value exchanged, like $1); scope of the use defined (as photo used in brochure only); duration (a set time period, not forever); words binding (heirs also have to be considered after death of person giving consent); and no other consideration involved (such as some sort of inducement or promise).[81]

Contracts with celebrities should spell out exactly what the celebrity is to do and what aspect of the public personality will be used. The following considerations are significant:

1. Is endorsement for the client by the public personality a factor?

2. Does the public personality expect to be paid for the use of his or her name?

3. Are the public relations activities on behalf of the client proprietary?

4. Are there any relevant contractual provisions?[82]

Model Release Serious legal problems can arise from failure to get a person's permission before using his or her photograph or other likeness in publicity or advertising. The photographer should always have the model sign a photo release form. Pads of model releases are available in most photo or stationery stores. If pictures of minors are used, the permission of parents or guardians must also be obtained. Notice that the permission for use extends to publicity for the organization only. This guarantees that the pictures will not be used to endorse a product or to further any other unspecified purpose.

Employee Contract A client has a right to expect loyalty and confidentiality from a practitioner. Some large PR firms have their employees sign a restricture covenant—and that means everyone, from the account executive to the file clerk. Ted Baron, president of a New York firm, recommended this "because they have access to insider information and documents, some of which your clients' competition or others would love to get hold of."[83] What are the penalties for breaking a covenant? Any sort of punishment management decrees—even firing, if the breach injures a big client or causes the company to lose clients unnecessarily. A covenant is a moral commitment as well as a psychological one (for, of course, you are less likely to do something if you publicly say you won't). Employers need to be especially careful with insider information, because "tippers" as well as "traders" are penalized for using any material nonpublic information.

Contracts are another matter. These are legal documents. They often have clauses about confidentiality and employers often include noncompete clauses in their hiring contracts. Then, when an employee leaves, there need be no discussion about the issue of competition. Contracts, of course, can be broken, or the noncompete clause can be negotiated.

Photo Agreement This is a contract between a PR practitioner or firm and a freelance photographer who is being hired to work on an assignment. Make sure that your agreement with the photographer spells out the limits of use for photographs. (Charges are usually higher when the photos will be used in ads than when they will be used in publicity.) You may want to use the photo more than one time or in different ways. Some photographers are willing to specify future use in one agreement. Many require one agreement per use. Remember that copyright protection begins for the photographer when the shutter is snapped. This will affect the agreement you draw up.

Work for Hire Occasionally a public relations practitioner in an organization (profit or nonprofit) or in a firm will hire a writer or artist for a specific job. It's common for a writer to be hired to handle an annual report, for example. Freelance writers may be hired for features or promotional materials, too. These cases are usually simple work for hire contacts where the employer owns the output but needs to specify any online use. Technical writers often are used for public relations jobs too and may require different contracts because they want to maintain control over their right to use the same information elsewhere in a different format. The work-for-hire letter of agreement sets the precise terms of the employment arrangement.[84]

Printing Contract In making a printing agreement, remember that no two situations are exactly alike, so the suggestions that follow will not always be appropriate. However, they may help you to develop your own contract or agreement. In addition to the contract, you will need to furnish the printer with specifications identifying how you want the publication to look. The following suggestions are often relevant for making a printing agreement:

1. **Dummy** in digital or physical format is a typical issue of the publication, showing the number of columns, widths of columns, number of pages and estimated ratio of advertising to editorial matter (if you intend to have advertising). Ask the printer for a quote on the price for a fixed number of copies of a certain number of pages. Ask for the price per hundred for additional copies. You also need to know how much it will cost to add pages or additional color. Many printers now have digital publishing capabilities using a digital press for quick jobs, with three to five days turnaround, because the printing process has fewer steps (7 compared with as many as 12 for offset printing and making only 1 pass through the printer). Digital printing allows the customer to see the finished product before the

press run, and corrections are easier to make, too. The cost, simplicity and speed of digital printing makes it ideal for customized printing pieces used in direct mail, special event programs (that dry quicker), sales announcements, posters and other such "print on demand" items.

2. **Deadlines** for the publication must be reasonable for you and for the printer. You might vary deadlines for certain pages in a large publication like a magazine, especially if the pages have color or a great deal of statistical matter (such as charts or graphs). But make sure the deadline for the final product, as in delivery date and time, is firm.

3. **Corrections** can be costly. The printer must agree to furnish **proofs** on all copy and advertising. Usually there is an extra charge for making corrections on **page proofs**.

4. **Makeup** troubles are often the reason for corrections. Make sure you provide the printer with legible dummies, correctly marked, and with copy you have checked for accuracy.

5. **Paper** is sometimes a problem. You and the printer must agree on the type and quality of stock you will use, and you should insist on a guarantee of continuity of supply (and price, if possible).

6. **Art** charges are usually specific. Get a list of art charges from the printer, and go over with the printer the types of art you are likely to use. Keep the information sheet on charges for reference in planning individual issues.

7. **Printing technique** is a basic decision and usually a primary one, because few printers can handle both **rotogravure** and offset and others handle only digital. In deciding on a printing technique, consider the quality of the job. If you have color covers, for example, with delicate shades, all the covers will not look alike when printed unless you pay extra for special handling— that is, for cleaning the press periodically to maintain color consistency. Don't put yourself in the position of demanding, after the fact, something you didn't arrange (and pay) for in the contract.

PR Services and Taxes In some states, services such as home repair and maintenance are not subject to sales taxes. Although Florida repealed its controversial sales tax on advertising when revenues began to plummet and boycotts were invoked, service industries are growing in an economy that is no longer heavily industrial. As tax bases are sought, efforts surely will be made to tax the service sector, including professional services such as those offered by accountants, lawyers and advertising and public relations practitioners. Watch for state laws in this respect and, of course, the laws of other countries if you do business abroad.

Working Across Borders Communication technologies often make working across borders appear to be seamless, but it's far from that, especially where the law is concerned. For example, while bribes are tax deductible in some countries, the USA has for years been virtually alone among major economies in making the paying of bribes illegal.[85] The USA has been working to level the playing field, and finally members of the top industrialized nations, through the Organization for Economic Cooperation and Development, have agreed to criminalize bribery by companies of foreign officials. They resolved to adopt this agreement as national law in each country, but that takes time.[86] In addition, some customs die a very slow death, even in the face of new laws.

Economic rules also differ from country to country, and although we talk of global markets, these really belong to countries. The decision of Glaxo Wellcome PLC to merge with Smith Kline Beecham PLC came after Glaxo had been talking about merging with American Home Products Corp. However, under London Stock Exchange rules, if a company's share price moves "significantly" on a true rumor, the company must make a decision. There's some speculation that this is what forged the merger and left American Home out of the deal.[87] Knowing a country's investment and banking rules is critical in doing business abroad.

Working abroad also means understanding how that nation's law enforcement agencies deal with terrorists. In the USA, the FBI strongly urges no cooperation with terrorists; in Russia, a USA systems analyst said if you don't pay off these criminals, you get blown up.[88] In some countries, kidnapping is so routine that it's almost like a criminal collection agency.

Laws affecting advertising are different too. Many companies ignore copyrights in countries where these are not usually enforced. Such a slip caused Procter & Gamble to sue Colgate-Palmolive in 1996 over toothpaste advertising in China. P&G says the Colgate ad using a seashell to illustrate the benefits of fluoride is the same ad that P&G used in 1989, only the shell was an egg shell. The suit was filed in New York, and both companies are U.S.-based, but usually the opponent or copycat of the copyrighted ad is from another country where the laws are different.[89] Knowing the law might have kept Philip Morris out of trouble in France, where the company launched ads that claimed passive exposure to cigarette smoke is no more a health threat than drinking milk or eating cookies. The case was brought by a cookie manufacturer. The judge's decision pleased the French antismoking lobby.[90]

International and multi-national companies are finding their operations challenged by courts in other countries, and generally losing. An example that got attention in 2007 was Microsoft's loss of a European Union ruling that in 2004 it had taken advantage of its position in bundling a media player with its Windows operating system then withheld from competitors information that would make their computers compatible. That likely would not have resulted in antitrust violations in the USA. You probably will be concerned mostly with laws in the country where your public relations operation is based. The laws in this chapter have dealt almost exclusively with the legal structure in the USA. When you are working in other countries, you must know the government and media systems well and know how the legal system relates to them. In many nations, the government owns and operates the media.

You'll need resident legal counsel if you are working in other countries. If you are doing only some of your work abroad, you can get reliable information at U.S. missions to those countries, especially the consulates. The U.S. Chamber of Commerce can be helpful, too, as can the State Department and the Department of Commerce. You can use many other resources to help stay out of legal trouble, such as affiliating with a resident PR firm or working with resident professional public relations associations. There also are books and current business journals to help keep you informed.

The important thing to remember is not to assume that a government that seems similar to the one you are familiar with has laws that are the same or even close. Assumptions can get you into serious legal difficulties.

Revisiting the Hypotheticals

To close this chapter, let's try to answer the questions posed at the beginning of the chapter. Although the Internet is still relatively free from the imposition of laws, one that does seem to be working in that environment is the copyright law. Because it's the library that is using "cyber cadet," a nonprofit, what you might want to do first is write a letter calling the infringement to the library's attention and ask for change. Otherwise you look like the corporate heavy threatening the poor little library.

The issue of drawing up a strategy to respond to another company's product is something you need to write with the idea that it may be made public at any time. Running it by the in-house attorney is not likely to make it qualify as privileged unless there's a substantial amount of legal advice that comes back to you based on what you suggested. Just having the attorney take a look does not make it safe under client/ attorney privilege.

Regarding the school buses, it's probably not a good idea to repeat in the school's newsletter information from the manufacturer touting the safety of the buses and the adaptability of the vans without obtaining verification of that information from one or more independent testing agencies. This is because you will be held legally responsible for checking out such claims before passing them on. Ignorance is no excuse for transmitting misleading information on which others may rely.

No, you can't write a publicity release that downplays the organization's financial crisis—unless, that is, you don't mind going to jail. You, individually, are responsible, regardless of who told you to do it. Moreover, it is not unthinkable that the person who approached you might, when faced with a lawsuit, deny having done so. Where does that leave you?

How you handle the question of the "copycat" logo depends on whether you registered your logo as a trademark. If you did, you can protect it better than you could have had you only copyrighted it. If you did nothing, you can count on a good logo being copied. If you didn't do anything and you see something similar in *The Wall Street Journal* that might confuse people, you might have a case anyway. But if a significant difference exists—say, the organization is in another field of business altogether—you don't have much of a chance.

With regard to the infomercial that you've been asked to script, you can't make it appear so much like a program that the audience is likely to be misled. The inclusion of quasi "commercial breaks" within a larger commercial presentation is not approved by the FTC. Again, you'd better check to make sure that the product/service being promoted in the infomercial can do all the things you are being asked to say

it can do in the script. Remember, the writer and the producer are the ones risking jail time, not the people who are offering the product/service for sale. Get a notarized statement from the marketer specifying what the product/service claims; and check with an attorney experienced in dealing with the FTC to see what your potential liability might be.

In the next hypothetical situation, if your lawyer client wants to include her certification on her letterhead, it could be interpreted as "advertising." Announcing a specialty is widely approved in medicine, but not in law, even though it is approved in some states. In fact, in some states you will find attorneys listed by state board certification of specialization in the business section of the telephone book (Yellow Pages).

The photo you are thinking about using in the special section for the outdoor sports event may not be usable, because most news photographers don't get model releases when they take pictures. But they do get names and addresses—or they are supposed to.

If you know the models' names and addresses, you can use the photo if you obtain their permission in the form of a signed release. Another reason to be careful about using such photos, even if you already have a release, is that one of the persons pictured might have died in the intervening period. You don't want to cause distress to the family by using the photo. When you have your own photographer shooting pictures during a special event, give the photographer a package of release forms to have the models fill out as the pictures are taken. This solves a lot of questions about use, and it helps with identifications, too.

The question from human resources about pictures of employees in the last magazine should always be answerable with a "Yes, there is a model release on file." You could be in trouble if there isn't one. You should always get model releases when you take employee pictures, because you don't know how you might use the picture later, and you don't know how long each employee photographed will be with you. If you have a publication in production, and a person whose picture you've taken leaves the company, it could cost a great deal to change the picture. In this case, because the magazine picture amounts to publicity, not advertising, you probably don't have a serious problem. But in situations like this one, a quick call to the organization's attorney is in order—to let the attorney know of a possible problem and to check the risk.

In the final hypothetical, your brother tipped off two colleagues at his company, and they made about $10,000 by purchasing put options on your company's stock. The SEC got all four of you. The two guys returned their profits and paid fines. Your brother got off with a $50,000 civil penalty. You had to pay a fine three times that amount and the illegal trading profits of the two guys, although you didn't earn a cent from the slip of the lip. The good news is the publisher decided it was an ethical breach that didn't affect your job performance so you got to keep your job. But you could have lost that too.

Discussion Questions

1. What is the impact of a legal battle on an organization's reputation? Think of some situations where the legal outcome was positive for the company and evaluate public confidence in the company. What about a negative outcome and public confidence?

2. How could a public relations practitioner get into trouble over violations of privacy?

3. What copyright issues could result in difficulties for the PR practitioner?

4. Where might problems arise because of plagiarism?

5. How can a global PR practice protect itself and its employer from litigation abroad?

Points to Remember

■ Although this chapter covers a great deal of material, areas that public relations people must know are libel, right of privacy, copyright and other permissions needed as well as contracts. Beyond that, each practitioner should know laws and regulations that govern the organization they represent.

■ The litigious climate in which public relations practitioners work means that any case, civil or criminal, can draw media attention.

■ Normal involvement with law for PR people falls into three general areas: normal legal exposure that any business might have, work-oriented exposure (or something peculiar to the client or organization's business) and extraneous legal exposure (such as testifying as an expert witness).

■ Legal involvement for public relations has increased due to outsourcing, which generates much more contract work for which the organization is held responsible.

■ Public relations has its functional roots in commercial speech, advertising, traditional speech and the press, and most of its freedom would not be available if some First Amendment guarantees had not been found to apply to commercial speech.

■ PR practitioners are more likely than the average citizen to get involved in criminal conspiracy charges, such as for bribery, price fixing, mail fraud, securities manipulation and perjury.

■ Four kinds of cases are likely to typify a PR person's legal involvement: the big case that can threaten the organization's existence, the human interest case that will capture media attention, the routine case that grows out of contract disputes and such and the case in which the PR person testifies as an expert witness.

■ Litigation journalism means that many trial lawyers and prosecutors are trying their cases in the court of public opinion as well as in the court of law, with or without public relations counsel.

■ PR conversations with legal counsel may not fall under the attorney/client privilege that keeps them from being made public, and simply having an attorney review documents without specifically getting legal advice also provides no protection from having them made public.

■ Watch danger zones and take individual responsibility because you personally are legally liable.

■ The key government regulatory bodies that PR practitioners are usually involved with, in addition to those specifically regulating the client's or organization's business, are the U.S. Postal Service (USPS), the Securities and Exchange Commission (SEC), the Federal Trade Commission (FTC), the U.S. Food and Drug Administration (FDA), the Federal Communications Commission (FCC) and the Internal Revenue Service (IRS).

■ Publicly held companies must comply with requirements about disclosure of their business operations as designated by the Securities and Exchange Commission.

■ If public relations people have knowledge of the publicly held company's business, they are considered "insiders" and may not trade on information that has not been made publicly available.

■ The Federal Trade Commission watches very closely claims for products that are made in advertising and publicity, and these must be supported by verification. Again, the PR person who prepared the copy is legally liable, as is the company.

- The Food and Drug Administration's job is to protect consumers. It monitors advertising, news releases, brochures and labels for material that could be deceptive. The FDA watches for any claims or even indications that a product is FDA approved when it isn't; or if it is approved for one use, they'll watch for claims about other uses.

- The FCC regulates broadcasting and telecommunications, including telephone and computer networks and satellite communications.

- The major defense for legal difficulties is provable truth.

- Court rulings on commercial speech have varied; while most recent cases are in favor of expanded commercial speech, there are important restrictions.

- Influencing juries—although it may bring contempt charges or cause other difficulties at trial—is exactly what some companies think needs to happen because litigation journalism/public relations on the part of the plaintiffs has portrayed them in such an unfair light.

- As individuals, PR people are responsible for registering their own activities as lobbyists and for vouching for the truthfulness of whatever they present in publicity or advertising.

- Areas of special legal vulnerability for PR people are defamation, invasion of privacy and misuse of copyrighted materials.

- The Internet has created some confusion about the absolute protection of copyrights and trademarks, but most companies are pursuing these infringements aggressively.

- Copyright infringement and plagiarism are not the same thing. The uncopyrighted work of another can be passed off as one's own, and that is plagiarism.

- Saying or writing anything that could injure the reputation of another is especially risky, even if that person is a "public figure"; and individual rights of privacy must be considered in all publicity and advertising.

- The Internet has been a place of free-flowing information, but individuals are increasingly pursuing libel claims for material on the Internet.

- Working across borders means understanding all the laws that govern the business you are involved

in outside of your homeland. Disobeying another nation's laws can have serious consequences.

- The most important protection for the PR practitioner consists of recognizing the danger signals and working with competent legal counsel to get through dangerous or potentially dangerous situations.

Go to the Web site for this book at **www. cengage.com/masscomm/newsom/ thisispr10e** to find more Web links on this subject.

Other Related Web Sites to Review

Federal Trade Commission
http://www.ftc.gov/bcp/consumer.shtm. This site has a list of consumer categories and you can order FTC publications from this site. The searches may be in English or Spanish.

Securities and Exchange Commission
http://www.sec.gov. Has a tutorial, types of filings and forms, regulations and staff interpretations, investor information, news, litigation and the SEC's divisions—all you need to know in one place. Sarbanes Oxley information also is on this site.

Internal Revenue Service
http://www.irs.gov. The Internal Revenue Service site has all sorts of guidelines, with lobby efforts on the part of charities included.

Tax-Exempt Status for Your Organization,
IRS Handbook
http://www.irs.gov

National Investors Relations Institute (NIRI)
http://www.niri.org

CBS MarketWatch
http://www.cbs.marketwatch.com. Has an editor and looks at chat and bulletin posting.

http://www.investorpackages.com. A news and information link to many publicly held companies.

Silicon Investor
http://www.siliconinvestor.com

Raging Bull
http://www.ragingbull.com

Motley Fool
http://www.fool.com

American Center for Law and Justice
http://www.aclj.org

Americans United for Separation of Church and State
http://www.au.org

Electronic Frontier Foundation
http://www.eff.org. Monitors technology and civil liberties issues.

FindLaw
http://www.findlaw.com. Offers free access to court decisions.

law.com
http://www.law.com. Some information is free, but not all.

Interesting, but not free:

eWatch
http://www.ewatch.com. Subscription service owned by PR Newswire will find the screen name behind the poster of bulletins that may be unflattering to the company.

CHAPTER 9

Strategic Management in PR Practice

OBJECTIVES

- To understand the environment of PR work.
- To appreciate the need to see or create the big picture and attend to details.
- To interpret PR's role in terms of the organization's purpose.
- To provide counsel and creative services as a member of the management team.

Don't just sell yourself and your ideas; sell the concept of public relations as a top management function—then prove that it works.

—**John W. Felton,** *retired vice president for corporate communications, McCormick & Company, Inc., and retired president of the Institute for Public Relations*

PR's Role in the Organizational Structure as Part of the Management Team

Public relations' value to an organization has grown with technology because of the increased value of communication skills and an ability to predict and handle crises. A field that used to be considered discretionary in organizational management is now essential. Some evidence is the explosion of jobs in the field, internationally, and the addition of public relations to business school syllabi and curriculum. In the business world, "goodwill" is considered an asset, financial media look for the "investor relations" person for comment, global media ask for a "spokesperson" in a crisis and boards of directors listening to reports of litigation ask management how the situation is going to play in the "court of public opinion."

Some observations about management differences in the profit and nonprofit sectors of public relations work follow. There are more parallels than real differences. In both situations you have a board of directors that sets policy, and the chief executive officer has to report to it and get both advice and consent from it. Public relations people need to know who these "super-managers" are, and what they think is important. Second, in both cases, your assets go out the door every day: employees. Public relations people have the job of helping employees understand the mission and expectations of the organization's management and giving them access to bring to the table and implement their own initiatives that can help achieve those goals. Employees cost real money in salary and benefits, but replacing them also costs a great deal in training and getting them functioning efficiently. Now the differences. For-profit organizations often have the means to implement changes immediately because they usually have the means to hire the help they need. Nonprofits have to find financial support for many initiatives in terms of patrons, sponsors or underwriters, donors and, usually, memberships or subscribers as well. Nonprofits rarely can hire as much help as is needed, especially for special events and campaigns, so volunteers must be persuaded to work, for no pay, just for recognition. Volunteers can't be hired, given orders or compensated, so they can do or not do whatever is asked of them. This affects the way projects are planned and implemented, but much of public relations management is just that—gaining and maintaining credibility through reliable, trustworthy relationships.

Public relations is valued for its strategic contributions. One is developing problem-solving strategies for the entire organization and helping to implement them through the PR department's own efforts to integrate and coordinate its work with other organizational units. Essential also is being attentive to issues as they emerge, monitoring them before they crystallize into public opinion, advising management how to handle the issues for a positive outcome to the organization and preserving organizational credibility in a crisis. (See Chapters 5 and 13.) In public relations positions, internally or externally from a firm or agency, two elements remain constant. First, attracting, advising, developing and retaining a talented, diverse staff that can work cooperatively and effectively across organizational divisions and disciplines. Second, managing resources—money, time and talent—to gain maximum effectiveness that you can document. ■

Role and Character of the Organization

To simplify the discussion, consider organizations falling into one of three categories: government, profit and nonprofit. Of course there are many variations in each of these. Dramatic differences are found in the levels and branches of government, the profit-making organization that deals directly with consumers versus one that does not, the nonprofit organization that is strictly charitable such as a foundation versus one that provides services.

There are some unifying characteristics, though. Government at any level is always involved with the public agenda because it serves a constituency. In democracies especially, it serves at the will of the people, which means power and politics are a part of all decisions. For profit-making companies, the key word is *profit*. The "bottom line" is always important because making money is the reason the company exists, and investors depend on getting some return. If the company is publicly held, there is a big difference, though, because of laws affecting the public obligations of these companies. (Refer to Chapter 8 on law.) If a company is a nonprofit, it is subjected to much more scrutiny than either of the other two types because people have contributed out of trust alone, without any expectation of services or products in return. Violation of public trust always damages an organization, but especially nonprofits. (See Chapter 13 on crises.)

The communication climate within each of these organizations is significant too. The communication climate is tied to top management style, rather than to the type of organization. Some top managers operate on a "need to know" basis and are reluctant to have open communication within the organization. They know information is power and want a tight hold on it. Top management at other organizations wants information shared throughout the organization so that informed decisions can be made individually and collectively. Communication at the first extreme is very top-down, with little communication coming from employees back up. Policies are likely to be strictly enforced. In the open communication environment, information comes from internal dialogue facilitated in many ways by management. Employees are empowered to make individual decisions, and although they are expected to report these decisions, management supports employees in taking the initiative. (For the effects these different styles have in a crisis, see Chapter 13.)

The communication climate is affected by the organization's core values, usually set forward in its mission statement. The corporate culture comes from this, again traceable to top management. The corporate culture affects everyone in the organization. Even the lowest-level employee is likely to be told, "This is the way we do things." What that may mean in a rigid communication system is "Don't dare deviate." In a looser one, it might mean "Go for it."

Internal public relations people, as employees, are most affected by the "tone" of management, but outside public relations practitioners working under contract are too. Even when a public relations firm has been hired at great cost, it may find it nearly impossible to get the information it needs in a closed communication system. If the PR firm is going to do the job, it has to depend almost entirely on outside information. In a more open communication climate, the firm can bring outside information inside for verification and find employees in all areas accessible and willing to say what they think. Needless to say, both planning and troubleshooting are much easier in that situation. The advantage the outside firm has, though, comes from having more independence. Although no firm wants to lose a valued client, an outside firm can "walk away" from a bad situation more easily than an employee can.

The Organization's Reason for Being and Place in Society

Mission statements are the origin for what an organization wants to accomplish, expressing what the organization sees as its reason for being and its role and place in society. Any organization's public relations efforts exist to support the overall mission of the organization. For that reason, any public relations department's development of an annual plan, either for the organization or for the PR department, has to start with the organization's mission statement or organizational purpose. The way the plan develops from there often depends on the nature of the organization, but the elements of the public relations plan remain the same.

One role of the public relations department is to assist with the evaluation of an organization's mission. This may include revising and rewriting or perhaps conceptualizing and writing a mission statement. In any case it must be done as part of PR's policy-making role as counsel to management.

Most organizations develop their mission statements early in their existence; but at least once every three to five years, the statement deserves a careful and systematic review by internal and special external publics. While calling for a mission statement review is the prerogative of top management, the PR department is responsible for organizing and planning the review. One outcome of a mission statement review is likely to be a rewritten or modified statement. Even if the mission statement is kept intact, internal publics and critical external publics must agree on this outcome of the review. The mission statement review is generally followed by a review of the long-range objectives by which the organization intends to implement the mission.

Mission statements set the tone for the organization, establish its character and define the parameters of its activities. They may be long, philosophical commentaries on the nature of the enterprise—as most university mission statements are—or they may consist of one or two simple paragraphs.

In addition to the mission statement, organizations write vision statements—descriptions about themselves indicating their self-image. These vision statements are the way organizations want their various publics to see them. Additionally, some organizations

PR in Practice

The concept of a spectrum from open to closed communication suggests that every organization's pattern falls somewhere between those two extremes. Closed systems mean not sharing information, often by management censorship, or simply by a process thinly disguised as "team-playing." In this process, management tolerates little or no dissent. You are either on the team, or you get booted off. The result is that management is surrounded by people who only know how to say "yes" and cheer management on, even if the direction is wrong.

Another indicator of a closed system is a highly competitive corporate culture. There's not much sharing because everyone knows information is power, so why share? Right? Wrong! An open, cooperative communication system means that someone is likely to offer a key to keeping the organization out of trouble, or to make a product highly successful or, well, you see the point.

Look at the economic and political failures, not just of the past few years, but of decades past. You'll find a great deal of evidence of closed or nearly closed communication systems. What you'll not be able to find are the missed opportunities from the lack of shared information.

have core value statements that suggest its ethics. Another statement you'll find is an identifying statement that is objective in substance and just tells what the organization is and does. If you are watching public television, you are likely to hear this identifying statement: "This is a public broadcast station, funded in part by viewers like you." You'll find publicly held companies' identifying statements in their annual and quarterly reports and in reports from analysts and brokers when you inquire about the company's stock. Many organizations use these identifying statements as the last paragraph in news releases, knowing the copy editor will often delete the last sentence but that sometimes it will appear. The idea is for repetition of this identification to help reinforce knowledge of the organization's role. Look for this in the last paragraph of stories about nonprofit organizations in your local newspaper.

All these public statements guide what the organization presents as what it wants to accomplish. The terms *goals* and *objectives* are defined as synonyms in the dictionary but are not used interchangeably by organizations. Organizations give the terms specific and different meanings, that is, one long-term and the other short-term. The origins of using goals as long-term and objectives as short-term and measurable came from advertising, the widely used Colley DAGMAR process. You'll find this in advertising management texts.

Organizational management books are a little less clear on whether it's goals or objectives that should be measured. The aspirations of individuals and different units of the organization are the collective from which organizational goals are agreed upon, set and achieved. The success of individuals and units is compared to how much each contributes to the organization's achievement of the tasks it has set for itself.

The "objectives" element came from revising a 1950s concept of "management by objectives" that mixed up the two terms. The 1980s revision includes the notion of setting goals that are worked toward as part of the process of arriving at some final assessment of accomplishment. While admitting that the terms are often used differently by different organizations, the Public Relations Society of America (PRSA) has concluded that goals should come first, with objectives following, as a simplification for use of the terms in its accreditation examination. In either case, the subset is what must be measurable.[1] Generally long-term efforts are the strategic ones while short-term represents the tactics.

With the integration of advertising and public relations efforts on the rise, to keep out of the conflict,

just think about what you want to have happen in the long term and about the short-term efforts that will get you there. The long-term measurement is obvious. You either get there or you don't, but how much you fall short has some qualities of measurement to it. Computer models often help organizations determine what the major contributing factors might be. Models are also useful in helping to determine what factors need to be considered in taking the steps to get there because they can weight different variables in different ways. The failure to get some short-term results, instantly measurable, is likely to have long-term consequences unless some compensating successes shore up the long-term results. Specifics in planning for a campaign or in a crisis are discussed in Chapters 12 and 13.

Publics and Organizational Relationships

Although the public relations department is not responsible for all of an organization's projects, programs and activities, PR is a source and resource for these, and has a concern because each involves relationships with different publics, an area that is PR's responsibility. The relationships with different publics are what give an organization its reputation. The consistency of good long-term relationships with publics is crucial.

Six components of a relationship are the major factors determining satisfaction, according to the work of PR researchers Linda C. Hon and James E. Grunig. These are: (1) control mutuality, or the degree to which parties have the right to exert some influence over the other; (2) trust, meaning the level of confidence and willingness to be open; (3) satisfaction, being the extent of favorable feelings due to positive expectations being reinforced; (4) commitment, which means both an emotional or affective commitment and a continuance commitment or a line of action; (5) exchange relationship, indicating the benefits one gives the other based on experiences or expectations; and (6) communal relationship, meaning both provide benefits because of a concern for the welfare of the other.[2]

While all are important, three deserve more explanation. Trust is founded in beliefs about the organization: in its integrity—that it will behave in a fair and just manner; in its dependability—that it will do what it says; and in its competence—that it has the ability to do what it says it will do. The idea of control mutuality is part of the concept of public relations as two-way, interactive communication and Grunig's theory of symmetry in relationships, not

PR in Practice

Similar to any other organization, universities share their reason for being and their view of their place in society. Texas Christian University (TCU), where one of your authors teaches, is a useful example because its mission statement was revised literally from the ground up when a new chancellor arrived. Everyone was involved in the year-long process—students, staff, faculty, administrators. Because the university was founded in 1873, remaining faithful to its origins was important, as was making it a part of the future. TCU is church-related, founded by the Disciples of Christ church, but it is not church-owned, so trustees from a number of faiths set the policies.

Although a long mission statement was developed, TCU uses a brief version on its Web site, on bookmarks, on cups, and so on.

Our Mission: To educate individuals to think and act as ethical leaders and responsible citizens in the global community.

Our Vision: To create a world-class, values-centered university experience for our students.

Our Core Values: TCU values academic achievement, personal freedom and integrity, the dignity and respect of the individual, and a heritage of inclusiveness, tolerance and service.

See http://www.tcu.edu.

always possible due to an imbalance of power. However, in any relationship, regardless of the power balance, both parties should feel that they have some opportunity to have an effect in the negotiation process. The notion of a communal relationship is more important in public relations than the idea of an exchange relationship because both should have a sense of empathy for the other.[3]

The affinity aspects are measurable using agree/disagree statements, thereby making it possible for management to get a more quantitative analysis of relationships with its various publics. Fractured relationships are usually due to one of two elements: people or policies. Employees can anger someone individually with all sorts of institutional consequences, or some thoughtless communication can create a whole category of angry people, as did a letter to parents about their children's obesity.[4] Policies that are seen as discriminatory or just thoughtless also can cause problems. Both people and policies can be the genesis of lawsuits that cause further damage to the organization because of loss of trust (see Chapter 7 on ethics).

Social media have become an important factor in making people alert to what is said and/or claimed by the organization in public statements by employers. Criticism and counter-claims can originate anywhere and have an impact. Employees participate in online social networks and can make postings of their own and certainly are affected by them, as are suppliers and regulators.

Monitoring, Measuring and Reporting

Even when many activities and countless forms of communication occur within an organization, the public relations department usually occupies the best position for monitoring what is or isn't happening and for evaluating how different publics are responding to various actions, messages and representatives of the organization. Technology is helpful in this process. Email messages can indicate responses, as can a look at alternative Web sites critical of the company. Blogs are another resource.

Many executives have been launching their own blogs to let their feelings as well as reasonings be known. Some of these, such as opinion page pieces and letters to the editor, come from the public relations department as a part of managing the institution's message. Checking for responses to these is another aspect of issues or environmental monitoring. Similar to other units in the organization, the public relations department is responsible for evaluating the results of its own efforts. At budget time, someone will always ask, "What did you do? How much did it cost? What did we get for the investment? How cost-effective was it? How did it contribute to the bottom line?" In its own evaluations, however, the public relations department is more interested in answering questions along the lines of: "What do our publics think of us? How does this match with what we think of ourselves? How are events, situations, attitudes, and so on going to

Theory and Research Perspective

Establishing and maintaining satisfactory relationships for an organization with its publics always has been a fundamental principle of public relations. When marketing began talking about relationships, the idea of branding developed to give instant identity to an organization and tie a relationship to identification with the brand, making it as personal as possible. This is fundamental to the concept of integrated marketing communications.

A corresponding development in public relations was the idea of reputation management. Part of that idea is that long-term satisfactory relationships of publics with a company are what give a company its reputation. A large part of the satisfactory relationship is trust—exactly the element in branding.

Now, consider the Internet and so-called global branding. Consumers are individual and local and are the reason products are changed for different markets. So branding is insignificant without performance that recognizes global differences. It has to work, or satisfy, the consumer of the product or service. The stronger the performance, the stronger the satisfaction, the better the relationship with brand and the more substantial the reputation of the providing company.

Branding and good performance both need to continue and both help the organization's leadership plan and give day-to-day direction to the organization. The inclusion of public relations in the process has built a stronger partnership between marketing and public relations, often still separate in organizations.

affect us in the future?" Both types of monitoring and evaluation need to go on, and both help the organization's leadership give day-to-day direction to the organization.

Several commercially available computer software programs can be used to conduct a public relations situation analysis—setting objectives, writing a budget, developing a strategy, deciding on tactics, then evaluating results and reporting them.

One of the more comprehensive studies of what constitutes good management in public relations was developed through work directed by James E. Grunig and supported by the IABC Research Foundation.[5] Since that work was published, a number of other countries have looked at their public relations practices using the "excellence study" as a guide. Most of the differences in studies from countries other than those included in the original study—USA, UK and Canada—come from six variables identified by the study: political system, level of activism, economic system, level of development, culture and media systems. Dr. Grunig and the research team found 10 principles indicative of good management: (1) the PR management is strategic; (2) PR reports directly to senior management or is empowered by management; (3) the PR function is an integrated one with all PR functions either in a single department or a mechanism exists to coordinate them; (4) the PR function is a separate management function; (5) the PR unit is headed by a manager, not a technician;

(6) the two-way symmetrical model for PR is used; (7) a symmetrical system of internal communication is used; (8) the staff comprises PR professionals who are educated in a body of knowledge, keep up with the literature and belong to professional associations; (9) there is diversity of gender, race and ethnicity in the PR staff; and (10) an organizational context for excellence exists that means participatory, rather than authoritarian, management cultures. The last point is important because activists in the organization push it toward being and doing its best.[6] A factor in all ten, though, is the role of public relations as a top management function, placing it at the management table with other counsel, such as legal and financial experts. Remember that all are staff counsel to management and not the final decision makers. Cooperation and collegiality among the management team is expected by top management. Your job is to work with others to understand what is possible, and the implications of taking the recommended action. Diversity of thought is important and isn't necessarily always a factor of gender, race and ethnicity. For the most part, although the A is now more diverse than ever before in its history, discrimination remains and if that is true in your organization, expect this discrimination to emerge, probably in online social networks. Be sure you do what you say you support; otherwise you jeopardize credibility.

In a global environment, there is another element that perhaps could be included as part of diversity but seems to stand alone because it involves understanding and respecting other cultures. This element is preparing practitioners for international assignments and sending them abroad for long-term stays. It isn't always easy to send public relations people on long-term international assignments, but these are valuable to the organization in two ways. The person builds relationships with individuals in the other country and personalizes the organization, thereby extending its reach and influence as well as giving it some resources on which to draw. The other benefit is the person comes back to the organization with some real insight into another culture to share internally in the decision-making process. This often prevents some costly errors in judgment. The critical factor in this process is proper preparation for the assignment and giving the person the long-distance support needed to make the experience a good one for the one assigned and for "trailing" spouses.[7]

Issue Monitoring and Managing for Organizations

Watching the global horizons for issues that seem to be developing is one of the most important functions of strategic public relations management. Sometimes it's just a news story about an incident or a proposed policy that catches a sharp practitioner's eye. It could be a rumor in an email or some comments in chat rooms. This kind of environmental scanning is both an overwhelming and necessary task. What a practitioner is looking for is something that could affect its products, one of its publics or its way of doing business. Proposed regulations or suggested policies, sometimes just political "trial balloons," can capture public attention. The PR person needs to notice first before the nugget of information becomes an issue around which public opinion has formed.

There's nothing new to what used to be called, from at least the 1950s, environmental monitoring. What is new is that the "environment" has changed dramatically and is now the world. A public relations practitioner can't depend on catching each warning, regardless of how sensitive that person's antenna. So PR people work with others in the organization to see the organization from their perspectives. Obviously the risk management division is helpful because experts there evaluate situations in terms of financial risks and insurance hazards. Attorneys are alert to rulings in new court cases that could affect the organization's regulatory environment. Because the law covers many specialties, it's important to touch base with all of the specialties that the company calls on periodically for representation. Marketing is always sensitive to competitive threats and new product challenges. Transportation keeps up-to-date on delivery systems, and this is much more complex now, because many "deliveries" cross borders. Human resources is another area because those managers worry about compensation, health costs, policies that affect families, recruiting practices and a host of other things that affect individuals such as fairness and equity issues. Depending on the organization, research may be yet another place where issues can be identified.

Finding the issues is just the beginning. After identification comes monitoring. Each of these issues has

PEANUTS reprinted by permission of United Feature Syndicate, Inc.

to be watched as its potential threat to the organization increases or decreases. Once the issue develops, publics line up on different sides of it, and even new publics form around the issue. This is a sensitive management area because what benefits one public may be a disadvantage to another. The best management can hope for is some honest brokering with the different publics so that even though one public is not willing to concede a position, at least it understands management's position and is sympathetic enough not to actively oppose it. A management model often used in both corporate and campaign management is called the SWOT analysis, an acronym for Strengths, Weaknesses, Opportunities and Threats. An internal analysis includes a look at the organization's strengths and weaknesses, and the external analysis involves an assessment of the opportunities and threats existing in the political, social and competitive environment.

The best PR managers keep top management aware of issues. The balance is to keep management from being blindsided without worrying them with constant warnings that fail to materialize. If PR managers are not judicious in their notices to top management, when they see a really serious issue that could precipitate a crisis, management may consider their warning just another alert with no substance.

Planning and Managing PR Work

Public relations' role in developing an organization's formal planning is significant. PR advisers help develop a mission statement for the organization—counseling on publics and on strategies to reach objectives, as well as on environmental monitoring—as part of determining the organization's one-year, five-year and ten-year goals and objectives. In addition, the public relations department must develop its own communication goals and objectives.

Two additional roles fall to the PR department's own responsibilities. One is hiring good public relations talent—full-time, part-time, interns and outside firms. Mentoring and nurturing is another role for internal people so that they can be promoted. Promotion means keeping in mind succession planning so that gaps in leadership roles don't occur. Diversity of points of view is important in hiring. If you hire only people who think like you do and have the same background as you, while it's likely to be a more peaceful environment, it is also a more dangerous one. You always need as diverse an array of

perspectives as you do skills. For outside PR assistance, the key is facilitating so that your company is seen as a good one to work with. The other major PR department role is budgeting.

In between these is the real job of developing and implementing PR work, planning strategies, solving problems and maintaining the department's reputation in the organization as a strong communication source and resource.

PR From Inside the Organization or Out

The PR practitioner's role is different on the inside as opposed to coming in as an outside resource. Outside resources might be an advertising agency that works with public relations and marketing, maybe merchandising and sales too, if these are part of the organizational structure.

The ad agency needs basic information from each of these units and should find it easy to work with all to coordinate message statements so that the organization as a whole "speaks with one voice." An ad campaign that is not seen as credible by employees, regardless of how effective it might be to outside consumers, is likely to cause problems. Nonetheless, the ad agency can't be just an order-taker or the organization loses the opportunity to get some outside input.

The PR unit also calls on designers, artists and photographers, and production people such as printers and audio and video companies. Although many of these capabilities are in-house, often there is a need to go outside. This is particularly true of audio and video, whether these are for employees or external audiences.

Research firms can also be an important resource. The reason is that research is time-consuming, and most internal public relations staffs don't have and can't dedicate the time to do that well. PR departments now allocate at least 10 percent of their budgets to research, and some go as high as 15 percent. Sometimes a research firm offers additional services, such as media planning, message distribution and other technological assistance. If so, that is usually a part of the contract because of the synergies involved.

The outside contractor may be a public relations firm that is expected, as an ad agency is, to offer research, planning, execution and evaluation. Usually the firm has a specialty for which it is hired: crisis management, health communication, public affairs, investor relations or such. The firm reports to the public relations manager, but also has access to top management. The ability of the outside firm to work comfortably

PR in Practice

The economy takes a turn for the worse. A new regulation is causing a crimp in business. A new competitor is taking a big share of your organization's profits. The result? Management decides that it can't afford the outside ad/PR assistance, so it brings everything in-house. Are you going to get more staff help with this deluge of details? No. So you have to take stock of the problem.

You have to decide what you can and cannot do. What you can do, you have to prioritize. You have to report to management what you can no longer do and offer some solutions. It may be that you have been doing newsletters for a number of different departments. Get the departments to submit their information to the intranet in a form you develop. Their information gets in. No one has to format it. One caveat: Be certain you monitor material on the intranet and let departments know what is needed. When everyone is over-worked, intranets often are neglected so that information is out-dated, or simply not there. The intranet is critical to keeping employees informed and offering management support on both project and personnel matters.

Other public relations responsibilities won't have such easy solutions or may have no solutions at all. They must be abandoned. Your report to management has to be endorsed, or you'll get blamed for not doing your job. That means your old job as well as your new one. Other departments have to understand why you can't be as helpful as you used to be so that you won't be seen as uncooperative. Most important, you have to work smarter.

Fortunately technology is a help if used creatively. The tendency is to imagine that technology will give you more time. While that is possible, you'll have to be careful about taking on anything new until your reconstructed department develops a sense of pace.

Managing your own time and disposition and that of the other PR staff is as big a challenge as the new responsibilities.

---

with the internal PR department is the key to success. The PR firm is usually willing to be flexible because this is a client relationship. However, the internal PR department has to be flexible enough to listen for challenging ideas and creative solutions to problems.

Advice you pay for and don't take is not a good investment. That means the PR department has to know exactly what it wants from an outside contractor and be able to conceptualize that clearly. Internal public relations practitioners also need to understand how the outside firms they contract for help handle their budgets so that they can anticipate billings. You don't want a surprise that is going to affect your budget, so before signing a contract, you need a statement of billing charges from the supplier.

PR Work—The Big Picture and the Devilish Details

An internal public relations department needs to have a clear view of its own mission and what it wants to accomplish. Furthermore, it needs its own priority listing of publics, the head of that list being top

management. Others include important sources of information and important service units inside the organization. The service units include the Web supervisor, email respondents for the Web site, technical staff that handle communication and the mailroom. Additional units are media personnel and special trade or government publics.

The internal staff has to set a timetable for activities, including deadlines and responsibilities, so that its own activities can be monitored and kept on schedule. This is especially critical in an organization that has a complex approval process because delays can be destructive.

Results of all activities are evaluated in an ongoing process so that end-of-the-year evaluation and reporting will be easier. A clear record needs to be kept of time spent helping other units of the organization to be sure credit is given to the PR department for these activities, such as producing a PowerPoint presentation for another division's manager. Budget considerations are a factor here, not just "credit."

PR is difficult to plan and manage because of high expectations, uneven levels of demand and the creative element. It calls for flexibility and entre-preneurship, often in environments that don't re-ward either. Many public relations problems arise from the failure of public relations practitioners to manage an internal situation, and this often turns on lacking approval to do whatever is necessary to accomplish the job.

Yet another management responsibility is un-derstanding legal issues, especially regarding management of employees and the nuances of contractual obligations. Internal human resources and legal departments can and should be consulted for advice.

Strategies for Planning and Problem Solving

One of the oldest formulas for problem solving is John Marston's R-A-C-E formula—an acronym for Research, Action, Communication and Evalua-tion.[8] But the concept is found earlier (without the acronym) in Scott Cutlip and Allen Center's 1952 edition of *Effective Public Relations*. Find the facts, establish a policy and/or plan a program, commu-nicate the story, and get feedback from internal and external publics to help determine modifica-tions or future planning.[9] A modification (with another acronym) appears in Jerry Hendrix's *Pub-lic Relations Cases*: R-O-P-E.[10] Like Marston, Hen-drix begins with research (R) but then he moves to objectives (O), of which he sees two: output ob-jectives and impact objectives. Output objectives are communications the public relations effort seeks to generate over the target period. Impact objectives are of three types: informational ob-jectives (message exposure, comprehension and retention); attitudinal objectives (creation, rein-forcement and change); and behavioral objectives (creation, reinforcement and change). The P in Hendrix's formula stands for planning and execut-ing a program (P) to accomplish the objectives. The final step, once again, is evaluation (E). The first part is monitoring and adjustment, and the second is an assessment of objectives achieved. The problem-solving procedure offered by Glen M. Broom and David M. Dozier is more complex.[11] The ten steps begin with defining or identifying the problem (1), followed by performing a situ-ational analysis that involves assessing background information and data and examining internal and external factors and forces (2). Problem identifica-tion and situational analysis are followed by setting program goals (3). The next steps are to identify

publics—who is affected and how (4)—and then to set program objectives (5) and plan action programs (6) for each public. Then each public's communi-cation program—message and media strategies—is determined (7). These steps are followed by pro-gram implementation—in which responsibilities, schedules and budget are assigned (8), evalua-tion (9) and, finally, feedback (10). A later model is R-O-S-I-E for research, objectives, strategies, im-plementation and evaluation.

The approach taken by one of the authors of this text is presented in Figure 9.1. Any problem-solving plan should take into consideration intervening situ-ations: how others will react (especially within the existing power structure), how the organizational culture affects the approach to problem solving, and how those who are not intended publics for messages—the **nimbus** groups—may interpret or respond to them.

Whatever the pattern used, the difficulty in han-dling public relations problems has to do with differ-ing perceptions of the problem and existing situations (Figure 9.2). The perceptions involved may be yours or those of others. The way you look at the problem has an effect, as does information you don't have. You may have some limitations yourself or some imposed on you by management, problems associated with upsetting the equilibrium of the organization.[12]

The way stakeholders view a problem can cause an organization to modify or change its reaction. Stake-holders view a situation from their own perspectives, not management's. From their view, the proposed solution might not even be reasonable.

The view of various individuals in the organiza-tion can have an impact too, especially if they are powerful or have strong persuasive powers. Some-times if a proposed solution affects a department in a negative way, it will react to defend itself.

Power structures outside the organization can have a major impact. Stockholders of publicly held companies are a good example. Many of the corpo-rate accounting problems of 2002 were attributed to companies thinking short-term instead of long-term to show increased earnings in each quarterly report to satisfy investors and analysts. Other power groups are activist organizations of all types, especially in-ternational ones because they can direct global at-tention to the proposed solution.

The corporate culture and the way decision groups function together also affect the approach to prob-lem solving. These two factors take problem solving out of the normal decision-making model because of

Figure 9.1   What Do You Do When There's a Problem?

What is the procedure for handling a problem? Where do you start?

1. Assemble readily available facts and background material. Have everything at hand relative to the problem; analyze and discuss these with executives. Background materials include four areas: organizational/client, opportunity/problem, audience, research.

2. Determine which publics are involved or affected.

3. Decide if additional research is needed to properly define the problem and evaluate its scope.

Where do you go from here?

4. Once the problem is defined and the publics determined, formulate a hypothesis, assemble facts to test the hypothesis and revise it if the hypothesis is disproved.

5. Elements to consider in this initial planning:

   a. What is the objective of the PR effort—what specifically do you want to accomplish? Be able to state this in concrete terms.

   b. What image of the organization do you want to present? (This should be a projection of the mission statement, but specifically adapted for this situation.)

   c. Which publics are targets? Why?

6. Who are other audiences whose opinions matter?

Now that you know whom you want to talk to and what image you want your actions to reflect, what do you say to accomplish that?

7. What message do you have for each public? These messages should have a particular slant for each audience, but they should convey the same basic theme and information.

8. What media can you use to carry these messages? Which media for each group are received and are credible? Will these media carry your message? If not, what other media can you use? Can you use conventional channels of communication (magazines, newsletters, closed-circuit TV, etc.) for internal audiences?

9. What response do you want from each audience?

10. What budget can you use for this—regular allocated budget or a special fund?

11. What is the best timing for actions? Develop a schedule and tie-in with other events to make news when appropriate or to avoid it if news coverage might prove detrimental.

12. Review problems or obstacles that might arise and make contingency plans for them.

13. Build in monitoring devices so you'll always know how you're doing.

Once it's all over, how do you know what happened?

14. Plan for evaluation.

15. Evaluate all aspects of the situation—the impact on and response from all audiences. Evaluation includes (a) impact—informational, attitudinal and behavioral—and (b) output (media efforts and results).

16. Communicate results.

In brief:

1. Find the central core of difficulty.

2. Check your total list of publics and note all of those who are involved in the problem, both centrally and peripherally.

3. Determine the problem's status in terms of potential harm to the organization.

4. List the related difficulties to be considered.

5. Explore the alternatives.

6. List the desirable objectives.

7. See how the solution fits into the long-range plans that are shaped toward what you see as the mission.

8. What are the immediate plans, and how do these fit with the long-range plans? Short-term solutions that don't fit long-range objectives and are not consonant with the mission statement are wrong. Don't do them. Start over.

Procedure for handling the problem internally:

1. Detail the plan and submit it to the policy executive for approval.

2. Get approval in writing.

3. Keep all people who are directly involved informed on a continuing basis throughout the move toward solving the public relations problem.

Figure 9.2 **Personal Perceptions and Problem Situations**

The way we look at a problem situation determines our approach to solving it. The complexity of our view is shown here. Other intervening factors arise when we attempt to communicate our perception—including how we want others to think of us.

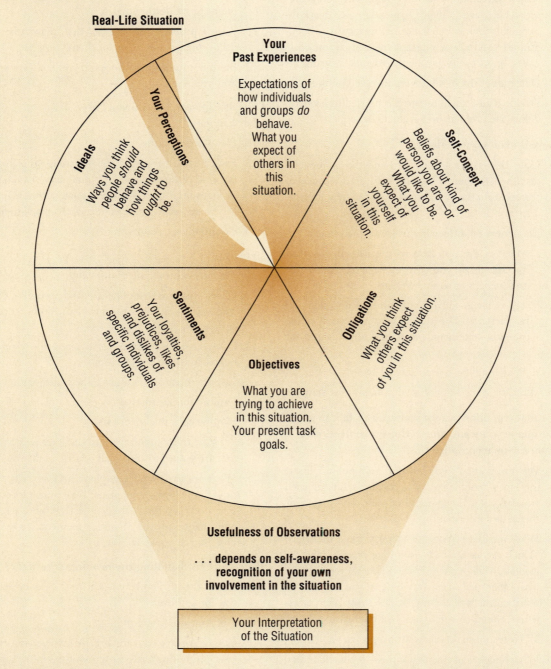

Real-Life Situation

Your Perceptions

Your Past Experiences

Expectations of how individuals and groups *do* behave. What you expect of others in this situation.

Self-Concept

Beliefs about kind of person you are—or would like to be. What you expect of yourself in this situation.

Ideals

Ways you think people should behave and how things *ought* to be.

Sentiments

Your loyalties, prejudices, likes and dislikes of specific individuals and groups.

Obligations

What you think others expect of you in this situation.

Objectives

What you are trying to achieve in this situation. Your present task goals.

Usefulness of Observations

. . . depends on self-awareness, recognition of your own involvement in the situation

Your Interpretation of the Situation

Source: Adapted and reprinted by permission of *Harvard Business Review*. An exhibit from "Human Relations Skills Can Be Sharpened," by Robert L. Katz, July/August 1956, p. 67. Copyright © 1956 by the President and Fellows of Harvard College; all rights reserved.

information control and power. The group with the most power in the collective decision-making process usually gets to interpret the problem in its own context, consider the choices and evaluate the effects of the proposed solutions.

Public relations people are involved in problem-solving situations almost constantly, and a good many of the eventual solutions to these problems are arrived at by groups. Occasionally, these groups include some people from outside and some from inside the organization; but most are arrived at internally, with much of the effort being exerted by the public relations department or outside PR counsel to the organization.

PR Departments as Source and Resource

Resources available in the public relations department are often needed by other divisions of the organization. PR can supply information on the organization's publics, on the socioeconomic and political climates in which the organization functions and on media.

Working at the management level means that public relations practitioners do a lot of listening to management as well as counseling. They are relied on for sound advice on the effects of events and policies on publics and how to solve problems with various stakeholders. Having the courage of one's convictions is needed from all of the management team, as is honesty and candor. Providing factual feedback is important from all managers, but the PR person also is expected to add the component of "feeling" expressed in public opinion.

Top management is not the only level that counts on public relations for counsel. Many other units call on PR for some evaluation of an event or issue, just as they count on them for technical support.

PR is often the source for publications and presentations. It provides information for the organization's Web site and its intranet. It sets policies for all communications, including use of the logo or corporate name to keep consistency in and control over the corporate image and to be sure the organization "speaks with one voice." Internally it prepares backgrounders, position papers, crisis planning and reports.

Externally PR provides news for all media, print and electronic, mass and specialized. The VNRs (video news releases) may be done in-house too, although these are usually out-sourced. Basic communication functions include initiating information for individuals, groups, organizations, and media, and also responding to each. Additionally public relations units are involved in developing, implementing and evaluating three different types of campaigns (internally, externally or both) for participation, opinion effects or behavior changes.

Because an internal PR department has to handle its own budget and be accountable for how the money is spent, it has to cost out each of these PR activities, including some allocation of employee time. When the PR department is hiring outside people, it can expect to be charged in one of three ways. A fixed fee sets a specific charge for all work and expenses on a particular project. A fee for services plus out-of-pocket expenses is a common billing practice. The contract needs to make clear what out-of-pocket expenses are included. A retainer arrangement covers counseling, supervision and overhead—the cost of doing business meaning secretarial and clerical costs, supplies and things such as utilities, rent, amortization of equipment and so on. Additional charges are made for services at hourly rates that reflect payroll costs plus out-of-pocket expenses supported by receipts.

Managing and Working with PR People

Internally a PR department head is responsible for sound management. To manage PR people effectively, you must first recognize that they are creative people who work under continuous pressure and face criticism from all fronts for whatever they do. Positive reinforcement from a supervisor provides encouragement and reinforcement. Next you must realize that they are individuals with professional attitudes that tend to make them more committed to their field than to the particular place where they may be working. Finally although most PR people are highly trained communicators, they often don't communicate as effectively with their colleagues as they do when they are working either with other departments or with outsiders at a communications task. Generational differences often impede understanding and complicate relationships. Global operations make this task more challenging because employees abroad are working in different time zones and may need information earlier that anticipated for resident staff.

Cultivating personal growth and keeping PR employees from getting bored with routine chores are challenges for PR managers. Offering continuing education in-house on company time helps everyone.

PR managers must see to it that their employees learn the organization's business thoroughly and keep up with developments in that business as well as their own field.

In managing PR personnel in global offices, value conflicts may occur. Value conflicts can occur over such concepts as time, status of women, regard for animals and ecology. All of these can put the organization at odds with its environment and can be sources of misunderstanding and resentment.

An organization may not be willing to compromise on some values, such as cleanliness, education, personal freedom and egalitarianism. Moreover, some ways of doing business in other parts of the world may conflict with laws governing the parent company—anything from standard bribes or kickbacks to the subordinate status of women to the employment of children. In these situations, some understanding must be reached with the host nation, and this can be accomplished only when the

organization's employees act with flexibility and sensitivity. While the organization faces unique challenges abroad, it also gains opportunities to learn and to incorporate new ideas from the host culture. Particular care must be exerted to ensure that internal publications and audiovisual presentations—some of which may be prepared at home but distributed to offices abroad—don't offend or violate cultural norms.

Of course, you don't have to go abroad to get into trouble by offending a cultural group. The stereotyping of people in any medium is likely to cause trouble, even when it's intended to be amusing; and language can offend, even at home.

Internal PR management also is responsible for hiring outside PR firms. Bids from the firms are based on their accounting structures. The cost of staff time spent on a project is measured in staff salaries, usually prorated to the nearest hour of time spent. The cost of executive time and supervision

Ethical Perspective

Being part of the management team makes it difficult for internal PR people to break bad news to employees. Part of the reluctance is top management's perception of that as a negative strategy. Often management wants to soften the bad news. The result is—if not outright lying to employees—misleading them.

Perhaps the Enron debacle awakened some employers to the need to let employees know directly, from management, what is going on, instead of making them rely on rumors and innuendoes that often originate with email messages from outside or even inside the company. The worst thing that can happen is that employees learn bad news from public news media.

One argument against sharing bad news is that it's bad for employee morale. That is not necessarily true. If there is an impending crisis, an organization's credibility is about all the organization has going for it. If employees don't trust management as the ultimate "insiders," why should anyone else, such as investors?

Misleading employees also destroys their confidence in management. The smart ones leave, often taking with them the experience and expertise the organization needs to weather the storm. On the other hand, if management explains the situation clearly and completely and asks employees for support, they are likely to get it. The critical ingredient there is that employees have to see management as taking the hits along with them.

If there will be layoffs, employees have to understand why and how these will be handled. One supervisor who was told to fire 300 people by the end of the week by sending them a blast phone message told management no. He called in each of the 300 people individually and told them what was going to happen at the end of the week and why. That's the good news. The bad news is that top management didn't understand or appreciate the need to do that.

The role of public relations is managing relationships with all of the organization's publics, especially employees. Handling internal communications is strategic management. Besides that, it's the right thing to do.

depends on the size of the agency: large agencies have executive oversight; small ones include the executive in the staff portion of the time. A PR business incurs chargeable and nonchargeable expenses. The following time and expenses can be charged to a client: (1) meetings with clients to prepare account material; (2) interviews, surveys and placement of materials; (3) supervision of mailing and distribution of releases, photograph assignments and other visual material prepared for the client; (4) travel time, including going to and from client's office, as well as time spent in off-hours (evenings and weekends) with client personnel on client matters. Nonchargeable expenses include the following: (1) keeping up contacts with media representatives; (2) meetings with office and staff and other group conferences related to PR business; (3) new business solicitation and preparation of materials for potential clients; (4) professional activities such as seminars, meetings and time spent on professional/firm matters; and (5) leisure time spent away from home in hotels, as well as purely social activities with clients, whether or not these occur in the evening or on weekends. Higher fees are generally charged for emergencies, special projects and delinquent accounts. Most PR firms give their retainer clients quarterly reports, with charges for extra services or credit carried over to the next quarter.

Externally the PR firm itself is another management issue, both for the PR department hiring it and the PR firm taking on the task of working for and with an internal PR department. For the internal PR people, hiring a firm means finding one the right size to do the job and with the right talent and experience to handle the project or problem.

A client looking for a PR firm must consider a small firm, a medium-sized one and large one—and among the large firms, whether the firm is international. Some small firms are really the offices of counselors who do strategic planning but little or no implementation. Other small firms may offer special services or be just generalists. The small firm often does a lot of networking to accomplish a task because it doesn't have a large staff. It is essentially a planner and contractor, hiring out work to freelancers and other contract workers. If a client represents too large a share of the small firm's business, there is the real economic danger of losing the client. This sometimes affects judgment. There is more of a tendency to just please the client instead of doing what the head of the PR firm knows needs to be done. The result is bad for both the firm and the client. Small firms have to be sure they aren't taking on a task too big for them, and that they don't become too dependent on a single client. Small firms have another problem. Occasionally they get

Global Perspective

Companies that have strong ties to countries other than where their headquarters are located have to make a special effort to keep relationships strong. Governments can change. Conflicts can erupt that draw the company into the circumstances. The company may have significant operations in countries that are not in favor with the country where it is incorporated.

One way to handle this is to publish information about the culture of these other countries and share that with opinion leaders and regulators so that some base of understanding is established. Safe subjects are the arts, foods, crafts and traditions of other countries. *Saudi Aramco World,* an elegant, well-edited bi-monthly publication of the oil company Saudi Aramco does just that. The Houston-based publication is distributed without charge to interested parties. Its distribution over a long period of time probably has done more than one can measure to help non-Arabs appreciate contributions by Arabs to knowledge, art and culture.

Another good illustration is the Ford Foundation, which not only has a quarterly *Ford Foundation Report* with articles on other countries, but also carries articles on its other projects such as documentary films. The *Report* is distributed without charge, and the publication allows use by others of any of its printed material without permission. Illustration and photo rights belong to the creators, who must give permission. The *Report* is on microfilm and also is available on the Foundation's Web site, http://www.fordfound.org.

a client who is exceptionally demanding, yet doesn't represent a large share of revenue. Smaller firms are sometimes reluctant to let clients go. Time is money, though, and there are fewer staff to provide that time.

A medium-sized firm usually charges more than the smaller firm because it sets aside part of the profits to solicit new business. Sometimes a new businessperson is hired just to generate new accounts. In that case, the person often works for a commission and doesn't do much else for the firm except make pitches and write proposals. The person then hands off the account to an AE (account executive). Where the small firm may just present a written proposal with a PowerPoint presentation, a medium-sized firm invests in some production to be competitive. These firms usually assign a person to work directly with the client, but that person may have a number of other clients to serve. Many of these firms are made up of generalists who rely on a few contract specialists to handle certain accounts.

Large firms are generally organized into groups composed of people who have the special expertise needed to handle a particular client's requirements. Larger firms normally have departments, such as media relations, that serve all groups. Groups usually make their own presentations, so the firm's principals are less in demand by the client than they are in the smaller and medium-sized firms. Large firms hire generalists and specialists and are more likely to hire outstanding people and then find work for them. New people are usually tested at skills-level jobs (such as writing releases or managing a news conference) to see what they can deliver, before they are given the chance to try management jobs.

International firms are among the largest of the large firms. They have to maintain offices and employees located around the world to serve their clients who need on-site representation. A large number of these international employees are public affairs specialists because much of their work is done with governments. The others, for the most part, are integrated communication specialists because they have to handle campaigns for products or services that combine PR, advertising and marketing communication. The local branches of the firm have their own clients and solicit business, but they also work with the parent firm and other international offices to coordinate global efforts.[13]

In all cases, what is important is a good fit between the firm and the client and most especially between the person servicing the account and the client contact.

Discussion Questions

1. What are the differences in handling public relations as an outside agency/firm or freelancer as opposed to working in an organization's PR department?

2. What effect does the type of the organization, its corporate culture and its communication environment have on PR practice internally? What effect do these factors have externally, if the organization is your client?

3. What is the impact of issue monitoring, managing and reporting on PR planning?

4. How significant are mission statements to organizations and their publics?

Points to Remember

- The PR department helps management develop and interpret the organization's objectives and goals, and the PR department plans programs to help the organization achieve those objectives and goals.

- The degree of involvement of PR in these activities depends on how management sees the public relations function.

- PR departments are involved in identifying and solving strategic problems for the organization, a multiphase activity that begins with the perception of the problem by management, by the PR department and by others.

- Solving the problem means recognizing the resources of the organization, the power structure, existing decision-making processes in the organization and the corporate culture.

- The most crucial role for public relations is acting as counsel to management; but to do so, public relations practitioners must understand the problems and needs of management and must win management's trust and confidence.

- To help identify and monitor issues, PR people work with others in the organization to see the organization from their perspectives.

- The best PR managers keep top management aware of issues. The balance is to keep management from being blindsided with something without worrying them with constant warnings that fail to materialize.

- People are PR's greatest cost and its greatest asset; however, because they are usually creative types, they are not always easy to manage.
- Adding to the challenges of managing PR people are the problems of maintaining offices abroad. PR managers must consider how their own cultural values can lead to conflicts in the resident culture.
- Culture conflict can also occur at home. Avoiding culture clashes in the workplace and in PR practice requires both strategic planning and sensitivity.

Go to the Web site for this book at **www.cengage.com/masscomm/newsom/thisispr10e** to find more Web links on this subject.

Other Related Web Sites to Review

For information about public relations firms, see trade association:

The Council of Public Relations Firms
http://www.prfirms.org

Also look for more information:

Internet PR Guide
http://www.internetprguide.com

Web sites with PR industry news:

PRWeek
http://www.prweek.com

O'Dwyer's PR Daily
http://www.odwyerpr.com

CHAPTER 10

Communication Channels and Media

Everything we know about entertainment and the forms it takes as "product" is up for grabs. The categories that seem so "natural" to us—TV, radio, albums, books, magazines, movies, and videos—are rapidly converging into one large digital data stream. . . . Beneath the media world lies our perceptual framework, and digital media may change how we know what we know.

—Chris Carlsson, *"The Shape of Truth to Come: New Media and Knowledge," in Resisting the Virtual Life*[1]

OBJECTIVES

- To appreciate the range of communication channels and media in the twenty-first century, consider the implications for public relations and examine how innovations in communication technology offer potential public relations opportunities, for example, in relationship building.

- To recognize distinctions between advertising and public relations messages and the channels and media that are appropriate for each type of communication.

- To understand the need for and use of strategies in preparing publicity messages.

- To develop a sensitivity about the unique strengths and weaknesses that each type of message and medium has for public relations message dissemination.

Channels of communication are public or private paths for messages to and from various publics. Media are conveyances for messages in those channels. **Public channels** are dominated by mass or specialized media available to anyone who chooses to subscribe, tune in or sign on. **Private channels** are more commonly used by media directed to a particular chosen individual or group. It's important to remember that although a medium may be a person, media generally are either print or electronic.

The frequently used classification of print and electronic media into **internal** and **external** types is somewhat artificial because it focuses on the medium's intended audience or public, not on the medium itself. As we noted in Chapter 5, however, publics don't necessarily accept those categories. Some members of external audiences, such as stockholders or university alumni, may see themselves as internal. And parts of the Internet, such as email, are more private than public, although unintended widespread dissemination of an email can be worldwide within minutes.

Another distinction frequently made in public relations regarding media is between **controlled** and **uncontrolled** types. When a medium is said to be controlled, there is some guarantee that the message crafted for that medium will be delivered to the audience as created, without modification, barring some kind of technical failure or human error. But with global access to messages through electronic technology, many messages now reach audiences for which they were never intended. For example, the commercials that accompany television programs are beamed by satellite to audiences all over the world; but often, they were designed for audiences in the country of origin of the products and services they advertise. Information available on electronic data banks is another example: Most of it is prepared with a specific audience in mind, but unintended audiences are receiving and using these messages in ways the preparers had never imagined.

The challenge today is to think of media as recognizing no borders and of messages as having the potential to reach unintended audiences who may misinterpret them or use them in ways that the sender never intended. Given that general guideline, the public relations practitioner must still try to design public-specific messages and media. ■

Choosing the Medium

All public relations efforts should have a specific objective. That objective, together with the audience, the message itself, the element of timeliness and your budget, should determine your choice of media. Generally, a mix of media is used, and one important consideration in this regard is the choice between controlled and uncontrolled media.

A billboard is an example of a controlled medium. You have complete control over its content and its appearance, and even where it is located because you buy a specific space. Television, on the other hand, is an uncontrolled medium, because—even when you control the content of a message (because it is an ad or public service announcement [PSA])—you probably do not control its context (what spot is shown immediately before or after it, and what content the surrounding program will have). Still, an advertisement or public service announcement could be considered controlled communication because the creator generally has control over the message. Other forms of communication are uncontrolled. For example, a news conference or a groundbreaking ceremony that receives TV coverage is an uncontrolled communication, because the PR person has no assurance that the cameras will videotape the event or focus the coverage in the desired way.

Of course, an element of uncontrollability lurks in every aspect of communication. There is no guarantee that the audience to whom a message is directed will pay attention to it or respond to it. You must carefully weigh the advantages and disadvantages of each medium before investing time, creativity and money in it. However, avoid the temptation to consider *production* costs instead of *cost-effectiveness*.

You should consider three questions in selecting the proper medium for your message:

1. What audience are you trying to reach, and what is its receptiveness to each medium?
2. When do you need to reach this audience, and by what date does it need to receive a message in order to respond to it?
3. How much do you need to spend, and how much can you afford to spend?

After you have answered and evaluated these questions, you need to ask four additional questions:

1. Which medium reaches the broadest segment of your target audience at the lowest cost?
2. Which medium has the highest credibility, and what is its cost?
3. Which medium can you count on to deliver the message within the necessary time constraints for the message to be effective?
4. Should a single medium be used? If a media mix is desirable, which media should be used to best complement one another in reaching your audience?

To make effective use of the media selected, you must know enough about the mechanics and technology of each medium to prepare the copy properly. Most students are surprised by the amount and different styles of writing demanded of PR practitioners. PR professors are not surprised, however, because in recommending students for jobs after graduation, they find the most frequently asked question is "Can they write?" The question implies *for all media*. In preparing messages for all media, you must consider the differences and the advantages and disadvantages of various media (see Table 10.1).

Choosing the Message—Advertising and Publicity

Confusion about what is advertising and what is publicity is natural because the line between the two is blurred. *The Wall Street Journal* observes that many advertisers are embedding their messages into TV shows, videogames, movies and other programming,

Table 10.1   Advantages and Disadvantages of Various Media

	Audience Size	Efficiency in Reaching Target Audience	Amount of Information	Inter-activity	Ability to Customize	Cost per Thousand	Shopping Experience	Ability to Demonstrate Product	Placement Lead Times	Control of Message	Control of Context	Longevity, Including Pass-Along Circulation
Magazines	varies	high	large	none	medium	medium	medium	low/med.	long	high	low	high
Telemarketing	varies	med./high	medium	high	very high	very high	medium	low	short	low/med.	low	low
Direct mail	varies	high	large	none	high	high	high	high	medium	high	medium	low
TV												
Ads	large	low	small	none	low	low	low	medium	medium	high	low	low
Infomercials	medium	high	large	none	low	low/med.	medium	very high	medium	high	high	low
Radio	medium	high	medium	none	low	low	low	low	short	high	low	low
Newspapers												
Major	large	low/med.	large	none	low	low	low	low	long	high	low	medium
Local	medium	med./high	large	none	medium	medium	low	low	long	high	low	low
Catalogs	varies	med./high	medium	none	low	med./high	high	medium	long	high	medium	medium
In-store (nonpersonal)	medium	medium	small	low	low	high	medium	medium	long	high	low	low
Personal selling	small	high	large	very high	very high	very high	high	very high	short	medium	low	low
Outdoor	medium	med./high	small	none	low	medium	low	low	long	medium	low	low
Internet	medium	med./high	large	high	high	medium	med./high	med./high	short	high	low	high
Ad specialties	small	high	small	none	medium	med./high	varies	low	med./high	high	high	high

Source: James G. Hutton and Francis J. Mulhern, "Marketing Communications: Integrated Theory, Strategy & Tactics," Hackensack, N.J.: Pentagram Publishing, 2002, p. 111. Reprinted with permission.

and some are attempting to mix advertising messages and editorial content in magazines as well, for instance by running ads next to stories about the same product, getting products mentioned in stories, creating contests that are linked to magazines and running advertisements that look like magazine layouts, all of which can blur the line between editorial and advertising.[2] Furthermore, although consumers of information may intellectually know the difference, they seldom remember whether the source of information was advertising or publicity unless the presentation was particularly memorable. For the discussion in this chapter, though, it is important to separate the two.

The major distinction is *economic*. Advertising has its own space in print and time in electronic media. That space and time is for sale. So *advertising is time or space that is paid for*.

There are two exceptions to this. One occurs when a medium uses its own time or space to promote one of its own products. For instance, a newspaper might run an ad for its own Web page or for blogs written by its reporters. It looks just like an ad, but it is for the same organization and no money has changed hands. In electronic media, you recognize these commercial messages as **promos**, or promotional announcements for something special in the programming, usually for that day or sometime later in the week. Another exception is when *the media give time or space* in their commercial slots *to nonprofit organizations* for messages that are prepared just like commercial messages. These messages are called **public service announcements (PSAs)**.

Publicity, on the other hand, *is news about a client, product or service that appears in the time or space that media reserve for "editorial copy"—news, features or other editorial content—or "programming" in broadcasting.*

Most programming is not wholly paid for because advertising is sold around the programs. However, some television stations do carry what is identified in viewing guides as "paid programming" or "infomercials." In that case, the entire program is really an ad. Print versions of such content are special sections that may look like the rest of the paper, but are really advertising; usually a disclaimer is printed on the section that says "Paid Advertising."

Types of Advertising Used in PR Practice

Three types of advertising are most common to public relations practice: house ads, public service announcements and institutional advertising used for issues, advocacy and identity. Three other types are

used less often, but do occur: specialty, cooperative and professional advertising.

House Ads   A **house ad** is what an organization prepares for use in its own medium or in another medium controlled by the same owner. For instance, a newspaper that is part of a chain of print and electronic media might promote a special subscription offer or announce a new "Lifestyles" section by running an ad or promo on the chain's television stations. No money is exchanged, although space allotments or "budgets" are established.

Public Service Announcements   PSAs are promotional pieces—not news stories—in the form of announcements. Generally, broadcast stations give unsold air time for PSAs, which are prepared just like commercials, from organizations such as the United Way, the American Heart Association or the local symphony. No money is exchanged, but the station may send the nonprofit organization an invoice for the amount of air time given, listing the number of hours and the commercial rate and bearing the notation "paid in full."

One word of warning if you work for a nonprofit organization that advertises: Just because your free public service time leaves some money in your advertising budget, don't splurge on sizable ads in print media. Those in electronic media can read. If you are buying ad space in a print medium while a broadcast medium is giving you PSA time, the station will notice and bill you for the "free" time at a commercial rate.

The release of radio PSAs on compact discs (CDs) was an effective format in the 1990s, according to News Broadcast Network's president Michael J. Hill. His firm had found wide acceptance for CDs, because most radio station libraries had converted to CDs, and the lower CD production cost also had made the format more affordable, Hill said.[3] However, many stations today may prefer electronic files over CDs, said Renee Rallos of WFAE 90.7 fm, a National Public Radio (NPR) station in North Carolina, with one reason being the "green factor" of not needing to dispose of CDs that are no longer being used. Print PSAs are generally, but not always, found toward the back of magazines and occasionally in newspapers. Leftover space is made available for free display ads (see Figure 10.1).

Commercial partnerships with nonprofits are not new, but they have increased dramatically as advertising costs have accelerated, whereas the

Figure 10.1 **Public Service Announcement of the National Congress of American Indians (NCAI)**

Reprinted by permission of National Congress of American Indians.

ability to reach audiences has dropped. These partnerships are sometimes confused with public service announcements.

The intent is to serve the public, but the commercial partnership takes the message statement out of the realm of public service announcements and into the area of cooperative **advertising** and promotion.

Institutional Advertising The objective of some **institutional advertising** is to convey a particular message. *Issue ads* are used by an organization as a forum for its views on a topic or problem. These ads are often called **advertorials** in print media and sometimes "infomercials" in electronic media, although infomercials on an issue are usually longer than a

60-second **spot**. Another type of longer infomercial, the "intermercial," appears on the Internet; it includes dialogue and video and may last up to 4 minutes. The name comes from "intersituals," which are the ads that pop up while a browser is downloading a page from a Web site, such as those displayed between Web pages.

Companies seeking public support for corporate policies and programs have begun to invest more in *advocacy advertising*. Advocacy ads are a form of lobbying to influence public opinion. They go beyond offering a general comment on issues to urging support for a position that benefits the organization specifically.

Corporate advocacy advertising often looks like editorial copy, although it may be clearly identified as an ad. Some corporate advocacy is done in partnership with a nonprofit organization and becomes a form of cooperative advertising.

Another type of institutional ad, which functions less as a persuasive message than as a reminder, is the type some companies call *sustaining* or *image ads*. **Image ads** are often used by companies seeking to modify their public image. They may present a redesigned logo or a change in policy. The image ad is also used by monopolies that wish to represent themselves as public servants. Companies frequently use this type of advertising to win favorable public opinion.

Nonprofit organizations, especially trade and professional organizations, may use image advertising, too. Because of an image ad's tone and content, it may be mistaken for publicity.

Some image advertising looks like product advertising and vice versa. A company may relate image to product if it is important to the company's reputation that its name be associated, in the public's mind, with a certain product. When image ads are not used, the company may begin to experience a decline in public approval and market share; after two years, the decline is quick and dramatic. If image ads are stopped when money is tight, the results can be disastrous.

A device similar to image ads is the *identity ad*, often used by nonconsumer product companies, or by consumer-oriented companies when takeovers or spinoffs have blurred public recognition.

Commercial Advertising by Nonprofits Not all advertising that nonprofit organizations do is public service advertising. Much is paid-for time or space. *The Wall Street Journal* carried a story about a campaign by the Episcopal Church to get people to return to church.

The television commercials were created by the St. Louis office of D'Arcy Masius Benton & Bowles for the Episcopal Radio-TV Foundation, a nonprofit Atlanta-based group that produces programming under the auspices of the Episcopal Church.[4]

Although many churches (Episcopal included) run ads around traditional religious holidays, this campaign in four states (Georgia, Tennessee, Ohio and Iowa) was aimed at getting people to return to the Episcopal Church on a regular basis. The target public was women between 25 and 45 years old because research showed these were more likely than other population subgroups to return to church and to bring their families. Other research, however, indicates that a much older generation is likely to attend church services on a regular basis. The investment was necessary to help reverse declining membership, according to the Rev. Canon Louis C. Schueddig of the Episcopal Radio-TV Foundation. He was quoted in *The Wall Street Journal* article as saying, "Materialism isn't the option it was five years ago."[5]

Creating and Solving Problems With Advertising Advertising can sometimes do more harm than good. For example, a spot on Peruvian television showed Africans ready to devour some white tourists until they were offered Nabisco's Royal Pudding instead. Peruvians saw it as fanciful and funny, but when the television show *Inside Edition* attacked the ad in the USA, Nabisco said the ad was inconsistent with the company's values and was a "mistake." Adapting sales pitches to foreign markets without offending home audiences is essential. Although many companies depend on local agencies to appeal to that market, some guidelines need to exist.[6]

One of the first considerations for global advertising is usually language, but it's also important to be sensitive to cultural preferences. Culture may be a more important consideration than language. In fact, often when English will work as a language, the culture where it is being used may be so different from U.S. culture that the graphics and even the "tone" of the writing won't be effective or may seem strange to that culture's readers. Advertising that creates a public relations problem is not money well spent. This is where research about publics is more than worth the investment.

Even in domestic settings, more thorough research won't hurt. In fact, it's the lack of research that dooms many corporate image ads. Most of the image ads are so "fact free" that they fail to persuade. This is especially the case among people such as investors who read *The Wall Street Journal*, where many such ads appear. Many of these corporate ads are not test-marketed for potential impact on stock price. What corporate image ads should be doing is building confidence.[7]

Ads are more often used successfully to do just that in time of crisis. Getting a message out about a problem is usually best in a controlled format that advertising offers. Ads showing Web site addresses and free-to-the-caller 800 numbers that people can call are often used to provide notices of some sort of difficulty or problem when access to the company is critical to bolster an audience's confidence in the organization or, in some cases, to offer information.

Advertising in Other Formats Sometimes the artwork for a print ad can be used in other formats. The most common of these is the *poster*, which in smaller form is called a *flyer*, and in larger form a *billboard*. Mail inserts are another type of format. Other versions are *transit* or *in-store* advertising. Some versions, usually of flyer size, are even sent as *fax* advertising. Fax advertising, which is usually from suppliers or service industries, has encountered some problems because the receiver pays for the paper on which the unsolicited message is printed.

There should be continuity between poster or billboard art, the packaging for a product and the store displays. An opera association, for example, may have a table flanked by posters set up in the lobby at performances to sell cups, tote bags, umbrellas and other items bearing the opera's logo. The purpose in this case is to raise money for the nonprofit organization. Some of these items, like pens with the opera logo, are the types of materials that profit-making organizations use in **specialty advertising**.

Without looking, can you recall the company whose name is on the pen you use or on your desk calendar? Advertising specialties are useful, inexpensive items, such as inexpensive laser pointers or baseball caps, imprinted with an organization's name, logo or message. These items are given away to customers or perhaps as souvenirs to those who attend a special event. Many opportunities exist to advertise on the Internet in addition to pop-up ads on the Web. While advertising on unpredictable blogs can be hazardous, advertisers have recognized the pervasive appeal of podcasts. Audio podcast listening increased significantly from 2007 to 2008, with 18 percent of Americans saying they have downloaded and listened to an audio podcast, while 16 percent of Americans consumed video podcasts.[8] This audience for "downloadable media" is more likely to be educated and affluent and to spend time and money online.[9]

Cooperative (Co-op) advertising offers almost as many advantages as advertising placed by a single organization. When one advertiser shares a message with another—such as when a cheese dip manufacturer combines with a potato chip manufacturer to buy advertising space and time—it also shares the production and space/time costs. This enables each to participate in both the production and the exposure.

Cooperative advertising also can involve commercial–nonprofit partnerships. One example is the actual endorsement of a product by a nonprofit organization in exchange for part of the proceeds of the sale. The first to do this was Johnson & Johnson's aspirin, which teamed up with the Arthritis Foundation, and the partnership was touted in the ads and on the product's bottles.

Advertising by Professionals Both advertising agencies and PR firms have learned to deal with advertising and promotion by lawyers, dentists, doctors and other professionals, who used to be prohibited by their professional codes of conduct from engaging in such commercial activities. As these professionals began putting their names in print and their faces on television, a new market for public relations practitioners opened.

In 1975 after the Federal Trade Commission (FTC) began attacking advertising restrictions on lawyers, doctors and dentists, self-promotional advertisements began to appear—particularly in local newspapers and on local television. Several Supreme Court decisions supported this trend among the professional groups. Although some PR practitioners are understandably pleased by the development, others consider handling some professional clients to be ethically questionable.

Languages and Advertising In the USA, advertisers are targeting their ads more frequently by using languages other than English. There are language-specific media—print and electronic—and neighborhoods where the language of preference is not English. In the latter case, mail to these zip code addresses and billboards and posters placed in these areas are not in English, but in the preferred language. For instance, Bank of America markets to and does business with customers whose preferred and sometimes only language may be Spanish (see Figure 10.2).

Figure 10.2   **Bank of America Web Site in Spanish**

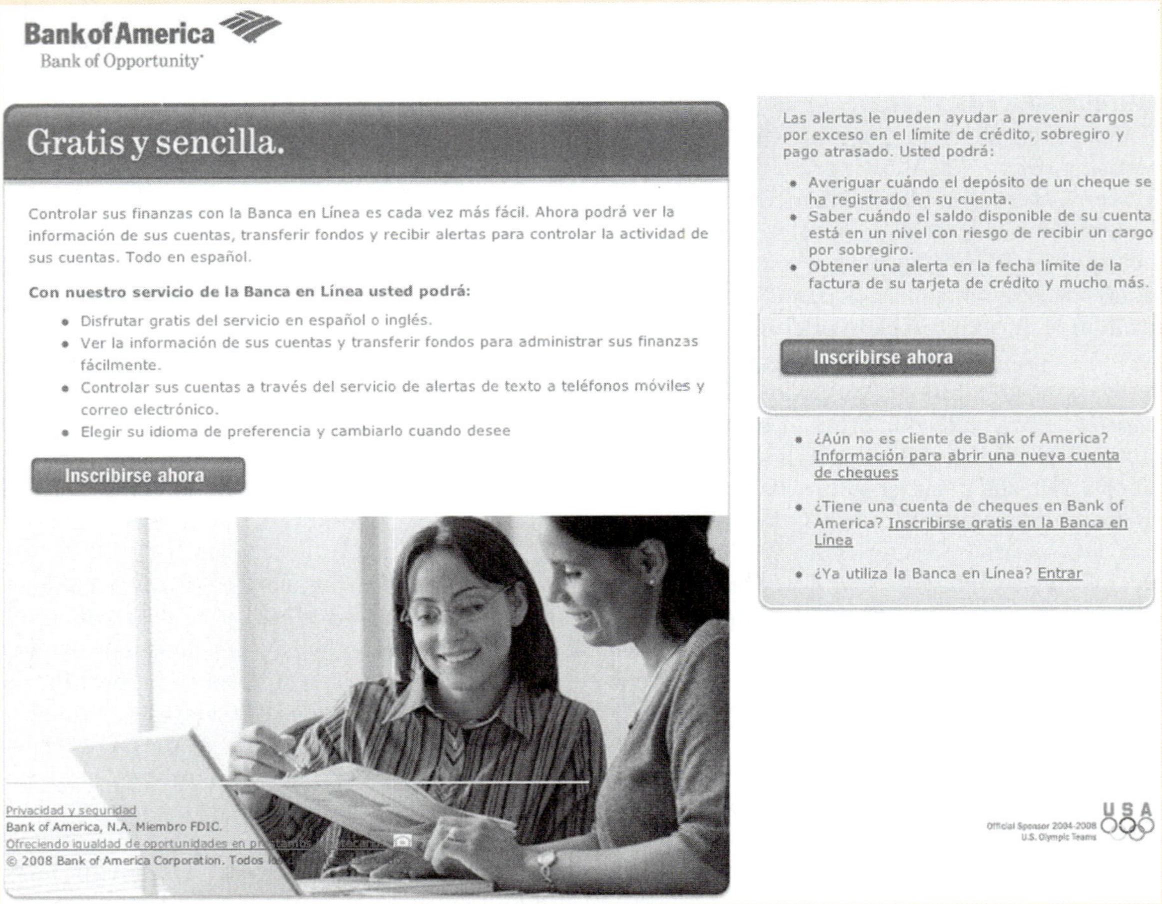

Source: http://www.bankofamerica.com/promos/jump/bankespanolenlinea/?cm_sp=OLB-General-_-SpanishBanking-_-SPA-HP-SO-Masthead_olb-111_mst_2span.jpg&adlink=000302072ch90000k275. Reprinted by permission of Bank of America, Charlotte, N.C.

Advertising as Controlled and Uncontrolled Communication

Controlled Advertising One significant advantage of using **controlled (paid) advertising** is that the advertiser nearly always has *total control*—over the message itself, over the context in which it will appear (size, shape, color) and over the medium in which it will run. And, of course, the advertiser knows approximately *when* an audience will receive the message. In addition, the advertiser has access to media research about the medium's audience, indicating *who* will receive the message and *how often* the audience will be exposed to it. Finally, media research may tell the advertiser with considerable degrees of accuracy the typical *impact* an ad schedule will have on the target audience's behavior.

Uncontrolled Advertising Uncontrolled advertising consists of PSAs prepared for use on radio and television stations. The message is controlled, but the delivery time is not.

Only nonprofit organizations qualify for free public service time. But because such time is scarce, the United Fund and local symphony season ticket drives, for example, must compete for it just as fiercely as any business competes for dollars. National nonprofit organizations send stations highly professional videos, either tape or DVDs, usually with a celebrity's voice-over. These are mailed far enough in advance to give station personnel time to find good slots in the daily programming for the announcements. In contrast, local organizations are more likely to put in a frantic call the day before a local blood drive asking the station to run some announcements starting immediately—with no DVD or tape and probably not even any copy. Or someone drops by with a dozen slides and two pages of copy and does not understand why this material can't be aired. Remember, however, that any PSA is used only if the station has time available to give, and even this slot may be sold and the PSA bumped at the last minute.

The amount of time and space for PSAs decreases as commercials and the media's own advertising—house ads and promos—fill up the vacancies. However, do not overlook the opportunities for PSAs on the Internet. Bill Goodwill and Ken Fischer of the PSA Research Center say that the combination of engagement opportunity, community building and viral referral can greatly amplify an original PSA with minimal cost and possible overall savings. They recommend posting your PSAs as an important part of your Web site.[10] Many people imagine that the stations already are required by the Federal Communications Commission (FCC) to devote a certain percentage of each broadcast day to PSAs. But a station is not compelled to do so by law. Furthermore, an FCC action in 1984 erased a guideline for TV that recommended devoting 10 percent of airtime to nonentertainment programming. The corresponding guideline for radio was abolished in 1981.

Station policies on PSA time are so diverse that they defy any general description. The effective practitioner simply learns and then meets the demands of each individual station.

Preparing Advertising Messages

A person writing advertising **copy** needs more than a list of details from marketing and sales describing what is supposed to be pushed. The copywriter must also know the purpose of the ad or commercial, the media it will appear in and its audience.

Copywriters must clearly define the purpose of an ad. Is the purpose to *inform?* Is it to introduce a new product, attract a new market, suggest a new use for a familiar product, give a corporate identity to a conglomerate or familiarize an audience with a new trademark? Is the purpose of the ad to *persuade?* Should the ad or commercial try to get its audience to think or do something? The following ad from a laundry company appeared in a British newspaper; its purpose is quite clear: "Strong, fat women who wish to lose weight wanted for hard but well-paid work."

Sometimes an ad's purpose is "positioning." Advertisers developed this technique as a way of finding a foothold in the marketplace, and public relations

strategists are now borrowing it. Positioning attempts to isolate a segment of the market in a highly competitive field by creating a unique image for a product that is fundamentally the same as its competitors. Thus, this technique artificially segments the audience.

After determining an ad's purpose, the next consideration is which media to use. Most ads go into a media mix, so the way the material can be interpreted for all sorts of media is important in crafting the message and planning the visuals.

Even if you hire others to write and produce the ads, you need to know a great deal about the media in which these ads will appear so that they will fit each medium's audience. In every case, you need to know about costs and estimated impact to make a useful presentation. You have to plan how to allocate resources so that you make the most of your budget.

Because advertising is so expensive, most organizations turn over actual ad development to a group of professional writers and artists. However, these people don't know the organization and its publics as well as someone who works with these publics all of the time. You need to help them convey the right tone in the ad, and you also have to get absolutely correct information to people who will be developing the ad, commercial or PSA. If a mistake winds up in an expensive production, and it's your mistake, the people who developed the ad don't have to make good on it. They will do it again, of course, but it has to be paid for again. Also, advertising deadlines are often tight, and there may not be time to redo the ad if the mistake is a major one. What happens then—when the media space or time is bought and there's no ad for it? Someone may be out of a job.

A special consideration in evaluating ads before they are approved for distribution is to reexamine the ad that has been produced in light of the purpose that was defined earlier. Sometimes ads are designed to win awards, and they often do. But the recognition for the award benefits the producer of the ad more than the organization paying for it. Award-winning ads are not always message-effective. The interests of the client compel you to keep the purpose in focus. Your responsibility is to evaluate carefully the best way to deliver your message within the constraints of time and budget.

Uncontrollable Problems

One of the biggest problems you will face in using advertising is that, if you get a good idea, it's likely to be imitated. Christian Brothers created a very successful ad campaign for its beverages using puns, only to see J&B, a competitor, launch a similar campaign.

Another seemingly uncontrollable problem that advertising campaigns frequently encounter involves the undesirable placement of ads in a newspaper or magazine relative to the adjacent copy. The same thing can happen in broadcasting, although it's fairly standard to have standing "kill" orders for, say, an airline commercial when the evening news carries the story of an airline crash. Most media try to avoid placement errors because it makes advertisers unhappy and can result in demands for compensation.

Yet another difficulty has to do with campaigns that attack the competition. These may take the form of a product-to-product confrontation, like soft drink taste tests, or one politician lambasting another. Some companies don't consider it much of a problem if the competition mentions their names in ads. They reason that consumers will forget which product was supposed to be better. They seem to respond like composer George M. Cohan, who said to a newspaperman in 1912, "I don't care what you say about me, as long as you say *something* about me, and as long as you spell my name right." But anyone who has watched some of the battles among the fast-food chains might question the validity of this viewpoint.

Election campaigning in the USA and elsewhere (perhaps due to either direct or indirect U.S. influence) continues to be negative. One perceived effect of this is lower voter turnout due to disgust with the whole affair—a rather dangerous trend in democracies, and even the highly contested and historic 2008 presidential elections had about the same portion of eligible voters cast ballots as in 2004. Some evidence suggests that negative advertising works for the attacker if a decision is forced within a time frame, as happens in the case of elections. But the decision to use negative advertising, either in an attack or in a counterattack, demands careful consideration because of its longer-term public relations costs, some of which may be intangible. Of course, new social media such as YouTube.com allow a proliferation of unendorsed advertisements and other political communication to confound what candidates are really saying, and in the 2008 presidential election, there was some confusion about what Republican vice presidential candidate Sarah Palin had said and what comedian impersonator Tina Fey was saying on the television show, *Saturday Night Live*.

Myths are the source of two other problems advertising must face. The first is the notion that one ad campaign can be effective across national boundaries and cultures. Evidence from an experienced agency, Gray Advertising, Inc., indicates that global campaigns only work when three conditions exist:

1. The market developed the same way from country to country.
2. Consumer targets are similar.
3. Consumers have the same wants and needs around the world.

If even one of the conditions does not exist, a global campaign will not work. For example, Gray says that Kellogg's Pop-Tarts failed in Great Britain because toasters aren't widely used there. The General Foods Corporation positioned Tang in France as a substitute for breakfast orange juice, but it subsequently found that orange juice was not popular among the French and that they drank almost none at breakfast.

The second myth is that a single advertising design or concept will work within a culture. Psychographics indicate the need for different appeals that might not be apparent from demographics. Whether the format is movie ads or paperback covers, it's important to adjust the advertising appeal to the audience. In many cases, different appeals must be designed to sell exactly the same product to different audiences.

Types of Publicity Used in PR Practice

A second major category of messages placed in various media by PR practitioners is publicity. What is publicity? Is it a column item in a local newspaper? A cover story in a national magazine? Thirty seconds on the 6 p.m. television news? A bit of chatter by a radio disc jockey? The mention of the company's name once or twice in a long story about the industry? A single photo in a newspaper or magazine? A 2-inch item in an association publication? An annual report? A house publication? A film? Postings on a Web page? It is all of these and more.

Publicity is information about an organization that is carried as editorial (not advertising) content in a publication or news medium. Often it's news, but it can also be a sales or promotional message.

Journalists rely on public relations people who know what the news media want, need and will use. The PR people must know their own organization thoroughly, have access to the top echelons (where they can get the information they need) and prepare it in a form that the news media can use (see Chapter 11). The news

Theory and Research Perspective

Two-way communication is essential in modern public relations practice. Feedback and dialogue are required to ensure good relationships with publics. In what has become a classic public relations debacle, Alcatel, a French telecommunications company, created negative public reaction when it put commercials on the air before testing them with a panel of consumers. In 2001 they aired an advertisement featuring Dr. Martin Luther King, Jr. Adcritic.com, which is a computerized library of TV commercials, posted a survey with five questions about the advertisement. People who visited the Web site were asked to watch a digitized version of the commercial online and to provide their opinions, which indicated some of the negative reactions that the advertisement created among the viewing public.

The offending commercial began with Dr. King delivering his "I Have a Dream" speech on August 28, 1963, to an empty Washington Mall. The advertisement's voice-over said, "Before you can inspire, before you can touch, you must first connect. And the company that connects more of the world is Alcatel, a leader in communication networks." A company executive said, "We had no idea that the media attention would be so great," commenting on the considerable negative reaction regarding the advertisement that actually had permission from Dr. King's estate to use his likeness. Many people thought this advertisement was inappropriate and offensive, objecting to the commercialization of one of the civil rights movement's most important moments (and perhaps implying that Dr. King had no audience). One critic said the advertisement cheapened the speech and the influence that it had on society.

Advertising agencies urge companies to "copy-test" advertisements in focus groups, and large advertisers like General Motors have strict rules about testing ads for offensive and controversial material before they are broadcast.

Source: Vanessa O'Connell, "Alcatel Has a Dream—and a Controversy," *The Wall Street Journal*, March 30, 2001, p. B5. Reprinted with permission.

---

media also depend on PR people because they never have enough reporters on a staff to cover everything going on in a metropolitan area. Much of the information the news media use comes to them from public relations sources. These are facts they did not have to gather, stories they did not have to write and pictures they did not have to take: information subsidies. But public relations representatives who expect to remain effective must justify the trust of the news media by being accurate, truthful and reliable.

Although much of the publicity information that PR people provide to the news media is "packaged" as news tip sheets or news releases, many other publicity tools are used to reach nonmedia publics. These include: publications, CDs, DVDs and videotape productions, speeches, various employee media, Web pages and other special media. Chapter 11 discusses tactical details of "how to do it."

Publications Three broad categories of publications carry publicity directly to audiences: organizational, industry and trade or association.

Organizational magazines, sometimes called **house publications**, are distributed to other stakeholders of a company. The distribution is usually vertical: Copies go to everyone in the organization, from top to bottom. Occasionally in a very large organization a publication may go to just one type of employee and thus get horizontal distribution—for example, a publication for supervisors. Some organizations' publications are intended for external audiences such as *Saudi Aramco World*. Others such as university alumni magazines are for stakeholder audiences, and still others are primarily internal.

A company or even a nonprofit organization may be a member of an industry organization. Such groups often produce periodicals, that is, **industry publications** aimed at bettering the entire industry. Industry organizations' magazines often gain wide distribution. They are received not only by industry executives but also by business editors, financial analysts, economics specialists, government officials and anyone else who has a particular interest in the industry.

Also distributed horizontally are **trade or association publications**—magazines, newsletters, newspapers or annual reports published at the national headquarters of a group whose members share common goals or interests. Among them are labor union publications, religious magazines and newspapers, and fraternal and professional publications.

Both profit-making and nonprofit organizations publish **sponsored magazines**. They are a costly venture, however, and some profit-making organizations have quietly folded their efforts, whereas others accept outside advertising for support. One magazine going to court personnel and attorneys in a large southwestern city focuses on issues that often underlie court cases (domestic violence, delinquency and the like) and is being published for a nonprofit, human-services organization.

Sponsored magazines published by profit-making companies may accept outside advertising, but charge less than newsstand magazines. Some companies seek co-sponsors because the venture is so expensive. These magazines differ from a company's own service magazines, although the latter are costly too. Examples of service magazines include various airlines' in-flight publications and American Express' *Departures*, which goes to its Platinum and Centurion Card holders. Sponsored magazines are "custom-published" by major media companies that want to expand their business. However, companies may find it impossible to sustain them during an

PR in Practice

In summer 2008, a video on YouTube.com showed musician Kid Rock announcing that illegally downloading music had "gone too far," but then encouraged kids to "steal everything." He ended with, "Remember, stay in school and stay off the drugs." His obvious sarcasm illustrated a long-standing problem that the music industry has attempted to correct through public relations campaigns and enforcement, as Kid Rock explained in a BBC News interview June 18, 2008. Asked whether he was worried about illegal downloading, he replied: "I don't agree with it. I think we should level the playing field. I don't mind people stealing my music, that's fine. But I think they should steal everything.

"You know how much money the oil companies have? If you need some gas, just go fill your tank off and drive off, they're not going to miss it."

A month earlier, a jury in Alexandria, Virginia, rendered a guilty verdict in the first ever criminal online music piracy trial. One estimate is that global music piracy causes $12.5 billion of economic losses every year, with 71,060 U.S. jobs lost, a loss of $2.7 billion in workers' earnings and a loss of $422 million in tax revenues, $291 million in personal income tax and $131 million in lost corporate income and production taxes. The Recording Industry Association of America (RIAA) conducted a full-scale public relations campaign in 2000 to discourage music lovers from downloading free music from the Web. The RIAA waged a public relations offensive, dispatching staffers to speak on college campuses and recording executives to testify on Capitol Hill, as well as having lawyers argue its case in courts. The public relations campaign included television and print ads that were sponsored by Artists Against Piracy, with artists speaking out against online piracy. A nationwide educational curriculum aimed at everyone from elementary school kids to adults encouraged people to think twice about taking songs off the Web for free.

Source: Kid Rock, "Kid Rock 'Steal Everything' PSA", accessed June 21, 2008 from http://www.riaa.com/newsitem; www.youtube.com/watch; Ian Youngs, "Kid Rocks Boycotts iTunes Over Pay," *BBC News*, June 18, 2008; "Jury Renders Guilty Verdict in First Ever Criminal Online Music Piracy Trial," *IRAA*, May 23, 2008; "Piracy: Online and One the Street," *RIAA* (n.d.), accessed June 21, 2008 from http://www.riaa.com; Anna Wilde Mathews, "Industry's Public-Relations Blitz Includes Pop Stars, Speeches, Appeals to 'Good Citizenship' ", *The Wall Street Journal*, June 20, 2000, pp. B1 and B4.

economic downturn, because they are so expensive to produce.

Newsletters can be internal, external or both. Some external newsletters are income generators, because their audiences pay for them through subscriptions.

Internal newsletters offer an effective means of communicating with employees. A newsletter should not be a collection of trivia, but it should contain items of interest. Many newsletter items later become subjects of fuller treatment in the institution's magazine. One company newsletter editor describes her publication as a "circulating billboard." In other companies it is much more, containing short articles, bits of humor, important announcements and notices. Some are also promotional. For instance, the Associated Press has used a broadsheet newsletter to sell its services and features to members.

External newsletters are also a publicity vehicle. Some are used for addressing issues. Others are created for and subscribed to by members of the public. Subscription to a newsletter can come through membership in an organization or through direct subscription, like a regular commercial magazine. The paid newsletter business is a big one. The Hudson Subscription Newsletter Directory lists more than 5,000 subscription newsletters.[11] Most cover highly specialized subjects and are obviously intended for a particular target public. Generally, they enjoy a high readership.

Desktop publishing and the World Wide Web have made newsletters of all kinds more attractive as a means of communication and have enabled them to resemble publications more than "letters."

Some newsletters are also (or only) delivered electronically; for example, the Web Marketing Association named the Web-based version of *Saudi Aramco World* the best magazine Web site for 2004.[12]

One major employee publication that PR departments produce is the employee **handbook**, which functions as both a reference work and an effective orientation tool. It should provide a definitive statement of what is expected from employees and what the organization offers them. The handbook should thoroughly explain policies, rules and regulations, and it should indicate how management helps to further the education and career development of the employee. The handbook should also detail how and under what circumstances the corporate name and logo can be used. Inclusion of a management organizational chart with the names of individuals whom employees need to know about or contact in various departments is essential. Workers at all levels should

be made aware of the way to get questions answered and problems solved. Most corporations find it necessary to produce handbooks annually to keep the information current.

Some organizations also publish handbooks for external use. Organizations with experts, such as universities, often publish a guide identifying those who are knowledgeable and willing to speak to media and others about their areas of expertise. Their names are also generally forwarded to ProfNet, a subsidiary of PR Newswire. ProfNet's Experts Database gives reporters profiles of professors seen as leading experts by their institutions so a reporter can get an immediate comment when needed for a breaking news story.

Video recordings remain excellent informational and publicity vehicles, despite the increasing number of Web-based options, and of course videos themselves can be placed onto Web sites.

One type of video to consider is the long feature, or **sponsored video**, which may be on a DVD. Such a production with or without movie stars or other celebrities is released by an organization or corporation and distributed free of charge. Such professionally produced digital videos and DVDs may be produced for as little as $15,000 or as much as $500,000. Most fall in the $50,000–$75,000 range. Large companies may have their own production units, but most hire independent producers. The customary audiences for sponsored videos and DVDs are schools, community organizations, television stations and (in some cases) movie theaters.

Another type of production to consider is the 1- to 5-minute production. Such short productions generally serve as fillers for feature programs, talk shows or local sporting events. To win acceptance, **feature fillers** must be newsworthy and timely, must show activity and must have only one mention or plug for the **sponsor**. They are generally presented in a news magazine format.

Various companies are making *corporate videos for external publics* (which of course may be reproduced on DVDs and placed on these companies' Web sites)—sometimes in years past for classroom use. Some of these drew criticism, for example, Exxon Corporation's videotape created for high-school science classes asserted that the *Valdez* oil spill did not destroy Alaska's wildlife. A Monsanto Company video discussed the uses of pesticides in increased farm productivity, and Union Carbide Corporation's video said chemicals contribute to more comfortable living.[13]

Some educators and environmental groups have challenged these messages, which usually look like documentaries. Corporate spokespeople counter by saying that the environmentalists are using the classroom, too. Indeed, some educators have used the videos as teaching tools, showing the corporate video and then one sponsored by an environmental group on the same issue. Despite the attendant criticism, companies and special interest groups evidently deem the videos sufficiently serviceable to justify their continued production and dissemination.[14]

Although some *internal videos*—such as video "newsletters" for employees—use the news magazine format, other formats are borrowed from television—such as MTV-style videos and game-show spoofs.[15] The videos are used to communicate the corporation's culture, to inform employees about corporate resources available for dealing with such problems as substance abuse, to instruct and train employees in new techniques or new jobs and to give employees the organization's side of controversial public issues in which it may become involved.

The reasons for using videos to reach internal audiences start with the fact that most employees now are products of total television and Internet immersion: They get most of their news from television and the Internet, and they use DVDs for home entertainment.

Employee information (training) remains the primary use for corporate videos, but they are also being used in employee relations (benefits) and crisis communication (informing employees of the organization's side of a controversial issue so that they can pass that view along to external audiences).

Some corporate videos are directed toward a combination internal/external audience such as investors who "own" the company but don't work there. Some crisis communication videos are specifically designed to reassure such audiences. Other videos deal with investor relations and address "recommenders" of corporate investment such as brokers and analysts. Videos focusing on community or environmental issues may be produced originally for internal audiences, but then may be adapted for special external audiences. The flexibility of the medium, which allows minor adaptations to be made on basically the same digital video, renders it especially useful for targeting messages to special audiences.

Intranets Just as the *Internet* is the major channel for global communication, computer systems within organizations make use of closed electronic systems called intranets. These intranets are used for all sorts of internal communication such as email, meeting notices and newsletters.

Speeches and Meetings Speeches are also publicity. When the president of an organization speaks to the local Monday club, the result is publicity, whether or not the local media cover the speech. This is because a person can also be a medium, as is the case with a speaker. The PR person usually gets the job of researching and writing speeches. To be well received, the remarks must be tailored for that particular group. The speech writer must also remember the personal characteristics of the speaker delivering the speech: The speech has to sound like the speaker, not like the writer.

Speeches are often published as brochures and sent to special audiences. This extends their usefulness as publicity tools. Sometimes, a copy of a speech is sent with just a special card (not a business card) attached. In other cases, the speech is reprinted with additional information.

Meetings often generate publicity, too, whether they are for internal or external audiences. Increasingly, meetings are used for external audiences as a proactive device to share concerns about an issue or environmental situation, and these are often covered by media. Internally, meetings are used to enable management to interact with employees and to gain feedback. Small-group meetings are seen as an effective management tool,[16] and they often generate publicity in internal publications.

Other Promotional Messages Another category of public relations messages used to promote organizations and individuals appears neither as editorial content nor as news in media. Examples of these promotional messages include exhibits and characters identified with the organization (Mickey Mouse appearing for Disney; the Cookie Monster from Sesame Street appearing for PBS). Other forms are books, multimedia presentations and closed-circuit television appearances. Other new media being used include material on CD-ROMs and information being made available 24 hours a day on special television networks.

Many presentations, like the ones this book's publisher sponsors, occur at trade shows or conventions. Some organizations invest in digital videos or PowerPoint slide shows, often on CDs, that can be used at display areas or meetings with little support from organization representatives. Your college's

admissions office probably uses such a traveling exhibit to recruit students.

In addition to using high-tech communications such as satellite broadcasts and computer networks, companies can rely on the old standby: print. Examples of self-promotion books abound—of historical note are Lee Iacocca's *Iacocca: An Autobiography*, Stanley Marcus's *Minding the Store*, John F. Kennedy's *Profiles in Courage* and Richard M. Nixon's *Six Crises*. A book gives prestige to the subject and can be worth the time invested in producing it. Organizations usually use promotional books for an anniversary or other special occasion. Some books miss being connected to an organization because they are written by a well-known author commissioned to prepare the manuscript. When a political figure, celebrity or executive's name is on the book as author, the chances are that a ghostwriter was employed. Much of the writer's time is devoted to tracking down elusive information, validating information given as fact and searching for illustrations. Nevertheless, a sincere effort, well done, often proves to be an asset.

Organizations also take advantage of their histories by opening museums. Museums are gradually replacing plant tours, which sometimes raise legal problems. Coca-Cola opened a museum in Atlanta in 1990, but it's a latecomer to the museum business. BMW and Mercedes Benz both have automobile museums in Germany. In the first 4 weeks of its operation, the John Deere Pavilion in Moline, Illinois, recorded 55,000 visitors. The John Deere Commons was developed as the centerpiece of the Quad Cities Riverfront Project, a $50 million civic renewal program that broke ground in 1993. The John Deere Pavilion has attracted more than 1.5 million guests from more than 50 countries and all 50 states since

it opened in 1997. Hormel Foods' SPAM Museum opened in September 2001 in Austin, Minnesota.

Books and museums have their limits. Much more pervasive are postal stamps. What could be better than getting people to stick a symbol of the organization on their mail, and pay to do that? The postal service in the USA has created a plethora of commemorative stamps in recent years. There's everything from opera stars to cartoon characters, but an organization can't just ask and have it happen. Proposals go to a panel that approves each suggestion. Some organizations go to considerable lengths to impress the selection panel because the identification would represent invaluable publicity.

Very effective publicity resulted when a PR practitioner had pictures made of children using milk cartons with the tops cut off as modeling clay forms. The publishers of a national children's educational book accepted the photo as showing an example of the creative application of everyday household items. The photo of the cartons subsequently appeared in the book, with the name of the milk company clearly visible. Such pictures, with the product in the background or foreground, are often used. If you ever wondered why hotels always have speakers' rostrums clearly labeled with the hotel's name and insignia, now you know.

An entire industry has developed around "product placement," making sure that identifiable brand-name products are used in television shows and in movies. The movie *Sex and the City* included promotion of a car, a fragrance and a vodka, among other products either in dialogue or on screen. And *Sex and the City* tie-ins were used in various product advertising and promotions. Thus, these product placements are not accidental choices of the prop department.[17]

Publicity as Controlled/Uncontrolled Communication

Determining where to place publicity demands an objective look at what is likely to happen to it, from creation to delivery. This means considering how much control you can exert over the delivery of the message by the medium.

Controlled Media Many specialized media, such as company, industry, trade and association publications, are under *their* editors' control. If you are the editor, it is a controlled publication; but if you are the PR director for a company submitting publicity to an industry or trade publication, your submissions are subject to editorial judgment and revision. Thus, if you are not the editor, specialized media fall into the uncontrolled category. Another person decides whether and how to use your material. On the other hand, magazines, brochures, newsletters and videos you produce and distribute are controlled, because you decide when, where and how to deliver the message. And this is certainly true of that mixed advertising/publicity medium, your Web site.

Uncontrolled Media News releases may be exceptionally well written; but once they are in the hands of an editor, anything can happen and you can't do much about it. An editor may run a release as you wrote it, give the release to a reporter to rewrite, give it to a reporter to use as a take-off point for an independently researched story or junk it entirely. The news media treat a professionally prepared release from a trustworthy source with respect, although it still may not be used if there is no space or time for it that day.

Editors get news releases from public relations wire distribution sources, from faxes, from email and through the mail. They may also pick them up from an organization's Web site, but this usually occurs when a news tip has gone out (unless reporters happen to be following the organization for a particular reason). However, the norm in recent years has been for public relations practitioners to send news releases by email, although it is most effective to follow up these news releases with a phone call, just to ensure that the public relations practitioner has contacted the appropriate writer or editor who can confirm receipt of the release. The University of Northern Iowa's marketing and public relations office does not send news releases as attachments; rather, staff paste 100 percent of their releases into the bodies of emails to avoid spam filters. James E. O'Connor,

assistant vice president for marketing and public relations, said the office doubles-up and faxes because some media ask for this delivery or because of a perceived need for a backup. But O'Connor warns, "Just because you send it doesn't mean the right person gets it." News media editors can also download accompanying JPG images and news releases from an FTP (File Transfer Protocol) site on the Internet; otherwise, these media's spam filters might block transmission of a release that has an attached photo. Also commonplace is public relations practitioners' use of RSS (Really Simple Syndication). An RSS channel can list headlines and descriptions of news releases as well as links to corresponding Web pages, or a full-text article can be accessed on the RSS channel's Web site through the RSS link. RSS feeds also can be used to keep employees informed. **News tip** sheets alert editors to possible news or feature stories. In addition, "calls for coverage" or queries may be used to elicit media coverage of PR events—a presidential press conference, the arrival of Santa to open a store's Christmas buying season, ribbon cuttings and groundbreakings. Whether these get any attention is up to the editors, who decide whether or not to assign reporters. Of course, even when reporters are assigned, they may not cover the event as the PR person would have wished. But if the event is well planned, the coverage will reflect it.

Preparing Publicity Messages

Some publicity messages go directly to audiences as controlled communications; others go to members of the news media, who constitute an intermediary audience.

Direct Publicity for Audiences Public relations offices frequently prepare material for audiences directly in print, electronic and digital video formats. It is quite common for newsletters and magazines to be developed by PR people, while most video production is done by production houses hired by the organization.

PR practitioners encounter two principal problems in putting out institutional *publications*, beyond the problem of justifying their existence to some dollars-and-cents-minded person in accounting. The first involves finding out what is going on in the organization. The second problem involves the tendency of management to view the publication as a propaganda organ for telling readers what it would like them to believe rather than what they would like to know.

Gathering information inside an organization is similar to what news reporters do—finding and cultivating sources. People who can be relied upon to provide timely and accurate information are priceless. It often helps to distribute forms that give people guidance in the type of information that would be useful. Within organizations, most PR publications people depend on meeting regularly with department heads, watching internal bulletins for newsworthy events in the making and talking to a lot of people.

Finding good information is not an easy job, and the second problem can make it more difficult. Management is justified in wanting to use publications to communicate, but the audience is often less interested in what management wants to say than in getting answers to problems they are encountering. What they want to know will usually make better copy than what management wants them to know. Surveys and readership studies give some guidance in determining what makes a publication worth its place in the budget.

Annual reports are still done in-house by some companies. Although these documents represent only a small part of the communications that go to the investors and analysts of a publicly held company, they are very important as public relations tools. Of all the publications produced by a company, the annual report is seen as the signature piece. For that reason, many privately held companies and some nonprofits also produce annual reports for institutional identity.

Some companies have almost no paper publications. In such companies, almost all communication is *electronic* and usually over an intranet. Departments may have their own publications, and task forces may be working together electronically without ever meeting. Chat rooms exist for discussion of issues. There's heavy dependence on listservs for getting the correct distribution of notices to people and reliance on people reading and responding to their email. Sophisticated electronic information users have systems managers who maintain these communication channels and create useful links of databases. For many companies, all of this internal electronic communication has become an integral, daily part of getting a job done.

Problems with these changes occur in organizations that have many unskilled workers, who are likely to be excluded from the employee communications because they are not comfortable with computers or don't even have access to a computer at work. However, this problem will decrease as new generations enter the workforce, because children are becoming computer users at a much younger age, and as organizations realize the importance of having computers available to all of their employees, not just those who use a computer for their jobs.

Digital videos are increasingly used for instructional and motivational communication within organizations, and some companies have their own closed-circuit television system. The medium is successful partly because of its familiarity, and in part because it is the closest thing to face-to-face communication. Satellites have increased the range of the digital video format, and some U.S. businesses have developed their own corporate networks. Even some annual reports have gone out as digital videos. And although most companies still publish an annual report, investor relations now depend heavily on electronic communication in general.

Publicity Through Mass Media In contrast to both advertising and publicity prepared directly for audiences, publicity prepared for the mass media generally is totally uncontrolled. Information about an

© Tom K. Ryan. Reprinted with special permission of King Feature Syndicate.

institution, product or person that appears as news in newspapers or magazines or on radio or television is used at the discretion of news editors. Thus it may be used in any context or not at all.

Information reaches the print news media through many routes, but three are basic: news releases, coverage of an event and interviews. To be acceptable, a *news release* must be written in the style used by the particular medium, and it must be presented in a form suitable to the technology of the medium. Awareness of the technological demands of each medium is also important if you expect *coverage of an event.* A speech may be an event, and certainly a news conference is, but an *interview* is not. The public relations person may formally arrange for a reporter to interview someone in a position of authority. Or the reporter may interview the PR person as representative or spokesperson for the institution. This informal situation—it may be a phone call or a visit by news media representatives—can be an organization's most significant source of publicity. Generally, it is the source preferred and used most often by the media, which often ignore events and throw away publicity releases.

More and more often, media interviews are handled by the chief executive officer (CEO) with the aid of the PR person. The PR person's job, therefore, extends to preparing the CEO to be an effective, efficient spokesperson. Some PR agencies, notably Burson-Marsteller, have become specialists in providing such training for their clients. Much of the bad publicity an organization gets can be attributed to errors by management: poor planning, ineffective communication or bad policies. Not getting any publicity at all, however, is probably the fault of the publicist. Newspeople say they throw away 80 to 90 percent of the news releases they get, because they are not usable. "Not usable" may mean the stories are incomplete (full of holes), inaccurate, not timely or just don't fit the news need.

Getting information to news media in a timely way usually means delivering the news electronically. It also means that the material in the release had better agree with other information on the same topic available to the editors online. To avoid bad publicity and nonpublicity, you should always observe the following six rules:

1. Make sure that the information you offer is appropriate to the medium in content and style, and is timely.
2. Check all facts carefully for accuracy, and double-check for missing information.

3. To deal with any questions that may arise, give the name and phone number of the person newspeople should contact.
4. An image, digital or printed, must be accompanied by the name, address and phone number of the supplier; most important, however, is the caption. However, because sending photos digitally has become the norm, the information/caption must be sent in a way that can be easily associated with the correct digital image (see Figure 10.3).
5. Never call to find out why a story or photo did not appear; and certainly don't ask, as you submit an item, when it will appear.
6. Do not send out a note with mailed releases asking for clippings. Newspapers do not run clipping bureaus.

Another mistake that publicity release writers commit involves failing to pay attention to the medium's audience. Trade publications often receive general "mass media" releases that can't be used because these releases are not tailored to the publication.

Some general media publications, although not technically trade publications, are by specialization much like trade or industry publications. One example is *TV Guide.* Some organizations would do well to pay attention to another type of specialized media—the so-called alternative media—especially if they need to reach activists and special interest groups. Examples of alternative newspapers include the *Boston Phoenix*, the *San Francisco Bay Guardian*, the *Chicago Reader*, Phoenix's *New Times* and the *LA Weekly.* These are often better read and have higher credibility (especially among activists) than traditional newspapers.

Other relevant recipients of publicity are activist networks like PeaceNet, WomensNet and the WELL in San Francisco. Each such network is run by grassroots activists concerned with civil rights, feminism, peace, ecology or some other issue. The opportunities are endless for public relations practitioners to reach their audiences if they think "micro" rather than "macro" in terms of publicity, and if they target releases especially for the audience of the medium selected.

Connecting an organization to hard news can work if there is really something to contribute. Organizations often "stretch" when trying to tie their organizations to something that has occurred and can look opportunistic. For example, some companies were criticized after 9/11 for trying to exploit the

Figure 10.3   **Wild Art: Photo Publicity**

An emperor in training

The Associated Press

An emperor penguin tends to his newly hatched chick at Sea World of California. The San Diego site is the only zoological facility in the world to successfully breed emperor penguins. The chick is the 16th hatched at the facility and will remain on its father's feet for the first few weeks of life. It was hatched Sept. 17.

catastrophe by bringing attention to themselves through their aid in or connection with the victims of the terrorist attack, which undoubtedly made many companies more cautious in promoting their relief efforts for tsunami victims as well as for the outpouring of aid for those left homeless by Hurricane Katrina as well as for more recent disasters globally.

In different parts of the world, handling the news media varies so widely that a local practitioner is often needed for guidance. Customs such as giving out free samples vary, and the style of the presentation in the releases is different too. In many cases, English-language releases work well, but even if the country uses English, it may not be American English. Spellings and word meanings may be different, even when the language is the same. Having releases available in the local language is good, as long as you are confident about the translation. This is especially critical with important documents, such as the releases that go with annual reports or other financial matters.[18]

You need a sophisticated knowledge of the medium to be able to prepare *broadcast-quality publicity*. Smaller market television may still use videotape cassettes, for example DVC Pro cassettes, with sound or satellite **feeds**, but larger markets are using digital video cameras that can download directly into a computer. Although TV news directors prefer to use their own staffs' material or something from another news source, they increasingly use publicity videos. VNRs (video news releases) usually cover hard news, not feature stories, and may be transmitted by satellite. It is also important to remember that different television broadcast standards exist throughout the world, so you must know and meet the technical standards that exist in a particular country if your publicity is to be used. Also, video cassettes and their players from one country may not be compatible with the system used in another country.

VNRs and **B-roll** (sent along so that news directors can create different versions of the piece) are so widely used now that the video distribution industry has grown exponentially. Media distribution agencies will send advisories to television news directors by newswire, fax or one of the computer networks and transmit the VNR by satellite to all the stations at once. Most production companies are able to provide the uplinks. The media distribution companies will also provide verification of station use. Some cassettes are still sent too, but it's cheaper to use the satellite.

One way to contain costs is to partner with another company. These co-op VNRs spread production and distribution costs and can result in a video with a broader appeal. Issues and events, such as holidays, are especially good for co-op VNRs because they can explore trends, offer different aspects or provide research information. In one example, a major producer of notebook computers cooperated with another electronics manufacturer to talk about home electronics during the Christmas buying season.[19] Some VNRs have been successfully used to support marketing campaigns, but this only works if the VNR precedes the commercial message.[20]

One use of VNRs can be to provide television stations with background they couldn't get and with quotes from experts not accessible to them. That's what happened when the *Journal of the American Medical Association* began offering VNRs on various topics, called *JAMA Reports*. Their producer, On the Scene Productions, said that if the story had broad consumer appeal, good production quality and an unbiased approach, then the opportunities for the videos to be used were good. When the report can be tied to a breaking story, of course, it's even more valuable to news directors.[21]

Educational TV often uses PR-produced feature videos if they contain no commercialism, and on rare occasions so does commercial TV. Frequently, television stations show a short feature video offered by a group. These are usually 90 seconds long, but some are 3 minutes long; most are entertaining, light and informative. Local stations use these most often on weekends, when news is slow and they have time they can fill with nonnetwork shows.

Publicity never supplants spot news—news recorded at the time an event occurs (usually by journalists)—but it is the best way to tell an advance story. However, such a video is just as subject to editing as a written news release is, and it too may not be used at all. This is definitely an uncontrolled area—nearly as uncontrolled as the spot coverage of news that results when a television crew is alerted to an event.

Sometimes an organization or profession is the subject of a television **documentary**. The PR practitioner can cooperate with those who are researching, writing and filming the documentary, but that is all that the PR person can do: help and hope for the best.

A form of television publicity that cannot be overlooked is the talk show. Daytime and evening talk shows continually present people promoting their latest book, movie, song or persona. Most local stations have a format that allows for local bookings.

Ethical Perspective

New communication channels and media mean new legal and ethical questions for public relations practitioners as well as for others in the organizations for which the practitioners work. Legal questions include: Is email treated legally like a phone call or a written note? Is a computer like a photocopier or a bulletin board? Is a password-protected folder in a computer like an employee's locker? Can a company legally enforce a complete ban on all nonbusiness use of email by employees? Email communication and Internet usage in organizations are raising many questions that public relations practitioners, as well as the courts, must continue to deliberate.[1]

How about court records, which in the past have been public, but actually were viewed by few people? Some courts are posting rulings and related documents on the Web, which could cause ethical privacy problems when, for example, people filing for personal bankruptcy must disclose Social Security, bank and credit card numbers, account balances and even names and ages of their children, or when court files contain medical and psychiatric records, tax returns and unproven allegations.[2]

The Internet, however, also provides a way to counteract unethical or incorrect information that is being disseminated by others. Against conventional wisdom, presidential contender Barack Obama decided in the summer of 2008 to fight rumors head-on with a dedicated Web site named FightTheSmears.com, on which the candidate hoped to easily refute "smears" with videos and photographs.[3]

Sources: [1]Michael, J. McCarthy, "Your Manager's Policy on Employee's E-Mail May Have a Weak Spot," *The Wall Street Journal*, April 25, 2000, pp. A1, A10.

[2]Jerry Markon, "Curbs Debated as Court Records Go Public on Net," *The Wall Street Journal*, February 27, 2001, pp. B1, B4.

[3]Karen Tumulty, "Can Obama Shred the Rumors?" *Time*, June 23, 2008, pp. 40–1.

In such events, the PR person should be sure of three things: (1) that the show fits the PR objective, (2) that the organization or sponsor gets credit and (3) that the spokesperson is well coached or skilled in television appearances. Some interviews also may be sent by a news distribution service such as Medialink via satellite. However, most stations still record the "send" for later use.

One of the myths that haunts public relations people is the notion that television exposure is critically important. This is not so. Television exposure is so fleeting and the audience is so fragmented that, unless all networks use the information, the impact may be minimal. Furthermore, television is becoming less important in an era of the Internet and its new social media. Most of the impact from local coverage comes from documentaries or news features.

Just as the possible benefits of being on television or in newspapers or magazines are exaggerated, so is the damage caused by negative stories. Some balanced stories that tell both sides of a story are seen within an organization as being "negative" because they say something against the organization. You can't avoid that, but you can be sure you tell the organization's side of the story successfully.

Traditional Hybrids: Direct Mail and 900 Phone Numbers

Direct mail is a hybrid of publicity and advertising. In certain instances (such as newsletters from politicians), direct mail can be considered publicity. On the other hand, direct mail that seeks magazine subscriptions, for example, most certainly is advertising. Direct mail is a form of controlled communication: The message can say anything that does not violate a law; it can be any size or shape the U.S. Postal Service will accept; and it can be sent any time its sender chooses. Mailing lists are available for almost any audience you might wish to reach (otherwise you can send it to "Occupant" at a particular address). However, just because the envelope arrives does not mean the message will be received.

Another form of direct mail is electronic mail (email), which is excellent for "perishable" messages that need instant delivery and a prompt response. "Spammed" direct mail messages delivered over the Internet are, however, becoming a nuisance and thus counterproductive, and "spam filters" have become increasingly effective in quarantining these messages.

Traditional direct mail has a high mortality rate, which is why so much is invested in designing appeals and in doing multiple mailings. The hope is that at least one effort will reach its intended audience.

The seven cardinal rules governing direct mail are as follows:

1. Know what the objective of the mailing is, and concentrate on it.

2. Use the correct mailing list. Remember that December through February is a significant job-change period; if you don't have time to check the accuracy of your list, mailings at this time should go to the title and not to the person.

3. Write copy that explains what the product or service does for the recipient.

4. Design the layout and format to fit the image of the product or service you are presenting.

5. Make it easy for the prospect to take the action you want taken.

6. Tell the story at least three times, and repeat the mailings two or three times.

7. Research all direct mail by testing the offer, package and list. Test to see if the offer is attractive to target audiences. Use alternative offers to make sure you have the best incentive. Test the package (presentation). Make sure respondents know what to do with the offer, and keep the directions simple and clear. Test the list with a sample mailing to ensure that it's accurate. Test the mailing even if it is as little as 1,000 pieces. Don't ever drop untested pieces in the mail. Figure 10.4 shows a direct-mail piece in multiple languages.

Three important considerations go into planning a direct mailing: recency, frequency and monetary matters. The *recency* of a direct mailing is significant in evaluating response; stories of delayed-action response are rare. *Frequent* mailings increase your chances of response by providing reminders. The *monetary* aspect—what you can afford to spend—influences the design and outcome of a direct mailing.

Usually direct-mail investments more than pay their way. The key to success is the mailing list you select. *Occupant* lists—lists organized by addresses—are easy to find and inexpensive but offensively impersonal. If you are mailing to a limited geographical

area, you can make up your own list from the criss-cross, or city, directory. *Specialized* lists are available according to age, income, educational status and almost any other kind of breakdown you want. Many organizations sell lists of their membership, and you can buy other lists from direct-mail list companies. Some base their lists on auto registrations, others on phone directories and others on complex sampling strata.

The price you pay for use of a list entitles you to use it only once. To protect its list, the mailing house actually sends out the material for you. The U.S. Postal Service reports that about 14 percent of the nation's population moves every year, generating more than 46 million address changes. Planning a periodic check of your list is the best way to safeguard the integrity of your basic mailing file. The U.S. Postal Service will help. The U.S. Postal Service provides a range of services, fully described in its Web site (www.usps.com), that helps its customers standardize addresses, make sure cities match zip codes, validate the zip codes and add four extra digits to each code. Your post office also will report any addresses that can't be coded. U.S. Postal Service employees are invariably helpful in answering any questions related to using their services, not only as policy, but also because informed Postal Service customers make their jobs easier.

Remember that every piece of correspondence going out of the office is an image-maker or -breaker. Careful attention to spelling indicates that you care about the recipient. Typographical errors suggest that the message was not important enough to command the writer's attention, and the person receiving the letter might wonder why it should deserve his or hers. Accurate spelling and syntax also imply knowledge and authority. Perhaps the most compelling reason for making every piece of copy perfect is that your letterhead is your signature.

Every bit as personal as a note bearing your letterhead is a telephone call. A premium-rate 900 telephone number charges the caller for calls to your organization. The voice information system offers callers access to a prerecorded message or other public relations information, if they have a touch-tone telephone. Callers can be charged anything from 50 cents to as much as $50 per call or more and may be billed at a flat rate or at a cost per minute. Although this service is intended to be legitimate, 900 numbers have gotten a bad reputation throughout the years because of the various scams and unsavory businesses that have used them.

Figure 10.4 Direct Mail in Multiple Languages

Service mark of AT&T

9-1-1 SPEAKS YOUR LANGUAGE

9-1-1 HABLA SU IDIOMA

9-1-1 Nói Tiếng Của Quý Vị

9-1-1 能說您的語言

СЛУЖБА 9-1-1 ГОВОРИТ НА ВАШЕМ ЯЗЫКЕ.

VIETNAMESE — Việt Ngữ

QUÝ VỊ CẦN LÀM GÌ KHI GỌI 9-1-1?

Khi quý vị cần giúp đỡ:

1. Gọi 9-1-1
2. Đừng cúp máy.
3. Báo cho 9-1-1 biết trường hợp khẩn cấp của quý vị cần:
   - CẢNH SÁT (POLICE)
   - CỨU HỎA (FIRE)
   - XE CỨU THƯƠNG (AMBULANCE)
   (Cố gắng học những từ này trong Anh ngữ)
4. 9-1-1 có thể đưa vào một thông dịch viên. Đừng cúp máy. Cứ giữ máy thoại.
5. Báo cho 9-1-1 biết ngôn ngữ của quý vị.
6. Nên bình tĩnh.
7. Cho 9-1-1 biết những tin tức của quý vị:
   - tên
   - số điện thoại
   - địa chỉ nơi đang cần giúp đỡ
8. Trả lời tất cả mọi câu hỏi.

9-1-1 **chỉ** được dùng cho các trường hợp khẩn cấp.

Ví dụ:
   - hỏa hoạn
   - tội ác
   - bị thương cần xe cứu thương
   - nguy hiểm đến tính mạng và tài sản

9-1-1 **không** phải là nơi hỏi tin tức

Nếu có gì nghi ngờ, gọi 9-1-1.

CAMBODIAN

(Cambodian script text)

SPANISH — ESPAÑOL

¿QUE DEBE HACER CUANDO LLAME AL 9-1-1?

Cuando necesite ayuda:

1) Llame al 9-1-1.
2) Manténgase en la línea.
3) Dígale a 9-1-1 cuál es su emergencia:
   - POLICIA (POLICE)
   - INCENDIO (FIRE)
   - AMBULANCIA (AMBULANCE)
   (Trate de aprender estas palabras en inglés).
4) 9-1-1 puede agregar un intérprete a la línea. Manténgase en la línea. **No** cuelgue. Escuchará un sonido de "click".
5) Dígale a 9-1-1 qué idioma habla.
6) Mantenga la calma.
7) Dele a 9-1-1 su:
   - nombre
   - número telefónico
   - la dirección en donde se necesita la ayuda
8) Conteste todas las preguntas.

9-1-1 es sólo para emergencias.

Por ejemplo:
   - incendio
   - crímenes
   - herido que necesita ambulancia
   - peligro para la vida o propiedad

9-1-1 **no** es un número de información.

En caso de duda, llame al 9-1-1.

RUSSIAN — РУССКИЙ ВАРИАНТ

ЧТО ДЕЛАТЬ, КОГДА ВЫ ЗВОНИТЕ 9-1-1?

Когда вам нужна помощь:

1) Звоните 9-1-1.
2) Дождитесь ответа.
3) Укажите диспетчеру службы 9-1-1 характер чрезвычайной ситуации:
   - ПОЛИЦИЯ (POLICE)
   - ПОЖАР (FIRE)
   - СКОРАЯ ПОМОЩЬ (AMBULANCE)
   (Постарайтесь выучить эти слова на английском языке).
4) Служба 9-1-1 может подключить к разговору переводчика.
   В этом случае вы услышите щелчок. Не вешайте трубку. Дождитесь ответа.
5) Скажите диспетчеру службы 9-1-1, на каком языке вы говорите.
6) Сохраняйте спокойствие.
7) Скажите диспетчеру службы 9-1-1:
   - ваше имя
   - ваш номер телефона
8) Ответьте на все вопросы.

Звоните 9-1-1 исключительно в случае чрезвычайной ситуации.

Например, в случае:
   - пожара
   - преступления
   - телесного повреждения, требующего скорой помощи
   - опасности для жизни или собственности

Служба 9-1-1 не является информационной службой.

В случае сомнения, звоните 9-1-1.

(continued)

Figure 10.4   Direct Mail in Multiple Languages (continued)

ENGLISH	KOREAN 한국말	LAOTIAN	CHINESE 中文	ARABIC اللغة العربية

WHAT TO DO WHEN YOU CALL 9-1-1?

When you need help:

1.) Call 9-1-1.

2.) Stay on the phone.

3.) Tell 9-1-1 what your emergency is:
- POLICE
- FIRE
- AMBULANCE

4.) 9-1-1 may add-on an interpreter. You will hear a clicking noise. **Don't** hang up. Stay on the phone.

5.) Tell 9-1-1 the language you speak.

6.) Be calm.

7.) Give 9-1-1 your:
- name
- phone number
- address where help is needed

8.) Answer all questions.

9-1-1 is for emergencies only.

For instance:
- fire
- crime
- injury needing an ambulance
- danger to life or property

9-1-1 is **not** for information.

If in doubt, call 9-1-1.

Developing Hybrids

Digital technology has created a whole new way of conveying information and interacting with publics. Some of you may be "attending" your public relations class online where you have assignments electronically delivered and returned, or perhaps you are sitting in a fiber optic distance education center far from your professor's classroom. This textbook has a Web site, and you may have class discussions in a "chat room," while you may get your academic counseling for the class in personal responses to your email messages from your instructor. You'll perform your academic research online, and your personal research too, such as finding the cheapest tickets for a trip home or a break from school and buying them online as well.

You may be using a CD-ROM with the class. Although not a new technology, more public relations people are using CD-ROMs now instead of brochures or in place of whole presentations such as media kits. There's more space for information, and the quality of the video is superb. You can use a CD, DVD or Internet RSS to deliver VNRs.

Computerized touch-screen kiosks offer interactive displays at trade shows. If you are selling an expensive item such as a house or car, prospective buyers can look at different options, select what they want and go as far with the transaction as the company allows, electronically.

The Internet offers Web sites that provide 24-hour-a-day global sources for news media. Reporters are likely to go to a Web site first for information and may or may not try the telephone or fax. All kinds of consumers of information use Web sites, and the news media have their own Web sites where users expect to find the latest information being processed by these news media.

The Internet

Organizations of all kinds, profit and nonprofit (including government), have Web sites, and when you access those pages, especially those of profit-making organizations, you are likely to get both advertising and editorial messages. That makes the Web site one of the most versatile of the new hybrids.

There are several ongoing tasks that are important for maintaining interest in a Web site. These include offering substantive content, keeping it updated and fresh, making it easy to use, providing a good text presentation for those who turn off graphics to save loading time and having all of the "basic" data such as you would expect to find on organizational "fact sheets," as well as the newsworthy items that would attract all of your publics, not just media.[22]

For that to happen, you might consider microsites for a number of functions, such as new campaigns, special offers, crisis communications and online sales. Although you can use a link from a home page, if special items aren't easy to find and use, people will give up. Microsites work in reverse. People put up special sites with their own addresses and the sites then offer a link to these people's home pages. The microsites typically don't last very long.[23] Their flexibility makes them an especially good publicity and promotion tool and a place reporters depend on for information.

The Internet is also turning out to be a reliable source for video news as well. While probably not the best way to distribute VNRs, online video is interesting not just to newspeople. TV producers can get RSS feeds off the Internet, and they may get story ideas there where they can see what is available. Also, VMS is able to send clips to subscriber clients electronically.

Of course, those opposed to your organization might post their own VNRs. In late 2007, CyberAlert, Inc. launched the first subscription service that automatically searches and monitors videoclips posted on video sharing Web sites and tracks news videos that are posted to online news sources.[24] The two-way interactive aspect is what makes the Internet so attractive as a new communication channel.

Benefits and Disadvantages of Interactive Audio/Text/Video

The Internet has dramatically changed public relations practice, in that publics can be defined more clearly and targeted more precisely. Furthermore, the interactive nature of the Internet allows for more reliable monitoring and evaluating. The down side to this change is that bad news may be instantly global, and email and chat room conversations can spread rumors and even pretend to originate from organizations. Organizations can also be attacked outright by rogue sites that mimic theirs.

Web sites are often created and then abandoned, reflecting badly on the organization. Some Web sites are simply too complex to use efficiently, and people don't return to them unless they find the technology

Global Perspective

The Internet offers a communication channel that is useful for public relations practitioners as well as for marketers. However, Internet messages from a variety of sources also can cause public relations problems for organizations; for example, no corporation wants its name to precede a rogue Web site, and these sites abound on the Internet. Public relations practitioners must constantly monitor the Internet to learn what online users are saying about their organizations and products and services.

The Internet also features many sites that may do little more than distract the millions of workers throughout the world who use their computers in their jobs, sites that have quickly become part of popular culture. This problem extends far beyond the USA; for example, young employees in Russia have their own diversion (found on YouTube.com) from office responsibilities—"Masyanya," an Internet cartoon whose 2-minute episodes quickly began getting 22,000 hits a day when the "multifilm" became available on the Web in late 2001. Popular among 20- to 30-year-old white-collar Russian workers, Masyanya's lines are quoted in after-hour bars as well as at office water coolers, whereas those higher in the corporate hierarchy criticize the cartoon character as an inappropriate role model for young employees. Masyanya is described as "a foul-mouthed, pot-smoking slacker living in St. Petersburg," a 20-something young woman who uses teenage slang, giggles a lot and has a particular fondness for alcohol, drugs and sex. The character's commercial appeal hasn't been lost on those ranging from political candidates who are interested in young people's votes to businesspeople wanting her to market condoms. The site is beginning to pay for itself with banner ads, related merchandising and other commercial spin-offs.

Source: Guy Chazan, "Internet Cartoon Transfixes Russia's Office Workers, to Bosses' Dismay," *The Wall Street Journal*, March 21, 2002, pp. B1 and B3. Reprinted with permission.

intriguing. Today, blogs constitute a greater threat—and perhaps a greater opportunity. Bloggers, some of whom may be reporters for news media, may enjoy considerable readership among people who also contribute their thoughts to the blog, but may have nothing nice to say about your organization or the products and/or services that it provides. Fortunately, search tools have become more sophisticated in searching for blogs and RSS news feeds. However, corporations are beginning to hire their own bloggers to keep Web logs for their customers and other publics.

A stand-alone unit for interactive use, such as a kiosk, can be a good teaching tool and an intriguing draw at a meeting or show. However, unless well conceived, it can be simplistic and boring as well as not really providing any information about the user.

Communication technology is moving so quickly that it takes conscientious effort on the part of public relations practitioners to keep up with the constantly evolving channels of communication and newly discovered ways to use these channels. Wiki software that allows "open editing" of Web page content by users, RSS feeds, FTP, podcasting and video blogging, HDTV (high-definition television), the world of Twitter—mid-career public relations professionals learned about none of these when they were studying to be practitioners. At no other time has public relations been so fascinating, so challenging and so important as it is today in a multicultural, global society that is linked so closely together through such communication technology.

Discussion Questions

1. What channels of communication do you think will evolve the most in the next two years? Five years? What new channels do you think will affect public relations practice as well as the way that members of a public can communicate with one another and with the practitioner's organization?

2. What, if any, are the disadvantages of Internet communication and such phenomena as text-messaging? Is faster communication always

better? Explain your answer. What media, if any, do you expect to become obsolete in the next few years?

3. What criteria should be used to determine public relations practitioners' choice of a channel and medium to communicate with a particular public?

4. How have new forms of communication affected the lives of college students today? How do you communicate with your friends? What do you do for recreation that you believe students in earlier generations couldn't or wouldn't do?

Points to Remember

- Channels of communication are public or private paths by which messages travel through media.

- Public channels are for the mass media, and private channels apply to the print and electronic media of organizations.

- The two principal types of public relations communication are advertising and publicity, both of which may take many media forms.

- In planning a public relations strategy, the practitioner chooses channels and media based on the purpose of the communication, the intended audience, the message to be delivered, the resources available and the credibility of the medium chosen to carry the message.

- A mix of media is generally used, and media can be categorized as controlled or uncontrolled.

- Public relations uses many types of advertising in various formats, which means that PR practitioners have to know how to prepare, place and evaluate ad copy.

- Creating most advertising messages of any kind—public service announcements or commercial messages—is a costly process, and evaluations of effectiveness are difficult.

- Advertising can create problems as well as solve them. Especially in a global environment, ads must be watched for their suitability in terms of language and culture for the intended audience as well as the unintended audience that might be exposed to them.

- Using ads may be especially important when a problem occurs, because it is a controlled format.

- Uncontrollable problems with advertising include undesirable placement, competitors' imitation of good advertising ideas and negative effects.

- Two myths associated with advertising are that a single concept can be used globally and that a single concept can work with all audiences within one culture.

- Messages that are not advertising generally are referred to as *publicity*—some form of news or information about the organization.

- Publicity can go directly to audiences or can be sent through mass and/or specialized media.

- Organizations generally produce publications such as magazines, newsletters and annual reports, and at least the last two are being made available electronically, usually through a Web site.

- Publications may be done in-house or externally. Most film and video work is produced by outside specialists unless the organization is large enough to support an in-house facility.

- Internet Web sites and intranets are often handled in-house by large organizations, but smaller ones use providers.

- Meetings and speeches are also a form of media, and speeches may be mailed for additional exposure.

- Other media for promotional messages include exhibits, characters identified with the organization, multimedia presentations, closed-circuit television, books, commemorative stamps and even cartoons.

- Publicity in the mass media and in specialized media outside the organization is uncontrolled and demands careful preparation to meet the demands of the medium.

- Use of video news releases (VNRs) by broadcasters and the video distribution industry has grown exponentially.

- Traditional hybrids (combinations of advertising and publicity) are direct mail and 900 telephone numbers. The success of direct mail depends on research to keep target audiences identified.

- Digital technology has created a whole new way of conveying information and interacting with publics. CD-ROMs and Web sites offer opportunities for profit and nonprofit organizations to send direct messages to specific publics.

- Web sites on the Internet provide sources of information and video for news media seekers as well as others.

- Along with the many benefits of the Internet, there are some down sides, such as the global spreading of bad news and rumors and outright attacks by rogue Web sites and misleading email.

- New technologies hold a lot of promise for public relations use, but such communication technologies' impact has to be carefully considered.

- Put news releases on your organization's Web site to reach those most interested in your organization.

Go to the Web site for this book at **www.cengage.com/masscomm/newsom/thisispr10e** to find more Web links on this subject.

Other Related Web Sites to Review

Advertising Association (British)
http://www.adassoc.org.uk/

American Advertising Federation (AAF)
http://www.aaf.org/

American Association of Advertising Agencies (AAAA)
http://www2.aaaa.org/Portal/Pages/default.aspx

Interactive Advertising Bureau
http://www.iab.net/

Nielsen/Net Ratings
http://www.nielsen-netratings.com

Reprinted by permission of Creators Syndicate, Inc.

CHAPTER 11

Tactics and Techniques

Details that Make PR Strategy Work

The explosion of media during the past few decades has led marketers to address many parts of the U.S. population that previously lacked audiovisual identities. Ethnic groups, racial groups, gender groups, and groups arrayed around political positions have seen versions of entertainment and news aimed at them. This sort of cultural diversity ought to be celebrated as the font of a strong, idea-rich society. . . . But to do that it ought to be shared among the population as a whole. The major problem with the emerging media world is its impulse to keep diversity hidden.

—Joseph Turow, in *Breaking Up America*[1]

OBJECTIVES

- To appreciate the distinctions among advertising, publicity, publications, annual reports and special events and understand the unique tactical and technical requirements for preparing messages in each.

- To recognize the best tactics and techniques for message presentation in the mass media that are available to public relations practitioners.

- To understand how media workers perform their jobs and the best ways that public relations practitioners can help them to do so.

- To develop sensitivity to how cultural differences among audiences can affect the way public relations messages are interpreted and perceived.

Public relations work is somewhat like a giant jigsaw puzzle: There are many pieces, and each must fit perfectly with the others to make the whole picture. In Chapter 9, you learned strategies to help you develop the picture. In Chapter 10, you surveyed the communication channels PR practitioners use as the framework for that picture. In this chapter, you get a look at the pieces. Have you ever worked a jigsaw puzzle by first separating what appeared to be ground from what looked like sky? Well, you can divide the major sections of the public relations puzzle—advertising and publicity—in the same way. In trying to sort out puzzle pieces by "sky" and "ground," however, you may sometimes have found pieces that included parts of both, and others that looked like one but were actually the other. That's also the case with advertising and publicity in public relations. ■

Advertising

Advertising has been defined as paid-for time or space, except in the case of public service announcements (PSAs), for which the time and space are donated to a nonprofit organization. But in some situations, advertising looks a lot like publicity. Usually when advertising takes on the appearance of publicity, there is no intention to deceive the careful viewer. Ads are supposed to be clearly labeled as such, but they can be labeled and still look very much like editorial copy.

Sometimes when a newspaper publishes a special section on something such as the opening of a hospital, the reader may not be aware that almost all of that section—even the news columns—consists of advertising that has been paid for.

The tendency of some public relations people to view PSAs as publicity, because no money changes hands, is confusing to most students and mystifying to others. Clearly, though, print PSAs look exactly like ads, and broadcast PSAs sound exactly like commercials. Moreover, they are handled through the advertising departments of print media and through public service directors at radio and television stations. Publicity, on the other hand, is handled by media news staffs and must compete for time or space with staff-generated news material. Perhaps the most clear-cut difference, however, is that PSAs, like other advertising, are controlled communications, the precise content of which is dictated by the originating organization. In contrast, publicity is subject to whatever revisions or editing the news media see fit to impose.

Ads as News Look-Alikes

Ads sometimes look like publicity. Although the copy is clearly marked as advertising, it may resemble a news feature and may be read as one by readers. These ads appear frequently in local publications and highlight products and services offered by local businesses. Some types of product advertising done by specialty houses look like a feature story or column. The line between advertising and publicity will blur further as traditional media are supplemented in creative ways using Internet and social media technology and as contemporary consumers of media lose their ability to distinguish between "fair and unbiased" news messages and information that has not been "vetted" by professionally trained journalists in their traditional role. Are bloggers, for example, just private citizens with an interest in a subject, or are they "citizen journalists"? Today, blogs are attracting and making money from advertisers, and public relations campaigns increasingly are pitching to bloggers.

Newspaper circulation has been dropping for more than 20 years simultaneously with increasing competition for advertising dollars, and most of the nation's largest newspapers saw circulation drop at an increased rate in early 2008, which was interpreted as a further migration of readers online.[2] Newspapers today have been trying to highlight a new measure to document their market penetration, that is, the total number of online and print readers instead of the number of print newspapers delivered each day.[3]

And while **Video News Releases** (VNRs) have been around a long time, criticism of their use and misuse remains. The Center for Media and Democracy reported in April 2006 that, over a 10-month period, it had documented television newsrooms' use of 36 VNRs, which it said was only a small sample of the thousands that are being produced each year. The Center identified 77 television stations that aired these VNRs or related satellite media tours (SMTs) in 98 separate instances without disclosure of their sources to viewers, and collectively these 77 stations reached more than half the U.S. population. In each case, these 77 television stations actively disguised the sponsored content to make the VNR appear to be their own reporting, and for more than one third of the time stations aired the pre-packaged VNR in its entirety. The Center noted that "Without strong disclosure requirements and the attention and action of TV station personnel, viewers cannot know when the news segment they're watching was bought and paid for by the very subjects of that 'report.' "[4] What all of this means is that such traditional dichotomies between news-editorial and advertising content are becoming indistinct, as are such categories as print journalism and electronic media. All such messages may be considered promotional pieces, however, and wouldn't pass muster as a news story if submitted to an editor in a traditional medium.

Sometimes public relations people have difficulty with ads that closely resemble publicity releases because unsophisticated managements don't know the difference between the two. Often, as in the "Homes" sections of Sunday newspapers, whole sections of copy may be involved, all consisting of display advertising (see Figure 11.1). In addition, newspapers sometimes run special sections—whole sections devoted to a special topic or event and built around the advertising that is sold.

The editorial copy in such a section is essentially written for those who have taken out ads. The amount of space purchased determines the length of the stories, as well as the amount of illustration material (art) that accompanies them. The only "free" copy in the section is what you write about the event or the topic itself, such as a historical feature, a current "what's going on" news item, profiles of people from previous events and photos related to the topical content of the section. The copy in most special sections, other than the Sunday real estate sections, looks like news but is not straight news.

Figure 11.1   **Advertisement that Resembles Publicity**

OB-GYN
Specialist

Your Health Advertorial

Nurse Midwife Offers Personalized Approach to Birth

By Kendra Richman
For OB-GYN Specialist

WATERLOO

When Sharon Kern was preparing for the arrival of her fourth child, she knew exactly what kind of birth she wanted.

"The more children I've had, the more I've realized I can be in control of what happens. I wanted to be able to do it at my own pace and not be controlled by the medicine," says Kern, who lives outside Traer. "We wanted to use a midwife, but I was afraid to have the baby at home."

Kim Boote, a certified nurse midwife with OB-GYN Specialists, provided the perfect option.

Boote sees patients throughout their pregnancy and delivers the baby in the hospital where medical services are available if needed. As a midwife, she focuses on empowering women to make choices about their health by educating them about the changes to their body during pregnancy. She works closely with each patient to create a personal plan for the birth of their baby. "I try to do whatever the patient wants, as long as it's safe for mother and baby," says Boote.

When the big day comes, Boote stays with her patient throughout the entire labor and delivery. Generally she keeps the room quiet and the lights low to create a relaxing environment. She encourages patients to manage their pain with breathing, movement or even warm showers. But she points out that it is a misconception that midwifes do not allow medical forms of pain relief. "I encourage my patients to use natural methods, but if they want an epidural or IV medication, I make sure they have it."

Kern embraces a natural approach to childbirth. She chose not to have pain relief for any of her deliveries. But she says her fourth delivery was the most enjoyable because of the atmosphere in the delivery room. "It seemed more relaxed because no one was telling me what to do, but instead followed what I was doing," she says. "Kim was quiet and let me concentrate and told me to push whenever I was ready."

A midwife delivery is not for everyone. Patients are carefully screened for any medical risk factors. For those patients who develop complications, Boote can call on the medical expertise of the physicians at OB-GYN Specialists. "Because I have a good relationship with the doctors, we can work together to provide the best care for the patient," she says. "If a C-section is needed, I can go in with the patient to offer support."

For patients with uncomplicated pregnancies and deliveries, a midwife offers a very personal approach to childbirth.

"A midwife is a great choice for a woman who knows what kind of birth she wants and needs someone to help her achieve it," says Boote.

"We wanted to use a midwife, but I was afraid to have the baby at home."
~Sharon Kern

Courtesy of the *Waterloo–Cedar Falls Courier* and Mathis, Earnest & Vandeventer, LLC.

Special sections may appear in many different forms. One on health care, for example, may look like a regular newspaper section, as might a *single advertiser* supplement for a new store. Alternatively, a store may use a magazine format to be inserted within a newspaper. A chamber of commerce annual report may look like a Sunday tabloid insert similar to *The New York Times Book Review* section (which is editorial matter, not advertising). Advertorials—magazine advertising supplements—often look like special features. Broadcast advertorials, or infomercials, though, look like editorials and deal with ideas or issues and not with products or services. Another area that invites confusion is broadcast news promos (the broadcast equivalent of house ads). These often sound like actual news sound bites and can mislead the viewer or listener.

Print and Broadcast PSAs

Public service announcements are examples of publicity-generating ad copy that are similar to special sections and display advertising. In all of these forms, you do *not* work with the publication's editorial staff in placing them. With print PSAs, you will probably deal with newspaper or magazine designers and layout artists in the publication's advertising department, who position ads and editorial matter. You might also work with a newspaper's advertising director to get a **drop-in ad** placed in a regular advertiser's space, with that advertiser's permission. Or you might work with a large regular advertiser to sponsor your space. Regular advertisers usually agree to do this only for nonprofit organizations or in conjunction with special civic events that are open to all, such as a Fourth of July fireworks celebration.

If your message is for the electronic media, you will deal with public service directors who are usually partial to general interest subjects such as health and safety or to specific social problems such as substance abuse. You can sponsor a PSA if you represent a profit-making organization as long as you are delivering a nonprofit organization's message that does not directly benefit your own organization.

When you are planning a PSA, you first need to consider its purpose. Then you must consider the budget: the amount of money you have to spend and the amount you can get from donations. You must also try to foresee problems you are likely to encounter in shooting, including actors, location, permissions, music and sound.

Preparing Successful Ads

Your most important consideration in preparing any type of advertising copy is effectiveness—achieving your purpose. The purpose must be clear because it's difficult for even the best copy to create awareness, convey specific information, get action and affect attitudes. You must decide where the public is in relation to the product or service (including a nonprofit organization's service) and go from there. The fact that memory is multidimensional means that, to be able to measure your ad's effectiveness with some degree of reliability, you have to know exactly what you wish to achieve and how prepared a specific public is to receive your message.[5]

Decisions about effectiveness include whether to use humor, whether to make comparisons and whether to use negative comments. Again, what you decide depends on what you are trying to accomplish and whom you are trying to reach. Humorous ads seem to get attention (see Figure 11.2), but they convey less information and don't always ensure recall of the advertiser.[6] There's a risk in comparative ads too, especially in credibility. Credibility also can be at stake in negative advertising, but you can usually count on recall. And although most people say they don't like negative advertising, they do respond to negative political advertising that seems to offer insight into an issue or an opponent's personal characteristics.[7] One of the most memorable parts of any ad is the organization's logo, designed not only for high recognition, but also for a positive attraction or reaction.

According to one study, "Successful corporate symbols will be those which effectively evoke the positive and powerful responses already present in the mind of the subject and those which were learned at a much earlier stage of their cultural education."[8] The latter point suggests that as organizations become involved in global communication, and as electronic channels of communication allow anyone in the world access to an organization's Web site, these logos should be pretested abroad to ensure that they meet with cultural acceptance. Organizations often change their logos so that they can "grow" with the organization and reflect a more modern look or encompass appreciation and understanding by a more diverse array of people. Sometimes logos change for a special occasion. Other organizations cling to an established logo for high recognition.

Figure 11.2   **Advertisement Using Humor**

1. **<u>Know thy enemy</u>.** (*Skiouros Rodentia*) Better known as the common ground squirrel. Often referred to as Nature's Perfect Killing Machine. Quick, nimble, agile. These are ferocious adjectives in the digital economy. Fear not, however. There are valuable lessons to be learned from the squirrel. Cold, hard, valuable lessons. And make no mistake, the squirrel does not grade on a curve.

2. **<u>Get nimble</u>.** That is, *Be the squirrel.* "To beat the squirrel, you must think like the squirrel." This all-out run for the glory that is the digital economy is no place for the meek or the sluggish. Quick response, efficiency, flexibility. These are the watch words of the successful competitor. More on that later.

3. **<u>Respect the squirrel</u>.** This is not a game. The squirrel means business. Serious business. As a great philosopher once said: "This ain't no party. This ain't no disco. This ain't no fooling around."

4. **<u>Run</u>.** Run like the wind. Run like the wind on performance-enhancing growth hormones. This is dangerous territory. You're going to need every advantage you can get. And every advantage is precisely what EDS is here for. Our intelligent Network Foundation is the first network infrastructure to deliver voice, video, and data on both wired and wireless platforms. Our EDS Digital CRM Solutions help you plan, implement, and operate comprehensive customer care programs. These are just some of the services designed to help beat the squirrel at its own game. Designed to help you run with grace and confidence, even with the beast breathing at your heels. In short, we have the services to make you quicker, more nimble, and more agile in today's digital economy.

This ad campaign for EDS is a take-off of "running with the bulls" in Pamplona, Spain. "Tips for Those Who Dare to Run with the Squirrels" is a humorous spoof that grabs attention, but also positions the company as offering services "to make you quicker, more nimble, and more agile in today's digital economy."

Reprinted by permission of Fallon Minneapolis and EDS.

Ethical Perspective

Product placements are commonplace in media, and federal regulators have become more concerned because television has been using more of these product placements to reach viewers who are using technology to skip commercials.

"You shouldn't need a magnifying glass to know who's pitching you," said Federal Communications Commission Commissioner Jonathan Adelstein. "A crawl at the end of the show shrunk down so small the human eye can't read it isn't really in the spirit of the law," which requires disclosure but which allows this disclosure at the end of the show. The FCC is also concerned about embedded advertisements on children's programming, which require a few-second break between the show and an ad. Cable programmers are exempt from product-placement rules. Product placements on broadcast TV shows rose almost 40 percent in the first quarter of 2008 compared to the same period a year earlier, and reality shows had the highest number of paid placements. The tactics and techniques of product placement have many implications for public relations practitioners in counseling their organizations. Public relations practitioners have available a range of tactics and techniques to communicate messages, and they also must examine the public relations ramifications of all of their organizations' messages that are being communicated by the organizations' marketers and advertisers.

Source: Amy Schatz and Suzanne Vranica, "Product Placements Get FCC Scrutiny," *The Wall Street Journal*, June 23, 2008, p. B3.

Publicity and Publications

Just as some advertising resembles publicity, some publicity and promotional pieces look like advertising. This is particularly true of brochures, which are as likely to be sales pieces as to be news or information pieces.

Brochures are one type of publication that organizations regularly produce themselves. Desktop publishing in the past several decades has increased the number and decreased the expense of such in-house publications. Except for brochures, house publications generally follow a magazine format, although some are designed as megapapers—oversized newspapers that are folded for a magazine or newsletter look.

One of the most important magazine-format publications an organization produces is its annual report. Although only publicly held companies are required by law to produce annual reports for their stockholders and for the Securities and Exchange Commission (SEC), many nonprofits publish annual reports for their stakeholders as well. But nonprofit organizations are less likely to produce quarterly reports. Publicly held companies must do so, and these often take the form of brochures of variable size and format. Sometimes speeches by top executives and reports by researchers are produced in brochure or magazine format and are sent to stakeholders as publicity.

Publicists often get extra mileage out of their newspaper and magazine stories by reprinting them for their own mailings. An organization's Web site should have a link to its online annual report, and the link should show the covers and inside pages of the annual report.

Producing Brochures and House Publications

Publishing is a highly technical part of public relations activity, and it has changed so much that the public relations practitioner who has not been paying attention over the past 20 years, 10 years or even 5 years would have a lot of catching up to do. However, the speed of the evolution of publishing has been inconsistent throughout the world, because cutting-edge technology that is used in some parts of the world is not so advanced in others. Some skills that were essential a decade ago are no longer needed, but new ones must be learned. Publishing is full of traps for the unwary—and unfortunately, mistakes are tangible and easily noticed. With desktop publishing, virtually all materials such as brochures and house publications have been computer-generated for decades, and the ease of doing this has meant that not all of these are prepared by the PR department. Indeed, Mary L. Taylor, publications coordinator in the University of Northern Iowa's office of marketing and public relations, says amateur use of such publishing software "is the bane of our existence." She means that nonprofessionals can master the software, but that doesn't mean they know anything about graphic design or writing or other components of such publications and thus their publications can appear amateurish and be ineffective. Therefore, the public relations practitioner may have to publish some guidelines for the publications' physical appearance so that they look as though they belong to the same organization, no matter who produces them. Publications from an organization should appear to belong to a "family." If the public relations practitioner doesn't control this family, working closely with marketing and advertising departments, the organization's image will suffer fragmentation.

Brochures The first decision you have to make in producing a brochure is to determine its purpose and its *audience.* This will suggest not only the number of copies to print, but also the distribution method to use. Distribution is critical to planning and can determine the brochure's format—for instance, whether it will be mailed as a self-mailer or whether it will need to fit into an envelope.

Brochures can come in all shapes and sizes, but these characteristics are mostly predetermined if the piece has to be mailed. If it is going in the mail, you must decide whether to enclose it in an envelope at additional expense or to send it as a self-mailer—that is, a folded piece with a tab closing and part of the surface reserved for the recipient's name and address. In either case, it is essential first to check with the U.S. Postal Service, particularly if your piece requires a specially designed and irregular envelope, because there are regulations governing acceptable envelope size. There are also regulations about sealing and addressing self-mailers and about sending a bulk mailing. Finding out all this in advance is important because this information affects brochure design, including the choice of paper stock. U.S. Postal Service workers are invariably friendly and helpful in explaining postal limitations because they want your publication to conform to their regulations.

Oftentimes an organization's mail center will have on staff highly knowledgeable people who can answer most questions, although they, of course, can't speak with the authority of those in the U.S. Postal Service about postal requirements that can and do change frequently. Larger public relations departments will have design staffs that include graphic designers (experts who may not necessarily be "artists" who can draw, but who know layout and design). In such departments, the public relations practitioner should have an initial consultation with design staff, that is, a "format discussion," and will in most cases let these graphic designers lay out and otherwise design the publication; choose its colors, paper stock and other design elements; and have them work with the outside or in-house printers—always in consultation and close communication with the public relations practitioner.

After determining the physical properties of the brochure and its envelope (if there is to be one), the designer might do a computer-generated **mockup** to discuss with the practitioner. Visualizing helps. You already know the basic message and theme of what you want to communicate, but now you need to decide more specifically what is to be said and how. Figure out what can be said with illustrations. Although the copy, that is, the text, will be most important in most brochures, nevertheless brochures often succeed or fail with readers in good part because of the strength or weakness of their graphics, so it is important to begin working early with design staff. Also, postage costs vary tremendously according to variables such as size and weight. The graphic designer responsible for the design must know the concept and the purpose, as well as the distribution method and how it affects the design. Together you must reach some decisions about color (ordinarily a financial, rather than an aesthetic, decision) and about the method of reproduction.

You might want to ask for rough layouts and may ask the artist to offer a choice of several different ideas. However, this adds cost, unless the extra work is done in-house and is not billed; designers and design agencies charge by the hour.

Once you have approved the design, you must decide on the exact paper stock, finish, weight and color; the precise color of ink; and the kind and size of type for each portion of the layout. The graphic design staff will often provide suggestions and advice, or you might leave such decisions to the graphic designers. Also, paper suppliers and printing companies usually have samples, which graphic designers keep on hand. Choose the printing company carefully, because an attractive **layout** that

Theory and Research Perspective

Research is a fundamental component of the public relations process, and research to understand publics is essential. Public relations practitioners might note some strategies of twenty-first-century marketers, some of whom are focusing not on tailoring products to fit local tastes, but on the strong sense of commonality of subcultures of global consumers who share similar outlooks, styles and aspirations despite where they live in the world or what languages they speak.

"We're seeing global tribes forming around the world that are more and more interconnected through technology," said the president of Global Health and Feminine Care at Procter & Gamble. Such tribes are teenagers worldwide who socialize with one another on the Internet and who like the same music and fashions, regardless of where they live. Working women and baby boomers also share many of the same concerns regardless of where they live, and they have many of the same needs and interests.

"Historically we used to be focused on discovering the common hopes and dreams within a country, but now we're seeing the real commonalities are in generations across geographical borders," said the brand franchise leader of Procter & Gamble's Global Always/Whisper brands.

"Going global isn't a big mystery," said the president of Global Health and Feminine Care. "There's so much common ground, so much universality among people."

Source: Carol Hymowitz, "Marketers Focus More on Global 'Tribes' Than on Nationalities", *The Wall Street Journal*, December 10, 2007, p. B1. Copyright (c) 2007 Dow Jones & Co. Reprinted by permission.

is carelessly printed is unusable. The number of brochures printed affects their cost: the more printed, the lower the cost for each.

The graphic designer can go ahead with production after all details are settled, copy has been written and supplied and either illustrations have been supplied or artwork has been approved.

Copyfitting and layout may fall to the graphic designer or another person skilled at layout, but public relations people should also master these techniques. It is generally accepted that the PR person can write the copy, design the format and produce a PDF or a CD to give to the printing company. Now it is time to begin work with the printer. Be sure to arrange with the printer to check with at least low-resolution (low-res) proofs before printing the publication and possibly high-resolution (high-res) proofs. Proofing is your last chance. Take it.

When a large printing run is complete and the folding is done, it may be worthwhile to have the stuffing and mailing handled by the printer or a mail service. Such mail service firms offer different services, but nearly all will work with a mailing list you provide electronically and either charge for labeling or use your labels. Virtually all labels are now printed directly onto the printed piece with ink jets. After the mailing, be sure to keep enough brochures on

hand to meet additional requests. Keep at least five as file copies as well as a CD. You may need them for reference.[9]

House Publications When you are producing a house publication, all production decisions depend on who the audience is. Because a house publication goes to employees or other organizational members only, it is likely to have quite a different design than that of a publication that receives broader distribution. What type of publication, then, is most likely to be accepted and read—a newsletter, a tabloid newspaper format or a **magazine format**? This decision is usually influenced by the budget allotted, which sometimes makes such a question moot.

The next decision involves frequency of publication. Frequency usually depends on the public relations department, and monthly issues are about all most PR departments can cope with. Some produce quarterly publications, whereas others publish simple and inexpensive daily or weekly "news sheets." The method of distribution is another consideration. If it is entirely internal, with distribution either in pick-up boxes or by supervisory personnel or in-house mail service, you need not be concerned about mailing regulations and labeling. However, many companies have found it advantageous to send the publication to the recipients' homes. Then employees won't read it "on company time" and won't throw it away at work because they are busy there. Furthermore, home delivery encourages other family members to read the publication. When home delivery is used, it is important to keep up with address changes, which the human resources department should have in its employee records, and it is critical to consult with the mail center so that delivery can be worked into a reasonable schedule, with consideration given for the mail center staff's other duties.

Once these policies are decided, content deserves the most careful attention. Enlightened management knows that what the employees want to know about the company is more important than what the company wants to tell the employees. Built into the publication should be ways to convey information and allowances for two-way communication—perhaps through letters to the editor or a response column that answers questions of general concern. Many employee publications give an intranet address also. The tone of the publication—which includes writing style, layout, artwork, type choice and general design—greatly affects the attitude the employees adopt toward it: whether they perceive it as their publication or as an authoritarian management tool.

To help determine content, and even type and frequency of publication, PR staffs have used questionnaires to find out what employees might like in the way of employee publications. The difficulty here is that some employees have no idea of what is possible. Choosing among unknowns is a bit of a problem. What seems to work better is to get a sample of house publications from others (not necessarily in the same type of organization), and select a representative panel of employees to meet on company time and discuss the type of employee publication that might be effective and that could be produced within budget, time and talent restrictions.

It is a good idea to retain the panel even after the publication appears, because panel judgments provide a check on whether the publication is being read, what part of it is best liked and what is missing.

Develop a dummy or mockup suggesting design and general type of content. Estimate how much copy and artwork will appear in each publication and approximately how many pages each will be; then determine how the publication will be printed. Learn what kind of presses will be used, because the number of pages (excluding cover) might have to be multiples of eight or at least four. Also, you will need

to decide whether you want a separate cover rather than a self-cover.

Larger organizations may have in-house printing plants; if you need to choose an outside printer, however, make sure to get bids from several. The printer will need to see the dummy, know how many copies are needed and know how often the publication will appear. Printers also need to know whether the publication will be coming to the shop electronically or whether the printer will be responsible for designing the publication. Together with the graphic designer or the printer, you have to decide on paper stock for the cover and inside pages and also headline and body type. The printer will have a price list for artwork and special effects to help in estimating the cost of each issue. Remember, the printer with the lowest bid might not provide as high-quality work and might have more expensive "alteration costs" for changes you might make as the process of printing proceeds.

Staff is a major concern in starting a house publication. Who will write and edit? Where can help and talent be found and put to work? Writers, photographers and graphic designers are all important to the success of a house publication, and some reasonable assessment of potential must be made before a publication can be launched. Again, budget is a factor in deciding how much talent can be bought. In the case of an employee publication, however, ego appeals, esprit de corps and gentle persuasion often work in lieu of remuneration.

A "beat" system and network of news correspondents for gathering information and preparing it for publication on schedule must be developed. Deadlines must be set for all copy and art, as must specifications for the way material is to be submitted. Some successful operations use reporting sheets, which are handled by a designated reporter rather than a person in each department. These are turned over to the editor and help in gathering news. Some departments ask that news be sent by email to an editor. Longer articles are generally determined by editorial/administrative decision and worked out on an assignment basis. Some editors plan a whole year's content; others plan one issue at a time, working only two or three months in advance on major stories.[10]

Some publications are prepared by institutions to be a customer or client service, offered at no charge. These bonus publications, from institutions such as insurance companies, are designed to make the customers feel good about the organization. The publications act as subtle ads suggesting that the company cares about its customers. Often the publications do not call attention to their sponsorship. An example is a fitness magazine sent out by a hospital group. Some organizations produce magazines that compete with consumer periodicals. Examples are *Smithsonian* (the Smithsonian Institution's magazine) and *Audubon* (an environmental club magazine that holds its own well against independent commercial environmental magazines).

Some organizations have abandoned their printed house publications in favor of CDs, DVDs and Web-based "magazines" that are readily available to their employees in their homes or elsewhere employees have opportunities to read or view these materials.

Producing Annual Reports

Responsibility for the annual report should be shared by two key people: a communications specialist responsible for deciding the *character* of the report and a high-level management representative (generally the chief financial officer or the chief executive officer) responsible for the *content*.[11] The design and the language of the report should be the province of the communications specialist, who should not have to yield to the style preferences of persons whose expertise lies in different areas.

To give these two individuals the authority they need, all key management personnel should be informed about who has the responsibility for the report and should be involved in contributing to the point of view the report ultimately reflects. Through meetings, a consensus may be reached on theme and approach.

The communications expert should prepare the first draft, working with content supplied by the other key person, and this document should be circulated for comment and contributions. Its impact on all audiences should be weighed, but specifically its *effect* on priority publics should be determined. For example, many annual reports contain copy that touts diversity in the workforce and professes a commitment to teamwork, but then these reports show disdain for employees in the illustrations or have pictures that clearly reveal power resting in the hands of a few white males. Annual reports going to many different countries must be carefully checked for culturally sensitive material. In addition to being sensitive to such representations while the report is being planned, the communications expert should suggest to other members of management how the published report might be used to communicate with various publics, because this could have some bearing on the presentation adopted.

Annual reports were once almost synonymous with complex and obscure prose, but some are now down-to-earth and occasionally even entertaining. Several companies have bought enough pages in magazines such as *Time* to present the entire annual report to an audience of millions.

Getting your report to "millions" may be overkill, but to make the most of the published report, it does need to be in the hands of all interested publics. Again, the communications expert should suggest to other departments the most effective use of the published piece.

Some annual report planning begins nearly a year in advance. It is common to begin at the end of the first quarter, and certainly work should commence no later than three to six months before the close of the fiscal year. The wise public relations person builds some padding into any schedule, and the annual report is the publication most likely to need it, because it is such a significant document (and for publicly held companies, it is legally required, with firm deadlines for its distribution). After all, it constitutes the organization's most comprehensive statement about itself.

The annual report is a process as much as it is a publication—a comprehensive review of the past year. Because approvals and participation are so important and because the report must be produced on a deadline, the schedule needs to be structured so as to prevent delays. You'll have to work with outside auditors, who are responsible for the financial content, and have the entire report reviewed by legal counsel as well as the company's audit committee of its board of directors. The chief financial officer generally has oversight of the annual report, as does the investor relations practitioner, who usually reports to the chief financial officer (CFO) and who may or may not be in the public relations department.

Every annual report normally contains the same kind of information, but reports differ from company to company as to the order in which the information is presented or to their headings. Most contain the following five elements: (1) a letter from the chairperson, (2) the auditor's report, (3) financial statements, (4) a longer section narrating pertinent facts about the past year's operation and (5) photos and charts.

Shareholders also get quarterly reports, and some companies package these attractively as newsletters.

Others use a brochure format or create packages that resemble thick statement stuffers. (Chapter 8 discusses SEC requirements for the annual report and the 10K quarterly reports.)

Ever since the SEC began requiring that a company publish its 10K and go online with it, the annual report has ceased to serve primarily as a financial document and has instead become primarily a public relations piece.

Even though annual reports have taken on a different significance, many remain hard for the shareholder (who may not be a financial expert) to understand. To many CEOs, therefore, the idea of an executive summary, or shortened version of the report, has seemed a good one. In 1987, the Financial Executives Institute devised the summary format, according to which financial information is relegated to the 10K and to the annual meeting proxy statement. Since then, businesses have come to use the executive summary format routinely, in addition to the annual report, although not all companies favor it.

Speeches as Publicity or Publications

For all the time and trouble that goes into preparing an executive's speech, you need to get more out of it than just one-time media coverage at the event. That's likely to be limited at best, even if the speaker is important.

A speech is one of many types of presentations that an organization may hold and use for further publicity (by sending speech texts or meeting transcripts to the news media). These events are often video recorded as an additional way to generate publicity. Some videos are made expressly for such publicity.

Most organizations reprint major addresses in brochure format and mail them to their special publics with a printed notice or a business card attached. Remember also to send copies to publications such as *Vital Speeches of the Day*. This prestigious and often-quoted periodical reviews and analyzes the speeches sent to it and reprints the best ones in its own pages.

You need to circulate copies of the speech internally as well. Remember that your employees are PR's front line. What would their response be if someone told them about a major speech by your organization's president that they were unaware of? Employees need facts to help you. You might even consider video recording the speech for internal use over closed-circuit TV or over other internal audiovisual communication systems. You can also refer to the video the next time you write a speech for that person, to ascertain what gestures the individual is comfortable with and what idioms she or he is likely to use. The question-and-answer session after a speech is especially helpful in these areas (see Figure 11.3).[12] Of course, the organization's Web site is an ideal place to have a link to a Web-based video of the executive's speech.

Special Events

Although a speech can be a special event, other events such as an open house are really just occasions or celebrations. Then there are big events such as a celebrity visit; a convention; or a trade, commercial or consumer show. Thorough planning for special events is the key.[13] Event planning software is available, and some firms do nothing but special events for organizations.

Setting up for Events There are nine steps or stages in planning for meetings or special events such as dedications, open houses and plant tours:

1. Start planning early. Depending on the size of your event, a year in advance is not too soon.

2. Make a blueprint and a timetable. Plan every detail, no matter how minor, and assign people to be responsible for each. Have alternates selected as "backups." These can be one or two extras—people without specific assignments but involved in planning so they can step in if necessary. Once you have all details listed, "walk through" the event mentally as a participant. That way, you will find what you overlooked.

3. Form as many committees as you deem feasible. By involving management and employees in this event, you spread the workload and get the employees enthusiastic and knowledgeable.

4. Use company professionals wherever possible: artists, design personnel, copywriters, exhibit specialists and the like.

5. Provide special attractions to ensure attendance and to make the event memorable. Examples: prominent personalities, parades, concerts, dances, films, exhibits of historical materials, citations or awards, prizes and drawings, product demonstrations and tours of the plant in operation.

Figure 11.3   **Meeting or Speech Checklist**

This is perhaps the most common arrangement asked of PR people and one that is often carelessly handled. The following detailed list may be adapted to suit particular situations.

1. Set up a day in advance when possible; if not, set up at least two hours before the program. Check the *podium* for proper height (short or tall speakers); test the podium light and microphone.

2. Find out what activity will be going on in the *room next to your speaker*; you don't want the speaker to have to yell to make him- or herself heard. When planning for a large group, it is important to see whether the hotel or restaurant expects another large group and, if so, what that group is. If your group consists of retired schoolteachers, they may not enjoy being housed in a hotel with a group of boisterous rodeo riders.

3. Check out the *sound system*, amplifiers and speakers. Find the cutoff switch for piped-in music.

4. Find access to the *lighting* controls.

5. Check access to *electrical outlets*. Have spare heavy-duty extension cords ready for broadcast media.

6. If visuals are to be used, check out the *projection system* for equipment being used, that is, VCR, CD player, computer and extra cables and cords. Test the proper distance for projection for VCR, CD player or computer. Make sure a table for the projectors is set up at the proper distance. Run two projectors, one on blackout so that it's ready if the other fails. Test the PowerPoint, computer and projector being used.

7. Have the proper number of *chairs and tables* on hand, and have them placed correctly. It may be desirable to cover the tables with cloths. Arrange the tables so that they are as close as possible to the speaker without crowding. However, a smaller room with some crowding is preferable to the yawning cavern of a big hall if attendance is light. If you get early enough warning about impending light attendance, most hotels can use screens to help "shrink" the room space.

8. Make arrangements for *water and glasses*; also, for coffee or other refreshments. Be sure there is a firm understanding about the *service*: when delivered, replenished and removed, and in what quantity.

9. Locate the *telephone*. If one is in the room, be sure to disconnect it or arrange for an immediate answer if a ring should interrupt the speaker, and remind those attending to turn off their mobile phones.

10. Make out *name tags* and have additional blank tags on hand. Remember that women guests may not have pockets for the pocket insert tags. Use pressure-sensitive tags, clips or pin-ons.

11. Set up a table for *guest registration* and name tags.

12. Maintain a *list of guests* invited, marked for those who confirmed their acceptance and for those who sent their regrets.

13. Have *place cards* or attendants to help guests to their seats.

14. Prepare a *program* of activities for the speaker and for guests, too, if possible.

15. Have *writing materials*, including cards, available in case the speaker wants to make last-minute notes.

16. Have *information kits* to give to guests.

17. Have an easy-to-read *clock* or stopwatch for timing.

18. Be sure all computer components are compatible.

6. Provide giveaways and souvenirs (they need not be expensive) for everyone. There should be different souvenirs for different target audiences. Personalize all items and tie them to the event. (Advertising specialty companies have catalogs filled with suggestions.)

7. To ensure smooth flow of traffic, arrange for parking; if the plant is some distance from the population center, provide bus transportation from points of departure. Train guides to conduct tours for visitors, and have knowledgeable employees positioned at strategic points to provide information and answer questions. Use signs and printed maps to direct visitors.

8. Publicize the event well in advance through all possible channels. Use all available controlled media to keep employees and other publics informed. Use the mass media for a broad appeal. If necessary, use advertising.

9. When the event is over, thank everyone who helped and participated. A successful dedication or open house requires the services of many—and hard work by quite a few—and their efforts should be gratefully acknowledged.

See Figure 11.4 for a checklist to use in preparing for events.

Handling Visual Presentations Public relations practitioners frequently plan presentations that involve the use of visual materials—a presentation to financial analysts, for example, or one to employees explaining a new benefits package.

Visual Devices You will be using various devices for visual presentations. Easel pads, overhead projectors, PowerPoint computer projection and slides are described here.

An **easel pad** and similar visual aids may seem primitive in an age of PowerPoint and other electronic communication, but these can still be used to help executives quickly generate ideas and to reach conclusions in the shortest time possible. An easel pad can stimulate group interest, help organize discussions, help explain or clarify and help summarize and review. Be sure to keep a supply of markers and masking tape on hand so that you can tape torn-off pages where they can be reviewed. (However, be careful to what you tape these pages, e.g., tape removed from wallboard might remove the wall's paint.

Overhead projectors are simple to set up and use, but make certain you understand how to operate the simple-to-use projector, and keep an extra light bulb handy. Traditional overhead projectors use transparencies, which can be quickly made on a photocopier. Much more common today is PowerPoint, a computer-generated presentation software that creates slide shows that are projected from a computer screen. You can project directly from the computer screen to the projector screen, much as professors commonly do from their classroom teaching stations.

Commonly, presentation rooms are equipped with interactive computers linked to wall-mounted high-resolution screens. Texts from laptops on the conference table can immediately be shown on the screen for all to see, and items for discussion can be quickly arranged categorically as participants generate new ideas. Always be careful not to clutter your presentation with too much material. The information put on the overhead must be clear and easy for anyone in the room to read. It should be the type of material that would be difficult to capture in words only and should include graphs, charts and statistics.

Not everything can be made into good **slides**. Poor color choice, intricate diagrams, cluttered charts and wrong-size type or lettering can leave your audience red-eyed and discouraged. Slides must have good color contrast, clear details that are kept to a minimum and type or letters of an appropriate size. You may want to provide handouts of the slide material for audiences to follow along with or take away.

A good four-step rule of thumb that almost always works can help you evaluate whether a given piece of material can be translated into a slide:

1. Measure the widest part of the material being considered for a slide.
2. Provide a reasonably wide border, and measure the border on both sides.
3. Add items 1 and 2 together.
4. Multiply the total by 6, giving you a total distance in inches (or feet, as the case may be) from your eyes or from the eyes of a person with 20/40 vision to the material. This is important. If someone with 20/40 vision can read the material easily and see all the pertinent details, then the material could make a good slide. If the material can't be easily read, it must be modified until it does pass the test.

Of course, most slides today are computer-generated, and your work computer most likely has this capability. Such slides can be very simple (which is oftentimes best), or they can be so elaborate that they give the impression of movement, resembling the animated art used in cartoons.

When you plan a slide presentation, you need to consider its eventual development into another format such as a CD. This is especially important if you intend to present it often. A video presentation requires more slides and more consideration of visual "bridges" established by transition slides. A CD has similar requirements but the images must be digitalized. Both benefit from the addition of audio.

Handling Audio Presentations A sound system can make or break a presentation. To avoid a major breakdown, you must pay attention to four key areas of sound system preparation: sound amplification, rented or company equipment, simple equipment and choosing components.

Never accept the word of a hotel that adequate sound amplification will be provided. Few hotels own acceptable professional equipment. Hotels' electronic rostrums, microphones and portable loudspeakers vary widely in age, quality and condition.

Figure 11.4   **Checklist for Facilities**

Organization is essential to ensuring that significant details are not overlooked. One of the easiest ways is to make a checklist far enough in advance—so that you can add those "middle of the night" thoughts to it in plenty of time to plan for and implement them.

One Week Before	Day Before	Day of Event	Following Week
Complete media kits, including speeches, bios and photos, with event timing indicated for broadcast news.	Have kits available for news media on request.	Meet with news media representatives; distribute kits.	Send follow-up letters to news media represented.
Advance release out.			
Find out what special facilities news media will need, and make arrangements to accommodate these needs. Order all supplies and equipment for newsroom or media use area. Check lighting, sound levels, electric outlets and so on.	Set up media area. Check out all equipment and special facilities. Check all visual displays and logos.	Recheck news media area to be sure all supplies and equipment are ready for use.	
Draft final guest acceptance list.			
Prepare guest information kits including program, brochures and the like.		Distribute guest information kits with badges.	
Prepare media, guest and host badges.	Set up physical facility and procedure for badge distribution.	Check badges and be sure badge issuance is recorded.	
Make arrangements definite. Be specific and agree on contingency plans. Plan cleaning of site and arrange for any special decorations. Remember logos, displays and so on.	Check eating area and order. Be sure time of service, place and cleanup are clear. Check site, grounds and all facilities.	Check food preparation, delivery and service.	

(continued)

Frequently, the components are not physically or electronically compatible with one another.

Do not check "sound amplification" off your list until a **dry run**—held in the meeting room itself—has demonstrated that every component in the system functions properly. Make certain that any assistant who must operate the equipment knows exactly how it works, knows the location of all switches and controls, knows the proper volume and tone-control settings and knows how to operate auxiliary equipment such as tape recorders or additional microphones. It exasperates both the audience and speaker to have to

Figure 11.4   **Checklist for Facilities (continued)**

One Week Before	Day Before	Day of Event	Following Week
Complete speeches and get adequate number of copies for kits, requests and files.	Have kits available for news media representatives who cannot attend.		
Assign hosts for VIPs.	Check with VIP host to confirm schedules.	Be sure all VIPs' needs are met.	Mail thank-yous.
Arrange for any citations or presentation materials.	Check to be sure special presentation materials are on hand.	Be sure persons making presentation have materials.	
Communicate individual responsibilities clearly and accurately.			
Detail any necessary safety precautions. Outline plan for emergency situation. Anticipate and be sure to communicate all emergency planning to all who might be involved.			
Arrange for message board for media and guests. Have local airline schedules, taxi numbers and hotel and restaurant lists, with times and phone numbers available.			
Make final transportation and hotel arrangements for guests. If remote, plan transportation and hotel accommodations for news media also.			

break the bond of communication to give mechanical instructions to an equipment operator.

Check out the loudspeaker system. Adjust its volume level to a point slightly higher than you would normally set it—recognizing that the room, when filled with people, will be much more sound-absorptive than when it is empty.

If you cannot rely on the hotel sound equipment, you can rent suitable gear from a nearby audio rental facility. Or you can bring it in and have your own firm set it up (subject to local union regulations and hotel convention requirements). The last approach is probably the most reliable—and the most economical.

When selecting the equipment you will use, remember the auto mechanic's maxim: You'll never have trouble with the accessories they *don't* include. A bewildering array of microphones, loudspeaker systems, amplifiers and accessory equipment are available for highly specialized uses and for startling effects. But keep your equipment basic and simple.

The technical information you need to make a wise choice regarding components is not great, and most manufacturers furnish helpful literature that even a novice can readily understand.

It's a good idea, nevertheless, to choose components to suit your individual needs. Microphones, for instance, are available in a great many types and prices, but no other element is so vital to the sound system. However good the other components are, they cannot compensate for a poor microphone. Be sure it is suited to the use for which it is intended. Price is no index to suitability.

Numerous evils commonly associated with poor sound amplification are actually side effects of unsuccessful attempts to offset microphone deficiencies. Amplifier hum or background noise may be caused by a microphone with a low output, inadequately compensated for by turning up amplifier gain (volume). Ear-splitting treble emphasis often occurs because an amplifier's treble control was turned up to overcome a loss of articulation at the microphone. When amplifier gain is held so low that the audience must strain to hear, the microphone is often to blame. In this case, if the gain were turned up, intolerable feedback would result because of the microphone's inability to distinguish wanted from unwanted sound.

Producing Institutional Videotapes and Films

Some annual reports are now produced on CDs or videotape as well as published in print. These are often used to introduce the firm to new audiences, such as securities analysts who have not previously followed the firm, communities in which the firm has not previously operated, large groups of new employees hired for specific tasks or successful job candidates who have been hired for high-level positions. Much postproduction video work is shifting to digital. With digital editing, a video story can be edited much the same way you use a word processing program in a computer to edit text.[14]

You'll need to be very specific in describing your video needs to the person who will be producing it. Many in-house and commercial producers use standard project proposal forms (see Figure 11.5).

Before looking at the video, be sure you know its subject, purpose and the nature of the audience it purports to reach. Only then can you judge whether it meets its goals, or is suitable.

As you look at the video, rate it on each of these ten points:

1. *Attention Span*: Is it "gripping," or "interesting," or just plain able to hold the audience's attention throughout? This is critical: if it is boring, nothing else really matters!

2. *Subject*: Does the video adequately cover the subject in a clear way and fulfill its expressed purpose? Is it too long? Or (seldom) not long enough?

3. *Audience Suitability*: Does it clearly address the audience it's aimed at . . . or the group you plan to show it to?

4. *Visuals*: Are the pictures in focus? Properly exposed? Are the colors true? If there are graphics, do they help to clarify and explain, or are they just there for effects?

5. *Timeliness*: Are the visuals up-to-date? (Nothing turns off an audience faster than an old-fashioned haircut or clothing style or any printed matter on the screen that shows the age of the video.)

6. *Talent*: Are the participants or actors real and natural? Do you believe them? Can you hear and clearly understand what they're saying?

7. *Sound*: Are the sound effects and/or music appropriate to the action? Is there proper balance among words, sound effects and music so that the message gets across in the most effective way?

8. *Editing*: Does the story flow naturally? Is the editing pace good, so the story neither drags nor moves too fast? Are you jolted by unusual angles, jumps in action, scenes that are too short or too long or by bad sound?

9. *Script Content*: Someone once said (or wrote) that the best script for a video is one with the fewest possible words. A well-done informational video should rely heavily on visuals to tell the story. Words should fill in, adding information that cannot be seen. Most videos have too many words. And words should be simple. Long words or cumbersome phrases are distracting.

10. *Believability*: Is the film "professional," in the sense that it moves along smoothly, in a logical fashion, and you're not distracted by the mechanics of the medium? In summary, did you find the video to be honest and believable?[15]

Figure 11.5   **Video Proposal**

Client _____ Dept./Co._____

Project _____

Address _____ Mail Code _____

Telephone _____ Fax _____ Email _____

- What is this tape expected to accomplish?

- Who is the target audience?

- After viewing the program, what should the audience:

  Know
  Think
  Feel

- What is their present knowledge toward the topic?

- Essential content (facts/ideas that must be included):

  I.
  II.
  III.
  IV.
  V.
  VI.

- Nonessential content (not critical but "nice to know")

  I.
  II.
  III.

- Video completion date _____

- Production begins _____

- Video length _____

- Presentation environment:

  Where will the video be shown?
  How many people will be in the audience?
  What type of equipment will be used (tape format, screen size)?

- Subject experts (names/titles/phone numbers) and other information sources:

- Budget _____

- The final script will be approved by _____

(continued)

Figure 11.5   **Video Proposal (continued)**

Time Line (to be completed by coordinator & client after review of Video Proposal Form)

	Date:	Duty:	Approved by:
• Script Outline	_____	_____	_____
• Script Draft 1	_____	_____	_____
• Script Draft 2	_____	_____	_____
• Final Script	_____	_____	_____
• Shooting Begins	_____	_____	_____
• Rough Cut Edit	_____	_____	_____
• Final Edit	_____	_____	_____

Signatures/Date: Client _____   Coordinator _____

TCP 9/96

Source: University of Northern Iowa, Office of University Marketing & Public Relations. Reprinted by permission of University of Northern Iowa Office of University Marketing and Public Relations.

Handling Celebrity Appearances

The presence of celebrities almost guarantees publicity, so luring them and making them glad they came is important. Arrangements for a celebrity's appearance may be made through an organization with which the celebrity is involved—for example, as the national chairperson of a charity. Or if the celebrity is a columnist or television star, contact may be made through her or his syndicate or network, using a local publication or network affiliate station as a starting point. Ultimately, though, you will probably deal with the celebrity's agent. It is important to remember that this person is a *business* agent.

Once you have the celebrity scheduled, you should request updated biographical information from his or her agent or public relations person and digital photographs of at least two different poses. Also get an appropriate digital version for Web sites and other electronic publication. The biographical data will give you a start in preparing the advance publicity. It is helpful if you can also get a telephone interview to fill in details, because curriculum vitae sheets are sometimes outdated or incomplete. Further, personal information and a personal contact offer insight into the celebrity's likes and dislikes and give some indication of what type of promotion would be best. It

is important to determine what that person likes to do and does best because this is where he or she will perform best for you. Recognize that some celebrities have unusual demands—for example, availability of multicolored candy with all the pieces of certain colors removed from the dish.

In planning the celebrity's schedule, you will probably work with the agent or with a person charged with scheduling. Make sure your communications with this person are clear, concise and definite. Your dependence is mutual, so you should try hard to establish rapport. Get off to a good start in your first contact by providing the following information: (1) travel arrangements, including who will be meeting the celebrity (and whether an airport arrival interview is planned); (2) where the celebrity will be staying; (3) what provision has been made for transportation; (4) what financial arrangements have been made (iron these out early!); (5) what the schedule of appearances is; and (6) what other group appearances have been scheduled and what special events the celebrity will participate in. Make multiple copies of the schedule so your staff and the celebrity's staff have contact information. Include phone numbers at various locations and mobile phone numbers.

Give the celebrity as much background as possible, not only on relevant groups and people, but also on the city. Personalize by tying the information into the celebrity's own background, career or special interests. This will help prepare the celebrity for the questions that he or she will have to field, and it will also make him or her feel comfortable and welcome rather than exploited.

Be sure all newsmaking events on the schedule are covered by your own staff reporter and photographer. In fact, don't go anywhere without your photographers. Some of the best picture possibilities can be missed if you depend on news media photographers working only on assignment. Moreover, the celebrity may want pictures, and these are easier to get from your staff than from the media. Someone in the office should keep a log of television appearances and clippings to present later to the celebrity, or to the accompanying PR person or agent.

Media information kits should be prepared and distributed in advance of the celebrity's appearance, but keep extra ones with you at all times. Reporters assigned to the story who have not seen the kit may ask you numerous questions that are already answered in the kit.

Arrangements should not only reflect the celebrity's star status, but also be personalized. One television actor found that the PR director at an affiliate station had keyed everything, even the fruit in his room, to the TV series in which he portrayed a teacher (the fruit was, of course, apples). For another celebrity, who was an art lover, pictures in the hotel suite were replaced with valuable paintings on loan from the local art museum.

The red-carpet treatment begins at the airport, where most major airlines maintain luxurious VIP rooms suitable for interviews. It may be the best place to have an initial press conference and have the celebrity greeted by a city official. Make arrangements through the airline's local public relations representative. Most airlines will also expedite baggage handling. The hotel's PR department is also eager to cooperate in seeing that the celebrity's room is specially prepared with flowers or fruit. You should check the celebrity in before arrival and have the room key in hand, to make this a smoother operation.

For transportation, a chauffeured limousine is almost a must for important celebrities; if this is impossible, try to get a new car on loan, say a demonstration model from a promotion-conscious dealer. Get a courteous driver who understands time schedules and knows the city. Be sure the celebrity knows how to contact the limousine service or driver in case of an emergency or a change in plans. One solution is to put up the driver in the same hotel as the celebrity so that immediate access is possible. Mobile phones—or at least a pager for the driver—can be helpful here.

Assign someone who is understanding and sympathetic to be with the celebrity throughout the schedule. This person should be able to handle special requests such as hairdressers at 6 a.m. or filet mignon at midnight. Be sure it is someone with patience, tact and diplomacy who also understands the significance of keeping on schedule. After a celebrity appearance is over, this person can probably suggest the best way to say thank-you.

Take care of all departure details such as checkout, bills, airline flight confirmation and baggage check-in. Attention to the celebrity cannot be relaxed just because the itinerary is closed. The farewell remarks of a celebrity are usually recorded and remembered too. One thought to keep in mind is that celebrities talk to other celebrities. A public relations director who was having difficulty "getting" a particular celebrity happened to mention it to another celebrity who had once been the organization's guest for the same event. To the PR person's surprise, the celebrity said, "Well, I'll just call and tell her she needs to be here. It's a good promotion vehicle, and you people know how to do things right."

Some celebrities you may be responsible for handling are relatively new at public relations appearances. For example, the book publishing business is so highly competitive that authors are frequently sent "on the road" to garner sales for their books. Some of these new celebrities may be more difficult to handle than more seasoned people because, while they are less likely to have high expectations of recognition, they are more likely to expect some privacy or time for themselves.

Preservation of talent may be necessary if the celebrity is a performer. Some performers are asked to make a number of appearances and play, sing or do whatever they do either too close to their performance schedule or in conditions that might jeopardize their being able to perform—soloists singing outside in cold night air, for example. You may be responsible for the schedules of some celebrities who are traveling without their own staffs, and you need to think of their needs in planning their appearances.

Publicity through the Mass Media

Good working relationships with media personnel are always important for smooth functioning, but they are particularly crucial when they can facilitate, impede or even destroy a public relations program. The secret of success in placing publicity is to develop a good working relationship by *knowing and anticipating the needs of the media.* Your PR efforts in handling publicity are usually a two-part operation: providing the information you want to convey to that medium's public and responding to inquiries. Your contacts are valuable as a source for placing stories or story ideas and as a resource for keeping you advised of media changes in personnel or procedures.

Fortunately, some things never change, and among them are the standards by which publicity is measured. Publicity is ranked by editors and TV news directors for news value. Publicity should meet three criteria:

1. Is it important to this medium's audience (readers, listeners or viewers)? For local media, it must be of local significance to be considered (i.e., it must have a local angle).

2. Is it timely? It must be news—something that just happened, is happening now or is scheduled to happen in the near future—not something the beat reporter had 3 days ago.

3. Is it accurate, truthful and complete?

One PR person, who had heard a newspaper's assistant metropolitan editor chew out an unfortunate publicist for offering copy with "more holes than a sieve," was later asked by the editor if the reaction had been too harsh. "Not at all," he replied. "Sloppy copy just makes it harder for the rest of us."

Strict news value is one yardstick of value. Another is human interest, a story or picture with humor, drama or poignancy. Humorous stories, especially, have an edge because so much of what editors must print is serious. A publicity piece that is genuinely funny or appealing is usually given good display.

In handling publicity, you are concerned with offering news releases to mass and specialized media, both print and broadcast. Your primary task is to interest the media in story and picture ideas they might cover. In doing this job, you must prepare materials that tell about the institution, such as newsletters, brochures and pamphlets, television and radio spots, slide presentations and perhaps films. When necessary, you must arrange for the media to talk directly to management in interviews and conferences. Therefore, you must master the styles of all media and develop working relationships with professionals in all of these fields.

A PR person must know, for example, the exact copy deadlines for all local media and the approximate deadlines for state and national media. If you are involved in international PR, you must be prepared to work late (in some cases very late) to reach your contacts abroad during their working day, because of time differences.

Knowing the media's working schedules will save you a great deal of grief. And it might be wise to call a sports, business or other section editor periodically to check on the possibility of new deadlines. Such attention to details separates the professional from the inept amateur.

Knowing whom to contact at the various media with your news is also essential. You need to make sure your releases get to the reporter or editor who covers your organization. Because media people change jobs and assignments frequently, your current media contact may not be the same person you dealt with last week.

If it is someone you need to call after normal working hours, be sure you have the bypass or after-hours and mobile phone numbers or you'll get stopped by a recording.

Technology and Public Relations

A PR person must keep current in the area of new technology for mass communications, and this knowledge must extend far beyond a knowledge of the software on his or her computer or his or her basic working knowledge of the Internet and social media.

PR Wire and Video Services Specialized wire and video services carry public relations news directly into the world's newspaper and broadcast newsrooms. This capability is especially important because the PR newswires provide copy from computer to computer so it can then be called up on a computer for editing and subsequent direct transmission to the typesetting equipment.

While television has arguably become less important, the medium still remains important, and a heightened need for Video News Releases exists because of the Internet. Satellite transmission has made the world's broadcast stations readily accessible to such releases, and videos can be placed on an organization's Web site as well as on a range of Internet sites, including those social media such as YouTube. Many public relations media services provide a complete publicity package of video news releases and satellite transmission.

The privately owned publicity services offer simultaneous transmission of Video News Releases and provide an efficient national network. Although they are membership organizations and charge for their services, they are run much like news bureaus, and their editors may reject copy as they try to exercise some judgment about what to send.

These PR suppliers provide journalists (via computer) with news releases, fact sheets, graphics and other information that PR people pay to have sent. Such publicity services charge clients an annual fee and then charge for each release. The price depends on the distribution ordered. A surcharge is usually added for larger-than-average releases (more than 400 words) and more complex ones with photos, graphics, spread sheets and audio. Video rates are more expensive. In addition to publicity, clients may send advisories and invitations, such as notifications of news conferences.

One particular advantage public relations wire services have for practitioners is the resulting national and international coverage now available for clients of a practitioner working from a single base.

Another advantage to the practitioner is editorial acceptance of the PR sources. Because copy is carefully checked before it is moved (even though the practitioners supplying the material are "clients"), news media are assured of a double check on details, timeliness and other elements that often make PR copy unacceptable. To preserve their own reputations, the PR news bureaus won't move inferior or inaccurate copy. One service even reminds clients: "Write to wire style and member newspaper computerization [constraints]. Following Associated Press (AP) style and keeping computer specifications in mind are marks of communications professionalism that improve your release's chances. Again, we'll be glad to help whenever you need us." The company has built a reputation for reliability with the media it services.

Yet another advantage of public relations wire services is that they are already in the newsroom. Many metropolitan dailies have a PR newswire feeding their computers right along with the AP, Reuters and other services' wires. Copy is pulled from that

source and considered for use on its merits. Broadcast releases are often a direct feed, after an advisory is wired. In contrast, many mailed releases (print and video) that reach reporters are never even opened. In addition, mail service may be delayed by lack of weekend delivery or by holiday closing. For all of these reasons, a newswire service is a good investment when broad coverage is desired, timing is significant and the budget allows.

Computer technology helps outside the newsroom as well. Reporters use laptop computers to cover news outside the office. At a special event, they can use a computer billboard service to keep up with what's going on from their hotel room. They can download a news conference release and work their stories from that information, if they wish, and then send the stories directly to the newspaper's computer.

A side benefit of PR distribution services such as Medialink is that most also supply basic news data banks for storing releases and published stories. These data banks can give a news story a longer shelf life.

Most of these services, as well as specialized clipping and monitoring services such as BurrellesLuce and VMS, provide an accounting of media use. Some users complain that the services (particularly some of the video services) are not exhaustive, but inflated figures are probably more of a concern than underreporting. Many organizations supplement their data services by hiring at-home workers to monitor video releases for them.

Following up on news releases yourself is more difficult, because you won't have the list of media that a service uses. Distribution and clipping services do maintain up-to-date media lists, because that's the heart of their business, but you will be given a copy of only a general distribution list.

You'll probably develop your own limited media directories. Lists of media abroad are now more readily available, with international directories. New software packages also offer solutions to building and maintaining media lists and measuring results. You'll also keep lists of where you placed your advertising, of course, and the monitoring services will trace your advertising as well as your releases if you want to purchase that additional service. The services will also perform an analysis of both. Television services that handle production for your PSAs sometimes monitor the use of your PSAs, too. But even the best services won't catch everything. They may misreport or misinterpret events. Use information from these services as a monitoring device; use your own research to measure results.

Media Electronic Systems   When a PR person gets a story of regional or national interest in a local paper, there is a good chance that the story will receive regular newswire service attention. The AP wire service uses a computer-to-computer hookup that allows newspapers to send copies of their local stories instantly into local AP bureau computers. Flow of stories from member papers to the bureaus increases the use by other papers of PR-generated stories of regional or national significance.

AP computers also can improve laser photos so that photo editors can crop, enlarge, reduce, brighten, darken or otherwise improve the quality of photos sent.

Newspapers' electronic information systems (EISs) are copy cannibals—devouring vast amounts of incoming material and immediately relaying facts, breaking news, sports scores, recent stock reports and such. EISs have enlarged the medium's "news hole" of available space for news. Cable is another cannibal, using programming 24 hours a day. Much of cable's programming gives PR practitioners special opportunities to reach some TV audiences with long video productions.

In-House Electronic Systems   Material that organizations can offer news media and other publics is much more sophisticated now. In particular, PR firms and departments have found that computers make preparing graphics much easier.

Computer-delivered photos are also available from digital cameras. These have built-in LCDs so images can be viewed as soon as they are shot, and with a direct connection to a computer, the images are immediately available for editing, processing and integrating into presentations.

PR and the Internet

You cannot effectively practice public relations today without using the Internet and its World Wide Web (referred to as the Web), and you must be intimately familiar with its uses by consumers, including knowledge about blogs and social media. Initially, the Internet was a text-based system that only connected academic institutions and government agencies; it was no more than a government-supported utility. With the arrival of Mosaic software, the Web began to feature graphics as well as sound and video content, and it quickly gained commercial attention. Of course, today both audio and video are ubiquitous on Web sites. The Internet became a "network of networks" that nobody owns or manages. Journals and most other mass media as well as even the smallest businesses and organizations throughout the world maintain a Web presence and announce their Web addresses in their promotions and advertisements.

What do public relations practitioners need to know about the Internet? As much as possible, and many mid-career and senior-level practitioners who never had a computer course in college have become experts who enthusiastically continue to learn more. However, if your organization does yet not have a Web page, the best choice would be a Web development agency. Knowledgeable staff will work with you to create a Web site that will attractively present your organization to hundreds of millions of Web users; will register a domain name for your organization, for example, http://www.uncc.edu; and will provide email addresses, for example, dkruckeb@uncc.edu. Such a consulting firm may not necessarily promote your Web site to search engines and Internet directories, but specialized companies do that. However, Web hosting providers, not development/design agencies, will use their servers to connect you to the Web, or you may have your own server and host it yourself or else host your own server with a hosting provider—depending on your needs and your budget. "Search engine optimization" means the company will attempt to improve your organization's ranking in search results for keywords or phrases related to your organization. However, some optimization practices are questionable, for example, attempting to "trick" the search engine in various ways. Google, for example, will exclude your URL from their database if they catch this being done.

A Web site is available 24 hours a day, 7 days a week, and can be a lot cheaper than many forms of comparable advertising and promotion. Of course, your organization can host its own server, design its own Web site and hire a Web manager. (A Web manager is usually responsible for Web content, whereas a Webmaster is responsible for the technical side, but in small companies one person often fills both roles, which is not very professional in some respects.) However, many public relations practitioners are learning and using economical software, such as Macromedia Dreamweaver, and others, to create and regularly update their organizations' Web pages. Companies are using their Web pages to accept customer orders 24 hours a day, 7 days a week, with no personnel needed to answer the phone. Credit cards are processed online, and the order goes straight to the shipping department. Furthermore, question-and-answer pages result in satisfied customers, and operations manuals on the Web save a lot of printing costs. A Web site's design should be user-friendly and interactive. Information should be compartmentalized, not cluttered, and links to other information should be simple and clear. The way out of various areas and access to the home page should be instant and easy.

An important advantage of a Web site for PR practitioners, said the late Gerald Anglum, former associate director of public relations at the University of Northern Iowa, is that corrections can be made in 5 minutes and at no cost (as opposed to a glaring error in a publication that had a 15,000-copy press run). However, Anglum noted that a Web page can be "horrible" if it implies that your organization is "out of touch" and appears to be poorly organized.

Preparing to Work with the Media

Because you must constantly sell ideas in stories or pictures to the media, you have to do advance work in gathering ideas and information.

Preparing the Story You should have some basic training as a reporter; this is because in order to write about news, you have to be able to recognize it when you see or hear it. In a large institution, where people may be too busy to bother giving you news tips, you must be enterprising enough to search out the news yourself. One way to encourage news cooperation in a large organization is to tell people exactly what you need and how and when to get it to you. Of course, once you have the information, you are often expected to make banner headlines with it.

Sometimes, a PR person's news sense becomes dulled by spending too much time reading company materials and too little time perusing outside news and newscasts—not to mention talking too much to company people instead of to newspeople. When this happens, he or she is likely to produce a three-page story in response to the boss's suggestion for a "great news story," when in fact the story deserves only three paragraphs. Although you should listen to the suggestion carefully (never discourage any news source), you should assess the story from a news editor's perspective, not from a company perspective.

Is it really worth three pages, is it simply a column item or does it deserve no exposure at all? Maybe the idea is good but the medium is wrong. Maybe the idea is good for the company publication but lacks appeal outside the institution. A publicity person must keep his or her sense of news value finely honed.

In gathering information for a release, a publicity writer must act the way a reporter would with the same access. Start with secondary sources, finding out if the company files contain anything written about the subject—any research or sales reports, any memos. Then seek out the primary sources, interviewing people to learn everything they know and are willing to share.

A good publicist keeps a basic file of the following:

- Statistical information
- Governmental information—regulatory and other
- Basic reference books for the field of interest and for related fields
- All legislation on problems—pending or proposed
- Trade association data
- Trade union literature—each union, and how it operates
- Records of the organization—a file copy of *all* your own publications
- File of ads run
- File of speeches by organization officials
- Clippings of all information about the company, with publication name and date for each
- List of individuals and organizations interested in the company, including civic groups appealing for contributions
- Biographies of top executives
- Pictures of stores, plants, products and other activities
- Lists of editors and publications
- People in all media to contact as potential recipients or sources of releases or information
- File on major competition and antagonists and their efforts
- Timetables of occasions for publicity, with some code for indicating news releases
- Keep material that you are likely to need quickly available electronically

Like a reporter, you should never begin work with some predetermined idea about the length of the story. Find out everything you can, because you must have complete information before you can properly condense it—otherwise news people won't later be able to get answers from you regarding questions you never anticipated (which they will ask). In doing your research, you may find that you have accumulated information for not one but several stories. You may find that, with a different emphasis, the story could be used by the newspaper, the local city magazine, an industry publication and your company's own house periodical. If your story focuses on a person, there may be even more opportunities for publication, because (again with a different emphasis) the story may be used in professional, religious or other publications of organizations in which that person is active. Research represents your principal investment in time. Make it pay off for you.

You should be familiar enough with the medium to which you are submitting copy to be absolutely certain the writing style you used precisely matches the style of the medium. For instance, it is important to know whether a newspaper has an "up" or "down" style—that is, whether it uses capital letters frequently (up) or seldom (down). Find out and accommodate. Beware especially of writing the way people from whom you got your information talk, because they often use jargon (business, professional, educational, governmental or whatever) that is unintelligible to outsiders. Don't write what someone says; write what the person means. Of course, this is impossible if you don't understand it yourself, so never be afraid to say to a source, "I'm sorry, that is out of my area. You'll have to explain. I don't understand." They probably don't know anything about communications either, so you're even. Most PR people emphasize the need to be creative and conceptual—to be able to see the "big picture." Although they agree with that idea, experienced PR people will tell you it is the details that matter.

News Releases Public relations people are news managers, whether they are dealing with news releases that they initiate (and subsequently distribute, mail or put on PR wires) or whether they are issuing responses to media inquiries. Sometimes these inquiries result from leaks of information that the PR person was trying to "manage." At special events, PR-sponsored newsrooms facilitate both news releases and response releases because a PR newsroom

manager is on duty who either has the information or knows where to get it promptly. The newsroom manager also knows the needs and schedules of the news media.

Whatever the circumstances, you have to be sensitive to media schedules. Your news schedules have to be worked out to fit the media served in each case. *Deadline* means just that. It is the *last* minute for handling new information, not the *preferable* time for doing so. When you are initiating news, you should let editors know your plans in advance, if possible, so that they can put your story on their schedules or in their "futures" books. One way to offer easy access to your organization's news releases is to offer them through your Web site.

Each story for newspaper and broadcast news should be prepared in a style and form appropriate to the particular medium. You must use the inverted pyramid or modified inverted pyramid format for news releases and accepted formats for features. In all cases, you must write the story as if you were a reporter.

Planning Publicity Photos and Illustrations A publicity story generally has a better chance of being accepted by a news medium if you can offer an illustration (line art or photos) to go with it. Many newspapers prefer to shoot their own photos, and the wire services almost always do. In such cases, you must work in advance of the day the newspaper intends to use the story to preserve its timeliness and still allow the editor to schedule a photographer at a time when you can set up the picture. You should have all the elements of the photo assembled—people, things or both—before the photographer arrives. But how the photographer arranges or uses the subjects is his or her business. Don't interfere.

If you have hired a photographer to take the picture for you, you may have to offer substantial guidance, depending on the photographer's background. If the photographer has news experience, you can probably trust the person's news judgment. But if he or she is a commercial photographer with no idea of newspaper requirements, you must make sure that the following five guidelines are observed: (1) keep the number of subjects down to four or less, (2) get high contrast and sharp detail suitable for publishing in print media, (3) avoid clichés (people shaking hands or receiving a plaque), (4) position your subjects close together and (5) keep the backgrounds neutral.

Make the most of the photographer you have hired and get the photos you need—not only for one particular story but for other possible versions of the story for different media. Once you have good photographs, you can use them in a number of ways. It is a good investment of your time to go with the photographer to ensure that you get the shots you want and to confirm spellings of names and other **cutline** information.

In ordering photographs, be sure to get some for your own digital files. Keep your photographic files up-to-date so you aren't caught offering an old photo to a news source when a news opportunity occurs. The news media often pull photos out of their own libraries to use, but they expect to get something new from someone seeking publicity—even if they initiate the request. Anticipate this with adequate digital photo files. In addition, do not give competing media the same picture, even if it only a photograph of a person.

Try to arrange with a photographer for your organization to buy the photographs for continued use. This is particularly important for high-cost assignments that involve color or aerial photography. Get a written contract. Otherwise, because of copyright law, the pictures belong to the photographer, and you have only bought specific rights. If the photographer will not sell the photographs or sign releases on "work for hire," you must anticipate all future uses of the photos you order for the digital file (publicity, ads, promotional materials) and identify those uses in the contract. If you own the photographs, you may for convenience ask the photographer to store them electronically for you at his or her studio.

The same is true for other artwork and video. If you plan to invest in elaborate schematics, maps, charts or graphs, make sure they become yours. Similarly, when you hire someone to shoot video to use in releases to television (although most TV stations and all networks prefer to shoot their own videos), it is all right to let the company that processes and duplicates the video keep the master, because they have a controlled environment to preserve it; but be sure you own that master. Make sure everyone knows and understands who the owner of a video is and how much duplication costs.

News photographers do not have time to make prints for you or send you photographs digitally; neither do the wire services. Both newspapers and wire services have photo sales departments to take care of such requests. Television stations may have commercial operations that can duplicate videos. Be prepared to pay for whatever you ask for. If you ask for videotape to be prepared at a station or for

illustrations to be handled by a newspaper's art department—whether it involves photo retouching or designing the cover for a special section—get your checkbook out. The news media are businesses.

When you hire a photographer or when one is assigned by a publication to cover some event, try to think of an original pose to replace unimaginative stock poses. Make sure all the people and the props the photographer will need are ready well before the time for the shot. Action shots are best because they help tell a story, but a "portrait" character study of a person whose face shows deep emotion is also desirable, especially when that person is in an interesting environment that relates to the accompanying story.

You should have at least two specific shots (including different camera angles) in mind before "shooting" the event. Discuss these with the photographer beforehand. Consider publication needs in terms of horizontal or vertical shots, the number of people to be included in the pictures and whether you need color or black-and-white photos. You also need to consider the event from the standpoint of the photographer, including how close the photographs can be taken. In some cases, the photographer needs to be unobtrusive. For that reason, many PR directors insist that their staffs have firsthand knowledge of photography, to understand how to use digital cameras and to control variables such as composition of the photograph's lighting. When you have a picture in mind, look through the lens to be sure it is there. If it isn't, work toward what you want. The more professional the photographer, the less direction he or she will need. Allow for travel time and rest periods while shooting, and be prepared to pay half or all the agreed-upon fee if you must cancel at the last minute.

Video News Releases (VNRs) Some organizations prepare their own video news releases, but others outsource this form of release. Many public relations services will handle video news releases for you, transmitting them worldwide by satellite. They also can monitor use of your **video news release**.

Video news releases continue to meet with resistance from media critics as well as from some news directors who feel they have less control over packaging news stories that come in this form from an outside source. However, it's so easy to edit videotape cassettes that many news directors accept video news releases, especially when they have B-roll (supplemental footage) to use. Public relations services that

Tribune Media Services, Inc. All Rights Reserved. Reprinted with permission.

produce and distribute video releases make it their business to know what the trends are, and they keep up with the preferences of network, cable and major station news directors. A telephone call or email to the stations you want to reach is important to learn their requirements, which can vary from market to market.

Promotions

The notion that media attention follows good promotions is not new. Edward L. Bernays said that the idea is to make news—to create really newsworthy events. Pseudo-events have earned some "bad PR" for promotions. And, of course, promotions themselves often earn a bad name for PR. In promotions, you see PR's closest ties to marketing—so close that some observers have called promotions "marketing PR." You are even likely to hear a component of marketing described as "advertising, selling and public relations." Sometimes you have to sell an idea or concept to sell a product, as Bernays promoted the "American breakfast" of bacon and eggs to sell his client's product.

When you see an ad that focuses on an event or a problem, look for the publicity. And when you see the publicity, such as stories about champagne around New Year's or exotic recipes using particular fruits in newspapers and magazines, look for the advertising. Sometimes there is also direct contact with the product itself, such as food samples in grocery stores. It's all promotion.

Often the only place you have to look is up. The skies are crowded with blimps, including ones you can see at night. The familiar Goodyear dirigible, a 195-foot ship, has smaller competitors, the 123-foot long Lightships that American Blimp Corporation began building in 1990. The design staff works on computers to build the airborne billboards that are lighted from inside. The new ships compete with the three Goodyear ships that the company made, a Fuji ship made in England and a Florida blimp builder's ship leased to H. P. Hood, a New England dairy products company. At sporting events, the ships have camera platforms for network crews, and the networks also insist that the blimp sponsor buy ad airtime. The floating ads are becoming increasingly popular, although certainly not for all products. A Miami corporate image consultant observed that you'll probably not see one advertising Weight-Watchers.[16] (See Figure 11.6.)

Image Marketing An image is the impression of a person, company or institution that is held by one or more publics. An image is not a picture; that is, it is not a detailed, accurate representation. Rather, it is a few details softened with the fuzziness of perception.

Image marketing reaches out to publics and tries to build a relationship beyond the product or service, but usually related to it. Sometimes customers develop their own relationships, and it's not always what the company had in mind. Examples are the nicknames customers give products or companies. For years Coca-Cola resisted being called "Coke." Its advertising even urged, "Call for it by full name. Nicknames encourage substitution." But by the 1940s, it gave up and decided not only to live with Coke, but to endorse it. In 1982, the company's new low-calorie drink was introduced as Diet Coke. Another nickname that was first resisted and then adopted is "FedEx." However, "Mickey D's" for McDonalds is still not exactly what the company prefers, but it is the way some customers have personalized their experience. If the nickname is negative, it may be best to ignore it, as Neiman-Marcus has done with "Needless Markup," and the abbreviated "Neiman's,"

Figure 11.6   **Floating Ad**

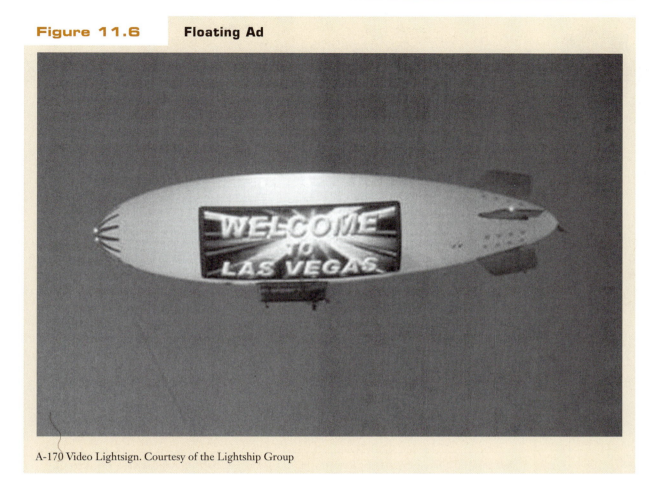

A-170 Video Lightsign. Courtesy of the Lightship Group

which the company doesn't like either. Stanley Marcus noted that "you give it more publicity by fighting it than by ignoring it."[17]

Publicity Spin-Offs Whenever a company engages in a conflict, the incident will be covered, and the publicity is likely to be negative. However, spin-offs that promote personalities and events are commonly used to generate positive publicity for people and events. IndyCar racer Danica Patrick was Rookie of the Year for both the 2005 Indianapolis 500 and the 2005 IndyCar Series season. Her win in the 2008 Indy Japan 300 made her the first woman to win an Indy car race. Her accomplishments might have been known primarily to racing fans and to those championing the achievements of women. However, when she appeared in the *Sports Illustrated* 2008 swimsuit edition, undoubtedly a lot more people learned about this type of motor racing and about Patrick's "#7 Motorola" car, as well as about Patrick's autobiography. Of course, some

critics would question whether such publicity was the best image to present.[18]

Celebrity Spin-offs Promotion planners often look for a "big name" to attract media attention. It's not a novel idea, but sometimes it can result in negative publicity that has nothing to do with the product. For instance, the celebrity's private life may make the news in a way that hurts the promotion, such as when professional athletes are involved in scandals, for example, Atlanta Falcons' quarterback Michael Vick's involvement with dog-fighting. Advertising has used celebrities frequently enough to have a long history of good and bad experiences. Although celebrities can increase recognition, they can't rescue a product, and the wrong celebrity, such as one exposed in compromising circumstances, may actually harm it.

These risks dictate that care be taken in choosing the celebrity. If you don't know much about the celebrity personally, you may need to contact

PR in Practice

Communication tactics and techniques don't always use traditional communication messages, channels or media, and some organizations use outrageous media events to publicize their causes. The world campaign by the People for the Ethical Treatment of Animals has enlisted the help of celebrities such as rock stars and bands and has staged over 12,000 protests at KFC restaurants and outside the homes of its senior executives. The campaign against KFC also featured an online video game called "Super Chick Sisters," in which players rescue celebrity Pamela Anderson.[1] The group has also identified horse-racing as a use of animals that it opposes. PETA noted after the race horse "Eight Belles" had to be euthanized on the track of the 2008 Kentucky Derby where she had fractured both of her front ankles after finishing the race, "The racing industry would have you believe that these horses are cared for and pampered. The reality is that this is an industry about speed and profit, and the horses are the tools to achieve that."[2] In 2006 two women in PETA staged a naked protest against wearing fur in Sydney, Australia. The director for PETA Asia Pacific said about PETA's common practice of protesting nude, "Naked is what gets people's attention and this is a funny way to talk about a serious issue." The women had covered their bodies with a banner.[3] This protest had followed a protest a few months earlier in Moscow by two bikini-clad activists, who had locked themselves in a cage near a KFC restaurant[4] and preceded a February 2007 protest in Dublin, where a nearly naked protester from France said, "I don't mind taking my clothes off if it means highlighting how wrong this industry is," referring to fur farming, which PETA wants Ireland to ban.[5]

Professional public relations practitioners do not use means that are unethical, inappropriate or illegal, or in this example arguably tasteless, but such tactics create media events that can be interesting to study because of the creativity of their originators. Without question, PETA gets considerable media attention from its protests.

[1]Hollie Shaw, "KFC Adopts Ethical Killing Standards; PETA Pressure," *Financial Post*, June 3, 2008, p. FP6, accessed June 23, 2008, from http://www.lexisnexis.com/us/lnacademic/results/docview/docview.do?docLinkInd=true&risb=21_T4020903281&format=GNBFI&sort=RELEVANCE&startDocNo=1&resultsUrlKey=29_T4020903285&cisb=22_T4020903284&treeMax=true&treeWidth=0&csi=257989&docNo=1.

[2]Andrew Strickler, "Animal Rights Group to Demonstrate at Preakness, Belmont for First Time in Wake of Death of Filly at Derby," *Newsday*, May 16, 2008, p. A06, accessed June 23, 2008, from http://www.lexisnexis.com:80/us/lnacademic/results/docview/docview.do?docLinkInd=true&risb=21_T4020911314&format=GNBFI&sort=&startDocNo=1&resultsUrlKey=29_T4020911367&cisb=22_T4020911366&treeMax=true&treeWidth=0&csi=306890&docNo=1.

[3]Claudia Ferraz, "Raw Emotion on the Streets in Fur Battle," *Hobart Mercury*, December 13, 2006, p. 21, accessed June 23, 2008, from http://www.lexisnexis.com:80/us/lnacademic/results/docview/docview.do?docLinkInd=true&risb=21_T4020929060&format=GNBFI&sort=RELEVANCE&startDocNo=1&resultsUrlKey=29_T4020929063&cisb=22_T4020929062&treeMax=true&treeWidth=0&csi=244810&docNo=1.

[4]Maria Levitov, "Bikini-Clad Activists Target KFC," *Moscow Times*, August 2, 2006, accessed June 23, 2008, from http://www.lexisnexis.com:80/us/lnacademic/results/docview/docview.do?docLinkInd=true&risb=21_T4020942357&format=GNBFI&sort=&startDocNo=1&resultsUrlKey=29_T4020942393&cisb=22_T4020942392&treeMax=true&treeWidth=0&csi=145252&docNo=1

[5]Aideen Sheehan, "Nude Protest Exposes Truth About Fur Trade," *Irish Independent*, February 14, 2007, accessed June 23, 2008, from http://www.lexisnexis.com:80/us/lnacademic/results/docview/docview.do?docLinkInd=true&risb=21_T4020959733&format=GNBFI&sort=RELEVANCE&startDocNo=1&resultsUrlKey=29_T4020959736&cisb=22_T4020959735&treeMax=true&treeWidth=0&csi=227171&docNo=1.

a major talent agency or one of the national services that tracks celebrities—where they have appeared, how they have been received and how they behaved. You want to find a celebrity who is a good "fit" for your event, and you want to be sure you

have a contract that covers all that you will want the celebrity to be involved in.

Celebrities' names and pictures are often used in the prepromotion of a special event. Be sure you have the celebrity's specific, written permission before using his or her name and picture in any advertising. Some who may agree to come to an event will not let their names or photographs be used in advertising because of previous advertising contracts for products or services. You must also make sure that any prior advertising association of the celebrity will not conflict with the image you want to create for your organization.

In using a celebrity for promotion, you may encounter the same problem that advertisers have when they use celebrities: People remember the celebrity, but not the message. You should also be aware that the celebrities are less concerned about the promotion than you are, and they are not under the same control in a publicity event as they are in producing a commercial. Don't expect them to be. Things that you didn't plan for can and do happen.

Publicizing Special Events

A special event may be any newsmaking situation—from a corporate open house to a freeway ribbon-cutting to the preview of an exhibition of rare paintings. The publicity for each event requires its own unique handling, but a few basic rules apply to virtually every case.

The Mechanics First, you must establish a timetable because so many events have to dovetail. The timetable should include the dates for the first announcement, which must be coordinated with any special invitations and advertising. Second, mailing lists must be prepared for both special activities and the news media. You must start early and set restrictive policies on handing out news media credentials. (You should not invite your PR colleagues to any media-day function, unless they had an active part in the planning.) Third, the promotion campaign itself must be planned in detail, with a theme selected that will carry through all advertising, publicity, letterheads, invitations and posters.

A media kit should be prepared for the event, and it should be one of the most carefully thought-out pieces of the entire promotion. Most media kits today are on CDs and are sent in advance to people who may not attend the special event but who may write something about it. They are also handed out at the event itself. Because the kits must serve a variety of media—specialized and mass, print and broadcasting—parts of the kits differ.

Media kits have to be tailored to each occasion; if mailed, they should also include a cover letter that briefly explains the event. The basic contents of media kits include:

- A fact sheet for the organization
- A fact sheet for the occasion
- Biographies and photos of the people involved
- A background on the organization and one on the event or situation
- A program or schedule of events
- A complete list of all participants
- A straight news story—summary
- A feature story
- A page of isolated facts about the event or organization
- Visual materials such as logos
- Information about cooperating organizations

Some news distribution services will prepare media kits for you and will coordinate their delivery. But you must provide the information the service needs to prepare the kits, along with any special instructions that you want them to have. For example, some have found it especially effective to put the guidance heads (suggested headlines for news releases) on the front of envelopes going to the news media. If you want something special like this, you have to tell the distribution service.

Setting Up a Newsroom The next most important planning should go into arranging the media facilities during the event. Find out from the local media what they will need, and then plan for the out-of-town reporters.

Setting up and maintaining a newsroom or media facility for a convention, meeting or any special event requires planning and constant attention. You will need three to four weeks for phone installations, although, in a crisis, you can get a portable phone bank installed at considerable extra cost. The phone lines are helpful for electronic transmissions. Most reporters will have mobile phones and laptop computers. The facility you set up is for people responsible for gathering the news and getting it out, so it must operate efficiently. When a newsroom is cramped, badly located or understaffed, it can result in poor coverage. The following elements are essential for a smooth-running operation.

First, have a sign-up sheet in the newsroom. Provide space for each representative's name, the medium that he or she represents and the local telephone number and address where the person can be reached.

Second, use a rack or display stand to keep media kits from falling apart and to let you know when supplies are running low. Have a separate place for the "news tips of the day," pick-up schedules, new fact sheets and new news releases. Daily news releases should list the day's events and summarize results of the previous day's events. All information must be easily available to media representatives. This means accessibility of news information, background material and releases, illustrations and people to be interviewed.

Third, select for the newsroom staff an experienced crew who is cognizant of the need to be helpful and friendly and who knows the importance of media deadlines. The number of staffers depends on the size of the event and the expected news coverage, as indicated by past occasions. The importance of having one well-qualified person in charge cannot be overemphasized. That person is an "anchor" who should always be available during regular hours and should be replaced by another "anchor" at other times. (When you have international coverage of an event, you have to run a 24-hour newsroom.) This person should be able to handle emergencies and opportunities and should know how to deal with delicate press and personal relations. Leaving the goodwill of an organization up to an inexperienced person can be damaging. Make sure all staffers know one another's mobile telephone numbers. In some situations key people may need hand-held radios so they can get messages instantly.

Fourth, separate the newsroom from the traffic of the convention or meeting.

Fifth, provide separate interview rooms for print and broadcast reporters. It is advisable to have an interview "set" for television coverage, another area for radio interviewing and a third location where newspaper and magazine reporters can talk with people. There should be plenty of wall plugs and extension cords for lights and other electronic equipment.

Sixth, plan for special equipment needs. Minicams and TV vans have made coverage easier for TV reporters, but large doors must be available nearby to allow equipment to be brought into the newsroom area. Get information in advance about any electrical outlets and other essentials that the TV crews might want. Murphy's Law (what can go wrong will go wrong) almost guarantees that someone will blow a fuse or trip a circuit breaker. At large news conferences, risers are usually necessary for each camera to have a clear shot.

Seventh, be aware that the overwhelming majority of journalists file their stories remotely to their newsrooms via laptop computers using wireless connections. Nevertheless, you should still provide a few plug-in telephones and *single* telephone lines, so make sure that at least some phone jacks are available to assure that as many journalists as possible can cover the event. Eighth, make certain that the newsroom has the following supplies: (a) for some events, such as sports events in press boxes, the press row should always have a phone for each seat, even though all journalists carry mobile phones; (b) copy machines; (c) computers and printers; (d) bulletin boards and pins or tacks and boards with erasable markers and erasers; (e) individual desks or tables with comfortable chairs and good lighting; (f) coat hangers and space to hang coats; (g) wastebaskets; (h) paper for the printers and copiers, shorthand spiral notebooks, envelopes and pencils; (i) drinking water in bottles and paper cups for hot and cold liquids; (j) paper towels; (k) an extra digital camera, batteries of all types, computer cables, jewelers' tools for quick repairs and basic tools such as hammers, pliers and flathead and Phillips-head screwdrivers in assorted sizes. Ideally, you would have an electrician available. The building may have one. If so, make special pay arrangements for the help you might need, and then be prepared to pay by the hour for actual work.

Ninth, darkroom facilities are no longer needed for photographers, virtually all of whom use digital cameras. However, some of these photographers might still appreciate computers and Internet access to transmit their photographs to their newsrooms.

Tenth, providing food and drinks in the newsroom is practically a must. Especially if the event that the journalists are covering is long, make sure there are plenty of food and soft drinks and coffee. As one journalist noted, "Journalists remember the experience of an assignment as much as what was said or what happened at the event that they were covering." Food is worth the cost because reporters expect it, and it keeps them from wandering away from the site. How elaborate the food table is depends on the budget and generosity of the organization operating the newsroom. The basic requirements are coffee with donuts or rolls in the morning, sandwiches for lunch and coffee and soft drinks throughout the day. Parties, however, should be held elsewhere. The distinction between working newspeople and partying newspeople is important to maintain. Never call a news conference unless it is a working session; never have a party for newspeople and expect them to work. However, it is customary at large conventions to have a cocktail hour or reception for the reporters at the end of the working day and to provide free tickets for evening meals. If lunchtime includes a regular session of the program, a media table should be set up in the eating area.

Eleventh, be sure restroom facilities are nearby and that they are kept locked, but keep several keys in the newsroom. Check periodically on restrooms' cleanliness and on the availability of supplies. Arrange for building maintenance people to help, and be prepared to pay them. It is useless to know that you need towels if you can't get to a supply.

Twelfth, to protect the equipment, secure the newsroom for use only by authorized media representatives. It cannot be a social lounge for curiosity seekers, people looking for a cup of coffee (or other nourishment) and registrants to the meeting, who always seem to prefer the newsroom but get in the way. Visitors and unaccredited persons—regardless of who they may be—should be handled firmly and not admitted to the news area, where they interfere with the news-gathering process and are resented by the working newspeople.

Finally, to ensure a good news operation, put yourself in the place of the reporter or editor. Update your Web page regularly and post news releases as well as other updates. Evaluate what you would need to cover the meeting properly, and then plan from that point. If your newsworthy event didn't get the proper coverage, it may be because the PR people didn't put the time, money and staff into a sincere effort.

Other Special Event Considerations

The day before the event, call local media as a reminder; you can check on their technical needs again at this time. If you have arranged for something like one of the blimps as a symbol of publicity, you don't want to miss getting coverage.

Plan **tie-ins** to the special event. Motels and businesses around town are usually willing to display special messages on their marquees, especially if the event is an annual attraction or has some civic interest. Exhibits and displays can be developed and placed with institutions such as banks, utilities, schools and libraries. The chamber of commerce usually has a list of simultaneous conventions and meetings, and a special offer might be made to the sponsors to show your exhibit or display at these, if attracting crowds is one purpose of the special event.

Gimmicks Some public relations people plan newsmaking gimmicks that will attract attention to their clients. At a groundbreaking for the SPCA (Society for the Prevention of Cruelty to Animals) of Texas, two trained dogs manipulated the shovel. Airplanes are available to tow banners over large crowd assemblies, such as football games and music festivals. Helium balloons, painted with **logos**, can be rented to float over the event, although make sure these are not released and will drift away to cause ecological damage or harm to animals. Even squadrons of aircraft that puff smoke on computerized command (called sky-typing) can be obtained, and there are always biplanes to do classic skywriting.

Stunts of this type are clever and are accepted for their general interest. Any stunt that misleads, however, or creates a hazard—such as a human fly who walks up the side of a building, tying up traffic and requiring rescue forces from the police and fire departments—is not generally regarded too highly by the news media.

Extending Publicity Coverage To get as much mileage as possible out of your publicity, you can send clippings and stories to special publications, such as trade magazines and newsletters, as well as to other media that serve special publics. If possible, it is always newsworthy to get a mayor, governor or state legislator to issue a proclamation to mark the event.

You can also produce your own magazines and books for a special event, such as a corporate anniversary or a merger. Banks and newspapers have been known to commission books from historians for their anniversaries, but most often the job falls to a public relations writer. Whenever possible, give the job to a historian. You will probably have many disagreements along the way, but the historian's reputation and desire not to compromise her or his scholarship will bring credibility to the publication. Management may not appreciate the historian's "warts 'n' all" approach, however; and management may also dislike the fees that will have to be paid.

Sometimes "extended coverage" of promotions and events is neither favorable nor desirable. Promotions that are tied to sales often turn negative, for several reasons. The promises stated or implied in sales promotions may result in some disenchanted consumers whose complaining can create negative

Global Perspective

Venezuelan-American scholar Juan-Carlos Molleda and Russian public relations scholar Alexander V. Laskin investigated trade press and academic articles on international public relations and related materials that were published by selected U.S. and UK academic journals, online publications of the Institute for Public Relations and articles in international association publications (i.e., those published by the International Association of Business Communicators and the International Public Relations Association) from 1990 to 2005. They learned that research in international public relations experienced a rise in the early 1990s, especially in 1992—possibly because of the breakup of the former Soviet Union in December 1991 and the sudden opening of new markets in the former socialist countries. However, after 1992, academic journals increased the number of articles on international public relations, while the number of articles in trade publications for practitioners went down and stayed level through 2005. The researchers also learned that international collaboration among authors was rare, with most trade and academic journal articles as well as book chapters having been written by one author or, if they were multi-authored, by authors from the same country. The majority of international public relations scholarship is concentrated in the USA, and the two countries that researchers most often focused on were the USA and the UK. Overall, the two most researched regions were Europe and Asia. International public relations research mostly focused on the public relations profession and public relations education and largely ignored image/reputation/impression, social responsibility or women's issues. The researchers observed, "... [W]hen a U.S. scholar studies public relations practices in the United States, we do not even attempt to call it an international research. However, if an Australian scholar writes an article about public relations practices in Australia, we would not be surprised to see it published in [the] international section of the journal." They concluded, "Such ethnocentric approach to defining international public relations is outdated in the modern century."

Source: Juan-Carlos Molleda and Alexander V. Laskin, "Global, International, Comparative and Regional Public Relations Knowledge," Institute for Public Relations, accessed June 24, 2008, from http://www.instituteforpr.org/research_single/global_international_comparative/.

---

media attention. Furthermore, business editors are likely to look for the bottom-line consequences of sales promotions, which are increasingly seen as unprofitable. (Some sales promotions are not intended to be profitable, especially when the product is new and the purpose is to introduce the product.)[19]

Sometimes news coverage can be negative in near-disastrous ways. For example, after journalist Ward Bushee wrote an editorial criticizing the dangers of ceremonial jet flyovers, he was invited to fly with a National Guard pilot. Special permission for a civilian to go along had to be cleared through the public affairs office at the Pentagon, so this wasn't a casual invitation. Nevertheless, the plane that Bushee was in collided with another, and his pilot had to push the eject button to save both of their lives. Fortunately, the journalist was not critically injured, and the Iowa National Guard said the accident wouldn't affect its

policy on public relations flights.[20] But the episode is something to consider.

On the Job with Media People

Successful publicity is often closely tied to the relationships you form in getting and disseminating information. Four groups are especially important to the publicist: (1) newspeople, (2) production people, (3) other PR people and (4) freelance writers. You need to know whom to turn to first in all four categories. Next you need to know the level of their skills, either by examining their work (when possible) or by checking their reputations (second best, but everyone seems to know everyone else in the media). Remember, you too will quickly become known by your degree of trustworthiness and by the quality of your work.

Relations with Newspeople

A good PR practitioner knows newspeople's jobs almost as well as they do, and is courteous and considerate toward newspeople. The PR professional also knows the importance of getting to know the newspeople and therefore initiates contact. One way is to hand-carry news releases to all the local media. It is time-consuming, and they might ask you to email them next time instead, but by occasionally hand-delivering hard-copy news releases, or a CD with the releases on them, the PR person establishes a working relationship with the media that permits extra consideration when the institution he or she represents may be under attack. Take the release to the particular editor or reporter who should receive it. Make sure no questions are left unanswered. Visits should not be long, and you must be alert for hints that you should leave. Minutes to a newsperson are precious. Don't engage in extended conversation unless the newsperson invites it (say, by offering you a cup of coffee), and then be sure to take the time. Plan a delivery schedule that gives you the needed flexibility but still allows you to get the releases to other media with deadlines. You probably will find that you have to call ahead to get in. Most media now have security checks, so you can only get in to see someone if the person knows you are coming.

Include on your list of local media not just the daily metropolitan newspapers but also television and radio stations and suburban newspapers. Include ethnic and alternative media, too.[21] If it is necessary to translate the release into a different language, call on the faculty of commercial language schools and local college or university language departments or on one of the relatively new firms of language specialists that handle business and industrial translations. (Be sure the translator knows current idiomatic use of the language.)[22]

When special events attract newspeople from outside the local area or members of the specialized media such as travel or outdoor publications, be sure to make personal contact while the opportunity is there. Contacts make smoother one of the more effective PR efforts—alerting news media to stories that might interest them. Usually this is a personal, individual effort, but organizations also send collections of news tips or story ideas for the state and national media. Most news releases are posted on Web sites, and media are alerted to the releases by an advisory.

If you are sending out many releases a week to the local media, you obviously cannot hand-deliver all of them, but it is important that you see all local newspeople on your mailing list at least once a month; there are no "little" or insignificant newspeople. James E. O'Connor, assistant vice president for marketing and public relations at the University of Northern Iowa, says he likes to visit all media to which the university routinely communicates, doing so at least once a year.

Most importantly, *be available*. PR people not only should not have unlisted telephone numbers, they should deliberately list their home phone numbers (as well as business phones) at the top of each release. A story may be processed after 5 p.m., and if you want it on the 10 p.m. news or in the morning paper, you should be available to answer questions. Often the caller is not an editor but someone from the copy desk who wants to check the spelling of a name in your story or to get some background to flesh out the story. You should immediately oblige them. The need comes at the time of the request, not later, when it is convenient for you.

In working with news photographers, never tell them how to take their pictures, because they know what their editors expect. But remember that, as the PR practitioner, you know the event, the institution and the people, so you may be able to think of other pictures that might be newsworthy and *suggest*—the word cannot be too strongly emphasized—these photo ideas to the photographer.

In working with television journalists, think and talk in ten-second sound bites, and remember the visual aspect of the coverage.

Relations with Production People

PR people need to work effectively with two types of production people: those in the media and suppliers. In the media, much of the technical work is handled electronically. However, knowing the production staffs and understanding production processes make it easier for you to avoid problems with the material you supply and to unsnarl problems that do occur. You need to know what is and is not technically possible in the various media, and it helps to be familiar with the terminology.

Knowing the terminology and production processes can be critical when you are dealing with suppliers. Technical suppliers produce your printed pieces, color separations for your artwork, PowerPoint, videotapes and sound. You also may be using a supplier to handle your Web site. You have to know what you want, and you have to appreciate and be able to pay for quality (or accept less if you don't have the budget). More importantly, your directions will be followed by the producers. Just as with other crafts people, if the mistake is the suppliers', they will correct it at no charge; but if it is your error or change of mind, they will charge for "alteration costs." Mistakes always cause delays, and the ones you make can be costly to fix. A PR project can go over budget quickly if it encounters technical problems.

When production people contribute to a nonprofit effort, as production houses and printers often do, you are likely to get a credit slip, like the ones you receive from broadcast stations after your PSAs have run. A gracious thank-you certainly is in order.

Relations with Other PR People

On occasion, you may work with PR people from other places. It may be in a cooperative promotion; it may be because you've hired a firm to help with a special event; or it may be that you have a longstanding relationship with an advertising agency.

Fiascos have occurred when a practitioner who is supposedly directing the agency's efforts has suddenly felt threatened by other PR people and has withdrawn his or her support and cooperation. To avoid such trauma, be sure to spell out in the beginning who has final approval over copy, and make sure deadlines and timetables are worked out to preserve your long-established relationships with the media. Then relax and manage. It is your job to supply the major source of information to the firm or agency and to see that work is expedited, that deadlines are kept and that quality is maintained. It should be a rewarding experience from which all participants benefit.

Relations with Freelance Writers

Although it may be time-consuming, you should try to cooperate with freelancers who may be using your PR department as a source of information for a story they hope to sell or for a book they are writing. The freelancer may have a contact you lack, and the writer's status as a free agent lends credibility to the material.

Of course, freelancers can also waste your time, especially if they are really nonwriters or writer "hopefuls" on a fishing expedition. There are a couple of ways to check, without offending them.

One is to ask them what and for whom they have written, and then look up the articles, which may be conveniently available in electronic databases. Another way is to ask them if they have sent a magazine or newspaper query on the article idea and received a response; if they say they have, you can call the editor for confirmation. (To make it seem like less of a "corroboration" check, you can suggest to the editor that you certainly are willing to cooperate but that perhaps you could help the writer better if you knew what direction the story would take and whether art might be needed.) Most editors will tell you immediately if the writer is working on assignment or on speculation. You should not dismiss the writer working without assignment, however; on the contrary, you may be able to help an inexperienced writer who may, in fact, sell the story.

Many magazines use staff for stories or assign writers. Working with a magazine's experienced people usually increases your own appreciation for what you are publicizing and is a pleasurable, albeit time-demanding, experience. One news bureau director and university magazine editor, contacted by a nationally syndicated Sunday supplement about a story on the university, found that three weeks of work with the magazine writers produced not only national coverage but a handsome reprint she could use as the primary portion of one of her magazines.

Sometimes a writer has malicious intent, but an experienced PR person can take the offensive to advantage. As one practitioner says, "I give them the straight stuff, and I try to keep them busy. Every time I say something, I try to think how it could be distorted, contorted, twisted beyond recognition, and if it still seems to shake out okay, I spit it out. One thing I do know, while they are talking to me they are not talking to the opposition or gathering facts against us." The key here is to anticipate how the truth might be used against you.

If a story seems unfair or distorted, employers are likely to blame the PR person, but the PR person cannot pass the blame on to the media without aggravating the situation. Most professional public relations people have never registered a complaint with any news medium in their entire careers. The standing rule with respect to the media is to call only if they have made a substantial error. If the story is libelous, let your institution's lawyer make the call. On the other hand, some PR practitioners think talking back gets attention, consideration and corrections.

Protecting Relationships: Contracts and Deadlines

One way to establish some understanding about what is to occur in PR–media relationships is to sign contracts and to keep to your written and unwritten obligations.

Contracts Trouble with some media arrangements, such as exclusive cover stories or special TV appearances, can be avoided through contracts. Contracts have enormous value as preventatives. The PR person also arranges contracts with suppliers of services. You should consider having contracts with an outside agency or studio, with a printer, with models and with any artists or photographers, even if they are your best friends or relatives. If your close friend, the photographer, has a contract, you can say, "The boss wants one of those color prints for his office," and your friend can say, "Well, it's not in the contract. How much do you think we ought to charge him for it?" A contract gives you the chance to suggest a fair price or say, "Forget it!" Bad feelings resulting from unexpected charges can be avoided if things are spelled out—in friendly but specific language.

Deadlines Meeting deadlines is essential to a smooth operation. Allow enough flexibility in planning for mistakes—yours and those of others. Once you have promised copy to the artist or typesetter or ads to the media, you *must* make that deadline. This is an unforgiving business, and either you function within the framework of allotted time segments or you don't function at all. Remember the significance of both contractual agreements and deadlines. The former may be invalid if the latter are not observed. Make sure that you get the ad or commercial to the proper person at the agreed-upon time in a form usable to the medium.

Direct Contact: Client or Boss and Newsperson

Public relations people usually have to prepare top management for an interview situation with the media. It may be one-on-one in the office of the executive, or it may be a news conference on familiar or unfamiliar ground with many reporters. In some instances, there may be a series of interviews on a "media tour," where the executive spokesperson is taken to different media that have accepted "bookings" (i.e., made arrangements) for the executive to talk with editors, specialized reporters or representatives of special-interest publications. The tour may also include visits with news departments of broadcast stations and perhaps appearances on talk shows. On the latter, the executive may appear alone, as part of a panel or as the guest of an on-air personality. In any event, the success of the interview depends less on the interviewee's personality (although that is certainly important) than it does on his or her preparation for the interview situation. The most efficient media "tours" today are by satellite, because it saves time for the interviewee and the media.

Some problems occur when the executive being interviewed has not done the necessary homework and is not fully prepared for questions. Not only must the interviewee be consistently ready with a brief, concise, clear and honest response, but he or she also must be aware of the interviewer's style and personal background. One exasperated PR executive said it was a problem to get his company's spokesperson to remember even an interviewer's name, much less his or her background and style. As a consequence, this PR person insisted on a role-playing exercise for the executive before any scheduled appearance. Although the executive was not ecstatic about submitting to the PR person's aggressive interviewing rehearsal, the spokesperson did prefer preparing in this manner to "reading all that dry stuff." Even if an executive is willing to prepare, however, it helps to have a run-through, with someone playing the devil's advocate and asking provocative questions. It is also important to have the executive listen carefully to the questions asked—a skill that can be learned in rehearsal.

In planning for an appearance, the executive and the PR director should develop some quotable material—ideally something carefully researched to appear fresh and newsworthy. Remember, the reporter is looking for a story, and it is wise to be able to offer one. If the reporter gets into a sensitive area, it is a mistake to mislead or skirt the truth, because most good reporters can spot such deceit quickly and then they move in for the kill. Rarely should one try to go "off the record" (although this is possible in certain circumstances with print media). It is usually better to say something, rather than "no comment." It is also a good idea to ensure that the reporter has follow-up access to the executive in case he or she needs to clarify something (see Figure 11.7).

The best way to get an accurate representation in the news media is to give a good performance. Does that mean a mistake-free performance? No, but it means correcting any mistakes immediately.

Figure 11.7   **Conducting Media Interviews**

The element of control that is present with written communications is far less so in an interview situation. As a consequence, the danger of looking bad in print is far greater when news is provided through this method. Certain ground rules, however, can make the interview more manageable and less burdensome to the person being interviewed. Following are guidelines for public relations people and executives to follow in conducting media interviews.

Rules for PR People

1. Select the place for the interview, one preferably on the home ground of the person being interviewed.
2. Be sure to allow sufficient time for the interviewer to complete an assignment.
3. Know the topic of discussion, and have supporting material at hand.
4. School the person interviewed beforehand as to what questions to expect. Be prepared to handle touchy questions.
5. Know your reporter's habits and interviewing style and give the person being interviewed a verbal sketch. At the same time, make sure the reporter is completely aware of the person being interviewed—background, hobbies and so on. These things can help establish rapport in preliminary conversation.
6. Set ground rules for the interview, and make sure both parties understand them.
7. Avoid off-the-record remarks. If it's off the record, keep it that way. Exceptions might occur if the reporter is known and trusted.
8. Help the reporter wind up the story in one day.

9. Make sure the reporter gets the story sought. In agreeing to do the interview, you have said in essence that you will give the reporter the story.
10. Stay in the background, and do not try to answer questions. If the question is one that requires an answer contrary to company policy and the person being interviewed starts to answer, remind him or her it is policy not to disclose that information. Or if the interviewee wants to hedge on a question that is perfectly all right to answer, say it is OK to answer.
11. Offer to answer further questions later.
12. Do *not* ask the reporter when the story will run or how big it will be.

Rules for Executives Being Interviewed

1. Know the topic you are to discuss.
2. Anticipate touchy questions.
3. Be completely honest.
4. Answer questions directly. If you cannot answer the question, say you cannot.
5. If you don't know an answer, say so and offer to get one. Follow up on this offer.
6. Keep the meeting as cordial as possible even in the face of bantering and pushing.
7. Avoid off-the-record remarks unless you know and trust the reporter. Explain that the information is not for public disclosure and politely decline an answer.
8. Be sure to answer questions that are matters of public record or not against company policy.
9. Use the personality that helped get you into a management position, and look professional.
10. Offer help later if the reporter needs it.

The role of the PR person in the interview is that of preparer, facilitator and clarifier. The public relations person who tries to inject him- or herself into the process during the actual interview is asking for a hostile reaction. The role of clarifier includes interpreting facts and technical language, offering background information, reminding the interviewee of questions that might have been overlooked and perhaps extending the interview if necessary.

Phillips Petroleum once printed on 2 × 3-inch cards its "golden rules" for handling newspeople and gave these cards to executives who took the company's media training class. The flip side of each card listed the company's public relations contacts, with

home and office numbers. Among the seven rules was the admonition to "*Be brief and to the point.* Be pleasant even when the reporter is hostile. Answer the question, then shut up. Dead air isn't your problem. Correct misstatements." Another rule states, "*Never answer hypothetical questions.* These get you into trouble with speculation." And still another good piece of advice: "*Never use expert talk.* Sharks are sharks, not marine life."[23]

Tape-record the interview yourself. Correct any inaccuracy or misrepresentation immediately.

You can hire a professional coach from a good firm such as News Broadcast Network to help prepare the executive to be interviewed. Some agencies such as Burson-Marsteller and Hill & Knowlton also prepare their clients for these experiences and for others, such as appearing as an expert witness or giving government testimony. People who are going to give depositions or appear on the witness stand can benefit a great deal from role-playing sessions in which they are questioned aggressively and challenged, because that's what's going to happen to them.

Some top executives haven't been seriously challenged face-to-face, much less insulted, in years. They may need some training in proper re-actions and responses under verbal fire. They also may need to be reminded of the different types of audiences who will respond to their remarks. These audiences include news media, employees, other industry or association people, consumers and various others. They need to think through responses to see how each sensitive public is likely to react.

Other recommendations include the following:

1. Go to the location prior to the interview if pos-sible, and get an idea about the physical setting.

2. Go early to get a seat so you can hear and see before you appear or before your client or boss appears. Get a seat for the person who will be interviewed.

3. If prepared testimony is to be given and if it is longer than two pages, attach a summary state-ment to the front.

4. Bring extra copies of the testimony and of your news release about it for the media's table at the hearing.

5. Know how to address the person in charge.

6. Dress conservatively and in your best outfit.

7. Be courteous and respectful, but stand your ground.

8. Thank the person presiding for giving you an opportunity to speak when you begin and when you finish.

9. Have an adequate supply of business cards to give to reporters.

10. Plan your schedule so that you will have time to meet with reporters afterward.[24]

When the client or the boss comes into direct con-tact with the news media, both sides probably have some misperceptions of the other. But the greater misperceptions probably are held by the client/boss. Most have had limited contact with newspeople, and some have had bad experiences. Your job is to see that all encounters are productive, if not altogether positive, experiences.

Again, two steps you can take will help you accomplish this. First, prepare your client or boss for the experience by going over the issues that are likely to come up, whether or not these are the main topics to be discussed. Be sure she or he understands how responses are likely to be inter-preted and reported. Second, make sure you are there to see what happens and to follow up with information, interpretation, pictures or whatever else is needed.

News Conferences and Results In general, don't call a news conference if you can avoid it, and never call one unless you are sure that what is to be said is newsworthy. But especially if there is a contro-versy, call a news conference in such a way that the organization doesn't appear to be hiding some-thing. Call a news conference if you have a celeb-rity whose time is severely limited, and you believe many newspeople would want to meet her or him. If you can, separate print and broadcast media by holding two news conferences; however, you may not be able to. If you do separate news conferences, be sure that deadlines do not give one medium an unfair advantage.

Some general rules to follow are these:

1. Choose a convenient (to the news media) loca-tion with adequate facilities. Try to choose a site that is appropriate to illustrate or provide an appropriate backdrop for the story—unless it's miles away from journalists' newsrooms.

2. Choose the right day and time, if you have a choice. Monday is good for coverage, and in some metropolitan locations Sunday is accept-able because news crews are working.

3. Plan to have the news conference covered for your own organization (video and audio—in ad-dition to and separate from the primary sound-on video—and also take still photographs). You need to be sure what was said, and you may be able to use some of the material later in your own follow-up story.

4. Take all of the background information on the person and the organization that you will need. Assign someone to get the names of reporters and media they represent, with phone numbers for callbacks.

5. To news media who didn't make it, offer a story and pictures (sound bites and video release when possible). Give them the same background material you prepared for those who attended. You should provide media kits for all news conferences.

6. Rehearse your spokesperson and be as aggressive in your drill as you can possibly be. Play devil's advocate.

7. Evaluate with your spokesperson the results right after the conference and again when the stories are in. Show him or her how the news media used what was said.

Media Tours: Print and Broadcast Although you can hire a PR news service or an agency to arrange a tour, you must be aware that, while your client or boss is providing information, he or she is also creating an image. A national business publication described an interviewee—an author on a book promotion tour—as looking like a "wrung-out politician." A newspaper columnist told how another interviewee asked him what day it was; this person, a film star riding the circuit to promote a new movie, did not know what city he was in either. The agenda is rigorous: one-night stands in major market cities talking with entertainment columnists, appearing on TV talk shows, opening new buildings and being the guest celebrity for special events in places such as shopping malls. The name of the game is *exposure*. Winning national exposure is a bone-wearying job. It requires a lot of calls and a lot of small efforts to create some momentum toward major recognition.

Politicians use the personal appearance as a media event to help create exposure. Candidates develop a message (called "The Speech" by media who travel with them) and present it as often as a dozen times in one day to different audiences. The most skillful emphasize some portion of it for a particular audience. The result of this single-message presentation is that the news media stop reporting on the speech and begin to report instead on audience reaction to it or on trivia of the campaign. One gubernatorial candidate, capitalizing on the scarcity of things to report once his campaign was underway, had media kits constantly updated with "The Campaign to Date," his own version of the varying emphasis he gave his speech in different towns or to particular audiences. A political columnist who was a member of the opposing political party admiringly called the update "useful to us and damn smart politics." What is being sold in tours by personalities is the image of the individual.

Here are some rules for on-the-road media tours to get the best results:

1. Become thoroughly familiar with the people you will meet on the schedule. Know their media. Be familiar with their work.

2. Be sure all physical arrangements are firm, and confirm these by letter. Call your office or agency daily to get changes and messages.

3. Take plenty of money and letters of credit. You may have to charter a plane to keep on schedule.

4. Be sure your person keeps on schedule and fulfills all commitments. Take advantage of any "down" time to make phone calls to let people know you are in town. Watch the person's health and personal appearance. Anyone going through this ordeal needs help and attention to his or her personal needs such as rest and diet.

5. Keep up with props, supplies of media kits, luggage and so forth.

6. Make notes at stops of what follow-up is needed. If some of it can be done by the office, pass along instructions in your twice-daily calls to staff.

7. Keep clippings if you are in town long enough to get them. In any case, take notes of who attended all sessions.

8. Be responsive and sensitive to both sides. Keep your client or boss from getting depressed or burned out. The satellite media tour is easier on the individual involved because the person can stay in one location and reach stations all over the nation.

More Informal Contacts Trade shows are in the category of special events, as are most PR parties. The problems that can arise from these are due to the less-controlled circumstances involved and the consequent increased opportunities for Murphy's Law (what can go wrong will go wrong) to operate. At trade shows, you must be alert to the presence of media people from specialized publications. Many feel that they deserve special attention, and they should get it. They certainly shouldn't be ignored.

Goofs and Glitches

Today world markets are the only markets, and translating materials is therefore a commonplace task. Perhaps in the future PR departments will consider as standard equipment the handheld computer that translates words and phrases into any language with the help of the appropriate audio recorder. Actually, few agencies handle their own translations, with or without language computer assistance. The problem involves the nuances of a language.

For example, a PR and advertising agency director in Mexico City tells about the agency's U.S.-based affiliate, which insisted on sending them billboards ready to put up for a client, Parker Pen. The Mexico City agency had wanted to handle the art and translations. When a billboard of 24 sheets arrived, a secretary in the office opened one package of poster duplicates of the billboard, gasped and began laughing. The Spanish translation had not taken into consideration local usage—and it was advertising that its new product would help prevent unwanted pregnancies! The Mexico agency's experience is not unique. Otis Engineering Company displayed a poster at a Moscow trade show saying that its oil-well completion equipment was effective in improving one's sex life. Ads for "rendezvous lounges" on an airline's flight in Brazil startled and offended patrons, because "rendezvous" in Portuguese translates as a place to have sex.

But you don't have to go abroad to get into trouble with sensitivities. In promoting its mouthwash Scope, Procter & Gamble just before Valentine's Day announced a list of "least kissable" celebrities, using names gathered from a survey. One of the least kissable was Rosie O'Donnell, who then repeatedly said, "Only dopes use Scope," on her popular talk show. Rival Listerine not only donated bottles of its product to the celebrity and the show's audience, but also sent $1,000 to For All Kids Foundation, her favorite charity, each time she kissed a guest celebrity on her show.[25]

Perhaps the worst goofs occur because of complacency, arrogance and "head-in-the-sand" denial that small problems can become big problems. Organizations are learning that they must continually monitor these little problems, and that's what is creating a market for services such as PR Newswire's eWatch, which tracks comments that are being made on the Internet's thousands of electronic forums and discussion groups.

Goofs and glitches have a way of creating problems, some of them serious. Sometimes you only find out about them when you get an early morning phone call, "Have you seen the morning paper or the news on the Internet?" or "Do you have the news on (radio or TV)?"

Talking Back and Correcting

The PR edict for years was "suffer in silence" when the news media made a mistake in their coverage. There was reason for such a decision: "You can't fight with a pen people who buy ink by the barrel." There were also adages such as, "Why spit in the wind?" and "I was taught not to kick jackasses." Today, for most PR people, the idea of talking back is still limited to demanding and getting their side of the story presented. Some, however, launch a campaign.

Ronald Rhody of The Rhody Consultancy offers several observations and postulates for responding to media, which he calls the Ben Franklin approach to the problem because they are based on this Franklin quote: "A little neglect may breed mischief: for want of a shoe the horse was lost; for want of a horse the rider was lost; for want of a rider the battle was lost; for want of a battle the kingdom was lost."[26]

The following are Rhody's principal postulates of the Ben Franklin approach:

1. No contest was ever won from the sidelines. Be players, not spectators.
2. The public has a right to accurate and balanced information about your operations.
3. The public's right to know is as much your responsibility as it is the responsibility of government or the media.
4. Fear of controversy or criticism is a luxury no institution in today's society can afford. Silence never swayed any masses, and timidity never won any ball games.
5. Take the initiative in all circumstances, whether the news is good or bad.[27]

Rhody thus disputes the conventional wisdom that is employed when dealing with this constituency (namely, remember that the news media represent a public). The only caution he considers appropriate in taking on the news media is the same one you would exercise with any other public: making sure you have documentable facts on your side.

Most PR people now endorse the notion that you can get substantial errors corrected—preferably editorially, and if not, by advertising. If redress seems necessary, file a lawsuit.

Global Perspective

The International Language of Gestures

On his first trip to Naples, a well-meaning American tourist thanks his waiter for a good meal well-served by making the "A-okay" gesture with his thumb and forefinger. The waiter pales and heads for the manager. They seriously discuss calling the police and having the hapless tourist arrested for obscene and offensive public behavior.

What happened?

Most travelers wouldn't think of leaving home without a phrase book of some kind, enough of a guide to help them say and understand "Ja," "Nein," "Grazie" and "Où se trouvent les toilettes?" And yet, although most people are aware that gestures are the most common form of cross-cultural communication, they don't realize that the language of gestures can be just as different, just as regional and just as likely to cause misunderstanding as the spoken word.

Consider our puzzled tourist. The thumb-and-forefinger-in-a-circle gesture, a friendly one in America, has an insulting meaning in France and Belgium: "You're worth zero." In parts of Southern Italy it means "asshole," whereas in Greece and Turkey it is an insulting or vulgar sexual invitation.

There are, in fact, dozens of gestures that take on totally different meanings as you move from one country or region to another. Is "thumbs up" always a positive gesture? Absolutely not. Does nodding the head up and down always mean "Yes?" Not in Bulgaria!

To make matters even more confusing, many hand movements have no meaning at all, in any country. If you watch television with the sound turned off, or observe a conversation at a distance, you become aware of almost constant motion, especially with the hands and arms. People wave their arms, they shrug, they waggle their fingers, they point, they scratch their chests, they pick their noses.

These various activities can be divided into three major categories: manipulators, emblems and illustrators.

In a manipulator, one part of the body, usually the hands, rubs, picks, squeezes, cleans or otherwise grooms some other part. These movements have no specific meaning. Manipulators generally increase when people become uncomfortable or occasionally when they are totally relaxed.

An emblem is a physical act that can fully take the place of words. Nodding the head up and down in many cultures is a substitute for saying, "Yes." Raising the shoulders and turning the palms upward clearly means "I don't know," or "I'm not sure." Gestures, called illustrators, in semantics are physical acts that help explain what is being said but have no meaning on their own. Waving the arms, raising or lowering the eyebrows, snapping the fingers and pounding the table may enhance or explain the words that accompany them, but they cannot stand alone. People sometimes use illustrators as a pantomime or charade, especially when they can't think of the right words, or when it's simply easier to illustrate, as in defining "zig-zag" or explaining how to tie a shoe.

Thus the same illustrator might accompany a positive statement one moment and a negative one the next. This is not the case with emblems, which have the same precise meaning on all occasions for all members of a group, class, culture or subculture.

Emblems are used consciously. The user knows what they mean, unless, of course, he uses them inadvertently. When Nelson Rockefeller raised his middle finger to a heckler, he knew exactly what the gesture meant, and he believed that the person he was communicating with knew as well. . .

In looking for emblems, we found that it isn't productive simply to observe people communicating with each other, because emblems are used only occasionally. And asking people to describe or identify emblems that are important in their culture is even less productive. Even when we explain the concept clearly, most people find it difficult to recognize and analyze their own communication behavior this way.

(continued)

Global Perspective (continued)

Instead, we developed a research procedure that has enabled us to identify emblems in cultures as diverse as those of urban Japanese; white, middle-class Americans; the preliterate South Fore people of Papua, natives of New Guinea; Iranians; Israelis; and the inhabitants of London, Madrid, Paris, Frankfurt and Rome. The procedure involves three steps:

1. Give a group of people from the same cultural background a series of phrases and ask if they have a gesture or facial expression for each phrase: "What time is it?" "That's good." "Yes." And so on. We find that normally, after 10 to 15 people have provided responses, we have catalogued the great majority of the emblems of their culture.

2. Analyze the results. If most of the people cannot supply a "performance" for a verbal message, we discard it.

3. Study the remaining performances further to eliminate inventions and illustrators. Many people are so eager to please that they will invent a gesture on the spot. Americans asked for a gesture for "sawing wood" could certainly oblige, even if they had never considered that request before, but the arm motion they would provide would not be an emblem.

To weed out these "false emblems," we show other people from the same culture videotapes of the performances by the first group. We ask which are inventions, which are pantomimes and which are symbolic gestures that they have seen before or used themselves. We also ask the people to give us their own meanings for each performance.

The gestures remaining after this second round of interpretations are likely to be the emblems of that particular culture. Using this procedure, we have found three types of emblems:

First, popular emblems have the same or similar meanings in several cultures. The side-to-side head motion meaning "No" is a good example.

Next, unique emblems have a specific meaning in one culture but none elsewhere. Surprisingly, there seem to be no uniquely American emblems, although other countries provide many examples. For instance, the French gesture of putting one's fist around the tip of the nose and twisting it to signify "He's drunk," is not used elsewhere. The German "good luck" emblem, making two fists with the thumbs inside and pounding an imaginary table, is unique to that culture.

Finally, multi-meaning emblems have one meaning in one culture and a totally different meaning in another. The thumb inserted between the index and third fingers is an invitation to have sex in Germany, Holland and Denmark, but in Portugal and Brazil it is a wish for good luck or protection.

The number of emblems in use varies considerably among cultures, from fewer than 60 in the USA to more than 250 in Israel. The difference is understandable, since Israel is composed of recent immigrants from many countries, most of which have their own large emblem vocabularies. In addition, since emblems are helpful in military operations where silence is essential, and all Israelis serve in the armed forces, military service provides both the opportunity and the need to learn new emblems.

The kinds of emblems used, as well as the number, vary considerably from culture to culture. Some are especially heavy on insults, for instance, while others have a large number of emblems for hunger or sex.

Finally, as Desmond Morris documented in his book *Gestures,* there are significant regional variations in modern cultures. The findings we describe in this article apply to people in the major urban areas of each country: London, not England as a whole; Paris, not France. Because of the pervasiveness of travel and television, however, an emblem is often known in the countryside even if it is not used there.

Source: Paul Elkman, Wallace E. Friesen and John Bear, "The International Language of Gestures," *Psychology Today*, May 1984. Reprinted with permission from *Psychology Today* magazine, Copyright © 1984 Sussex Publishers, Inc.

Discussion Questions

1. Find an advertisement that looks like publicity, that is, one that appears to be a news story, in the editorial portion of a newspaper, magazine or other periodical publication. What are the ethical implications of such advertisements? Are they always ethical? If not, under what circumstances would they not be ethical?

2. How many companies or products and services can you recognize just from their logos? Find a logo with which you were unfamiliar. How does it communicate the image of the company or other organization that it represents?

3. What should be the editorial objectives of an employee publication? What purposes can such a publication serve?

4. What are some of the obvious goals of an annual report? What other functions can an annual report fulfill? What components or information in an annual report would give you confidence in investing in that company? In buying products from that company?

5. Can you think of situations in which people of one culture might not understand a public relations message that was effective in another culture? What are some of the misunderstandings that could occur in such cross-cultural message dissemination?

Points to Remember

- Advertising is paid-for time or space, except in the case of public service announcements (PSAs), for which the time and space are donated to a nonprofit organization or cause. Usually when advertising takes on the appearance of publicity, there is no intention to deceive.

- PSAs are handled through the advertising departments of print media and through public service directors at radio and television stations. Publicity, on the other hand, is handled by media news staffs and must compete for time or space with staff-generated news materials.

- The purpose of advertising must be clear because it's difficult for even the best copy to create awareness, convey specific information, get action and affect attitudes.

- One of the most memorable parts of any ad is the organization's logo, which is designed for high recognition and positive attraction.

- As organizations become involved in global communication, logos should be pretested abroad to ensure that they meet with cultural acceptance.

- Except for brochures, house publications generally follow a magazine format. Some, however, are designed as megapapers—oversized newspapers that are folded for a magazine or newsletter look.

- The first decisions to make in producing a brochure are to determine its purpose and its audience.

- Because a house publication goes to employees or members only, it is likely to have a different design from a publication that receives broader circulation.

- What employees want to know about a company is more important than what the company wants to tell employees. A house publication should make allowances for two-way communication.

- Although only publicly held companies are required by law to produce annual reports, many nonprofits publish annual reports for their stakeholders.

- Responsibility for the annual report should be shared by two people: a communications specialist responsible for the character of the publication, and a high-level management representative responsible for the content.

- Most annual reports contain the following five components: (1) a letter from the chairperson, (2) the auditor's report, (3) financial statements, (4) a longer section narrating pertinent facts about the past year's operation and (5) photos and charts. Some annual reports are now produced on video formats as well as in print.

- Visual presentations include easel pads, overhead projectors and slides, and PowerPoint and other computer projections and slides projected directly from the computer to the screen. Not everything can be made into a good visual, however. The function of a visual is to illustrate a point and to clarify and fix a factor or image.

- A video should have an objective—a specific, stated purpose. It cannot "tell the whole story."

- The secret of success in placing publicity is to develop a good working relationship with journalists by knowing and anticipating the needs of the media. Efforts usually have two parts: providing the information you want to convey to that medium's public, and responding to inquiries.

- Specialized wire and video services directly link public relations news to the world's newspaper and broadcast newsrooms. The privately owned publicity services offer simultaneous transmission of news releases and national or even global networks.

- PR people use the Internet for external publicity and intranets for internal communication. Posting information and news releases at a Web site makes such information available 24 hours a day and allows for instant updating.

- Computer graphics for three-dimensional color designs can be made either with an electronic pen or directly by a computer; laser graphics provide movement and three-dimensional effects.

- In-house PR use of technology includes access to data banks, word processing, computer generation of art, desktop publishing and communication by video conferences and electronic mail systems.

- Public relations people are news managers when they deal with news releases they initiate and when they issue responses to media inquiries.

- A deadline is the last minute for handling news information; when you are initiating news, let editors know your plans in advance so they can put your story on their schedules. Each story should be prepared in a style and form appropriate to the particular medium.

- A publicity story generally has a better chance of being accepted by a news medium if you can offer an illustration to go with it.

- Keep your graphic and photographic files up-to-date so that you aren't caught offering old artwork to a news source when a news opportunity occurs.

- You should have at least two specific shots in mind before going to shoot the event.

- Don't call a news conference if you can avoid it, and never call one unless you are sure that what is to be said is newsworthy.

- Words, emblems and gestures all have cultural connotations. Be aware of meanings, especially taboos.

- For most PR people, the idea of talking back to media is limited to demanding and getting their sides of their stories presented. However, some PR people aggressively reply to media when they think media have wronged them.

Go to the Web site for this book at **www. cengage.com/masscomm/newsom/ thisispr10e** to find more Web links on this subject.

Other Related Web Sites to Review

Direct Marketing Association (DMA)
  http://www.the-dma.org/

Tactics
  http://www.prsa.org

Web Content Report
  http://www.ragan.com/wcr

CHAPTER 12

Campaigns

Experience keeps a dear School, but Fools will learn in no other, and scarce is that; for it is true, we may give Advice, but we cannot give Conduct as Poor Richard says: However, remember this, They that won't be counselled, can't be helped, as Poor Richard says: and farther, That if you will not hear Reason, she'll surely wrap your Knuckles.

—Benjamin Franklin, "The Sayings of Poor Richard"[1]

OBJECTIVES

- Know the types of campaigns public relations practitioners typically perform for their organizations.
- Understand the campaign process and be able to identify the characteristics of a successful campaign.
- Understand how to prepare a campaign, including planning, goal-setting, timetables and budgets.
- Understand the need for campaign evaluation and be able to identify types of evaluation appropriate for public relations campaigns.
- Develop a sensitivity toward cultural distinctions throughout the world, and an understanding of how different campaign strategies, tactics and techniques for different publics may be needed when planning a public relations campaign that is worldwide in scope.

The interactions of organizations with their publics provide the setting for specific efforts such as public relations campaigns; such interactions also form the background against which all case studies must be examined. The study of campaigns is more than a shared learning experience or the basis for developing a public relations repertoire; it is ongoing research into what gives an organization viability and credibility in a fluid socioeconomic and political environment that is global in scope. In this chapter we look at the planning, implementation and evaluation of campaigns. ■

Types of Campaigns

Campaigns are coordinated, purposeful, extended efforts designed to achieve a specific goal or a set of interrelated goals that will move the organization toward a longer-range objective expressed as its mission statement (see Figure 12.1).

Campaigns are designed and developed to address an issue, to solve a problem or to correct or improve a situation. They accomplish these purposes by changing a behavior; by modifying a law or opinion; or by retaining a desirable behavior, law or opinion that is being challenged.

A campaign may be constructed around a *positioning statement*—an objective operating statement for the organization. Communication planning is then structured to help the organization achieve its mission, in light of how the organization has positioned itself.

Figure 12.1   **Model of the Successful Organization**

Model of the Successful Organization

Begins with, and invests much energy in, a

1. Definitive Mission Statement (Values)

   ■ the distilled essence of the organization's reason for being
   ■ implies its positioning, goals, policies.

This is carried out by

2. Corporate Culture (Shared Values)

   ■ demonstrated by role models, heroes
   ■ reinforced by rituals, stories
   ■ the source of teamwork, morale, productivity.

This in turn lets the organization speak with One Clear Voice to penetrate the changing and competitive environment by building

3. Positive Public Relationships (Expressed Values)

   ■ more than marketing or communication
   ■ the source of loyalty, credibility, trust.

Over time this creates

4. Reputation (Understood Values)

   ■ generates latent readiness to like, accept, trust, believe
   ■ a serendipitous, self-powering force that lies at the core of all human interface
   ■ epitomized in the old Squibb motto, "The priceless ingredient of every product is the honor and integrity of its maker."

Source: "Opportunity '85: Bring Rigor and Process Management to Building Public Relationships by Creating an Easily Applied and Simple to Explain Conceptional Framework." Reprinted with permission, *pr reporter*, 28(1), January 7, 1985.

The term *positioning* is often used in marketing to refer to a competitive strategy—a way to identify a niche in the market for a product or service. Public relations people tend to talk about positioning in terms of the entire organization and to build a communications effort around a statement that describes the organization's positioning of itself. When the positioning is to set a new course, it calls for a campaign.

Of course, there are many other reasons for a campaign. Indeed, most organizations have more than one campaign going on at a time. But not all of these campaigns are so central to the organization as to change its positioning or alter its corporate culture.

Various types of PR campaigns exist. Six were described by the late Patrick Jackson, who was senior counsel and cofounder of Jackson, Jackson and Wagner, an international firm located in New Hampshire, and former president of the Public Relations Society of America (PRSA). Jackson, who was one of the leading public relations counselors and practitioners in the USA, identified these types of public relations campaigns: (1) public awareness campaign; (2) public information campaign, which provides information together with awareness and is totally different from a simple awareness campaign; (3) public education campaign, in which members of a public

are emotionally and attitudinally comfortable enough that they can apply what they learn to daily behavior; (4) reinforcement of attitudes and behavior of those who are in agreement with your organization's position; (5) changing or attempting to change attitudes of those who do not agree; and (6) behavior modification campaign, for example, to wear seat belts.[2]

Characteristics of Successful Campaigns

Regardless of how you categorize campaigns, experience suggests that successful ones share some basic principles and characteristics. Five principles of successful campaigns can be identified: (1) assessment of the needs, goals and capabilities of priority publics; (2) systematic campaign planning and production; (3) continuous monitoring and evaluation to see what is working and where extra effort or changes need to be made; (4) consideration of the complementary roles of mass media and interpersonal communication; and (5) selection of the appropriate media for each priority public, with due consideration for each medium's ability to deliver the message.

Studies of successful campaigns indicate that five elements or characteristics are always present.

NON SEQUITUR

Reprinted with permission of Universal Press Syndicate.

First is the *educational* aspect of a campaign. A campaign should always enlighten its publics—telling them something they didn't know or giving them a different perspective or way of looking at something they already knew, or thought they knew.

The second element is *engineering*—a factor critical to behavior change, which is the objective of almost all campaigns. Engineering involves ensuring that the means are there (and convenient) for publics to do what you want them to do. Thus, if you want them to throw trash into containers instead of on the ground, the containers must be conveniently located. (One city placed its trash barrels on the median at left turn signals at a convenient angle so that drivers waiting for the green arrow could dump trash there instead of pitching it out the window.) Asking women in developing nations to have their children inoculated against disease can achieve the desired result only if the medical personnel and the serums are readily available—probably taken to women and their children in the villages. You can't expect a woman who works from daylight to dusk, and often beyond, to take a day off to walk miles carrying an infant to get a shot and then to walk miles back carrying the same, now unhappy, child.

The third element of successful campaigns is *enforcement*. There must be something beyond incentive to underscore the significance of the campaign. Many automobile seat-belt campaigns went through the education and engineering phases but failed to elicit behavior change until laws approved fines for noncompliance. The same has been true for campaigns in favor of wearing motorcycle helmets, and in many developed nations for campaigns to inoculate children. Today children are not allowed to attend school until they can prove that they have had certain inoculations.

The fourth element in successful campaigns is *entitlement*, which is also a form of *reinforcement*. **Entitlement** means that publics are convinced of the value of the appeals of the campaign and in a sense "buy into" the message. This helps with reinforcement, because it extends the message statement by having others outside the campaign give it voice. Such reinforcement is needed not only because people forget, but because new members of a public are added daily, and continuing messages have to be available for them. Those who are complying also need the reinforcement so that they will continue to do what they have been doing. The "Smokey Bear" (*the* isn't Smokey's middle name) campaign in the USA to prevent forest fires is one of the most successful information campaigns ever; created in 1944, it's still going. Its first forest fire prevention message remaining unchanged until April 2001, when the Ad Council updated Smokey's message from "Only you can prevent forest fires" to "Only you can prevent wildfires."

Evaluation of a campaign is the fifth significant element. In ongoing campaigns such as Smokey, there are annual evaluations, as well as three- and five-year checks. The evaluation is a campaign's report card. It identifies what kind of desired behavior change occurred, when and in which publics.

Planning a Campaign

As discussed in Chapter 9, the first task in planning a campaign is to look at the organization's mission statement to clarify the objectives and goals of the PR program. Within the limits of the organization's objectives and goals, you must set those for the PR program that your research suggests are needed. Define the goals—what you want to accomplish—as precisely as possible and in long-range terms. Then attach measurable short-range objectives. A clear statement of goals and measurable objectives means you will be able to evaluate the success of your campaign because you can measure how close you came to achieving them or by how much you surpassed what you had expected.

Look critically at the goals and objectives you've set, and ask some probing questions. Are they compatible with the current PR program? Where are they headed, ultimately? Would any conflict with your institution's mission statement and policies? Is there possible conflict with a primary public? With any particular public, including secondary publics? How significant is the conflict? Could it destroy a program? More pragmatically, how will you measure success along the way?

You must clearly define your publics before planning your strategy. The demographics and psychographics of your publics will give you insight into the tactics and techniques you should employ to make your strategy succeed. Demographics comprise objective, statistical data such as age, sex, education and income. Psychographics comprise the value statements you can make about audiences, their lifestyles, their likes and their dislikes. Part of your strategy involves deciding the most effective ways to reach each public, which could include a range of mass media as well as interpersonal communications. What do you want to have happen as a result of this communication? How far do you need to take a public to get that to happen? Because there are six steps in the persuasion process, a public is likely to be at *one* of these six levels. You have to reach them at that level and bring them along through the other levels to the acting level (see Chapter 6).

Setting Goals, Timetables and Budgets

Results can be identified on several levels. Suppose, for example, that you are in charge of public relations for the local public library system. Your first goal may be to get a bond issue passed for a new library. But you also want to increase awareness of specific areas of library service and, perhaps, to stimulate demand for more bookmobiles to serve more distant locations of the library's service area. You may lose the bond issue, but if results are positive with the other two objectives, you will have accumulated good will that can help at future budget hearings to increase services and to provide more bookmobiles.

Estimates or timetables for achieving results need be no more elaborate than a marked calendar, but the deadlines must be realistic, given the objectives involved. Allow for foul-up time, and try to finish work ahead of schedule. Avoid the need to explain continually why you are behind. Contingency planning means deciding in advance who will pick up the ball if someone drops it and what effect the substitution will have. Downtime from mistakes can be reduced considerably if you have a realistic timetable. Don't crowd yourself or your staff. Consider how to integrate the project into the overall schedule of PR activities so that it won't conflict with regular duties such as writing the annual report or preparing for a stockholders' meeting. If necessary, allow for calling in extra clerical help when there is an overload.

You have to know at this point whether you are working from your department's regular allocated budget or from a special project budget. If it is a special project budget, you must know its size and be aware of conditions or restrictions that are being placed on it. Alternatively, the budget may be a mixture of your regular budget plus specific additional amounts for specific purposes. It might also be that additional money must be allocated before your budget is complete. Accurate knowledge of your budget will allow you to see what extra help you can contract for, how creative you can get, which media you can use and how often you can use these media.

Setting Creative Strategy: Choosing Theme and Media

The success or failure of a PR campaign depends largely on your problem-solving ability and creativity—in deciding on the theme, in choosing the media and in using the media. Go back and ask yourself what you expect to achieve. How will you monitor progress toward that expectation, and how will you measure results? What does each public need to know? What is the best way to present and deliver this message? What would be the most likely way to get that public's attention? This is where creativity—in use of words or symbols in an original approach to the medium—makes the difference.

The theme may be determined in a number of ways—from several persons brainstorming together, from one person's new idea or from adaptation of someone else's successful idea. It is important to entertain *all* ideas without prejudging them. Criticism kills creativity and may snuff out a potentially good idea at birth. Stimulate people to share ideas—no matter how wild—by offering encouragement and enthusiasm. A good theme won't save a poorly executed campaign, but well-oiled campaign machinery won't save a bad idea either. You also need to pretest ideas as well as completed materials, getting feedback from the publics with whom you want to communicate.

Your choice of media depends both on the publics you want to reach and on the message you want to deliver. You should be able to make a preliminary decision as to which media are right once your goals are determined; however, the *creative choice* of media is something different. What is a unique way to reach a special public? What media have not been used before but could be? Someone, after all, was the first to use bumper stickers, skywriting and silk-screened T-shirts, and today's communication technology allows—indeed encourages—much creativity with unprecedented opportunities to communicate effectively and relatively inexpensively with a range of publics without limitations of time and space.

The *creative use* of media is also important. A media schedule that lists which media to use and when can be the key to a campaign's success—and also to its failure. Cereal companies that began advertising in the comics might have been laughed at by those who advertised in women's pages, but the comic-page advertisers knew who their real consumers were and how to reach them. Today's advertisers reach children through "advergames," that is, video games on Web sites. Although a TV commercial may last only 30 seconds, children spend on average 5 to 7 minutes playing an advergame.[3] A PR person has to be careful about the complementary use of advertising and publicity. Advertising is definite, scheduled communication that appears along with whatever planned activities it is designed to promote. Publicity is indefinite communication that cannot be guaranteed except in controlled media. If the planned activities are newsworthy enough, mass media attention may result.

In both advertising and publicity, you are presenting a message—information. People either seek information or just process it. If involved enough in the subject to seek information, they are not likely to turn to mass media, says PR researcher James E. Grunig.[4] Grunig found that only people with extra time to spend are exposed to mass media. The more active people are, the less time they spend with mass media. To reach the involved, you need to use specialized publications because that is where people go who are actively seeking information on the subject. However, if you are aiming for low public involvement and perhaps just want exposure to an issue, then a mass medium is appropriate, especially one such as television that forces audiences to process information. Remember, though, that the public you most want to reach might not be there, and your effort (if publicity) or expense (if advertising) may be wasted.

Your budget has a great deal to do with how much flexibility you have in choosing media, and with how many publics you can reach effectively.

Contingency Planning

One cheerful PR person says his smile is the result of always anticipating the worst that could happen, and then being pleasantly surprised when it doesn't. Undesirable possible outcomes always have to be kept in the back of your mind. What if a billboard company confuses dates, and your ads don't go up on time? Can you use newspaper advertising and radio or TV commercials to take up the slack or rely on people to access the information on your Web site? What if your publicity is pushed off the news by a disaster or other breaking story, such as a 500-year flood or a Hurricane Ike? What if your TV time is preempted to cover such an event? Flexibility and contingency plans are needed.

A PR director can get help in contingency planning from his or her staff. Not only will the staff make creative suggestions and come up with good alternative proposals, but they will support the project, particularly when it is likely to consume a lot of their time. The director should evaluate accurately and honestly what each individual can best contribute to the project (and should think about the talents of individuals rather than just about the jobs each has done before). After the project proposal is accepted by management, the director must write down everyone's duties and responsibilities to avoid misunderstandings over who does what and when.

Remember to allow for contingencies in the timetable too. Build in some leeway, or one missed deadline will jeopardize the entire effort. Elasticity in the schedule will also allow you to take advantage of opportunities and make changes.

You will undoubtedly experience having some critical element in a project barely make it—event programs delivered from the printers with the ink barely dry, artwork delivered only an hour before it is needed for printing production. But if a PR director allows this to happen often, his or her staff will find the work environment too harrowing and unpleasant, and the PR practitioner will risk his or her mental and physical health as well as job and reputation.

Setting Internal Strategy: Selling Programs within the Organization

After you have set your goals, you must plan the strategy you will use to achieve them. One of your first tasks in mapping your strategy is to sell your plan to management. You do this with a carefully reasoned and well-designed presentation, based at least in part on what has received approval in the past.

People doing a job tend to get so caught up in their enthusiasm that they forget that others, including top management, may not know what they are supposed to be doing or why. In addition, some CEOs demand to know more than others, and some are more quantitatively oriented than others. Cultural differences can complicate matters, too. One U.S. employee in a Japanese company was excited by some successful promotions, but in reporting these to his Japanese boss, he had his enthusiasm considerably dampened by questions such as: "How much are you going to spend? What are you going to accomplish? How much more are you going to sell next month, next quarter, next year as a result?" He resisted, but finally was pushed into putting numbers on the board for the demanding manager.[5]

The greatest danger in presenting a plan rests in failing to anticipate questions and challenges. Listen to opposing points of view, but maintain control and do not allow "a good plan to get nibbled to death," as one PR director put it, before you have a chance to test its effectiveness. One PR director who had to work in a hostile climate made a practice of duplicating her presentations and circulating them to management instead of calling a conference, because she said people will approve ideas on paper that they would never approve in an open meeting. If necessary, show your plan to several important people first so that you can anticipate the reception it will get, before you actually present it formally. The whole process is not unlike caucusing in politics before calling for a committee vote. Much verbal battle can be eliminated by careful listening in the planning stages.

Implementing the Campaign

Implementing the project involves adapting and applying tactics to strategies while adhering to the timetable and budget, keeping people informed and solving problems positively.

Adapting and Applying Tactics to Strategies

The framework for your whole campaign must be suited to its institutional environment (either a closed or an open communication system), as determined by top management. This is not synonymous with proaction and reaction. A campaign *is* proactive. But some campaigns are mounted by closed communication organizations.

You will choose messages and messengers for *each* public, drawn from what your research tells you are the best choices. You will select a master communications strategy—a functional strategy based on differentiation, segmentation or modification. This, with other factors such as what your image research tells you is the goal to be achieved, will determine your campaign's emphasis—publicity, advertising and/or promotion. You will set persuasive strategies for your publics because you want to make sure that something happens.

You will use tactics to shape specific messages for delivery to each public in order to achieve the purpose you have determined. You have to keep on a schedule and within the budget in making these choices. If the publicity writer says it is impossible to get the information needed for a story in time for it to go into the media kit as scheduled, determine how long the delay may be, set an absolute deadline and make sure it is one you can live with. Most importantly, keep people informed of changes as well as of first plans. Most foul-ups occur because one person does not know the problems besetting another person whose work is related.

Keeping People Informed

There are many ways to solve internal communications problems. The head of one small PR firm, noting that his staffers headed for the coffeepot between 9:30 and 10:00 a.m., scheduled a coffee-break conference time with free doughnuts. In persuading his staff members to sit for a while and discuss their successes and problems, he helped them integrate their staff work. Staffers, hearing the problems of others, discovered how their own timetables were going to be affected.

The chief executive of a larger PR operation, after observing the most horrendous arguments among his staff over who was to blame for a delay, insisted that written communications be sent to everyone.

Although he admits that sometimes snafus still occur, he says it is only because someone did not read a communiqué.

A multibranch operation has another alternative: a weekly speaker phone conference (telecon) where it may be brought out that someone from Dallas and someone from Chicago are both heading for, say, a plant in Montreal. The PR corporate director can then tell the Chicago person to take care of both assignments, thereby reducing costs in travel expenses and staff. Videoconferencing is likewise common in organizations having geographically dispersed offices and plant operations.

Solving Problems Positively

Still, even in the most carefully planned and well-managed effort, complications and confusion do occur. The important thing is to resolve each problem and get the job done successfully. Placing blame wastes time and energy and can damage working relationships. Good working relationships are imperative for smooth functioning any time, but particularly where personal relationships can facilitate or impede (or even destroy) the public relations program.

Whatever the PR projects, all internal publics should be kept informed. This is easy to overlook, especially when there is dynamic leadership.

Pleasing everyone is impossible, but the PR practitioner who works according to policy—real policy, not "unwritten policy"—is usually safe. Unwritten policies may seem as compelling as written ones, but persistence and diplomacy can often change them— although this may be difficult if they represent the principal interests of the major stakeholders. Written policy generally is much less flexible and should be followed carefully until changes are adopted. Policies can be changed by those who are bold enough to do so, but you must first devise a strong justification for any change and then determine how to sell it to the publics involved, anticipating how they will perceive it.

Evaluating the Campaign

Two types of evaluations have to occur in a campaign: monitoring and postmortems.

Monitoring

You need an ongoing system for monitoring all major activities. Some measures can be unobtrusive, such as counting the number of color-coded tickets collected for an event, the number of gift certificates redeemed or the number of Web site "hits." Other areas require the more careful monitoring of formal research (see Chapter 4). Monitoring is important in a campaign because you may need to change directions, re-allocate resources or redefine priorities to achieve your objective. Monitoring makes it possible, for instance, for political candidates during a campaign to increase television exposure in an area where their name recognition or support is low, or to arrange for an unscheduled appearance in the area.

Although results of such monitoring are less visible in other types of campaigns, the need to monitor remains. Think about it on a personal level. You wouldn't want to plan a party, send out invitations and not know if anyone was coming. You would be buying food or guaranteeing a certain turnout for a caterer. Before you did these things, you would certainly want to know how many people to expect.

Postmortems

Every PR campaign deserves a thorough and honest autopsy. What worked, what didn't and why? What was accidentally a success? What could have been done better?

Formal research is needed here. You need to uncover some solid evidence that objectives were achieved or not achieved. You need to establish what missed the mark and by how much. Anecdotal evaluation is useful and often insightful, but it does not make a good budget defense or tell you whether the public relations problem was resolved through the campaign.

To make a postmortem successful, you must keep all analyses on a professional level; no witch-hunts should be permitted. If something did not work, there is usually more than one reason for its failure and more than one person responsible. Use constructive criticism to suggest, "If we had attempted to do this, would it have worked better than what we did try?" Egos, especially creative egos, are fragile things, yet no one minds looking into the mirror unless she or he sees someone in the background pointing an accusing finger.

As mentioned in Chapter 4, you need to evaluate several results. These include the impact on publics; the effect on the organization's goals and mission; the effect on the attitudes of publics toward the organization and on their perception of the organization; and the effects on the organization's financial status, ethical stance and social responsibility.

© Tom K. Ryan. Reprinted with special permission of North America Syndicate.

The most effective evaluations are continuing programs—for instance, annual surveys of what audiences like or dislike, surveys of employee attitudes and measurements of consumer attitudes. Informal evaluative research may be done by reading letters and taking phone calls from happy and unhappy publics and by talking with representatives of various publics to ascertain their attitudes. These give you benchmarks against which to measure a campaign's effects. If you say after a campaign, "It's all over, we can forget it," instead of initiating an ongoing evaluation program, you will put yourself in the position of, as one astute advertising executive put it, "constantly reinventing the wheel."

Although this discussion has addressed campaigns mounted for a specific purpose and for a specific period of time, an organization should have an overall public relations program tied to its fundamental mission and goals. This should be a written program complete with rationale, policy support statements, listed priorities, identified publics and illustrations of the tools to be used. It should be reviewed regularly and modified as needed. Most importantly, it should receive top management endorsement, just as budgets do.

In each campaign you need to look for the "self-interest" appeal being made to each target audience— the key to all effective communication to this public. Search out the other communication strategies in message structure and media delivery that have proved successful (or unsuccessful) in informing and influencing the target audience.[6] Look beyond the specific strategies to find their base in some general concept that you can apply to other campaigns. Then plan your program by integrating all of these elements into a flexible and feasible timetable, and secure management and staff support. Select media that will ensure successful and on-time

implementation of the program. Finally, evaluate the results or effectiveness of the program through formal post-program research and through less formal methods of responses and reactions from staff and publics. Post-program research should always include measurements of success or failure for not only financial impact, but also for ethical impact and social responsibility.

Campaign Outline

Before narrowing our focus to the issue of changing behavior, let's review the steps involved in the whole process of developing and executing a campaign. In summary:

- Define the problem. Set goals for the campaign within an organizational framework.

- Evaluate the impact of the problem on publics and on the organization, and define clearly the issues involved in the problem.

- Develop an organizational strategy consonant with the mission.

- Determine a communication strategy to reach the stated goals and objectives.

- Plan actions, themes and appeals to publics. In developing a functional strategy, plan where the emphasis will be—ads, publicity and/or promotion.

- Develop an organizational responsibilities plan, with budgets and timetables.

- Decide which tactics and techniques fit the strategy best and how you will monitor each aspect.

- Evaluate the results or effectiveness of the program.

Changing Behavior

Public relations practitioners are often depicted as masters of manipulative techniques designed to get people to think or act in a certain way, and in fact most campaigns do strive to produce behavior changes. This is the case even when campaigns start at the awareness level, because the purpose of a campaign to create awareness (of a problem, of a product or service or of a person) is ultimately to get a response to the campaign that is action. The same goes for "information campaigns" as well: What is desired is action, which may mean getting people to behave differently from how they usually behave.

The ethical question of the propriety of such campaigns is not always raised, especially when the campaign appears to reflect majority social values. But sources behind the campaign pay for it, and their values or "social agenda" may not match that of individuals who lack the means and (in some cases) the access to communicate through public and private media.

PR in Practice

Public relations students are commonly taught that there is no "general public"; rather, to practice public relations, an organization's "publics" must be identified and segmented. In his 2007 thesis for his master of arts degree in communication studies at the University of Northern Iowa, graduate student Sergei Golitsinski questions this fundamental principle that organizations should focus their communication only on those publics that have been identified as having the potential to cause these organizations negative consequences and that a general public is insignificant and, in fact, nonexistent.

Rather, Golitsinski argues that new communication technologies have given the "general public" the power to cause direct negative consequences for organizations. To evaluate this hypothesis, his study examined the October 2006 Edelman/Wal-Mart crisis that was caused by the "Wal-Marting Across America" blog. The blog was launched by Edelman, an independent global public relations firm, as a publicity stunt on behalf of Wal-Mart, yet it was presented as an independent blog that was being maintained by a couple who were traveling in their recreational vehicle and were writing stories about happy Wal-Mart employees. The truth was revealed in a *Business Week* article, which triggered a massive discussion in the blogosphere and in mainstream media.

The methodology of Golitsinski's study involved quantitative and qualitative analysis of blog posts and mainstream media articles. Relevant blog posts were collected and processed with the help of a computer science approach (Golitsinski was concurrently earning his master of science degree in computer science), which consisted of automatically exploring the Web and discovering blogs participating in the conversation and constructing a chronological model of this conversation for further analysis, represented as a graph, with nodes denoting blog posts and the edges—the links between these posts. The final data set consisted of 18 mainstream media articles and 156 blogs containing 201 relevant posts, connected by 1,548 links.

The results of the study demonstrate that Edelman suffered significant negative consequences that were caused by the blogosphere. The negative consequences included significant negative publicity, as well as a negative public opinion about Edelman, which was formed through the discussion on the blogosphere. The study demonstrates that the consequences were caused by collective action on behalf of all blogs that were involved in the conversation. Golitsinski argued that the individuals and groups behind these blogs represent multiple publics, which can be described in the context of this study as the "general public." Therefore, the hypothesis of this study was supported: New communication technologies, such as the blogosphere, have given the "general public" the power to cause direct negative consequences for organizations.

Source: Summary of 2007 thesis about the general public from Significance of the General Public for Public Relations: A Study of the Blogosphere's Impact on the October 2006 Edelman/War-Mart Crisis by Sergei Golitsinski, Unpublished master's thesis, 2007. University of Northern Iowa, Cedar Falls, IA. Reprinted by permission of Sergie Golitsinski.

Imbalances of means and access are part of the concern over development campaigns in some countries. These "public information campaigns" usually are handled by the government, which may not allow much input from those who are the objects of the campaign. All information campaigns, Charles T. Salmon says, represent weapons in conflicts of interest, and social intervention involves conflicts of values.[7]

A successful campaign—one that changes behavior—has three elements, according to the U.S. Forest Service: education, engineering and enforcement.[8] The educational part consists of telling people what you want them to do, which in the case of the U.S. Forest Service was to refrain from destroying the forest and, since April 2001, all of the nation's wildlands. The second step, engineering, enables people to accomplish what you are asking. To this end, the Forest Service built "fire-safe" campsites and put up steel signs that were difficult to vandalize. The third step is enforcement, where the will of the people begins to get restricted. Laws were enacted to protect the national forests, and people who failed to obey the laws became subject to fines. Regulations also permit access to forests to be restricted if the U.S. Forest Service determines that the danger of damage to the forest is too high.

But laws can be overturned, or people can flagrantly violate them. What is it that makes people accept and obey? William Paisley says that, because people in the USA accept the notion of a "free marketplace of ideas," campaigns (even conflicting ones) are common. But to gain public support, a social issues campaign must get on the public agenda of issues, and the issue must be seen as having some public merit.[9]

Then, in addressing the merit of an issue, a fourth "E"—entitlement—is added to the list of campaign elements.[10] Some public issues are seen as obligations and others as opportunities, but entitlement involves laws, public policy and public acceptance. Laws can be upheld or changed, and laws tend to change with society's social agenda, as drinking-age laws illustrate. Public policy becomes a part of the entitlement consideration when more than one group or agency claims a social issue; and certainly environmental issues of all kinds have multiple sponsors who usually carve out their own part of the issue and try to make their identification with it distinctive. The final part of entitlement, as Paisley

Global Perspective

Public relations scholars Dean Kruckeberg and Marina Vujnovic argue that U.S. public diplomacy needs public relations rather than propaganda in today's world. They note that, while propaganda was central to U.S. public diplomacy in earlier times, and remains central today, the USA must now practice *true* public diplomacy, which should rely not only on political theory and the theories of international relations, but also on theories and models of public relations that are based on two-way symmetrical communication and community-building.

The core problem, they say, is that U.S. public diplomacy today is best characterized as "marketing communication" that focuses on "building bridges" by filling information gaps between other countries and the USA, that is, messages that give citizens throughout the world *more* of us and *more* of what *we* see as America: music, entertainment and Hollywood dream-factory movies, without any sensitivity to the fact that this is exactly how people of many other countries interpret cultural imperialism.

The authors say that U.S. public diplomacy must recognize that U.S. constituents are "publics," not "markets," and that an effective public diplomacy model must be one that is not propaganda or market-oriented advocacy, but one that is based on two-way symmetrical communication and community-building. A propaganda model centers the USA at the hub of the global milieu in its relationships with other nations, that is, a diplomatic worldview in which the "spokes" of the USA's communication and relationships radiate outward to satellites of stakeholders (other nations and their people). This Cold War model is inferior to a community-building model that recognizes that the USA is only one part of a global social system.

Source: Dean Kruckeberg and Marina Vujnovic, "Public Relations, Not Propaganda, for U.S. Public Diplomacy in a Post-9/11 World: Challenges and Opportunities," *Journal of Communication Management*, 9(4), 2005, pp. 296–304.

sees it, is public acceptance. In the USA, the issue requires association with first-party stakeholders—those whom the issue affects directly—to have credibility and thus win widespread public support. The fifth "E" is evaluation.[11]

Changing behavior works best when the people who are being asked to change are encouraged to participate in formulating the behavioral goals. Top–down information campaigns in most countries are doomed to failure. On the other hand, if members of the public become partners in the planning, they share ego involvement in the push for successful outcome. Self-persuasion is a major ingredient.

Billboards often play an important role in development communication campaigns, and they often rely on drama and symbols more than on words. That's important, given the communications problems of a high rate of illiteracy and/or a multiplicity of languages. Language problems make radio an important campaign medium, as well. Unfortunately, many development campaigns have depended on mass media and top–down message construction, with no development of infrastructures to make carrying out the messages possible. The result has been some information or education about what the government wants people to do, but not much

Ethical Perspective

Wal-Mart is the biggest company in the world and a global symbol of business power. Observers said founder Sam Walton, who died in 1992, disdained the press, publicists and government relations, focusing instead on customers. After the successful merchandiser was accused of destroying small-town America, it drew other critics in its newer global role. The company has hired publicists and lobbyists as well as lawyers, and its top executives give speeches to defend Wal-Mart from problems ranging from sex-discrimination litigation, wage and pay disputes and fights with unions to a multimillion-dollar settlement with immigration authorities over illegal workers and resignation of a top company officer after allegations of financial improprieties (which *Fortune* magazine writer Andy Serwer calls a management and public relations quagmire and what one financial analyst called "headline risk"). The company now has 2 million "associates" (employees) worldwide (with 1.4 million in the USA), and its global marketing penetration has resulted in the company being one of the largest employers in the USA, the largest employer in Mexico and one of the largest in Canada.

Wal-Mart, by all appearances, has learned to take its public relations more seriously. It publicizes the millions of dollars it contributes to community organizations, runs a TV image-advertising campaign, has a Web site (WalMartFacts.com) to counter criticisms and has engaged a major public relations firm and has hired dozens of communications specialists in regional offices, state capitals and in Washington, D.C.[1] Wal-Mart, which also operates in Argentina, Brazil, China, Costa Rica, El Salvador, Guatemala, Honduras, Japan, Nicaragua, the UK and India, as well as in all 50 states in the USA, donated $17 million for Hurricane Katrina relief and establish mini Wal-Mart stores in areas impacted by the hurricane. Items such as clothing, diapers, baby wipes, food, formula, toothbrushes, bedding and water were given out free of charge to those with a demonstrated need, and the company also collected contributions at its 3,800 stores and Web sites.[2] In 2007 the company and its foundation gave $296 million to charitable causes, a $24 million increase over 2006.[3] By mid-June 2008 Wal-Mart had already made a $500,000 commitment to assist with relief efforts needed because of the floods in the Midwestern USA.[4]

Sources: [1]Andy Serwer, "Bruised in Bentonville," *Fortune*, April 18, 2005, pp. 84–9; "Corporate Facts: Wal-Mart By the Numbers," accessed June 24, 2008, from http://walmartstores.com/FactsNews/FactSheets/.

[2]"Katrina Relief: Wal-Mart Commits Additional $15 Million," Wal-Mart news release dated September 1, 2005, and "International Operations," accessed June 24, 2008, from http://walmartstores.com/FactsNews/FactSheets/.

[3]"Wal-Mart Gives More than $296 Million in 2007," Wal-Mart news release dated February 25, 2008, accessed June 24, 2008, from http://walmartstores.com/FactsNews/newsroom/7991.aspx.

[4]"Wal-Mart Commits $500,000 to Support Flood Relief Efforts," Wal-Mart news release dated June 11, 2008, accessed June 24, 2008, from http://walmartstores.com/FactsNews/NewsRoom/8385.aspx.

in the way of engineering to see that it's feasible, and very little interactivity and feedback, although this is improving as governments realize that even authoritarian governments need "entitlement" to gain compliance.

One type of campaign that has received widespread mass media attention is the campaign for population control. Although various countries' experiences could be cited, the pattern is the same for many. Billboards and radio spots carry slogans and jingles. In some countries, television is also used, especially soap operas. A few countries have tried taking folk media, puppets and plays to outlying villages.

These campaigns encounter at least two basic problems. First, the message of having few children appears to make little sense in a rural community where many hands are needed and mortality rates are high. Second, too few family-oriented clinics or health programs may be available for follow-up counseling and materials, and in any case the male typically makes most of the family-planning decisions.

Women living in these societies could tell the planners why their messages won't work, but while many people might talk to them, few people ask them anything and even fewer listen. One difficulty in getting useful interaction with or feedback from people in many countries relates to their social relationships. Recognizing this problem, Hernando Gonzáles has offered a revised interpretation of the interactive model that doesn't look at the flow of information up or down in situations where status and power are likely designators.[12] Instead, his model

Theory and Research Perspective

Barbara M. Burns, APR, Fellow PRSA, said companies everywhere are portraying themselves as social movements, but ironically it is the "hip" companies that the antiglobal people hate. They hate them because these companies have made a mockery of these people's values. In the 2001 Atlas Award Lecture on International Public Relations at the International Conference of the Public Relations Society of America, Burns provided insights into "The NGO War Against Globalization: Implications for International Public Relations." Burns noted that Web sites are devoted to exposing what is "fake, false, and façade" about companies, including those whose sport utility vehicle (SUV) ads pretend to bring their drivers closer to nature, while these gas guzzlers are used mostly to go to shopping malls.

Indeed, said Burns, an international movement has grown up against "branded life." Burns said that, in rethinking corporate social responsibility, public relations practitioners must make their messages more authentic because corporate reputations can't rest on cosmetic slogans or advertising. "In the corporate world . . . as public relations professionals, we have to do a much better job of explaining our traditions and values. We have to stop the spin," she said.

In addition to structuring clearer, honest messages in English, Burns said more American public relations professionals should also be studying foreign languages. This is because language opens up the door to culture and understanding so that public relations practitioners can understand how native speakers arrive at their view of the world. Burns further recommended taking a more scientific approach to structuring public relations messages. Burns said, "We know that opinion differs from culture to culture, within cultures and also from media to media. In order to structure clear messages, we need to understand our reputation on a global and local scale."

Formal research helps practitioners be more accurate in their assessments. Burns noted that public relations can have a much greater influence on events than the media can. Public relations practitioners are the persuaders working behind the scenes, influencing what bosses and clients do and say. Although the media have a crucial role, they don't have the same influence as public relations does.

Source: Barbara Burns, "The NGO War against Globalization: Implications for International Public Relations," speech presented at the International Conference of the Public Relations Society of America on October 30, 2001.

looks at the already established norms of interactivity, with a view toward building coalitions so that power can accrue to these groups, which can then act as representative voices.

Government Campaigns

Most countries have some sort of government agency responsible for conducting campaigns for the country as a whole. These often deal with issues of population control in countries such as China and India, economic restructuring in newly democratized countries such as Romania and Bulgaria and tourism in Mexico and many island nations.

In addition to those major campaigns, different units of central governments may be involved in special efforts to correct problems or make improvements. In the USA many government agencies form coalitions in areas where their interests coincide, and they often create alliances with nonprofit groups that have similar purposes. Sometimes they are joined by corporations.

National coalitions like this are mirrored in international campaigns such as conferences on population control and the environment. The United Nations is a focal point for many international efforts that benefit multiple countries.

Global Campaigns: Does One Fit All?

The nations of the world always have engaged in a great deal of economic interaction, but something quite different happened after World War II. First, many national economies were shattered, and the USA invested heavily in the Marshall Plan to rebuild them. As the various nations began to recover their economic strength, they turned to the USA first as a marketplace for their goods and later as a place to invest their new wealth.

Along with the increase in international economic activity came the need for help in dealing with different governments, with the languages and customs of foreign and unfamiliar customers and with the effects of two new technologies—aviation and television. This need existed both in the USA and in the foreign countries. The USA was rapidly expanding its political and commercial involvement abroad, and the foreign nations were discovering the USA as an eager customer. The borders between countries

seemed to vanish, and businesspeople talked of "jet lag." Later the micronization of electronic technology and the advent of the computer made virtual face-to-face contact such as videoconferencing possible throughout the world. Going global is even more necessary today, but it is still an untidy and uncertain business. The PR firms that got in early (in the 1960s, 1970s and 1980s) are still at the top of the heap: Burson-Marsteller, Hill & Knowlton and Ogilvy & Mather. They control a campaign—"a seamless campaign" as Burson-Marsteller calls it.

Although PR firms and networks are available to do the job, some companies handle their own PR/advertising/marketing/sales campaigns at home and abroad. Their PR and marketing people may or may not work together. The U.S. Department of Labor Bureau of Labor Statistics reports that in 2006, there were about 48,000 advertising and public relations services establishments in the USA. About 4 out of 10 wrote copy and prepared artwork, graphics and other creative work, and then placed the resulting ads on television, radio or on the Internet or in periodicals, newspapers or other advertising media. Within the industry, only these full-service establishments are known as advertising agencies. About 1 in 6 were public relations firms. Many of the largest agencies are international, with a substantial proportion of their revenue coming from abroad.[13] Public relations in full-service agencies commonly is used for publicity and promotion. With today's global economy and instant communication, together with global tensions over problems related to everything from nuclear arms to worldwide fuel and food shortages, public relations for corporations, civil society organizations and governments is even more important, indeed essential, and can no longer be marginalized as a support function of marketing and advertising.

One of the most intensive global campaigns is the World Health Organization's AIDS campaign. In addition to experiencing the problems of any campaign (language barriers, government regulations and media), the AIDS campaign suffers from a lack of infrastructure—a problem not limited to nonindustrialized nations. Add to that the cultural taboos of many societies regarding any discussion of sexual matters, as well as the objections of social conservatives in all cultures, who fear that sex education encourages promiscuity, and you have a real campaign challenge.

Global Perspective

Media Relations at a Russian Luxury Hotel

By Natalia Ermashova

Personal Assistant to General Manager and Media Relations Manager

Grand Hotel Europe

St. Petersburg, Russia

During the past several years, the hotel business in Russia has been booming. More and more world-famous hotel brands have expressed their interest in expanding to the Russian Federation. This interest also has to do with relative stability of the political and economical environment at the present moment, so investors do feel confident committing to expensive projects.

In modern Russia, especially in the large metropolitan areas such as Moscow and St. Petersburg, the market for luxury products of all kinds is undergoing rapid development. As more and more people are able to afford expensive consumer goods and services, the supply is also growing at a steady pace.

Like any enterprise offering services, we at the Grand Hotel Europe are depending heavily on the hotel's relations with the mass media, and we spend a lot of time and effort to build good working communication with them.

Because Russians present the majority and the largest target audience for our hotel, and because they are notorious for being ready to spend a lot of money, the Grand Hotel Europe pays special attention to the Russian media, and the modern glossy press is one of our major targets.

The market of mass media that are aimed at wealthy people is also growing fast. While on the one hand competing for advertisers, the media on the other hand is extremely spoiled by the tremendous demand, and getting your enterprise's point across free-of-charge is a quite challenging task. For a commercial organization, getting free coverage is always a problem, as every mentioning can be considered advertising and, thus, those in the media think it should be paid for.

So, on the one hand, the hotel goes out of its way to amaze and surprise its customers, because nowadays people are not looking just for a comfortable place in which to sleep in—they crave an unforgettable experience, and this is true for both leisure and business travelers. But, on the other hand, we need to perform a double effort to amaze the press, which wants only astonishing news and facts. It is not enough to host a journalist for a weekend in the best room with meals included—we must surprise him with a midnight boat trip, or with an exclusive cocktail on our roof while watching the sunset, or we must present an in-room dinner accompanied by a live string trio. There must be something to talk about, something which is an experience. Or an unusual fact—for example, how many lamp bulbs a hotel uses per year? How much washing detergent? How is the waiters team preparing for a major catering—including by actually rehearsing serving the dishes? Did you know that our hotel has Europe's largest fleet of brand-new BMW limousines? Our hotel is lucky, because, apart from everything else, we are a protected historical building, and we boast plenty of live art and antique items in rooms and guest areas. So we have more to talk about for media that specialize in the arts and interior design.

So we brainstorm and send teasers to media with interesting facts, trying to draw their attention, because a mere "Our Chef has come up with a new salad" does not get the coverage anymore.

Over the last three years, we were successful in becoming THE luxury hotel in St. Petersburg, and not just "one of the 5 star hotels." A lot of work has been put into building this distinction, but it pays back—both with demanding customers who perceive us as the only place to stay in the city and with increased coverage in media.

Apart from regular hotel activities, we do a lot of social work and have our own "Grand Hotel Europe Charity Foundation," which engages in assisting children in need. We hire young girls and boys from

(continued)

Global Perspective (continued)

orphanages and give them their first jobs with a full package of benefits, which also spells out the future for them. We do support many charity causes and events, fully understanding our social responsibility in this city, and it is very rewarding to see our activities very well-covered in the mass media, both locally and internationally, as well as being noted by local authorities for our efforts.

The World Health Organization has responded by creating basic educational materials that it furnishes to health authorities in various countries to adapt to the cultures of the country. Many countries have turned the development of their plan (and the funds to implement it) over to public relations firms. Although many nations have taken aggressive action, others have not, perhaps because they face too many other issues that demand immediate attention. But the problem is global and involves essentially the same facts everywhere, so at some point the campaigns tailored for various countries and for the ethnic and cultural groups within those countries will offer a remarkable case study.

Discussion Questions

1. Think of five or six public relations campaigns with which you are familiar. Identify which kind of campaign each is, that is, (1) public awareness campaign, (2) public information campaign, (3) public education campaign, (4) reinforcement of attitudes and behavior of those who are in agreement with your organization's position, (5) changing or attempting to change attitudes of those who do not agree and (6) behavior modification campaign. What about "advertising campaigns" and "health campaigns" and other types of communication campaigns? Are these public relations campaigns? Identify how these might be alike or different from other types of public relations campaigns.

2. What are some of the ethical questions you have to consider when conducting a public relations campaign?

3. Can you think of an example of a campaign that has been effective in one country or culture but that failed in another country or culture? Why do you think this was? What could have been done to make the campaign more effective in the other country or culture?

4. Can you think of a public relations campaign that influenced your behavior, for example, a campaign to encourage caution with fires when camping, or use of car seat belts, or consumption of healthy foods? What was it about that campaign that influenced you, do you think?

Points to Remember

- Campaigns are designed to accomplish specific organizational objectives.

- A campaign's foundation is the organizational mission, and its roof or containing factor is the budget. The elements are research, publics, action and evaluation.

- Planning for a campaign involves setting goals, creating timetables and developing budgets.

- Setting the creative strategy means choosing a theme and media to use in communicating with the designated publics.

- Internal strategy is critical to establishing organizational support for the campaign.

- Implementation has three major components: (1) adapting and applying tactics to strategies, (2) keeping people informed and (3) solving all problems positively.

- While a campaign is in progress, all elements have to be monitored so goals are achieved. After the campaign, a review or postmortem to determine what worked and what didn't is important for future planning.

- Governments conduct comprehensive campaigns to make improvements or to solve problems. Like other organizations, governments often conduct several campaigns at the same time. Some of these are handled by government departments.

- Often campaigns are undertaken by coalitions.

- Most global campaigns, even those for a product being sold around the world, do not work well across cultures. The cultural aspect is more important than are national borders or languages, although laws can affect certain campaign tactics.

- Campaigns are usually built around a desire to establish, change or modify behaviors. The five *Es* of a successful campaign are education, engineering, enforcement, entitlement and evaluation.

Go to the Web site for this book at **www. cengage.com/masscomm/newsom/ thisispr10e** to find more Web links on this subject.

Other Related Web Sites to Review

Ascribe: The Public Interest Newswire
  http://www.ascribe.org/

Advertising Age
  http://www.adage.com

Adweek
  http://www.adweek.com

Brandweek
  http://www.brandweek.com

Free Publicity
  http://www.PublicityInsider.com

PRJobSeek.com
  http://www.prjobseek.com

O'Dwyer's PR Daily
  http://www.odwyerpr.com

O'Dwyer's PR Services Report
  http://www.odwyerpr.com/pr_services_report/ current.htm

PRWEEK
  http://www.prweek.com/

The Business Communicator, Corporate Responsibility Management and Strategic Communication Management
  http://www.melcrum.com

The Strategist
  http://www.prsa.org

CHAPTER 13

Crisis and Credibility

Corporations have challenges that they have never faced before. This presents global opportunities for those who practice public relations.

—Harold Burson, *Burson-Marsteller*

OBJECTIVES

- To create awareness of situations that could become crises.
- To plan strategies and implement policies that help an organization through a crisis.
- To recognize the triggering event that precipitates a crisis.
- To understand management's likely response to a crisis and plan a coping strategy.
- To be sensitive to the needs of all publics, including nimbus publics, when a crisis occurs.

Crises challenge organizations to live up to their reputations, and the way a crisis is handled determines the outcome, both in the court of public opinion and in terms of an organization's credibility. Crises and credibility go hand in hand, and the first few years of the twenty-first century have had a high level of crises and low level of credibility—a history of damage control.

The impact of globalization has hit the world hard and fast, creating crises in dramatic climate change, energy, food and housing—all basic to human life. Climate change due to global warming has disrupted growing seasons, wildlife habitats (plants and animals) and the somewhat predictable occurrence of natural disasters such as floods, hurricanes, tornadoes and earthquakes. An interlocking world economy has spread the contagion of financial misdeeds and energy demands. Conflict around the globe has brought world hunger to the forefront along with refugee issues that involve not only food but also shelter, consequently creating impositions on the infrastructure of many nations.

The interrelatedness of these issues only exacerbates the difficulty of solutions. Although much attention has been given to the conflict of different value systems being at the root of these problems, tension created by the issues themselves cannot be discounted as a major contributing factor.

Look at the food crisis, for example. Weather changes have made some areas arable while others have become barren. There is more food in some places, less in others. The solution has been to move food to where it is needed. Energy is required to both produce and distribute food. The major source of energy, fossil fuels, is being depleted at record rates as populations increase and more nations become industrialized. Among the many solutions are to use food products for fuel, especially corn. The unintended consequences are less food for both people and animals.

Scarcity drives up prices so food, even when available, is priced beyond the budgets of so many people that social unrest then contributes to conflict.

Ethical issues everywhere often provide the triggering event for crises. The lack of product supervision in China caused a wave of crises involving imported prescription drugs, pet food and toys. Another example is the USA, where a financial crisis in 2007 and 2008 in the mortgage industry caused more people to lose their homes than at any other time in the nation's history. Adding to the economic crisis caused by homeowners no longer able to meet monthly payments is the loss of jobs. Some of the job loss is tied to higher energy costs that industries are trying to meet by shedding employees. Crises often beget crises. That makes planning for the inevitable essential. ■

Anticipating a Crisis

There is some structure to anticipating and planning for a crisis. Issues management, discussed in Chapter 9, is a major factor in anticipating a crisis. The problem is deciding which issues are likely to engage publics or contain triggering events that will precipitate a full-blown crisis.

Public relations practitioners routinely inform top management of issues and situations that could escalate. They recommend that some attention be given to those issues that might need action now and that others only bear watching. The corporate culture and the attitude of management have a lot to do with how executives respond to these warnings. Time is also a factor for top executives.

Learning how to approach particular executives with potential problems is a skill that has to be relearned with management changes. Often the public relations person will be working directly with the manager of a particular division where the crisis might develop rather than with top management, but top management needs to be kept informed so as not to be surprised if a crisis does occur.

Sometimes crises are not new, but recurring. Urban myths often resurrect old crises, as Proctor & Gamble discovered when the myth about satanic symbolism in a logo it had long since discontinued reappeared on the Internet. The Internet was also a source of difficulty for Coca-Cola, accused of environmental damage and possible product contamination with pesticides in India. The accusations circulated on the Internet were created by activists, many associated with nongovernment organizations (NGOs) or, as they sometimes are designated, CSOs (civil society organizations). Occasionally success stimulates activists' attention to an industry. In 2008 that happened to Unilever, widely celebrated in 2004 and 2005 for its Dove campaign that championed natural beauty. The Dove campaign moved quickly through the social media. Now those same media have sparked criticism of the company for its use of palm oil in its beauty products. Greenpeace launched its 2008 campaign in Britain and put parodies of Dove's award-winning ads on YouTube to call attention to the depletion of Indonesian rain forests to get that palm oil. The activist organization claimed victory when Unilever issued a promise not to use palm oil except from suppliers who could provide proof that the origin was not endangered forest areas.

New events related to old issues also revive crises, such as mad cow disease—a problem in the UK since the 1980s—appearing in the USA. This caused a ban in the USA on importing cattle from Canada, the supposed source of the sick animal in a U.S. herd, and a ban on accepting U.S. beef exports by other countries. In 2008 a rumor circulating in South Korea was that Americans were exporting their beef because no one in the country would eat it. Rumor often is more difficult to deal with than reality.

Often it is continuing action on a crisis that keeps it in the news, as with protesters staging events in 2004 on the twentieth anniversary of the Bhopal disaster in India that killed at least 5,000 people. Two events brought that disaster back to the public agenda. One was India's Supreme Court ruling that $330 million in compensation held by the Indian government would be distributed directly to the victims. The other event resulted from the BBC's falling for a hoax in which a fake corporate spokesman for Dow Chemical claimed responsibility for the incident. Dow now owns the plant that belonged to Union Carbide. Both companies blame the disaster on a disgruntled employee. Natural disasters, too, are recalled, especially on

PR in Practice

Every disaster situation presents a major challenge to the crisis communication-handling skills of corporate communication professionals. Not only do they need to provide the media with clear, well-informed and timely messages that take account of the sensitivities involved in life and death situations, but they also need to be genuine in their support of the local communities affected by the disaster. When an earth tremor caused the collapse of an Australian gold mine, 14 miners escaped safely, but one was killed in the cave-in. Two other miners were found five days later after having spent a total of 14 days trapped inside a small wire work cage.

Within hours of the disaster, the small community of Beaconsfield in northern Tasmania had become swamped with worldwide media attention. In a relatively rare move, all Australian television news anchors broadcast live from the mine site. Interest from American media was also strong, given two mining disasters just two months earlier in West Virginia that had resulted in the deaths of 15 miners. The homes of the trapped miners became fortresses, with a report of one very determined journalist scaling a fence to offer one of the wives a check for an exclusive interview.

The fortunes of Beaconsfield Mine Joint Venture (BMJV), the company at the center of this crisis, could have been easily ruined by the mine collapse and resulting adverse, critical or negative media attention. However, BMJV fully understood the need for ongoing, transparent information and positioned itself as a company "with heart," sympathetic to the concerns of the families of the miners involved and swiftly responding to the constant media interest. Essentially, BMJV managed to successfully turn attention away from the death of miner Larry Knight, and any potential underlying health and safety issues that could have resulted in the closure of the mine with the consequent loss of hundreds of jobs for the local community. The focus turned to what became known as "The Great Escape" of the two miners trapped in the wire cage, Brant Webb and Todd Russell.

The two official spokespeople, Bill Shorten from the Australian Workers Union and the resident manager of the Beaconsfield mine Joint Venture, Matthew Gill, were both well briefed, credible and surprisingly accessible. The selection of unionist Shorten was a wise choice because not only was he able to speak credibly about the situation from the miners' point of view, but he also symbolized the collaborative relationship between the company and the community. Both spokespeople used straightforward, direct and friendly language to describe this complex and difficult situation.

The eventual release of the trapped miners was stage-managed well for the media. All of Australia watched on as both miners surfaced, dramatically clocked off, and dodged the media circus to make their way to the hospital for full medical check-ups. The Great Escape coverage lived on when the two survivors hit the talk show circuit and even accepted an invitation by USA chat show queen Oprah Winfrey. However, despite extensive media interest, Webb and Russell have kept largely to themselves, avoiding harsh criticism of BMJV. With approval of the workers union and endorsement by the two survivors, the mine has since re-opened, effectively ensuring employment opportunities for the community of Beaconsfield.

Even the most extensive crisis communications plan at the time could not have anticipated that the Beaconsfield Gold Mine would make global front page news. The management team successfully and smoothly handled this highly complicated and emotion-laden incident, by being visible and transparent. The communications team remained calm and avoided any speculation or blame games. Furthermore, the team fully understood the need for regular communication with all key stakeholders. Most importantly, BMJV remained in control at all times, managing to channel the media's interest onto their preferred stories and angles, which focused on survival rather than casualty. Today the mine is remembered for the cave-in and the death of Knight, but predominantly for an amazing story of survival against the odds.

Source: "The Great Escape: Crisis Communication Following the Collapse of an Australian Goldmine," by Kathatrina Wolf, Curtin University of Technology, Australia.

anniversaries of floods, fires and earthquakes. Crises come in many forms, but public relations people for the most part deal with public crises. These can be described, categorized and usually (in general form at least) predicted.[1] Crises are like plays; there are only so many basic plots. Everything else is a variation. Two factors are always present: crises involve people, and they interrupt the normal "chain of command."

Causes of crises are either physically violent or nonviolent. The physically violent ones come to mind immediately—earthquakes, fires, storms, plane crashes and terrorist acts, to name but a few. The permission of courts in the USA to allow financially troubled institutions to cut or dramatically reduce their pension obligations is an example of a physically nonviolent crisis.

Each of these broad categories, violent and nonviolent, has subsets with more specific descriptors. Some violent crises are created by acts of nature, such as lightning that sparks a forest fire or a hurricane or typhoon that sweeps a coast. Some nonviolent crises, too, are created by acts of nature—crises such as viral epidemics, insect plagues and droughts. These may take lives, but they are not cataclysmic or overwhelmingly violent. That factor alone calls for a different type of crisis management.

Some crises result from intentional acts committed by a person or group. Violent intentional crises are due to acts of terrorism that result in loss of life or freedom, such as hostage-taking. This category also includes product-tampering, when it results in loss of life or destruction of property. Nonviolent intentional crises include bomb and product-tampering threats, hostile takeovers, insider trading, computer viruses, malicious rumors and other malfeasance.

The third subcategory of crises includes unintentional events that are neither acts of nature nor deliberate acts of individuals or groups. This category includes violent unintentional accidents, such as explosions, fires and chemical leaks. On the nonviolent side are process or product problems, which often have delayed consequences such as stock market crashes, business failures or hostile takeovers. Table 13.1 provides an outline and summary of the various kinds of crises.

Whatever organization you are working in or with, you can predict and thus anticipate most possible crises. This means that you can plan for crises.

In responding to the notion that crises could be planned for, one corporate PR director said, "Research and planning sound great, but that's academic. I'm too busy fighting alligators to drain the swamp." Often such a response is a form of denial or simply an excuse—one

that public relations counselors often hear, especially when they are called on a weekend and asked to put out a bonfire that had been smoldering for months. When the fire is either contained or extinguished, the alligator comment often follows. The problem for the PR person is that the CEO, who the counselor is also dealing with, is asking how the fire got so big so fast. The key to good crisis management is anticipation.

Imagining the Worst

Part of anticipating crises is listing the kinds of crises your organization is most likely to face and preparing for the worst. Many crisis managers use a descriptive typology.[2] Once they have put a name to a type of crisis, such as "technological," it helps to think about the company in terms of the different types of problems in this area that could arise. Planning includes eliminating some risks by examining policies that might be put in place to prevent crises in that category. An example is policies that airlines have in place for customers with medical conditions that make it necessary for them to use oxygen all the time, including in flight. With the airlines the issue is safety. They want the passengers who need oxygen to use the plane's supply. But arrangements to do this have to be made in advance, and access is limited to just a few seats. Many passengers may not know to call ahead or may suddenly have plans changed. They can't fly if they arrive at the gate expecting to use a portable oxygen supply onboard.

Many policies develop from a risk assessment process. Risk assessment comes from interpretations of data from a number of sources, many of them scientific, to determine safety levels. An example is evaluating risks from exposure to pesticides used on foods—processed or unprocessed. Research helps policy makers develop some risk assumptions and these govern policy, including government regulatory decisions.[3]

An important part of assessing any potential crisis is evaluating the vulnerability of the organization to the worst-case scenario of that crisis. For very serious potential crises, many managers use simulations to test vulnerability and the potential success of their crisis plans. In 2003 London First issued a 30-page action plan, "Expecting the Unexpected," telling how to plan for different types of crisis, which ones to anticipate and how to provide for a continuity of business operations regardless of the crisis. London First is an organization of businesses wanting to improve and promote the city and develop action plans to cope with crises for both small and large businesses. The brochure lists five steps to provide for

Table 13.1	Crisis Typology	

Use this as a guide to classify crises in current news reports.

Source of Crisis	Violent: Cataclysmic—Immediate Loss of Life or Property	Nonviolent: Sudden Upheaval but Damages, if Any, Are Delayed
Act of Nature	Forest fires, floods such as those in England in 2007, the Myanmar cyclone in 2008, hurricane Katrina in the USA in 2005, and earthquakes on land and under the sea, such as the underwater one that created a tsunami in 2004.	Droughts, epidemics, disease, such as avian flu (bird flu) and mad cow disease, now seen as a threat to North American deer and elk, and reemergence of hoof and mouth disease in the UK in 2007.
Intentional	Acts of terrorism, including product tampering, when these result in loss of life or destruction of property, such as the mass transit bombings in London in 2005 and attempts in 2006.	Bomb and product-tampering threats, hostile takeovers, insider trading, malicious rumors and other malfeasance, such as the Société Générale French bank trader scandal of 2008. China claimed terror plots targeting the Beijing Olympics tried to discourage attendance and spoil the games.
Unintentional	Explosions, fires, leaks and other accidents, such as the crash of a TAM plane attempting to land in a rainstorm in São Paulo, Brazil in 2007 that hit a building, taking 200 lives on and off the plane.	Process or product problems with delayed consequences, as with Chinese-made products in 2007 and 2008, stock market crashes, business problems such as the home mortgage crises in the USA in 2007 and 2008.

continuity: (1) analyze your business, (2) assess the risks, (3) develop your strategy, (4) develop your plan, and (5) rehearse your plan. The booklet also offers seven points to include in planning: (1) make it clear who needs to do what: (2) use checklists that people can follow easily; (3) include clear, direct instructions for the crucial first hour after an incident; (4) agree how often you will check your plan to ensure it is always a "living document"; (5) update it to reflect changes in personnel and the risks you may face—a good plan is simple without being simplistic (you can't plan in detail for every event); (6) remember that people need to be able to react quickly in an emergency— there will be no time to read lots of detail; (7) plan for worst-case scenarios. If your plan covers how to get back in business if a flood destroys your building, it also will work if just one floor is flooded.[4]

Crisis management is also immeasurably aided when top executives accept an integrated two-way symmetrical model of public relations. When channels of communication are open and two-way, warnings about potential crises often come from employees or suppliers. This can occur, though, only when the corporate culture permits openness and two-way symmetrical communication. When that model is used with proactivity and symmetry—along with issues management, planning, prevention and implementation—resolving conflicts that a crisis might cause is likely to be easier, because the organization and its publics have been talking to each other all along.[5]

An organization confronted with a crisis is concerned with its own behavior and with the behavior of its members and of all of its other publics.

Reprinted with permission of United Feature Syndicate.

Some publics tend to be neglected in the planning process—unintended (often global) audiences of communication about the crisis. Such publics, known as nimbus publics,[6] often receive information about the crisis because of the global nature of technology. Every crisis plan needs to take into account the potential global impact of crises, even when these are viewed as being essentially domestic. Organizations experience a crisis, not as an isolated event or series of events, but as one or more occurrences that develop in the total environment of public opinion in which the organization operates. That total environment encompasses various nimbus publics that the organization may not have recognized as being affected by the crisis and by the organization's response to it.

Sometimes a crisis creates a nimbus public, as in the case of the response of Roman Catholics around the world to public attention in the USA on priests accused of sexual abuse. Other nimbus groups may be identified for the first time as the result of a crisis. An example is the declared "war on terrorism" as defined by the USA. Although this drew support from some traditional allies, such as Britain, others were not as supportive and criticized U.S. State Department policies as precipitating the crisis. Handling such nimbus publics means considering the environment of global public opinion in the planning process (see Figures 13.1 and 13.2).

A crisis gets your attention and demands the immediate attention of top management. It may or may not come with preliminary hints or warnings. But whether the crisis involves violent or nonviolent dangers created by natural events, deliberate acts or accidents, it can be anticipated with good imaginative powers that are exercised through brainstorming.

Various departments within the organization should participate.[7] You need to hold brainstorming sessions with various departments because someone may be aware of a possibility that you couldn't imagine without having that person's special job-related knowledge. Look at all aspects of the organization.

The "imagining" process in which you want to engage management involves taking the role of an intelligent and resourceful adversary and asking, "What's the best way to wreck this company?" Then you assume the role of corporate management and ask, "What is the best response?"[8]

Some places to start with the imagining process are money, people, products or services, processes and locations of operations.[9] Being accountable for money is important to all stakeholders, and being able to explain where the money came from and where it went is important to all organizations, not just commercial operations. People can cause all sorts of problems, which is the reason they need to be well trained and why they need to be listened to when they have issues or complaints. Health is also an issue here because of exposure to environmental contamination or contagious disease. Products or services always have to be considered in terms of their convenience, safety and effect on the environment. Processes are especially important to regulators, customers and suppliers. The location of an organization is often an element of crises, especially in other countries when the political or economic climate goes downhill.

Because these areas are so diverse, it is important to ask those "how to wreck" and "how to recover" questions of management at all levels. CEOs will tell you that it's impossible for them to know all the details of their organization, and the devil often is in the details. When a crisis occurs, management calls

Figure 13.1   Public Opinion Node in Crisis Management

The minimum objective of crisis management with respect to public opinion is to maintain the positive public opinion the organization enjoyed before the crisis and to limit negative public opinion, collectively or from any single public, to precrisis levels. The public opinion node itself contains all opinions (positive or negative) held by all members of a specific public.

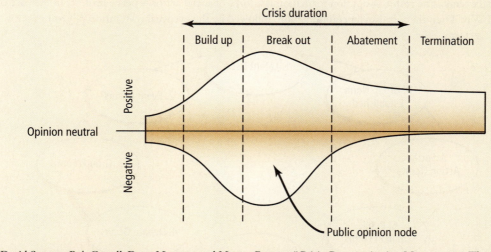

Source: David Sturges, Bob Carrell, Doug Newsom and Marcus Barrera, "Crisis Communication Management: The Public Opinion Node and Its Relationship to Environmental Nimbus," *SAM Advanced Management Journal*, 56(3), Summer 1991, pp. 22–27. Reprinted with permission.

together the management team to do some fast fact finding to determine how to respond. The response, according to one, is "Tell the truth and tell it fast."[10]

While you are imagining the worst, consider the impact that each event you can identify will have on each public individually. When you do this, you can anticipate possible chain reactions—that is, for example, what an explosion that contaminates your product will do to your stock and how you are perceived by important publics.

A crisis doesn't occur in a vacuum. It occurs in an operational environment that includes all publics central to the organization. An indirect environment encompasses all other readily identified publics that usually are involved in the organization's ongoing relationships with constituencies. Those two are operating in yet another environment that includes nimbus publics, groups not ordinarily thought of as publics central to the organization, but which have become so due to the crisis or publics that have developed as a result of the crisis.[11] Keeping all of those publics in mind is particularly difficult during a crisis, but it is important to at least consider them because any one of these publics, or a group of them, can complicate the crisis

situation and further test the credibility of the organization. The way you handle a crisis while it is occurring can lessen or increase its impact significantly. Planning can help you develop strategies out of the intensity of a crisis. It also helps you to clarify or modify a management response, depending on whether management operates in a closed or open climate.

An organization's communication climate has a great impact on how management handles crises. Of all the wrong decisions an organization can make in a crisis, deciding to shut off the flow of accurate information is probably the worst. Closed and open communication systems have been described earlier; but, in terms of crisis management, the open system is much easier to operate in. Rumors are less likely to start when information is openly available and a residue of trust exists inside and outside the organization. You must always consider an organization's communication climate when you undertake crisis planning.

Planning and Materials

Planning for a crisis today includes anticipating being a potential target for a terrorist attack, thanks

Figure 13.2   **Stages of Public Opinion in a Crisis**

Latent issues should be detected by environmental monitoring, but when a crisis occurs, groups tend to form in relation to the event and to responses to it by the organization and by other publics. The result may be public debate of issues, as occurred after the USA and its allies went to war in the Persian Gulf in 1991. As time elapses after an event, public opinion forms. It does so more dramatically if the crisis, like the Persian Gulf conflict, involves daily changes and additional events. The result of opinion formation is a form of social action—peace protests in the case of the Persian Gulf War. Then there is usually counteraction, followed by the eventual restoration of group norms.

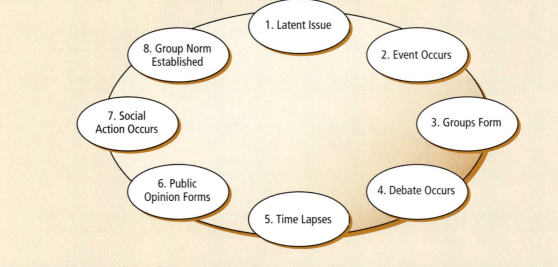

Source: David Sturges, Bob Carrell, Doug Newsom and Marcus Barrera, "Crisis Communication Management: The Public Opinion Node and Its Relationship to Environmental Nimbus," *SAM Advanced Management Journal*, 56(3), Summer 1991, pp. 22–27. Reprinted with permission.

to the ongoing attacks, especially bombings, that have been occurring. Although attacks are as old as stagecoach holdups, 9/11, the aftermath in Europe and certainly all over the Middle East put terrorist attacks on a large scale. For example, since 9/11, the USA government has issued warnings from time to time about particular industries when the government has received information that indicates an industry might be a target: nuclear plants and petroleum refineries, for example.

In planning for a crisis, you must always recognize that information is going to be in great demand. Unfortunately, you won't be able to get much information about the crisis itself ahead of time. You can make a crisis easier to handle, though, if you organize the information you can obtain in advance. You should collect information on products/services, processes, locales, people and the policies that govern the organization. Keep all of this information readily available to those most likely to need it, and keep it in a form that is most likely to be usable in a

crisis. Information is useless if the people who need it don't know it is available or don't understand how to use it.

What kind of information should be gathered, and in what form should it be kept?[12] You need details and descriptions of products or services, product contents and product development processes or service processes, as well as a list of general operating procedures. You should also have current safety and instruction manuals and copies of all recent inspection reports. In case of an explosion or a fire, you will have to describe contents and processes, with full awareness of potential danger areas—that is, the explosive nature of stored grains or the use of inflammable chemicals in a cleaning operation. You need a full description of all locations, including what is kept in surrounding areas and specifics such as acreage, street names, and the location of nearby homes, businesses or nonprofit organizations.

For every operation, you need a list of personnel and the times that specific personnel are likely to be occupying an area. If the organization has clients or customers who are likely to be on the premises, you need that information, too. In 24-hour operations—for example, mines, manufacturing plants, some retail stores, medical facilities and residential educational or care-giving institutions that operate with shift changes—you must set up a system with your personnel or human resources department so that you have at your fingertips an up-to-the-minute record of which employees are working where and at what particular time. This information must be kept remote from the location. For example, at the time of a disaster, one mining company had to call all families and ask which family members were missing to determine who was trapped in a mine. This occurred because an explosion close to the opening of the mine blew up the shack in which miners had signed on for the shift. You should also keep a list of personnel benefits that employees receive in the event of death or injury on the job.

Keep separation policies on hand in the event that an employee or employees are responsible for the crisis. You should have policies and processes governing access to facilities, because many crises are caused by disgruntled employees or former employees. You also need access to as much information as your human resources office has on all employees and officers in the event of a crisis that involves them. You may not use all of the available information, for reasons of privacy, but the undisclosed facts available to you may help you to put a situation into perspective.

Part of being prepared is routine and consists of maintaining current corporate fact sheets containing all necessary basic information in the files at all times. Such information should include the following:

1. Addresses of the home office and all branches or subsidiaries (if any) and all telephone numbers, including the numbers of security people and night numbers that override the main control and put you through to the person on duty.

2. Descriptions and schematics of all facilities, in detail, giving layouts and square footage and the number of people in each area (very important facts in case of fire or cave-ins).

3. Biographical information on all employees, and long, in-depth pieces on key executives. Often called "current biographical summaries," these are useful for speeches and introductions, but here they might become standing obituaries,

material ready to use with only the addition of cause of death.

4. Photos of all facilities and all principals (recent photographs; not the architects' rendering of the 10-year-old building or the CEO's favorite photo from several years past).

5. Statistics on the facilities and the institution: number of people employed now; cost of buildings and equipment; annual net (or gross) earnings; descriptions of products or services, or both if that is the nature of the institution; major contracts with unions and suppliers; details of lawsuits pending or charges against the institution; information on regulatory or accrediting agencies with some sort of oversight covering the institution, its products and its services (for instance, the Food and Drug Administration over products in that area or hospital accreditation over health care institutions).

6. A history of the institution, including major milestones, prepared like a fact sheet.

7. Emergency information such as nearest hospital, police and fire chief's direct numbers, best access routes, hazardous substances identification and potential threat, local government officials' direct numbers and numbers for contacts at regulatory agencies.

8. Ways to check personnel to see who might have been involved—a format for accounting for each member of the workforce.

9. The organization's mission statement and related documents, such as values and positioning statements.

10. Position papers.

11. Key publics and contact information, including bypass information for media and strategic suppliers and regulators.

12. Digitalized video.

Simply keeping all these materials up-to-date is a major undertaking, but it is vitally important. Most institutions handle them piecemeal, updating employee biographies annually and photos less frequently, and gathering new and relevant facts once the base is established. A periodic review of these materials is essential. Make a checklist and use it, marking the date of the most recent check next to it.

The crisis plan itself should be a guideline rather than a heavily detailed process, for two reasons: ease of recall and flexibility. Both features aid in the creative handling of a specific crisis.

Dealing with a Crisis

Dealing with a crisis requires an ability to keep an eye on the objective—to maintain corporate credibility, even if the organization is at fault, and attend to even the smallest details, not only for accuracy, but also to maintain trust. The most valuable asset a PR person can offer an organization in a crisis is helping management understand the perspective of the critic or opponent. Management's tendency is to dismiss the attack and the attacker out-of-hand. Not only is that not useful, but it is also dangerous.

Communication Before and During a Crisis

Some crisis plans are thorough and comprehensive, but they are never communicated. Then, when a crisis occurs, employees either don't have a copy of the plan or don't know how to follow its instructions. A good plan should include an easy-to-use fact sheet and background information.[13]

Having a **dark site** on the organizational intranet, password-protected, is one way to provide instant access to information in case of a crisis.[14] Dark site materials are updated regularly and systematically because crises can come without warning. They are activated as soon as the crisis occurs. On the site should be an internal crisis manual with step-by-step action items, a list of suggested procedures and all the information and materials mentioned in the planning and materials section. In addition, an external dark site to serve as a crisis channel for the public needs to be created so that it can be activated immediately for the public. Frames can be prepared in Word-HTML to be uploaded as needed. For visuals, as well as text, you can prepare materials in PDF or JPEG formats. Current information and news releases can be added when the site is activated.

You should hold regularly scheduled meetings with all managers and supervisors likely to have to deal with a crisis, to review crisis response procedures. "Regularly" really depends on an organization's structure. In an organization with high turnover, quarterly review meetings may be appropriate. An organization with more stable employment and a system for giving information to new hires may prefer annual reviews. Reviews not only renew familiarity with procedures, but they also allow planners to review the procedures themselves to ensure that they are relevant. Reviews spaced more than a year apart court trouble.

One reason to discuss crisis planning in advance is to get management involved in handling various publics before a crisis occurs. You may be able to alter some management tendencies toward procrastination by offering hypothetical examples of the effects of such behavior and by encouraging role playing. In organizations such as hospitals and banks, employees should be crisis-trained for the possibility that they may either have to negotiate with a hostage-taker or survive as hostages themselves.[15]

Three key elements promote successful communication during a crisis: (1) the existence of a communication plan as a part of the overall crisis plan, taking into consideration that normal channels may not be open; (2) the ability to assemble a crisis team when a crisis occurs; (3) the use of a single spokesperson during the crisis.

In developing a communication plan, remember that employees are going to talk to neighbors and to casual acquaintances whether authorized to do so or not. Consequently, your communication plan must include strong internal as well as external communication. Determine the best system to use: memos, closed-circuit TV, computer terminals, telephone. Identify people likely to be the principal participants in a communication plan, and develop a system for checking message statements before these are disseminated through the media.

The message statements will be generated by the crisis management team that you assemble from staff. This team will be instructed by outside PR counsel (when you decide to retain outside help) and by the organization's legal counsel. Isolate the crisis management team from normal day-to-day business affairs during the crisis. If day-to-day business is interrupted, the company will appear to be consumed by the crisis and unable to manage the situation. Management of communication during the crisis is not the same as managing the crisis itself.

Designate members of the crisis team as fact finders—people who will dig out facts, organize facts, resolve conflicting data and control and direct the flow of information to the team members and the spokesperson. Designate a person to evaluate the effects of the crisis on all publics and to monitor how the messages from the organization are influencing various publics and the factions within these publics.

Ethical Perspective

In business, the legal question asked is: "Can we do this?" If the legal answer is "yes," the ethical question that may not get asked is, "*Should* we do this?" A partner to this question is, "What are the consequences to all stakeholders?" The Federal Aviation Authority (FAA) has the responsibility to ensure air safety in the USA, and the authority to order whatever is necessary to guarantee that safety.

The FAA knew of a wiring problem near the main landing gear in MD-80 airliners in 2003, perhaps as early as 2001. However, evidence in the agency's records show the process for issuing an airworthiness directive was in progress by June 2003. A year before that the plane's manufacturer McDonnell Douglas merged with Boeing, and had issued a service-alert bulletin, filed with the FAA. Evidence of this problem, which results in chafed and burned wires in the plane's wiring bundle, has existed since the 1980s. Earlier in March 2008, the FAA called attention to the problem with Southwest Airlines, which grounded its planes to fix the faulty wiring. Subsequently a whistleblower revealed some camaraderie between the FAA regulators and Southwest that appeared to have resulted in nothing being done about the problem earlier, resulting in bad publicity for both. However, Southwest, a regional carrier based in Dallas, Texas, got its planes repaired and back in the air with minor interruption to its schedule. The consequences were that the FAA began auditing all inspection and maintenance records.

American, with a regional hub at Dallas–Fort Worth International (DFW), was not so fortunate. When the inspectors arrived at DFW, they found some differences in interpretation of the directive by American mechanics. The first warning resulted in American's taking its MD-80s out of service for the repairs with minor schedule interruptions. However, the subsequent FAA inspection resulted in the agency's finding that American had used some replacement parts that did not meet FAA standards. American officials decided to ground 300 of its MD-80 planes, anticipating that the FAA was going to demand that anyway.

The result was a cancellation of 3,279 flights that inconvenienced an estimated 300,000 passengers, many of whom were stuck in the airport for more than a day, a good many without luggage. Many slept on the floor because there were not enough cots. And because concessions closed at night, many did without food.

American CEO Gerard Arpey took personal responsibility for the crisis and did not blame either the FAA or the airline's mechanics. Most passengers complained largely about not being told about flight cancellations, and even being advised, when they called to ask, to come to the airport to see if their flight had been cancelled. Other planes landed during this time, subsequently stranding many passengers expecting connections. The furor resulted in a Senate subcommittee holding an aviation safety hearing in April and on April 18, the Department of Transportation announced measures to improve the FAA.

Source: The Fort Worth Star-Telegram's coverage of the crisis.

You must include legal counsel in all planning because, when a crisis occurs, legal advice and PR advice to top management often conflict. Legal counsel tends to advise "no comment," while PR counsel urges "openness." The reasons underlying both tendencies are justified by what occurs. Because the opposition seizes upon every word, lawyers understandably believe that it is better to say very little. Openness clearly creates more difficulty for lawyers who are trying to defend an organization. As a PR practitioner, you must accept that fact. But at the same time, the openness of an organization in a crisis also affects public opinion favorably. Whether the situation involves a jury trial or a Supreme Court hearing, the proceedings occur within the climate of public opinion.

Internet crises require immediate attention because online activists can damage a reputation, affect stock prices, create mistrust among consumers and/or suppliers, alert regulators with untrue information, cause internal discontent or lower employee morale, even inspire lawsuits. A prompt response is a brief but succinct email to all identified with copies to those the message would impact. The email should offer documentation through connections to existing information. Intercepting the electronic mischief in a timely way is critical. That's why good management assigns people to do this. (See Chapter 9.)

The way the crisis story is told is important too because it must be credible and acceptable. For that reason, public relations educator Robert L. Heath advocates using a narrative format while recognizing that the news media need the who, what, when, where, why and how. Heath says, "First, people need to recognize that crisis response entails the telling of a story—the enactment of a crisis narrative. The next consideration is the critical and strategic selection of the specific narrative account for and report on that event. . . ." It is essential that the story be truthful, that key publics are able to relate to the story and that the narrative demonstrates that the organization has control of the situation for a successful resolution to the story.[16]

After developing a plan for responding to a crisis and making people in the organization familiar with it, the next most important part of dealing with a crisis is designating the (that is, the *single*) most credible spokesperson. Some authorities say that choosing the spokesperson is the most important part of dealing with a crisis, because that person sets the style for handling the crisis. It may or may not be the CEO. Frequently the CEO is involved in making critical decisions to resolve the crisis if that responsibility has not been delegated to someone else. In any case, the person designated should be someone who is perceived by the organization's publics as knowledgeable and who is kept up-to-date on all developments.

The spokesperson must know all aspects of the crisis, must understand their implications and must have sole responsibility and authority for speaking in the name of the organization. The appropriate spokesperson may be different in different crises. When a university was dealing with a football scandal, the designated spokesperson was the coach. The same school, when faced with an academic crisis, used the academic vice-president. Each had been previously trained to deal with the news media. The spokesperson is usually a member of the crisis team and functions as your key contact for all media. If for some reason (probably time pressures) you decide to use a different spokesperson inside for employees than for the news media, you must be sure that the

two present exactly the same information. The only difference should be the inside slant that the spokesperson for employees gives. Using an inside slant does not mean presenting biased information; it means taking into consideration the special concerns of employees. You might also choose an inside person because that person has greater credibility with inside audiences. But the external spokesperson must be someone respected and highly credible to inside audiences as well, or you will damage the credibility of the inside person in the process. The spokesperson should not be an outsider, even if that outsider is a quasi-insider, such as a staff member from the public relations firm of record or from a law firm. Corporate response to the crisis is as important as the outcome.[17]

Employee and Management Roles in a Crisis

As "insiders," employees are the most trusted sources for information, more so than management, especially if the crisis involves management actions or inactions.

Employees' Critical Role   You must truly believe your employees are the front line in public relations to use them effectively in a crisis. They are the organization's most credible representatives to the people outside the organization with whom they come in contact; and when you think about it, those people constitute all the rest of your publics—from media to customers, from clients to suppliers. People will develop perceptions from the way employees respond to their questions and from their behavior. Unfortunately, most organizations in crises tend to neglect their employees. This not only mistreats personnel, but also harms the organization.

Employees get depressed during a crisis. They worry first about themselves and then about the organization (see Table 13.2). They become overly dependent on internal networks fed by rumors and on the news media. Employees should never first learn something about their organization from the news media unless it is something that has just occurred, such as a fire. "Employees may hold the key to the organization's ability to survive and then recover from life-threatening crises," according to two researchers who have looked at the stress that crises cause employees.[18]

Management's Behavior   In planning for crises, you need to be able to anticipate the communication

Table 13.2	**Employee Crisis Communication Model**

Employees personalize their organization's crisis, and, if their needs are not attended to through appropriate communications, their responses to external publics and their interactions with each other can impede the organization's recovery from the crisis.

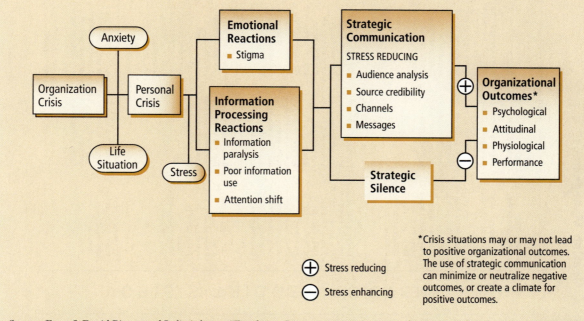

*Crisis situations may or may not lead to positive organizational outcomes. The use of strategic communication can minimize or neutralize negative outcomes, or create a climate for positive outcomes.

Source: From J. David Pincus and Lalit Acharya, "Employee Communication Strategies for Organizational Crises," *Employee Rights and Responsibilities Journal*, 1(3), 1988, p. 190. Reprinted by permission of Springer Science and Business Media.

climate by predicting how management is likely to act and react as the drama of a crisis unfolds. Relying on case studies and Hazel Henderson's pattern for typical management responses to problems, Bob Carrell developed some guidelines for anticipating management reactions in the three stages of crisis management: (1) prior to the crisis during normal day-to-day operations, (2) at the moment some event triggers the crisis, and (3) during the crisis situation that follows the event (see Table 13.3).[19]

Carrell acknowledged that the crisis management effort can be hampered by the following elements:

1. The extent of a crisis may not be known immediately.

2. Persons or audiences affected by a crisis may be difficult to identify.

3. The cause of a crisis may be difficult to identify, and its cause(s) may never be fully known.

4. A crisis is always traumatic to audiences affected directly by it.

5. Accurate and appropriate information about a crisis is an expectation—sometimes rising to unreasonable levels—of audiences, especially by those directly affected.

6. Information decisions are made under conditions of high stress.

7. Because the situation is a crisis, the credibility of the organization is suspect among audiences directly and indirectly affected by it.

8. A crisis incites emotional behavior by everyone related to it. Physical exhaustion also takes a toll on everyone involved.

Carrell also noted that the tendency of management toward an open or closed communication style, along with the corporate culture that the style creates, has a great deal to do with the way the organization responds both internally and externally.

One of the worse management behaviors in a crisis is not telling the truth or simply remaining silent. When an organization is in trouble, top

Table 13.3   Toward a Matrix of Crisis Communication Management

RESPONSIBLE MANAGEMENT BEHAVIOR	ONGOING			CRISIS-TRIGGERING EVENT → SITUATIONAL			
	Assessment of Environment	Development of Crisis Management/Communication Plan	Proaction	Activate Crisis Communication Plan	Arrest Triggering Event	Recovery	Evaluation
LEVEL 4 (++)*	• Prudent evaluation of all categories of potential crises • Evaluates risks • Considers, prepares strategies and plans to prevent, minimize impact of crisis • Management is optimistic, confident, open-minded and aggressive	• Identify management team • Assign specific duties • Designate one person only to convey information to internal and external audiences • Train spokesperson, other members of crisis team • Plan viewed as positive way of meeting private and public responsibilities • Plan reviewed and revised regularly	• Implements, within capacity to do so, policies and strategies to prevent or minimize impact of crisis • Lobbies for government/public support for changes in laws and regulations • Aggressive, proactive communication program to prepare audiences for crisis • Believes in principle of inoculation	• Spokesperson takes charge of communication function • Timely, consistent, candid information to internal and external audiences • Conveys information vital to public safety • Allays fears • Stifles rumors by supplying appropriate, factual information	• Inspires wholesome exchange of information with internal and external audiences • Seeks support as necessary • Makes adjustments in policies and strategies to arrest crisis	• Makes changes in policies and strategies to enhance recovery • Makes slight (if any) changes in organizational structure or personnel • Chances of recovery and turnaround are good	• Evaluates causes of recent crisis, responses to it, and outcomes • Reviews, revises crisis management/communication plan for future use in light of recent experience
LEVEL 3 (+)*	• Evaluates some potential crisis categories, ignores others, myopic • Control systems questionable • Wants to prevent/minimize potential crisis but not fully committed to doing everything they can • Management often complacent	• Communication function regarded as defensive necessity • Communicates only as much and as often as required by internal and external pressure • Does some training but not much follow-up to keep plan current	• Selective implementation of policies/strategies designed to prevent/minimize impact of crisis, but could do more • Sporadic participant in lobbying programs • Little, if any, commitment to communication program to educate, prepare audiences for crisis	• Posturing messages with little substance • Face-saving approach • Rumors and propaganda often go unchallenged or uncorrected • Group think creeps in • Grudgingly admits crisis but often denies culpability • Offers plausible excuses	• Exchanges only limited information with internal and external audiences • Fears ridicule • Makes policy and strategy changes only sufficient to arrest crisis, no more • Audiences view organization with skepticism	• May make changes in policies and strategies, but usually these are very few • May make some changes in personnel but organizational changes are rare • Chances of recovery and turnaround are fair	• May change crisis management/communication plan, but changes often not taken very seriously
LEVEL 2 (–)*	• Lip service to planning and preparation for crises • Management more concerned with sustaining power/status • Lacks sense of public responsibility	• Group think is common • Plan fully protectionist • Short-term solutions to long-term problems • Plan rarely reviewed and updated • Little or no training	• Does only what is demanded by law	• Often denies crisis exists • Rarely admits culpability • Places blame on others • Feelings of invulnerability are common	• Bunker mentality • Digs in and is often recalcitrant, inflexible • Communication channels are plugged up	• Reluctant to make changes in policies and strategies; changes usually made to conform to new public policies • In-fighting increases • Loss of confidence in leadership • Low morale • Loss of public confidence	• Existing plan remains unchanged • Rarely changes made in top management or in policies or strategies
LEVEL 1 (– –)*	• Unable or refuses to recognize potential crises • Can't or won't develop a crisis plan	• Crisis management/communication plan does not exist	• Grudgingly does what is demanded by law	• Self-postulating as victim of circumstances, incompetent personnel	• Ostrich syndrome • Admits nothing • Does no more than is absolutely necessary • Relies on short memory of audiences	• Searches for persons to be offered publicly as sacrificial lambs • Changes in policies and strategies are only those mandated by law • Chances for recovery are very poor	• Organization may collapse • Replacement of top and some middle management is probable • Restructuring is common

* (++) = Open; (+) = Mostly Open; (–) = Mostly Closed; (– –) = Closed

Source: Reprinted with permission of Bob Carrell.

"It's all according to your point of view. To me, you're a monster."

Recognizing different perspectives is critical in a crisis. Finding the right person in a public to deal with is almost as difficult as locating Nessie, who has appeared here to represent her view of who is the "monster."

From *Modern Maturity*, now called *AARP Magazine* 1995.

management has to offer a clear definition of the situation and take responsibility for coming up with recommendations for solutions. It doesn't hurt to ask the board for help, either.[20] Crisis counsel James E. Lukaszewski says, "Codes of silence are ethical impediments to the truth." He also says, "Overcoming codes of silence is often the critical element in achieving successful crisis management."[21] All of an organization's stakeholders need and deserve the truth. Furthermore, the tone of the immediate response to the crisis affects the reputation. A defensive response can be damaging to the organization's reputation, especially if its reputation already is weak or unfavorable.[22]

Crisis Constants Five communication elements that remain constant in any crisis help explain how people who do not directly experience the crisis will evaluate it. First, people learn about crises primarily from personal networks, if the situation is geographically close or if there is some relationship between the crisis and the network. An example would be an explosion in a nearby plant where employee networks carry the news to other employees faster than the mass media carry it. Second, people tend to interpret the seriousness of a crisis in terms of personal risk, or risk to people important to them. This perception may be based more on subjective than objective factors, so public and official perceptions of risk sometimes differ considerably. Third, government sources are relied on as the most authoritative. Fourth, the amount of mass media coverage indicates the significance of the

crisis to a global public. Fifth, the availability of information in an open-communication environment reduces rumor and increases the accuracy of others' assessments of the situation.

Any crisis involves many more entities than just the organization that is experiencing the damage and is most responsible for the remedy. Developing an image that suggests the organization is successfully handling the situation depends on two factors: the reality of the organization's being able to cope with the problem, and how well the organization communicates its successful handling of the problem to those who didn't experience the crisis. An organization's inability to cope with a crisis or the perception that it is bungling its efforts to cope can dramatically damage its credibility.

One thing to remember is that the major issue is not so much when a crisis disappears but how it leaves, which is the mark of success or failure. A corporate communications expert offers 10 guidelines. The first, again, is to take responsibility, and the second is to recognize the difference between bad publicity and a real crisis, and adjust your response accordingly. A third rule is to use research to determine how you are going to respond to both the facts of the situation and to what major publics are thinking about the situation, and a fourth rule is to recruit some credible third parties to speak on your behalf. A fifth rule is to treat the news media as conduits of information, not enemies, and the sixth rule is to assume you will be sued whatever you do, but openness may be a factor in your favor in litigation.

Seventh, watch the Internet as closely as you watch traditional news media to get some insight into how the situation is being perceived, and eighth, demonstrate empathy and concern. Rule nine is to take the first 24 hours very, very seriously because this is when the issues are framed and the company is judged by its response. The tenth rule is to begin building corporate assets in the area of public opinion—corporate reputation—right away because you will need to draw on these in a crisis.[23]

PR's Responsibility for a Crisis

When the advent of a crisis catches an organization unaware, this may bring criticism of public relations people. It is often seen as the PR person's responsibility to forewarn and prepare management. In some respects that's true. One invaluable contribution that PR makes is issue monitoring. (See Chapter 5.) Another significant factor is the PR person's continuous monitoring of publics, which should again offer an opportunity for PR to be a bellwether of potential problems. If crisis anticipation is to remain a recognized role for PR, ignorance cannot be a good excuse. But even when warnings are given, PR does not run an organization; it is only a part of the management team.

It is the PR person's responsibility to convince management to act. Often when you wonder where the PR person was when a crisis escalated, it's a sign the PR person probably lost an internal battle. A way to avoid that, according to crisis specialist James E. Lukazewski, is to approach your discussion from a management perspective.[24] Discuss management objectives and the impact of the crisis situation on all the publics, instead of dwelling on the news media. Talk about the organization's mission statement, its reputation, its objectives and its business strategy. Take management through a comparison of peer companies in similar situations and help management see opportunities in the crisis instead of just negatives.

Your job is public relations, and your responsibility in a crisis is to give the rest of the management team insight and information they don't have because of their backgrounds and training. When you present it in terms they understand and are comfortable with, you'll be more likely to persuade them to make some decisions you can communicate so that everyone in the organization is speaking with one voice and has focused on the issue and an appropriate response to it.

When an organization fails to respond to a crisis in the making, it's often due to management's reaction to predictions or forewarnings. At least one response that usually causes trouble is arrogance. Arrogance leads to making some assumptions about the vulnerability of the company or the significance of the perceived problem. Ignoring nimbus publics is another difficulty that arises from arrogance, a feeling that some publics are just not important enough for consideration.

Another management mistake that causes trouble is the failure to get objective information from all publics that might be involved in a potential problem. Just asking a few people in a public won't work. If there is a potential problem, all the publics involved need to be targets of good information gathering and listening. When a public has some misinformation that is causing the problem, a crisis might be averted by correcting misperceptions or misunderstandings before something erupts. This is often the case with employee relations issues, supplier problems or customer complaints.

Yet another cause for crises going undetected before they really develop is using bad judgment. An example of bad judgment that may be lethal is failing to alert employees to problems or potential problems. Even if employees can't be completely taken into confidence, they need to know enough to be helpful. One thing this accomplishes is making employees, especially line managers, aware of the public relations impact of events, actions and issues. They are then more likely to alert PR staff to potential or developing problems. They may become willing collaborators, because any crisis is seen as their crisis too. This kind of involvement also ensures their support and cooperation when the unpredictable crisis does occur. They are even better equipped to anticipate and make decisions on their own that will be useful in responding to the crisis at their level.

Getting employees involved and alerting them to issues is quite useful because they have information the management team may not even know exists. A case in point. When the jury began its decision-making on Arthur Andersen LLP's culpability in the Enron case, they ignored issues raised by the prosecution, such as the shredding of significant documents, and focused on one email sent by Andersen attorney Nancy Temple that read, in part, "I suggested deleting some language that might suggest we have concluded the release is misleading."[25] Internal documents can not only be legally damaging, but also reflect badly on the company.

An inability to convince management to act immediately and responsibly is at the crux of the 1989 *Exxon-Valdez* case that remains a topic of the "wrong way" to handle a crisis to this day. When the supertanker *Exxon Valdez* ran aground on Bligh Reef in Prince William Sound off Alaska, many people in the oil industry said among themselves, "Thank goodness it happened to Exxon." It wasn't that they wished the company ill, and certainly no one was pleased about the accident, which promised to draw renewed scrutiny to past oil spills and the question of whether the industry's current safety measures were adequate. What the industry people had in mind was that Exxon had enough staff and crisis "know-how" to handle the spill swiftly and professionally. Such assumptions turned out to be unsound. The reaction of Exxon's chairman of the board, Lawrence G. Rawl, was to remain silent for two days and to stay in New York. Exxon president William Stevens later conceded that some of what he and other company executives considered one-sided reporting of the accident was partly the organization's fault. Stevens said that the coverage from the reporters onsite was well-balanced and fair.[26] When Rawl died in 2005, although he had done many laudable things in his life, this event was part of his obituary, not officially, but added by newswriters.

Responding Internally and Externally in Crises

Every crisis produces an initial management consultation that occurs face-to-face, by telephone conference call or through a satellite teleconference. It is important to keep comprehensive notes of this meeting. After the meeting, you should write a response release, clearing it first with top management and the organization's attorney. You need a recorded actuality simultaneously with the spokesperson's statement. Depending on the status of the crisis, you may need to call a news conference. If so, you must prepare a list of points you want to make; and of course, you must be prepared for the reporters' questions (see Chapter 11).

As news develops, you will issue bulletins to keep all publics informed. Some of these may be put on an electronic system, such as a Web site or email. Others will be written news briefs or taped actualities. All will quote the spokesperson.

Web sites help in managing requests for information. The media can get updated quickly with information and digitized images. Interested publics also have access to this information that can be put on the usual Web site or on an activated dark site linked to the home page. Employees have access to that information as well as special information that can be put on their intranet.

Often the telephone must be used, too. It may be necessary to get an 800 number with a recorded message that is updated as necessary, as well as a way for callers to get to an operator if necessary.

Constraints of the crisis situation will keep you from communicating as freely as you would like, but all responders must understand that responses should never be misleading or deceptive in any way. Most of the demands will be from the news media, especially broadcasters because they need live coverage. PR practitioners encounter a number of difficulties when working with mass media to communicate the reality of a crisis. One is the inclination of reporters to be more interested in the rare and unusual, especially in communicating risk. For example, a volcanic eruption, which is sudden and dramatic, may get more attention than dangerous water pollution, awareness of which often develops slowly and undramatically. In the latter instance, it may be difficult even to get access to communication channels.

As demonstrated dramatically by the 9/11 crisis and in 2005 by the London train and subway bombings, both of which provided dramatic evidence of the difficulty of using traditional channels of communication, communication channels are usually disrupted by crises. The disruption may be mechanical (especially if the crisis is a natural disaster), or it may result from demands that the crisis makes on personnel who ordinarily would be taking care of the communication functions. In either case, extra efforts have to be made by the organization to get information to mass media.

Media representatives usually seek authoritative information about a crisis, primarily from government sources. When a crisis occurs, though, people in positions of authority are generally absorbed in helping solve the crisis. Therefore, they seldom see the value of setting aside time to communicate information about the crisis. In addition, those involved in solving the crisis may be a mix of government and nongovernment personnel, such as in a natural disaster or terrorist act, when law enforcement, fire and safety groups work with others from the government. These may also interact with nonprofit relief groups such as the Red Cross. All must work with the organization at the center of the crisis, which may be a privately owned business.

Global Perspective

A network of activists, with one very active stimulant, is using the Internet to deal Coca-Cola some grief in India, an important market for the company, and one with a troubled history. Coke was popular in India until 1977, when a new government demanded that it turn over its formula and dilute its ownership stake in its India unit. A change in 1993 brought the company back in as the government tried to attract foreign investment.

The problem now is that the company is being accused by U.S.-born Amit Srivastava, who lives in northern California and is the single employee of his activist group, of doing extensive environmental damage in India. The son of a management professor in India, Srivastava dropped out of Southern Illinois University to devote his energy to activism. He has aroused NGOs to his cause so that now there is an ongoing global campaign, one that has cost Coke millions of dollars in legal fees and lost sales in India.

Srivastava used to work for Corp Watch, a nonprofit corporate watchdog based in Oakland, and in 2002 posted an article on its Web site about Coke's overuse of ground water in India drying up wells used by citizens. In 2003 Corp Watch lost funding and Srivastava lost his job, so he began his own company, bringing Corp Watch India with him, and called the new company Global Resistance. Global Resistance is a very small company. Srivastava is the only full-time employee, keeping his office in a home that he shares with friends in California. However, there is a part-time Web site editor located in New Delhi who helps to maintain his ties with India. His Web site is a resource for all the NGOs in India and elsewhere, and he gets funding from several private foundations. The company's budget last year was $60,000. His Web site, www.indiaresource.org, gets about 20,000 hits a month versus Coke's counter site, www.cokefacts.org, which draws only about 800 a month.

Srivastava compares what Coke is doing in India to the Bhopal disaster. One issue is Coke's discontinued practice of giving away waste that had toxic materials to farmers. One NGO has succeeded in getting a court order in Rajasthan requiring pesticide residues to be listed on its labels. The company is resisting, saying the levels are safe. In Kerala, activists claimed that it drained and polluted the local water supply and had the $16 million bottling plant there shut down in 2004. Coke is trying to get the plant reopened and that case is in India's Supreme Court.

In Varanasi, a local water official blamed the Coke plant for polluting ground water by releasing wastewater into surrounding ground. Coke's response to the Varanasi situation is that drainage had been a problem there until the company built a pipeline. And it said the problem with the water supply in Kerala was a drought, and a court there agreed, saying water tends to dry up in the summer, according to a study it ordered. But the court said that although Coke had aggravated the situation, the major factor was a lack of rainfall. The NGO's response is that Coke shouldn't have sites where water is scarce at any time during the year.

Coke's Asia communication director, David Cox, based in Hong Kong, has spent months in India trying to respond to the NGO's allegations. The lack of success prompted Mary Minnick, former president of Coke's Asia Division and now head of global marketing, innovation and strategy, to say in a conference call with analysts in April 2005 that the company was "still feeling the residual effects of the unfounded pesticide scare in 2003."

The turmoil continued in India for Coke and Pepsi when in 2006 studies of pesticides in the beverages by the Centre for Science and Environment (CSE) were released to the news media. The India Soft Drink Manufacturer's Association responded for Coke and Pepsi by sending out a news release challenging the validity of the CSE study. When Coke responded with its own study that said their beverages were safe, public outcry resulted because the two scientists involved in the study had been working for Coca-Cola at the UK-based independent laboratory, Central Science Laboratories (CSL)

Global Perspective (continued)

for years. The media flurry and public response was such that the central government put together a panel to study the issue, but in the meantime, the beverages had been banned in educational and government institutions as well as hospitals, influenced by state political parties opposing the national government. The issue involved corporate, government and nongovernmental groups who played out their various agencies in the public forum of the news media. At least the public got informed of the issues. (See Chapter 2 for more on this situation.)

Sources: Steve Stecklow, "Virtual Battle: How a Global Web of Activists Gives Coke Problems in India," *The Wall Street Journal*, June 7, 2005, p. A1, 6. Reprinted with permission.

Although each group involved may have its own traditional methods of dealing with the news media as a single organization, they are less effective in responding to media inquiries when forced to do so as a loosely organized unit brought together by the crisis. Lines of authority are blurred, and some of the personnel may be out of their usual geographic boundaries. Beyond that, even the best-prepared organizations—and there aren't many of those—can seldom cope with the demands of the news media for information once the media have been attracted to the crisis. The more experienced an organization is with handling crises, the better the response will be (see Figure 13.3 and the Theory and Research Perspective box on page 336.

Another problem is the tendency to close down the normal communication channels discussed earlier in this chapter. Often the crisis is such a threat to an organization that either the organization itself or others with control over it, such as the government, severely limit information about the crisis.

Even in the best of circumstances, a crisis generates contradictory information. So much occurs at the same time, and so many people have different pieces of information, that it is difficult to present a clear picture. The situation is even more complicated if the crisis is the result of an adversarial action such as a hostile takeover. In an adversarial situation, the crisis is complicated by counter rhetoric that also helps to shape the reality for all publics. In such situations, the most credible source often wins the battle for public opinion.

Sometimes a crisis situation turns around for a while but then resurfaces because of an accident, investigative reporting or legal action. Some crises continue for years, so you need to plan for short- and long-term crisis management. The key is to maintain credibility.[27]

Credibility is always at stake. Public perception of an organization's honesty and openness in the beginning is essential. Observations in news reports that someone was unavailable or refused to comment erode confidence quickly. Failure of an organization to be prepared is also an issue. This is not easily forgiven in most cases in which there was opportunity to discover the problem. Even in sudden and unpredictable situations, though, a company can still look bad. A good example is when cities fail to warn residents of impending natural disasters such as storms. Not anticipating such acts of nature and failing to prepare for them cause a loss of confidence and credibility. Responses from a company or organization that seem self-centered and devoid of sympathy for victims are among the most serious mistakes. How to find the proper emotion in a response to a given situation or crisis has been studied by academician and researcher W. Timothy Coombs, who developed a typology of responses. His guidelines are useful because he examines the crisis, considers the management-response strategy and looks at the various factors that influence the type of response, such as whether the organization is truly at fault or if there is a misunderstanding.[28]

A model of mass media behavior in a crisis has been developed by Joseph Scanlon and Suzanne Alldred of the Emergency Communications Research Unit, Carleton University, Ottawa, Canada. Drawing on their research and experience, they have concluded that reporters respond to hearing of a crisis by trying to get information by "whatever ingenious

Figure 13.3 Crisis PR: Media Headquarters in Emergencies

Your operation must contain two specific areas that serve as a central clearing point for reporters and company PR personnel in a serious emergency. These areas should be equipped with several telephones and with someplace for the people to sit and write.

If the emergency is centered in the area of one of the headquarters, the alternate location should be used. Additionally, company employees should be informed of this fact so that they are able to direct reporters to the area from which news will be forthcoming.

At least two secretaries should be made available to the staff member handling public relations if the emergency takes place during working hours, because there will be times when this individual will, by necessity, be away from news headquarters.

If no news headquarters needs to be established, all calls from news media should be directed to one or two designated lines. While the PR person is out assessing the situation, names and phone numbers of callers should be taken.

Handling PR in an Emergency

1. Need for establishing the news headquarters will be determined by the PR person. News headquarters will keep all visitors to the site under control and out of the way of any emergency work being done. Also, having a news service indicates the company's desire to be cooperative. The size of the emergency will determine whether there is a need for a headquarters.

2. The person handling public relations will maintain contact with reporters, making sure they stay in approved locations while on plant property, and provide as quickly as possible all information determined to be in the company's best interests.

3. The person handling public relations will check with a designated representative of management on the text of announcements and help formulate answers to questions.

4. The person handling public relations will be responsible for guiding reporters into the disaster area, if company management will permit such a visit.

5. The fundamental responsibility for which facts are to be given to the press and ultimately to the public must remain with top management. It is the responsibility of the person handling public relations to operate with the approval of top management.

6. Maintain close contact with members of media. More often than not they will be able to tell you things you don't already know. This is a great way to stem the flow of false information.

7. Keep a log of all facts given out, with times they were released. This avoids duplication and conflicting reports, if new developments should change facts.

8. Do not release the names of victims until you know for a fact that the families involved have been notified. Tell the reporters that the name of the victim will be made available as soon as the next of kin has been told of the mishap.

9. When it is necessary to admit a fact already known to the press, be sure confirmation is limited only to definite information that will not change. If firefighters carry a victim from the plant in a body bag and the reporter sees it, say only that one body has been recovered. DO NOT SAY that you "don't know how many are dead." Never speculate as to the cause of accidents, amount of damage, responsibility, possible downtime, delays in shipments, layoffs and so on.

In other words, say no more than to confirm what is already known, and yet give the reporters the impression the company will give all the assistance it possibly can. As facts that won't be harmful become known, clear them and give them to news media people.

Questions to Look for in Emergencies

What Reporters Can Get from Other Sources if Forced To

1. Number of deaths
2. Number of injuries
3. Damage (fire chief will give estimate in dollars; give yours in general terms of what was destroyed as soon as known)
4. What burned and/or collapsed
5. Time
6. Location within plant (paint locker, press room, etc.)
7. Names of dead and injured, following notification of relatives
8. Their addresses, ages and how long with company, as well as occupation
9. How many people employed; what activities

(continued)

Figure 13.3   Crisis PR: Media Headquarters in Emergencies (continued)

Facts Desired but Not Necessarily Desirable to Give

1. Speculation about anything
2. Any delivery delays or such (accentuate positive as soon as course is sure)
3. How caused (let city officials release this; chances are story will die before report is completed)
4. Specific damage estimate as well as what was destroyed (this information might be extremely valuable to competitors)

Dealing with the Media During Emergencies

In meetings with the press at the scene of emergencies, several things should be remembered. Basic is the fact that the public is represented by the press, and this medium has a recognized right to information that may vitally concern the community, employees, their friends and families and the victims. It is also common knowledge that the best way to prevent the spread of false rumors and misinformation is through issuance of factual information. At the same time, the company must guard its own interests and insist on relaying factual information only in an orderly, controlled manner.

Remember

1. Speed in reply to a query is all-important. All reporters have deadlines to meet.
2. Keep cool. If reporters get snappy, chances are it's because they are under considerably more pressure at the moment than you. Try to cooperate to the extent possible.
3. If you don't know the answer, attempt to get it for the reporters.
4. Eliminate obstacles wherever possible. Most reporters agree that the more obstacles they find in their way, the harder they will work to ferret out the real story—from any source possible. They will almost always use something they have uncovered, and you have no control over what they might uncover.
5. Never ask to see a reporter's story. Time is usually a factor. If you feel the reporter may be misinformed, check back with him or her on the point to make sure.

6. There's seldom a reason you should not be quoted by name. As a member of the management team and one charged with public relations, you are speaking for the company.
7. Never argue with a reporter about the value of a story.
8. Any information that goes to one source in the emergency is fair game to all. Don't play favorites. They listen to and read each other's copy anyway.
9. Never flatly refuse information. Always give a good reason why it isn't available. Be sure facts are, indeed, factual.
10. Always know to whom you are talking. Get the reporter's name and phone number in case you need to contact him or her later.
11. Never give an answer that you feel might not stand up. It can embarrass you later.
12. Never falsify, color or slant your answers. A reporter is trained to see a curve ball coming a mile away and has fielded them before. If a reporter thinks you are pitching one, he or she will remember it a long time and tell colleagues and other members of the news media over coffee. This will also set him or her off quicker than getting no information at all.
13. Be especially alert about photographs. You have no control of photos taken off company property, but you have every right to control photos taken within the plant. Consider the possibility of pool photos and film/video where it is impractical to have several photographers on the scene at once. Remember, photos can be as harmful as words.
14. Be sure no time lag comes into play between the time you get information that can be put out and the time it is actually given to news media people.
15. Have safety, labor and employee records available for your reference if possible.
16. Be quick to point up long safety records and any acts of heroism by employees.
17. If damage must be estimated for the press immediately, confine statements to general descriptions of what was destroyed.
18. Always accentuate the positive. If your public relations is good, so are your chances of receiving an even break.

or technical means are available, and use their background files to fill in the gaps."[29] In making the point that editors assign people so that the breaking story receives continuous coverage, to ensure that information is released as soon as it is gathered, Scanlon and Alldred note that the coverage consists of periods of high drama followed by lulls. Reporters often share information and attempt to fit it into a deadline-driven framework. Trends for coverage, the researchers say, are set by the prestige media, but, while the national and international media cover the story only at its height, the local news media stay with it all the way through to resolution of the situation. The role of the public relations person is important (1) in conducting the delicate negotiations that have to go on between source and media about what to use and what not to use; (2) in providing enough opportunities, such as news conferences, for information to be given to the media; and (3) in educating as well as informing so that reporters don't fall back on stereotyping to explain the incident itself or the people involved in it.[30]

When media are involved in direct coverage of a crisis, some slanting is expected due to the factors mentioned such as timeliness, deadlines and competition. Bias is likely to enter the reporting of crises in any case, something to keep in mind if your company is a multinational one. The bias is likely to represent the political-economic position of the reporter's country. In cases of religious states, tenets of the faith may also become an important factor. The amount of attention paid to a crisis and the approach to the story are both influenced by such bias.

So, what happens when the media get it wrong?

Talking Back in a Crisis

Organizations used to take their lumps in the news media silently when negative publicity occurred, especially if they had tried to be open and cooperative and the policy had backfired.

Hostility levels between business and the news media go up and down, and the PR person usually tries to ride the tide without drowning. Organization officers often admit that they rely on their PR person to handle all contact with the news media because their rage wouldn't permit civility. Of course, when PR people get along well with news media representatives—as they must—their internal loyalty sometimes becomes suspect. Nevertheless, the

---

Theory and Research Perspective

Richard Hyde set up four criteria for messages in 1980 when he was handing the leak at the Three Mile Island nuclear plant: "1. Tell it all, tell it fast and tell it accurately; 2. Make provisions for information sources to speak from a common platform at the same time; 3. Cover all the bases on all important subjects; 4. Provide regular updates to all important internal and external publics."

Mapping those messages is a concept developed for New York City's Center for Risk Communication by Vincent T. Covello, who says the exercise involves a team of experts (scientific) on the subject, and another team that includes communications specialists and people with both legal and management expertise. In a paper for the World Health Organization's conference on bioterrorism and risk communication in 2002, Covello listed seven duties for the teams, recognizing that the two teams may have different approaches to the problem that would have to be reconciled: "1. Identify stakeholders; 2. Determine specific concerns for each group of stakeholders; 3. Analyze specific concerns to find underlying general concerns; 4. Conduct structured brainstorming with input from message mapping teams; 5. Assemble supporting facts and proof for each key message; 6. Ask outside experts to systematically test messages; 7. Plan delivery of resulting messages and supporting materials." The outcome, Hyde says, should be that all message maps adhere to three standard requirements: "1. Three key messages; 2. Seven to 12 words per message; 3. Three supporting facts for each key message." These can be combined, sometimes, in a single sentence. One illustration that Hyde offers is a single sentence of 27 words.

Source: Richard C. Hyde, "In Crisis Management, Getting the Message Right Is Critical: Considerations for Effectively Handling a Crisis Today," *The Public Relations Society of America*, New York: The Strategist, Summer 2007, pp. 32–35.

advice PR people gave for years to irate CEOs who wanted to talk back (or worse) to the news media was "let me handle them." And they handled them with kid gloves.[31] However, the public relations stance is different now and more companies are talking back. The difficulty is that, as more aggressive action is taken, public credibility is severely strained.

Legal counsel often is on the side of aggressive action. Lawyers also don't want anyone to apologize in a crisis that involves payment of damages. MIT (Massachusetts Institute of Technology) did issue a public apology in the hazing death of an undergraduate student. The mother also got a hug as she was given the $6 million dollar check MIT paid to settle the negligence suit. Lawyers and insurance carriers fear that any soothing words are likely to cause them problems in defending the organization.

Apologies and/or expressions of regret, however, give a human face to the organization and occasionally soften demands. Remember the case probably will go to court anyway, and trials are open to the public. Angry, abused people may and will say anything if they feel they've been ill-treated or discounted.

Perception is also an issue now that crises are instantly global.[32] The impression of witnessing crises firsthand through the media is simply a perception drawn from what the media choose to show or are able to show. People act on those perceptions—sending aid to crisis sites with sympathetic appeals or avoiding areas that appear to be dangerous due to natural or political crises.

In addition to problems of perception versus reality that instantaneous coverage creates, "crisis while it happens" coverage raises credibility problems because, in any breaking news situation, information is sketchy and conflicting. When the information is released without benefit of editing (which involves checking), it places a heavy burden of responsibility on the news staff providing the coverage.

When the crisis involves confidentiality, the difficulty of getting accurate information to the public through the news media is increased. The role of the public relations spokesperson becomes more crucial, and the spokesperson is often subjected to intense media criticism. The military spokespeople who handled briefings during the Persian Gulf crisis were subjected to intense grilling. And even though the media had unprecedented access to the field in the 2003 Iraqi war because of the military's authorization of "embedded" reporters, there was criticism of the U.S. command's control over media briefings. But despite government censorship and controls, the instantaneous coverage

that is transmitted globally has circumvented the traditional editing process, and editing now is left to reporters who often don't have the luxury of time to check and confirm their information.

Instant coverage has always been a source of difficulty in terrorist attacks, which, because of mounting problems in the Middle East, have been elevated there to the level of constant risk from the lower level of isolated incidents. There is some evidence that the news media, like witnesses, are less likely than government sources to use sensationalist, judgmental or inflammatory words in describing acts of terrorism, although they do often use inflammatory characterizations of the perpetrators of terrorism.[33] Presumably the political nature of government sources influences them to characterize terrorism as political violence. When an organization (whether a nonprofit group or a company) is the victim of terrorism, especially in the case of hostage-taking, witnesses should be made available to the news media, when possible, because they have credibility and are less likely than government sources to use inflammatory words. It is also important to try to control the tendency of news media (and often of government officials) to use the victims of terrorism as symbols.[34] For example, if the hostage is depicted as representing the USA or American citizens, the hostage's value to a terrorist who is acting out a protest against the USA or its policies increases. The same could be said for employees of financial institutions, taken hostage to protest economic disparities.

There is a fine line between keeping a hostage from becoming a valuable symbol and projecting an uncaring attitude about the person's fate. The role of the public relations spokesperson in working with the news media in this situation is critical. The media's contribution in a crisis as interpreters and educators could be enhanced in many instances if media personnel were dealing with adequately prepared and trained public relations spokespeople who could supply accurate background information.

Some of the most serious issues that occur in reporting global crises arise from a conflict of opinion about the function, role and responsibility of the mass media. In some countries, news media are privately owned and function with few government restraints. In other countries, news media are under considerable government regulation and supervision. There are differences in government oversight among the media, with broadcast media being the most highly regulated, even in the USA. Media roles are interpreted differently, too, with some countries seeing them as

Reprinted by permission of United Feature Syndicate.

representative spokespersons for the country. Even more controversial is the view of media "responsibility," which varies individually among journalists as well as collectively among media organizations, and is closely tied to values.

The way news media representatives interpret the function, role and responsibility of the news media affects how they report a crisis, how they interact with news sources in a crisis and how their media offices present information from reporters to their audiences. Regardless of where these media are situated, technology has made their reports potentially accessible to audiences all over the world. Accounts of crises are evaluated for the timeliness and usefulness of the information they contain. That information is the result of cooperation between the news media and the spokespersons for the organization in crisis.

When the organization sees news media coverage as a threat and withholds information or makes it difficult for news media to obtain information, reports of the crisis are much more distorted and the organization's perceived ability to cope with the crisis is much reduced. Fear that disclosure will damage an organization's image virtually ensures that the crisis will be reported in greater depth, over a longer period of time and with added sensationalism, because media will turn to outside sources that often deliver speculation and rumor rather than facts.

Increasingly, electronic bulletin boards, which have no editors and are global with little regulation, are being used as a source of information (with impact) and rumor.

Reacting to Special Crisis Situations: Rumors, Recalls, Whistleblowers, Takeovers and Litigation Journalism/PR

Rumors can start anywhere. If an organization is involved in a long-term crisis, rumor control headquarters must be set up and staffed. In the absence of fact, there will be fabrication. Because rumors feed on anxiety, emotional topics such as threats to physical or emotional well-being are always an integral part of them. And the people most distressed by the "news" are the ones most likely to pass it on. The following advice on handling rumors comes from communications specialist Walter St. John.[35] First, try to avoid situations like these, which encourage rumors to grow:

1. Authentic and official information and news are lacking.
2. Authentic information is incomplete.
3. Situations are loaded with anxiety and fear.
4. Doubts exist because of the existence of erroneous information.
5. People's ego needs are not being met (satisfaction from possessing the "inside dope").
6. Prolonged decision-making delays occur on important matters.
7. Personnel feel they can't control conditions or their fate.
8. Serious organizational problems exist.
9. Organizational conflict and personal antagonism are excessive.

The following strategies should be used to combat rumors:

1. Analyze the scope and seriousness of the nature and impact of the rumor before planning and engaging in any active correction.
2. Analyze the specific causes, motives, sources and disseminators of the rumors.
3. Confer with persons affected by or being damaged by rumors. Level with them and assure them

of your concern and of your sincere attempts to combat the rumors effectively.

4. Immediately (and massively, if it appears advisable) supply complete and authentic information regarding the matter.

5. Feed the grapevine yourself with counter rumors placed by trusted colleagues and confidants.

6. Call the key status and informal leaders, opinion molders and other influential people together to discuss and clarify the situation and to solicit their support and assistance.

7. Avoid referring to the rumor in disseminating the truth. You don't want to reinforce the rumor itself, unless it already is in wide circulation. In that case you must go public so that those passing on the rumor will be discredited.

8. Conduct meetings with the staff and others at the grassroots level to dispel the rumors, if necessary.

Once rumors begin to travel, they spread with considerable speed, and it is extremely difficult to stop them. The best way to combat rumors is preventively—restricting the need for them in the first place by keeping people promptly and accurately informed and by maintaining good two-way communication. But when rumors start, you need to act immediately to control them.[36]

Almost immediately after the 9/11 attacks, rumors were proliferating on the Internet, and some of them were hoaxes perpetrated by people trying to profit from the tragedy. For example, a spam email campaign with a bogus cause tried to attract contributions. The American Red Cross sent a news release directing email recipients to its official Web site or online partners. The release warned about spam and said the organization would work with officials to prosecute offenders and ensure that only legitimate causes were promoted.[37] The leading global investment bank, Bear Stearns, in 2008 blamed rumors for creating a crisis of confidence about the liquidity of its assets and its ability to do business. The floundering bank was bought by JPMorgan.

Sometimes a rumor starts from rogue Web sites. Some decisions have to be made about responding. Engaging the operator of the Web site might not only be ineffective and a waste of time, but what you say could be distorted and used against you. The complaints need to be examined, though, for any possible truth and then addressed on your Web site in an interactive way. If the site is something

that infringes on your name, it can be shut down under the Uniform Domain-Name Dispute Resolution Process (UDRP), which comes from the Internet's managing authority, Internet Corporation for Assigned Names and Numbers (ICANN). Filing a complaint does cost money but could be worth it. See www.icann.org/udrp/udrp-rules-24oct99.htm for more information.[38]

Sometimes the cost of refuting rumors can be high. Procter & Gamble was the victim of chain emails that said its product Febreze would poison a pet. The company got 1,500 emails and calls a day during one month, and total contacts of more than 25,000. The company spent $100,000 in a targeted letter campaign to stop the rumor.[39]

Rumors also can almost cause recalls, as Pepsi-Cola learned when a syringe was reportedly found in a can of Diet Pepsi. Specialists in the company at every part of the process cleared up the rumor immediately, and Pepsi brought the public into the plant with video news releases. The crisis lasted only four days because of the swift response and Pepsi's focus on tampering as the only possible excuse behind the rumor.[40]

Recalls can be a response to tampering, as in the case of Tylenol, or a product problem, as in the case of Bridgestone/Firestone. The legal battle between the tire company and Ford, first to recall Firestone tires, severed the relationship between the two and damaged credibility and consumer confidence. Although Tylenol's recall is a classic case of good public relations, Firestone didn't come off so well and found itself not only the subject of editorial cartoons, but also appeared in a negative light in the comics. You know your reputation is in trouble when that occurs. Determining when to recall a product can be difficult, and you might be too hasty, as Merck has considered in its recall and temporary taking of Vioxx off the market. The call on a whistleblower case can be difficult too.

Deciding on the right thing to do in a whistleblower case starts with determining the validity of the accuser and the accusations. A whistleblower usually is an insider with access to information that is being withheld. The whistleblower knows that if this information is made public, it could damage an organization's reputation, precipitate litigation or regulatory action or require costly changes in a product.

The term *whistleblower* often invites memories of the Karen Silkwood case that resulted in a book and a film. Normally whistleblowers are legally challenged by the company, not physically attacked. However, that is risky, too, because whistleblowers have high credibility because of their inside information.

An organization's first job is to ask for the whistleblower's evidence and determine whether the accusation is real or contrived. Because the whistleblower generally is known by the company, there is often an initial reaction to that person's credibility based on her or his reputation. When a person with a solid work reputation goes public, or, as is often the case, threatens to go public with some information, wise management investigates the accusation and fixes it.

The best companies avoid the whole issue by inviting and rewarding employees who find flaws and suggest repairs. Now, as a result of the Sarbanes-Oxley law, whistleblowers have a direct line to corporate boards of directors, so management has to discuss the issue with the board (see Chapter 8). What often happens, though, is that an unhappy employee goes public with some information, either by reporting a complaint to a regulator or by going directly to the news media, sometimes going to the Internet first. That is what provokes a crisis. Whatever the organization does looks defensive. If it tries to counter the information, it has to avoid attacking the individual, not only for legal reasons but because it looks like a giant crushing an ant trying to carry food to the colony. The best defense, the only defense, is the truth. Unfortunately that often takes some time to determine. From a public relations standpoint, the best initial response is to acknowledge the information without any judgment and report back as soon as possible with the facts. Failure to investigate the accusation and report the findings will damage credibility. Public opinion is likely to be based on the axiom, "Where there's smoke, there's fire."

Mergers and acquisitions often get talked about as though they are the same. That's not the case. Mergers are when two organizations decide to become one, and there is some determination, beyond the financial arrangements, of the union's structure. Sometimes the names are hyphenated, at least initially, to preserve identity and signify balance. The boards are balanced with representatives for each entity, and decisions are made about management before agreements are signed. Because of all that is involved to provide such balance, it is no wonder that mergers often fail before being completed. Acquisitions are another matter. One company is buying another. Usually it is a larger company buying a smaller one, the AOL–Time Warner situation being something of a surprise. The acquirer holds more power, although usually every effort is made to retain key employees because that is part of the value of any purchase. The problem with both of these situations, though, is that the process invites unwanted entry of an outside company in the form of a hostile takeover. The crisis begins.

To manage the crisis, a message statement has to be crafted that is clear and understandable, no matter how complex the situation. Telling someone that the issue is "complicated" makes eyes glaze over and suspicions surface. What you can be sure of is vilification, accusations, rumors, wildly inaccurate stories in the media (including, and maybe particularly, on the Internet) and lawsuits of all sorts.

The risk in dealing with takeovers is that people will resort to name-calling, waste energy on anger and fall for false issues that seemingly need to be addressed. Expending your organization's energy and resources is part of a takeover strategy. Keep on the message, stay positive and be open, assertive and aggressive. Be honest and timely in responses. Sometimes getting the attorneys to agree to let you do that may be your first battle, although more and more they are seeing the wisdom in hiring outside PR counsel in such battles because there is too much pressure on the inside PR staff who must manage day-to-day business to keep confidence in the organization's ability to handle the situation.

Lawyers are using public relations tactics themselves, and what was first called litigation journalism is now often called litigation/PR. What occurs is that attorneys try their cases in the court of public opinion before they get to trial. That is not a crisis unless you have a court case with some strong human interest elements that can be exploited before the trial. As an organization you may be hamstrung legally to respond if it is an individual suing. There will be misrepresentation of your position, unquestionably, and facts in your defense suppressed. Remember this is prosecution and you are the defendant. The way you defend your position without attacking an individual is key to handling this crisis. Incidentally, avoiding this public display is the reason many cases are settled out of court, even if the company is certain it has done nothing wrong. It saves money for continued litigation, and saves the company's reputation from continued exposure to the accusations. (See Chapter 8.)

Crises are evaluated in terms of the damage done or the risk of future damage. Evaluations not based on experience are based entirely on communication, and even people involved in a crisis rely heavily on communication in interpreting the crisis. Because many people depend on the mass media for information, those attempting to handle the crisis must try to get the most accurate information to the news media. This must be done not only to quiet rumors that exaggerate the situation and later damage credibility, but also to instill confidence in priority publics regarding the organization's ability to manage the crisis.

Recovery and Evaluation

For help in recovering from a crisis, the late Bob Carrell, professor emeritus of advertising at the University of Oklahoma, suggested looking again at the first phase in his matrix of crisis communication management—a phase before the crisis event occurs. He made these recommendations for getting a crisis under control:

1. Determine the cause(s) of the crisis. It is important to undercut rumors and speculation that may have been rampant.

2. Decide which strategies and policies can be developed that will prevent similar or related crises. Direct experience with a crisis, although painful, teaches more than even the best scenario ever could. A crisis is the most severe test of existing strategies and policies.

3. Ask whether the crisis plan itself worked and whether changes should be made to it.

4. Evaluate the performance of all personnel in the crisis situation. Any failures in the crisis plan may have been caused by faulty provisions in the plan or by poor execution.

Figuring out a good way to apologize for creating a crisis and selecting good timing for the apology are other aspects of recovery. Exxon's apology was more too late than too little. Firestone didn't apologize. American Airlines didn't waste any time before apologizing for a ground crew's decision to order a change of pillows after a gay-rights group left one of its airplanes, and it probably saved itself some difficulties. When Martha Stewart was sent to jail for perjury (not insider trading, but lying about it), she served her term as soon as she could and not only helped restore her own credibility but also got some positive publicity from her time in jail. Certainly it didn't hurt her, because she got a new television show when she got out, and her companies were helped too.[41]

Whatever the strategy a company decides on, it needs to have the following outcomes to be considered a success in crisis handling, according to two management theorists: early detection, incident containment, business resumption, lessons learned/policies implemented, improved reputation as a result of appropriate response, stakeholder resources readily available for response and timely decisions made on the basis of facts.[42]

Discussion Questions

1. Think of recent crises (total of six) to illustrate each crisis in the typology.

2. List three situations that are likely to cause a crisis and name an organization that would be vulnerable in each situation.

3. For one of these situations, develop a comprehensive list of publics, noting the impact of the crisis on them.

4. In that same situation, what plans would you make now to ward off the crisis or prepare for it if you think it can't be prevented?

Points to Remember

- Crises challenge organizations to live up to their reputations, and the way a crisis is handled determines the outcome, both in the court of public opinion and in terms of an organization's credibility.

- Public relations people deal with crises, usually played out in the mass media, although more and more the "media" of cyberspace are becoming influential.

- Crises never truly go away. The way a company handles a crisis becomes a part of its reputation.

- Due to technology, word of a crisis is usually communicated globally.

- Two broad categories of crises are violent and nonviolent. Within each of these two are subcategories for acts of nature, intentional acts and unintentional events.

- Anticipation through imagining crises that could occur is part of planning. It is especially important to determine the vulnerability of the organization to different types of crises.

- The crisis may involve "nimbus" publics—publics that were not designated recipients of messages, activities or products/services of the organization.

■ There are three key elements for dealing with a crisis: having a plan, assembling a team and using a single spokesperson.

■ Employees are the most critical public in a crisis because they affect the way the crisis is interpreted by others.

■ Some feel that dealing with crises openly is likely to create litigation, but you should expect to be sued anyway. If you've been open and honest in your communication, that probably will be an asset in litigation.

■ The role of the CEO in a crisis is especially important. Historically, if the CEO has been involved in or responsible for the crisis, the organization has had greater difficulty in recovering.

■ Crises that originate on the Internet require an immediate response.

■ In a crisis, the media will be there to cover it, but the organization's own channels of communication may be disrupted or difficult to reach.

■ The credibility of an organization is always at stake, and that's why working with the news media is so critical. However, expect bias to occur in the coverage. This often is rooted in economic-political reasons, especially in global situations.

■ Crises usually provoke rumors because there is a vacuum of information, and rumors can create crises that are difficult to quiet.

■ Recalls of products are an important part of crisis communication, and the way they are handled affects public confidence in the organization.

■ Some crises can be avoided through effective communication. All can be better managed. Good communication without action in dealing with the crisis, however, is not effective.

Go to the Web site for this book at **www.cengage.com/masscomm/newsom/thisispr10e** to find more Web links on this subject.

Other Related Web Sites to Review

CyberAlert
http://www.cyberalert.com

Market360
http://www.biz360.com/products.html

NetCurrents' PressClipper
http://eservices.ccnmatthews.com/ccnnewswire/clients-netcurrents.html

PR Newswire's eWatch
http://www.ewatch.com

Reprinted by permission of Universal Press Syndicate.

CHAPTER 14

Public Relations Practice and a Worldview

OBJECTIVES

- To understand that we all look at the world, its people and its situations through different lenses.

- To realize that to function in a global society, it is necessary to understand different perspectives.

- To be aware that you will be working with public relations practitioners all over the world and, in some cases, competing with them for jobs and business.

- To initiate opportunities to learn about other cultures and other languages, and to experience the "worlds" others inhabit.

The challenge in this era of globalization— for countries and individuals—is to find a healthy balance between preserving a sense of identity, home and community and doing what it takes to survive within the globalization system. . . .

[N]o one should have any illusions that merely participating in this global economy will make a society healthy. If that participation comes at the price of a country's identity, if individuals feel their olive tree roots crushed, or washed out, by this global system, those olive tree roots will rebel. They will rise up and strangle the process.

—Thomas L. Friedman, The Lexus and the Olive Tree[1]

In your life experiences, you've no doubt had something like this happen. You go to a movie you especially enjoy, and later you are sharing your reactions with a friend, anticipating the same enthusiasm and perhaps even the same reactions to and appreciation of particular scenes or lines. You're dismayed when your friend either says at the outset, "I hated that movie!" or, perhaps, that he or she liked the movie but really didn't like the parts you thought were especially meaningful. What's going on here? Perhaps it is a difference in values.

Where do we get our values? We get them from many places, but primarily from our family environment. Second, we acquire values from our faith. We also get values from our culture, which embraces faith and family as well as the social, political, economic and moral climate in which we were reared. There's enough diversity in all but a few countries in the world today that you are likely to encounter others with a dramatically different view of the world from yours. No one's view is "wrong." It is just different, and there's a rational as well as emotional reason for an individual's perspective.

Other factors also enter into our values. If you grew up in a part of the world where water is scarce, you learned to conserve water, which to you is a very precious, not always available, commodity. Other people from places where it not only rains, but floods, have a wholly different view of water. So your environment is yet another factor in your values.

What about language? You have what the Singaporeans mandate and call a "mother tongue," which is the language of your heritage, the language you first learned to speak. That language has a strong influence on your view of the world. Some words in that language are not only untranslatable; they are not even interpretable. That is because they represent some realities and some values inherent in the linguistic culture.

Now take this into our current global experience where we send email messages to friends around the world with the click of a mouse. We watch earthquakes in real time as they occur in regions remote from us, not only geographically but also culturally. Sometimes we lack the knowledge or experience to place what we are seeing into perspective. What we do is try to understand what we are watching from our own perspective. How correct we are in our assessment depends on our breadth of knowledge and experience, as it is an individual assessment.

Now that we have public relations colleagues in every nation in the world, there is a good chance we may be involved in some sort of mutual effort—a health campaign, for example, or the launch of a new product or service. What occurs when you find yourself working with someone who is not only in another part of the world, but culturally and emotionally in "another world"? The real possibility is some sort of disconnection. For one thing, you need to know what the practice of public relations is like in that country and the status of public relations practitioners. You also need to do research on the country: culture and customs, religions, laws, media ownership and freedom. This will help you in planning with your colleague appropriate messages and illustrations. You need to let the local person you are working with know that you are sensitive to the economic, social, political and cultural environment there. The situation gets especially complex if you are planning a global campaign where you may be working with colleagues all over the world.

This chapter has two purposes. The first is to make you aware of the hazards and opportunities of working with public relations colleagues around the world. The second is to make you especially sensitive to the way your organization's actions and messages may be viewed from another worldly perspective— the audiences in all of the countries your efforts will reach. You'll need to be prepared for feedback from other parts of the world that can be mystifying unless you understand the context. The combined experiences of your authors represent 18 countries, other

than the USA, in which they have lived and worked. Most of what is included here comes from firsthand experiences.

A global communications community combined with a global marketplace has created both necessities and opportunities for public relations people to work across borders. The solution most often endorsed by public relations professionals has been to find a "partner" born into the culture. Being a native, the colleague will realize immediately problems that could arise from illustrations, wording or suggested media use. Although selecting a local in the culture remains a good solution, you need to be sure that your PR partner is approaching public relations practice from the same perspective that you are. For example, in only a few countries is public relations practiced at the strategic level where the PR person has the power and authority to affect policy. That can be critical in getting a communication campaign underway and keeping it on course, so the role of public relations in the country is important, as is respect for the discipline.

Next, remember that just because media relations is a special practice in many parts of the world, in some areas it is not. You cannot make the assumption that all news media operate in a "free" environment. A change of government or even a change of leadership in a democracy can make the word *free* a relative term. A change in ownership, too, can change the approach to news gathering and reporting. There are also cultural influences on the media.[2] In many such countries, even where the media are free from government control, the reporters and editors expect to receive "compensation" for "information subsidies," material submitted from public relations sources. Because public relations practitioners use media, both mass and specialized, you have to know the rules and conditions of the country for media operating there. Another possible arena for misunderstanding, besides freedom of expression, is right of assembly. Think about the campaigns in the USA that involve getting groups of people together to hear a speech or presentation and then, perhaps, having those attendees call other meetings to take the campaign message to special groups. That won't work in a large number of countries where there is no legal right of assembly. You have to know what freedom individuals have in another nation before you plan any public relations activities there.

While taking all of this into consideration, you need yet another piece of information when you are working with a PR "partner" in a global effort. You need to know what education and preparation that person has for the job. In many parts of the world, on-the-job training is all the training people get, and the quality and depth of that training matters a great deal. The person may have had some continuing education through a professional public relations association, because such programs do exist in most countries today. This, however, is not a "shared experience" because the person probably learned public relations as it is practiced in her or his country. It may be that your colleague attended a university or technical school and took courses in public relations, perhaps even got a degree in public relations. That still is not the same experience as yours, because the public relations field still lacks an international body of knowledge from which to frame education for public relations in any sort of international model.

Even if you think your colleague is practicing from a Western public relations model, that does not mean it is the same as yours. Given all these differences that you are likely to find in working with a partner or many partners in a global effort, you can imagine the multiplicity of publics with which you both will interact. The worldviews of various publics are the perspectives from which these publics will look at all your public relations initiatives. ■

Global Variables Affecting PR Practice

Characteristics and variables of an organization's environment—the political, social, cultural and economic characteristics of where it does business—influence how it practices public relations.

Three variables affecting public relations practice the most, which were isolated by K. Sriramesh and Dejan Verčič, include a country's infrastructure, its media environment and its societal culture.[3] Infrastructure ingredients that are key to global public relations are a nation's political system, its level of economic development and the level of activism prevalent in that country. Media ingredients include who controls the media, media outreach and levels of saturation and media access. Variables of societal culture that influence public relations include stratification, uncertainty, collectivism, interpersonal trust and deference to authority.

Another three variables that seemed to explain the differences in how public relations is practiced from one country or culture to another were noted by Culbertson and Chen in the preface to their book,

International Public Relations: A Comparative Analysis. These include:

- A nation's political structure—stratification, nature of personal relationships, media credibility, economic development, stage of nation building, emphasis on personal loyalty and the presence or absence of elites—shapes the practice of public relations.

- There is a movement throughout the world from one-way to two-way communication and more emphasis on knowledge and persuasion as a part of relationship building.

- Women public relations practitioners are becoming both more numerous and more influential, despite persistent gender stereotyping, male-oriented cultural artifacts and discriminatory treatment and salaries.[4]

As these studies show, certain influences on how public relations functions are specific to a particular locale in the sense that where a PR practitioner is on the globe makes a big difference in how public relations is viewed and practiced.

Political Ideology and PR Practice

Although it is useful to know the 23 different forms of government in the world and what the related terms mean, the names tell you only something, not everything, about the way a particular country works.[5] What you need to know is where the power really lies. For example, the USA is a federal republic, and so is the Sudan, India and Nigeria, yet the governments in these countries are not exactly the same. So we began to use fuzzy terms like *democracy* to differentiate. The problem is that democratic principles are interpreted within cultural and religious contexts. The largest democratic country in the world, India, practices democracy in a different way from, say, Brazil or Mexico or the USA. So how do we understand the practice of public relations in these different political environments?

Four elements that affect public relations significantly in any country are: (1) right to assemble freely and to organize; (2) freedom of speech, including the right to criticize government in any public forum; (3) freedom of ordinary citizens to leave the country and return as they choose; and (4) access to legal relief for the prompt hearing and redress of grievances.

PR in Practice

In Panama, Rare, a U.S.-based conservation organization, has a success story to tell in one of its Rare Pride social marketing campaigns. For each country, Rare selects an indigenous animal that is the source of local pride around which to focus its campaign for the protection of wildlife and its native habitat. The choice in Panama is the quetzal, the colorful bird that is the pride of Cerro Punta, a farming community with a population of 7,000 in the Talamanca mountain range.

Rare has partners there in the local environmental group, Fundación para el Desarollo Integral del Corregimiento de Cerro Punte (FUNDICCEP) and the U.S.-based Nature Conservancy.

Primary responsibility for the success of the Cerra Punta campaign was with its dedicated director, Luis Sánchez Samudio. Sánchez, who has a business degree from a local university, skillfully uses Rare's tools such as posters, a human-sized costumed quetzal, songs, puppets, buttons, school fairs and radio to spread the message of conservation and preservation to the farming community, persuading them to use natural, rather than chemical, protection for their crops.

Cerro Punta's 875 farms, covering about 12,300 acres, produce 80 percent of all the vegetables and tubers consumed by the 3.2 million population of Panama. The soil is rich enough for four growing seasons, but because much of the land is on steep inclines, soil preservation is a challenge in the rainy season. Sánchez teaches farmers to use organic substitutes for chemicals so that run-off doesn't threaten wildlife, and he encourages natural soil conservation measures to avoid expanding fields, often using two local farmers' fields for demonstrations. The farmers, José Abdiel and Hehofilio Gonzales, are enthusiastic participants and early adopters of the changes.

Sánchez also has enlisted teenagers from a catechism class he teaches to help spread the messages of the campaign. In the process the youngsters learn computer skills and information that could help them become ecotour guides in this area located near a forested area between Panama's Barú Volcano National Park and Costa Rica's La Amistad international park.

In the quetzal mascot campaign, Sánchez combines his business education with what he learned at Rare's Guadalajara's university-based training center about ecology, conservation and taking surveys. It was there, too, that he was introduced to the techniques of social marketing.

The polite and quiet director of the campaign has a small staff and works long hours, but he believes that the land and its natural inhabitants are important to preserve. A 2007 survey indicated that the campaign had increased awareness among the farmers of the benefits of living near a protected area from 15 percent to 52 percent. Now 85 percent of the landowners, up from 61 percent before the campaign, are willing to petition the Panamanian government for more controls on the use of agricultural chemicals. However, there is still work to be done in that area because the survey shows that farmers' knowledge of natural alternatives to the chemicals remains at only 30 percent.

Source: Tristram Korten, "The Pride of Cerro Punta," *Nature Conservancy*, Winter 2007, pp. 58–64.

Much of public relations is organizing publics directly or facilitating their organization, whether in formal organizations such as activist groups or simply with audiences for presentations of any kind, from speeches to fine arts. A parallel to this is the freedom to say whatever you need to say, within some published and well-defined legal limits, because public relations needs the recognition of corporate and individual freedom of expression. The ability to move freely within the global community is another critical need for public relations people so that they may attend to clients or address problems in any part of the world.

Much public relations work for clients involves creative projects, from developing logos and campaigns to preparing longer works for books and CD-ROMs. Without protection within the country where these are developed, there is no hope for protection outside its borders. Another aspect of needing access to legal relief is in resolving conflict—this is part of defending a corporate reputation. While that is the professional responsibility of attorneys, any PR person who has ever been involved in an organization's crisis will understand the need to get a fair and impartial hearing in a court of law. Transparency of government is a measure of how likely it is for hidden practices to be discoverable and punished in a court of law untainted by corruption and bias.

Economic Systems/Levels of Economic Development and PR Practice

Where a nation has most of its goods and services under government control, the practice of public relations in that country is mostly public affairs. There is little opportunity or freedom for private enterprise. The practice of public relations is limited to internal government campaigns directed toward its population and to outside relationships with other governments and external tourists.

When countries like this began to privatize, the practice of business-to-business public relations developed, often on a global basis. The need for customer relations also increased because there was now a marketplace and choice. Competition meant developing good relationships so that favorable public opinion would contribute to the company's competitive edge.

In a free-market economy, the competition is global, and the need for a full array of public relations activities opens up: advertising and marketing services certainly, as well as integrated communication, business-to-business, investor relations, international business and international media relations, Web development and other high-tech communication. In addition, strategic planning and management issues mean the development of specialties such as counseling and consulting; research—both market and strategic—including media analysis; consumer relations; community relations; corporate communications; and crisis and issue management. Arts, entertainment and culture communications increase, which often means an increase in fundraising, sponsorships and special events. Employee relationships are especially important in a competitive environment, and often that means training employees and management to

respond to media inquiries. Political communication also increases—lobbying, speech writing, public affairs and health care and environmental communications. The need for public relations talent always increases in a more diversified economy.

Levels of Activism and PR Practice

Activism can have several levels of intensity and can take many forms, ranging from the mere verbal expression of an alternate point of view to indiscriminate violence. Indeed, the techniques used by activists tell much about a particular activist public, and an organization's response to the activism against it tells much about its public relations practice as well as about the society within which the organization exists. Larissa A. Grunig says, "An activist public is a group of two or more individuals who organize in order to influence another public or publics through action that may include education, compromise, persuasion, pressure tactics, or force."[6]

As obscene as it may seem, a terrorist group that attempts to indiscriminately kill and maim innocent civilians in its efforts to disrupt and ultimately destroy a government, its society and institutions is an activist group. This extreme example illustrates why some problems do not yield entirely, or even primarily, to public relations solutions. Rather, stakeholders must rely on opposing force and the law. However, the public relations practitioner has particular responsibilities in such a situation.

In a free and democratic society with a high level of individual rights, and especially in countries with diverse populations, public relations practitioners must accept particular responsibilities as educated and reasoning citizens, as well as professional communicators. Their actions must ensure that innocent people who share ethnic or cultural similarities with terrorists are not harmed or discriminated against, and that their rights are not abridged. Also communications must be directed toward the protection of the rights of all citizens to be sure these are not compromised at a time when fear and emotions are high. The public relations practitioner must separate the activists and their actions from the issues.

That is being illustrated dramatically by acts of terrorism around the world. Jessica Stern of Harvard says that to understand terrorists, any terrorist, from anti-abortion activists who bomb clinics and shoot physicians to Islamic suicide bombers, common traits exist among these people who feel they have "a moral mandate to murder." She found from interviews with "retired" or confined terrorists that they want to transform themselves and simplify life because they feel marginalized by society and seek identification and recognition as martyrs to some noble cause. In doing so, their world becomes simply divided between good and evil, just and unjust.[7]

Activism can range from actions that must be considered abhorrent in any civilized society, to a situation in which laws are broken and people's livelihoods are damaged, to one in which people peaceably show solidarity in their value judgment. Political, social, cultural and economic characteristics of countries will determine the type of response to such scenarios. While terrorism must be viewed as obscene in any civilized culture, lesser civil disobedience might be met by a range of responses in one culture, while other cultures would not even endure the seemingly innocuous peaceful protest of citizens. Cultural awareness is a significant part of successful communication, but few organizations do the necessary research on the publics they want to reach and with whom they expect to build relationships and understanding.[8]

An example of a recent product introduction in the Middle East illustrates just how nimble and flexible public relations practitioners need to be in this new global environment. A public relations firm based in Dubai, United Arab Emirates, with branches throughout the Middle East and in London and Europe, won new product introduction business from a major American manufacturer of shaving razors. The manufacturer wanted to increase market share in the Middle East (its shavers were sold there) by introducing to the Middle East a new line of shavers for women that had been quite successful in the USA and Europe. The firm was asked to develop a communications message that would effectively reach women in the Middle East through publicity and advertising messages.

The publicity and advertising that had been done in the USA and Europe when the product was launched focused on the primary benefit American and European women received from using the new shaver: a clean, close shave that left legs and underarms smooth and sleek. But that would not work in the Middle East; in fact, taking that approach would have been a major affront to a traditional Muslim culture in which women go to great lengths to protect their modesty. They never would publicly speak about, or admit to, anything as private and personal as shaving. So to feature the shaver itself, and to tout the benefits from using it, would have been a major cultural mistake.

The public relations firm knew this, so instead they focused on the brand name rather than the specific shaver. The message in news releases, store promotions and advertising in the Middle East was much less specific than it had been in the West. "Beauty," not "shaving," became the central benefit of using the product.

The particular societal and religious culture of the region clearly influenced this public relations campaign. So did the media culture: It is doubtful that any newspaper or television station in the region would have carried either news or advertising about the new product if the focus had been on shaving. "Going global" is clearly about more than transcending national or regional boundaries. It is about understanding culture and ideology, and using that understanding to communicate effectively with target audiences.

Culture and PR Practice

Culture not only influences how public relations is practiced, but ultimately it defines what public relations is. Today's practitioners have to reconcile how the organizations for which they work relate not only to their own indigenous cultures but also to an emerging global culture. Tomorrow's practitioner will have to help people with different values and beliefs live in harmony and with mutual respect in a society that is, at least technologically, global. Which of these scenarios do you think will occur?

- One culture will overwhelm all others in a world in which time and space will be largely irrelevant because of rapid means of communication and transportation.

- All of the world's cultures will together form a new "global" culture, that is, a "melting pot" culture different from previous cultures.

- Multiple cultures desiring to keep their own identities nevertheless will recognize the importance of tolerance and create a "salad bowl" of cultures that will coexist peacefully.

- A fourth, less attractive, choice is the development of extreme nationalism or some other "ism" by those who want to preserve and persevere. If they don't want to conquer or overwhelm other cultures outright, at least they will want their own corner of the world to be of their design—even at the price of war or ethnic cleansing.

Theory and Research Perspective

Public relations techniques and campaigns are frequently used to raise awareness and change attitudes about social issues and problems, but the techniques most appropriate in each instance and of course the specific issues and problems to be addressed vary widely across borders. A campaign in Lithuania to position deaf people as successful and happy members of society and to raise awareness of Lithuanian Sign Language as well as its use in families of deaf children illustrates a culturally sensitive approach.

In Lithuania, one of the former Soviet Union countries in the Baltic States, Lithuanian Sign Language (LSL) was officially recognized as the native language of the deaf in 1996. However, the deaf and their families, and those who work with the deaf, have not had sufficient opportunities to learn LSL. Training had not been available, so parents of deaf children—90 percent of whom live in hearing families—did not have the opportunity to learn LSL to enable them to communicate with their own children. There was an underlying cultural stigma associated with deafness: sign language was not a necessary means of communication because the deaf can learn lip reading and use spoken language, making them more like hearing people.

The Center for Lithuanian Sign Language (CLSL) used public relations techniques accepted by and appropriate to its culture to raise awareness of LSL usage and training. With the support of the European Community, CLSL established training courses for the hearing parents of deaf children. And working with the firm Saatchi & Saatchi, it set out to persuade the deaf community, hearing parents of deaf children, teachers of deaf children, the hearing society and the mass media that deaf people were contributing, productive members of society and that LSL could improve the integration of the deaf into society.

In some cultures, particularly those in the West that are considered most advanced, the mass media are not a key public relations audience. But in Lithuania, which is undergoing a period of national development during which the mass media are trusted and valued institutions, media relations is a very important and effective public relations tool. Therefore, media relations on the national level was critical to change the attitudes of parents and of the hearing society. Press releases, press conferences and opportunities to interview experts were essential tactical tools. Third-party endorsements also lent credibility to the campaign.

But other tactics were used as well. The overall campaign slogan was "Tell me a story, too . . ." which implied that little deaf children wanted the same kind of story-telling experience their hearing counterparts enjoyed at bedtime. To reach both children and their parents, the campaign enlisted the cooperation of the Children's Theatre, which translated several performances into LSL. And it convinced an independent director, playwright and group of deaf teenagers to develop and present a play in which deaf teenagers acted and in which LSL along with dance were the means of communication.

The campaign's goals were achieved: More LSL courses for the parents of deaf children were offered and a larger number of parents attended the courses.

In many cultures, sign language for the deaf would not even have been an issue deserving of a public relations campaign. And even if it were, the tactics and techniques most appropriate to reach necessary audiences might not have been predominantly media relations tactics and techniques. But successful public relations relies on doing what is culturally relevant and effective.

Source: Ieva Burneikaite, "Tell Me a Story, Too," in *The Evolution of Public Relations: Case Studies from Countries in Transition*, 2nd ed. (Gainesville, FL: Institute for Public Relations, 2004), published on the Institute's Web site, www.instituteforpr.org.

Public relations practitioners need to help resolve complex relationships of their organizations with a range of publics having cultures, traditions, beliefs and values far different from those of their organizations. As problem solvers, the practitioners will be called on to ensure that people who may be different from one another are able to live with each other.

In our global community, people are looking at the world through individual prisms. The major barrier in this for public relations practice is that social responsibility is based on ethical codes of behavior that have their roots in values, which come from learning and experience. The challenge then is the question of "truth." In practicing social responsibility

Global Perspective

It is not only large corporations and organizations that use public relations tactics to achieve goals and influence. Activist publics do, too.

CAPS (Community Alliance for Positive Solutions), based in the southwest of Western Australia, is one such group, using various public relations tactics to enforce change at a local alumina refinery owned by Alcoa World Alumina Australia.

Consisting of over 150 paid members and more than 360 supporters, CAPS aims to "hold Alcoa accountable" for the impact it has on the local community. CAPS formed in June 2004 out of concern for the effects of Alcoa's pollution and general impact on the local community. CAPS was later incorporated (in March 2005), and its members include refinery neighbors, concerned residents and local businesspeople coming together around a common cause and representing a number of different towns and localities close to the refinery operations.

The mission of CAPS is to create a collaborative effort between the communities of Yarloop, Hamel, Wagerup, Cookernup, Waroona, Harvey and other impacted areas to maintain the integrity of these communities and preserve the quality of life required by their citizens, while supporting Alcoa in creating positive, viable solutions for environmental and community sustainability.

CAPS use many public relations tools and tactics—including lobbying of politicians, media relations and community relations. CAPS communicates with its members through various means including its own Web site (www.caps6218.org.au), a regular newsletter and public meetings.

In late 2007 CAPS joined with the high profile antipollution campaigner Erin Brockovich. Ms. Brockovich, with her lawyers and CAPS, investigated complaints of health problems alleged by the local community against Alcoa. Support and involvement from Ms. Brockovich assisted CAPS in its program of public relations to gain further support and raise the profile of its cause. Although CAPS has already achieved a great deal of successful media coverage, plus support from many local politicians, the help of Ms. Brockovich enabled CAPS' agenda to gain even more coverage not only in Western Australia but also overseas. For example, in the UK, the *Guardian* headline stated: "Erin Brockovich in Australian sequel as she takes on case of stricken hamlet."

Public relations professionals are taught to scan the environment and to create corporate strategies to communicate to key publics. However, they need to be mindful that those key publics can organize themselves to become activist publics, and many will develop their own campaigns of public relations tactics to achieve goals that may clash with those of the corporation.

In the case of CAPS, its aim is to get its case of health complaints to be heard and acted on. Through its use of, and relationships with, local politicians, the media, the local community and other like-minded activist groups, it continues to be able to get its issues raised in the public sphere not only locally but globally.

Source: Used with permission, "When Activist Publics use PR: CAPS and Alcoa World Alumina Australia," by Lorelei Campbell, Curtin University of Technology.

in a global society, practitioners have to live with the ambiguity of different versions of truth. Practitioners have to probe the depths of publics to ferret out value systems that determine behavior and weigh ethical decisions about what their organizations or clients should do to find the most socially responsible strategy.

Media Environment and PR Practice

Several factors create the environment in which the media function. The first is the role the government thinks the news media should play, and which it allows them to play, in the society. Another factor is ownership of the media. The third is the education, experience and ethics of the editors and writers. In nontraditional media, such as the Internet, where, except for media Web sites, there are no editors and anyone qualifies as a writer-contributor, anything goes.

The basic division for media is between authoritarian and libertarian, with that depending on their degree of self-determinism, according to John Merrill.[9] These are the first two concepts in what have been called the four theories of the press, the other two being communism and social responsibility.[10] The latter, social responsibility, is now the dominant one and implies that the news media must perform a public service.[11] The problem is that what is socially responsible is subject to interpretation. Many authoritarian systems, for example, think they are more socially responsible than freer media. However, as Merrill notes, "a libertarian press is contentious, pluralistic, even mischievous," because it is free to mirror a society that is "contentious, pluralistic, controversial, outspoken and mischievous."[12]

The first two concepts, authoritarianism and libertarianism, are fundamental. They are closely tied to the type of government and affect the content of the news media. The government also affects the ownership of the news media. Some governments own and control all of the news media. In other countries, the print media may be relatively free, but not so the electronic media. In many countries the wire services for the traditional media also may be owned and controlled by the government. In such cases, getting information into tightly controlled, highly regulated media means it must meet the goals and standards of the government, not the interested group trying to get information about itself into public view.

Even in the USA where media are considered the "freest" in the world, the concept that the public owns the airwaves means that broadcast media are regulated, but not controlled by the government. Print media are governed only by laws that apply to other types of companies. When the ownership is unrestricted except by laws governing business, public relations firms are free to offer any type of information for editorial consideration. The advertising columns are open for consideration of public service announcements, and certainly for purchase, as long as the advertising content meets the publication's standards.

No one expects to be "charged" for anything except contract advertising, and certainly not for information to be published. Nor is there any expectation of "subsidizing" publicity by compensating the reporters or editors. In fact, news media in the USA have their own codes of ethics that not only condemn such behavior but also guarantee some punishment, usually firing, in such cases of ethical breaches. Beyond that, journalists belong to professional groups that also have codes of ethics, which, although not enforceable, carry professional sanctions.

Global media have had to adjust to various media practices, even the Internet to some extent. A few governments have tried to block access to the Internet, but without much success, so far. Satellite broadcasts can be blocked, and have been by a few countries. Authoritarian governments maintain that media controls are needed to keep their cultures from being "contaminated." In such restrictive environments, public relations practitioners experience considerable difficulty and often face high levels of frustration in trying to participate in public discourse on the part of their clients or employers.

Conclusion

There is no question about it: Increasingly, those who work in public relations will be communicating across political, economic, social and cultural boundaries as the target audiences and market for products and services become more global. Successful "straddling" of these boundaries will require great sensitivity and an ability to think globally while acting locally.

Additionally, public relations may be called on more often to function in the arena of public diplomacy. The USA attempted this by establishing in

Ethical Perspective

One reporter says he'll publish a news release if he gets cash, but another reporter says she won't publish a negative story the paper has scheduled if she's paid a bribe. An advertising sales manager from a local newspaper shows up at a media conference, helps himself to a media kit, then presents an invoice for the ad he says you must run before you'll get any news coverage from the media conference.

In some countries, such as the USA, such practices would be considered unethical. But in other countries they are standard practice in dealing with the news media. How PR practitioners and media representatives interact can vary significantly from country to country. The nature of the "transaction" between PR practitioners and journalists that results in the printing or broadcasting of stories based on news releases or other public relations materials varies greatly across the globe.

The International Public Relations Association (IPRA) released the results of an online study in 2002 that showed "cash for editorial" and other practices generally considered unethical in the USA are very common in both print and broadcast media of many countries, especially in Southern and Eastern Europe and in Central and South America. This study—part of IPRA's Campaign for Media Transparency—asked public relations practitioners in 52 countries if certain ethical standards were normally followed by media in their country. Respondents included editors and journalists.

The most common problems were (1) asking for cash or other inducements to publish news releases or feature stories, (2) publications asking for payment not to publish certain stories, (3) company news releases appearing in exchange for paid advertising and (4) advertising disguised as editorial material, or material appearing because of influence or payment from a third party. Cash for copy was the most significant problem. In an update of the media transparency issue, one in three public relations practitioners and one in five journalists said it is common and considered acceptable in their countries for national media to accept such payments. This most recent report is from an international online survey in 2007 by Dr. Katerina Tsetsura, published by the Institute for Public Relations and done in partnership with four other international professional associations that include the International Public Relations Association (IPRA), the International Federation of Journalists, the International Press Institute and the Global Alliance for Pubic Relations and Communication Management.

IPRA has proposed a Charter on Media Transparency that it hopes media around the globe will sign. The five provisions are: (1) Editorial material appears as a result of editorial judgment of the journalists involved, and not as a result of any payment in cash or in kind or barter by a third party; (2) Editorial matter that appears as the result of any such consideration will be clearly identified as paid promotion or advertising; (3) Journalists or other members of the media should not suggest that editorial coverage will be given except by editorial merit; (4) Only products being examined so journalists can express an opinion about them should be accepted, and these should be returned after sampling, the time frame for the loan being set in advance; (5) All editorial providers—newspapers, magazines, Web publications, radio, television and other news transmitters—would prepare a policy statement regarding the receipt of gifts or discounted products or services from third parties by journalists and others on their staffs. All employees would be required to sign the policy, which would also be made available to the public.

IPRA and the Institute for Public Relations, the latter located in the USA, are collaborating in the development and publication of a biennial international index of bribery and the media that will rate and rank countries and regions based on ethical media practices. The 2007 report, published in 2008, "An Exploratory Study of Global Media Relations Practices," by Dr. Katerina Tsetsura, is available online in a PowerPoint presentation from www.instituteforpr.org.

its State Department an under-secretary for public diplomacy and public affairs. When Karen Hughes left the job in December 2007 her efforts to improve the nation's globally poor reputation met with mixed reviews. What most commentators observed about the effort is how essential it is for public policy changes to reflect the public affairs efforts.

Spokespeople for different countries have the opportunity and the responsibility to raise awareness of situations that threaten international harmony and to speak out on national issues of concern, especially types of crises with international implications such as droughts, disease, repercussions of climate change, internal changes in trade and commerce and laws that affect interactions with other parts of the world.

Areas of commonality may be as diverse as social marketing projects, health and education campaigns, information exchange such as transparency and global responses to providing assistance on immigration and refugee situations.

Discussion Questions

1. If you found out that you were going to have to work on a PR project with someone from another country, also a PR practitioner, what questions would you want answered about that person?

2. What questions would you want answered about that person's country?

3. What decisions about the project should the two of you, as PR practitioners, reach agreement on before you begin the project?

Points to Remember

■ Some words in a language are not only untranslatable, they are not even interpretable. That is because they represent realities and values inherent in the linguistic culture.

■ Sometimes we lack the knowledge or experience to place what we are seeing on television or in photos into perspective. What we do is try to understand what we are watching from our own perspective.

■ Because of different cultures, religions, life experiences and socioeconomic and political environments, there may be some intellectual and emotional "disconnects" in attempts to work with colleagues from another country.

■ Three variables of an organization's environment, regardless of country and culture, affect how PR is practiced: a country's infrastructure, its media environment and societal culture.

■ Three other variables that seem to explain the differences in public relations practice from country to country are: the political structure, two-way communications trend away from one-way and gender stereotyping.

■ Four elements that affect public relations significantly in any country are: (1) right to assemble freely and to organize; (2) freedom of speech, including the right to criticize government in any public forum; (3) freedom of ordinary citizens to leave the country and return as they choose and (4) access to legal relief for the prompt hearing and redress of grievances.

■ Public relations practitioners must accept particular responsibilities to ensure that innocent people who share ethnic or cultural similarities with terrorists are not harmed or discriminated against, and that their rights are not abridged, and to ensure that the rights of citizens are not compromised during a time when fear and emotions are high.

■ The need for public relations talent always increases in a more diversified economy.

■ Public relations practitioners will need to help resolve complex relationships of their organizations with publics whose cultures, traditions, beliefs and values are far different from those of their organizations. In a global society, practitioners will have to live with the ambiguity of multiple "truths," a major consideration in efforts at practicing social responsibility.

■ The environment in which the media function is created by the role the government thinks the news media should play in the society; media ownership; and the education, experience and ethics of the editors and writers. A nontraditional medium, the Internet, has fewer internal restrictions but may be blocked by governments.

Go to the Web site for this book at **www.cengage.com/masscomm/newsom/thisispr10e** to find more Web links on this subject.

Notes

Chapter 1

1. Robert I. Wakefield, "Effective Public Relations in the Multinational Organization," in Robert L. Heath, ed., *Handbook of Public Relations* (Thousand Oaks, CA: Sage, 2001), p. 642.

2. Lucien Matrat, "The Strategy of Confidence," *International Public Relations Review*, 13(2) (1990), pp. 8–12. The quoted language is on p. 8.

3. *PR News*, October 10, 1994, p. 3.

4. Fraser Likely, "The Knock and the Roles in Public Relations/Communications," *Journal of Corporate Public Relations* (1994–1995), pp. 7–13.

5. Lisa M. Keefe, "What is the Meaning of 'Marketing'?," *Marketing News*, 38(15) (Sept. 15, 2004), pp. 17–18.

6. Tom Duncan, Clarke Caywood and Doug Newsom, "Preparing Advertising and Public Relations Students for the Communications Industry in the 21st Century," Report of the Task Force on Integrated Communications (December 1993).

7. Joe McGinniss, *The Selling of the President, 1968* (New York: Trident Press, 1968).

8. Frank Wylie, "The New Professionals," Speech to the First National Student Conference, Public Relations Student Society of America, Dayton, Ohio (October 24, 1976); published by Chrysler Corporation, p. 6.

9. Ibid., pp. 6–11.

10. Daniel Goleman, "The Electronic Rorschach," *Psychology Today* (February 1983), p. 43.

11. Civil Society Team, "Issues and Options for Improving Engagement Between the World Bank and Civil Society Organizations," The World Bank (March 2005).

12. Task Force on Stature and Role of Public Relations, "Report and Recommendations," Public Relations Society of America (November 1980).

13. Stephen A. Greyser, "Changing Roles for Public Relations," *Public Relations Journal*, 37(1) (January 1981), p. 23.

14. Philip Lesly, *Managing the Human Climate*, 54 (January–February 1979), p. 2.

15. James E. Grunig, "What Kind of Public Relations Do You Practice? New Theory of Public Relations Presents Four Models," *pr reporter*, 27, *Purview* (April 9, 1984), p. 1.

16. Lalit Acharya, "Public Relations Environments," *Journalism Quarterly*, 62(3) (Autumn 1985), pp. 577–84.

17. Glen M. Broom and George D. Smith, "Testing the Practitioner's Impact on Clients," *Public Relations Review*, 5(47) (1979), pp. 47–59.

18. Joey Reagan, Ronald Anderson, Janine Sumner and Scott Hill, "A Factor Analysis of Broom and Smith's Public Relations Roles Scale," *Journalism Quarterly*, 67(1) (Spring 1990), pp. 177–83.

19. Michael Ryan, "Participative vs. Authoritative Environments," *Journalism Quarterly*, 64(4) (Winter 1987), pp. 853–57.

20. Ibid., p. 855.

21. Ibid., p. 856.

22. Henderson is quoted by William A. Durbin, "Managing Issues Is Public Relations' Responsibility," in "Tips and Tactics," biweekly supplement of *pr reporter*, 16(9) (May 15, 1978), pp. 1, 2.

23. Durbin, "Managing Issues," pp. 1, 2.

24. David G. Clark and William B. Blankenburg, *You & Media* (San Francisco: Canfield Press, 1973), p. 175.

25. Frederick Andrews, "Puzzled Businessmen Ponder New Methods of Measuring Success," *The Wall Street Journal* (September 9, 1971), p. 1. Reprinted with permission of *The Wall Street Journal*, © Dow Jones & Company, Inc., 1971.

26. Joann S. Lublin, "'Green' Executives Find Their Mission Isn't a Natural Part of Corporate Culture," *The Wall Street Journal* (March 5, 1991), pp. B1, B6.

27. Ginny Carroll, "Green for Sale," *National Wildlife*, 29(2) (February–March 1991), pp. 24–28.

28. Philip Lesly, "Effective Management and the Human Factor," *Journal of Marketing*, 29 (April 1965), pp. 1–4. Reprinted by permission of the American Marketing Association.

29. Andrews, "Puzzled Businessmen Ponder New Methods," p. 1.

30. Philip Lesly, "Challenges of the Communications Explosion," *The Freeman* (October 1973), pp. 607–8.

31. Ibid.

32. David Finn, "Modifying Opinions in the New Human Climate," Ruder & Finn Papers no. 1, reprinted from *Public Relations Quarterly*, 17 (Fall 1972), pp. 12–15, 26.

33. Ibid.

34. John Cook, "Consolidating the Communications Function," *Public Relations Journal*, 29(8) (August 1973), pp. 6–8, 27–8.

35. David Shaw, "'Spin Doctors' Provide New Twist," *Los Angeles Times* (August 26, 1989), sec. 1, p. 24.

36 Claudia H. Deutsch, "Media Manipulation 101," *New York Times* (January 21, 1990), sec. 3, part 2, p. 29.

37 Herb Greenberg, "Banking Blues," *San Francisco Chronicle* (January 14, 1991), p. C1.

Chapter 2

1   Labor Party media adviser to Great Britain's transport secretary on September 11, 2001, an hour after the first hijacked plane crashed into the World Trade Center in New York.

2   According to a report by Professor Eric Goldman of Princeton University, referred to by Edward L. Bernays in *International Public Relations Review*, September 1977, p. 4 of reprint. However, according to Sanat Lahiri, International Public Relations Association (IPRA) president in Kolkata, India, in *pr reporter* (December 17, 1979), the phrase *public relations* was used much earlier by Thomas Jefferson, and this reference appears in the first edition of Scott Cutlip and Allen Center's *Effective Public Relations* (Englewood Cliffs, NJ: Prentice Hall, 1952), p. 40.

3   Ibid.

4   Irwin Ross, *The Image Merchants* (Garden City, NY: Doubleday, 1959), p. 51.

5   Edward L. Bernays, *Public Relations* (Norman: University of Oklahoma Press, 1952), p. 84.

6   Based on Ross, *The Image Merchants*, pp. 51–64.

7   J. A. R. Pimlott, *Public Relations and American Democracy* (Princeton, NJ: Princeton University Press, 1951), pp. 235–41.

8   Alan R. Raucher, "Public Relations in Business: A Business of Public Relations," *Public Relations Review*, 16(3) (Fall 1990), p. 19.

9   Theodore Lustig, "Great Caesar's Ghost," *Public Relations Journal* (March 1986), pp. 17–20.

10 Theodore H. White, *Caesar at the Rubicon* (New York: Atheneum, 1968), p. 9.

11 Marcus Lee Hansen, *The Atlantic Migration: 1607–1860* (New York: Harper & Row, 1961), p. 30. Also see E. I. McCormac, *White Servitude in Maryland: 1634–1820* (Baltimore: Johns Hopkins University, 1904), pp. 11–14.

12 Cutlip and Center, *Effective Public Relations*, p. 49.

13 Richard Bissell, *New Light on 1776 and All That* (Boston: Little, Brown, 1975), p. 26.

14 Frank Luther Mott, *American Journalism* (New York: Macmillan, 1950), pp. 179–80.

15 Jerome Mushkat, *Tammany: The Evolution of a Political Machine* (Syracuse, NY: Syracuse University Press, 1971), pp. 373–74. "Public opinions" are noted, not "polls" specifically, in this reference. See also Gustavas Myers, *The History of Tammany Hall* (New York: Gustavas Myers, 1901).

16 Stanley L. Jones, *The Presidential Election of 1896* (Madison: University of Wisconsin Press, 1964), pp. 276–96.

17 Ibid., p. 295.

18 Deborah J. Warner, "The Women's Pavilion," in Robert C. Post, ed., *1876: A Centennial Exhibition* (Washington, D.C.: Smithsonian Institution, 1976).

19 Vernon L. Parrington, *Main Currents in American Thought* (New York: Harcourt Brace, 1938), pp. 31–43, especially p. 40.

20 Cutlip and Center, *Effective Public Relations*, 4th ed., p. 49. See also John Walton, *John Filson of Kentucky* (Lexington: University of Kentucky Press, 1956). Also in Cutlip, Center and Broom, 7th ed. (1994), p. 107.

21 Bernays, *Public Relations*, pp. 36–39.

22 Cutlip and Center, *Effective Public Relations*, 4th ed., p. 83.

23 The rest of the remark, made in 1882 in his private railroad car while being interviewed by reporters, was: "I don't take any stock in this silly nonsense about working for anybody's good but our own because we're not. When we make a move we do it because it is in our interest to do so." Roger Butterfield, *American Past* (New York: Simon & Schuster, 1947), p. 476.

24 Richard Bissell, *The Monongahela* (New York: Rinehart, 1952), pp. 184–91.

25 John Brooks, "From Dance Cards to the Ivy League Look," *The New Yorker* (May 18, 1957), p. 74.

26 Vail also sought third-party credibility by subsidizing the writing of favorable editorials and by giving newspaper editors free long-distance service. For more on this aspect of Vail, see Marvin N. Olasky, "The Development of Corporate Public Relations 1850–1930," *Journalism Monographs*, 102 (April 1987) (Columbia, S.C.: Association for Education in Journalism and Mass Communication, 1987).

27 William R. Faith, "The American Public Relations Experience: 400 Years from Roanoke to Reagan" (New York: Institute of Public Relations Research and Education) unpublished manuscript.

28 Scott M. Cutlip and Allen H. Center, *Effective Public Relations*, 5th ed. (Englewood Cliffs, NJ: Prentice Hall, 1978), p. 73. Also in Cutlip, Center and Broom, 7th ed. (1994), p. 98.

29 Forrest McDonald, *Insull* (Chicago: University of Chicago Press, 1962), pp. 44–45.

30 Ronald A. Fullerton, "Art of Public Relations: U.S. Department Stores, 1876–1923," *Public Relations Review*, 16(3) (Fall 1990), p. 69.

31 Ibid., p. 71.

32 Ibid., p. 72.

33 Sherman Morse, "An Awakening on Wall Street," *American Magazine*, 62 (September 1906), p. 460.

34 Faith, "The American Public Relations Experience."

35 W. A. Swanberg, *Pulitzer* (New York: Scribner's, 1967), pp. 73–122.

36 Cornelius C. Regier, *The Era of Muckrakers* (Chapel Hill: University of North Carolina Press, 1932).

37 Douglas Ann Johnson Newsom, "Creating Concepts of Reality: Media Reflections of the Consumer Movement" (Austin: University of Texas, unpublished Ph.D. dissertation, 1978).

38 Ross, *Image Merchants*, pp. 29–30.

39 Cutlip and Center, *Effective Public Relations*, 4th ed., p. 72. In 7th ed., p. 101. See also Scott M. Cutlip, "The Nation's First Public Relations Firm," *Journalism Quarterly*, 43 (Summer 1966), pp. 269–80.

40 William Kittle, "The Making of Public Opinion," *Arena*, 41 (1909), pp. 433–50.

41 Cutlip and Center, *Effective Public Relations*, 4th ed., p. 83. In 7th ed., pp. 107–08.

42 Scott M. Cutlip, *Fund Raising in the United States: Its Role in America's Philanthropy* (New Brunswick, NJ: Rutgers University Press, 1965).

43 Ibid.

44 Ibid.

45 Ibid. (letter from Pendleton Dudley to Major Earl F. Storer).

46 Howard Weeks, "The Development of Public Relations as an Organized Activity in a Protestant Denomination" (Washington, D.C.: American University, unpublished master's thesis, 1963).

47 McDonald, *Insull*, p. 3.

48 David L. Lewis, "Pioneering the Film Business," *Public Relations Journal* (June 6, 1971), pp. 14–18.

49 Cutlip and Center, *Effective Public Relations*, 4th ed., p. 82.

50 Ibid.

51 Lewis, "Pioneering the Film Business," pp. 14–18.

52 Stephen Ponder, "Progressive Drive to Shape Public Opinion: 1898–1913," *Public Relations Review*, 16(3) (Fall 1990), p. 95.

53 Ibid.

54 Alan R. Raucher, "Public Relations in Business: A Business of Public Relations," *Public Relations Review*, 16(3) (Fall 1990), p. 21.

55 L. L. L. Golden, *Only by Public Consent: American Corporations Search for Favorable Opinion* (New York: Hawthorn Books, 1968), pp. 37–39.

56 George Creel, *How We Advertised America: The First Telling of the Amazing Story of the Committee on Public Information That Carried the Gospel of Americanism to Every Corner of the Globe* (New York: Harper & Row, 1920), especially pp. 18–19.

57 Bernays volunteered to help on the Foreign Press Bureau and had to have his loyalty investigated by military intelligence, because he was Austrian-born.

58 *Who Was Who in America*, vol. 3 (Chicago: Marquis, Who's Who, Inc., 1960), p. 129.

59 Bernays, *Public Relations*, p. 84.

60 Walter Lippmann, in Clinton Rossiter and James Lare, ed., *The Essential Lippmann* (New York: Vintage Books, 1963), p. 96.

61 Golden, *Only by Public Consent*, pp. 37–39.

62 Cutlip and Center, *Effective Public Relations*, 4th ed., p. 91. See also George Griswold, Jr., "How AT&T Public Relations Policies Developed," *Public Relations Quarterly*, 12 (Fall 1967), pp. 7–16.

63 Golden, *Only by Public Consent*, p. 386.

64 Cutlip and Center, *Effective Public Relations*, 4th ed., pp. 674, 675.

65 Philip Meyer, *Precision Journalism* (Bloomington: Indiana University Press, 1973), pp. 144–45; see also George H. Gallup and Saul Forbes Rae, *The Pulse of Democracy* (New York: Simon & Schuster, 1940), pp. 41–56.

66 George Juergens, *News fom the White House: The Presidential Press Relationship in the Progressive Era* (Chicago: University of Chicago Press, 1981), p. 29.

67 Rodger Streitmatter, "The Rise and Triumph of the White House Photo Opportunity," *Journalism Quarterly*, 65(4) (Winter 1988), pp. 981–86.

68 Ibid.

69 Ross, *Image Merchants*, p. 102.

70 Charles S. Steinberg, *The Creation of Consent* (New York: Hastings House, 1975), p. 27.

71 Bernays, *Public Relations*, p. 145.

72 Richard Meran Barsam, *The Nonfiction Film* (New York: E. P. Dutton, 1973), p. 129.

73 Ibid., pp. 151–56.

74 Golden, *Only by Public Consent*, pp. 163–72.

75 Ross, *Image Merchants*, p. 93.

76 Ibid., pp. 87–88.

77 Cutlip and Center, *Effective Public Relations*, 4th ed., p. 673. See also comments in Golden, *Only by Public Consent*, pp. 347–50, and the Public Relations Society of America.

78 Richard W. Darrow et al., *Public Relations Handbook* (Chicago: Dartnell Corporation, 1967), pp. 55–56.

79 *Facts on File*, Vol. 17, "National Affairs" (New York: Facts on File, 1957), p. 116.

80 PRSA *Blue Book*. See also Golden, *Only by Public Consent*, pp. 347–50.

81 Ibid.

82 Stephen A. Greyser and Steven L. Diamond, "Business Is Adapting to Consumerism," *Harvard Business Review* (September–October 1974), p. 38.

83 Public Relations Society of America, "Frustration Shock," slide presentation script, 1974, p. 2. [Hereafter cited as PRSA, 1974.]

84 Greyser and Diamond, "Business Is Adapting," p. 38.

85 Rebecca Smith, "Before Nader, There was Helen Nelson," *Dallas Morning News* (September 24, 1995), p. 7F.

86 PRSA, 1974, p. 7.

87 Smith, "Before Nader," p. 7F.

88 Ralph Nader, "A Citizen's Guide to the American Economy," in Robert R. Evans, ed., *Social Movements* (Chicago: Rand McNally College Publishing, 1973), p. 217.

89 Edgar Chasteen, "Public Accommodations," in Robert R. Evans, ed., *Social Movements* (Chicago: Rand McNally College Publishing, 1973), p. 379.

90 PRSA, 1974, pp. 3–4.

91 D. J. Aulik and L. J. Saleson, "Client Satisfaction: Conceptualization, Measurement, and Model Development—A Perspective," paper presented at School of Business, University of Wisconsin at Madison, May 12, 1975.

92 Nader, "A Citizen's Guide," p. 220.

93 PRSA, 1974, p. 3.

94 According to the 1970 U.S. Census, this age group accounted for 11 percent of the population.

95 Louise Cook, "Consumer Voices Being Heard," *Fort Worth Evening Star-Telegram* (May 18, 1976), p. 7A.

96 Anthony M. Orum, ed., *The Seeds of Politics: Youth and Politics in America* (Englewood Cliffs, NJ: Prentice Hall, 1972), p. 3.

97 Robert Glessing, *The Underground Press in America* (Bloomington: Indiana University Press, 1970), p. 51.

98 *1966 Facts on File*, p. 526.

99 Bo Burlingham, "Popular Politics," *Economic Working Papers* (Summer 1974), pp. 5–14. See also Cook, "Consumer Voices," op. cit.; Richard Flacks, "The Liberated Generation," in Orum, ed., *The Seeds of Politics*, pp. 267–68; Orum, *The Seeds of Politics*, p. 3.

100 PRSA, 1974, p. 1.

101 Ibid., p. 3.

102 *1967 Facts on File*, p. 85.

103 *1971 Facts on File*, p. 801.

104 Aulik and Saleson, "Client Satisfaction," p. 2.

105 Sylvia Porter, "'Fair Deal' Wanted: Anybody Listening?" *Dallas Morning News* (May 18, 1977), p. 5C.

106 David G. Clark and William B. Blankenburg, *You and Media* (San Francisco: Canfield Press, 1973), p. 175.

107 *1970 Facts on File*, p. 830.

108 *Facts on File*, Vol. 29, "U.S. Developments" (New York: Facts on File, 1969), pp. 266–67; see also Vol. 28, p. 625.

109 Ibid.

110 Andrew Hacker, "Survey of the 70s," *Britannica Book of the Year*, 1980, pp. 129–37.

111 Dave Montgomery, "A Texan Meets the Press (and Says a Little Prayer)," *Fort Worth Star-Telegram* (April 10, 1983), p. 29A.

112 Sidney Blumenthal, "Brave New World: Marketing the President," *Dallas Morning News* (September 20, 1981), p. G1.

113 Ibid.

114 Streitmatter, "Rise and Triumph of White House Photo Opportunity," p. 985.

115 Howard Greene, "USIA's TV Network Could Be 'Most Powerful' Propaganda Instrument in History of World," *TV Guide*, 1987, news release, pp. 27–29.

116 Randall Rothenberg, "Brits Buy Up the Ad Business," *New York Times Magazine* (July 2, 1989), p. 14.

117 Tom Duncan, Clarke Caywood and Doug Newsom, "Preparing Advertising and Public Relations Students for the Communications Industry in the 21st Century." Report of the Task Force on Integrated Communications (December 1993), Appendix C.

118 Carolyn Cline, Hank Smith, Nancy Johnson, Elizabeth Lance Toth, Judy VanSlyke Turk and Lynne Masel Walters, "The Velvet Ghetto" (San Francisco: IABC Foundation, summary report, 1986).

119 Bureau of Labor Statistics, U.S. Department of Labor, "Public Relations Specialists," *Occupational Outlook Handbook, 2008–09 Edition* (Washington, D.C.: U.S. Department of Labor, n.d.) Retrieved June 18, 2008, from http://bls.gov/oco/ocos086.htm.

120 Edelman Global Press Release, "Business, Media Now More Trusted than Government," retrieved June 20, 2008, from http://www.edelman.co.uk/trustbarometer.

Chapter 3

1 Staff and contributors, "Thinking About Tomorrow: Technology: The Journal Report," *The Wall Street Journal*, Monday, January 28, 2008.

[2] Thomas L. Friedman, *Longitudes and Attitudes: The World in the Age of Terrorism* (New York: Anchor Books, 2003), p. 395.

[3] Gavin Anderson, 2000 Atlas Award Lecture, p. 9. Presented at the Annual Conference of the Public Relations Society of America, Chicago, Illinois, October 23, 2000. Published by the International Section of the Public Relations Society of America (PRSA), K. Anderson Crooks, APR, editor, December 2000.

[4] Muhammad I. Ayish, "Beyond Western-Oriented Communication Theories: A Normative Arab-Islamic Perspective," *The Public*, 10(2) (2003), pp. 79–92. Also see Radhika Parameswaran, *The Other Sides of Globalization: Communication, Culture, and Postcolonial Critique, Communication, Culture & Critique* (2008). Publication of the International Communication Association, pp. 116–125.

[5] For some insight into convergence in the reporting of news, see *Global Journalism Research: Theories, Methods, Findings, Future*, eds. Martin Löffelholz and David Weaver (Malden, MA: Blackwell Publishing Ltd., 2008). For current information on media transparency issues and public relations practice, see Katerina Tsetsura's, "Does the Level of Public Relations and Journalism Professionalism Influence Media Bribery? An Exploratory Study of Global Media Relations Practice." Paper presented at the 11th International Public Relations Research Conference: Research That Matters to the Practice, March 8, 2008, available on the Web site for the Institute for Public Relations. In *The Wall Street Journal's* special section "Technology: The Journal Report" on pp. R3, 4, see "How We Get News" by Michael Totty.

[6] John Paluszek, "Public Affairs' Troubled Global Reach: What the 'Voices From Elsewhere' Are Telling Us," *Public Affairs Review* (5) (2000. Publication of the Public Affairs Council and the Foundation for Public Affairs, Washington, D.C.), pp. 7–12.

[7] Laurence Evans, *Edelman Trust Barometer 2008* (New York: Edelman), p. 13.

[8] Tim Traverse-Healy and John Gordon, "21st Century Issues and Trends," *FrontLine* (21) pp. 5–13. For some insight into what leaders in the UK think, look at this compilation of issues and trends identified by UK executives through their speeches, focus group sessions, a Delphi study of executives and phone interviews with academics, public policy executives and leading business and industry journalists and commentators.

[9] Doug Newsom, *Bridging Gaps in Global Communication* (Malden, MA: Blackwell Publishing Ltd., 2007), Part 1, pp. 1, 2.

[10] See Doug Newsom's chapter on the global practice of advertising and public relations in *Global Journalism*, 4th ed., edited by John Merrill and Arnold S. de Beer. Esher, UK: IPRA FrontLine Ltd. (2001), vol. 23, pp. 5–13; reprinted by Centre for Public Affairs Studies Xtreme Information Group.

Chapter 4

[1] Don W. Stacks, Preface, *Primer of Public Relations Research* (New York: Guilford Press, 2002), p. vi.

[2] For new research information, contact The Institute for Public Relations, POB 118400, Gainesville, FL 32611–8400, Phone: 352AC 392.0280, Michelle Hinson.

[3] Mary McGuire, Linda Stilborne, Melinda McAdams and Laurel Hyatt, *Internet Handbook for Writers, Researchers and Journalists* (New York: Guilford Publications, 2002).

[4] "Discover the Web's Hidden Treasures," *Sunday (New York) Times*, May 30, 2004, Doors, p. 13.

[5] John Markoff and Edward Wyatt, "Google Is Adding Major Libraries to Its Database," Dec. 14, 2004. http://www.technewsworld.com.

[6] "Do Search Engines Offer Objective Results on Your Company? Maybe Not, IPR Learns," *Ragan's Interactive Public Relations*, 6(11) (November 2000), pp. 1–2, 7.

[7] For a good description of research sources, see Jacques Barzun and Henry F. Graff, *Modern Researchers*, (6th ed)., (Wadsworth, Blemot, CA, 2003).

[8] Roger D. Wimmer and Joseph R. Dominick, *Mass Media Research* (8th ed). (Belmont, CA: Wadsworth, 2005).

[9] See Herbert J. Rubin and Irene S. Rubin for *Qualitative Interviewing: The Art of Hearing Data*, 2nd ed. (Thouand Oaks, CA: Sage, 2005). Although the book is about interviewing, useful there, but especially valuable to all types of qualitative research are Chapter 10, "The First Phase of Analysis: Preparing Transcripts and Coding Data," and Chapter 11, "Analyzing Coded Data."

[10] Bernard Berelson, "Content Analysis in Communication Research," in Bernard Berelson and Morris Janowitz, eds., *Reader in Public Opinion and Communication*, 2nd ed. (Glencoe, IL: Free Press, 1953), p. 263.

Chapter 5

[1] James Carey, "The Communications Revolution and the Professional Communicator," in Eve Stryker Munson and Catherine A. Warren, eds., *James Carey: A Critical Reader* (Minneapolis: University of Minnesota Press, 1997), p. 247.

[2] Wilbur Schramm, *Men, Messages, and Media: A Look at Human Communication* (New York: Harper & Row, 1973), pp. 243–45.

3 Andrea Gerlin, "Jury Pickers May Rely Too Much on Demographics," *The Wall Street Journal* (December 16, 1994), pp. B1, 8.

4 SRI International, VALS Program, 333 Ravenswood Ave., Menlo Park, California 94025.

5 Tom Miller, Roper Starch Worldwide, reported in "New Psychographic Study Covers 1.5 B People Worldwide," *pr reporter*, 40(49) (December 17, 1997), pp. 1–3.

6 For insight on the consequences of this, see David Buckingham, "News Media, Political Socialization and Popular Citizenship: Towards a New Agenda," *Critical Studies in Mass Communication*, 14 (1997), pp. 344–66.

7 See special Technology section of *The Wall Street Journal*, "The Corporate Connection" (November 18, 1996), and special Internet section of *The Wall Street Journal* (December 8, 1997).

8 Scott McCartney, "Society's Subcultures Meet by Modem" and Jared Sandberg, "Fringe Groups Can Say Almost Anything and Not Worry About Getting Punched," Marketplace, *The Wall Street Journal* (December 8, 1994), pp. B1, 4, 5, 10.

9 Don Middleberg, "How to Avoid a Cybercrisis," *Public Relations Tactics*, PRSA, 3(11) (November 1996), pp. 1, 15.

10 Richard R. Mau and Lloyd B. Dennis, "Companies Ignore Shadow Constituencies at Their Peril," *Public Relations Journal*, 50(5) (May 1994), pp. 10–11.

11 Carol Hymowitz and Rachel Emma Silverman, "Can Workplace Stress Get *Worse*?" *The Wall Street Journal* (January 16, 2001), pp. B1, 4. Also look at research through 2007 available from http://www.one2xl.com/stress.html. Many companies that offer counseling to individuals and organizations have a wealth of data on the issue.

12 Daniel Costello, "Incidents of 'Desk Rage' Disrupt America's Offices," *The Wall Street Journal* (January 16, 2001), pp. B1, 4.

13 Sue Shellenbarger, "Employers Are Finding It Doesn't Cost Much to Make a Staff Happy," *The Wall Street Journal* (November 19, 1997), p. B1.

14 Leon E. Wynter, "Group Finds Right Recipe for Milk Ads in Spanish," *The Wall Street Journal* (March 6, 1996), p. B1.

15 W. Timothy Coombs and Sherry J. Holladay have a good discussion of this in *It's Not Just PR: Public Relations in Society* (Malden, MA: Blackwell, 2007), pp. 109–11.

16 John Bitter, "A Basic Training Document: Following a Problem Solving Cycle Steadies the Course in a Crisis," *pr reporter* (January 24, 1983), pp. 1–2.

17 Otto Lerbinger, ed., "Issues Management Strategies Suitable for Different Lifecycle," *Purview* (March 26, 1990), p. 277. From John F. Mahon, "Corporate Political Strategy," *Business in the Contemporary World*, 2 (Autumn 1989), pp. 50–62. For a comprehensive look at issues management and its implications, see Robert L. Heath, "Corporate Issues Management: Theoretical Underpinnings and Research Foundations," in Larissa A. and James E. Grunig, eds., *Public Relations Research Annual*, vol. 2 (Hillsdale, NJ: Lawrence Erlbaum, 1990), pp. 29–65. For a good discussion of the application of theory to the process, see Gabriel M. Vasquez, "Testing a Communication Theory–Method–Message–Behavior Complex for the Investigation of Publics," *Journal of Public Relations Research*, 6(4) (1994).

18 Richard K. Long, "Understanding Issue Dynamics," in Darden Chambliss, ed., *Public Affairs in the New Era* (New York: PRSA, 1986), pp. 22–4.

19 Wayne A. Danielson, speech to Sigma Delta Chi, University of Texas at Austin, October 26, 1967.

20 Philip Lesly, "Turning Over an Elephant with a Shoehorn," *Managing the Human Climate*, 90 (January–February 1985). For the ethnoecology approach to corporate culture, see James L. Everett, "Organizational Culture and Ethnoecology in Public Relations Theory and Practice," in Larissa A. and James E. Grunig, eds., *Public Relations Research Annual*, vol. 2 (Hillsdale, NJ: Lawrence Erlbaum Associates, 1990), pp. 235–51.

21 Melvin L. DeFleur and Sandra Ball-Rokeach, *Theories of Mass Communication*, 5th ed., (New York: Longman, 1989), p. 159. "Mass society refers to the relationship that exists between individuals and the social order around them. In mass society . . . individuals are presumed to be in a situation of psychological isolation from others, impersonality is said to prevail in their interaction with others, and they are said to be relatively free from demands of binding social obligations."

22 Stephen M. Downey, "Corporate Identity's Role in Economic Recovery," *PRSA Newsletter*, 11(4, 5) (April–May 1983), p. 1.

23 Keith L. Alexander, "American Airlines Apologizes for Manual," *USA TODAY* (August 21, 1997), p. 2B.

24 *pr reporter*, 40(32) (August 18, 1997), pp. 1, 2.

25 Bernard Hennessy, *Public Opinion*, 4th ed., (Monterey, CA: Brooks/Cole, 1981), p. 4. Social scientist Ithiel de Sola Pool also said: "An opinion is a proposition, while an attitude is a proclivity to be pro or anti something." For his discussion of public opinion, see "Public Opinion," *Handbook of Communication* (Chicago: Rand McNally, 1973), pp. 779–835.

26 Hennessy, *Public Opinion*, pp. 4–8.

27 Daniel Katz, "The Functional Approach to the Study of Attitudes," *Public Opinion Quarterly*, 29 (1960), p. 163.

28 Maureen Honey, *Creating Rosie the Riveter: Class, Gender and Propaganda During World War II* (Amherst: University of Massachusetts Press, 1984), p. 212.

29 Walter K. Lindenmann, "An 'Effectiveness Yardstick' to Measure Public Relations Success," *Public Relations Quarterly*, 38(1) (Spring 1993), pp. 7–9.

30 Philip Meyer, *Precision Journalism* (Bloomington: Indiana University Press, 1973), p. 184.

31 Charles W. Roll, Jr. and Albert H. Cantril, *Polls: Their Use and Misuse in Politics* (New York: Basic Books, 1972), p. 117.

32 Carroll J. Glynn, "The Communication of Public Opinion," *Journalism Quarterly*, 64(4) (Winter 1987), pp. 688–97. See also Charles T. Salmon and Hayg Oshagan, "Community Size, Perceptions of Majority Opinion, and Opinion Expression," in *Public Relations Research Annual*, vol. 2, pp. 157–71.

33 Melvin DeFleur and Sandra Ball-Rokeach, *Theories of Mass Communication* (New York: Longman, 1989), p. 192.

34 Elizabeth Noelle-Neumann, "Turbulences in the Climate of Opinion: Methodological Applications of the Spiral of Silence Theory," *Public Opinion Quarterly*, (1977), pp. 143–58, and *The Spiral of Silence—Public Opinion, Our Social Skin* (Chicago: University of Chicago Press, 1984).

35 Fred L. Palmer, "Opinion Research as an Aid to Public Relations Practice," address at International Conference in Public Opinion Research, Eagles Mere, Pennsylvania, September 13, 1948.

36 Hadley Cantril, *Understanding Man's Social Behavior* (Princeton, NJ: Office of Public Opinion Research, 1947), p. 31.

37 Jolie Solomon and Carol Hymowitz, "Team Strategy: P&O Makes Changes in the Way It Develops and Sells Its Product," *The Wall Street Journal* (August 11, 1987), p. 12.

38 Bob Davis, "Scholastic Work, Many Forces Shape Making and Marketing of a War Schoolbook," *The Wall Street Journal* (January 3, 1985), p. 1.

39 Douglas Quenqua, "The Trust Timeline," *PR Week* (June 13, 2005), p. 11.

Chapter 6

1 For more on this, see Melvin L. DeFleur and Sandra Ball-Rokeach, *Theories of Mass Communication*, 5th ed. (New York: Longman, 1989), pp. 29–43.

2 To understand the use of system theory in public relations, you need to go to theory books for mass communication and interpersonal communication. For interpersonal, go to the latest edition of Stephen W. Littlejohn's *Theories of Human Communication* and for mass communication, go to the latest edition of *Communication Theories* by Werner J. Severin and James W. Tankard, Jr.

3 Daniel Katz and Robert L. Kahn, *The Social Psychology of Organizing* (New York: Wiley, 1978; from the initial 1966 publication).

4 Norman Wiener, *Cybernetics: On Control and Communication in the Animal and the Machine* (New York: Wiley, 1948) and later his *The Human Side of Human Beings: Cybernetics and Society* (Garden City, NY: Doubleday Anchor, 1954).

5 For more on grounded theory, see Barney Glaser and Anselm L. Strauss, *The Discovery of Grounded Theory* (Chicago: Aldine, 1967).

6 Jurgen Habermas, *Knowledge and Human Interests*, translated by Jeremy J. Shapiro, (Boston: Beacon Press, 1971), p. 192.

7 See Jean-Francois Lyotard's *The Postmodern Condition: A Report on Knowledge* (Minneapolis: University of Minnesota Press, 1984) and Jean Baudrillard's *Simulations*, (New York: Semiotext, 1983).

8 See Michael Foucault, *Madness and Civilization*, 1967, and *The Order of Things*, 1972, both published by Tavistock in London.

9 Behavioral Model Replacing Communications Model as Basic Theoretical Underpinning of PR Practice," *pr reporter*, 33(30) (July 30, 1990), p. 1.

10 Ibid., p. 2.

11 See Denis McQuail and Sven Windahl, *Communication Models for the Study of Mass Communications* (New York: Longman, 1981). For integrated communication models see the "Drivers of Brand Relationships" and "the integration triangle" as well as a cross functional chart for internal organizational structure to facilitate integration in Tom Duncan and Sandra Moriarty's book, *Driving Brand Value* (New York: McGraw-Hill, 1997).

12 Somewhat different motivational patterns are given by Daniel Katz and Robert Kahn in *The Social Psychology of Organizations* (New York: John Wiley, 1966), p. 341. Given as "motivational patterns for producing various types of required behaviors" are the following: (1) legal compliance; (2) the use of rewards or instrumental satisfactions—either individual rewards or "system" rewards such as earned memberships or seniority, earned approval of leaders or affiliations with peers that win social approval; (3) internal patterns of self-determination

and self-expression; and (4) internal values and self-concept.

13 William J. McGuire, "Persuasion, Resistance, and Attitude Change," in Ithiel de Sola Pool et al., eds., *Handbook of Communication* (Chicago: Rand McNally, 1973), p. 221.

14 Ibid., p. 223.

15 Herbert I. Schiller, *The Mind Managers* (Boston: Beacon Press, 1973), pp. 134–35.

16 William L. Rivers, *The Opinionmakers* (Boston: Beacon Press, 1965), p. 1.

17 Zimbardo et al., *Influencing Attitudes* (Reading, MA: Addison Wesley, 1977), p. 156.

18 Robert B. Cialdini, Joyce E. Vincent, Stephen K. Lewis, José Catalan, Diane Wheeler and Betty Lee Darby, "Reciprocal Concessions Procedure for Inducing Compliance: The Door in the Face Technique," *Journal of Personality and Social Psychology*, 31 (1975), pp. 206–15.

19 Stephen W. Littlejohn, *Theories of Human Communication* (Belmont, CA: Wadsworth, 2002) pp. 126–8.

20 Ibid., pp. 128–30.

21 Cialdini et al., "Reciprocal Concessions Procedure for Inducing Compliance."

22 Ibid.

23 Ibid.

24 Ibid.

25 From Earl Newsom's published speeches: "Elements of a Good Public Relations Program," presented to public relations conference of Standard Oil (New Jersey) and affiliated companies, December 3, 1946; "A Look at the Record," presented to Annual Public Relations Conference of Standard Oil (New Jersey), December 16, 1947; "Our Job," presented to Reynolds Metal's executives, March 21, 1957.

26 Philip Lesly, "Guidelines on Public Relations and Public Affairs," in *Managing the Human Climate*, no. 24, adapted from *The People Factor: Managing the Human Climate* (Homewood, IL: Dow Jones-Irwin, 1974).

27 "Another Propaganda Technique," *Glimpse*, 39 (March 1987), p. 2.

28 Leon Festinger, "The Theory of Cognitive Dissonance," in Wilbur Schramm, ed., *The Science of Human Communications* (New York: Basic Books, 1963), pp. 17–27. See also Festinger's *A Theory of Cognitive Dissonance* (Stanford, CA: Stanford University Press, 1982); and Philip B. Zimbardo, Ebbe B. Ebbesen and Christina Maslach, *Influencing Attitudes and Changing Behavior: An Introduction to Theory and Applications of Social Control and Personal Power* (2d ed). (Reading, MA: Addison-Wesley, 1977).

29 Earl Newsom, "Elements of a Good Public Relations Program."

30 Charles U. Larson, *Persuasion Reception and Responsibility* (Belmont, CA: Wadsworth, 1998), pp. 31–2.

31 Mary John Smith, *Persuasion and Human Action* (Belmont, CA: Wadsworth, 1982), pp. 320–22.

32 H. D. Lasswell, "The Structure and Function of Mass Communication in Society," in *The Communication of Ideas*, Bryson, ed. (New York: Harper and Brothers, 1948). As a political scientist, Lasswell was primarily interested in propaganda and in 1927 wrote a book on propaganda used in World War I. To review his communication model and some modifications on it, see Denis McQuail and Sven Windahl, *Communication Models, For the Study of Mass Communication* (New York: Longman, 1981), pp. 10–11.

33 McQuail and Windhahl, pp. 13–4.

34 Summaries at the first of each section are from Alexis S. Tan, *Mass Communication Theories and Research* (New York: Allyn & Bacon/Longman, 1985), pp. 141–3, 164–5, 176–7, 204–5.

35 Jay A. Conger, "The Necessary Art of Persuasion," *Harvard Business Review* (May–June 1998), pp. 84–95.

36 Michael D. Slater and Donna Rouner, "How Message Evaluation and Source Attributes May Influence Credibility Assessment and Belief Change," *Journalism & Mass Communication Quarterly*, 73(4) (Winter 1996), pp. 974–91.

37 See the chart on page 55 of William McGuire, "Theoretical Foundations of Campaigns," in Ronald E. Rice and William J. Paisley, eds., *Public Communication Campaigns* (Thousand Oaks, CA: Sage, 1981).

38 Maxwell McCombs, *Setting the Agenda: The News Media and Public Opinion* (Cambridge, England: Polity Publishers, 2002).

39 Jian-Hua Zhu, James A. Watt, Leslie B. Snyder, Jingtao Yan and Yansong Jiang, "Public Issue Priority Formation: Media Agenda-Setting and Social Interaction," *Journal of Communication*, 43(1) (Winter 1993), pp. 8–29. See also Samuel Coad Dyer, "Descriptive Modeling for Public Relations Environmental Scanning: A Practitioner's Perspective," *Journal of Public Relations Research*, 8(3) (1996), pp. 137–50. Dyer operationalizes an agenda-setting model for research in public relations issues monitoring.

40 Edward L. Bernays, "Down with Image, Up with Reality," *Public Relations Quarterly*, 22(1) (Spring 1977), p. 12.

[41] Philip Lesly, "Another View of the Communications Gap," *Managing the Human Climate*, newsletter published by the Philip Lesly Company, Chicago, IL, 44 (May–June 1977). For the information on truthful and deceptive persuaders, see James W. Neuliep and Manfran Mattson, "The Use of Deception as a Compliance-Gaining Strategy," *Human Communication Research*, 16(3) (Spring 1990), pp. 409–21.

[42] Abraham Maslow, *Motivation and Personality* (New York: Harper & Row, 1954). See also Maslow's *Toward a Psychology of Being* (New York: Van Nostrand Reinhold, 1962).

[43] Don Fabun, *Communications: The Transfer of Meaning* (Encino, CA: Kaiser Aluminum and Chemical Corp., distributed by Glencoe Press, 1969), p. 19. Copyrighted 1968 by Kaiser Aluminum and Chemical Corp., and reissued in 1987 by Macmillan Publishing Company.

[44] For further information about readability indexes, see (1) Robert Gunning, *The Technique of Clear Writing*, rev. ed. (New York: McGraw-Hill, 1968); (2) Rudolph Flesch, *How to Test Readability* (New York: Harper & Row, 1951); *The Art of Plain Talk* (New York: Harper & Row, 1946), p. 197; and "A New Readability Yardstick," *Journal of Applied Psychology*, 32 (June 1948), p. 221; (3) Edgar Dale and Jeanne Chall, "A Formula for Predicting Readability," *Educational Research Bulletin*, 27, Ohio State University (January–February 1948); (4) Wilson L. Taylor, "Cloze Procedure: A New Tool for Measuring Readability," *Journalism Quarterly*, 30 (Fall 1953), pp. 415–33; and "Recent Developments in the Use of 'Cloze Procedure,'" *Journalism Quarterly*, 33 (Winter 1956), pp. 42–8. You might also want to read Irving E. Fang, "The Easy Listening Formula," *Journal of Broadcasting*, 11 (Winter 1966–1967), pp. 63–8; B. Aubrey Fisher, *Perspectives in Human Communication* (New York: Macmillan, 1978); Rudolph F. Flesch, "Estimating the Comprehension Difficulty of Magazine Articles," *Journal of General Psychology*, 28 (1943), pp. 63–80, and "Measuring the Level of Abstraction," *Journal of Applied Psychology*, 34 (1950), pp. 384–90; Davis Foulger, "A Simplified Flesch Formula," *Journalism Quarterly*, 55(1) (Spring 1978), pp. 167, 202.

[45] Robert Blood, "Icons and the Influence of Public Opinion," *Journal of Communication Management*, 2(1) (1997), pp. 83–91.

[46] "The Discipline of Language," newsletter, Royal Bank of Canada.

[47] Steven H. Chaffee, Keith K. Stamm, Jose L. Guerrero and Leonard P. Tipton, "Experiments on Cognitive Discrepancies," *Journalism Quarterly Monograph* (December 1969). Illustrations are as follows: (1) Deadline pressures affected the selection of wire copy by wire editors; when under such constraints their biases affected the selection of material whereas on other occasions, with no time pressures, they were impartial. (2) In an election campaign there are one-sided exposures early and late that attempt to persuade voters of the opposition to cross over; these should be timed to coincide with the period when they are likely to listen to arguments that run counter to their loyalties—certainly not at the last minute, however, such as an election eve telethon.

[48] John C. Meyer, "Humor as a Double-Edged Sword: Four Functions of Humor in Communications," *Communication Theory*, 10(3), pp. 310–31.

[49] "Message Strength Withers When Borders Are Crossed," *PR Week*, May 6, 2002, p. 9.

[50] Judy Motion, "Personal Public Relations: The Interdisciplinary Pitfalls and Innovative Possibilities of Identity Work," *Journal of Communication Management*, 5(1), 2000, pp. 31–40.

[51] "A Respectful Approach To Solving Problems and Achieving Behavior Change," *pr reporter*, 45(20), May 20, 2002, pp. 1–2. (Reporting on a speech by Jerry Sternin, assistant dean, Harvard Business School.)

[52] Liz Yeomans, "Does Reflective Practice Have Relevance for Innovation in Public Relations," *Journal of Communication Management*, 5(1), 2000, pp. 72–80.

[53] Ursula Stroh and Miia Jaatinen, "New Approaches to Communication Management for Transformation and Change in Organizations," *Journal of Communication Management*, 6(2), pp. 148–65.

[54] Douglas Kiel and Euel Elliott, *Chaos Theory in the Social Sciences: Foundation and Applications* (Ann Arbor: University of Michigan Press, 1996).

[55] Juan-Carlos Molleda, "Exploratory Research About Integration of the International Corporate Public Relations Function," paper presented at the International Communication Association, May, 2001, Washington, D.C.

[56] Gregg A. Payne, Jessica J. H. Severn and David M. Dozier, "Uses and Gratification Motives as Indicators of Magazine Readership," *Journalism Quarterly*, 65(4) (Winter 1988), p. 909.

[57] Walter Siefert, personal communication.

[58] "Seventy-six Percent Trust What They Read in News Publications According to Simmons' Affinity Study Pilot Test," *PR Newswire* (Oct. 8, 1997).

[59] Aileen Yagade and David M. Dozier, "The Media Agenda-Setting Effect of Concrete Versus Abstract

Issues," *Journalism Quarterly*, 67(1) (Spring 1990), p. 3. For a good summary of agenda-setting theory and an insight into the role of persuasion, see Ellen Williamson Kanervo and David W. Kanervo, "How Town Administrators' View Relates to Agenda Building in Community Press," *Journalism Quarterly*, 66(2) (Summer 1989), pp. 308–15.

60   Maxwell McCombs, *Setting the Agenda: The News Media and Public Opinion*.

61   For the evolution of the two-step flow theory, see Elihu Katz and Paul Lazarsfeld, *Personal Influence: The Part Played by People in The Flow of Mass Communications* (New York: Free Press of Glencoe, 1955), pp. 15–42; Katz, "The Two-Step Flow of Communication: An Up-to-Date Report on a Hypothesis," *Public Opinion Quarterly*, 21 (Spring 1957), pp. 61–78; Paul Lazarsfeld and Herbert Menzell, "Mass Media and Personal Influence," in Wilbur Schramm, ed., *Science of Human Communication* (New York: Basic Books, 1963); Johan Arndt, "A Test of the Two-Step Flow in Diffusion of a New Product," *Journalism Quarterly*, 45 (Autumn 1968), pp. 457–65; Melvin L. DeFleur and Sandra Ball-Rokeach, *Theories of Mass Communication*, 5th ed. (New York: Longman, 1989), pp. 192–95, 318.

62   Charles Russell, "Culture, Language and Behavior: Perception," *ETC, A Review of General Semantics*, Spring 2000, pp. 4–27.

63   Albert Mehrabian, *Silent Messages*, 2nd ed. (Belmont, CA: Wadsworth, 1981).

64   Patti Wood, "Nonverbal Cues That Show Credibility and Deception," *tips & tactics* supplement to *pr reporter*, 40(5) (April 29, 2002).

65   Walter Lippmann, "Stereotypes," in Morris Janowitz and Paul M. Hirsch, eds., *Reader in Public Opinion and Mass Communication* (New York: Free Press, 1981), pp. 29–37.

66   See G. T. Cameron, "Does Publicity Outperform Advertising? An Experimental Test of the Third-Party Endorsement," *Journal of Public Relations Research*, 6 (1994), pp. 185–207. Kirk Hallahan, "Product Publicity: An Orphan of Marketing Research," in Esther Thorson and Jeri Moore, eds., *Integrated Communication: The Search for Synergy in Communication Voices*, Mahwah, NJ: Lawrence Erlbaum Associates Publishers, 1996, pp. 305–30 and Hallahan, "No Virginia, It's Not True What They Say About Publicity's 'Implied Third-Party Endorsement' Effect," *Public Relations Review*, 25 (1999), pp. 331–50.

67   The history of the magic bullet or hypodermic needle theory is in Jeffery L. Bineham's "A Historical Account of the Hypodermic Model in Mass Communication," *Communication Monographs*, 55 (1988),

pp. 230–46. For a chronology of the effects debate, see Denis McQuail, *Mass Communication* (Thousand Oaks, CA: Sage, 1987) pp. 252–56. For an update look at Tara M. Emmers-Sommer and Mike Allen, "Surveying the Effect of Media Effects: A Meta-Analytic Summary of the Media Effects Research," *Human Communication Research*, 25 (1999), pp. 478–97.

68   Alexis S. Tan, *Mass Communication Theories and Research*, 2nd ed. (New York: John Wiley, 1985), pp. 124–25.

69   Kurt Lewin, "Studies in Group Decision," in Dorwin Cartwright and A. F. Zander, eds., *Group Dynamics* (Evanston, IL: Row Peterson, 1953); and *Group Dynamics, Research and Theory*, 3rd ed. (New York: Harper & Row, 1968).

70   Jose L. Guerrero and G. David Hughes, "An Empirical Test of the Fishbein Model," *Journalism Quarterly*, 49 (Winter 1971), pp. 684–91.

71   Martin Fishbein, "Investigation of Relationship Between Belief About an Object and Attitude Toward That Object," *Human Relations*, 16 (1963), pp. 233–39. While the illustration used here, for simplicity, involves individuals, the validity of the Fishbein model as a predictive tool for *individual* attitudes is disputed by Guerrero and Hughes, op. cit., who see its best application as being to *group* attitudes—certainly a significant observation for PR.

72   Solomon E. Asch, "Effects of Group Pressure upon the Modification and Distortion of Judgment," in H. Guetzkow, ed., *Groups, Leadership and Men* (Pittsburgh, PA: Carnegie Press, 1951), pp. 177–90; R. S. Crutchfield, "Conformity and Character," *American Psychologist*, 10 (1955), pp. 191–98. See also Asch and Crutchfield, quoted in Rex Harlow, *Social Science in Public Relations* (New York: Harper & Row, 1957), pp. 64–69.

73   Michael Burgoon, Marshall Cohen, Michael D. Miller and Charles Montgomery, "An Empirical Test of a Model of Resistance to Persuasion," *Human Communication Research*, 5(1) (Fall 1978), pp. 27–39.

74   Carl I. Hovland, Irving L. Janis and Harold H. Kelley, *Communication and Persuasion: Psychological Studies of Opinion Change* (New Haven, CT: Yale University Press, 1953), p. 270.

75   Stuart Henderson Britt, "Are So Called Successful Advertising Campaigns Really Successful?" *Journal of Advertising Research*, *335* (June 1969), pp. 3–9. Also in Britt's *Consumer Behavior in Theory and Action* (New York: John Wiley, 1970), pp. 46–48.

76   M. Beth Heffner and Kenneth M. Jackson, "Criterion States for Communication: Two Views of Understanding," paper presented to Theory and Methodology Division, Association for Education in

Journalism convention, Carbondale, Illinois, August 1972.

77 James E. Grunig, "Communication Behaviors and Attitudes of Environmental Publics: Two Studies," *Journalism Monograph*, 81 (March 1983).

78 Elizabeth Wolfe Morrison, "Information Seeking Within Organizations," *Human Communications Research*, Vol. 28, No. 2, April 2002, pp. 229–42.

79 Kelly Doyle Duncan, "Strategic Uses of Intranets, in High-Tech Companies: Connecting IMC Theory to Systems Development Best Practices," *IMC Research Journal* (Spring 2001), pp. 27–32.

80 *pr reporter* (January 6, 1986), p. 2.

81 Min-Sun Kim, "Attitude-Behavior Relations: Meta-Analysis of Attitudinal Relevance and Topic," *Journal of Communication*, 43(1) (Winter 1993), pp. 101–42.

82 B. F. Skinner, "Origins of a Behaviorist," *Psychology Today* (September 1983), p. 31.

Chapter 7

1 Robert W. McChesney, *Rich Media, Poor Democracy: Communication Politics in Dubious Times* (Urbana and Chicago: University of Illinois Press, 1999).

2 Deon Binneman, "The Two Wolves Story," *Power Lines*, 5(57) (July 7, 2005).

3 Ivan Hill, *Common Sense and Everyday Ethics* (Washington, D.C.: American Viewpoint, Ethics Resource Center, Incorporated, 1980), p. 95

4 John A. Koten, "Moving Toward Higher Standards for American Business," *Public Relations Review*, 12(3) (Fall 1986), p. 3.

5 "New York, New Governor," *The Economist* (March 19, 2008), accessed June 18, 2008, from http://www.economist.com/world/na/displaystory.cfm?story_id=10880961.

6 Skip Rozin, "Let's Go to the Patriots' Videotapes," *The Wall Street Journal* (May 31, 2008), p. W9.

7 Marina Vujnovic, "A Reconceptualization of Journalistic and Public Relations Professionalism: The Case of Armstrong Williams," unpublished paper.

8 Julie Rawe, "Coming Clean on Student Loans," *Time* (April 11, 2007), accessed June 18, 2008, from http://www.time.com/time/nation/article/0,8599,1609251,00.html.

9 Ron Winslow and Avery Johnson, "Merck's Publishing Ethics Are Questioned by Studies," *The Wall Street Journal* (April 16, 2008), p. B4.

10 Hugh M. Culbertson, "How Public Relations Textbooks Handle Honesty and Lying," *Public Relations Review*, 9(2) (Summer 1983), pp. 65–73 (especially pp. 67, 68, 72).

11 Sissela Bok, *Lying: Moral Choice in Public and Private Life* (New York: Pantheon Books, 1978).

12 Shailagh Murray and Bryan Gruley, "On Many Campuses, Big Brewers Play a Role in New Alcohol Policies," *The Wall Street Journal* (November 2, 2000), pp. A1 and A10.

13 Rachel Zimmerman, "Wrangling over Abortion Intensifies as RU-486 Pill Nears the Market," *The Wall Street Journal* (November 14, 2000), pp. B1 and B4.

14 Arthur W. Page, "The Page Philosophy" (Arthur Page Society, Inc., Room 19A, 225 West Randolph St., Chicago, Illinois 60606).

15 Marvin Olasky, "Public Relations vs. Private Enterprise: An Enlightening History Which Raises Some Basic Questions," *Public Relations Quarterly*, 30(4) (Winter 1985–1986), pp. 6–13.

16 "Wal-Mart Commits $500,000 to Support Flood Relief," news release issued by Wal-Mart June 11, 2008, accessed June 19, 2008, from http://walmartstores.com/FactsNews/NewsRoom/8385.aspx.

17 Remi Trudel and June Cotte, "Does Being Ethical Pay? Companies Spend Huge Amounts of Money to Be 'Socially Responsible.' Do Consumers Reward them for It? And How Much?" *The Wall Street Journal* (May 12, 2008), p. R1.

18 Hadley Cantril, *Understanding Man's Social Behavior* (Princeton, NJ: Office of Public Opinion Research, 1947), p. 60.

19 Earl Babbie, *The Practice of Social Science Research*, 8th ed. (Belmont, CA: Wadsworth, 1998), pp. 438–46.

20 Bobby White, "New Gear Lets ISPs Track Users and Sell Targeted Ads: More Players, Privacy Fears," *The Wall Street Journal* (December 6, 2007), p. B1.

21 Christina Binkley, "Casino Chain Mines Data on Its Gamblers, and Strikes Pay Dirt," *The Wall Street Journal* (May 4, 2000), pp. A1 and A10.

22 Michael Ryan, "Organization Constraints on Corporate Public Relations Practitioners," *Journalism Quarterly*, 64(2, 3) (Summer–Autumn 1987), pp. 473–82.

23 *Loyalty Report Executive Summary* (Indianapolis: Walker Information, September 2007), p. 3.

24 David C. Korten, *When Corporations Rule the World* (West Hartford CT and Berrett-Koehler Publishers, San Francisco), p. 212.

25 Ron Alsop, "At M.B.A. Programs, Teaching Ethics Poses Its Own Dilemma," *The Wall Street Journal* (April 12, 2005), p. B4.

26 For a discussion of personal responsibility in professional PR ethics, see Dean Kruckeberg, "Ethical Decision Making in Public Relations," *Public Relations Review*, 15(4) (1992), pp. 32–37.

27 Mark Cobley, "Norway Fund May Widen Ethics-Based Investing," *The Wall Street Journal Europe* (January 18, 2008), accessed June 19, 2008, from http://online.wsj.com/article/ SB120061108879898973.html?mod=djem_jiewr_be.

28 Philip Mattera, "The New Business Watergate: Prosecution of International Corporate Bribery Is on the Rise," *CorpWatch* (December 18, 2007), accessed June 19, 2008, from http://www.corpwatch. org/article.php?id=14859.

29 "Is Corruption an Asian Value?" *The Wall Street Journal* (May 6, 1996), p. A14.

30 For articles discussing these issues, see *Public Relations Review*, 19(1) (Spring 1993).

31 Katerina Tsetsura, "An Exploratory Study of Global Media Relations Practices," Institute for Public Relations, accessed June 20, 2008, from http://www. instituteforpr.org/research_single/an_exploratory_ study_of_global_media_relations_practices/.

32 Geoffrey A. Fowler, "Beijing Tightens Olympics-Ad Grip," *The Wall Street Journal* (June 4, 2008), pp. A17.

33 "TV Ads: Advertiser and Network Campaign," accessed September 19, 2005, from http://www. parentstv.org/ ptc/campaigns/TVads/main.asp

34 Richard B. Schmitt, "Can Corporate Advertising Sway Juries?" *The Wall Street Journal* (March 3, 1997), pp. B1, 8.

35 Sarah Ellison, "Food Makers Propose Tougher Guidelines for Children's Ads," *The Wall Street Journal* (July 13, 2005), p. B1.

36 Suzanne Vranica, "Controversial Snickers Ad Prompts GLAAD to Ask for Meeting with NFL," *The Wall Street Journal* (February 7, 2007), pp. A1, 8.

37 Jennifer Levitz and Emily Steel, "Boston Stunt Draws Legal, Ethical Fire," *The Wall Street Journal* (February 2, 2007), p. B3.

38 Allyce Bess, "E-Mail Crusade Against Intel: Is It Trespass?" *The Wall Street Journal* (August 14, 2002), pp. B1 and B4.

39 Karen Tumulty, "Can Obama Shred the Rumors?" *Time* (June 23, 2008), pp. 40–41.

40 Emily Steel, "Multimedia Games Create TV-Show Buzz," *The Wall Street Journal* (December 7, 2007), p. B4.

41 Julie M. Donohue, Marisa Cevasco and Meredith B. Rosenthal, "A Decade of Direct-to-Consumer Advertising of Prescription Drugs," *New England Journal of Medicine* (August 16, 2007), accessed June 20, 2008, from http://content.nejm.org/ cgi/content/full/357/7/673.

42 "AMA Calls for Tighter Drug Ad Oversight," *ConsumerAffairs.com*, accessed June 20, 2008, from http://www.consumeraffairs.com/news04/2008/05/ ama_drug_ads.html.

43 "Post-It Scam Continues to Strike," *pr reporter* (March 4, 1996), p. 4.

44 Hazel Warlaumont, "Blurring Advertising and Editorial Photographic Formats," *Visual Communication Quarterly* (Summer 1995), pp. 4–10.

45 David Lieberman, Fake News, *TV Guide* (February 22–28, 1992), pp. 10–16, 26.

46 "FCC Mulls Expanding Regulation for Prepackaged News, PRSA Calls for Vigorous Application of Existing Industry-Wide Disclosure Standards," news release issued by PRSA 24 June 2005, accessed Sept. 18, 2005, from http://media.prsa.org/ article_ print. cfm?article_id=481.

47 Doug Levy, "What Kids Read About Smoking," *USA TODAY* (October 11, 1994).

48 "Doctored Images Now Common," *pr reporter* (April 10, 1995), p. 1.

49 Tom Wheeler and Tim Gleason, "Photography or Photofiction: An Ethical Protocol for the Digital Age," *Visual Communication Quarterly* (Winter 1995), pp. 8–12.

50 Shiela Reaves, "The Unintended Effects of New Technology (and Why We Can Expect More)," *Visual Communication Quarterly* (Winter 1995), pp. 11–15.

51 Public Relations Society of America, *Public Relations Tactics: The Blue Book: PRSA Member Directory* (New York: Public Relations Society of America, 2002), p. A3.

52 Carl Parkes, *Travel Writing Subsidies*, (April 11, 2007), accessed June 20, 2008, from http://travelwriters. blogspot.com/2007/04/travel-writing-subsidies.html.

53 William B. Blankenburg, "The Adversaries and the News Ethic," *Public Relations Quarterly*, 14(4) (Winter 1970), p. 31.

54 Andrew Buncombe, "There's Beef in Your French Fries, Says McDonald's," *Independent* (London) (May 25, 2001), p. 18.

55 Alix M. Freedman, "As UNICEF Battles Baby-Formula Makers, African Infants Sicken," *The Wall Street Journal* (December 5, 2000), pp. A1 and A18.

56 Amar Bhide and Howard H. Stevenson, "Why Be Honest if Honesty Doesn't Pay?" *Harvard Business Review*, 67(5) (September–October 1990), pp. 121–29.

57 Joseph L. Badaracco, Jr., "The Discipline of Building Character," *Harvard Business Review* (March–April 1998), pp. 114–19.

58 David Finn, "Medium Isn't Always the Message," *Dallas Morning News* (May 21, 1981), p. 4D.

Chapter 8

1 Morton J. Simon, speech to North Texas Chapter of the Public Relations Society of America, Dallas, Texas, August 29, 1978.

2 Marian Huttenstine, "New Roles, New Problems, New Concerns, New Law," *Southern Public Relations Journal*, 1(1) (Spring 1993), p. 5.

3 Ibid.

4 Morton J. Simon, Public Relations Law (New York: Appleton-Century-Crofts, 1969), pp. 16–17. Also see Joseph F. McSorley, *A Portable Guide to Federal Conspiracy Law: Developing Strategies for Criminal and Civil Cases* (Washington, D.C.: The American Bar Association, 1996).

5 Edward Felsenthal, "Justices Rule People Fined by U.S. Also Can Be Criminally Prosecuted," *The Wall Street Journal* (December 11, 1997), p. B14.

6 Simon, 1969, pp. 16–17.

7 Carole Gorney, introductory remarks, Symposium on Litigation Journalism, Austin O. Furst, Jr., Series at Lehigh University, Bethlehem, Pennsylvania, May 5, 1994.

8 Jaxon VanDerbeken, "A Lawyer's Media, Simpson's Attorney Follows Own Strategy in Manipulating News Coverage," *Fort Worth Star-Telegram* (June 26, 1994), p. A6.

9 Huttenstine, "New Roles," p. 5.

10 Ibid., pp. 5–7.

11 Ibid., pp. 7–8.

12 Ibid., p. 8.

13 Ibid., p. 10.

14 Morton J. Simon, speech to North Texas PRSA.

15 David H. Simon, "Lawyer and Public Relations Counselor: Teamwork or Turmoil?" *American Bar Journal*, 63 (August 1977), pp. 1113–16.

16 James E. Lukaszewski, "Litigation Communication Management," *Executive Action* (January/February/March 2000), p. 1.

17 "PR Communications Not Privileged, Can End Up in Court," *pr reporter* (July 21, 1997), pp. 1, 2.

18 Morton Simon, *Public Relations Law*, pp. 16–17.

19 "The ABCs of Dealing with Whistle-Blower Suits," *tips & tactics* supplement of *pr Reporter* (May 27, 1996), pp. 1, 2.

20 *Rowan v. Post Office Department* 397 U.S. 728 (1970), appeal of U.S. District Court for Central District of California, January 22, 1970, decided May 4, 1970.

21 For complete law visit the U.S. government Web site or see the Sarbanes-Oxley law.

22 For more information on Sarbanes-Oxley costs to Ad/PR conglomerates, see the editorial by Jack O'Dwyer posted Aug. 2, 2004, "PR Commentary," at www.odwyerpr.com.

23 See Carol Hymowitz's column in the Lead section, "In Sarbanes-Oxley Era, Running a Nonprofit Is Only Getting Harder," for *The Wall Street Journal*, June 21, 2005, p. B1.

24 "Compliance Update, Reg FD Sparks Smart, Interactive Outreach to Investors, Consumers and Media," *Interactive Public Relations* (April 2001), 7(4), pp. 1–2, 4.

25 Two major cases are *SEC v. Texas Gulf Sulphur*, 344 F. Supp. 1983 (1972), and *Financial Industrial Fund v. McDonnell Douglas*, 474 F. 2d 514 (1973).

26 *SEC v. Texas Gulf Sulphur*, 344 F. Supp. 1983 (1972).

27 Richard S. Seltzer, "The SEC Strikes Again," *Public Relations Journal*, 28(4) (April 1972), p. 22.

28 *SEC v. Pig 'N' Whistle Corp.*, 359 F. Supp. 219 (1973).

29 Ibid.

30 *SEC v. Pig 'N' Whistle*, CCH Fed. Sec. L. Rep. (1972), pp. 34–38, 42–43.

31 For additional information, see Bryon Burrough, "SEC Bid for Full Merger Disclosure Begs Question: What Is Disclosure?" *The Wall Street Journal* (August 12, 1978), p. 17.

32 See *Greenfield v. Heublein*, 742 F. 2d 751 (1984), a decision that did not settle the matter of whether boards of directors have to approve agreements in principle prior to the announcement. The failure to settle caused a class action lawsuit in 1985 over the RCA–GE merger. Compare *Levinson v. Basic, Inc.*, 786 F. 2d 741 (1986), where the court ruled that meetings occurring over a couple of months (during which time the company issued releases insisting it didn't know why trading was heavy) on a possible merger were material and should have been disclosed. The current Supreme Court rule is that materiality depends on the probability that the transaction under consideration will be consummated (99 L. Ed. 2d 220).

33 Paul Beckett, "Lack of SEC Rules Irks Appeals Courts," *The Wall Street Journal* (April 14, 1998), p. B11.

34 Cassell Bryan-Low, "New SEC Rules Will Aid Firms' Insiders," *The Wall Street Journal* (October 18, 2000), p. C15.

35 Joanne Lipman, "FTC Zaps Misleading Infomercials," *The Wall Street Journal* (June 19, 1980), pp. B1, B6.

[36] Ibid.

[37] Facts on File (September 15, 1978), p. 22; also see 1979 *Encyclopedia Book of the Year*.

[38] Michael Waldholz, "Prescription-Drug Maker's Ad Stirs Debate over Marketing to Public," *The Wall Street Journal* (September 22, 1987), p. 39.

[39] Joe and Losana Boyd, "Prescriptions for Preapproval," *Public Relations Journal*, 44(4) (April 1988), p. 14.

[40] William Power, "A Judge Prescribes a Dose of Truth to Ease the Pain of Analgesic Ads," *The Wall Street Journal* (May 13, 1987), p. 31.

[41] Peter Fritsch, Allanna Sullivan and Rochelle Sharpe, "Texaco to Pay $176.1 Million in Bias Suit," *The Wall Street Journal* (November 18, 1996), pp. A3, 6.

[42] "ValueJet Holders File Suit Alleging Carrier Deceived Investors," *The Wall Street Journal* (June 25, 1996), p. B7.

[43] Charles Gasparino with contributions from Deborah Lohse, "NASD Fines Firm, 2 Executives in Case of Misleading Ads," *The Wall Street Journal* (February 20, 1996), p. B9.

[44] Douglas Quenqua, "Nike CSR in Limbo as APCO Wins the Work," *PR Week* (June 17, 2002), p. 1. For a thorough discussion of the ethical basis justifying regulation of corporate speech, see Robert L. Kerr, "Impartial Spectator in the Marketplace of Ideas: The Principles of Adam Smith as an Ethical Basis for Regulation of Corporate Speech," *JMC Quarterly*, 79(2) (Summer 2002), pp. 394–415. See Stephanie Kang, "Nike Settles Case with an Activist for $1.5 Million," *The Wall Street Journal*, September 15, 2003, p. A10.

[45] Sandy Davidson, "Supreme Court Strengthens Commercial Speech Protection, Media Law Notes," newsletter of the Association for Education in Journalism and Mass Communication, 23(3), (Spring, 1996), p. 10.

[46] Rosalind C. Truitt, "The Cases for Commercial Speech," *Presstime* (March 1996), pp. 29–31.

[47] Ibid. For a good discussion of the issue, see Catherine A. Pratt, "First Amendment Protection for Public Relations Expression: The Applicability and Limitation of the Commercial and Corporate Speech Models," in Larissa A. and James E. Grunig, eds., *Public Relations Research Annual*, vol. 2 (Hillsdale, NJ: Lawrence Erlbaum Associates, 1990), pp. 205–17. For background on the issue, see two publications by Robert L. Kerr: "Justifying Corporate Speech Regulation Through a Town-Meeting Understanding of the Marketplace of Ideas," *Journalism Communication Monographs*, 9 (Summer 2007) (Columbia, SC: Association for Education in Journalism and Mass Communication) and "Subordinating

the Economic to the Political: The Evolution of the Corporate Speech Doctrine," in *10 Communication Law & Policy*, pp. 63–99. For the ethics aspect see individualistic and collectivist political philosophies in Elizabeth Blanks Hindman, "The Chickens Have Come Home to Roost: Individualism, Collectivism, and Conflict in Commercial Free Speech Doctrine," paper presented to the Law Division of the Association for Education in Journalism and Mass Communication, Kansas City, July/August 2003.

[48] Richard B. Schmitt, "Can Corporate Advertising Sway Juries?" *The Wall Street Journal* (March 3, 1997), pp. B1, 3.

[49] *First National Bank of Boston v. Bellotti*, 435 U.S. 765. Supreme Court ruling, Attorney General of Massachusetts is No. 76–1172, argued Nov. 9, 1977, decided April 26, 1978.

[50] "Washington Wire," *The Wall Street Journal* (January 2, 1976), p. 1.

[51] Public Relations Society of America National Newsletter (April 1974), p. 4.

[52] George E. Stevens, "Newspaper Tort Liability for Harmful Advertising," *Newspaper Research Journal*, 8(1) (Fall 1986), pp. 37–41.

[53] Advice and policy guidance on FOIA is available through the Executive Branch's Office of Information and Privacy. The FOIA Counselor service can respond to inquiries at (202) 514-FOIA. Additionally, the Justice Department can make available a list of all the principal FOIA administrative and legal contacts at all federal agencies that deal with FOIA matters. For a discussion of the tension created by privacy and public interest, see Martin E. Halstuk and Bill F. Chamberlin's "The Freedom of Information Act 1966–2006: A Retrospective on the Rise of Privacy Protection Over the Public Interest In Knowing What the Government Is Up To," 11 *Communication Law & Policy*, pp. 511–64.

[54] For a monograph on the implications of the interpretation of copyright law for public relations, see Harold William Suckenik, "Copyright Rights Just Changed Forever—Do You Know What You're Buying and Why?" from the Institute for Public Relations, University of Florida, POB 118400, Gainesville, FL 32611-8400. The American Society of Journalists and Authors' Code of Ethics and Fair Practices has a position on work for hire and on model agreement. The Society's address is: 1501 Broadway, Suite 302, New York, NY 10036.

[55] Write the U.S. Government Printing Office for copies of the copyright law that went into effect January 1, 1978, and for interpretations of the new applications. See also Kent R. Middleton, "Copyright and the Journalist: New Powers for the Freelancer," *Journalism Quarterly*, 56(1) (Spring 1979),

pp. 38–42. Information on the World Wide Web is a mix of copyrighted work and work that is in the public domain. Just because it is available on the Web doesn't mean it can be used. For some assistance in checking on copyright restrictions, see the list of Web sites with information that appears in the *Instructor's Manual* for this text.

56 *Sony Corporation of America et al. v. Universal City Studios, U.S. Law Week*, 52 LW 4090. Supreme Court case No. 81–1687 was argued Jan. 18, 1983, and was decided Jan. 17, 1984.

57 *Harper & Row Publishers, Inc. v. National Enterprises*, 105 S. Ct. 2218 (1985). Supreme Court case No. 83–632 was argued Nov. 6, 1984, and was decided May 20, 1985 (88 L. Ed. 2d 588).

58 Ross Kerber, "Vigilant Copyright Holders Patrol the Internet," *The Wall Street Journal* (December 13, 1995), pp. B1, 5.

59 Nicole B. Casarez, "Penny-Wise, Pound-Foolish: What Public Relations Professionals Must Know About Photocopying and Fair Use," *Public Relations Quarterly*, 42(3) (Fall 1997), pp. 43–7.

60 Anne Fadiman, "Nothing New Under the Sun," *Civilization* (February/March 1997), pp. 86–87.

61 Marshall Leaffer, "An Overview of Copyright Law for Journalists and Other Media Artists," speech to Association for Education in Journalism and Mass Communication, San Antonio, Texas, August 1987.

62 Ibid.

63 Junda Woo, "Government Paper on Copyrights in Cyberspace Vexes Some Firms," *The Wall Street Journal* (September 2, 1994), p. B3.

64 Ann Davis, "'Invisible' Trademarks on the Web Raise Novel Issue of Infringement," *The Wall Street Journal* (September 15, 1997), p. B12.

65 Robert Sack, *Libel, Slander and Related Problems* (New York: Practising Law Institute, 1980). The new edition of this volume is: Robert D. Sack and Sandra S. Baron, *Libel, Slander and Related Problems* (New York: Practising Law Institute, 1994).

66 *New York Times v. Sullivan*, 376 U.S. 254 (1964).

67 *Gertz v. Robert Welch Inc.*, 418 U.S. 323 (1974).

68 Amy Dockser Marcus, "'False Impressions Can Spur Libel Suits," *The Wall Street Journal* (May 15, 1990), p. B1. This case is *Diesen v. Hessburg*, SCM, 455 N.W.2d 446. U.S. The Supreme Court citation for this case is SCUS, 498 U.S. 1119, Feb. 25, 1991.

69 Susan Caudill, "Choosing the Standard of Care in Private Individual Defamation Cases," *Journalism Quarterly*, 66(7) (Summer 1989), pp. 396–434.

70 Kyu Ho Youm, "Survivability of Defamation as a Tort," *Journalism Quarterly*, 66(3), (Fall 1989), pp. 646–52.

71 Paul M. Barrett, "Author Who Sued Over Scornful Review Is Now Scorned by the Publishing World," *The Wall Street Journal* (April 17, 1994), pp. B1, B2.

72 Alex M. Freedman and Amy Stevens, "Philip Morris Is Putting TV Journalism on Trial in Its Suit Against ABC," *The Wall Street Journal* (May 23, 1995), pp. A1, 14.

73 Paul Holmes, "An Extension of Public Relations by Other Means," *Reputation Management* (March/April 1996), pp. 10–17.

74 Scott Andron, "Scratched Car Saves ABC," *Quill* (September 1997), pp. 14–15.

75 Linton Weeks, "Testing the Legal Limits of Cyberspace," *Washington Post National Weekly Edition* (September 8, 1997), p. 29.

76 Evan Ramstad, "Putting News on Internet First Seen as Protective," *The Wall Street Journal* (March 5, 1997), p. B8.

77 Sondra J. Byrnes, "Privacy vs. Publicity," *Public Relations Journal*, 43(9) (September 1987), pp. 46–9.

78 "Nun Not Laughing at Greeting Card," *Fort Worth Star-Telegram* (August 12, 1985), p. 7A.

79 Constance Johnson, "Anonymity On-Line? It Depends Who's Asking," *The Wall Street Journal* (November 24, 1995), pp. B1, 10.

80 Thomas E. Weber, "New Lexis Database of Names Sparks Outcry on Privacy," *The Wall Street Journal* (September 19, 1996), p. B2.

81 Frank Walsh, "Elements of a Consent Release," *Public Relations Journal* (November 1983), p. 8.

82 David M. Coronna, "The Right of Publicity," *Public Relations Journal* (February 1983), pp. 29–31.

83 Ted Baron, "Legal Protection for the PR Agency," *Public Relations Journal* (September 1971), p. 33.

84 For additional examples of model releases as well as copyright and trademark registration forms, see Roy L. Moore, Ronald T. Farrar and Erik L. Collins, *Advertising and Public Relations Law* (Mahwah, NJ: Lawrence Erlbaum, 1998).

85 Dana Milbank and Marcus W. Brauchli, "How U.S. Concerns Compete in Countries Where Bribes Flourish," *The Wall Street Journal* (September 19, 1995), pp. A1, 14. Since 1977, bribing by U.S. companies has been prohibited under the Foreign Corrupt Practices Act, which is rigidly enforced.

86 Neil King, Jr., "Bribery Ban Is Approved by OECD," *The Wall Street Journal* (November 24, 1997), p. A14.

87 Steven Lipin and Sara Calian, "Did U.K.'s Strict Rules Spur Deal?" *The Wall Street Journal* (February 2, 1998), pp. C1, 16.

88 Patrick M. Reilly and Joann S. Lublin, "Should Businesses Negotiate with Terrorists?" *The Wall Street Journal* (September 20, 1995), pp. B1, 5.

89 Raju Narisetti, "Where's a Good Place to Put Toothpaste? On Seashells or Eggs?" *The Wall Street Journal* (December 5, 1996), p. B5.

90 Matthew Rose, "French Court Blocks Philip Morris Ads That Liken Passive Smoke to Cookies," *The Wall Street Journal* (June 27, 1996), p. B3.

Chapter 9

1 Because this is a public relations text and not an organizational management text, for a fuller discussion of these topics, go to the following sources. For advertising, see DAGMAR, "Designing Advertising Goals for Measured Advertising Response," in Don E. Schultz and Beth E. Barnes, *Strategic Advertising Campaigns*, 4th ed. (Lincolnwood, IL: NTC Business Books, 1994), p. 324. For organizational theory, see "MBO, Management by Objective," pp. 177–78 in the discussion of Goal-Setting Processes and also p. 6 where goals are described as "narrowly defined" and p. 8 where coordinating activities in organizations are discussed, in Katherine Miller, *Organizational Communication: Approaches and Processes*, 4th ed. (Belmont, CA: Wadsworth, 2005). For a public relations interpretation from PRSA for accreditation examinations, a goal is a "more specific expression of a mission or purpose, and commonly described as the desired outcome of a plan of action *designed to solve a specific problem* over the life of a campaign." (Italics added.) An objective is defined as "a specific aspect of the problem with each of several objectives contributing toward achieving the goal." For a discussion of these under strategies, see pp. 247–51 in Robert Kendall, *Public Relations Campaign Strategies, Planning for Implementation*, 2nd ed. (New York: HarperCollins, 1996). PRSA acknowledges that the debate over which comes first, goals or objectives, varies with organizations, but it decided on this application to simplify evaluating responses to its accreditation exam. If you're interested in history, you can find a discussion of the 1950s mix-up in Russell L. Colley, *Defining Advertising Goals for Measuring Advertising Results* (New York: Association of National Advertisers, 1961).

2 Linda Childers Hon and James E. Grunig, "Guidelines for Measuring Relationships in Public Relations," The Institute for Public Relations, 1999.

3 Ibid.

4 See the full story in "Handling Sensitive Subjects With Stakeholders: One Approach Shows Various Pitfalls," *pr reporter*, 45(15) (April 15, 2002), pp. 1–2. In trying to do what one public wanted, school nurses in a school district in Pennsylvania

made a whole batch of parents unhappy by sending them a letter talking about obesity in their children. The letters went to some parents who didn't have an obese child, or who maybe had one obese child and one that wasn't. The "public clamor" resulted in media coverage as far away as London and Australia.

5 See James E. Grunig, *Excellence in Public Relations and Communication Management* (Hillsdale, NJ: Lawrence Erlbaum Associates, Inc., 1992).

6 Ibid.

7 See Alan R. Freitag's article "Ascending Cultural Competence Potential: An Assessment and Profile of USA Public Relations Practitioners' Preparation for International Assignments," where he points out that preparation is limited, but when it is given, it pays large rewards in increased cross-cultural competencies on the part of the individual. His article is in *Journal of Public Relations Research*, 14(3) (2002), pp. 207–27.

8 John E. Marston, *The Nature of Public Relations* (New York: McGraw-Hill, 1963), pp. 161–73; also in his *Modern Public Relations* (New York: McGraw-Hill, 1979), pp. 185–95.

9 Scott M. Cutlip and Allen H. Center, *Effective Public Relations* (Englewood Cliffs, NJ: Prentice Hall, 1952), p. 87.

10 Jerry A. Hendrix, *Public Relations Cases* (Belmont, CA: Wadsworth, 1998), pp. 5–6.

11 Glen M. Broom and David M. Dozier, *Using Research in Public Relations* (Englewood Cliffs, NJ: Prentice Hall, 1990), p. 25.

12 Adapted from Robert L. Katz's article, "Human Relations Skills Can Be Sharpened," *Harvard Business Review*, July/August 1956. Look at his chart on page 64, still as useful today as then, which is usually the case with sound theory.

13 See Barbara DeSanto, Danny Moss and Andrew Newman, "Building an Understanding of the Main Elements of Management in the Communication/Public Relations Context: A Study of U.S. Practitioners' Practices," *J&MC Quarterly*, 84(3) (2007), pp. 439–54.

Chapter 10

1 Chris Carlsson, "The Shape of Truth to Come: New Media and Knowledge," in James Brook and Iain A. Boal, eds., *Resisting the Virtual Life: The Culture and Politics of Information* (San Francisco: City Lights, 1995), p. 235.

2 Brian Steinberg and James Bandler, "Blurring the Line?" *The Wall Street Journal* (August 9, 2004), pp. B1 and B3.

3 "News/Broadcast Network Studies Usage of PSAs on Compact Disc," *PR News* (October 23, 1993), p. 5.

4 Laura Bird, "And They're Very Good at Praying for Success," *The Wall Street Journal* (October 15, 1993), p. B1.

5 Ibid.

6 Leon E. Wynter, "Global Marketers Learn to Say No to Bad Ads," *The Wall Street Journal* (April 1, 1998), p. B1.

7 Terry Haller, "Corporate Ads Doomed," *Ad Age* (January 25, 1982), p. 47.

8 Tom Webster, "The Podcast Consumer Revealed 2008," *Edison Media Research* (n.d.), accessed June 21, 2008, from http://www.edisonresearch.com/home/archives/2008/04/the_podcast_con_1.php.

9 Roxanne Darling, "Podcasting Listeners Are Paying Attention," *Bare Feet Studios* (May 1, 2008), accessed June 21, 2008, from http://www.barefeetstudios.com/2008/05/01/podcasting-listeners-are-paying-attention.

10 Bill Goodwill and Ken Fischer, "New Media–New Audiences–New Technologies: Social Media Is Changing the PSA Landscape," *PSA Research Center* (n.d.), accessed June 21, 2008, from http://www.psaresearch.com/.

11 Newsletter & Electronic Publishers Association, "How Many Subscription Newsletters Exist?" accessed June 17, 2008, from http://www.sipaonline.com/about/newsletter/FAQs.htm.

12 *Saudi Aramco World*, accessed 28 September 2005, from http://www.saudiaramcoworld.com/issue/200504.

13 Suzanne Alexander Ryan, "Companies Teach All Sorts of Lessons with Educational Tools They Give Away," *The Wall Street Journal* (April 19, 1994), p. B1.

14 Ibid., p. B2.

15 Adam Shell, "Reaching Out to the TV Generation," *Public Relations Journal*, 46(11) (November 1990), pp. 28–32.

16 Zoe McCathrin, "The Key to Employee Communication: Small Group Meetings," *Professional Communicator* (Spring 1990), pp. 6, 7, 10.

17 David Allen Ibsen, "'Sex and the City' Movie: A Product Placement Bonanza," *Five Blogs Before Lunch* (March 17, 2008), accessed June 21, 2008, from http://daveibsen.typepad.com/5_blogs_before_lunch/2008/03/sex-and-the-cit.html. For a discussion of the ethics of product placement, see Dean Kruckeberg and Kenneth Starck, "The Role and Ethics of Community Building for Consumer Products and Services," in Mary-Lou Galician, ed., *Handbook of Product Placement in the Mass Media: New Strategies in Marketing Theory, Practice, Trends and Ethics* (New York: Best Business Books, 2004), pp. 133–146.

18 Aimee Stern, "Overseas Sales Hype," *International Business* (February 1993), pp. 64, 66.

19 Judy L. Roberts, "Co-op VNRs Distribute Messages and Costs," *Tactics, PRSA* (June 1997), pp. 20–21.

20 Douglas Simon, "VNRs Support Corporate Image Campaigns," *Tactics, PRSA* (June 1997), p. 26.

21 Sally Jewett, "Health Care VNRs: Alive and Well," *Tactics, PRSA* (June 1997), p. 23.

22 David Gumpert of NetMarquee Online Services, "Challenge for Web Site Managers: Now That You're a Publisher, What Will You Publish?" *tips & tactics*, supplement of *pr reporter*, 35(2) (February 24, 1997); and see "Planning Powerful Electronic Publications," *tips & tactics*, supplement of *pr reporter*, 35(14) (October 27, 1997).

23 Greg Hansen of Cyberactive Services, "Smaller May Be Better for Web Marketing," *tips & tactics*, supplement of *pr reporter*, 35(16) (December 8, 1997).

24 Bill Comcowich, "New Video Monitoring Service Automatically Searches Consumer Video Sharing Sites Each Day for Video Clips About Companies or Brands: Free Trial Offered," *CyberAlert* (November 14, 2007), accessed June 21, 2008, from http://www.cyberalert.com/r_111407.html.

Chapter 11

1 Joseph Turow, *Breaking Up America: Advertisers and the New Media World* (Chicago: University of Chicago Press, 1997).

2 Andrew VaValle, "Newspaper-Circulation Drop Sharpens," *The Wall Street Journal* (April 29, 2008), p. B1, accessed June 23, 2008, from http://online.wsj.com/article/SB120938966488449473.html.

3 Sarah Ellison, "Newspapers Try New Math on Circulation," *The Wall Street Journal* (November 6, 2007), p. B10, accessed June 23, 2008, from http://online.wsj.com/article/SB119427904477182611.html?mod=djem_jiewr_jm.

4 Diane Farsetta and Daniel Price, "Fake TV News: Widespread and Undisclosed," *PR Watch.org*, accessed April 6, 2006, from http://www.prwatch.org/fakenews/execsummary.

5 Victor V. Cordell and George M. Zinkhan, "Dimensional Relationships of Memory: Implications for Print Advertisers," *Journalism Quarterly*, 66(4) (Winter 1989), pp. 954–59.

6 Bob T. W. Wu, Kenneth E. Crocker and Martha Rogers, "Humor and Comparatives in Ads for High- and Low-Involvement Products," *Journalism Quarterly*, 66(3) (August 1989), pp. 653–61, 780.

7 Karen S. Johnson-Cartee and Gary Copeland, "Southern Voters' Reaction to Negative Political Ads in 1986 Election," *Journalism Quarterly*, 66(4) (Winter 1989), pp. 888–93, 986.

8 Frank Thayer, "Measuring Recognition and Attraction in Corporate, Advertising Trademarks," *Journalism Quarterly*, 65(2) (Summer 1985), pp. 439–42.

9 For production details, such as copyfitting, see Doug Newsom and Jim Haynes, *Public Relations Writing: Form & Style*, 8th ed. (Belmont, CA: Wadsworth, 2008).

10 For a full discussion of this topic, see Newsom and Haynes, *Public Relations Writing*, pp. 381–88.

11 William Ruder and David Finn, *How to Make Your Annual Report Pay for Itself*, second booklet in *Management Methods*, a series on public relations by members of Ruder and Finn, Inc.

12 "Formal Guidelines for Reviewing Information Films or Videotapes," *pr reporter* (February 23, 1982), p. 4. For information on writing scripts and speeches Doug Newsom and Jim Haynes, *Public Relations Writing: Form & Style*, 7th ed., pp. 319–35.

13 Details by Jim Haynes on planning an event appear in the *Instructor's Guide* to this text.

14 Jodi B. Katzman, "Interactive Video Gets Bigger Play," *Public Relations Journal*, 51(1) (May 1995), pp. 6–8, 10, 12.

15 "Formal Guidelines for Reviewing Information Films or Videotapes," *pr reporter* (February 23, 1982), p. 4.

16 Bill Richards, "Bright Idea Has Business Looking Up for Ad Blimps," *The Wall Street Journal* (Oct. 14, 1997), pp. B1, 8.

17 Andy Dworkin, "Lighthearted Nicknames Have Serious Side," *Dallas Morning News* (March 15, 1998), pp. H1, 2.

18 "Danica Patrick's Q&A," accessed June 23, 2008, from http://sportsillustrated.cnn.com/ features/ 2008_swimsuit/danica-patrick/qa.html.

19 Some negative financial aspects of promotions are detailed in two articles: John Philip Jones, "The Double Jeopardy of Sales Promotions," *Harvard Business Review* (September–October 1990), pp. 145–52; Magid M. Abraham and Leonard M. Lodish, "Getting the Most Out of Advertising and Promotion," *Harvard Business Review* (May–June 1990), pp. 50–60. The latter carries this observation: "Managers must cut back on unproductive promotions in favor of hard-to-imitate promotion events that directly contribute to incremental profitability. And they must use the new data to shape distinctive promotional efforts for specific local markets and key accounts" (p. 50).

20 Associated Press, "Flyover Foe Gives Ride a Try and Nearly Dies," *Fort Worth Star-Telegram* (June 4, 1990), sec. 1, p. 3.

21 Andrew Patner, "Papers Take Alternative Path to Success," *The Wall Street Journal* (June 19, 1990), p. 31.

22 Many U.S. publics do not recognize English as their language of choice, and the variety of languages in the USA alone can present a challenge. *PR News* reports that some 100 languages are spoken daily in the southern part of California alone. *PR News*, 66(46) (November 26, 1990), p. 3.

23 *pr reporter* (September 20, 1982), p. 3.

24 John Martin Meek, "How to Prepare Your Client for Government Testimony," *Public Relations Journal* (November 1985), pp. 35–37.

25 Yumiko Ono, "Mouthwash PR Bad-Mouths Star and Other Zlutzy Campaigns," *The Wall Street Journal* (December 23, 1997), p. B8.

26 Ronald E. Rhody, "The Conventional Wisdom Is Wrong," *Public Relations Journal* (February 1983), pp. 18–31.

27 Ibid., p. 19.

Chapter 12

1 Benjamin Franklin, *"The Sayings of Poor Richard": The Prefaces, Proverbs, and Poems of Benjamin Franklin Originally Printed in Poor Richard's Almanacs for 1733–1758*, Paul Leicester Ford, ed. (New York and London: G. D. Putnam's Sons: The Knickerbocker Press, 1889), p. 282.

2 Patrick Jackson, speech for Vern C. Schranz Distinguished Lectureship in Public Relations, Ball State University, Muncie, Indiana, 1984.

3 Chicago Tribune, "As Fat Fears Grow, Oreo Tries New Twist," *Courier* (August 29, 2005), pp. A1 and A7.

4 *pr reporter* (May 29, 1978), p. 1.

5 John E. Rehfeld, "What Working for a Japanese Company Taught Me," *Harvard Business Review*, 68(6) (November–December 1990), pp. 167–76, especially p. 171.

6 Ronald E. Rice and William J. Paisley, eds., *Public Communication Campaigns* (Beverly Hills, CA: Sage, 1981), p. 7.

7 Charles T. Salmon, ed., *Information Campaigns: Balancing Values and Social Change* (Newbury Park, CA: Sage, 1989), p. 47.

8 William Paisley, "Prologue," in Ronald E. Rice and Charles K. Atkin, eds., *Public Communication Campaigns*, 2nd ed. (Newbury Park, CA: Sage, 1989), p. 17.

9 Ibid., p. 21.

10 Ibid., p. 23.

11 Ibid., p. 23.

12 Hernando Gonzáles, "Interactivity and Feedback in Third World Development Campaigns," *Critical Studies in Mass Communication*, 6 (1989), pp. 295–314.

13 U.S. Department of Labor Bureau of Labor Statistics, "Advertising and Public Relations Services," accessed June 24, 2008, from http://www.bls.gov/oco/cg/cgs030.htm.

Chapter 13

1 Doug Newsom, "A Crisis Typology," paper presented at the Latin American and Caribbean Communication Conference, Florida, February 5, 1988.

2 Lerbinger describes crises as natural, technological, confrontation, malevolence, skewed management values, deception and management misconduct. He has a strategy for dealing with each. See Otto Lerbinger, *The Crisis Manager: Facing Risk and Responsibility* (Mahwah, NJ: Lawrence Erlbaum Associates, 1997).

3 James D. Wilson, "Connecting Risk Assessment to Risk Management: The Center's Risk Analysis Program," *Center for Risk Management Newsletter*, No. 9 (Winter 1996).

4 Rupert Steiner, "Office Disaster? It's All in the Planning," *Sunday Times* (London) June 29, 2003, section 3, p. 12. For more details on physical preparation for planning, see chapter 2, "Crisis Communication and the Planning Process," in *Writing for Public Relations: Form and Style*, 8th ed., by Doug Newsom and Jim Haynes (Belmont, CA: Wadsworth, 2005), pp. 395–420.

5 Alfonso Gonzales-Herrero and Cornelius B. Pratt, "An Integrated Symmetrical Model for Crisis-Communications Management," *Journal of Public Relations Research*, 8(2), pp. 79–105.

6 David L. Sturges, Bob J. Carrell, Douglas A. Newsom and Marcus Barrera, "Crisis Communication: Knowing How Is Good, Knowing Why Is Essential," paper for Third Conference on Corporate Communication, Global Communications: Applying Resources Strategically, Fairleigh-Dickinson University, Madison, New Jersey, May 23–24, 1990.

7 Newsom, "A Crisis Typology."

8 Nancy Jeffery, "Preparing for the Worst: Firms Set Up Plans to Help Deal with Corporate Crises," *The Wall Street Journal* (December 7, 1987), p. 23.

9 Donald R. Stephensen, "Are You Making the Most of Your Crises?" *Public Relations Journal* (June 1984), pp. 16–18.

10 Norman R. Augustine, "Managing the Crisis You Tried to Prevent," *Harvard Business Review* (November–December 1995), pp. 147–58.

11 David Sturges, Bob Carrell, Doug Newsom and Marcus Barrera, "Crisis Communication Management: The Public Opinion Node and Its Relationship to Environmental Nimbus," *SAM Advanced Management Journal*, 56(3) (Summer 1991), pp. 22–7.

12 One of the most comprehensive crisis planning books is *The Emergency Public Relations Manual*, 3rd ed. (1987), by Alan B. Bernstein, president of PASE, Inc., printed by PASE, POB 1299, Highland Park, NJ 08904. Another is *Crisis Communications Planning Guide* by Skutski & Associates, Inc., 100 First Avenue, Suite 800, Pittsburgh, PA 15222.

13 Doug Newsom and Jim Haynes *Public Relations Writing: Form and Style*, 7th ed. (Belmont, CA: Wadsworth, 2005), pp. 394–420.

14 Freda Colburne, "The Dark Side of Management," *PR News*, March 20, 2000, p. 4.

15 A good reference for rehearsing negotiations in a hostage situation is "The Structure of Communication Behavior in Simulated and Actual Crisis Negotiations," by Paul J. Taylor and Ian Donald in *Human Communication Research*, 30(4) (October 2004), pp. 443–78.

16 Robert L. Heath, "Telling a Story: A Narrative Approach to Communication During Crisis," Speech Communication Association Conference (now National Communication Association), San Diego, California, 1996.

17 Colburne, "The Dark Side of Management."

18 David Pincus and Lalit Acharya, "Employee Communication During Crises: The Effects of Stress on Information Processing," paper presented at the Association for Education in Journalism and Mass Communication, San Antonio, Texas, August 1987. Published as "Employee Communication Strategies for Organizational Crises," in *Employee Responsibilities and Rights Journal*, 1(3) (1988), pp. 181–99.

19 Bob Carrell, "Predicting Ethical and Responsible Communication Behavior of Organizations in Crisis Situations," paper presented at International Association of Mass Communication Research conference, New Delhi, India, August 27, 1986.

20 Carol Hymowitz, "Should CEOs Tell Truth About Being in Trouble, Or Is That Foolhardy?" *The Wall Street Journal*, February 15, 2005, p. B1.

21 James E. Lukaszewski, *Executive Action Newsletter*, April-May-June, 1999, p. 1.

22 Lisa Lyon and Glen T. Cameron, "A Relational Approach Examining the Interplay of Prior

Reputation and Immediate Response to a Crisis," *Journal of Public Relations Research*, 16(3), pp. 213–41.

23 Harlan Teller, Hill & Knowlton Executive Managing Director of U.S. Corporate Communications Practice, "Communicating During a Crisis Includes Research: 10 Rules of the Road," *tips & tactics*, a supplement of *pr reporter*, 35(11) (September 8, 1997).

24 James E. Lukazewski, "Getting the Boss to Listen," *Executive Action* (January/February/March 2002), p. 1.

25 Jonathan Weil, Alexei Barrionuevo and Cassell Bryan-Low, "Auditor's Ruling, Andersen Win Lifts U.S. Enron Case, Shredding Wasn't Factor in Verdict, Jurors Say: A Single E-Mail Was," *The Wall Street Journal*, June 17, 2002, pp. A1, A10.

26 Staff of Management Review, "The Alaskan Oil Spill: Lessons in Crisis Management," *Management Review* (April 1990), pp. 12–21.

27 See Newsom and Haynes "Crisis Communication and the Planning Process." Chapter 20, *Public Relations Writing: Form & Style*, 7th ed., pp. 394–420.

28 W. Timothy Coombs, "Choosing the Right Words," *Management Communication Quarterly*, 8(4) (May 1995), pp. 447–76. The typology referred to ranges from defensive (attack, deny, excuse, justify) to accommodative (ingratiation, corrective action, full apology). Coombs's modification strategy is for the organization to admit the situation is not good and everyone is working hard to make it better. The approach is humble with no admission of responsibility. For additional Coombs research, see "An Analytic Framework for Crisis Situations: Better Response from a Better Understanding of the Situation," *Journal of Public Relations Research*, 10 (3) (1998), pp. 117–91.

29 Alan B. Bernstein, "Handling the Press Under Stress," *Enterprise* (October 1984), p. 26–7.

30 Ibid.

31 Public affairs/PR people often differ from CEOs on issues. Some research indicates that the major factor is age, because people tend to become more conservative as they grow older, and the longer a person is in corporate public affairs, the more likely he or she is to reject the interests of the CEO. These two factors are discussed, along with other research on the topic, in Fred J. Evans, "Business: Attacked from Without and Undermined from Within?" *International Public Relations Review* (November 1983), pp. 27–32.

32 See Doug Newsom, "Crisis, No Longer Local, Always Global," *Public Relations Voice*, 8(2) (2005) (India), p. 12.

33 Robert G. Picard and Paul D. Adams, "Characterization of Acts and Perpetrators of Political Violence in Three Elite U.S. Daily Newspapers," Terrorism and the News Media Research Project, funded by the Gannett Foundation, sponsored by the Association for Education in Journalism and Mass Communication, Robert G. Picard and Lowndes (Rick) Stephens, directors.

34 Jack Lule, "The Myth of My Widow: A Dramatic Analysis of News Portrayals of a Terrorist Victim," Terrorism and the News Media Research Project, funded by the Gannett Foundation, sponsored by the Association for Education in Journalism and Mass Communication, Robert G. Picard and Lowndes (Rick) Stephens, directors.

35 Walter D. St. John, *A Guide to Effective Communication* (Keene, NH: Department of Education, Keene State College).

36 For additional information, see Nicholas DiFonzo and Prashant Borda, "Corporate Rumor Activity, Belief and Accuracy," *Public Relations Review*, 28 (2002), pp. 1–19.

37 "Corporate Communicators Respond to Rumors, Email Scams," *Ragan's PR Intelligence* (November 2001), p. 9.

38 "Cybersquatter Problems? Here's Your Cost-Effective Way to Handle 'em," *Ragan's Interactive Public Relations*, 6(12) (December 2000), p. 1.

39 "Use Targeted Letters to Refute Web Site Rumors," *Interactive Public Relations* (October 1999), 5(9), p. 7.

40 Pepsi, *The Pepsi Hoax: What Went Right?*, brochure from the company published by Pepsi-Cola Public Affairs, 1993.

41 See Laurie P. Cohen, "Stewart's Latest Project: Advocating for Prisoners," *The Wall Street Journal*, January 14, 2005, p. A4.

42 Otto Lerbinger, "Theorists Discuss Management Crisis Successes and Failures," *purview*, a supplement of *pr reporter*, 436 (March 9, 1998).

Chapter 14

1 Thomas L. Friedman, *The Lexus and the Olive Tree: Understanding Globalization* (New York: Farrar Straus Giroux, 1999), p. 35.

2 For a thorough discussion on the political, economic and cultural influences on the gathering and presentation of news, see "International Media Systems: An Overview," by John Merrill, Chapter 2 in *Global Journalism: Topical Issues and Media Systems* by Arnold S. deBeer and John Merrill (Boston: Allyn and Bacon, 2004).

3 K. Sriramesh and Dejan Verčič, eds., *A Handbook of International Public Relations* (Hillsdale, NJ: Lawrence Erlbaum Associates, 2003).

4 H. M. Culbertson and Ni Chen, eds., *International Public Relations: A Comparative Analysis* (Mahwah, NJ: Lawrence Erlbaum Associates, 1996), pp. ix–x.

5 Forms of government (23): republic; people's republic; socialist republic; cooperative republic (Guyana); Islamic republic (Iran); federal republic (Argentina); federal state (Austria); federal parliamentary state (Australia); socialist state (Liechtenstein); parliament coprincipality (Andorra); monarchy (Bahrain); constitutional monarchy (Antigua and Barbuda); federal constitutional monarchy (Belgium); dependent territory (Bermuda, UK); overseas territory (Aruba, Netherlands); territory (American Samoa); overseas department (French Guiana); overseas country (New Caledonia [French]); department collectivity (Mayotte); part of a realm (Greenland, [Danish]); crown dependency (Guernsey, UK); commonwealth (Puerto Rico, U.S.); federation of emirates (United Arab Emirates). For an explanation, go to the glossary of any major reference book.

6 Larissa A. Grunig, "Activism: How It Limits the Effectiveness of Organizations and How Excellent Public Relations Departments Respond," in James E. Grunig, ed., *Excellence in Public Relations and Communication Management* (Hillsdale, NJ.: Lawrence Erlbaum Associates, 1992), p. 504.

7 "How Terrorists Think," *Financial Times*, Weekend, June 12–13, 2004, pp. W1, 2, from an interview with Jessica Stern about her book *Terrorism in the Name of God* (Emerald Grouop Publishing, Ltd., London, England: HarperCollins, 2003).

8 Jim R. McNamara, "The Crucial Role of Research in Multicultural and Cross-Cultural Communication," *Journal of Communication Management*, 8(3) (2004), pp. 322–34.

9 John C. Merrill and S. Jack Odell, *Philosophy and Journalism* (New York: Longman, 1983), p. 153.

10 Ibid, p. 158.

11 Ibid, p. 162.

12 Ibid, p. 163.

ABC Audit Bureau of Circulations; an organization giving accurate circulation data on U.S. print media.

A–B rolling Used in editing video tape and other media. A-roll is laid into the non-linear editing system first. It consists of Sound on Tape (SOT) or called Sound Bites, and the narrator's audio track. B-roll, or video gathered during the taping of the story is layered on top of the A-roll. B-roll often matches the narrative being communicated on the A-roll.

academy leader A specifically marked film with numbers one second apart, used for cueing film in the projector.

accidental/convenience sampling A type of nonprobability sampling that involves the selection of happenstance, as opposed to planned, samples. Standing near the information booth at a shopping mall and asking questions of shoppers who happen to walk by is an example of using an accidental or convenience sample.

account A contract agreement with a client.

acetate A transparent plastic sheet used in layouts, called "cell" for cellulose acetate; it also serves as a base for photographic film and is used for magnetic tape too important to risk stretching. Acetate does not stretch and breaks cleanly.

across the board A show aired at the same time daily at least five days a week; also called a strip show.

adjacencies Broadcast term referring to programs or a time period; usually means commercials placed next to specific programming.

advance News story about an event to occur in the future.

advertising Paid-for time or space, except in the case of public service announcements (PSAs) where the time and space are donated to a nonprofit organization.

advertorial (1) In broadcasts, an organization's use of commercial time to state a point of view on an issue, often called an *infomercial*; (2) in print, a simulated editorial text with advertising content, usually run in consumer publications—product- or service-oriented copy.

advocacy advertising Advertising that is a form of lobbying to influence public opinion.

AE Account executive; the liaison between the firm and the client.

aerial shot A photo taken from a helicopter or plane. In movie film production and printing, the term refers to a particular effect.

affidavit A sworn statement; proof that commercials were aired at specific time periods.

affiliate A radio or TV station that is part of a network but is not owned and operated by the network.

AFM American Federation of Musicians; a union.

AFTRA American Federation of Television and Radio Artists; a union whose membership consists of anyone who performs live on videotape; filmed TV shows require membership in SAG—Screen Actors Guild.

agate Typographic term for 5 1/2-point type, the standard unit of measurement for advertising lineage; 14 agate lines to the inch.

air brush An artist's brush that operates with compressed air; it is used to retouch photos or create special effects in illustrations.

air check Tape made of a radio or TV program or a commercial when it is aired.

airtime Time when a radio or TV program starts.

alignment (1) Straightness or crookedness of letters in a line of type; also refers to the positioning of the elements in an ad for a desirable effect. (2) "Setup" of the head on an audio- or videotape machine.

alphanumeric A set of characters used in computer programming that includes letters, digits and other special punctuation marks.

AM May mean either a morning newspaper or standard radio broadcasting—amplitude modulation of 535 to 1605 Kilohertz (kHz).

angle Particular emphasis of a media presentation; sometimes called a slant.

animation Process of filming cartoon drawings, with each sequential drawing slightly different from the preceding one, to create the illusion of movement.

annual report Financial statement by management, used as a communication to all stockholders, security analysts and other interested publics; required by Securities and Exchange Commission for publicly held companies.

answer print In 35-mm film, the first print off a negative (or in 16-mm, off a reversal) after the work print is completed; used to check quality.

AOR Album-oriented rock music; designation for a type of radio station format.

AP Associated Press; a cooperative or membership news-gathering service, dating from 1848, serving both print and broadcast media with stories and pictures. AP is international in scope and has its own

---

*For a comprehensive book (679 pages) of communications terms (to 1996), see *NTC's Mass Media Dictionary*, by R. Terry Ellmore (Lincolnwood, IL: National Textbook Company, 1996).

correspondents, in addition to receiving material from member media.

Arbitron Ratings company and sales research organization for broadcasting; also known as ARB.

arc To move the camera in an arcing motion about a subject.

A-roll The portion of a video news release (VNR) that has sound. This first clip in a double chain of video is used by television news directors who do not wish to edit the VNR.

art General term for all illustrations in any medium.

art-type Adhesive-backed, paste-on type used for special effects.

ASCAP American Society of Composers, Authors and Publishers; a licensing clearing house that sets fees and controls artistic performance activity. *See also* BMI.

ascender The element of a lowercase letter extending above the body of the letter, as in *b, d* and *h. See also* descender.

ASCII (ask-ee) American Standard Code for Information Interchange; a code that makes text easier to transfer over networks.

aspect ratio TV picture measurement—three units high and four wide; also used for film measurement, varying with the format.

assemble mode Adding shots on videotape in a consecutive order.

attitude A predisposition to behave in a certain way. People exhibit their attitudes by what they do or say; knowing someone's attitude often helps predict how that individual will act.

audience Group or groups receptive to a particular medium.

audio Sound.

audio mixer (1) Control room technician who mixes sound from different sources; (2) equipment for mixing sound.

audit In communications, a review analyzing perceptions of key publics (usually with an emphasis on internal publics), evaluating disparities between the two and formulating recommendations for improving the flow of communications.

author's alterations (AA) Composition term for changes made on proofs by the author after type has been set. *See also* printer's errors.

availabilities Unsold time slots for commercials.

back light (1) Diffused illumination from behind the subject and opposite the camera; (2) in three-point lighting, a light opposite the camera to separate the subject from the background.

back of the book In magazines, the materials appearing after the main editorial section.

backroom or backshop The mechanical section of a newspaper plant.

backtiming (1) In broadcasting, a method of determining the time at which various program segments must begin to bring a program out on time. (2) In a PR campaign, scheduling to determine completion dates for various component parts to climax.

backup (1) In newspaper assignments, a second reporter or photographer used as a backup in case the first does not or cannot complete the job. (2) In printing, when one side of a sheet has been printed and the reverse side is being printed.

backup lead-in A silent lead-in to a sound film or videotape recording when the original recording preceding the sound is uncut; lead-in sound may be blooped or faded out by audio mixer.

bad break In type composition, an incorrect word division at the end of a line of type.

B&W Black-and-white (monochrome) photograph (as opposed to color photo).

bank (1) Composing-room table for galleys; (2) a strip of lights.

banner A long line of type; also called a streamer.

banner head Headlines set in large type and usually stretching across a page.

barter Paying for advertising through goods, rather than money, or airing programs with commercials or time availabilities without paying directly for the program.

BASIC Beginners All-Purpose Symbolic Instruction Code; a common time-sharing and business computer language for terminal-oriented programming.

baud Channel speed for data transmission.

beat A reporter's regular area of coverage, such as "city hall beat."

beeper (1) Recorded telephone conversation or interview; (2) device frequently attached to the telephone that "beeps" every 14 seconds as required by the FCC to indicate that a recording is being made.

beep-tape Magnetic tape reproducing a continuous beep.

belief A conviction firmly grounded in the bedrock of one's value system.

Ben Day Process carrying its originator's name that makes possible a variety of shadings in line plates through photoengraving rather than the more expensive halftone.

bicycling Transporting film or audio or video recording from one station to another instead of making a duplicate.

bit Binary digit, either a 0 (zero) or 1 (one); smallest unit of data handled by a computer; eight bits (a byte) stand for one text character.

black leader Three seconds of black video that precedes the beginning on a VNR. This helps the editors determine where to edit the story.

blanking out Breaking or separating forms, and placing spacing material where lines or illustrations have been lifted, in order to print in different colors; also called breaking for color.

bleed Running a picture off the edge of a page. The printed image is intended to extend beyond the trim edge of the sheet or page. Allow additional space on all bleed sides of an illustration to be sure it bleeds after trimming.

block programming Scheduling the same types of shows back to back; the opposite of magazine format, which is varied.

blog Weblog that carries the opinion of the creator to anyone with access to the Web.

bloop To erase sound track—by degaussing (wiping out) if magnetic, or by opaquing (blocking out) if optical.

blow up To photographically enlarge the visual size of any item.

blurb A short promotional description of a story or article.

BMI Broadcast Music, Inc.; a copyright-holding organization from which permission for using musical selections may be received without asking individual copyright holders. Permission from BMI (or ASCAP) is obtained through a license fee. The copyright covers anything broadcast that exceeds four bars. Noncommercial stations get special consideration.

board The audio control board, which sends programming to the transmitter for broadcast or to the tape machine for recording.

body type Type used for text matter, as distinguished from display (headlines or headings) type.

boldface type (BF) Blacker, heavier type than the regular typeface, so it stands out from surrounding copy.

booklet A compilation of six-plus pages, printed with a paper cover and bound.

boomerang effect When a person affected by public opinion reacts in a way opposite from that which is expected.

border The frame around a piece of typed matter.

box or boxed Type enclosed within printed borders.

bps Bits per second; how fast data can be moved.

break (1) Story available for publication; (2) stopping point—may designate a commercial break.

breaking for color *See* blanking out.

break up To kill or break up a type form so it cannot be used to print from again.

bridge (1) A phrase or sentence connecting two stories; (2) in broadcasting, transitional program music.

bright Light, humorous news story.

broadside Message printed on one side of a single sheet no smaller than 18 × 25 inches, designed for quick reading and prompt response.

brochure A printed piece of (usually) six or more pages. More elaborate than a booklet, but without a backbone; differs from a pamphlet by its use of illustrations and color.

B-roll Second clip in a double chain of video. News directors use B-roll footage to make their own versions of a video news release (VNR) that has been sent by a public relations practitioner.

brownlines Lithographer's proofs.

browser A system that facilitates searching the Internet; the three major browsers are Netscape, Explorer, and Safari.

BTA Best time available; commercial aired at the best time available for the station.

bulletin (1) Important news brief; (2) wire-service message to kill or release a story.

burnishing Spreading dots in a halftone to deepen certain areas; also rubbing down to make pasteups stick.

business publications Periodicals published by and/or directed toward business.

bust shot Photographic framing of a person from the upper torso to the top of the head.

busy Too cluttered, as in a print illustration, still photograph or TV scene.

butted slug Type matter butted together to make one continuous line.

byline Reporter's name preceding a newspaper, magazine or broadcast story.

byte A set of adjacent bits considered as a unit. *See also* bit.

cable television *See* CATV.

CAD/CAM Computer-aided design and computer-aided manufacturing; systems of special hardware and software used in architectural or mechanical design that produce working blueprints or drawings from which the structure or product can be manufactured.

cameo lighting Foreground figures are lighted with highly directional light, with the background remaining dark.

camera chain TV camera and associated equipment, including power supply and sync generator.

camera copy Copy ready for reproduction; also called repros.

camera negative Original negative film shot by a film camera.

camera-ready Material for a publication or printed piece that is in final form, ready to make a plate for printing.

campaign An organized effort to affect the opinion of a group or groups on a particular issue.

caps Capital letters.

caption or cutline Editorial material or legend accompanying an illustration.

casting off Estimating the space required for copy set in a given type size.

cathode ray tube (CRT) An electronic vacuum tube with screen, on which information, news stories and so on can be displayed.

CATV Community antenna television, also called cable TV; a system in which home receivers get amplified signals from a coaxial cable connected to a master antenna; CATV companies charge a monthly fee for this service.

CCTV Closed-circuit TV; programs telecast not to the public but only to a wired network of specific TV receivers.

CD-ROM Compact disc, read only memory; electronic publication that makes much information available for research and offers an opportunity for publicity materials to be made available electronically.

CDs Compact discs that can carry text, photos and music for use with a computer.

cell or photocell Optical reader.

cell phone *See* mobile phone.

census Counting or asking questions of all elements or members of a population, rather than taking a sample of that population.

center spread Two facing center pages of a publication, printed on a single, continuous sheet.

central tendency The "average" direction or "middle ground" of data, usually expressed as the mean, median or mode.

CERP Confederation Europeenne Des Relations Publiques, based in Brussels, comprises four separate organizations: CERP consultants, CERP education, CERP PRO (public relations officers) and CERP students. This organization has consultative status with the Council of Europe and UNESCO and is recognized and supported by the European Commission.

CFO Chief financial officer for any organization, profit or nonprofit.

chain *See* double chain; film chain.

channel (1) In broadcasting, a radio spectrum frequency assigned to a radio or TV station or stations; (2) in computer science, a path for electrical communication or transfer of information—an imaginary line parallel to the edge of tape along which lines are punched.

channels of communication Public or private paths for messages to and from various publics.

character Any single unit of type—letter, number, punctuation mark.

character generation Projection on the face of a CRT of typographic images, usually in a high-speed computerized photocomposition system. The series of letters and numbers appears directly on the television screen or is keyed into a background picture.

cheesecake Photographs that depend for their appeal upon display of sexual images.

chroma key Electronic process for matting (imposing) one picture into another; called "shooting the blue" because it generally uses the blue camera signal of color TV cameras, but it may use any color.

circular Flier, mailing piece, free distribution item, usually one sheet and inexpensive.

circulation (1) In broadcasting, refers to the number of regular listeners or viewers of an area regularly tuned to a station; (2) in print, subscribers plus street or newsstand sales.

class publications Periodicals designed for well-defined audiences, with a focus limited to certain subjects.

CLC Capital and lowercase letters; used to designate a typesetting format.

client An institution, person or business hiring PR services.

clip (1) Newspaper clipping; (2) in broadcasting, a short piece of digital matter or tape used as a program insert; (3) to cut off high and low audio frequencies of a program; (4) to compress the white and/or black picture information, or to prevent the video signal from interfering with the sync signals.

clip art Graphic designs and illustrations sold with permission to use, so designers of advertising or publications don't have to create their own artwork; some of this art is sold in books of camera-ready line art, while other types come suitable for electronic scanning or already in electronic form for computerized desktop publishing.

clipping returns Clippings mentioning a specific subject from newspapers, magazines, trade journals, specialized publications and internal publications. Commercial services supply clippings from numerous publications for a monthly charge and a per-clipping charge or for a flat rate per clipping. "Clips" also include TV.

clipsheet Stories and illustrations formerly printed on one page and sent to publications, now set electronically.

close-up (CU) An object or any part of it seen at close range and framed tightly. The close-up can be extreme (XCU or ECU) or rather loose (MCU; medium close-up).

cluster samples Clusters or groups of elements in a population, such as particular cities or geographic regions, from which smaller samples are drawn. The population is first divided into clusters reflecting various traits, and then a sample is drawn from each cluster.

coated paper Paper with an enameled coating to give it a smooth, hard finish suitable for best halftone reproduction.

cohort study Multiple samples drawn from the same population are studied longitudinally over time and then compared or contrasted.

coincidental interview Method of public opinion surveying in which a phone interview is conducted to gain information.

cold comp Type composition by various "cold methods"—from typewriter to high-speed computerized photocomposition systems.

cold light Fluorescent light.

cold reading Broadcasting copy read by an announcer without prior rehearsal.

colophon (1) Credit line at the end of a book for the designer and printer that tells what typefaces and paper stock were used; (2) publisher's logo. *See also* logo.

color (1) "Mood" piece to go with a straight news story; (2) lively writing; (3) exaggerate, falsify; (4) colored ink or art.

column rule A vertical line separating columns of type.

combination plate A halftone and line plate combined in one engraving.

commercial protection Specific time between competing commercials granted by a station.

Committee on Public Information Committee headed by George Creel that was dedicated to gaining popular support for the U.S. war effort during World War I.

community The immediate area affected by company policy and production.

community relations A function of public relations that involves dealing and communicating with the citizens and groups within an organization's geographic operating area.

compact disc (CD) Digitally encoded storage medium for sound or text, decoded by scanning with a laser beam (CD-I is an interactive disk).

comparative ethics (descriptive ethics) A study of how different cultures observe ethical standards.

composition (1) Typesetting and makeup; (2) art arrangement of words into a stylistic format.

compositive or composite (1) In broadcasting, a sound track with the desired mix of sounds; (2) in photography, mixing elements from different negatives to create false images.

computer network Two or more interconnected computers.

computer program A set of instructions that, converted to machine format, causes a computer to carry out specified operations to solve a problem.

condensed Type that is narrower than regular face.

conservation Support of an existing opinion held by a public to keep it from changing.

console Part of a computer through which the operator or repair person communicates with the machine

and vice versa; normally it has an entry device such as a keyboard.

content analysis A research method that involves objective description or analysis of the language content of news releases, newspaper stories, speeches, videotapes and films, magazines or other publications.

continuity Radio and television copy.

continuity strip An ad in comic strip format.

control group Group composed of members chosen for particular characteristics or opinions; used as a comparison to a *test group.*

controlled advertising Usually paid advertising in which the advertiser has total control over the message, the context in which it will appear and the medium in which it will run.

controlled media There is some guarantee that the messages crafted for those media will be delivered to the audience as created, without modification.

control track The area of a videotape that is used for recording synchronization information (sync spikes), which is essential for videotape editing.

control unit In a digital computer, the parts that retrieve instructions in correct sequence; the unit interprets each instruction and then applies proper signals to the arithmetical unit.

conversion Influencing opinion away from one side of an issue toward another.

co-op advertising Sharing costs of advertising between two advertisers. In broadcasting, it nearly always refers to a national/local share.

coppering Revising old news to give it a feeling of currency.

copy (1) Any broadcast writing, including commercials; (2) any written material intended for publication, including advertising.

copy desk The news desk at a newspaper, magazine, radio or TV station where copy is edited and headlines are written.

copy fitting Determining how much copy is needed to fill a certain amount of space in a design or publication, or figuring how much space is needed to accommodate a given amount of text.

copyreader A newsroom employee who reads and corrects (edits) copy and writes headlines.

core (1) The "memory" of a computer; (2) a small hub on which film is wound for storage or shipping.

corrections Changes made to ensure accuracy.

correspondent Out-of-town or nonemployee reporter.

cost per thousand (CPM) (*M* means "thousand"); the cost to an advertiser to reach 1,000 listeners or viewers with a given message; figured by dividing time cost by size of audience (in thousands).

cover (1) To a reporter, getting all available facts about an event; (2) outer pages of a magazine—specifically, the outside front (first cover), inside front (second cover), inside back (third cover) and outside back (fourth cover).

cover shot Shot of the scene used as a reserve if you miss the action with the first shot.

cover stock Sturdy paper for magazine covers, pamphlets, booklets, tent cards, posters and other printed matter where weight and durability are important.

CPI (1) In typesetting, characters per inch; (2) in computer science, the density of the magnetic tape or drum.

CPM Cost per thousand (*M* means "thousand"); the ratio of the cost of a given TV segment to the audience reached (in thousands).

CPS Characters per second; relates to paper tapes or typewriter speeds.

CPU Central processing unit; the main frame of a computer, with circuits that control operations.

crawl graphics Usually credit copy that moves slowly up the TV or cinema screen, often mounted on a drum (or crawl). More exactly, an up-and-down movement of credits is called a roll, and a horizontal movement a crawl. Both the roll and the crawl can be produced by the character generator.

credits List of people who participated in a TV or film production.

cropping Changing the shape or size of an illustration to make it fit a designated space or to cut out distracting or undesirable elements.

cross-fade (1) In audio, a transition method in which the preceding sound is faded out and the following sound is faded in simultaneously. The sounds overlap temporarily. (2) In video, a transition method whereby the preceding picture is faded to black and the following picture is faded in from black.

CSO Civil Society Organization an activist group that monitors public and private organizations especially regarding civil rights violations (see Chapter 7).

CRT *See* cathode ray tube.

crystallization Creating an awareness of previously vague or subconscious attitudes held by a public.

CTC or CTK Copy to come.

CTG Copy to go to printer/and or production, which could be digital.

CTR Computer tape reader; attached to a phototypesetting device when needed.

CU Close-up; usually head and just below shoulders of a person in TV, film or still photograph. *See also* close-ups.

cue (1) In TV, film or radio, a signal to initiate action; (2) a mark in a TV script for technical and production staffs; (3) white or black dots on film indicating the end; (4) to find the proper place of a transcription.

culture crowding A number of cultures existing side-by-side. The USA is becoming much more diverse than at any time in its history. PR people not sensitive to this can unintentionally offend Americans who feel their cultures are not represented.

cumulative audience (cume) The audience reached by a broadcast station in two or more time periods or by more than one station in a specific time period (such as a week).

custom-built network A network temporarily linking stations for a special broadcast.

cut (1) To delete part of some copy or to end a program suddenly; (2) a track or groove in a transcription; (3) in engraving, a metal plate bearing an illustration, either lined or screened, to be used in letterpress printing (with a raised printing surface made from a matrix); (4) instantaneous transition from one film or video source to another. *See also* engraving.

cutaway shot A shot of an object or event peripherally connected with the overall event and neutral as to screen direction (usually a straight-on shot); used to intercut between two shots in which the screen direction is reversed; also used to cut between two takes with the same shot, avoiding a jump cut.

cutline The caption or legend accompanying an illustration.

cybernavigation Finding your way around the World Wide Web to find the electronic information accessible by computer.

cyberspace The abstract location of the electronic information superhighway which makes the transmission and reception of information available through computer technology.

daisy wheel A type head used in letter-quality printers that contains a font of type on a circular wheel.

dark sites Web sites on the intranet that are dormant or "dark" but ready to be used when an organization has a crisis. One site should be reserved for internal instruction, and the second can be activated for public access.

data Information, often in numerical form and often obtained through systematic observation and surveys, that helps describe, explain or predict relationships, attitudes, opinions or behavior. *Data* is plural; the singular term is *datum*.

database/data bank A collection of data used by an organization, capable of being processed and retrieved.

dateline The line preceding a story, giving date and place of origin; usually only the location is printed.

deadline The time a completed assignment is due and must be delivered.

dealer imprint The name and address of the dealer (such as automobile) printed on a leaflet, pamphlet, poster or similar matter, usually in space set aside for this purpose.

deck (1) Part of a headline; (2) a recording machine only (audio or video).

deck head A headline having two or more groups of type.

deckle edge A ragged edge on a sheet of paper.

DELPHI technique A research method that elicits an interactive exchange of ideas and information among a panel of experts to arrive at a consensus; several rounds of questionnaires usually are involved, each incorporating and reporting responses from earlier rounds of questioning.

demographics Certain characteristics in the audience for any medium—sex, age, family, education, economics.

department Regular section on a particular subject in a newspaper or magazine.

depth of field The measure in which all objects, located at different distances from the camera, appear in focus. Depth of field depends on the focal length of the lens, the f-stop and the distance between object and camera.

DES Data Encryption Standard; provides security for electronic messages.

descender Bottom part of a lowercase letter that extends below the body of the letter, as in *p, q* and *y*. *See also* ascender.

digital video Used for instructional and motivational jobs within organizations; some companies have their own closed circuit television.

dirty copy Written material with considerable errors or corrections.

disk Record or transcription.

display type Type or hand-lettering for headlines; usually larger than 14 points.

dissolve In TV or film, a gradual transition from shot to shot whereby the two images temporarily overlap; also called lap-dissolve, or lap.

documentary An informational film presentation with a specific message.

dolly To move the camera toward (dolly in) or away (dolly out or back) from the object.

domain The part of Web address that comes after the @ sign and is separated from it by a dot (period).

donut A commercial in which live copy runs between the opening and close of a produced commercial, usually a musical jingle.

dope News information or background material.

dot coms High-tech companies with Web listings; name of company.com (period = dot).

dot-matrix printer A printer that forms type characters by arranging dots of ink in a grid, or matrix, pattern.

double chain A film story using two film chains simultaneously. *See* film chain.

double-page spread Two facing pages; may be editorial material or advertising, with or without illustrations.

double projection Shooting and recording sound and pictures separately for later simultaneous productions; gives higher-quality reproduction.

double-spot Two TV commercials run back to back.

double system sound In film and TV, picture and sound portions are recorded separately and later may be combined on one film through printing (married printing).

double truck Center spread, or two full facing pages.

downlink To receive audio and video signals or digitized computer information from a communication satellite, which acts as transmitter.

download To feed a news release from the organization's computer directly into the medium's computer, for example, for typesetting purposes.

dress (1) The appearance of a magazine; (2) in broadcasting, a final dress rehearsal in which people rehearse wearing what they will wear on camera; (3) set dressing, properties.

drive out In type composition, to space words widely to fill the line.

driver A program that assists a computer with operating a device or interface.

drop folio In books and publications, page number at bottom of page.

drop-in ads Small advertising messages added to or "dropped in" regular advertisements of a different character, such as a 1-column-inch ad for a community fund drive in a department store's regular half-page ad.

dry A "slow" or "dry" news day when not much is going on.

dry brush drawing A drawing, usually on coarse board, made with thick ink or paint.

dry run A rehearsal, usually for TV, before actual taping or airing, if live.

dub Duplication of an electronic recording or an insertion into a transcription. Dubs can be made from tape to tape or from record to tape. The dub is always one generation down (away) from the recording used for the dubbing and is therefore of lower quality.

dubbing Transcribing a sound track from one recording medium to another, such as from film sound to audiotape.

dummy The suggested layout for a publication, showing positions of all elements. A hand dummy is rough and general. A pasteup dummy has proofs carefully pasted in position.

duotone Two-color art. Two halftone plates are made from a one-color illustration and etched in two different colors to produce a two-tone effect.

dupe Duplicate proof.

ears Boxes or type appearing at the upper left and right corners of publications alongside the flag (newspaper nameplate).

easel pad A large pad of paper that is held by a tripod. The public relations practitioner uses marking pens to write on a sheet of paper, which can then be flipped over or torn off so a clean sheet can be used. Easel pads can be used in small meetings and are particularly useful in recording "brainstorming" ideas or other thoughts of those attending a meeting.

easel shots or "limbos" Still pictures or models videotaped by a TV camera.

edge key A keyed (electronically cut-in) title whose letters have distinctive edges, such as dark outlines or a drop shadow.

edit To modify, correct, rearrange or otherwise change data in the computer.

editing Emphasizing important matter or deleting the less significant: (1) in live TV, selecting from preview monitors the pictures that will be aired and the assembly of shots; (2) in print media, the collection, preparation, layout and design of materials for publication.

edition Identical copies printed in one run of the press.

editorialize To inject opinion into a news story.

editorial matter The entertainment or educational part of a broadcast program or publication, exclusive of commercial messages.

EDP Electronic data processing.

electronic editing Inserting or assembling a program on videotape without physically cutting the tape.

electronic film transfer Kinescoping a program from videotape to film by filming the images that appear on a very sharp television monitor.

electronic newspaper A system in which the individual becomes his or her own gatekeeper, selecting online a tailored mix of news and other information from a newspaper web site.

electros or electrotype Printing plates made by electrolysis from original composition or plates. Made from wax or lead molds, they are much cheaper than original and duplicate photoengravings; used when long runs or several copies of plates or forms are required. If the expense of shipping is an additional cost factor, mats or flongs should be used instead of electros; replaced mostly by digital versions.

em The square of any given type body, but usually refers to the pica em, which is 12 points square. A common method of measuring type composition is to multiply the number of ems in a line by the number of lines.

email Electronic mail delivery through a browser; sometimes hyphenated (e-mail), but increasingly used without the hyphen following the style of other listings such as ecommerce, eCollege (name of an electronic learning program) and eBay (name of an online shopping place).

embossing Making an impression by pressing a piece of paper between two metal dies so that it stands above the surface of the sheet.

en Half an em, a unit of measure in typesetting. Equal to the width of a capital *N* in the particular typeface and size of typeface being used.

enameled stock *See* coated paper.

end rate The lowest rate for commercial time offered by a station.

engraving (cut) Zinc or copper plate that has been etched, generally with acid, to get a raised surface that, when inked, will print on paper. Engravings are reproductions of either line illustrations or halftones (screened); also called photoengravings, because they are made by being brought into contact with film negatives of illustrations. In commercial usage, *engraving* refers almost solely to letterpress printing, although in the past it referred to the intaglio processes.

entitlement A form of reinforcement in which publics are convinced of the value of the appeals of a campaign and "buy into" the message because they believe the organization has a "right" to ask.

equal-time provision This provision has been ruled unenforceable by the FCC. It stated that if a licensed broadcaster permits any person who is a legally qualified candidate for any public office to use the broadcasting station, the licensee has to give equal opportunity to all other such candidates, and the licensee has no power of censorship over the candidate's material that is broadcast.

essential area The section of the television picture, centered within the scanning area, that is seen by the home viewer, regardless of the masking of the set or slight misalignment of the receiver; sometimes called critical area.

establishing shot An orientation shot, usually a long shot with a wide angle giving a relationship of place and action; sometimes called a *cover shot*.

ET Electrical transcription; like a record, but produced only for broadcast stations.

etching proofs Sharp, clean proofs from which zinc etchings can be made.

ETV Educational TV.

evaluation Measuring the relative success of a program or activity in terms of the goals and objectives set for it. Evaluation is a form of research, and may use various research methodologies to answer two basic questions: "Did we do what we set out to do?" and "How well did we do it?"

exclusive A correspondent's report or story limited to a single station, network or periodical.

experiential reporting Storytelling that gives audiences the sense of participation through computer-generated reality. One method is an interactive program with audio and video being used for armchair "tours." Another is a system for experiencing virtual reality that requires wearing electronic "glasses" and using handheld devices or "gloves."

extended or expanded Extrawide typeface.

external publication Publication issued by an organization to people outside its own employee or membership groups, such as to customers, the local community and the financial world.

external publics Exist outside an organization and are not directly or officially a part of the organization, although they do have a relationship with it.

extra condensed Compressed, very thin type.

face The printing surface of type; also used to identify one style of type from another, such as plain face, heavy face and so on.

fact sheet Page of significant information prepared by PR people to help news media in covering a special event.

fade (1) In audio, the physical or mechanical decrease of volume, either voice or music, to smooth a transition between sounds; (2) in video, the gradual appearance of a picture from black (fade-in) or disappearance to black (fade-out).

family Complete series of one typeface, with all variations (bold, italic, small caps, and so on).

fax Shorthand for *facsimile*; exact reproduction of printed matter (words and photos) by telephone or radio transmission.

FCC Federal Communications Commission; the government regulatory body for broadcasting.

feature (1) To play up or emphasize; (2) a story that is not necessarily news but usually is more for human interest.

feature filler (1) In broadcast, a one- to five-minute segment, sometimes on videocassette, that serves as a filler for feature programs, talk shows or local sporting events; (2) in print, a small feature item, often called a "bright."

feed Electronic signal, generally supplied by a source such as a network from which a station can record; also, what one station sends to another station or stations.

field study Observation or experimental study in a natural setting.

file To send a story by wire, or other means. In computer language, information on a related record, treated as a unit.

fill (1) In broadcasting, additional program material kept ready in case a program runs short; (2) to fill out for timing or space.

fill copy Pad copy; relatively minor material used to "fill out" a broadcast or page.

filler A short, minor story to fill space where needed in making up the pages of a publication; copy set in type for use in emergencies.

fill light An additional direction light, usually opposite the key light, to illuminate shadow areas.

film chain A motion picture film projector, slide projector and TV camera, all housed in single unit called a "multiplexor," used to convert film pictures and sound or still pictures mounted on slides into electronic signals.

film clip A short piece of film.

film counter A device used to measure film length while editing.

film lineup A list of films in broadcast order.

film rundown A list of cues for a film story.

Financial Accounting Standards Board Sets and enforces rules on accounting for postretirement benefits other than pensions.

financial relations A function of public relations that involves dealing and communicating with the shareholders of an organization and the investment community.

financial responsibility An organization's fiscal soundness and how the organization interacts with investors and investment advisers; also, how an organization gets and spends its money.

fixed position A spot delivered at a guaranteed time.

fixed service Short-range TV transmission on the 2,500-megacycle band; generally used for closed-circuit TV.

flack Slang for a press agent or publicist, primarily those in the entertainment fields; apparently first recorded by writer Pete Martin in the April 1, 1950, issue of *Saturday Evening Post*. Martin defined the term in a May 5, 1956, issue of the *Post* with these words, "And since 'flack' is Hollywood slang for publicity man. . . ." This word has a few meanings from obsolete provincial English usage: as a verb, to palpitate, to hang loosely, to beat by flapping; and as a noun, a stroke or touch, a blow, a gadding woman. The word *flak* came into use during World War II and is an acronym for the German Flieger Abwehr Kanone, an aircraft defense cannon, literally translated to mean "the gun that drives off raiders." The Old English word and the military word may or may not have anything to do with the inspiration of its application to PR. Some sources say the entertainment industry's magazine *Variety* began using *flack* for publicist or press agent as a tribute to the motion picture industry's publicist, Gene Flack. This could account for the spelling, since the German cannon was spelled *flak*. (Source: Wes Pederson, Director of Communications and Public Relations, Public Affairs Council, letter to PRSA's *The Strategist*.).

flag (1) The front-page title or nameplate of a newspaper; (2) a device to block light in film lighting.

flagship station The major network-owned station or the major station in a community-owned group of stations.

Flash drive *See jump drive.*

flier *See circular.*

flighting Broadcast advertising technique for interspersing periods of concentrated advertising with periods of inactivity; usually six-week patterns help a small advertiser get results.

flong *See electros; matrix.*

floppy disk A disk on which computer-generated copy or graphics can be stored, largely replaced by newer storage devices such as CDs and jump drives. *See jump drive.*

FM Frequency modulation; radio broadcasting (88 to 108 megacycles) with several advantages over standard (AM) broadcasting such as elimination of static, no fading and generally more consistent quality reception.

focus group A test panel of people, usually 20 or fewer at a time, selected and interviewed as representative of a particular public likely to have views and opinions on an issue or product.

fold Where the front page of a newspaper is folded in half.

folder A printed piece of four pages or a four-page, heavy-paper container for other printed materials.

folio Page number.

follow copy Instruction to the typesetter to set type exactly like the copy in every detail.

follow-up A story presenting new developments of one previously printed; also known as a second-day story.

font Typeface in one size and style.

for general release Notifies an editor that other news media also have been given the story.

format (1) The size, shape and appearance of a magazine or other publication; (2) the skeletal structure or outline of a program, or even of the kind of programming a station does.

four-color process Reproduction of full-colored illustrations by the combination of plates for yellow, cyan (blue), magenta (red) and black ink. All colored illustrations are separated photographically into these four basic colors.

frame (1) A single picture on a storyboard; (2) a single picture in film footage; (3) 130 seconds in TV, 124 seconds in film; (4) a command to a camera operator to compose the picture; (5) a single screen on a computer.

Freedom of Information Act Federal law that gives individuals access to certain types of government information. The media derive their right to that information from the public's right.

freelancer An unaffiliated writer or artist who is available for hire, either on retainer or for specific projects.

Freenet Free access computer Internet network, usually from some part of the community.

freeze frame Arrested motion, which is perceived as a still shot.

frequency discount A lower rate available to volume advertisers.

fringe time Broadcast time is generally considered to be 5:30–7:00 P.M. and 10:30 P.M.–1:00 A.M., the early and late fringes bracketing prime time.

front of the book The main editorial section of a magazine.

front timing The process of figuring out clock times by adding given running times to the clock time at which a program starts.

f-stop The calibration on a lens indicating the ratio of aperture diameter or diaphragm opening to focal length of the lens (apertures control the amount of light transmitted through the lens). The larger the f-stop number, the smaller the aperture or diaphragm opening; the smaller the f-stop number, the larger the aperture or diaphragm opening.

fully scripted A TV script that indicates all words to be spoken and all major video information.

fundraising Working with donor publics to solicit funds, usually through benefits, for charitable groups.

futures research Research designed to anticipate and predict future events. Organizations often engage in futures research to help anticipate and prepare for changes in their political, social and economic environments.

gain Amplification of sound.

galley proofs Originally proofs reproduced from the type as it stood in galley trays before being placed in page form but with cold type as photocopied from the master print or repro.

gel or cell A sheet of transparent colored plastic used to change the color of a still photo, key light or graphic, or clear material used in film animation. It is inserted in front of key lights, on top of art.

geodemographics Audience characteristics having to do with their geographic location.

ghost writer An anonymous writer who writes copy for which someone else takes credit, that is, under the byline of another person.

gigabyte Data storage unit equivalent to about 1,000 megabytes.

gimmick A stunt that is designed to draw attention to an issue or a cause.

glossy print A smooth shiny-surfaced photograph; also called glossy.

GONGOs These organizations are voluntary grassroots groups that affect public policy and may be government-sponsored, even government-initiated and sometimes part of the bureaucracy. CSOs are Civil Society Organizations that are also voluntary grassroots groups. Both generally are less formally organized than NGOs, non-government organizations.

government relations A function of public relations that involves dealing and communicating with legislatures and government agencies on behalf of an organization.

grain (1) Direction in which paper fibers lie, and the way paper folds best. Folded against the grain, paper is likely to crack or fold irregularly. (2) Unwanted silver globs in a photograph.

graphics (1) All visual displays in broadcasting; (2) art, display lettering and design in print media.

gravure A form of intaglio printing. *See also* intaglio printing.

greeking Pasting dummy, "pretend" text set in the desired typeface and size onto a layout. The type on the layout gives the appearance of what the finished publication will look like, even though the words or characters are nonsensical.

gross rating points The combined quarter-hour ratings for a time period when each scheduled commercial for a single, specific advertiser was aired.

guanxi A Chinese business custom that has no real English translation but results in using a well-connected person of higher status and greater power to get something done. Reciprocity is understood, with that returned favor being an even more significant one.

GUI Graphical user interface; the icons or symbols that make interaction with a computer's system easier.

guideline Slugline; the title given to a news story as a guide for editors and printers.

gutter The space between the left and right pages of a printed publication.

halftone A screened reproduction (composed of a series of light and heavy dots) of a photograph, painting or drawing.

handbook A publication that functions as both a reference work and as an orientation tool. An employee handbook provides a definitive statement of what is expected from employees and what the organization offers them.

hand composition Type set by hand.

handout Publicity release.

hard disk A piece of computer hardware capable of storing large quantities of computer-generated copy or graphics.

hardware Physical equipment of the computer.

HDTV High-definition television; high-definition electronic production, or sometimes used to include any advanced TV system.

HDEP High-definition television; advanced television system with 1,125 scanning lines, 60 fields, an aspect ratio of 16:9 and a 90 mHz bandwidth.

head The name, headline or title of a story.

headnote Short text accompanying the head and carrying information on the story, the author or both.

headroom The space left between the top of the head and the upper screen edge in a television display.

Helsinki Charter Union of IPRA, CERP and ICO, all of which signed a charter agreeing on quality and quality development for public relations.

highlight halftone A halftone in which whites are intensified by dropping out dots, usually by hand-tooling.

hold News not to be published without release or clearance.

hold for release (HFR) News not to be printed until a specified time or under specified circumstances.

holdover audience Listeners or viewers inherited from a preceding program.

Home Box Office (HBO) A company that supplies pay TV programs to cable systems.

Home Information System (HIS) A computer-based electronic information system that links the home to a variety of databases; the individual consumer controls the information mix delivered.

hometown stories Stories for local newspapers of individuals participating in an event or activity, usually written so the names and perhaps addresses can be filled into a general story.

horsing Reading a proof without the original copy.

host The server computer linked to the Internet.

house ad An ad either for the publication in which it appears or for another medium held by the same owner.

house magazine House organ or company magazine; an internal publication for employees or an external publication for company-related persons (customers, stockholders, dealers) or the public.

house publication Periodical publication that is distributed to employees and perhaps to other stakeholders of an organization.

HTK Head to come; information telling composition that the headline is not with the copy but will be provided later.

HTML HyperText Markup Language; formatting instructions and codes for interactive online Internet documents.

http Hypertext Terminal Protocol; used as a prefix to URLs (Uniform Resource Locators).

human interest Feature material appealing to the emotions—drama, humor, pathos.

HUTs Households using television; the number with sets in use at one time.

hypertext Links electronic documents to provide additional information about a topic.

ID Identification; in broadcasting, includes call letters and location in a 10-second announcement that identifies the station, usually in a promotional way.

image A public's perception of an organization or individual, which is based largely on what the organization or individual does and says. The term is derived from art, where it refers to the actual or mental likeness of somebody or something.

image marketing "Selling" a positive impression of a person, company or institution.

impose To arrange pages so they will be in sequence when the printed pages are folded.

independent station A broadcast station not affiliated with a network.

indicia Mailing information data required by the Postal Service.

industry publication A periodical that is designed to serve an entire industry and that is published by an organization of industry members.

industry relations A function of public relations that involves dealing and communicating with firms within the industry of which the organization is a part.

infomercial Advocacy advertising in the broadcast media that may be as long as program length. *See also* advertorial.

information subsides Information used by the news media that comes from PR sources.

initial letter First letter in a block of copy, usually two or three copy lines deep; used for emphasis; frequently in another color.

inline Letter with a white line cut in it.

I-pod® Handheld device for electronic communication, including games and movies.

input Information entered into a computer by typing, scanning, drawing, talking, singing or transfer from another computer.

insert (1) New material inserted in the body of a story already written; (2) printed matter prepared for enclosure with letters; (3) in film, a matted portion of a picture or an additional shot added to a scene.

institutional ads, commercials and programs All productions planned for long-term effects rather than immediate response.

intaglio printing A process in which the design is scratched or etched below the general level of the metal and filled with ink, so the transfer in printing will show only the design. Gravure, for example, rotogravure, is intaglio printing.

integrated commercial An "actor-delivered" commercial incorporated into a show, or a multiple-brand announcement for a number of products by the same manufacturer.

integrated marketing communications Focused on branding to give instant recognition for a product or company.

intercut TV film technique of cutting back and forth between two or more lines of action.

intermercials Ads on the Internet that include dialogue and motion video and last up to four minutes.

internal communications Communications within a company or organization to personnel or membership.

internal publication A publication directed to personnel or membership of a company or organization.

internal publics Persons who share the institutional identity of the organization, including employees, management and many types of supporters, such as investors.

Internet The home of thousands of electronic information networks—some of them begun by news media organizations for profit and by public relations people or by nonprofit organizations to provide instant information, some of them highly specialized—on a 24-hour basis.

interstitials Web advertising that appears to a user while a browser is downloading a page within a site.

interval measures In social science, constructed measures based on experiences with distributions, rather than a true zero.

interviewee A person being interviewed.

interviewer (1) A person who seeks information by asking questions either formally or informally; (2) one who asks respondents the questions specified on a questionnaire in an opinion or market survey.

interviewer bias A form of survey error that occurs when the interviewer asks questions slanted to get a response to support a particular point of view.

intranet Internal network for organizations.

investigative reporting Searching below the surface for facts generally concealed.

IPOs Initial public offerings; when a company offers shares to investors for the first time.

IPRA International Public Relations Association; a global professional organization, based in London, representing senior practitioners in more than 70 countries.

ISDN Integrated Services Digital Network; offers voice and digital network services.

island An ad surrounded by editorial material.

ISP Internet service provider; an organization or a company such as America Online that provides gateway access to the Internet.

issue advertisements Used by an organization as a forum for its views on a topic or problem.

issues management A function of public relations that involves systematic identification and action regarding public policy matters of concern to an organization.

italic Type in which letters and characters slant.

item A news story, usually short.

jingle A musical signature or logo used for broadcast identification and as a vehicle for a message.

job press A press taking a small sheet size, normally under 25 × 38 inches.

jump (1) To continue a story from one page of a publication to another; (2) in film, to break continuity in time or space. *See also* jump cut.

jump cut Cutting between slots that are identical in subject yet slightly different in screen location. As a result, the subject seems to jump from one screen location to another for no apparent reason.

jump drive A device on which digitially produced text, audio and video can be stored externally from a computer hard drive. Sometimes called a flash drive or thumb drive.

jump head The title or headline over the continued portion of a story on another page.

jump lines Short text matter explaining the destination of continued text.

jump the gutter To continue a title or illustration from a left to a right page over the center of the publication.

justify To arrange type and spacing so that all type completely fills the line to the end of the designated column width and is the same length as lines above and below the line; also called block style.

keying An electronic effect in which an image (usually lettering) is cut into a background image.

key light The principal source of illumination.

kicker (1) A short line over the source of directional illumination; (2) a headline; (3) a type of television light.

kill (1) To strike out or discard part or all of a story; (2) in films or TV, to stop production.

kinescope Film of a TV program film taken directly from a receiving tube; also called a transfer.

LAN Local Area Network; group of computers in close location connected by cable.

lapel mike Small microphone worn as a lapel button.

laser printer A printer that uses a laser beam of light to create the printed image at a level of quality often equal to that of mechanical printing.

lavaliere mike (lav) A small microphone suspended around the neck, or worn on a tie, collar, or another part of clothing.

layout Dummy.

LC Lowercase (uncapitalized) letters.

lead ("led") Spacing, formerly metal, placed horizontally between lines of type to give more space between lines. Leads can be 1, 2 or 3 points thick. Ten-point type lines separated by 2-point leads are said to be "10-point leaded 2 points" or "10 over 12." *See also* slug.

lead ("leed") (1) The introductory sentence or paragraph of a news story; (2) a tip that may develop into a story; (3) the news story of greatest interest, usually placed at the beginning of a newscast or in the upper right corner of a newspaper, although some papers favor the upper left position.

leaders (1) In print, dots used to direct the eye from one part of the copy to another; (2) in broadcasting, a timed visual used at the beginning of sequences for cues. *See also* academy leader; black leader.

lead-in line A section of film, videotape or copy, such as the first sentence used by a newscaster, to cue the technical staff or news anchorperson.

leaflet A printed piece of about four pages, usually from a single sheet, folded.

leg Part of any network; usually a principal branch off the main trunk.

legend Cutline. *See also* caption.

letterpress A printing process in which raised type and plates are inked and then applied to paper through direct pressure.

letterspacing Putting narrow spaces between letters.

level (1) In audio, volume; (2) in video, number of volts.

Lexis Database.

lighting ratio The relative intensities of key, back and fill light.

light level Measured in foot-candles or in lumens.

light pen A penlike tube containing a photocell, which, when directed at a cathode ray tube display, reacts to light from the display. The response goes to the computer, and text in the data store can be deleted or inserted.

limbo Any set area used for shooting small commercial displays, card easels and the like, having a plain light background. The floor and the background appear to go on forever.

lineprinter A drum, chain or cathode ray tube printer that usually is capable of printing a complete line of characters in one cycle of operation. The whole line is composed in the computer.

linotype A typesetting machine that casts lines or letterpress type instead of single characters. Seldom used now.

listserv An Internet mailing list of members of special interest groups who agree to have their names on a list that sends messages to all members, and passes on their responses to all.

lithographic printing Chemically transferring an inked image from a smooth surface to paper, as in offset lithography, offset printing or photo-offset.

lithography Printing from a flat surface.

live Performed at broadcast time.

live copy Copy read by station announcer, in contrast to electronic transcriptions or tapes.

live tag A message added to a recorded commercial by the announcer, usually to localize the spot.

localize To stress the local angle.

log A second-by-second daily account of what was broadcast.

logo Logotype or ligature; (1) a combination of two or more letters, for example, *fl*.; (2) a company trade name or product identification; (3) in broadcasting, a musical or sound signature used for identification.

long shot An object seen from far away or framed very loosely. The extreme long shot shows the object from a great distance.

loop (1) In audio, a technical way to keep up special sound effects or a background noise like rain by constant transmission from one spot of tape; (2) in video, loops used with videotape may replace kinescope pictures and sound recordings for national dissemination of TV programs. Loop feeds allow the affiliated local station's programs and news reports to be picked up by the network. Film loops permit continuous repetition of the picture.

LS Long shot, as with a TV or film camera.

Mac and PC platforms Personal computers use a different technological base, or platform. Microsoft software for PCs is different from Microsoft for the Macintosh, which uses an Apple platform. Some software is available to work across platforms, but not everyone has the software.

machine format A broadcast format in which elements are not prefixed by time or relative position, but are varied; opposite of segmented.

Macintosh Operating Systems and Windows Computer programs, which may cause problems with communication if the receiver cannot open attachments.

magazine format *See* block programming.

mainframe A fast computer usually programmed with several software packages and programming languages. Individual terminals may be linked to a mainframe for access to software and for manipulation or storage of data.

make good When an ad or commercial is not run because of media error or when it is run with a misprint or malfunction, the media must publish or broadcast it free at a later date.

make ready To prepare for printing.

makeup (1) Getting type and art in printing form correctly; (2) placing information and pictures on a publication's page; (3) planning a group of pages; (4) in film, putting several films on one big reel.

manifest In content analysis, the visible, surface content.

marketing An organizational function and a set of processes for creating, communicating and delivering value to customers and for managing customer relations in ways that benefit the organization and its stakeholders. Including activities (ideas and services) of nonprofit organizations, as well as those sold for profit.

markup Proof with changes indicated.

mass publications Periodicals with wide appeal and large, general circulation.

master The original of a film or videotape.

master positive Positive film made from an edited camera negative and composite sound track with optical effects.

masthead Name of publication and staff that appears in each issue of magazine or paper, usually on the editorial page in a box that also gives information about the paper such as company officers, subscription rates and address.

material In investor relations, a term applied to any event that is likely to affect the value of stock. In the financial community, the word means any information or event that could affect the price of the stock, causing it to go up or down.

matte (1) Imposition of a scene or title over another scene, excluding background (not a blend or a super); (2) name for a box placed in front of a lens to shade and hold filters and effects; (3) dull finish needed for still photos used by TV so lights will not be reflected.

Mbone Multicast (back)bone sends video over the Internet.

mean The mathematical "average" calculated by dividing the sum of values or scores by the total number of scores; one measure of central tendency.

media (singular: medium) Conveyances for messages in channels of communication; media generally are either print or electronic.

median The exact midpoint of an array of values of scores; one measure of central tendency. Half of the values or scores are above the median, and the other half are below.

media relations A function of public relations that involves dealing with the communications media in seeking publicity for, or responding to, media interest in an organization.

Mediastat A broadcast rating service.

medium shot An object seen at medium distance, neither close up nor far away.

memory Same as storage.

merchandising Focused on the packaging of a product, idea or person; concerned with presentation.

meta search engines Do not have their own databases but have the ability to search multiple databases at one time.

MICR Magnetic ink character recognition; automatic reading by a machine of graphic characters printed in magnetic ink.

microwave relay Use of UHF radio relay stations to transmit television signals from one point to another in a line of sight, usually about 25 miles.

midcourse evaluation Evaluative research undertaken while a program or project is ongoing to determine whether any adjustments should be made in the original plan to account for changing public, media or environmental conditions.

milline A unit of space and circulation used in advertising to measure the cost of reaching an audience. The milline rate is the cost per million for a one-column line of agate type.

MIME Multipurpose Internet Mail Extensions; permits addition of nontext data such as video and audio to email text.

minicam A highly portable TV camera and videotape unit that can easily be carried and operated by one person.

minority relations A function of public relations that involves dealing and communicating with individuals and groups of racial or ethnic minorities.

mixer (1) Audio control console; (2) person working this console.

mixing (1) In audio, combining two or more sounds in specific proportions (volume variations), as determined by the event (show) context; (2) in video, combining various shots via the switcher.

mobile phone Or cell phone that carries voice, text and sometimes images and runs on rechargable batteries.

mockup A scale model used for study, testing or instruction.

mode The most common or frequently found value or score in a data set; one measure of central tendency.

model release A document signed by a model allowing use of photographs or art in which he or she appears.

modem Modulator/demodulator; a device that translates computer signals for dissemination over a telephone line, and vice versa.

monitor (1) To review a station's programming and commercials; (2) a TV set that handles video signals.

montage In TV and film, a rapid succession of images to stimulate idea association. *See also* compositive or composite.

MOO Multi object oriented; an environment that permits blending of texts, graphics and meetings (used for online instruction).

MOR Type of radio station programming that is "middle of the road."

more Written at the bottom of a page of copy to indicate that a story is not complete, that there is more to come.

morgue A newspaper library for clippings, photos and reference material.

MOS "Mitout sound"; film recorded without sound.

mouse A handheld computer input device that propels a pointer or cursor around the computer screen to select commands, functions or text.

movieola A device used to view film during editing.

MS Medium shot, as with a TV or film camera.

mult box A portable electronic box (usually resembling a large travel case) that allows dozens of tape recorders to be plugged in at once to record off the public address (PA) system so the speakers' remarks will be captured and transmitted to all simultaneously. *See also* multiplexer.

Multigraphing A trademarked process for making numerous copies of typewritten or hand-drawn material; more closely resembles hand-typing than does mimeographing.

multiplexer (1) A system of movable mirrors or prisms that takes images from several projection sources and directs them into one stationary television film camera; (2) an instrument for mixing signals.

must Written on copy or art to designate that it must appear.

NABET National Association of Broadcast Employees and Technicians; a union for studio and master control engineers; may include floor personnel.

nameplate The name of the publication appearing on page one of a newspaper. *See also* flag.

national rate A rate offered to advertisers in more than one market.

NET National Educational Television.

network Any link, by any technology, of two or more stations so they can each separately broadcast the same program.

network option time Broadcast hours when a network preempts on its affiliates and the stations it owns.

new lead Replacement for a lead already prepared, usually offering new developments or information. *See also* lead.

newsletter A periodical that contains news items of interest to a public or publics. Newsletters can be internal, external or both.

newsprint A rough, relatively inexpensive paper, usually made from wood pulp, used for many newspapers and for other inexpensive printed material.

news release A news story written in print or broadcast style for use by a news medium.

news tip A news story idea not in story format given to a news medium for that medium's staff to write if the story idea is deemed to have merit.

news wheel A news show in which content is repeated with some updating.

Nexis Database.

NFS Network File System; allows one to work on files from a remote host.

NGOs Nongovernmental organizations; may include anything from charities to activist groups; a term used more in other countries than the USA.

Nielsen The A. C. Nielsen Company, the biggest name in broadcast ratings; reputations and shows literally live or die on their Nielsen ratings.

nimbus publics Those who are outside of the organization's traditional list of publics that sometimes form when a crisis occurs. An example would be expatriates responding to an issue or event that affects their homeland or members of a religious, ethnic or racial group responding in sympathy to an event or situation happening to their constituency, although not directly to them.

9/11 September 11, 2001, the date of a three-pronged attack on the USA, attributed to the al-Qaeda organization.

nominal measures Used in ordering data, these variables have attributes that are mutually exclusive or exhaustive.

nonparametric In statistics, a method or test that is not based on distributions.

nonprobability or nonrandom sample A sample selected in such a way that it's not possible to estimate the chance that any particular member of the population will be included in the sample. Using nonprobability samples results in the risk of over- or underrepresenting certain segments of the population.

normative ethics Generally the domain of philosophers and theologians who study such questions as whether ethical behaviors are a part of human nature.

NPR National Public Radio.

obituary News biography of a dead person.

OCR Optical character recognition; electronically reading printed or handwritten documents.

offset Lithographic process.

ombudsman/woman Someone who researches complaints and problems brought by individuals or groups against an organization.

online In direct communication with the computer central processing unit (CPU).

on the nose (1) On time; (2) correct.

OPEB Postemployment benefits other than pensions, such as stock options.

open-ended A recorded commercial with time at the close for a "tag."

open spacing Widely spaced letters and other characters.

opinion An expression of an attitude, belief or feeling, usually in writing or orally, held at a particular moment.

optical center A point equidistant from the left and right sides of a sheet of paper and five-eighths of the way up from the bottom; where the reader senses the center is, although this is not the true mathematical center.

optical reader An electronic reader of copy.

opticals In film, any variations to the picture achieved after or during filming, such as mattes or dissolves; may be done during filming or by control board when multiple cameras are used.

optical scanner A visual scanner that scans printed or written data and generates their digital representation.

ordinal measures Used in ordering data, these variables have attributes that can be rank-ordered.

orphan In publishing, an indented opening line of a paragraph that appears as the bottom line on a page or column of type; these are to be avoided.

outline The gist of a written article or program.

output The information that comes out of a computer or other device, such as a printer, linked to a computer; may be in hard copy form on paper, or may be digitized information stored on a floppy or hard disk.

outtakes Filmed or taped scenes or sequences not used in the final production.

overdubbing Recording separate channels on a multichannel tape separately, and then adding and synchronizing so the original sound track is supplemented. This allows a few voices to become a chorus and a few instruments to become an orchestra.

overhead projector Equipment that projects a light onto a screen; a transparency placed on the overhead projector is projected onto the screen. Although still used, the overhead projector has been replaced to a great extent by PowerPoint projectors that project computer-generated slides.

overline Kicker headlines, above and at the left, and smaller in size than the main headline.

overrun Established printing trade practice that permits delivery of and charge for up to 10 percent more than the quantity of printed matter ordered.

overset More type set than there is space to use.

PAC (political action committee) A clearly identifiable legal organization registered and incorporated in states to raise money for politicians whom they favor.

pace The overall speed of a show or performance.

pad Fill.

page proof A proof showing type and art as they will appear in the printed piece unless subsequently altered.

pamphlet A printed piece of more than four pages with a soft cover; differs from a brochure in its size, simplicity and lack of illustrations.

pan Horizontal turning of the camera.

panel (1) An area of type sometimes boxed but always different in size, weight or design from the text and partially or entirely surrounded by text; (2) in broadcasting and other communication research, a group brought together to discuss one subject or several related subjects.

paper Various types and quality of stock that will be decided in the printing agreement.

paper tape A strip of paper on which data may be recorded, usually in the form of punched holes. Punched paper tape can be sensed by a reading head used to transfer the data. Each charge is represented by a pattern of holes, called a row or frame.

parametric In statistics, a method or test based on distributions that make different assumptions about the population from which the sample was taken.

participation spot Shared time in a program for spot commercials or announcements.

pasteup *See* dummy.

patch (1) In broadcasting, a temporary equipment connection. Patch panels or patch boards are assemblies of jacks into which various circuits are permanently tied and into which patch cords may be inserted. They are essential at "on-site" special events. (2) In publishing, a block of repro—usually one or more full lines—that is inserted in a mechanical in place of earlier material that contained an error or otherwise required updating.

PBS Public Broadcasting System.

personal A brief news item about one or more persons.

photo composition A photographic method of setting type to produce proofs on paper.

photoprint Reproduction of art or a printed or written piece by one of many different photographic copying processes.

Photostat A trademarked device for making photographic copies of art or text.

pica Standard printing measure of 12 points. There are slightly more than 6 picas to the inch.

pied type Type that is all mixed up.

PIQ Program Idea Quotient; annual study by Home Testing Institute to get reactions to new program ideas. Ratings are on a 6-point scale from "favorite" to "wouldn't watch."

pix Pictures.

place Any type of printing surface, engraving or electrotype.

play up To emphasize, give prominence.

plug A free and favorable mention.

PM Afternoon paper.

PMT (photo mechanical transfer) A positive (as opposed to a negative) that can be printed by offset lithography.

point Printers' standard unit of measure equal to 0.01384 inch. One inch equals slightly more than 72 points. Sizes of type and amounts of leading are specified in points.

poll Survey of the attitudes and beliefs of a selected group of people.

position Where elements in any publication appear; usually indicates relative significance.

postdubbing Adding a sound track to an already recorded (and usually fully edited) picture portion.

poster type Large, garish letters.

pot Potentiometer; a volume-control device on audio consoles.

power structure Those who are socially, politically and economically advantaged.

PR Public relations.

precinct principle Organization of a campaign through delegation of local responsibilities to chosen leaders in each community. These may be opinion leaders and are not necessarily political leaders.

preempt In broadcasting, to replace a regular program with a commercial or a news event of greater importance.

preemptible spot Commercial time sold at a lower rate by a station, which has the option of taking it back if it has a buyer at full rate, unless the first purchaser pays to keep it at full rate.

presentational TV performance format where camera is addressed as audience.

presidential patch Portable sound system with outlets for amplifiers to be connected; unity gain amplifier with numerous microphone-level outputs used in pool remotes to cut down on the number of microphones needed.

press agentry A function of public relations that involves creating news events of a transient, often flighty sort.

pretesting Testing a research plan, any of its elements or any elements in a campaign before launching the entire program.

primary publics Each organization has its particular primary publics, all or many of whom are priority publics. At any time, depending on the issue or situation, one or more of these primary publics can become a target, or priority, public.

printer's errors (PE) Typographical errors made by composition when setting type. *See also* author's alterations.

printing technique A basic, primary decision in the printing contract regarding the quality of the job.

priority publics Can be described nominatively, that is, by name; demographically; or psychographically. *See also* target publics.

private channels of communication Channels that are used by media to communicate with a particular individual or group.

privilege Constitutional privilege granted the press to print with immunity news that might otherwise be libelous—for example, remarks made in open court.

probability sample A sample selected in such a way that the chance that any particular member of the population will be selected for the sample is known. Using a probability sample enables the researcher to calculate the chances that the sample accurately represents the population from which it was selected.

process plates and progressive proofs Each of the color plates printed singly so they may be laid over each other for effect. In progressive prints, in addition to the single prints of each color, the colors are shown in proper color combination and rotation to suggest the final printed result.

product placement commercial products easily identified that are used in news or entertainment.

program A set of instructions that makes the computer perform the desired operations.

program trading When large investors, usually funds, have their computers set to sell automatically if a stock they are holding drops below a specified level.

promo Broadcast promotional statement, film, videotape/recording, slide or combination.

promotion A function of public relations that involves special activities or events designed to create and stimulate interest in a person, product, organization or cause.

proof A trial impression of type and engraved matter taken on paper to allow the writer and publisher to make corrections.

propaganda A function that involves efforts to influence the opinions of a public in order to propagate a doctrine.

propaganda devices Specific devices—spoken, written, pictorial or even musical—used to influence human action or reaction.

PR quotient A way to evaluate and prioritize publics.

PR wires Commercial wire services that send public relations news releases to media.

pseudoevent An event created to bring attention to an issue or cause.

psychographics The attitudes, lifestyles and interests shared by publics.

public (publics) Any group of people tied together by some common bond of interest or concern. *See also* audience.

public affairs A function of public relations that involves working with governments and other organizations that help determine public policies and legislation.

public channels of communication Mass or specialized media available to anyone who chooses to subscribe or tune in.

publicity A function of public relations that involves disseminating purposefully planned and executed messages through selected media, without payment to the media, to further the particular interest of an organization or person.

public opinion Preferences expressed by a significant number of persons on an issue of general importance. Public opinion must be expressed to be measured.

public relations The various activities and communications that organizations undertake to monitor, evaluate, influence and adjust to the attitudes, opinions and behaviors of groups or individuals who constitute their publics.

public service announcement (PSA) Promotional pieces, not news stories, in the form of advertisements carrying a nonprofit organization's message and aired or published free.

public television Noncommercial broadcasting; stations are financed by federal grants, private donations and public subscriptions.

puffery Unsubstantiated and exaggerated claims that appear in either advertising or publicity.

pulp Magazines printed on rough, wood-pulp paper, in contrast to "slicks," which are magazines printed on coated or calendared stock.

punch To give vigor to the writing or editing process.

PVI (public vulnerability index) An informal way of estimating the impact of a public on an organization; designed to help organizations identify target or priority publics.

quads A type of videotape recorder.

query A letter addressed to an editor that summarizes an article idea and asks if the piece might be considered for publication.

questionnaire The body of questions asked of subjects in a research effort.

Quicktime A computer-based video format for encoding and playing video files.

quoins ("coins") Triangular wedges of steel used in locking up a type form.

quote A quotation or estimate of costs.

RADAR Radio's All Dimension Audience Research; a survey conducted by Statistical Research Inc., for NBC, CBS, ABC and Mutual networks.

radio-TV wire (1) Broadcast wire; (2) the news services wire copy written in broadcast style.

ragged right (or left) In typography, when the left side of the text is justified and the right side varies in length. In ragged left, the right side is justified.

RAM Random access memory; a storage device in which the time needed to find data is not affected significantly by where the data are physically located.

random sample A sample in which each person or element of a population has an equal chance of being selected. A table of random numbers, sometimes generated by a computer, often is used to select sample members randomly from a population.

raster The scanned area of the CRT tube; line scans traced across the face of a CRT tube by a flying spot.

rating service A company that surveys broadcast audiences for total homes or individuals tuning in or gives percentages of total listening audience for specific stations and specific shows.

ratio Measures based on a true zero point (such as age, as opposed to temperature, which is an internal measure).

raw stock Unexposed film; called camera stock when it is unexposed film for use in a motion picture camera; called print stock when it is unexposed film for making copies of still photographs.

reach The number of people or households that a station, commercial or program is viewed or heard by in a given time period; used with frequency to measure a station's audience for evaluation of worth, generally for advertising pricing.

real time Online processing, with data received and processed quickly enough to produce output; interactive.

rear screen projection Projection of positive transparencies onto a translucent screen.

rebate An extra discount on ads earned by using more time or space than the contract specifies.

recap A recapitulation of news.

reduce To decrease the size of anything visual when reproducing it.

register (1) The correct position for a form to print in so that the pages, when printed back-to-back will be in their proper places; (2) in color printing, the precise position for superimposition of each color in order for the colors to blend properly.

rejection slip A letter or printed form from a publication's editor accompanying a manuscript returned to its author.

release print In TV, a film print made from a negative and given to stations to use.

relief printing Letterpress; letters on the block or plate are raised above the general level so that, when an inked roller is passed over the surface, the ink can touch only the raised portions.

remote A videotape recording or live broadcast originating outside the regular studios.

reprint A second or new impression of a printed work, either text or art.

repro *See* camera copy.

research The foundation of all good public relations strategy. Involves publics and public opinion, also the marketplace and the social, economic and legal climate in which a public relations activity is centered.

respondents Those to whom questions are directed in a survey.

retail rate The local rate (or lower) for advertising.

retouch To improve photographs before reproduction as artwork.

reversal print A copy made on reversal print stock.

reverse To print text or art in white on a dark background, or, in making a cut from a picture, to turn over or "flop" the negative so that everything appears as a mirror, not a true, image.

review A critique or commentary on any aspect of human events—politics, society or the arts.

rewrite person A newspaper staff member who rewrites stories and takes phoned-in reports but does not leave the office to cover news.

rim On newspapers, the outer edge of a copy desk where copyreaders work under the direction of a "slot" person or copy chief.

ROP Run of press; means that an ad may be placed on any page of the publication.

ROS Run of station or run of schedule; costs less and is usually preemptible.

rotary press A press that prints from curved stereotypes or a plate attached to a cylinder.

rotogravure Printing by means of a sensitized copper cylinder on which is etched the image to be reproduced.

rough A preliminary visualization of art.

rough cut The first editing of a film, without effects.

roundup A comprehensive story written with information gathered from several sources.

router Routes data on alternative paths if part of a computer network is busy.

routing Cutting out part of a plate or engraving to keep it from printing.

rule A thin strip of type-high metal that prints as a slender line.

run in To join one or more sentences to avoid making an additional paragraph.

running foot Identification information printed in the bottom margin of a magazine.

running head Identification information printed in the top margin of a magazine.

running story or breaking story A fast-breaking story usually written in sections.

saddle stitching Binding pages by stitching with wire through the fold.

SAG Screen Actors Guild.

sample The portion of the total population queried in a survey, intended to be representative of the total population.

sample error The degree to which a sample lacks representativeness; this can be measured and is reduced by having large samples or more homogeneous ones.

sandwich or donut In broadcasting, a commercial with live copy between the musical open and close.

sans serif Typeface without serifs, which are the cross lines at the end of the main strokes of many letters.

scaling Measuring and marking illustrations for engraving to ensure that the illustration will appear in the appropriate, designated size and in proper proportion.

scanner Optical scanner.

scanning Movement of an electron beam from left to right and from top to bottom on a screen.

scanning area The picture area scanned by a television camera's pickup tube; more generally, the picture area actually reproduced by the camera and relayed to the studio monitors.

search engine A service such as Google, Yahoo!, Excite or Infoseek that catalogs or indexes Web sites and allows users to search by using key words; a system that has databases and searches them to find topics.

segue An audio transition method whereby the preceding sound goes out and the following sound comes in immediately after.

server *See* host.

service provider Company offering connection to Internet.

set close To thin spaces and omit leads.

set open To open spaces using slugs as leading.

sets in use Rating service term for the percentage of total homes in the coverage area in which at least one radio is on at any given time; the radio equivalent of HUTs (households using television).

set solid To set without extra space between horizontal type lines.

setwise Differentiates the width of a type from its body size.

7/24 A shortcut to saying the work is seven days a week, 24 hours a day; also sometimes referred to as 24/7.

shared ID When an organization or institution appears on the TV station's channel identification.

share of audience or share The percentage of the total audience tuned into each station at any given time.

shelter books Magazines that focus on housing or related subjects.

short rate A charge back to an advertiser for not fulfilling a contract.

show Program.

side stitching A method of stitching thick booklets by pressing wire staples from the front side of the booklet and clinching them in back.

SIG Special interest group.

sig Signature file such as sender's name, address, phone, fax.

silhouette or outline halftone A halftone with all of the background removed.

silk screen A stencil process using fine cloths painted so that the surface is impenetrable except where color is supposed to come through.

simulcast Simultaneous transmission over radio and television.

situational ethics Seeing ethical standards as varying or flexible in their application to specific occasions or situations.

sizing Scaling.

skip frame A process in which only alternate frames are printed, to speed up action on film.

slant Angle: (1) the particular emphasis of a media presentation; (2) to emphasize an aspect of a policy story.

slanting (1) Emphasizing a particular point or points of interest in the news; (2) disguised editorializing.

slick A publication, usually a magazine, published on coated, smooth paper.

slicks Glossy prints used instead of mattes in sending releases or art to offset publications.

slidefilm Filmstrip; a continuous strip of film with frames in a fixed sequence, but not designed to simulate motion. A recorded sound track usually is synchronized with the succession of the film frames.

slides Individual film or digital frames, usually positive but sometimes negative transparencies, projected either in the room where an oral presentation is being given or from a TV control room. Individual film or digital frames. Slides seldom are used and not at all in television stations.

slip sheet Paper placed between sheets of printed paper to prevent smudging.

slot In newspaper rooms, the inside of a copy desk where the copy chief or copy editor sits.

slow motion A scene in which the objects appear to move more slowly than normal. In film, slow motion is achieved through high-speed photography (exposing many frames that differ only minutely from one another) and normal (24 frames per second, for example) playback. In television, slow motion is achieved by multiple scanning of each television frame.

slug lines The notation placed at the upper left of a story to identify the story during composition and makeup of a publication.

slushpile A collection of unsolicited manuscripts received by magazines.

social responsibility Another term for good citizenship; means producing sound products or reliable services that don't threaten the environment and that contribute positively to the social, political and economic health of society, as well as compensating employees fairly and treating them justly.

SOF Sound on film.

soft news Feature news or news that does not depend upon timeliness.

software The programs and routines associated with the operation of a computer, as opposed to hardware.

SOT Sound on videotape.

special to . . . Notifies an editor that no other news medium in that circulation area has received the news release.

specialty advertising Advertising that appears on such items as pens and desk calendars; advertising specialties are useful, inexpensive items on which an organization's name, logo or message is imprinted; they are given to customers or to those attending a special event.

spin Putting a slant on a story so that it shows the organization or individual in a favorable light, even if the situation is much to the contrary. Someone "spinning" or "putting a spin on" a story may be called a "spin doctor." The deception involved in this practice and the deceit associated with the term should be distinguished from the standards of practice endorsed by most public relations people.

splice The spot where two shots are actually joined, or the act of joining two shots; generally used only when the material (such as film or audiotape) is physically cut and glued (spliced) together again.

split run The division of a publication before printing to accommodate advertisers desiring to reach a specific regional market and often with regional editorial emphasis.

split screen A divided screen that shows two or more pictures; often used in TV titles and commercials.

sponsor (1) The underwriter of broadcast programming whose messages are presented with the program. Most advertisers buy spot time and are not sponsors. (2) The underwriter of an event or activity, who gets publicity for participation.

sponsored film Film or video sponsored by an organization and distributed free of charge. Film or video audiences include schools, community organizations, television stations and sometimes movie theatres.

sponsored magazine A periodical that is published by an organization whose primary purpose is not to publish this magazine, but to provide another product or service. Both profit-making and nonprofit organizations may publish sponsored magazines— for example, a magazine by a special interest group or an airline's in-flight magazine.

spot announcement or spot A broadcast commercial that usually lasts less than one minute.

spread (1) A long story, generally illustrated; (2) a group of related photographs; (3) copy that covers two facing pages in a publication, generally without gutter separation and usually printed from a single plate.

SPSS Social science statistical package; used in research.

stakeholder One who has an investment (time, money, other resources) in an organization.

stand-by The signal given in a broadcast studio before the on-air signal is given.

standing head A regularly used headline or title in a publication.

standing matter Type kept set from one printing to another, such as staff names on a newspaper.

stat The repro-quality version of line art or other material produced to specified size by a stat machine; also called photostat.

station break Break to a station for a contracted local spot; may include on-the-hour legal identification required of broadcasters by the FCC.

stereotype A plate cast by pouring molten metal into a matrix or flong; an inexpensive form of duplicating plates generally used by newspapers.

stet A proofreader's designation indicating that the copy should stand as originally written, that the change marked was an error.

stop-motion A slow-motion effect in which one frame jumps to the next, showing the object in a different position.

storyboard (1) Artwork that shows the sequence of a TV commercial; (2) in film work, drawings and text showing major visual changes in a proposed show. The storyboard grew out of animated film, which was pioneered by Walt Disney.

straight matter Plain type set in conventional paragraph form, as opposed to some kind of display.

straight news Hard news; a plain recital of news facts written in standard style and form.

stratified sample The population is divided into strata (groups or subpopulations with common traits), and the sample chosen contains the same proportion of desired traits as the population strata from which it is drawn.

stuffer Printed piece intended for insertion into bills and receipts, pay envelopes, packages delivered to customers or any other medium of delivery.

stylebook A manual setting standards for handling copy and detailing rules for spelling, capitalization, abbreviations, word usage and such.

subhead A small headline inserted into the body of a news story to break up long blocks of type.

summary lead The beginning paragraphs in a news story, usually including the *H* and five *W*s (who, what, when, where, why and how).

super In film or TV, superimposition of a scene or characters over another scene; also called a take-out or add videotape.

supercard A studio card with white lettering on a dark background, used for superimposing or keying a title over a background scene. For chroma keying, the white letters are on a chroma key blue background.

surprint In printing, superimposing type or lettering on an illustration so the type remains solid, unbroken by a screen.

survey An analysis of a market or of opinions held by a specified group.

suspended interest A news story with the climax at the close.

sync Synchronization; keeping one operation in step with another (1) between sound and picture, or (2) between a scanning beam and a blinking pulse.

synchronization rights Rights granted by a mechanical rights agency to use music licensed by them.

system cue Network identification.

tabloid A newspaper format, usually five columns wide, with each page slightly more than half the size of a standard newspaper page. A tabloid format often involves the use of just a picture and headlines on page one.

tag (1) The final section of a broadcast story, usually stand-up (personally given rather than taped) following a film or VTR; (2) an announcement at the end of a recorded commercial or music at the end of live copy.

tailpiece A small drawing at the end of a story.

take (1) In print, a portion of copy in a running story; (2) in broadcasting, a complete scene; (3) to cut.

talent Any major personality or model for ads or publicity photos. In TV or radio, anyone in front of the camera or on the air.

tally light The red light on a video camera that indicates which camera is on air or being recorded.

target publics Often called priority publics, these publics are so designated because of their impact on the organization, and vice versa.

TCP/IP Transmission Control Protocol/Internet Protocol; rules about transferring data over the Internet.

teaser (1) In print, an ad or statement used to build anticipation that piques interest or stimulates curiosity without giving away facts; (2) a technique in which the beginning of a film has scenes and sounds related to the theme of the program rather than a title.

technological transparency Global media, print and electronic, make what happens in one part of the world immediately visible and accessible, almost simultaneously, around the world.

telecommunications Long-distance transmission of signals by any means.

teleconference Use of various telecommunication devices (computers, telephones, television and video systems) to permit three or more people at multiple locations to communicate with each other in a "live" and often interactive format.

tele line The equipment room where film and slide projectors are located.

teleprocessing Information handling in which a data processing system uses communication facilities.

teletext A one-way electronic information system; noninteractive.

terminal Any point in a communication system or network where data can enter or leave.

test group People selected and used to measure reactions to or use of a product or idea.

testing Sampling the opinions, attitudes or beliefs of a scientifically selected group on any particular set of questions.

text Written material; generally used in referring to editorial rather than commercial matter; excludes titles, heads, notes, references and such.

TF Till forbid; advertising to run until advertiser terminates or contract expires.

thirty (30) In newspaper code, "that's all." A reporter writing a story places this at the last of the written material to signify the end.

thumb drive *See* jump drive.

tie-back Previously printed information included in a story to give background or a frame of reference and to refresh the reader's memory.

tie-in (1) Joint or combined activities of two or more organizations on a single promotional project; (2) a promotional activity designed to coincide with an already scheduled event.

tight In broadcast and print media, having little time or space left for additional material.

time base corrector An electronic accessory to a videotape recorder that helps make playbacks and transfers electronically stable; helps maintain picture quality, even in dubbing.

time classifications Broadcast time rated by audience level and priced accordingly, as Class AA, Class A, Class BB, Class B, and so on.

timesharing Use of computer hardware by several persons simultaneously.

tint block A solid color area on a printed piece, usually screened.

tip Information offered that could lead to a story.

tipping in Hand insertion or attachment of extra pages in a publication, usually of a different stock than other items.

title slide A graphic giving the name of a TV show.

TIVO Service that allows taping of TV programs without commercials.

total audience plan A spot package designed to reach all of a station's audiences.

track The physical location on magnetic tape where the signal is recorded for a specific source—the channel 1, 2, and so on, of audio; the video signal; the control signal.

trade or association publication A periodical published by a group whose members share a common goal or interest, for example, a labor union or a professional association.

traffic The department in ad agencies that handles production schedules; in broadcasting, traffic handles everything that goes on the air.

trial balloon Getting reaction to an idea before trying it out on the public; used by politicians who aren't certain what public reaction to an idea will be.

triggering event An event, which might be a speech or even an untimely remark distributed by media, that is, in effect, the needle that bursts a crisis balloon and precipitates a crisis.

trim (1) In newspapers, to shorten copy; (2) in printing, the final process that cuts all pages to the same size.

turnover In advertising, the ratio of *net unduplicated* cumulative audience over several time periods to average audience per time period.

TWX (TWIX) A teletype machine.

typeface A particular type design; may carry the name of the designer or a descriptive name.

type family The name given to two or more type series that are variations of the same basic design.

type page The printed area on a page bordered by margins.

type series The collective name for all sizes of one design of typeface.

typo Typographical error.

UC and LC Upper- and lowercase—capitals and small letters.

UHF Ultra high frequency; TV channels broadcasting at higher frequencies.

uncontrolled advertising PSAs prepared for use on radio and television stations. The message is controlled, but the delivery time is not.

uncontrolled media There is no guarantee that the messages that are crafted for those media will be delivered to the audience as created without modification.

under and over In broadcasting scripts, using sound dominated by (under) or dominating (over) any other sound.

underrun Printing practice that permits an allowance of 10 percent less than the total printing order as completion of an order when excessive spoilage in printing or in binding causes a slight shortage. *See also* overrun.

upcut In TV or film, to unintentionally overlap a sound picture with another sound.

update To alter a story to include the most recent developments.

UPI United Press International began as an international wire service to which any media could subscribe for news copy and photos, unlike AP, which is a membership cooperative. UPI was bought in 1992 by MBC, a London-based company.

uplink The transmission of audio, video or digitized computer information to a communications satellite, which relays the information to other receivers.

uppercase Capital letters.

urban myths or legends Fabricated rumors that start as hearsay and are distributed so widely, usually through emails, that they acquire an aura of truth. There are Web sites where you can check for credibility.

URL Uniform Resource Locator; an Internet address.

Usenet User Network; computer forums or discussion groups.

VALS 2 A system that designates categories of publics by their values, attitudes and lifestyles.

varitype A typewriter with alternate type fonts.

VDT Visual or video display terminal; an electronic device used in type composition and word processing, with a television-type screen to display data.

vertical saturation Scheduling commercials heavily one or two days before a major event.

VHF Very high frequency TV channels.

video All television visual projection.

video conference A teleconference in which full video is transmitted, as well as voice and graphics. The video signal can be from one point of origin to many receiving points, or two-way, simultaneously connecting two or more points, each of which can both originate and receive video.

video news release (VNR) A scripted news release that is fully produced and sent to television news directors on a videocassette, usually with some B-roll (background footage) to make editing possible; often sent by satellite.

videotex An interactive electronic data transmission system; establishes a two-way link from an individual's television set or home computer to a database.

vidicon A special camera tube often used in closed-circuit operations and TV film cameras.

vignette A story or sketch, often a "slice of life" drama.

vignetted halftones A halftone with edges that soften gradually until they completely fade out.

virtual reality A computer-generated environment that can be experienced by wearing special equipment.

virus Invasive destructive computer software program masked as normal communication.

visual scanner Optical scanner.

VO Voice over; broadcasting or film script designation for a narrator's voice to be used at a certain time in the production.

VTR (1) In TV, videotape recording. It is cheaper and more flexible than film, but less permanent. (2) In radio, voice transmitter and receiver—a small device attached to the phone, enabling a reporter to call in a story and preserve broadcast quality.

war file Pronounced "ware" file; a type of digital audio file.

wash drawing A watercolor or diluted India ink brush drawing requiring halftone reproduction.

watermark An identification mark left in the texture of quality paper stock; revealed when the paper is held up to light.

Web site Connected Web pages, usually from one organization.

when room Designation on copy or art that means it is usable at any time.

wide open A publication or news script with ample room for additional material.

widow (1) A short line (one word or two) at the end of a paragraph of type; this is to be avoided, especially in the first line of a page or column and in captions. (2) In publishing, any less-than-full-measure line ending a paragraph that appears as the top line of a page or column; again, this is to be avoided.

wild track Related footage with a sound track not intended to be in sync with the picture.

wipe A transitional television technique in which one scene gradually replaces another.

woodcuts Wooden printing blocks with the impression carved by hand. Now an art form, these were the forerunner of zinc engravings.

woodshedding In broadcasting, reading and rehearsing a news script.

working drawings Final drawings, usually black-and-white, prepared for use by an engraver, show how final art will appear.

work print The film print used in first editing. Usually one "light print," not printed for full-quality reproduction.

workstation A group of linked computer equipment used in accomplishing word processing or design tasks. A workstation often consists of a computer terminal with keyboard and monitor linked to a printer and sometimes to a scanner.

World Wide Web (WWW) A collection of computers connected on the Internet.

wow Pitch distortion or variation caused by changes in the speed of film or tape; also sound distortions in records.

WPD Work product doctrine; material prepared directly for an attorney that is privileged as long as it is kept confidential and secure.

wrap-up Summary or closing.

wrong font A letter from one font of type mixed with others of a different font.

WTO World Trade Organization; a United Nations organization of member nations that send delegates to meetings to make decisions about global markets.

XCU, ECU In TV or film, an extreme close-up; for a person, this might show eyes and nose only.

yak Narration.

Z-axis The imaginary line that extends in the direction the lens points from the camera to the horizon. Z-axis motion is movement toward or away from the camera. This is not a standardized term in the industry.

zinc etching A line engraving etched in zinc.

Index